P9-DTW-578

CRITICAL GERONTOLOGY:
Perspectives from Political and Moral Economy

Edited by
Meredith Minkler
and
Carroll L. Estes

POLICY, POLITICS, HEALTH AND MEDICINE Series
Vicente Navarro, Series Editor

Baywood Publishing Company, Inc.
Amityville, New York

Copyright © 1999 by the Baywood Publishing Company, Inc., Amityville, New York.
All rights reserved. Printed in the United States of America on acid-free recycled paper.

Library of Congress Catalog Number: 97-37071
ISBN: 0-89503-185-X(Paper)
ISBN: 0-89503-184-1 (Cloth)

Library of Congress Cataloging-in-Publication Data

Critical gerontology : perspectives from political and moral economy /
   edited by Meredith Minkler and Carroll L. Estes.
         p.   cm. - - (Policy, politics, health, and medicine series)
   Includes bibliographical references and index.
   ISBN 0-89503-184-1 (cloth). - - ISBN 0-89503-185-X (paper)
   1. Gerontology.   2. Gerontology- -Moral and ethical aspects.
I. Minkler, Meredith.   II. Estes, Carroll L.   III. Series : Policy,
politics, health, and medicine series (Unnumbered)
HQ1061.C69   1999
305.26- -dc21   97-37071
                                                                      CIP

Table of Contents

Acknowledgments

Many people have helped make this book a reality, and we are particularly grateful to our coauthors who believed in this effort and contributed substantially to the final product. We are indebted as well to the many friends and colleagues who have provided encouragement and intellectual stimulation, and whose own work has deeply influenced our thinking in critical gerontology and related areas. Notable among the latter are Alvin Gouldner, Jim O'Connor, Patricia Hill Collins, Peter Townsend, Vicente Navarro, Randall Collins, and Joe Gusfield.

We are fortunate to count among our role models in aging and feminism three older women—Lillian Rabinowitz, the late Maggie Kuhn, and the late Tish Sommers—whose passion and activism, and whose commitment to social change based on critical reflection, have inspired us and countless others both within gerontology and beyond disciplinary boundaries.

Special thanks are due our faculty colleagues and graduate students in the Schools of Public Health and Social Welfare at the University of California, Berkeley, and at the Institute for Health and Aging and the Department of Social and Behavioral Sciences, School of Nursing, at the University of California, San Francisco. By sharing their ideas and challenging our own thinking, they too have contributed much to this volume.

Our sincere gratitude is extended to those staff members and research colleagues and assistants who helped move this project forward—Janney Skinner, Jennifer Dresen, Diane Driver, Susan Alward and the library reference staff at Berkeley, and Karen Linkins, Grace Yoo, Roxie Kellam, Kappa Bixon, Patrick Henderson, and Marie Christine Yue at UCSF. Finally, Patsy Wakimoto is deserving of special acknowledgment, as her organizational skills, time, and commitment played an invaluable role in enabling this project to become a reality.

Vicente Navarro at Johns Hopkins University and Stuart Cohen at Baywood Publishing Company both are deserving of special thanks for their encouragement of this third coedited volume on critical gerontology. Our copy editor, Linda Strange, also contributed much to the final production, and we are grateful to her, and to the Baywood staff, for their assistance along the way.

Finally, our deepest thanks go to our families—to our parents and late parents who believed in us and provided a lifetime of support and encouragement, to Meredith's husband Jerry for his love, support, and the loan of the dining room table, and to our children, Duskie and Jason, for enriching our lives beyond measure.

Introduction

Meredith Minkler

In any discipline, or sub-discipline, a mainstream or orthodoxy develops which is often conservative and rarely self-critical. There is a need, particularly in a relatively young field of study, for a constant reappraisal of concepts and ideas in order to prevent the orthodox approach becoming stultifying.

Phillipson and Walker (1, p. 12)

With these words, British scholars Chris Phillipson and Alan Walker well articulated the growing need for a critical gerontology—an approach to social gerontology that provokes and challenges assumptions, and that is grounded in a commitment "not just to understand the social construction of aging, but to change it."

Since the publication of our earlier volume, *Critical Perspectives on Aging* (2), in 1991, the field of critical gerontology has continued to evolve primarily along two paths—paths that have sometimes intersected and moved in common directions, but that have tended to remain distinct (3). The first path, and the one with which this book is chiefly concerned, embraces a broad political economy of aging framework. Critical gerontology in this sense views the "problem" of aging in structural rather than individual terms. Such an approach, in the words of Carroll Estes and her colleagues, "starts with the proposition that the status and resources of the elderly, and even the trajectory of the aging process itself, are conditioned by one's location in the social structure and the economic and social factors that affect it" (4).

The political economy path in critical gerontology provides multidisciplinary lenses through which to examine such themes as the social creation of the dependent status of the elderly, and the management of that dependency through public policies and health and social services. To borrow John Myles's (5) phrase, it helps bring to light the many ways in which "politics, not demography" determines how old age is defined and approached in a society.

One of the strengths of a broad political economy framework lies in its ability to highlight the intersections between race, class, gender, and aging (2). By stressing those "interlocking systems of inequality" (6) that help shape and determine the experience of aging and growing old, it offers important insights into the social construction of aging on multiple levels. Critical gerontology in the tradition of

1

political economy, in sum, offers a rich and multiperspectival framework within which to view and better understand old age as a "problem" for societies "characterized by major inequalities in the distribution of power, income and property" (7, p. 79). As such, it provides a much needed supplement to the study of the biological and psychological aspects of aging, which, for all their contributions, reveal little about the social construction of aging in a broader sociopolitical context (8).

The second path in critical gerontology, while not the focus of this book, provides an important supplement to political economy perspectives in putting a human face—and a human body and spirit—on aging and growing old (3, 8–14). This second path emerges from a humanistic orientation and critiques what Harry Moody describes as the ever more technical and "instrumental" orientation of academic gerontology, within which "the problems of later life are treated with scientific and managerial efficiency, but with no grasp of their larger political or existential significance. The last stage of life is progressively drained of meaning (15, p. 82). A number of authors have provided excellent illustrations of and commentaries on the humanistic approach (9–14).

Although this volume is designed to help us travel the first path in critical gerontology, it recognizes and is enriched by the movement of a number of its contributors across the two pathways. Further, in continuing to develop and refine the notion of moral economy in relation to aging and intergenerational relations, the book seeks to offer a conceptual perspective that can enrich the political economy of aging by enabling a deeper exploration of such issues as the current and increasingly contentious debates over social security and resource allocation between the generations. Defined by Kohli as "the collectively shared moral assumptions underlying norms of reciprocity in which a market economy is grounded" (16, p. 125), moral economy helps to surface and make explicit the often implicit cultural beliefs and values underlying societal policies and practices affecting the old. In the words of Phillip Clark (Chapter 8), "The moral economy approach encourages—indeed, requires—us to look beyond the 'appearance of things' at the underlying foundational assumptions, facts, loyalties, and values that undergird and shape the 'superstructure' of public policy" (page 148).

As noted in Chapter 2, political and moral economy perspectives share some important similarities, among them the fact that both ground their analyses of topics such as aging within considerations of broader sociohistorical processes. While political economy focuses in particular on the social structural context of aging, moral economy is primarily concerned with the related context of popular consensus defining norms of reciprocity as these affect the old and resource allocation across age groups. The explicit integration of a moral economy perspective within a broader political economy framework, therefore, makes possible a richer and more thorough analysis than either can achieve independently.

Within this combined political and moral economy context, the goals of this volume are twofold. First, the book attempts to complement, update, and extend *Critical Perspectives on Aging* by applying a political economy perspective to the analysis of such diverse problems and issues as the complex interplay of race, class, gender, and aging; the transformation of health and welfare policies for the old; the gendered nature of work and retirement; and the myths and realities of "senior power." Although most of these and other topics will be explored primarily within the context of the United States, others will be examined in cross-national perspective, with special attention to Canadian and British experiences in these domains.

The book's second goal, like that of our earlier volumes, lies in theory building. As Carroll Estes notes in Chapter 1, "The central challenge of the political economy of aging is to understand the character and significance of variations in the treatment of the aged and to relate them to broad societal and global forces and conditions" (page 17). Toward this end, the book begins by looking at the state of the art of the political economy of aging as a theoretical approach, highlighting such recent developments as the latter's increased attention to the phenomenon of culture and suggesting areas for further development and refinement. Subsequent chapters once again build on this base by providing new political economy analyses within the broad field of aging which may themselves contribute to the further conceptual development of this approach, as well as to its concrete application in gerontology.

The theory-building purpose of this volume also extends to its efforts to further refine and expand our thinking in the realm of moral economy. As noted above, moral economy may provide a useful adjunct to political economy, particularly as we attempt to understand such topics as the vastly different approaches to health care for the old in Canada and the United States, recent efforts to justify attacks on entitlement programs for the elderly within an "intergenerational equity" framework, and the increasing popularity of concepts such as "productive aging" (see Chapter 20).

In Chapter 1 of this volume, Estes provides a comprehensive introduction to the political economy of aging, suggesting that the central task of this theoretical approach is "to locate society's treatment of the aged in the context of the economy (global and U.S.), the state, the conditions of the labor market, and the class, sex, race, and age divisions in society" (page 28). Unlike psychological and other micro-level approaches that legitimate "incremental and individualistic approaches to public policy," political economy perspectives suggest that issues such as health and the dependency of the old are embedded within the structure of the labor market and other macro-level considerations.

Estes demonstrates the special relevance of such an approach for understanding how the elderly have come to be "homogenized" and labeled a social problem; how the social status and treatment of the old and of subgroups within the elderly population have developed; and how resource allocation policies affecting the old have been determined.

Chapter 1 devotes special attention to several critical areas within the political economy of aging—the state, social class, gender, and the symbolic and cultural dimensions of the political economy of aging—that continue to be underdeveloped. In contrast to the many scholars who view questions of aging as peripheral to state and class theorizing (since the old are no longer in the "productive" workforce), Estes places aging squarely within the domain of both state and class interrogations. The power of the state in allocating resources and shaping and reproducing social patterns, and the continuing role of pre-retirement social class in shaping the experience of old age, are thus used to underscore the importance of further developing state and class analyses with specific reference to aging.

Yet as Estes goes on to suggest, "theories of the state and class that do not explicitly and adequately address the subordination of women and the 'privileging of men' fail as comprehensive frameworks for understanding social phenomena" (page 26). Attention therefore is devoted in Estes's chapter, and throughout this volume, to aging and gender, as well as to the intersections of age, class, gender, and race/ethnicity as these influence the experience of aging on both the macro and the individual or micro levels.

The multiperspectival nature of political economy and its consequent ability to move across narrow disciplinary boundaries enable it to integrate related conceptual approaches. In Chapter 2, Meredith Minkler and Thomas Cole propose one such integration, introducing the concept of moral economy and suggesting its usefulness as an adjunct to political economic analyses. British historian E. P. Thompson's (17) view of moral economy as the shared assumptions underlying reciprocal relations is employed in this chapter and in many subsequent parts of the book. Following a consideration of the ambivalence surrounding moral questions that has tended to characterize the "Scientific Marxism" tradition in political economy (18), Chapter 2 reviews the development and evolution of the notion of moral economy, noting its relevance as an analytical tool in gerontology. The authors then highlight promising new scholarship that has occurred over the past decade in explicitly applying a combined moral and political economy framework to understanding recent developments in aging and aging policy. The creation and evolution of pension systems, the reality versus the rhetoric of "generational inequity," the senior revolt against the ill-fated Medicare Catastrophic Coverage Act, and recent claims by the New Right of a "historic mandate" to drastically restructure Medicare and Medicaid are briefly discussed as areas in which a combined political and moral economy perspective has deepened our understanding and enriched our analyses. On another level, constructs such as "productive aging," which Martha Holstein critiques in detail in Chapter 20, also are seen as lending themselves to the kind of combined analysis illustrated in many subsequent parts of this text.

The utility of a combined political and moral economy framework within critical gerontology is perhaps best demonstrated in Part II of this volume. Chapters 3 and 4 begin a dialogue to which other authors contribute in subsequent chapters of the book. Malcolm Johnson (Chapter 3) initiates the discussion by examining structural shifts on both the family and governmental levels that have combined to "place at risk" the intergenerational support that elders both require and anticipate. Arguing that governments have scaled back their commitments to the old "more in panic than in thoughtful response," Johnson notes that the shift to market provision of care, when coupled with longer life expectancies and changing family formations, provides "a picture of change with profound moral dimensions." Although Johnson goes on to critique what he sees as the postmodern world view of "disintegration and disorder," he nevertheless makes the case for "a revolution in economic and political action" which is "essentially moral" in nature and which embraces a recommitment to intergenerational solidarity on multiple levels.

Johnson's call for moral transformations in economic and political action is addressed by Ann Robertson in Chapter 4. Critiquing the rhetoric of "apocalyptic demography" (frequently expressed in terms of "dependency ratios" and skyrocketing health care costs), Robertson examines the social construction of dependency which increases the perceived neediness of the old. She describes the Catch-22 experienced by elders "caught between a social ethic of independence . . . and a service ethic which constructs them as dependent" (page 82), with attention to the ways in which the false dichotomy between dependence and independence ill serves both individuals and the broader society. Robertson argues that the postmodern "therapeutic ethic," combined with a legacy of radical individualism, has worked to depoliticize need in a way that contributes to this false dichotomy. She concludes by arguing for a "moral economy of interdependence" that repoliticizes need, transcends the dependency/independence dichotomy, and expresses through our public policies a recognition that we are indeed all part of the same community.

The importance of moving in this direction is well demonstrated in the area of aging and disability, as the "decline and loss" paradigm (19) commonly invoked tends to ignore the broader needs and aspirations of the elderly disabled, reinforcing in the process their marginalization. In Chapter 5, Jae Kennedy and Meredith Minkler examine different definitions and models of disability, and stress the contribution of newer approaches that give prominence to the role of broader environmental factors in the disablement process. The social production and distribution of disability is then examined, as is the problematic tendency of our public policies to focus on disability almost exclusively in terms of its role as an impediment to work. The authors explore age, gender, and race biases in disability programming, as well as some of the historical roots of our attitudes and consequent policies toward the elderly who are disabled. The chapter concludes by highlighting some of the principles put forth by the independent living movement and their salience for achieving what Robertson described in Chapter 4 as a new "moral economy of interdependence" over the life course. Such an approach, which moves us far afield from the contemporary tendency to dichotomize "dependence" and "independence" in old age, is seen as providing us with a far better way to address the dramatic social and economic inequities that accompany aging and disability.

Although one set of images of the elderly tends to focus on their high rates of chronic illness and disability, another conjures up visions of an active, wealthy, and powerful voting bloc whose costly government programs and "single issue voting" are directly responsible for many of the problems facing younger generations and the national economy (20–23). The increasingly popular rhetoric of "generational equity" or "justice between generations" is based in part on such images, and this rhetoric, unfortunately, is not limited to the right. In the recent words of liberal economist Lester Thurow (21, p. 46):

> A new class of people is being created . . . a large group of affluent, economically inactive, elderly voters who require expensive social services like health care and who depend upon government for much of their income. It is a revolutionary class, one that is bringing down the social welfare state, destroying government

finances, altering the distribution of purchasing power and threatening the investments that all societies need to make to have a successful future.

In the last chapter of Part II (Chapter 6), Debra Street critically examines such arguments and attempts to separate the myths from the realities of "senior power" and the voting behavior of older Americans. Contrary to the rhetoric, for example, she finds little substantive evidence that the elderly constitute a voting bloc; rather, their voting decisions appear to be based on "the same complex criteria" that help to determine the voting patterns of other age groups. Further, while noting the political power of such senior organizations as the American Association of Retired Persons (AARP) in protecting programs like Social Security, Street demonstrates that the "elderly lobby" has been far less effective in initiating new programs. Indeed, as she points out, "the special interest perspective of the politics of aging hides more than it reveals"—obscuring, among other things, the transclass and transgenerational nature of the politics surrounding programs such as Medicare and Social Security. With the other contributors to Part II, Street advocates for incorporating moral economy perspectives within a broad political economy framework if we are to meet the challenges of understanding our increasingly heterogeneous—and increasingly aging—societies.

Among the greatest challenges of our aging societies are, of course, those concerned with the provision of humane and affordable health and social services in ways that empower, rather than disempower, their recipients. And nowhere is the debate over such provision more wrenching than in the United States as it continues to experience a profound politics of retrenchment. Carroll Estes begins Part III by offering a "second look" at her classic conceptualization, over two decades ago, of the "aging enterprise"—that vast array of bureaucracies, interest groups, providers, and programs that has contributed to the commodification and treatment of the needs of the elderly in ways that often work to benefit professionals and organizations more than they do the elderly (24). In Chapter 7, Estes views social constructions of the elderly as a "problem" and as "special and different" as providing the rationale for age-segregated categorical services, and the biomedicalization of aging as contributing to fears of aging on both the individual and the broad societal levels. She examines the restructuring of community care and the rapid ascendancy of managed care against a backdrop of fiscal austerity and social constructions of the "problem" of old age, and makes a case for policies that are universalistic and empowering of the old and other generations and social groups.

Chapter 8 next focuses specifically on health care, and uses a comparative approach to examine the "crisis" of aging and health care in Canada and the United States. Phillip Clark uses a moral economy and "public ethics" framework to examine the values and moral underpinnings of health and social service policy in the two nations, how these may be changing, and how a moral economy perspective can help predict the likely evolution of health care policy in Canada and the United States. Although the two countries share concerns about the health care costs of their aging societies, and although both are engaged in struggles to preserve their Medicare systems, the high value placed on collectivism in Canada (as witnessed in the universalistic nature of its "Medicare" program) provides a sharp contrast to the individualistic orientation that reigns in the United States. The playing out of current debates over how to respond to the health needs of their aging populations is likely, as Clark notes, to be heavily influenced by these divergent underlying values and moral assumptions.

This broad overview of aging health care policy is followed in the remainder of Part III with a more detailed look at specific aspects of the current efforts to transform health care policy for the elderly in the United States. In Chapter 9, Carroll Estes and Karen Linkins explore the major reductions in the role of the federal government that have taken place over the last two decades in terms of their impacts on health and human services policies. Building on the analysis introduced in Chapter 8, they use a political economy framework to explore the states' "race to the bottom" in long-term care. A new wave of tax revolts on the state level, block granting, managed care, welfare reform, and continued attacks on the nonprofit sector all are seen as boding ill for the future of long-term care in the United States. Lost in the shuffle, Estes and Linkins suggest, is the "larger goal" of long-term care policy—one addressing social, not merely economic objectives, and concerned with such forgotten ideals as empowerment, universality, and social justice.

Marty Lynch and Meredith Minkler (Chapter 10) provide a case in point, examining the proposed restructuring of Medicare and Medicaid and its implications for the elderly, with special attention to older women, people with disabilities, the low-income elderly, and elders of color. Employing both a political and moral economy framework, this analysis of the major alternative proposals for transforming U.S. health policy vis-à-vis the old makes special use of Katz's (25) notion of perceived "deservingness" as a major criterion undergirding our public policies. Despite their differences, both the Democratic and the Republican proposals examined in this chapter are seen to reflect an accelerated movement of government away from its legitimation functions and toward an increasing emphasis on capital accumulation. They reflect, as well, an increasing "bifurcation of care" (26), often along lines of perceived deservingness, that bodes ill for the most vulnerable groups within the elderly population.

Of the many options being discussed for restructuring Medicare in the United States, one that has enjoyed increasing popularity—including the recent endorsement of the American Medical Association—is that of transforming this federal insurance program into a voucher system. In Chapter 11, Jonathan Oberlander describes how a Medicare voucher system would operate and lays out the primary advantages (e.g., enhanced consumer choice and fiscal control) claimed by its proponents. As he goes on to suggest, however, the realities of a Medicare voucher system would often be just the opposite of what is promised, severely limiting choice and unfairly penalizing those who enroll in more expensive health plans. Finally, and of particular importance from a political economy perspective, a Medicare voucher system would exacerbate existing inequalities in medical care access and fragment "the universal and cross-class political coalition" that has been instrumental in supporting this popular program. Although Oberlander's analysis is focused on the implementation of a voucher system in relation to health care for the elderly in the United States, the implications of this discussion for European countries interested in applying principles of "managed competition" to their own health care systems are clear.

As the chapters in Part III illustrate, most of the current discussion of curbing the high costs of health care for the elderly in the United States has tended to focus on Medicare and its coverage of hospitalizations. Yet of far greater concern to many elderly and their families is the growing problem of a long-term care system that, for the most part, is not covered by Medicare, operates at a profit, and directly affects one in four American families. In Chapter 12, Charlene Harrington updates her earlier structural analysis of the U.S. nursing home industry (27) and looks at features of both the nursing home market and the industry itself in an effort to identify factors related to continuing poor quality of care. Second only to the drug sector of the health care industry in terms of proprietary and chain ownership (27), the nursing home industry stands as a highly visible reminder of the problems plaguing a market economy approach to health care in the United States. As Harrington points out, implementation of the Nursing Home Reform Act of 1987 produced some improvements—for example, in substantially lowering the number of patients who were physically restrained (28). Yet despite these changes, and the massive infusion of public funds, nursing homes have the poorest quality-of-care record of any segment of the health care industry. This continuing legacy, along with recent efforts to eviscerate nursing home reform legislation in an industry that is heavily for-profit and increasingly chain-owned and operated, strongly underscores the need for structural rather than piecemeal reform.

As suggested in Part III, many of the proposed changes in health care policy for the old have the effect of reinforcing already pronounced inequities based on race, class, and gender within the elderly population. In Part IV, we turn our attention more directly to these "interlocking systems of inequality" (6) and how our public policies work, wittingly or unwittingly, to reinforce and exacerbate them. Steven Wallace and Valentine Villa begin in Chapter 13 by examining the relative invisibility of minority elders with respect to our health and social policies and juxtaposing this against the increasingly powerful role of the corporate health sector and other elite interests. Using political economy as a conceptual framework, Wallace and Villa examine changes in the economy and in popular perceptions (e.g., that immigrants cause economic crisis) which have resulted in anti-immigrant and other recent policies that directly affect elders of color. At the same time, increasing out-of-pocket costs under Medicare, the shift to managed care, and financial and other barriers to both nursing home and in-home supportive services are taking a particularly heavy toll on the minority elderly.

Like race, ethnicity, and social class, gender remains a major stratifier in society, and one that takes on increasing salience in old age, which, as Butler notes, is indeed "a territory populated largely by women" (29, p. 794). The disproportionate representation of women in the peripheral or secondary sector of the labor market, wage discrimination, the sexual division of labor, and the devaluation of caregiving are among the structural inequalities that help explain the economic dependence of women on men and the continued economic vulnerability of many older women. Joanna Weinberg (Chapter 14) uses a political economy framework to examine in detail one of these factors—the marginalization of caregiving in the rapidly devolving "welfare state"—which remains in large part a gender issue. Weinberg presents contrasting theories and meanings of caregiving and examines its contested social value in both the historical origins and evolution of welfare policy and recent efforts to "end welfare as we know it." She views the gendered division of caregiving for and by the elderly through several lenses, including the legislative structure of the welfare state; the disjuncture between the health care needs of older women and a Medicare reimbursement system that corresponds primarily to a male pattern of illness; and a division of labor that largely "confines women to the private sphere and constrains access to resources and to independence." Weinberg stresses the need for recognizing and attending to the political nature of the public/private spheres of caregiving, as well as to "the essentially subjective nature of the character of care." She then proposes the restructuring of social policies to provide compensation for caregivers, the affording of increased visibility and legitimacy to this role, and the restructuring of caregiving so that men and women participate more equally in caregiving tasks.

As noted earlier, a major contribution of the political economy perspective lies in its ability to highlight the intersections of race, class, gender, and aging as they help shape and determine the experience of growing old. To date, however, much of the social science theory and research on race, class, gender, and aging has tended to reflect what Margaret Andersen (30) has called the "add and stir approach to oppression." Using this approach, scholars examine a topic, such as poverty in old age, primarily through one lens or prism, such as gender, and subsequently add the effects of other stratifiers, such as race and class, into the mix. Comparisons of dominant and subordinate groups often add to the confusion, inadvertently reproducing problems of marginalization in the process.

In Chapter 15, Paula Dressel, Meredith Minkler, and Irene Yen take a critical look at the state of gerontological research with regard to race, class, and gender, noting the limitations of the dominant "double jeopardy" and "age as leveler" hypotheses (31), as well as the add-and-stir and other between-group comparison approaches typically used in this research. The authors highlight promising approaches that move beyond these positions, such as placing previously neglected groups at the center of investigation (32), using culturally relevant theoretical tools (33), and considering gender, race, class, and age as interlocking phenomena. The relevance for critical gerontology of promising new developments in epidemiology, sociology, and other fields is further examined, with special attention to the notion of gender, race, class, and age as sources of self and/or social identity whose salience varies with political and interactional context.

A theme running throughout this book is that socially constructed classifications of gender, race, class, and age are both shaped by and, in turn, help to shape not only individual actions and interactions but also institutional arrangements. In the final part of the book we explore in more detail the institutions of work, retirement, and social security, with special attention to the gendered, racialized, and classed nature of these phenomena. We begin in Chapter 16 by examining women's retirement income in the United States with the presentation of an updated version of a special "Mother's Day Report" produced by the Older Women's League (OWL). Noting that "for many women, the path to poverty in old age begins the first day of work," OWL examines disparities in the incidence of poverty among men and women by age, race, and ethnicity, as well as the prominent role of marital status as a risk factor for poverty in later life. Gender-based inequities in both the Social Security and private pension systems are explored, as are the serious limitations of the government's SSI (Supplemental Security Income) program, which continues to leave recipients well below the poverty line. More than any other portion of this book, this chapter is filled with statistics capturing the precarious economic position of older women and other vulnerable groups. In the words of public health leader Victor Sidel, it serves as a stark reminder that "statistics are people with the tears washed off," and hence as a call for collective action.

This telling case study of women's retirement income in the United States is followed in Chapter 17 by a more theoretical look at the social construction—and reconstruction—of work and retirement in postmodern societies. British scholar Chris Phillipson draws on both critical theory and political economy to examine the changing nature of work and retirement as we approach the 21st century. He argues that retirement "both developed and was constrained within the framework of an industrialized society," which located this experience within the context of structured dependency. With the "loosening of the contours" of advanced industrialized societies by the late 1960s, however, new definitions and visions of retirement began to emerge, and the very idea of a modal "retirement experience" was called into question. While this change has some important positive features (e.g., in making more visible the experience of older blacks and others for whom traditional notions of retirement have historically been ill-suited) (34), it also poses serious threats to the identity of the old. Phillipson stresses the need for a new political economy of retirement that would consider both the emancipatory possibilities of retirement in postmodern societies and the new types of structural inequality to which it may give rise.

From Phillipson's conceptual analysis of work and retirement, we move to Robert Hudson's cross-national perspective on the evolution of social security and the welfare state (Chapter 18). Building on earlier chapters, Hudson reviews key trends in the assault on the welfare state (e.g., shifting values and the movement from national public programs to a heightened emphasis on the private sector) as these affect the old and the debates on aging policy. Drawing on data and examples from numerous and advanced industrialized societies, Hudson demonstrates how remarkably similar trends and concerns are resulting in severe challenges to aging policies and the principles and commitments in which they are grounded. The chapter concludes by laying out a "social contingency framework" to guide discussion as we rethink how to weigh and assess the different risks facing the old, without losing sight of such "bedrock concerns" as universalism and adequacy.

As is clear from Hudson's analysis, many nations are now grappling with shifting notions of "the rights and responsibilities of the old," with potentially profound effects on their public policies. In the United States, the crisis rhetoric surrounding Social Security has reached a feverish pitch and has enabled policymakers to begin "marketing radical reform" of the system in a way that would, until recently, have been unthinkable. In Chapter 19, Eric Kingson and Jill Quadagno take a critical look at the "entitlement crisis framework" which is enabling proposals previously relegated to the far right to gain a serious hearing. Means-testing Social Security, radically reducing benefits, and privatizing the system are among the reforms under consideration—reforms whose legitimacy rests in large part on "inflated claims of impending fiscal crises." As the authors go on to suggest, however, far more modest adjustments could restore the long-range solvency of the system. Echoing a theme that appears often in this volume, Kingson and Quadagno remind us that Social Security is, in the last analysis, a critical expression of our moral commitment as a society to caring for its members, and one we should not lose sight of.

In the final chapter, Martha Holstein shifts our gaze from formal systems of provision for the economic needs of the elderly to the mind-sets within which later life is conceptualized. She sees the popular notion of a "productive aging society," embodying images of healthy, energetic elders, contributing to society largely through gainful activity, as a well-meaning but dangerous paradigm and one deserving of careful scrutiny. Pointing out that political and economic forces tend to reduce "enriched" notions of productivity simply to paid work, Holstein uses feminist, cultural, and contextual analysis to explore the deleterious effects that this narrowness of vision may have on older individuals, and especially older women. Work-related definitions of productivity thus detract from important social roles (e.g., in volunteerism, community leadership, and caregiving) in which older women in particular are likely to be engaged. Such conceptualizations may further intensify already strong prejudices against the disabled elderly.

Although the notion of productive aging has some advantages—for example, in underscoring the strengths of older people—Holstein sees it on balance as feeding into the already strong tendency to define problems such as poverty in individual terms, and to reinforce negative images of many older women and disabled and low-income people who may fail to fit comfortably within a narrow vision of what constitutes "a good old age." Further, as Holstein notes, visions of a "productive aging society" can, all too easily, become "the unintended handmaidens for a political agenda" that delegitimates crucial health and social policies for the old.

This Introduction began by citing Chris Phillipson and Alan Walker's articulation of the need for an approach to gerontology that provokes questions, challenges assumptions, and is committed not only to enhancing our understanding of how aging is socially created, but also to bringing about changes in that social construction. Critical gerontology in this sense is committed to overcoming what Peter Townsend (35, p. 19) once described as the attempted disassociation between social science research and policymaking which "falsely neutralizes scientific practice" and is a luxury we can ill afford. We are hopeful that in addition to meeting its goals in the areas of theory building and critical analysis, this book will stimulate readers to take action, based on critical reflection, that will help create the conditions needed for empowerment and high quality of life in old age and across the life course.

REFERENCES

1. Phillipson, C., and Walker, A. The case for critical gerontology. In *Social Gerontology: New Directions,* edited by S. DeGregorio, pp. 1–15. Croom Helm, London, 1987.
2. Minkler, M., and Estes, C. (eds). *Critical Perspectives on Aging: The Political and Moral Economy of Growing Old.* Baywood, Amityville, N.Y., 1991.

3. Ovrebo, B., and Minkler, M. The lives of older women: Perspectives from political economy and the humanities. In *Voices and Visions of Aging: Towards a Critical Gerontology,* edited by T. Cole et al., pp. 289–308. Springer, New York, 1993.
4. Estes, C. L., Swan, J. H., and Gerard, L. Dominant and competing paradigms in gerontology: Toward a political economy of ageing. *Ageing Soc.* 2(Pt 2): 151–164, 1982.
5. Myles, J. F. Conflict, crisis and the future of old age security. *Milbank Mem. Fund Q./Health Soc.* 61(4): 462–562, 1983.
6. Stoller, E. P., and Gibson, R. D. *Worlds of Difference: Inequalities in the Aging Experience,* Ed. 2. Pine Forge Press, Thousand Oaks, Calif., 1997.
7. Kart, C. S. The end of conventional gerontology, *Sociol. Health Illness* 9: 76–87, 1987.
8. Minkler, M. Critical perspectives on ageing: New challenges for gerontology. *Ageing Soc.* 16: 467–487, 1996.
9. Cole, T. *The Journey of Life: A Cultural History of Aging in America.* Cambridge University Press, New York, 1992.
10. Cole, T., Van Tassel, D., and Kastenbaum, R. (eds). *Handbook of Aging and the Humanities.* Springer, New York, 1992.
11. Cole, T., et al. (eds). *Voices and Visions of Aging: Towards a Critical Gerontology.* Springer, New York, 1993.
12. Holstein, M. Taking next steps: Gerontological education, research, and the literary imagination. *Gerontologist* 34: 822–827, 1994.
13. Moody, H. R. Toward a critical gerontology: The contribution of the humanities to theories of aging. In *Emergent Theories of Aging,* edited by J. Birren and V. Bengston, pp. 19–40. Springer, New York, 1989.
14. Featherstone, M., and Hepworth, M. Images of ageing. In *Ageing in Society: An Introduction to Social Gerontology,* edited by J. Bond, P. Coleman, and S. Peace. Sage, London, 1993.
15. Moody, H. *Abundance of Life: Human Development Policies for an Aging Society.* Columbia University Press, New York, 1988.
16. Kohli, M. Retirement and the moral economy. *J. Aging Stud.* 1: 125–144, 1987.
17. Thompson, E. P. *The Making of the English Working Class.* Vintage Books, New York, 1966.
18. Gouldner, A. *The Two Marxisms: Contradictions and Anomalies in the Development of Theory.* Seabury Press, New York, 1980.
19. Minkler, M. Aging and disability: Behind and beyond the stereotypes. *J. Aging Stud.* 4(3): 245–260, 1990.
20. Binstock, R. H. The aged as scapegoat. *Gerontologist* 23: 136–143, 1983.
21. Thurow, L. C. The birth of a revolutionary class. *New York Times Magazine,* May 19, 1996, pp. 46–47.
22. Minkler, M., and Robertson, A. The ideology of age/race wars: Deconstructing a social problem. *Ageing Soc.* 11: 1–22, 1991.
23. Peterson, P. B. Social insecurity. *Atlantic Monthly,* May 1996, pp. 56–86.
24. Estes, C. L. *The Aging Enterprise.* Jossey-Bass, San Francisco, 1979.
25. Katz, M. *The Undeserving Poor: From the War on Poverty to the War on Welfare.* Pantheon, New York, 1990.
26. Hudson, R. Newt Federalism: The Contract with America, Aging Policy and the Fraying Safety Net. Symposium comments at the Annual Meeting of the Gerontological Society of America, Los Angeles, November 15, 1995.
27. Harrington, C. The nursing home industry: A structural analysis. In *Critical Perspectives on Aging: The Political and Moral Economy of Growing Old,* edited by M. Minkler and C. Estes, pp. 153–164. Baywood, Amityville, N.Y., 1991.

28. Kane, R. L., et al. Restraining restraints: Changes in a standard of care. *Annu. Rev. Public Health* 14: 545–584, 1993.
29. Butler, R. N. On behalf of older women: Another reason to protect Medicare and Medicaid. *N. Engl. J. Med.,* March 21, 1996, pp. 794–796.
30. Andersen, M. L. *Thinking about Women: Sociological and Feminist Perspectives.* Macmillan, New York, 1983.
31. Dowd, J. J., and Bengston, V. L. Aging in minority populations: An examination of the double jeopardy hypothesis. *J. Gerontol.* 33: 338–355, 1978.
32. hooks, b. *From Margin to Center.* South End Press, Boston, 1984.
33. Burton, L., Dilworth-Anderson, P., and Bengston, V. Creating culturally relevant ways of thinking about aging and diversity: Theoretical challenges for the 21st century. In *Diversity: New Approaches to Ethnic Minority Aging,* edited by E. P. Stanford and F. M. Torres-Gil, pp. 129–140. Baywood, Amityville, N.Y., 1992.
34. Gibson, R. C. The subjective retirement of black Americans. *J. Gerontol. Soc. Sci.* 46: S204–S209, 1991.
35. Townsend, P. Ageism and social policy. In *Ageing and Social Policy,* edited by C. Phillipson and A. Walker. Gower, London, 1986.

PART I.
THEORETICAL FRAMEWORK

Numerous conceptual perspectives are used by the contributors to this volume to help explicate the diverse topics under investigation. Critical theory in the tradition of Habermas (1), Giddens (2), and others, feminist theory (3, 4), and what Burton and her colleagues (5) have called "culturally relevant ways of thinking" about aging and diversity are among the conceptual approaches employed to help illuminate such topics as the social construction of retirement, gender and caregiving, and the impacts of the current politics of retrenchment on minority elders.

Yet despite this conceptual breadth and diversity, two bodies of theory will be seen to form the book's overarching frameworks for analysis. Part I provides an introduction to these primary theoretical traditions—the political and moral economies of aging—which, we argue, offer different yet highly complementary approaches to understanding both the experience of aging and the factors shaping aging-related program and policy development.

In Chapter 1, Carroll Estes provides an in-depth look at the political economy of aging, which rejects the notion that aging—or any other complex social issue—can be understood in isolation from larger political, social, or economic realities. In Walton's words, "the central problem of the political economy perspective is the manner in which the economy and the polity interact in a relationship of reciprocal causality affecting the distribution of social goods" (6). As noted in the Introduction, such a perspective of necessity views the "problem" of aging in structural rather than individual terms. And it urges us to examine such issues as the sociopolitical nature of how our society views the elderly; the social, political, and economic bases of policies that determine how benefits, privilege, and power are distributed; and both the social creation of the dependent status of the old and the management of that dependency through our public policies and health and social services.

Following an overview of the political economy of aging as an alternative to mainstream theoretical frameworks for understanding aging and aging policy, Estes examines in more detail four topics which she views as "particularly promising areas of investigation and theorizing": the state and state theory as they relate to aging, social class, gender, and symbolic and cultural dimensions, especially as these relate to race and ethnicity. Chapter 1 concludes by laying out the key assumptions underlying a political economy approach to the study of aging—premises that serve as threads which help weave together many of the subsequent chapters of this volume.

In Chapter 2, Meredith Minkler and Thomas Cole introduce the book's second major theoretical framework, using as a jumping-off point historian E. P. Thompson's (7) notion of moral economy as popularly shared moral assumptions underlying certain societal practices, such as treatment of the poor or care of the elderly. Following a brief historical review of the etiology and development of the concept of moral economy, the authors describe its special relevance as an adjunct to the political economy of aging. They then suggest the utility of moral economy for sharpening and deepening our understanding of such topics as the evolution of retirement and why our health care policies for the elderly look the way they do. Minkler and Cole end by providing several snapshots of recent efforts to enrich the study of aging through the combined application of political and moral economy perspectives. Yet the main aim of this chapter is to set the stage for the more in-depth illustration of such integrative analyses in subsequent chapters of this volume.

REFERENCES

1. Habermas, J. (ed.). *Observations on "The Spiritual Situation of the Age,"* translated by A. Buchwalter. MIT Press, Cambridge, Mass., 1984.
2. Giddens, A. *Modernity and Self-Identity.* Policy Press, Cambridge, England, 1991.
3. Andersen, M. L. *Thinking about Women: Sociological and Feminist Perspectives.* Macmillan, New York, 1983.
4. Gilligan, C. *In a Different Voice: Psychological Theory and Women's Development.* Harvard University Press, Cambridge, Mass., 1982.
5. Burton, L., Dilworth-Anderson, P., and Bengston, V. Creating culturally relevant ways of thinking about aging and diversity: Theoretical challenges for the 21st century. In *Diversity: New Approaches to Ethnic Minority Aging,* edited by E. P. Stanford and F. M. Torres-Gil, pp. 129–140. Baywood, Amityville, N.Y., 1992.
6. Walton, J. Urban political economy. *Comp. Urban Res.* 7(1): 5–17, 1979.
7. Thompson, E. P. *The Making of the English Working Class.* Vintage Books, New York, 1966.

CHAPTER 1

Critical Gerontology and the New Political Economy of Aging

Carroll L. Estes

Building on our earlier work on critical gerontology (1), the political economy of aging emphasizes the broad implications of political, economic, and social relations for the aging and for society's treatment of older persons. It is a systemic view predicated upon the assumption that old age can only be understood in the context of problems and issues of the larger social order. Older Americans are viewed as a heterogeneous category. A pivotal element is the analysis of the implications of social class, gender, generation, and racial and ethnic status for all aspects of the definition, experience, and management of the elderly.

Public policy is understood as the outcome of the social struggles and the dominant, competing, and repressed interests of the period (2). Policy represents the structure and culture of advantage and disadvantage embodied in social class, racial, ethnic, gender, and age relations (3). Just as public policy both reflects and stimulates various social struggles, policy is a crucial determinant of the life chances, condition, and experience of elders in different structural locations in the society (4).

The central challenge of the political economy of aging is to understand the character and significance of variations in the treatment of the aged and to relate them to broad societal and global forces and conditions. A major task is to understand how the aging process itself is influenced by the treatment and location of elders in society. The political economy perspective requires an interdisciplinary and sociohistorical approach that draws upon anthropology, sociology, economics, political science, epidemiology, history, and health services and health policy research. It employs a multilevel analytical framework (5) of: (a) financial and industrial capital (e.g., multinational corporations); (b) the activities of the state; (c) the "aging enterprise" (3) and the medical-industrial complex; and (d) the public. This framework emphasizes structural influences upon the aging experience and recognizes the relevance of societal institutions and social relations for understanding how aging and old age are socially constructed and processed in society. Social class, race, ethnicity, and gender are seen as directly related to the resources upon which persons may draw in old age (4).

In building toward a comprehensive gerontological framework, the political economy of aging offers a theoretical and empirical perspective on the socio-economic determinants of the experience of aging and old age and on the policy interventions that emerge in the context of capitalist society. The lived experience of aging is to be understood in relation to the lives of other generations and segments of society, and these in relation to the broader material and symbolic order. The political economy perspective proposed here examines (6, p. 19):

> interrelationships between the polity, economy, and society, or more specifically, the reciprocal influences among government . . . the economy, social classes, strata, and status groups . . . [and] the manner in which the economy and polity interact in a relationship of reciprocal causation, affecting the distribution of social goods.

Work on the political economy of aging has begun to specify how the meaning and experience of old age and the distribution of resources to the aging are directed by economic, political, and sociocultural factors (3, 7–26). A major contribution of this work is its illumination of how social policy for the aged mirrors the structural arrangements of U.S. society and the distribution of material, political, and symbolic (e.g., ideological) resources within it. Public policy reflects and reinforces the "life chances" associated with each person's social location within the class, status, and political structures that comprise society (27). The lives of each succeeding generation, or subgroups within them, are similarly shaped by the extent to which social policy maintains or redistributes those life chances.

The sociohistorical, political, and economic context in which persons age and become a "problem group" is crucial for understanding the relative influence of the state and social class, gender, racial, and ethnic relations as they impinge upon the resources allocated to different subgroups of elders. Social class is broadly conceived to include the impact of economic relations and especially the relations of production and the distribution of wealth.

Questions concern the social-structural features that manifest change and elevate concepts of "private troubles" to the level of public issues at particular historical moments (28); how the definition of public issues reflects the dominance and structural location of specific interests, institutions, and classes; and how the health and subjective experiences of individuals in old age are shaped by these social forces. The structure and operation of the major societal institutions (e.g., family, workplace, and medical and welfare institutions) are of particular interest as they shape both the subjective experience and the objective condition of individual older persons.

Particularly fruitful areas of work on the political economy of aging include studies of:

- The socially and structurally produced nature of aging and the lived experience of old age as these vary by class, gender, generation, race, and ethnicity.
- Ideology as a central element in the social, economic, and political processing of the old and old age in society.

- The social construction, social control, and management of dependency by organizations and institutions, including the state.
- The types of social interventions that are legitimated and delegitimated by the dominant social construction(s) of aging.
- The role, function, and social relations of the state, employers, and employees, and how these affect the aging as they impinge upon social policy (public and private).
- The nature and consequences of social policy for the elderly, with particular attention to the effects of societal divisions of social class, gender, and racial/ethnic status.
- The "aging enterprise" (3) and its largest component, the medical-industrial complex, as industries that have enormous financial interests in controlling the definition and treatment of aging (4).
- The critical and reflexive examination of gerontological knowledge and the role of intellectuals and practitioners in the field (4, p. 347).

The focus is on aging status and social class and the intersections between them as they are structurally embedded and conditioned by economics, politics, and cultural values and beliefs in society. This approach is distinguished from other gerontological perspectives by viewing the situation of aging as the product of social structural forces rather than natural or inevitable individual biological and psychological processes. These latter perspectives, by definition, either do not explicitly address the effects on individual aging of existing structural arrangements and the import of the market in distributing rewards in old age, or take them for granted (7). In contrast, the focus of life-course and other theories of aging oriented to the individual level tends to explain the dependency status of the elderly according to individual life-course behavior or "choices" (29–31).

In contrast, the structural view of aging commences with the proposition that the status, resources, and health of the elderly, and even the trajectory of the aging process itself, are conditioned by one's location in the social structure and the relations generated by the economic mode of production and the gendered division of labor. These relations are sociohistorically framed through the interaction of economic, political, and ideological forces and the social struggles they create. The dependency of the elderly is understood as a social product of the market and the social relations it produces. Policy interventions consistent with the political economy perspective would address institutionalized structures of society such as the labor market, patriarchy (32), and racial discrimination, in contrast to interventions that would address problems on an individual level (e.g., with counseling or individual services). Four particularly promising areas of investigation and theorizing are the state, social class, gender, and racial and ethnic status and aging.

THE STATE

The political economy perspective draws heavily upon state theory; however, questions of aging are seen as central, not peripheral, to the investigation of society and the state. A central dynamic is the examination of the contradictions between the social needs of persons throughout the life course and how the organization of work (capitalist modes of production, their transformations and struggles around them) and state actions around them interact and affect these social needs. An example is in the current intensified struggles over the role of the federal government versus the market and the devolution of power to the states via welfare reform, raising questions of the right or entitlement to income or health security in old age.

Older persons are more dependent on state policy than are younger persons. Older minorities and women are more dependent upon the state than are older white men because of social disadvantage more likely to occur earlier in their life course (33, 34). Over the past several decades, women's dependence has shifted from private relations with men to public dependence on the state. Women are linked to the state in three types of status: as citizens with political rights, as clients and consumers of welfare services, and as employees in the state sector (33–36). For racial and ethnic minorities, economic disadvantage and discrimination are a jeopardy throughout the life course. These opportunity structures are profoundly important in shaping their dependency on the state through compromised life chances, including lower economic status and higher morbidity and mortality in old age.

The role and power of the state, constraints on state intervention, and state legitimacy functions in the distribution of benefits have, with few exceptions (17, 32), not been examined in direct relation to the aged, although Ginsberg (37), O'Connor (38), Gough (39), and others have indirectly addressed these issues. In the health field, however, more work within a political economy framework has been done (2, 40–47).

The study of the state is central to the understanding of old age and the life chances of elders since it has the power to (a) allocate and distribute scarce resources to ensure the survival and growth of the economy, (b) mediate between the different segments and classes of society, and (c) ameliorate social conditions that could threaten the existing order. The power of the state, moreover, extends beyond the distribution of resources to the formation and reformation of social patterns (48). For example, the state does more than regulate institutions and relations such as marriage and motherhood since it manages them (48). The state actually constitutes "the social categories of the gender order," as "patriarchy is both constructed and contested through the state" (48). Similarly, relations associated with age, racial/ethnic status, and class are constructed and contested in the state. Recent battles around affirmative action exemplify how both racism and sexism are being contested in the state.

The state is comprised of major social, political, and economic institutions, including the legislative, executive, and judicial branches of government; the military and criminal justice systems; and public educational, health, and welfare institutions (49). Although there are many theories of the state (38, 50–53), most theorists agree with Max Weber's contention that the first role of the state is to assure the survival of the economic system (54).

Within the political economy perspective, state theory (55, 56) assumes the conflict paradigm, which conceives of the social order as held together by the dominance of certain groups over others. The outcomes of conflict and power struggles are posited as explanations for how society is organized and functions, and society is seen as held together by constraint rather than consensus (57). Societal institutions such as work organizations and medicine organize and operate in the ways they do because some manage to successfully impose their ideas, material interests, and actions on others. Indeed, it is argued that consent is manufactured (4, 58, 59). Within the conflict paradigm, the state is seen as actively participating in these struggles, and as reflecting various forms of interests of the most powerful. A variety of neo-Marxist and neo-Weberian theories of the state fall within this perspective.

A contrasting view of the state emerges from the social order paradigm, built on consensus theories which posit that society is held together by shared values and agreement about the way it functions (60). The liberal political and pluralist theories within the social order paradigm portray the state as a neutral entity, operating in the universal interest of all members of society. The social order paradigm has been faulted for idealizing democracy and "public choice" while overlooking the power of large-scale vested interests and the "mobilization of bias" built into interest group politics (61).

Offe and Ronge (50) identify four characteristics of the state in capitalist societies: first, property is private, and privately owned capital is the basis of the economy; second, resources generated through private profit and the growth of private wealth indirectly finance the state (e.g., through taxation); third, the state is thereby "dependent on a source of income which it does not itself organize . . . thus [it] has a general 'interest' in facilitating" the growth of private property in order to perpetuate itself (62, p. 192); and fourth, in democracies such as the United States, political elections disguise the basic fact that the resources available for distribution by the state are dependent on the success of private profit and capital reinvestment, rather than on the will of the electorate. A fifth attribute of the state is its accountability for the success of the economy; the state bears the brunt of public dissatisfaction for economic difficulties.

Elite/managerial and class theories of the state gained prominence in the 1980s. The former, sometimes called independent state theory (9), argues that state managers act, not as direct agents of the ruling class, but in the interest of preserving their own bureaucratic power (63), and that in doing so they contribute to the maintenance of the political and economic order. The state is seen as neither completely autonomous nor a tool of the capitalist class, but instead as a mediating body between power blocs (55, 64, 65). In Offe's view, "the state is an 'independent' mediator of the class struggle inherent in the capital accumulation struggle, independence hinging on the inability of both capitalist and working class to organize themselves as classes" (quoted in 55, p. 251).

Important developments in class theorizing on the state include structural and capital logic (66, 67), instrumentalist, and class struggle theories (38, 52). Structural theories emphasize the economic role of the state as "a self-contained institutional system guided by the interests of political officials and organizations" in the context of deep structural forces at work (68, p. 907; 69); structuralists theorize that no intervention is needed by capital to ensure that the state will act to maintain the system. Instrumentalist theories emphasize the state as a neutral arena for reconciling upper-class interests (70). Class struggle theories are the most fertile of recent developments in state theory, with at least three theoretical strands: mass turmoil thesis, elite dominance thesis, and power resource theory (55, 64). Each of these theories shares a vision of the state as the "material condensation of class forces," in Poulantzas's words (67). State structure incorporates the results of previous struggles and policy subject to class forces.

Significantly, much of this literature suggests that the state, rather than the mode of production, is the principal site of class struggle, hence the principal focus of analysis. This is a revision in recent Marxist thought, with politics assuming a new primacy (55). Recent efforts to revise and improve class struggle theory include the work of Jenkins and Brents (68) on political struggle theory, that of Pampel (71) on class and demographic theories, and Quadagno's work (64) on race, class, and gender. Jenkins and Brents underscore "the distinctive logic of the political struggles defined by liberal democratic capitalism" (68, p. 907), emphasizing the role of social protest and intercapitalist political competition. Pampel, building on a political resources framework developed by Hicks and Misra (72) that incorporates class, political, and demographic theories, finds that the explanation for welfare state policy toward the aging and children in the United States and elsewhere requires both demographic and class theories. Quadagno faults class theory for its inattention to the role of state policy in mediating race relations and for its blindness to "a defining feature of social provision: its organization around gender" (64, p. 14).

Pascall (73) notes that the state sustains the subordination of women through social policy based on a particular family form: the nuclear family with a male breadwinner and a dependent wife. Dependent relations are sustained by Social Security and other agencies of the welfare state that lock women into a spousal wage relationship. The state also supports this relationship through the labor market and the refusal to pay for the caring work of women (74) (see also Chapter 14). As a result of no pay or low pay to predominantly female caregivers, "the price of such caring work is economic dependence . . . [which] amounts to the exploitation of one kind of dependency to deal with another" (73, p. 29). Any comprehensive theory must articulate not only the relations between state and economy, but also those with the household (75). Thus, the role of the state in social reproduction must be examined from the position of the aging, and particularly that of women (73) and its effects on older women.

In the 1990s there has been increasing attention to the state and the generations (76), almost in direct proportion to the strength of the crisis constructions of population aging, the baby boom, and the need to balance the budget. The popularized versions of this work are being manufactured by politicians, Wall Street (77), and think tanks following the establishment of the Concord Coalition and the Bipartisan Commission on Entitlement and Tax Reform. The power struggles surrounding entitlements such as Social Security and Medicare highlight the import of research on the challenged and changing role of the state in the context of ongoing struggles between business and labor as well as social movements across the political and ideological spectrum.

Theorists explicitly working on aging and the state include John Myles in Canada (15); Anne Marie Guillemard in France (23, 24); Jill Quadagno (64, 70, 76, 78) and Carroll Estes and her colleagues (1, 3, 4, 32, 79, 80, 81) in the United

States; and several British scholars including Alan Walker (82, 83) and Chris Phillipson (84).

The state and state policy on aging need to be examined more closely in terms of how each promotes and reproduces the dominant institutions. One example is the consideration of how state policies that treat aging issues as individual and medical problems (e.g., requiring medical services that are sold for a profit through managed care corporations) are ideologically and practically consistent with state roles in the process of capital accumulation and in legitimation of capitalist social relations through processes of social control (e.g., welfare and middle-class entitlements such as Medicare) and social integration (e.g., democratic processes). The political economy perspective renders the aged and state policy intrinsic parts of the broader phenomenon of crisis construction and management in advanced capitalism and considers how the aged and old age policy are used in these processes (81). The task is to specify how the aged and state policy are implicated in crisis formation and trajectory and the role of ideology therein.

SOCIAL CLASS

According to Giddens (85), there is widespread confusion and ambiguity in use of the term, "class." This seems particularly so for those who have attempted analysis of aging and class (25, 86–88). Gerontology from a political economy perspective demands attention to social class; nevertheless, work on the topic is surprisingly underdeveloped. James Dowd remains one of the few who has examined exchange, power, and class issues in the negotiation of exchange rates between the aged and others in society. Dowd notes that "the individual experience of growing old and the nature of age relations vary so significantly by social class that there is a need for unified analysis in which both age and class are considered" (25, pp. 21–22).

One difficulty in applying class theory to the aged is that the elderly are no longer in the socially defined "productive" sector of the economy (25). Yet, this is precisely the point of examination critical to the political economy approach (8, 9, 21, 22). In capitalist society, the relation of social class and age is profoundly influenced by the fact that being old is characterized by disattachment from the productive process. Although retirement alters class dynamics by removing the aged from the immediate relations of the workplace, these relations continue to "live" as part of the individual retiree's everyday life and in the relationships among retirees with common work histories. They are extremely important in old age (21), affecting post-retirement life expectancy and multiple aspects of quality of life. Nevertheless, this disattachment from the productive process, as defined in the traditional Marxist sense, means that the relations of the workplace do not constitute the primary dynamic of class relations for the aged.

One particularly useful concept of class is the Ehrenreich and Ehrenreich definition of class in terms of a "common relation to the economic foundations of society" (89). Class is "characterized by a coherent social and cultural existence; members of a class share a common life style, educational background, kinship networks, consumption patterns, work habits, and beliefs" (89, p. 11). This conceptualization of class may be of special importance to the study of age and class because it is concerned with dynamics that continue operating for elders when they are no longer in the workplace. In particular, it is a concept that embraces the relationship between the aged who receive state benefits and the agents of public and private social welfare bureaucracies. Although the Ehrenreichs note that there is no easy way to define class for some categories of professional workers as a group, certain professional–client relationships can be seen as inherently class relationships. In this sense, the professionals, bureaucrats, and service providers who constitute the "aging enterprise" (3) and the medical-industrial complex contribute to the dependency of the aged, and both exert social control over them. The resulting systems of services reinforce preexisting class relationships (90). Similar observations can be made for the design and delivery of services and the resulting gender and racial/ethnic hierarchies imposed through social welfare services in which "the professionalization and bureaucratization of care has made room for men at the top" (73, p. 31). By extension, the policies that have created and sustained the "aging enterprise" and the medical-industrial complex (3, 14, 91) constitute an important part of class relations and of the reproduction of class relations among the elderly and different subgroups of the elderly.

The dependent status of many older persons subjects them, to a greater degree than younger persons, to the social relations of subordination to public and private service agencies that act to reproduce capitalist culture and class relations. Analyses of class and age need to be concerned with understanding how individual elders, given their unique biographies and historical moment, are made differentially dependent according to their pre-retirement social class, gender, and racial and ethnic status. For example, a "differential process of devaluation" occurs based on class and gender (91). Working-class elders, and particularly minority elders, are more rapidly devalued in the labor market and in the society as a whole than are the aged of other classes. Similarly, women, whose labor is not generally considered productive, are more devalued than men in old age (92).

Property ownership and income sources continue to serve as the basis of class divisions in old age just as they do earlier in the life course, and these divisions are reinforced by social welfare policy. However, according to Wright's (93) definition of class, the ownership of wealth without effective control over investment and physical means of production leaves even the wealthy elderly on the periphery of the class dynamics of the larger society. Several important issues are raised. For example, how is the social class of elderly men to be assessed when retirement severs connection to the means of production and their economic status deteriorates with fixed incomes and advancing age? With the loss of work (94) and major workplace restructuring that is touching white males, this is particularly relevant.

Questions of age and social class are further compounded when we explicitly take gender into account. Are older women in their own, or their husband's class? And is this class of pre-retirement "origin" (e.g., in younger age) or the social class of "destination" in old age, based on retirement income and assets? When an older male spouse dies, the economic status of the surviving female spouse often changes dramatically, usually negatively (95). A similar result is likely to occur with divorce. For an older woman who experiences such a change in marital status (widowhood or divorce), is her social class derived from (i.e., mediated by) the class of her (former or late) husband, or from her own (likely, downwardly mobile) direct relation to productively derived resources? The issue of direct and mediated class location is profoundly important (96) and has implications both for social class identification and for the "treatment" of the condition of older women through state policy.

Consideration needs to be given to both the differential implications of retirement and old age by social class and the implications of retirement and old age for class relationships—and both according to gender and racial and ethnic status. The fact that most of the aged must face life on a fixed income is itself both a reflection of class relations and a factor in the analysis of class and aging. While the analysis of social class and aging may present different problems than does a more general analysis of the class dynamics of society, the consideration of class theory needed to "account for" the aged is likely to shed light on class analysis in general, especially as it deals with other "nonproductive" groups.

A promising area of inquiry concerns how the state uses social policy for the elderly to deal with the cross-pressures on the state to promote conditions favorable to business, while also providing sufficient benefits to those left behind by the market to ensure loyalty to the existing system. It is important to differentiate conditions under which class-based coalitions emerge and override age interests, and those under which status issues such as age or generation account for state policy outcomes. This work will illuminate the interconnections between class and status in political movements and their consequences for societal treatment of the aged.

GENDER

A major underdeveloped area of great significance in the political economy of aging concerns the differential gendered consequences of aging from a life-course perspective. Substantial developments have occurred in the past two decades in feminist theoretical and empirical work relevant to social policy (35, 73, 75, 97–99).

Joan Acker (100) asks to what extent the overall institutional structure of the state—and, by inference, the major policy of Social Security—has "been formed by and through gender." A crucial question is: "How are men's interests and masculinity of certain kinds intertwined in the creation and maintenance of particular institutions [such as the state], and how have the subordination and exclusion of women been built into ordinary institutional functioning?" (100, p. 568). Contributing the concept of "gendered institutions," in which "gender is present in the processes, practices, images and ideologies and distributions of power in the various sectors of social life" (100, p. 567), Acker contends that gender is a dimension of "domination and discrimination [that is] neither obviously discrete nor structurally analogous [to social class and race]. Class relations do not function in the same way as gender relations; race relations are still another matter. All of these come together in cross-cutting ways" (100, p. 566). She observes that both the state and the economy, among other institutions, have been developed and dominated by men; therefore they have been "symbolically interpreted from the standpoint of men [as they have been] defined by the absence of women" (100, p. 567).

An important contribution to feminist theory and race is the work of Collins (101) on "standpoint" in black feminist theory that acknowledges the struggle of oppressed persons for self-definition, involving "tapping sources of everyday, unarticulated consciousness [that is] traditionally denigrated in white male controlled institutions" (101, p. 28). Collins's description of the interlocking systems of race, class, and gender oppression (101, p. 68) and their linkage to the work on standpoint theory illustrates the approach of the political economy perspective that is advanced in this chapter. It seeks to address and link the personal experience of age and aging from the subject's standpoint to the various complex and interrelated dimensions of the structural locations in which we find the individual older person.

The relationships between and among social class, gender, race, ethnicity, and age are significant theoretical and empirical problems (102) that must be addressed at the macro, meso, and micro levels in present and future work on the political economy of aging.

Acker maintains correctly that theories of the state and class that do not explicitly and adequately address the subordination of women and the "privileging of men" fail as comprehensive frameworks for understanding social phenomena (98). She observes that (a) "understanding class and gender discrimination and exploitation is integral to understanding the place (and oppression) of women [and, we would add, older women] in industrial capitalist societies," and (b) the relations that produce class are gendered processes, structured through relations of distribution as well as relations of production. Personal relations (particularly marriage), the wage, and the state are all locations of gendered distribution. Distribution is vitally affected by the dominance of market relations as the basis of distribution and the indifference of the economic system to the reproduction of the working class and the demands of working-class daily life (98, p. 479).

The focus on reproductive relations has at least two major redeeming features for the political economy of aging. First, it places the gendered division of labor and the unpaid (informal) work of women throughout the life course squarely at the center of analysis, explaining much about the condition and situation of older women in the United States (92). Second, attention to the concept of social reproduction offers the potential of casting a new and more accurate light on the role of both women and the elderly (men and women) in the daily activity of the productive sphere, since it moves beyond the traditional labor market concept of production with its inherent age and gender bias (103). With the concept of social reproduction, the elderly may be seen as contributing to the creation and use of new medical technologies (a form of created consumption) that are instrumental in the development and expansion of a large and profitable medical-industrial complex. The commodification of the needs of the elderly (3) and the state role in underwriting this complex (e.g., state-financed third-party reimbursement) illustrate how the elderly support the economy (i.e., in reproducing the capitalist system).

Caregiving and the ideology of community care legitimate minimal state activity in long-term care by defining this type of care as the private sphere of home and family (73, 83, 104, 105). Thus, under state policies of devolution (see Chapter 9), even more caring work may be transferred from the formal to the informal sector when the state is pressured to redirect its resources from meeting human needs to underwriting various aspects of capital accumulation (85) and to the interstate competition to attract and maintain capital investment (106) (see Chapter 9). Examples are the case of hospital cost containment under Medicare prospective payment, when the lengths of hospital stays were reduced and millions of days of hospital care were transferred to the labor of families and the community (107); and, more recently, for-profit managed care, which is further compressing hospital days of care. In place of ignoring these costs, Burggraf (108) describes the "feminine economy of care-giving" that operates in U.S. society and recommends a model of investment and incentives that recognize the enormous value and cost (time, labor, and opportunity costs) of women's unpaid labor in nurturing and protecting society's human capital.

THE SYMBOLIC AND CULTURAL

The sociology of culture has become an influential part of the study of social institutions such as the state (109–112). The classic theoretical opposition of culture versus structure has given way in the 1980s and 1990s to an understanding of the importance of the interplay of structural and cultural factors (109, p. 103). The cultural and symbolic are reflected in the ideas, beliefs, ideologies, and meanings that are part of the construction and definition of aging as a problem that societies produce. An essential factor affecting the state and aging is the nation's cultural commitment to individualism, which blames problems on individuals rather than the system (109, p. 96). Consciousness is a product of culture (110–112) that profoundly shapes the experience we have in aging and all stages of the life course. One's identity in terms of age, gender, and race is an essential element of this conscious-ness and experience. The symbolic and cultural elements of the political economy of aging are incorporated in the development of the constructionist perspective on aging (3) and the moral economy approach to aging (see Chapter 2).

The power of symbols, language, concepts, and labeling is repeatedly demon-strated (113, 114). Symbolic interactionist, labeling, and deviance theories delineate the significance of social perceptions in the processing and treatment of individuals as members of collective groups in society (114–116). The experience of growing old is socially "produced" in that it is neither immutable nor "given" by the character of external reality (3, 117).

How old age is regarded by members of a society is also socially constructed by the attributions and imputations of others, which are differentially influenced by those with sufficient power to impose their constructions of reality (3), thereby controlling the dominant reality. These attributions, in turn, shape how old age is processed and treated by society. The conceptualizations of old age as an illness and as an economic crisis for society are socially created in the sense that they are not determined solely by objective facts. Two processes create these construc-tions: first, the interpretation and ordering of perceptions of "facts" into ways of thinking, and second, the relative power and influence of those who interpret and disseminate the facts (118). In this sense, the problems of the elderly are only those that experts, policymakers, and the media define as "real" (3). Such attributions are framed by available theories, methodologies, and research data that channel the conceptualization, conduct, analysis, and interpretation of data, as well as by the dominant cultural, economic, and political forces and intellectual fashions of the period (118).

An important aspect of the link between the micro and the macro is found in the different ways in which the aged are defined and treated, and their relation both to one's interpersonal relations and self-concept (119–122) and to the structural arrangements and resource disparities in the society. Problem-definitions and policy solutions are best understood in terms of power relations (123). Much labeling of the aged involves a focus on physical debility and physiological decline (3). Elders are expected to adopt the characteristics of the sick role even when there is no medically diagnosed pathology (124). Sick role expectations (60) applied to old people include withdrawal from the social world, reduction of normal social and occupational responsibilities, and dependency on others in an imbalanced power relationship (124).

Those who control the definitions of aging used in public policy in effect control access to old age benefits such as medical care as well as the costs and structure of care (125). Currently, public money and professional effort are disproportionately expended on acute rather than chronic care and on institutional (hospital and nursing home) rather than social supportive services for the elderly. Both reflect a definition of health and health care in old age that is a product of the professional dominance of medicine and consistent with a profitable medical care industry.

The myth of pervasive debility in old age persists and may become self-fulfilling in the loss of effectiveness and personal control (121). Insinuations of loss of competence and mental illness in old age are two vehicles that usher the elderly into productive custody and long-term care institutions where they are particularly susceptible to external management. Attributions of physical decline and personal incompetence to the aging process effectively depoliticize (126) issues related to institutionalization and legal control, while focusing attention on the individual and individual treatment rather than the social situation creating the need for treatment.

CONCLUSION

The political economy of aging directs attention to the relationship of the treatment and experience of old age in the capitalist economy in a global context involving worldwide economic and political conditions (127–129). The task of the political economy of aging is to locate society's treatment of the aged in the context of the economy (global and U.S.), the state, the conditions of the labor market, and the class, sex, race, and age divisions in society. Serious consideration of the relationship of capitalism to aging is required (84, 130). Issues to be examined include the dilemmas and contradictions in maintaining both a market economy and democracy—that is, jointly advancing public interest in a democracy and private profit through capitalism.

Social policy on aging is a product of the tensions between the state, capital, and labor in working through the contradictions of capital and the crisis tendencies they create (81). Aging policy is a major battleground on which the social struggles presently engulfing the state are being fought as the nation attempts to address the tensions between capitalism and democracy. Important considerations are the ways in which state policies are ideologically and practically consistent with the state role in the process of capital accumulation and its legitimation through processes of social control and social integration. It is equally important to consider how the aged and aging policy contribute to problems of the state, capital, and/or labor, and in what respects. Aging policy needs to be examined more closely in terms of how it promotes and reproduces the dominant institutions and the role of ideology in these processes. The moral economy approach proposed in this volume (see Chapter 2) will contribute to understanding the role of cultural beliefs, values, and norms undergirding societal institutions and practices vitally affecting the old.

The construction of population aging as a crisis reflects aspects of two ideological dimensions. First, the concept of the "demographic imperative" created a rallying point for those who argue that the elderly are living too long, consuming too many societal resources, and robbing the young—an argument used to justify rollbacks of state benefits for the aged (131–133). Additional anti-statist sentiments have been expressed in the unfounded contention that state policy to provide formal long-term care will encourage abdication of family responsibility for the aging, which, it is then erroneously argued, will bankrupt the state. This line of reasoning is consistent with continuing refusal of the state to provide for long-term care, reinforcing the nation's long-term care policy that such care is (and should remain) the responsibility of the informal sector and the unpaid labor of women. In addition, managed care is accelerating pressures on unpaid caregivers for post-acute care, as "drive by" mastectomies and other such outpatient procedures require increased care in the home for very sick patients.

Second, the projected chronic illness burden of pandemic proportions (another version of the crisis) has been useful in the Reagan administration's and subsequent ideological warfare on health care as a right and has contributed to the social production of another crisis construction—the unaffordability of the baby boom generation and the intergenerational tensions that presumably go with it. One result of this construct is that the elderly have been accused of crippling the state and capital with unsupportable demands. Daniel Callahan's (134) argument that society must "set limits" on the aged is a case in point, for it indicts those who advocate for elderly rights as encouraging "unreasonable," "unfair," and "selfish" expectations in the old concerning life expectancy, quality of life, and societal allocations. One aspect of this intergenerational struggle is the battle for the intellectual high ground in constructing and researching resource and equity issues for the elderly (133). The seriousness and import of this struggle are reflected in the crucial role played by intellectuals both in maintaining the status quo and in advocating meaningful sociohistorical change (135).

The political economy approach to aging is based on the following premises:

- Coercion and social struggles between the more and less powerful are the means by which the status quo and, conversely, social change are imposed and/or maintained.
- The social structure shapes how older individuals are perceived and how they perceive themselves, affecting their sense of worth and power.
- Attributional labels applied to the elderly shape not only the experience of old age, but also societal decisions concerning public policy for the elderly.
- Social policy and the politics of aging mirror the inequalities in social structure and the outcomes of power struggles around those structured arrangements. As

such, policy is neither neutral nor quixotic, it reflects the advantage and disadvantage of business and workers, whites and nonwhites, and men and women in society.

- Social policy reflects the dominant ideologies and belief systems that enforce, bolster, and extend the structure of advantage and disadvantage in the larger economic, political, and social order.

In summary, the political economy of aging is attendant to the sociostructural and cultural forces that underlie the conditions and dynamics of aging and aging policy. It is essentially concerned with class, gender, generational, and racial and ethnic divisions in society as these explain resource distributions in old age as a function of the relations of capital and the state. The political economy perspective is, by definition, sensitive to the integral connections between macro-structural conditions and the cultural and micro-level dimensions of the private and most intimate experiences of old age.

Acknowledgments — This chapter is built in part upon a number of my earlier co-authored books, chapters and articles on the political economy of aging. I gratefully acknowledge my co-authors on this earlier work, Karen W. Linkins, Elizabeth Binney, James H. Swan, Lenora Gerard, and Jane Zones, for their many contributions.

REFERENCES

1. Estes, C. L. Toward a sociology of political gerontology. *Sociol. Symp.* 26: 1–18, 1979.
2. Alford, R. The political economy of health care: Dynamics without change. *Polit. Soc.* 2: 127–164, 1972.
3. Estes, C. L. *The Aging Enterprise.* Jossey-Bass, San Francisco, 1979.
4. Estes, C. L., Linkins, K. W., and Binney, E. A. The political economy of aging. In *Handbook of Aging and the Social Sciences,* Ed. 4, edited by R. Binstock and L. George. Academic Press, New York, 1995.
5. McKinlay, J. B. (ed.). *Issues in the Political Economy of Health.* Methuen Tavistock, New York, 1984.
6. Walton, J. Urban political economy. *Comp. Urban Res.* 7(1): 5–17, 1979.
7. Walker, A. The social creation of poverty and dependency in old age. *J. Soc. Policy* 9: 49–75, 1980.
8. Walker, A. Towards a political economy of old age. *Ageing Soc.* 1(1): 73–94, 1981.
9. Townsend, P. The structured dependency of the elderly: A creation of social policy in the twentieth century. *Ageing Soc.* 1: 6, 1981.
10. Townsend, P. *The Last Refuge.* Routledge and Kegan Paul, London, 1962.
11. Townsend, P. *Poverty in the United Kingdom.* Penguin Books, Harmondsworth, Middlesex, 1979.
12. Townsend, P., and Wedderbum, D. *The Aged in the Welfare State.* Bell, London, 1965.
13. Estes, C. L., Swan, J., and Gerard, L. Dominant and competing paradigms in gerontology: Toward a political economy of ageing. *Ageing Soc.* 2(2): 151–164, 1982.
14. Olson, L. *Political Economy of Aging.* Columbia University Press, New York, 1982.
15. Myles, J. F. The aged, the state, and the structure of inequality. In *Structural Inequality in Canada,* edited by J. Harp and J. Hofley, pp. 317–342. Prentice-Hall, Toronto, 1980.

16. Myles, J. F. Income inequality and status maintenance. *Res. Aging* 3: 123–141, 1981.
17. Myles, J. F. The Aged and the Welfare State: An Essay in Political Demography. Paper presented at the International Sociological Association, Research Committee on Aging, Paris, July 8–9, 1981.
18. Myles, J. F. *The Political Economy of Public Pensions.* Little, Brown, Boston, 1984.
19. Nelson, G. Social class and public policy for the elderly. *Soc. Serv. Rev.* 6(1): 85–107, 1982.
20. Tussing, A. The dual welfare system. In *Social Realities,* edited by L. Horowitz and C. Levy. Harper and Row, New York, 1971.
21. Guillemard, A. M. Retirement as a Social Process: Its Differential Effects upon Behavior. Communication presented at the 8th World Congress of Sociology, Toronto, Canada, August 21, 1974.
22. Guillemard, A. M. State, society and old age policy in France: From 1945 to the current crisis. *Soc. Sci. Med.* 23(12): 1319–1326, 1986.
23. Guillemard, A. M. The making of old age policy in France. In *Old Age and the Welfare State,* edited by A. M. Guillemard. International Sociological Association, Sage, New York, 1983.
24. Guillemard, A. M. *Le Decline du social, formation et crise des politiques de la vieillesse.* Presses Universitaires de France, Paris, 1986.
25. Dowd, J. *Stratification Among the Aged.* Brooks/Cole, Monterey, Calif., 1980.
26. Evans, L., and Williamson, J. Social security and social control. *Generations* 6(2): 18–20, 1981.
27. Weber, M. Class, status and party. In *From Max Weber: Essays in Sociology,* edited and translated by H. H. Gerth and C. W. Mills. Oxford University Press, New York, 1946.
28. Mills, C. W. *The Power Elite.* Oxford University Press, New York, 1956.
29. Henretta, J., and Campbell, R. Status attainment and status maintenance: A case study of stratification in old age. *Am. Sociol. Rev.* 41: 981–992, 1976.
30. Samuelson, R. J. Benefit programs for the elderly: Off limits to federal budget. *National J.* 13(40), 1981.
31. Baum, M., and Baum, R. C. *Growing Old.* Prentice-Hall, New York, 1980.
32. Estes, C. L., et al. *Political Economy, Health and Aging.* Little, Brown, Boston, 1984.
33. Hernes, H. *Welfare State and Woman Power.* Norwegian University Press, Oslo, 1987.
34. Markides, K. S., and Black, S. A. Race, ethnicity and aging: The impact of inequality. In *Handbook of Aging and the Social Sciences,* Ed. 4, edited by R. Binstock and L. George, pp. 153–170. Academic Press, New York, 1995.
35. Sassoon, A. *Women and State.* Hutchinson, London, 1987.
36. Estes, C. L., Gerard, L., and Clark, A. Women and the economics of aging. *Int. J. Health Serv.* 14(1): 55–68, 1984.
37. Ginsberg, N. *Class, Capital and Social Policy.* Macmillan, London, 1979.
38. O'Connor, J. *The Fiscal Crisis of the State.* St. Martin's Press, New York, 1973.
39. Gough, I. *The Political Economy of the Welfare State.* Macmillan, London, 1979.
40. Kelman, S. (ed.). Special Section on Political Economy of Health. *Int. J. Health Serv.* 5(4): 535–642, 1975.
41. Renaud, M. On the structural constraints to state intervention in health. *Int. J. Health Serv.* 5(4): 559–571, 1975.
42. Renaud, M. Special Issue on the Political Economy of Health. *Rev. Rad. Polit. Econ.* 9, Spring 1977.
43. Lichtman, R. The political economy of medical care. In *The Social Organization of Health,* edited by H. Dreitzel, pp. 265–290. Macmillan, New York, 1971.
44. Navarro, V. *Medicine Under Capitalism.* Prodist, New York, 1976.

45. Navarro, V. (ed.). *Health and Medical Care in the U.S.: A Critical Analysis.* Baywood, Amityville, N.Y., 1973.
46. Navarro, V. *Why The United States Does Not Have a National Health Program.* Baywood, Amityville, N.Y., 1996.
47. Bond, P., and Weissman, R. The costs of mergers and acquisitions in the U.S. health care sector. *Int. J. Health Serv.* 27(1): 77–87, 1997.
48. Connell, R. W. *Gender and Power.* Stanford University Press, Stanford, Calif., 1987.
49. Waitzkin, H. *The Second Sickness: Contradictions of Capitalist Health Care.* Free Press, New York, 1986.
50. Offe, C., and Ronge, V. Thesis on the theory of the state. In *Classes, Power and Conflict,* edited by A. Giddens and D. Held, pp. 249–256. University of California Press, Berkeley, 1982.
51. Frankel, B. On the state of the state: Marxist theories of the state after Leninism. In *Classes, Power and Conflict,* edited by A. Giddens and D. Held. University of California Press, Berkeley, 1982.
52. O'Connor, J. *Accumulation Crisis.* Basil Blackwell, New York, 1984.
53. Gough, I. *The Political Economy of the Welfare State.* Macmillan, London, 1979.
54. Navarro, V. The political economy of medical care. *Int. J. Health Serv.* 5(1): 65–94, 1975.
55. Carnoy, M. *The State and Political Theory.* Princeton University Press, Princeton, N.J., 1984.
56. Vincent, A. The nature of the state. In *Theories of the State.* Basil Blackwell, New York, 1987.
57. Collins, R. Comparative approach to political sociology. In *State and Society,* exited by R. Bendix et al. Little, Brown, Boston, 1968.
58. Gramsci, A. *Selections from the Prison Notebooks,* edited and translated by Q. Hoare and G. Nowell Mith. Lawrence and Wishart, London, 1972.
59. Buroway, M. *Manufacturing Consent: Changes in the Labor Process under Monopoly Capitalism.* University of Chicago Press, Chicago, 1979.
60. Parsons, T. *The Social System.* Free Press, New York, 1951.
61. Schattschneider, E. E. *The Semi-Sovereign People.* Holt, New York, 1960.
62. Giddens, A., and Held, D. (eds). *Classes, Power and Conflict: Classical and Contemporary Debates.* University of California Press, Berkeley, 1982.
63. Skocpol, T. *States and Social Revolutions: A Comparative Analysis of France, Russia, and China.* Cambridge University Press, Cambridge, England, 1979.
64. Quadagno, J. Race, class, and gender in the U.S. welfare state: Nixon's failed family assistance plan. *Am. Sociol. Rev.* 55: 11–28, 1990.
65. Block, F. The ruling class does not rule: Notes on the Marxist theory of the state. *Socialist Revol.* 33: 6–28, 1977.
66. Althusser, L. *Lenin and Philosophy and Other Essays.* Monthly Review Press, New York, 1972.
67. Poulantzas, N. *State, Power, Socialism.* Verso, New Left Books, London, 1980.
68. Jenkins, J., and Brents, J. Social protest, hegemonic competition, and social reform: A political struggle interpretation of the origins of the American welfare state. *Am. Sociol. Rev.* 54: 891–909, 1989.
69. Gold, G., Lo, C., and Wright, E. O. Recent developments in Marxist theories of the state. *Monthly Rev.* 5(6): 29–43, 1975.
70. Quadagno, J. Welfare capitalism and the Social Security Act of 1935. *Am. Sociol. Rev.* 49: 632–647, 1984.

71. Pampel, F. C. Population aging: Class context and age inequality in public spending. *Am. J. Sociol.* 100(1): 153–159, 1994.
72. Hicks, A., and Misra, J. Political resources and the growth of welfare in affluent capitalist democracies, 1960–82. *Am. J. Sociol.* 99: 668–710, 1993.
73. Pascall, G. The family and women's work. In *Sociol Policy: A Feminist Analysis.* Tavistock, New York, 1986.
74. Finch, J., and Groves, D. *A Labour of Love: Women, Work and Caring.* Routledge and Kegan Paul, London, 1983.
75. Dickinson, J., and Russell, B. (eds). *Family, Economy and State.* Garamond Press, Toronto, 1986.
76. Street, D., and Quadagno, J. The state, the elderly, and the intergenerational contract: Toward a new political economy of aging. In *Societal Impact on Aging,* edited by K. W. Schaie and W. A. Achenbaum. Springer, New York, 1993.
77. Peterson, P. G. *Will America Grow Up Before it Grows Old?* Random House, New York, 1996.
78. Quadagno, J. *The Transformation of Old Age Security: Class and Politics in the American Welfare State.* University of Chicago Press, Chicago, 1988.
79. Estes, C. L. Crisis, the welfare state, and aging. *Gerontologist,* 1997, in press.
80. Estes, C. L. The politics of ageing in America. *Ageing Soc.* 6(2): 121–134, 1986.
81. Estes, C. L. The Reagan legacy: Privatization, the welfare state and aging. In *Old Age and the Welfare State,* edited by J. Quadagno and J. Myles. Temple University Press, Philadelphia, 1990.
82. Walker, A. Intergenerational Relations and Welfare Restructuring: The Social Construction of a Generational Problem. Paper presented at the Conference on the New Contract Between the Generations: Social Science Perspectives on Cohorts in the 21st Century. University of Southern California, Los Angeles, 1991.
83. Walker, A. Community care and the elderly in Great Britain: Theory and practice. In *Readings in the Political Economy of Aging,* edited by M. Minkler and C. L. Estes. Baywood, Amityville, N.Y., 1984.
84. Phillipson, C. *Capitalism and the Construction of Old Age.* Macmillan, London, 1982.
85. Giddens, A. *The Class Structure of the Advanced Societies.* Harper and Row, New York, 1975.
86. Atchley, R. C. Social class and aging. *Generations* 6(2): 16–17, 1981.
87. Streib, G. Social stratification and aging. In *Handbook of Aging and the Social Sciences,* edited by R. Binstock and E. Shanas, pp. 339–368. Van Nostrand Reinhold, New York, 1985.
88. Riley, M. W. Social gerontology and the age stratification of society. *Gerontologist* 11(1, Pt. 1): 79–87, 1971.
89. Ehrenreich, B., and Ehrenreich, J. The professional managerial class. In *Between Labor and Capital,* edited by P. Walker, p. 5. South End Press, Boston, 1979.
90. Sjoberg, G., Brymer, R. A., and Farris, B. Bureaucracy and the lower class. *Sociol. Soc. Res.* 50: 325–334, 1966.
91. Nelson, G. Social class and public policy for the elderly. *Soc. Serv. Rev.* 56(1): 85–107, 1982.
92. Estes, C. L., and Binney, E. A. Older Women and the State. Unpublished manuscript. Institute for Health and Aging, University of California, San Francisco, 1990.
93. Wright, E. O. *Class, Crisis and the State.* Verso, London, 1978.
94. Rifkin, J. R. *The End of Work.* Putnam's Son, New York, 1995.

95. Burkhauser, R. V., and Smeeding, T. M. Social Security Reform: A Budget Neutral Approach to Reducing Older Women's Disproportionate Risk of Poverty. *Policy Brief,* 2. Maxwell School Center for Policy Research, Syracuse, N.Y., 1994.
96. Wright, E. O. Women in the class structure. *Polit. Soc.* 17(1): 35–66, 1989.
97. Abramovitz, M. *Regulating the Lives of Women.* South End Press, Boston, 1988.
98. Acker, J. Class, gender, and the relations of distribution. *Signs* 13(3): 473–493, 1988.
99. Redclift, N. The contested domain: Gender, accumulation, and the labour process. In *Beyond Employment,* edited by N. Redclift and E. Mingione. Basil Blackwell, New York, 1985.
100. Acker, J. Gendered institutions. *Contemp. Sociol.* 21(5): 565–595, 1992.
101. Collins, P. H. *Black Feminist Thought.* Unwin Hyman, London, 1990.
102. Jones, V. J., and Estes, C. L. Older women: Income, retirement, and health. In *Women's Health: Complexities and Differences,* edited by S. B. Ruzek, V. L. Olesen, and A. E. Clarke. Ohio State University Press, Columbus, 1997.
103. Binney, E. A. Personal communication, 1990.
104. Binney, E. A., Estes, C. L., and Humphers, S. Informalization and community care. In *The Long Term Care Crisis,* edited by C. L. Estes et al. Sage, Newbury Park, Calif., 1993.
105. Estes, C. L., and Swan, J. H. No care zone and social policy. In *The Long Term Care Crisis,* edited by C. L. Estes et al. Sage, Newbury Park, Calif., 1993.
106. Peterson, P. E., and Rom, M. L. *Welfare Magnets.* Brookings Institution, Washington, D.C., 1990.
107. Estes, C. L., et al. *The Long Term Care Crisis.* Sage, Newbury Park, Calif., 1993.
108. Burggraf, S. P. *The Feminine Economy and Economic Man.* Addison Wesley, Reading, Mass., 1997.
109. Griswold, W. *Cultures and Societies in a Changing World.* Pine Forge Press, Thousand Oaks, Calif., 1994.
110. Wuthnow, R. *Poor Richard's Principle: Recovering the American Dream through the Moral Dimension of Work, Business and Money.* Princeton University Press, Princeton, N.J., 1996.
111. Wuthnow, R. State structures and ideological outcomes. *Am. Sociol. Rev.* 50: 799–821, 1995.
112. Wuthnow, R., and Witten, R. New directions in the study of culture. *Annu. Rev. Sociol.* 14: 49–67, 1998.
113. Estes, C. L. Construction of reality: Problems of aging. *J. Soc. Issues* 36(2): 117–132, 1980.
114. Becker, H. S. *Outsiders.* Free Press of Glencoe, New York, 1963.
115. Matza, D. *Becoming Deviant.* Prentice Hall, Englewood Cliffs, N.J., 1969.
116. Conrad, P., and Schneider, J. W. *Deviance and Medicalization: From Badness to Sickness.* Mosby, St. Louis, 1980.
117. Gusfield, J. Literary rhetoric of science. *Am. Sociol. Rev.* 41: 1–33, 1976.
118. Gouldner, A. *The Coming Crisis of Western Sociology.* Basic Books, New York, 1970.
119. Thomas, W. I. *The Unadjusted Girl.* Gannor, Santa Fe, N.M., 1970.
120. Scott, R., *The Making of Blind Men.* Russell Sage Foundation, New York, 1970.
121. Rodin, J., and Langer, E. Aging labels: The decline of control and the fall of self esteem. *J. Soc. Issues* 36(2): 12–29, 1980.
122. Rodin, J. Sense of control: Potentials for intervention. *Annals* 503: 29–42, 1989.
123. Friedson, E. *Profession of Medicine.* Dodd, Mead, New York, 1970.
124. Arluke, A., and Peterson, J. Accidental medicalization of old age and its social control implications. In *Dimensions: Aging, Culture, and Health,* edited by C. L. Frye. J. F. Bergen, Brooklyn, N.Y., 1981.

125. Estes, C. L., and Binney, E. A. The biomedicalization of aging: Dangers and dilemmas. *Gerontologist* 29(5): 587–596, 1989.
126. Zola, I. K. *Disabling Professions.* Marion Boyers, Boston, 1977.
127. Amin, S., et al. (eds). *Dynamics of Global Crisis.* Monthly Review Press, New York, 1982.
128. Mandel, E. *The Second Slump: A Marxist Analysis of Recession in the Seventies.* New Left Books, London, 1978.
129. Castells, M. *The Economic Crisis and American Society.* Princeton University Press, Princeton, N.J., 1980.
130. Myles, J. F. Conflict, crisis and the future of old age security. *Milbank Mem. Fund Q.* 61: 4, 1983.
131. Minkler, M. Blaming the aged victim: The politics of retrenchment in times of fiscal conservatism. In *Readings in the Political Economy of Aging,* edited by M. Minkler and C. L. Estes. Baywood, Amityville, N.Y., 1984.
132. Binney, E. A., and Estes, C. L. The retreat of the state and its transfer of responsibility: The intergenerational war. *Int. J. Health Serv.* 18(1): 83–96, 1988.
133. Binney, E. A., and Estes, C. L. Setting the wrong limits: Class biases and the biographical standard. In *A Good Old Age? The Paradox of Setting Limits,* edited by P. Homer and M. Holstein. Simon and Schuster, New York, 1990.
134. Callahan, D. *Setting Limits.* Simon and Schuster, New York, 1987.
135. Gramsci, A. *Prison Letters.* Pluto Press/Unwin Hyman, London, 1988.

CHAPTER 2

Political and Moral Economy:
Getting to Know One Another

Meredith Minkler and Thomas R. Cole

As we have seen in the preceding chapter, political economy provides a valuable framework for understanding how polity, economy, and society shape the conditions, experiences, treatment, and health of older people. "The central problem of the political economy perspective," writes Walton, "is the manner in which the economy and polity interact in a relationship of reciprocal causation, affecting the distribution of social goods" (1, p. 9). The trajectory of growing old, from this perspective, is intimately tied to one's class position or location in the larger social order.

Political economy has contributed a great deal to the development of social gerontology, whose early social and psychological theories were insufficiently attuned to issues of social structure, power, ideology, and history (2). In particular, political economy has helped explain variations in the treatment of the old and has explicated the influence of race, class, gender, and labor market conditions on aging (3–5). By acknowledging the importance of historical context and social/political processes, it enables social gerontology to "tap into the dynamic interrelationships of individual and structure" (6, p. 53).

Because political economy is multiperspectival and moves across narrow disciplinary boundaries, it retains the ability to integrate related conceptual frameworks. Many political economists have taken advantage of this flexibility by including in their work careful considerations of the sociocultural dimensions of phenomena under study (cf. 7–12). Particularly over the last two decades, as Estes notes in the preceding chapter, "The classic theoretical opposition of culture versus structure has given way . . . to an understanding of the importance of the interplay of structural and cultural factors" (page 27). At the same time, however, certain mechanistic versions of political economy have continued to treat culture as a mere reflection of social structure, ignoring the elusive and contingent aspects of historical process.

We believe that cultural questions such as individuality, subjectivity, spirituality, or morality are not simply "dependent variables" to be explained by material factors (13, 14). To avoid the dangers of reductionism, political economy must make increasing conceptual room for understanding moral and existential issues not as mere epiphenomena but as necessary and irreducible elements of social processes.

37

Especially in the study of aging, where humanistic interest in these questions is growing (15–17), it has become increasingly important to tear down invisible Berlin-like walls and encourage rapprochement if not reunification. By exploring the concept and uses of moral economy, this chapter suggests one line of thought that can enrich the political economy of aging.

This chapter begins by examining the uneasiness around moral questions that has tended to characterize Marxist political economy in the tradition of "Scientific Marxism" (18). We suggest that concerns with justice, rights, fairness, and obligations—which Marx rejected in his later writings as illegitimate and ideological—serve some positive functions (e.g., in protecting against certain forms of oppression), which should not be overlooked. We then introduce the concept of moral economy, or collectively shared assumptions defining norms of reciprocity (19), as a useful complement to political economy, making possible a richer and more thorough analysis than either can achieve independently. The origins of the concept of moral economy and its applications will be highlighted. The chapter ends with a discussion of the usefulness of this concept in enriching our understanding of aging. We make a case for integrating moral economy into a broader political economy perspective, and for applying Marx's ideas about "emancipated morality" to the political economy of aging.

MARXISM AND MORAL QUESTIONS:
A CASE STUDY IN AMBIVALENCE

In the Marxist tradition of political economy, moral questions in general have been treated with ambivalence, if not repression (20, 21). This treatment derives from a paradox embedded in Marx's own idea about morality (20–22), particularly in his later years when, as Gouldner suggests, Scientific Marxism "counterposed determinism to voluntarism" and held philosophy in general as "suspect and demode" (18).

On the one hand, Marx believed "that morality is a form of ideology, and thus social in origin, illusory in content, and serving class interests; that any given morality arises out of a particular stage in the development of the productive forces and relations and is relative to a particular mode of production and particular class interests" (9, p. 3). The later Marx saw his critique of capitalism as scientific rather than moral; and it is said that whenever "anyone started to talk to [him] about morality, he would roar with laughter" (22, p. 22). On the other hand, both Marx's early work and his later writings are filled with compelling moral judgments and fueled by powerful commitment to a more just society. Marxian political economy bristles with outrage at the evils of capitalism: exploitation, alienation, and the moral degradation of an economy ruthlessly driven by the search for marketplace advantage and the extraction of surplus value. How could Marx reject morality yet still make moral judgments?

Lukes (20) answers this question by helping us see that Marx distinguished between what he considered the ideological morality of *Recht*—a form of false consciousness—and the true morality of *emancipation*. The German word *Recht* has no direct English translation. It refers to aspects of law and morality such as justice, fairness, rights, and obligation (20). Hegel used the word broadly to refer to civil law, morality, ethical life, and world history (23). In particular, Hegel saw private property rights and principles of contractual justice as a means of restraining competitive, egoistic relations in an emerging bourgeois society (23). Marx, however, argued that the morality of *Recht* was neither an objective nor a fair means of ordering social relations (24). He argued instead that the principles of *Recht* simply governed and stabilized capitalist social relations while claiming to protect the rights of man in general. He appealed to a morality of *emancipation,* based on an imagined harmony of social unity and individual self-development. For Marx, human emancipation required emancipation from the morality of *Recht* and from the conditions of exploitation and wage-slavery that called it into being (20, 24).

It is beyond the scope of this chapter to discuss the complex philosophical issues involved in Marx's ideas about morality. Nor can we discuss the implications of the recent integration of socialist criticism into liberal political theory, which Scientific Marxists traditionally dismiss for its alliance with the morality of *Recht* (20). We welcome, however, the revival of moral questions in the Marxist tradition of political thought and practice (9–12). And we are pleased that moral economy, understood as part of an expanded conception of *Recht,* is increasingly being used to shape promising new research in the political economy of aging.

MORAL ECONOMY:
HISTORY AND CURRENT USAGE

Since understanding the evolution of moral economy is necessary for appreciating its contemporary relevance to the study of aging, we begin here with a brief historical note.

In his seminal work, *The Making of the English Working Class,* the British historian E. P. Thompson (25) first built on the work of Durkheim (26) and others to develop the concept of moral economy, or popular consensus concerning the legitimacy of certain practices based on shared views of social norms or obligations. In particular, Thompson uncovered the collectively shared moral assumptions that empowered artisans, peasants, and laborers who rioted in response to scarcity and soaring food prices in the late 18th and early 19th centuries. Workers of this period held that, especially in times of shortage, the price of bread should not be based solely on impersonal market forces but also in considerations of fairness and custom. The riots "were popularly regarded as acts of justice" (25, p. 65) legitimated by an old moral economy which an emerging working class carried into a new capitalist economy.

Belief in the God-given and hence communal nature of land was fundamental to the notion of moral economy, and was reasserted by Christian moral philosophers as an important rationale redressing social inequalities (27). By the end of the 18th century, however, increasingly secular justifications of private property, declines in government regulations, the popularity of laissez-faire, and changing attitudes toward labor combined with rising poverty rates, the food riots, and other factors to greatly increase hostility toward the poor.

In this climate, the old moral economy in many parts of Western Europe quickly unraveled and "a fundamental watershed in our thinking about poverty" occurred (27, p. 19). Malthusian population doctrine, and the hated Poor Law Amendment Act of 1834 that it helped spawn, thus denied that the poor had any claim on society for subsistence, beyond what their labor could buy. The functioning of natural economic laws became, in Claeys's words, "the supreme arbiter of all questions of social welfare" (27, p. 21) and, together with Malthusian population principles, took priority over notions of Christian charity and the rights of the poor to a living. Moral economy, in this sense, was seen by Thompson (25), Claeys (27), and others as having collapsed under the weight of these changes, to be followed and replaced by the market economy.

Current usage of the concept of moral economy has tended to reflect this historical interpretation. Most contemporary applications thus involve anthropological and sociological studies of premarket societies in Asia, Africa, and elsewhere (28–32). On the one hand, such applications have considerable relevance for our understanding of aging in many parts of the Third World. Scott (28), for example, demonstrates that the moral economy of the subsistence ethic in precapitalist peasant societies dictated that all members of a community had a right to a living, including sufficient provision to carry out such culturally and economically dictated roles as caring for elderly parents. On the other hand, however, to limit the usage of the concept of moral economy solely to analyses of aging and other phenomena in premarket economies is to ignore its larger relevance. Indeed, as Kohli (33) argues, the dichotomy between moral and market economy that these scholars erect is in fact a false dichotomy and one that robs the concept of moral economy of some of its contemporary usefulness in understanding advanced Western societies. In his view, the market economy should be viewed instead as (22, p. 277):

> a new form of economic organization giving rise to its own moral economy, on which it depends for functioning. . . . What occurs is not a collapse of the moral economy but a shift of the main arena of moral conflict from the consumption market to the labor market: it concerns no longer the price of goods, but the "just reward" for work.

It is a premise of this book that the concept of moral economy is indeed a useful one today for examining the place of consensual assumptions about reciprocal obligations, not only in attitudes toward and treatment of elders in peasant societies in the Third World, but also within the market economy in the United States and other advanced industrialized nations. Moreover, as Kohli suggests, by looking to new "arenas of moral conflict" such as the labor market, social security, and resource allocation among different age groups, the particular usefulness of a moral economy approach employed in conjunction with a political economy framework becomes apparent.

While the remainder of this chapter will focus on the moral economy of aging, it should be noted that applications of this concept in the United States have often tended to focus not on aging per se, but on the history of labor organizing around the age-related issue of seniority (34–36). Indeed, unions have been characterized in the United States as "instruments for implementing a moral economy of the working class" (31) that challenged a "possessive market economy," unrestrained by custom or status (35, p. 272). Using the U.S. automobile industry as a case in point, Gersuny and Kaufman (34) demonstrate how seniority became the cornerstone of the workers' moral economy and a key demand in disputes between the auto industry and the United Automobile Workers (UAW). Without underemphasizing the significant social control functions of seniority systems (e.g., in reinforcing dependency and increasing the pool of older, more disciplined workers), such analyses illuminate other, often overlooked, aspects of the evolution of labor practices in the United States. Further research is needed, however, to better answer such questions as why seniority, rather than pensions, constituted the centerpiece of the workers' moral economy in the United States (37).

MORAL ECONOMY AND THE STUDY OF AGING

The past decade has witnessed a number of intriguing applications of the concept of moral economy to our understanding of aging and aging policy. Among the first and best known of these applications was Kohli's (33) historical analysis of the creation and evolution of the world's first pension system in Germany, over 100 years ago. Without negating traditional political economy explanations of emerging pension systems, Kohli offered moral economy as a complementary lens through which to more fully examine this development. Within this broad theoretical framework, he described Germany's welfare system as having developed in part as an attempt to construct a reliable life course by covering illness, disability, and old age—the risks associated with the organization of work—and thus providing workers with a stake in the existing social order. The norms of reciprocity, or "taken for granted beliefs regarding fairness" inherent in such a system, are, Kohli argues, "informal and somewhat vague" but at the same time "a powerful reality" undergirding modern work societies.

A major contribution of Kohli's analysis lies in his conceptualization of the "moral impact" of pensions and other forms of welfare in terms of their creation of "lifetime continuity and reciprocity." Retirement thus meant "the emergence of old age as a distinct life phase, structurally set apart from active life and with a clear chronological boundary (33, p. 277). With its emergence, the "moral universe" moved beyond the family or local community to the formal work sector of the market economy— with profound political implications.

Several other analysts have examined pension systems within a life-course context in which norms of reciprocity are implicitly embedded (37–39). Myles's comparative examination of pension systems, and particularly his notion of a "living wage" based on substitutive benefits, thus is consonant with a moral, as well as a political, economy perspective. As Myles suggests, the belief that pension benefits should be set at "a level sufficient to allow continuity in living standards" is one of the hallmarks of the modern welfare state. And embedded in this notion of substitutive benefits are strong moral economy notions concerning what is due the "deserving elderly" (40)—those who have contributed to the economy through their "productive" lives and therefore are believed to merit a decent, living wage in their later years. In Vincent's words, the notion of "a fair return for a fair life . . . becomes a possible and indeed dominant attitude when living a full life span becomes a relatively predictable occurrence" (41, p. 148).

The evolution of pension systems in North America and Western Europe nicely illustrates the fit between moral and political economy approaches, and the ways in which their joint application may enrich our understanding of other phenomena within social gerontology. A key tenet of moral economy, for example, is that the shared moral assumptions underlying norms of reciprocity serve and reflect the values not only of the subordinate, but also of the dominant groups. In this way, the demands of the subjugated group—whether of English peasants for a just price for bread or of older workers and the elderly for a pension system—also have important social control functions that serve the interests of the dominant class. In the latter case, retirement in advance of physiological necessity enabled employers to rid themselves of their most expensive workers and further served a social control function by creating and reinforcing dependence and reducing dangerously high levels of unemployment in young men (39). Thus, while achieving a pension system was a primary goal of older workers and elders grounded in moral economy notions of fairness, its institutionalization had a flip side which worked to the benefit of employers, and of larger capitalist interests (39).

Political economy has traditionally helped examine and explain such factors as the social control functions of social security systems. Yet as this example illustrates, the use of moral and political economy perspectives together enables a more thorough analysis of the significance of such developments than either can achieve independently.

It is tempting to use moral economy as a kind of ethical trump card to be played against one's political opponents. But intellectual integrity requires a more nuanced mix of discourses in moral economy. In the long run, there are several ongoing and superficially contradictory tasks. We must (a) analyze the empirical reality of actual moral economies; (b) provide rational arguments for the superiority of any particular moral economy; (c) provide pragmatic and strategic arguments for achieving a more preferable moral and political economy of aging; and (d) continue to develop utopian ideals of emancipatory moral economies in which individual self-development and communal well-being are harmonized.

In his comparison of health care for the aged in Canada and the United States in Chapter 8, Clark takes up the first of these tasks. He shows that Canada's particular moral economy is reflected in its far greater concern with equity and access to health care for the old, and indeed all members of society. The notion of moral economy may in fact be a useful one for analysts exploring further the preoccupation, particularly in the United States, with distinguishing between "deserving" and "undeserving" elderly, poor, and so forth, as this continues to shape public policy (40). For example, the particular moral economy embedded in much U.S. public policy has limited the notion of "deservingness" (those who are considered worthy of entitlements; others receive less generous welfare benefits or none at all) mainly to individuals who have been able to participate in primary labor markets. This limitation does not exist in Canada, the United Kingdom, and other Western societies (38–40).

The concept of moral economy further provides a helpful conceptual framework within which to access recent claims by the Republican Congress of a "voter mandate" for its proposed radical restructuring of many entitlement and safety-net programs. As Lynch and Minkler discuss in Chapter 10, the Republicans couched their claims, in part, in terms of shifting societal norms concerning the deservingness of the elderly, the poor, and other subgroups. Yet the reality of such a shift has not been borne out by opinion polls and other data.

While most scholars to date have tended to employ a unitary concept of moral economy in relation to aging, an alternative perspective has been offered by Hendricks and Leedham (6). These analysts suggest that because the norms implicit in moral economy vary with changing cultural and social contexts, several forms of moral economy may exist side by side in highly fragmented societies, competing for hegemony. Hendricks and Leedham propose two "ideal types" of moral economy. Moral economies grounded in use value are characterized as meeting human needs and creating social arrangements that maximize life chances for all. In contrast, moral economies grounded in exchange value are seen as taking a utilitarian approach to the public good and ignoring both problematic issues of distributive justice and the existence of goods not easily measured in economic terms. In Chapter 20 of this volume, Holstein thus illustrates how the popular concept of "productive aging" is embedded in other social meanings such that less value is ascribed to caregiving, volunteerism, community leadership, and other activities seen as less "productive" than paid work.

The perspective offered by moral economy also is helpful in explicating recent debates over what has been termed "justice between generations" or generational equity. For as Vincent points out, the question of generational equity "is not simply a demographic or economic one. It is also essentially a political and moral question" (41, p. 147). While the concept of generational equity is a flawed basis for public policy, proponents of this perspective do a service in pointing to the necessity for far greater attention to meeting the needs of impoverished children, low-income workers, and other non-elderly segments of society (42).

On the one hand, the moral economy of the life course may be seen as forming an unspoken historical foundation for the views of some scholars (e.g., Callahan (43) and Daniels (44)) concerning justice among young and old in an aging society. Such analysts underscore the need to rethink moral obligations among age groups and to reformulate the moral economy of the life span in a new demographic context (45). On the other hand, such characterizations tend to overlook how much has been lost by the secularization and modernization of the life course. If indeed it was once the case that "To every thing there is a season, and a time to every purpose under the heaven," one must question whether this holds true for the season of old age in late 20th century America. The demeaning of old age and the marginalization of the elderly that are now embedded in the bureaucratized life course of the welfare state (45) must be considered in any attempt to understand alienation within, and potentially between, generations.

In spite of the trivialization of old age, however, and despite the media rhetoric of conflict between generations over the high cost of Social Security and Medicare, there is in fact relatively *little* support among young people in the United States for cutting back entitlements for the old. Instead, opinion polls and other data suggest strong continued societal and cross-generational support for programs directed at the elderly, even among those "baby boomers" who are under the erroneous notion that Social Security will be bankrupt before they are old enough to reap its benefits (46).

The cross-generational stake in old age entitlements is discussed elsewhere in this volume (see Chapters 3 and 4). Of particular relevance here, however, is the persistence of strong moral economy notions of reciprocity and of what is "due" the old as reflected in young people's continued support for these programs. As Hendricks and Leedham (6) suggest, such support is consistent with a moral economy grounded in use value, in which human needs are envisioned as being met across time and over the life course, rather than through isolated exchanges.

In a related way, a moral economy approach also is helpful in examining the periodic calls for "setting limits" on medical care for the old, and in understanding the strong societal reactions against such proposals. In a controversial book, ethicist Daniel Callahan (43) argues in part for setting limits on government-funded, life-extending treatment for the very old, suggesting instead that scarce resources be diverted to improving quality of life for the elderly and to a world "worthy of bequest" for the young. While stating that such limit-setting is necessary to add meaning to old age, Callahan also invokes the concept of a "moral community," to suggest that elders should see their primary role as one of stewardship on behalf of future generations and service to the young. Callahan's attempt, in short, was to suggest a reordering of the moral economy and a reassessment of society's unquestioned allegiance to such principles as unlimited high-technology treatment regardless of the age of the recipient. Ironically, however, the strong opposition he and others (47) have encountered for advancing such notions has itself been firmly rooted in moral economic arguments. In particular, Callahan's original call for setting limits for life-extending treatment for the very old had been criticized for ignoring basic principles of equity, equality, and social justice which dictate that citizens shall not be denied the right to medical care on the basis of age.

Moral economy considerations around distributive or economic justice in later life also are implied in the work of Tindale and Neysmith (48, 49). Neysmith (49) thus examines the "shoulds" or moral bases of alternative principles guiding social distributional policies for the elderly in Canada. In demonstrating the inherently contradictory nature of these principles (which in turn rely on contradictory notions of equity), she offers an analysis that bridges political and moral economy considerations in the complex area of resource allocation in an aging society.

The above examples have focused on the utility of a combined political and moral economy perspective for examining and understanding broad questions on such issues as the evolution of pension schemes and societal attitudes toward and policies for the old. On another level, however, notions of reciprocity and fairness, and collective moral assumptions regarding what is "due" the old, also are helpful in explaining such developments as the dramatic "senior revolt" against the Medicare Catastrophic Coverage Act passed in the United States in 1988 and quickly repealed the following year. As Holstein and Minkler (50) note in their analysis of this debacle, the primary reason for the elderly backlash against the catastrophic coverage legislation was a combination of misinformation and grave concerns over fairness. In particular, the "seniors only" nature of the Medicare surtax was deemed a radical and unfair departure from the notion that taxes should be spread throughout the society, not simply imposed on special subgroups. It was, in short, the Act's perceived disregard for popular consensus on what constituted legitimate and illegitimate taxation that in large part led to the downfall of this landmark decision.

Still another area within the political economy of aging that may lend itself to investigation partially through a moral economy lens is that of gender justice and care of the elderly. As Campbell and Brody (51) demonstrate, while women in the United States and Japan have increasingly expressed egalitarian attitudes toward parent care, comparable shifts have not occurred in practice. Consequently, women in both countries, and indeed in most of the world (52), have retained primary responsibility for care of elderly parents.

The importance of viewing care of the elderly and gender justice within a political economy perspective has, of course, been well demonstrated (see Chapter 14). At the same time, however—and to the extent that there is indeed a popular consensus on norms of reciprocity vis-à-vis unpaid care of the old by women—moral economy considerations, and possible shifts in such underlying norms, are deserving of study. Moreover, as Neysmith (52) suggests, such analyses are needed not only in advanced industrial societies, but in Third World countries as well. In the latter nations, she notes, policy and programmatic reforms focused on the needs of the old "will be isolated unless micro-macro connections [become] central rather than peripheral to our analyses" (52, p. 320). The latter would include explication of not only the political economic forces underlying gender inequality in caregiving, but equally important, the assumptions and underlying norms of reciprocity in care for the old that assign responsibility to a society's adult daughters, but not its sons. The limitations and inequities underlying moral economy notions in this and other areas indeed represent an important area for further research.

In sum, as the above examples illustrate, whether we are examining the experience of aging in Third World countries, in advanced industrialized socialist economies, or in capitalist nations, shared moral assumptions about reciprocity and fairness, and collective visions of what is due the old, should form an integral part of the database we are exploring. A more thoughtful integration of moral economy with political economy perspectives on aging requires uncovering, critically analyzing, and historically interpreting such assumptions.

While we have examined in this chapter the possible role of moral economy perspectives in enriching political economy of aging analyses, a fundamental similarity between these approaches also must be underscored. Both moral economy and political economy thus examine topics such as aging in terms of their embeddedness in a larger whole. Both ground their analyses in a sociohistorical context, with political economy focusing in particular on the social structural context of aging, and moral economy on the related context of popular consensus defining norms of reciprocity as these affect the old and resource allocation across age groups.

Further, both political and moral economy provide important alternatives to the "increasingly technical and instrumental orientation of academic gerontology" (53). In this regard, and building on Habermas's (8) notion of the colonization of the life world of old age, Moody argues that "The problems of later life are treated with scientific and managerial efficiency but with no grasp of their larger political or existential significance. The life world of the last stage of life is progressively drained of meaning" (53, p. 82). By examining the last stage of life with attention to these larger issues of significance and meaning, political and moral economy approaches to aging greatly enrich academic gerontology.

CONCLUSION:
TOWARD A MORALITY OF EMANCIPATION IN LATER LIFE

We began this chapter by criticizing Marx's tendency, particularly in his later writings, to dismiss questions of justice, fairness, rights, and obligations—the morality of *Recht*—and we argued that popular norms of reciprocity and fairness in fact played an important role in the evolution of a self-conscious working class. We also argued that moral economics of the life course in Western welfare states provide strong cultural justification for public pensions and other policies affecting the old. Finally, we noted that in contrast to the later Marx's narrow and harsh view of the "rights of man," his vision of a morality of emancipation was both broad and inspiring. We believe that it holds particular promise with reference to individual and societal aging.

As we have seen, Marx's notion of the morality of emancipation was based on an ideal of individual self-development achieved through mutual identification and community with others. Marx saw life under capitalism as alienating in part because it encouraged conflict and mutual indifference, which in turn stunted the possibility of human development for all members of society. He looked forward to the time when human social relations and economic productivity would create a society in which human development could take place unhindered by alienation and the struggle to eke out a living.

Marx's view of freedom and alienation has special relevance for our aging society, where mass longevity has created a new abundance of later life that is plagued by the absence of vital cultural meaning. As Moody puts it, the "collapse of meaning and the erosion of quality of life in old age reflect a deeper failure unacknowledged by the optimistic prophets of postmaterialist abundance: namely a failure of communication and legitimation in the social order as a whole" (53, p. 81). Confronting this crisis will mean building a new moral economy of the life course and the institutions that support it. The need to create a just distribution of goods and services remains central: "as long as the political economy is organized in ways that prevent abundance from actually becoming available to all" (53, p. 81), the emancipatory possibilities of our new abundance of life cannot be realized.

We believe that the challenge to aging societies lies not only in creating a just distribution of resources between and within age groups but also in moving beyond the alienated form of old age common in advanced industrial society, where old people are pressured into retirement and encouraged to opt for trivialized leisure or _free time = human development_

the consumption of professional services. Marx's morality of emancipation was predicated on the idea that free time would be spent for genuine human development. A new moral economy of later life requires attention to quality-of-life issues in education, work, productivity, and health care at each stage of the life course. It requires social support for higher forms of activity; education, new forms of paid and unpaid work, and new arenas that bring old and young together. It requires, too, a vision of the whole life course that reaffirms the intimate interdependence of generations.

REFERENCES

1. Walton, J. Urban political economy. *Comp. Urban Res.* 7: 1, 9, 1979.
2. Estes, C. L., Swan, J. H., and Gerard, L. E. Dominant and competing paradigms in gerontology: Toward a political economy of aging. In *Readings in the Political Economy of Aging,* edited by M. Minkler and C. L. Estes. Baywood, Amityville, N.Y., 1984.
3. Walker, A. Toward a political economy of old age. *Ageing Soc.* 1: 73–94, 1981.
4. Olson, L. K. *The Political Economy of Aging.* Columbia University Press, New York, 1982.
5. Guillemard, A. M. Old age, retirement and the social class structure: Toward an analysis of the structural dynamics of the latter stages of life. In *Aging Midlife Course Transitions: An Interdisciplinary Perspective,* edited by T. K. Kamen and R. J. Adams. Guilford, New York, 1982.
6. Hendricks, J., and Leedham, C. A. Dependency or empowerment? Toward a moral and political economy of aging. In *Critical Perspectives on Aging: The Political and Moral Economy of Growing Old,* edited by M. Minkler and C. L. Estes, pp. 51–64. Baywood, Amityville, N.Y., 1991.
7. Gramsci, A. *Selections from The Prison Notebooks,* edited and translated by Q. Hoare and G. Nowell Smith. Lawrence and Wishart, London, 1971.
8. Habermas, J. Introduction. In *Observations on "The Spiritual Situation of the Age,"* edited by J. Habermas, translated by Andrew Buchwalter, pp. 19–20. MIT Press, Cambridge, Mass., 1984.
9. Frazer, N. *Unruly Practices: Power, Discourse and Gender in Contemporary Social Theory.* University of Minnesota Press, Minneapolis, 1989.
10. Walzer, M. *Spheres of Justice.* Basic Books, New York, 1983.
11. Mouffe, C. Hegemony and new political subjects: Toward a new concept of democracy. In *Marxism and the Interpretation of Culture,* edited by C. Nelson and L. Grossberg, pp. 89–104. University of Illinois Press, Urbana, 1988.
12. Sandel, M. J. *Liberalism and the Limits of Justice.* Cambridge University Press, New York, 1982.
13. Bolough, R. W. *Dialectical Phenomenology: Marx's Method.* Routledge and Kegan Paul, Boston, 1979.
14. Schmidt, A. *History and Structure,* translated by J. Herf. MIT Press, Waltham, Mass., 1983.
15. Spicker, S., Woodward, K., and Van Tassel, D. D. (eds.). *Aging and the Elderly: Humanistic Perspectives in Gerontology.* Academic Press, New York, 1978.
16. Cole, T. R., and Gadow, S. A. *What Does It Mean to Grow Old? Reflections from the Humanities.* Duke University Press, Durham, N.C., 1986.
17. Cole, T. R., Van Tassel, D. D., and Kastenbaum, R. (eds.). *Handbook of Aging and the Humanities.* Springer, New York, 1991.

18. Gouldner, A. *The Two Marxisms: Contradictions and Anomalies in the Development of Theory.* Seabury Press, New York, 1980.
19. Thompson, E. P. *The Poverty of Theory and Other Essays,* pp. 363–364. Merline Press, London, 1978.
20. Lukes, S. *Marxism and Morality.* Oxford University Press, Oxford, 1985.
21. Marx, K., and Engels, F. *Manifesto of the Communist Party.* Marx Engels Collected Works, 6, translated by R. Dixon. Lawrence and Wishart, London, 1975–1994 [1848].
22. Vorlander, K. *Marx und Kant.* Vortrag genhalten in Wien am 8 April 1904. Verlag der Deutschen Worte, Vienna, 1904.
23. Hart, H. L. A. Are there any natural rights? *Philos. Rev.* 64: 177–178, 1955.
24. Marx, K., and Engels, F. *The German Ideology.* Marx Engels Collected Works, 5, translated by R. Dixon. Lawrence and Wishart, London, 1975–1994 [1845–1846].
25. Thompson, E. P. *The Making of the English Working Class.* Vintage Books, New York, 1966.
26. Durkheim, E. *The Division of Labor.* Macmillan, New York, 1933 [1893].
27. Claeys, G. *Machinery, Money and the Millennium: From Moral Economy to Socialism, 1815–1860.* Polity Press, Cambridge, England, 1987.
28. Scott, J. C. *The Moral Economy of the Peasant Rebellion and Subsistence in South East Asia.* Yale University Press, New Haven, Conn., 1976.
29. Evans, G. From Moral Economy to Remembered Village. Working Paper No. 40. Center for South East Asian Studies, Monash University, Australia, 1986.
30. Ravallion, M., and Dearden, L. Social security in a moral economy: An empirical analysis for Java. *Rev. Econ. Stat.* 70: 36–44, 1988.
31. Brocheux, P. Moral economy or political economy? The peasants are always rational. *J. Asian Stud.* 42: 791–803, 1983.
32. Bates, R. H., and Curry, F. Community v. market: A note on corporate villages. *Am. Polit. Sci. Rev.* 86(2): 457–463, 1992.
33. Kohli, M. Retirement and the moral economy: An historical interpretation of the German case. *J. Aging Stud.* 1(2): 125–144, 1987.
34. Gersuny, C., and Kaufman, G. Seniority and the moral economy of U.S. automobile workers, 1934–1946. *J. Soc. Hist.,* Spring 1985, pp. 463–475.
35. McPherson, C. B. *The Political Theory of Possessive Individualism.* Clarendon Press, Oxford, England, 1962.
36. Perlman, S. *A Theory of the Labor Movement (1928).* Macmillan, New York, 1949.
37. Quadagno, J. Organized labor, state structures and social policy: A case study of old age assistance in Ohio, 9116–1940, *Soc. Prob.* 36(2): 181–196, 1989.
38. Myles, J. *Old Age in the Welfare State: The Political Economy of Public Pensions.* University Press of Kansas, Lawrence, 1989.
39. Graebner, W. *The History of Retirement.* Yale University Press, New Haven, Conn., 1980.
40. Katz, M. B. *The Undeserving Poor: From the War on Poverty to the War on Welfare.* Pantheon Books, New York, 1989.
41. Vincent, J. A. *Inequality and Old Age.* University College London Press, London, 1995.
42. Minkler, M., and Robertson, A. The ideology of age/race wars: De-constructing a social problem. *Aging Soc.* 11: 1–22, 1991.
43. Callahan, D. *Setting Limits: Medical Goals in an Aging Society.* Simon and Schuster, New York, 1987.
44. Daniels, N. *Am I My Parents Keeper?* Oxford University Press, Oxford, England, 1988.
45. Cole, T. The spectre of old age: History, politics and culture in America. *Tikkun* 3: 14–18, 93–95, 1989.

46. Minkler, M. Scapegoating the elderly: New voices, old theme. *J. Public Health Policy,* 18: 8–12, 1997.
47. Lamm, R. Long time dying. *New Republic,* August 27, 1984, pp. 20–23.
48. Tindale, J. A., and Neysmith, S. M. Economic justice in later life: A Canadian perspective. *Soc. Just. Res.* 1: 461–476, 1987.
49. Neysmith, S. M. Social policy implications of an aging society. In *Aging in Canada,* Ed. 2, edited by V. Marshall. Fitzhenry and Whiteside, Toronto, 1987.
50. Holstein, M., and Minkler, M. The short life and painful death of Medical Catastrophic Coverage Act. In *Critical Perspectives on Aging: The Political and Moral Economy of Growing Old,* edited by M. Minkler and C. L. Estes, pp. 189–206. Baywood, Amityville, N.Y., 1991.
51. Campbell, R., and Brody, E. M. Women's changing roles and help to the elderly: Attitudes of women in the United States and Japan. *Gerontologist* 25(6): 584–592, 1985.
52. Neysmith, S. M. Dependency among third world elderly: A need for new directions in the nineties. In *Critical Perspectives on Aging: The Political and Moral Economy of Growing Old,* edited by M. Minkler and C. L. Estes, pp. 311–321. Baywood, Amityville, N.Y., 1991.
53. Moody, H. R. *Abundance of Life: Human Development Policies for an Aging Society.* Columbia University Press, New York, 1988.

PART II: RETHINKING DEPENDENCE, INTERDEPENDENCE, AND THE POLITICAL POWER OF THE OLD

Investigators in the field of critical gerontology on both sides of the Atlantic have expressed increasing concern over what Ann Robertson (1) calls "apocalyptic demography" and what Alan Walker (2) terms "the alarmist demography of despair." Within this bleak scenario, the rapid aging of populations, with its attendant health and social costs, is seen as being on a collision course with overall societal well-being. An alternative perspective, however, and one well articulated in this second part of the book, suggests that "old versus young" predictions and the "bankruptcy hypothesis of aging" be replaced by a broader vision stressing the intimate interdependence of generations.

In Chapter 3, Malcolm Johnson introduces this vision and reaffirms the need for "personal and social solidarity as the foundation for trust and reciprocity between generations." He begins by highlighting the dramatic changes in family arrangements and expectations regarding late life that have occurred against a backdrop of official policies shifting the provision of care to the private sector. Johnson then brings together several different bodies of theoretical and analytical work in areas such as family and generational studies, the philosophy of solidarity, obligation and reciprocity, and the political economy of aging for the light they may shed on interdependence and the compact between generations. In sharp contrast to postmodern visions of "disintegration and disorder" which have become increasingly popular among intellectuals, Johnson proposes a vision premised on "a renewal of citizenship," in which moral considerations are brought to center stage. Among these moral considerations is what he calls "the central promise" of the contract between generations—the notion that an adequate income and care of the old are not luxuries we can ill afford but "an enduring right" critical to a caring society.

Using Johnson's thoughtful analysis as a jumping off point, Ann Robertson begins Chapter 4 by revisiting the notion of "apocalyptic demography" which she introduced in her earlier examination of the social construction of Alzheimer's disease (1). Central to catastrophic scenarios of the aging of populations, she argues, is the social construction of dependency with its heavy accent on the relative "deservingness" of different groups in need. Building on the work of Mary Ann Glendon (3) and others, Robertson examines how discussions in this arena have tended to be dominated by a therapeutic, "we know what's good for you" language of need and an accompanying "rights talk" that effectively diminishes public discussion about need. As an alternative to these limiting discourses, Robertson proposes "an alternative language of need" framed in terms of "the moral economy of interdependence." The latter notion, she argues, moves us beyond the false dichotomy of dependence/independence. Further, it involves elders and their communities in determining their own needs and the best means for addressing them, and places a heavy accent on the common good.

From Robertson's theoretical discussion of the need for movement beyond the dependence/independence dichotomy and toward an increased appreciation of our interdependence, we move in Chapter 5 to a concrete application of some of these ideas. Jae Kennedy and Meredith Minkler begin by examining the different definitions and models of disability, as well as its social production and unequal distribution within cultures. As in Chapter 4, notions of deservingness and needs-based distributional systems are seen as heavily influencing who receives what forms of assistance from whom, and under what conditions. Further, gender, race, class, and age biases in disability programs are seen as profoundly disadvantaging many of those most in need of benefits.

The historical roots of contemporary ambivalence toward elders with disabilities are briefly explored in this chapter, with particular attention to the Victorian-era tendency to "split" old age into negative and positive poles. Like their early predecessors, contemporary efforts to separate out and glorify "healthy" and "successful" aging are seen as having lost sight of a more thoughtful, dialectical vision of aging which respects health *and* disease, able-bodiedness *and* disability, as equally valid parts of the aging experience.

Chapter 5 concludes by looking to the Independent Living Movement for an alternative and more robust vision of aging and disability. As Kennedy and Minkler point out, despite its emphasis on the language of independence, the independent living movement is, in fact, philosophically in tune with the moral economy of interdependence described in Chapter 4. Recognizing the stake that all people have in policies that respect the rights of the disabled to full integration and participation in society, the Movement's philosophy is viewed as providing an important blueprint for our aging societies.

In the final chapter of this section, Debra Street turns our attention to yet another aspect of the social construction of aging, namely the myths and realities that surround the political power of the old in the U.S. welfare state. The conventional view that "special interest politics" explain the durability of Social Security and Medicare is contrasted with a political economy perspective tying these programs instead to notions of citizens' rights. Arguing that "elderly citizens' political interests do not derive activities from class, race/ethnicity, gender, or age in isolation," Street underscores the overlapping statuses and identities of older persons whose voting patterns and other political activities reflect their heterogeneity.

Street also critically examines the political power of age-based interest groups, such as the 33 million member American Association of Retired Persons (AARP), which commonly are perceived as constituting a formidable "gray lobby" with tremendous influence on policy-making. Using examples such as the passage and quick repeal of the Medicare Catastrophic Coverage Act under President Reagan, Street demonstrates that "an interest group politics of aging offers, at best, only partial explanation of policy interests and outcomes." The politics surrounding programs like Medicare and Social Security indeed are seen as crossing class, race, and generational lines—a fact that will take on even greater policy significance with the growing diversity of the elderly population in the years ahead.

Several of the contributions to Part II are steeped in theory and philosophy and may prove difficult for readers who are not familiar with these bodies of thought. We include them early on in the book, however, as they introduce important themes and perspectives that are illustrated in subsequent chapters and which, we believe, make major new contributions to critical gerontology.

REFERENCES

1. Robertson, A. The politics of Alzheimer's disease: A case study in apocalyptic demography. In *Critical Perspectives on Aging,* edited by M. Minkler and C. L. Estes. Baywood, Amityville, N.Y., 1991.
2. Walker, A. The economic 'burden' of ageing and the prospect for intergenerational conflict. *Ageing Soc.* 10: 377–396, 1990.
3. Glendon, M. A. *Rights Talk: The Impoverishment of Political Discourse.* The Free Press, New York, 1991.

CHAPTER 3

Interdependency and
the Generational Compact

Malcolm L. Johnson

INTRODUCTION

The moral foundations of human societies, the characteristics and qualities of citizenship, and the role these two underpinning concepts perform in binding together civic society are long-established scholarly concerns. Yet the combination of a permanent demographic reconstruction and the loosening of established patterns of family living present new and pressing reasons for developing fresh under-standings of what constitutes the bonds which link human beings, inexorably, together. In short, old age and the family encompass the center ground of a major political and policy discourse which brings together intellectual, research-based, and practical debate. It also raises important questions about resource allocation in both the public and private spheres.

One of the positive features of recent discussion has been the active re-engagement of philosophers who in the path of Rawls (1) have taken a close interest in social justice in health care and social services issues. These voices are largely new to gerontology and bring with them a skill in conceptual analysis which is greatly needed. Within this band of socially committed scholars is David Selbourne. His muscular examination of contemporary society published as *The Spirit of the Age* (2) was followed immediately by *The Principle of Duty* (3). Further reference to this work will be made later. Here we need only note his observations that (3, p. 6):

> I take it to be my obligation, so deep is the present moral crisis of the liberal civic order in particular, once more to explain, justify and defend both logically and intuitively the *civic bond,* the very expression of human organization for mutual security and well-being.

This chapter is reprinted with permission from *Ageing and Society,* Volume 15, Number 2, Pages 245–265, June 1995. © 1995, Cambridge University Press.

A Moral Enterprise

Selbourne brings a passion to his intellectual writings which puts his own values on display. Whether or not we share his conviction, it is difficult to resist the motivation to reconsider the nature of duty in relation to not only ourselves and our kin, but also the citizen-stranger. From a different political standpoint Richard Titmuss brought the same deep commitment to his empirically based essay on social exchange between strangers, *The Gift Relationship: From Human Blood to Social Policy* (4).

Were Titmuss writing today he would be as exercised about justice between age groups and the inescapable need to retain gift relationships between generations as he was about the commercialization of the giving and receiving of blood and a health service that is free at the point of need. Yet there is no set of categorical criteria which can reliably delineate the presence of serious moral decline. Nonetheless I align myself with those who are profoundly disturbed by the consequences of unfettered individualism. Its product appears to be the elevation of self and the denial of social obligation. As Nozick (5) puts it, the individual has a moral right to absolute control over himself and his possessions, a right not only to buy and sell but to abuse and destroy, provided only that such a right does not interfere with the rights of others. By his lights the past decade has been one of progress and fulfillment. Selbourne called it "a hooligan's charter" (3, p. 10).

Significant changes in family formations and in the life expectation of all who survive into mid-life represent two of the most fundamental changes in social structure. Together these shifts, against a backcloth of official policy to relocate the provision of care in the market, provide a picture of change with profound moral dimensions. However, it is vital that the several discrete topics and discussions should be brought together. So this chapter sets out to consider whether or not present-day family arrangements continue to include a delivered sense of obligation toward older people. It also reflects on the empirical effects of sociological and ethical changes, observable through research, on contemporary social behavior and the extent to which ethical imperatives are still powerful influences.

The Postmodern Disorder

These debates take place alongside, rather than in intimate association with, others which deal with the supposed disintegration of social order and personal practice. In particular the ultimate theory of dissolution embodied in notions of postmodernism and the subset of them, post-Fordism, has served to create a climate of despair about the continued willingness and capability of future generations to sustain the old and the infirm. MacIntyre posits the central problem of the age, as the consequences of "the Enlightenment Project" (6, p. 63n) which ostensibly freed the individual from hierarchy and teleology to conceive of himself or herself as morally sovereign. Yet this very release from theological dominance led to the excessive rationalism of Taylorian (7) industrial processes which led to Henry Ford's production line systems—which in turn yielded new forms of differentiation, conflict, and inequality (8).

The story line of this progression (or is it regression?) is that since the secularization of human values, individual rights have been through a series of reformulations which have been shaped by the modern state in league with organized religion. Industrial capitalism gives way to post-capitalism (9) and to forms of economic and social disorder. Baudrillard extends the argument by claiming that the end of modernity is simultaneously the end of the social, and the termination of bourgeois democracy, including the institutions of free speech and human rights (10, 11).

Translating these interpretations of social fragmentation into the social welfare of older citizens requires a willingness to accept them as explanatory frameworks—which I do with great reluctance. But it is less difficult to accept Williams's (12) view that Fordist influences created a post World War II welfare state which was essentially male, white, and geared to mass employment. Thus major changes in employment patterns by gender, class, age, and race will have a marked and fairly rapid impact on health and social care provision and pensions. She concludes—and I concur—"that these issues and debates need to take account not only of the changing conditions of work but the changing conditions of the family, culture and nationhood" (12, p. 72).

Families of Ideas

The persistence of nuclear-family forms is indisputable; but mutations and new forms in the past two decades have caused serious doubts about the capacity and commitment of domestic units to support all their members. So inevitably much of what follows will focus on the changing family. There is, however, as we have already noted, another level of social obligation beyond that of kinship, which is also influx. It exists at the societal level and is embedded in economic structures. On the one hand there are reasons for some analysts to fear that the costs of the current arrangements for old and other dependent people are too great for governments to meet. On the other there is a progressive individualism in the political atmosphere which manifests itself in the work setting. Together these perceived shifts away from formerly agreed obligations have stimulated a set of agitated responses. Our task is to assess the veracity of the argument that changing social structures, demographic patterns, and ideologies of personal conduct have undermined the solidarity between people of different ages both at any point in time and across time. Such a discussion must start from a base. No assessment of the positive or negative consequences of change can be made without a point of reference.

In this case we may start (as do Daniels (13), Walker (14), and Johnson and Falkingham (15), among many) from the belief that there has operated in the past a generalized obligation on those who were young and fit enough to be economically active to make provision for those too young or too old to join them in the creation of income and wealth. In turn these workers could expect that future cohorts of producers would sustain them in their need for income and services, to ensure their physical and social well-being. Such a statement would readily embrace the essence of the contemporary debate in North America, Western Europe, and Japan, which focuses on the threatening inability of producers to go on delivering sufficient resources to maintain the level of economic transfer necessary to meet the rising claims of health, social security, and pension budgets for the retired population. But despite its resonances of history and political economy, there are important missing dimensions. It makes too many assumptions about the sociology of the family and of the philosophical foundations of a contract between the generations. Nor is there any hint of the seminal influence of the changing perceptions and roles of women as the principal caregivers. Even further away are the most recent environmentalist arguments, the prognostications of political economists, and the emergence of a subgroup of better-off older people for whom the obligations to their children's inheritance is subsumed by an intent to consume their own accumulated wealth. In parallel, there is perceived by some observers a growing unwillingness of young people to accept their traditional dependence on parents, leading to a generational contest for a better share of private and public resources. So it must be recognized that the reciprocity in families can also lead to coercion—of the very old by the young. It may also result in the unreasonable restriction of the young unemployed, who are captured in a new dependency.

FAMILIES AND GENERATIONS

Structural functionalist propositions of universal family forms (16, 17) in the fifties quickly led to a large body of empirical work (18, 19) which demonstrated a wide variety of patterns. These challenges to the universality thesis included Bettelheim's (20) and Spiro's (21) studies of kibbutzim which presented both the strengths and the shortcomings of de-familied communal living. A range of anthropological research highlighted functioning matrifocal lone-parent families in the West Indies and Central America (22, 23).

By the late sixties the debate had moved first to a series of powerful assaults on nuclear-family living (24–26) which depicted it as pathological and harmful. In his Reith Lectures, Leach (24) said "Far from being the basis for a good society, the family with its tawdry secrets, is the source of all discontents." Then came a sustained focus on the role of women (27, 28) which gave rise to a new canon of feminist literature and gender studies that have both recorded and materially changed social perceptions of women. Running concurrently with the mass extension of paid employment among women, the two processes have affected the quantity, availability, and style of their contribution to household and caring activities (29). Such gender issues have become an important part of the generational debate because of the greater part played by women in the care of old and disabled people. More latterly it has prompted further attention to the social and economic role of grandparents in continued support of younger people (30). In particular, studies signal either a disenfranchisement brought about by divorce of the grandchildren's parents or what Arber and Ginn (31) describe as "the continued domestic exploitation of older women."

Specifically gerontological interest in generational relations began to take form in the United States during the sixties. It was prompted by the student uprisings based on protest movements concerning civil rights, student rights, anti-Vietnam War, rights for women, and the (hippie) counter culture. As Bengtson and Mangen (32) put it "These movements seemed to pit the young against the old. 'Don't trust anyone over 30' because a rallying cry that directly emphasized the counter culture's mistrust of the older generation." Leonard Cain (33) had registered an early interest in the equity of a common retirement age for people of manifestly different life expectations, which led him to a broader examination of the new cohorts of older people in America. By the time Bengtson and Cutler (34) came to review the literature for the first *Handbook of Aging and the Social Sciences,* the current shape of the dialogue had largely formed. Tracing ideas from Mannheim (35), whose focus was on the understanding of what he called "generation units" as components of social change; they started with questions of definition and moved on to issues related to age-group differentiation, family and socialization, cohorts, political alienation of the young, age-connected patterns of Medicare usage, lineage and helping relationships, solidarity, and dependency ratios.

Solidarity of Care

The list of topics also formed the framework for the seminal studies conducted by Vern Bengtson and David Mangen, which began in 1970 and have continued up to the present day. They rely on two clear premises (*a*) that solidarity in intergenerational relations is a complex and multidimensional rather than a unitary construct and (*b*) that the measurement tools for observing these phenomena required further elaboration. The emphasis on methodological refinement, using the LISREL statistical modeling technique, has characterized the research. Such responses can be seen both as a natural progression in the sophistication of empirical research methods and as a reaction against the tide of opinion which had formed in that time as a result of the work of Townsend (36) in the United Kingdom, Shanas (37) in the United States, and their associates in Denmark (38). These studies highlighted the high degree of family support to elderly people. Townsend goes as far as to say "that family obligations are taken more seriously than before." Yet the indications of increasing loneliness and the uneven patterns of family support fueled an anxiety that these traditional caring arrangements were beginning to break down.

Bengtson and colleagues (39) saw the need for a more clinically precise assessment that would enable a clearer differentiation of family and relationship types to emerge—and be studied over time, rather than at a fixed point in time. By 1988 he and his team had identified 13 family types which emerged from cluster analysis of their data. They fell into four main groups: (*a*) the "moderates," 50.1 percent of the sample; (*b*) the "exchangers," 12.6 percent; (*c*) the "geographically distant," 15.7 percent; and (*d*) the "socially distant," 18.5 percent. Falling into a kind of league table for helpfulness to the older generation, these groupings also represent clearly different formations. Families may be cohesive on one dimension but fragmented on others. The researchers conclude that, by their definitions of solidarity, only about half would exhibit solidarity.

While acknowledging that family solidarity is a multidimensional concept, of particular significance in this review is the extent of functional social exchange—the transfer of labor and helping skills—between the generations and within generations. On this dimension the latest studies continue to confirm very high levels of commitment, even when the family has fractured in some way. Money flows largely from the old to the young, but care and support is given across the generations in all directions, with women in late middle age being the major givers. Linda Chatters and Robert Taylor (40) in their report of levels of assistance to elderly parents amongst American blacks conclude: "These findings are consistent with previous work that indicates that intergenerational support is characteristic of black families." In making this statement, they too found diverse patterns, based on region, physical proximity, marital status, and the degree of affectual closeness. Moreover they highlight the emergence of widowed daughters as major caregivers to parents.

Barry Wellman's sequence of studies on Canadian samples extending over two decades provides further understanding of what kinds of help are provided by what kinds of kin. His main contribution is twofold: the identification of density and clustering in kinship networks (41, 42), and the delineation of five basic "dimensions" of support (43). The latter consist of Emotional Aid, Services, Companionship, Financial Aid, and Information, supplied by close kin in that sequence of intensity. His longitudinal studies of East Yorkers reveal extensive networks of kin and friends which supply high levels of aid. Sixty-one percent of network members provided emotional support and services, with the most immediate relations being primary providers. The cumulative impact of the data enabled Wellman to conclude (42, p. 211):

> While noting the strains in parent/adult child ties, my interest is in the high level of supportive resources they convey. The bond between parent and adult child is the most supportive of all intimate and active ties, providing high levels of both material and emotional support.

A similarly rigorous study in England by Jane Finch and Hilary Mason (44) came to equally categorical conclusions. After pointing out that kin relations were a significant source of assistance for many people, they try to sum up the vast array of qualitative data (44):

> However, our main point is not so much that these experiences of giving and receiving help within families were *common* experiences (though many of them were) but that they were treated as *unremarkable* experiences by many people who talked to us. They were seen as a characteristic part of family life.

Despite the powerful endorsement of family as a source of many kinds of help to older people—and in the reverse direction—we should retain a proper skepticism. Most studies, still, report only one side of the transaction, usually that of the giver. When both sides are surveyed there is usually a dissonance, with the younger generation providing a more solid account of their giving than the older people feel they have received. There are as yet few longitudinal studies, so plotting trends over time in different countries and regions is difficult to achieve. Similarly, male contributions to caregiving are poorly documented, but recent studies indicate higher contributions than were previously reported, and marked shifts as domestic roles modify in response to female employment and the re-gendering of work (45). Yet any reading of the long-term trend of the whole body of data indicates the remarkable persistence of family support and the very high level of personal responsibility accepted by family members. What we need to be aware of is the likely influence of secular changes in the population that could undermine these patterns, and they are addressed in the final section.

SOLIDARITY, OBLIGATION, AND RECIPROCITY

We have established that wherever people live in society with each other, they do so in relationships of differing types which bind them together both within and across generations. Whether these arrangements are properly labeled families or kinship systems is a technical issue. But what universally characterizes them is a set of rules or laws, guidelines, and conventions which set patterns of obligation involving differing degrees of reciprocity. The nature of this solidarity between individuals and within the fabric of organized society has been the subject of philosophical examination throughout recorded history. In modern times we look to the formative work of Locke and Rousseau.

When Locke wrote of the social contract (46) in the late 17th century, he drew on existing work concepts of popular consent (47). He refined them to provide an explanation of the legitimacy of government and the proper relationship between governments and their subjects in terms of the latter's obedience. Believing that government could only exist on the basis of consent, Locke declared that rulers were entitled to obedience but only if their subjects had actually consented to obey, and so were committed to showing that they had consented, that they had voluntarily agreed, even when it looked as if they had not. By linking consent with obligation as integral features of civil society, his writings served to fashion contemporary liberal political philosophy. In the context of the subject of this chapter, his contribution was to give greater credence to contractarian thinking which Bentham and the utilitarians reinforced in the 19th century and John Rawls (1) used as the point for departure of his *A Theory of Justice.*

As Peter Laslett (48) points out in his book with James Fishkin, *Justice Between Age Groups and Generations,* there are profound difficulties in articulating the contractual nature of intergenerational exchange, which in turn are magnified by attempts to consider the processional nature of justice over time. This is the essential conceptual element in the discourse about an intergenerational compact and the consequent issues of equity, which lie at the heart of this chapter. There are, of course, practical concerns about the willingness and capacity of governments and economic systems to deliver the resources to support elderly populations (see below). In advanced societies, these are questions more of political conviction than of economic possibility. What will unlock the political uncertainty, based as it is on short-term strategies and misconceptions about the "burdens" of an aging population, is a newly refurbished notion of generational solidarity.

As Harry Moody points out, the character of generational giving and receiving is transitive: "We 'repay' the generosity of the preceding generation by giving in turn to our successors" (49, p. 229). Indeed, this apparent paradox is virtually universal. It is to repeat Laslett's term "processional." But even if life can be metaphorically depicted as a procession, it is also one which stops at points in the life path to engage in a series of ritual exchanges. Following nurture to adulthood there may be a period of dependent "apprenticeship"—college, or low earnings early in a career—and a parental transfer to enable the establishment of an independent household, perhaps through marriage. The appearance of grandchildren may prompt further gifts, as might financial misfortune or ill-health (13). But as the journey leads the older generation to their last years, the often unspoken dialogue of emotional support and services in kind in the unspecified expectation of inheritance is acted out. Empirical evidence of this is to be found in long-term care where relatives seek to restrict expenditure to minimize diminution of their inheritance (50).

Callahan (51) has addressed these issues at the macro level by proposing a set of criteria for delimiting the resources older people might claim from the health care system. For him the bond between generations must respect limits that are at once humanistic, normative, and economically feasible. While the fear he exposes is the unnecessary and undesirable use of scarce resources needlessly to extend life, it too is a metaphor for the boundaries which now exist in the gift relationship between generations.

Callahan's book provoked widespread criticism and hostility. Binstock and Post (52) called it scapegoating. Moody (53) called it a blunder. Many others were indignant. The American media were righteously angry. Yet on maturer reflection many of the critics have mediated their reactions with reflection and recognize, as I do, that Callahan has served us well by breaching the death taboo we persist in sustaining despite Aries's (54) equally controversial analysis of it nearly two decades ago. *Setting Limits* is not only a compassionate book, it is intellectually courageous, for it gives systematic attention to the issue which could divide the young and the old, were it not honestly addressed. In his digest and response Callahan makes few concessions to his critics, noting that the most vociferous of them (55, 56) review the alternatives "and find them full of problems too" (57, p. 398).

Where I take issue with Callahan is with the prudentialism he shares with Rawls. It may make good sense for the custodians of society not to put its future well-being at risk by adopting rash policies which might undermine its cultural and financial wealth. But prudence should not extend to despair: that the currently unfathomable problem is an unsolvable problem. However, I too am simply expressing a value-based judgment and reveal myself as more of an optimist than he. Indeed the essence of the whole debate has not been about the quality of analysis but about the *politics* of generational equity—an issue taken up in the next section.

What seems to have escaped attention in the welter of disagreement is the cultural message which Callahan offers. He invites us to look at human life as an experience which has clear limits. It suggests (to adopt a term I gained from Joep Munnichs) a metaphor of finitude. It is the discomfort presented by the finality of death that brings such wrath. It has no place in the Enlightenment/Modernist realm, nor in the self-indulgent confusion of the postmodern. By contrast the image of a procession is progressive, optimistic, and modern.

Also at risk in the intergenerational debate is another metaphor: that of the contract. Human societies that are not subject to totalitarian regimes are founded on contracts written (in law) and unwritten. The principal ingredients are consent and trust. There is an inescapable recognition of social exchange and reciprocity in those wider contracts between strangers. The compact between the generations is not only between unknown parties, it is between the dead and living and the unborn. It is a moral responsibility to maintain the core of trust, even when the details of the agreement are under review—as they must be in the world of rapid and global change. So if we are to join Laslett's procession, its value base needs to be reaffirmed.

Michael Ignatieff puts it elegantly (58):

> We want to know what we have in common with each other beneath the infinity of our differences. We want to know what it means to be human, and we want to know what the knowledge commits us to in terms of duty. What distinguishes the language of needs is its claim that human beings actually feel a common and shared identity in the basic fraternity of hunger, thirst, cold, exhaustion, loneliness or sexual passion. The possibility of human solidarity rests on this idea of natural human identity. A society in which strangers would feel common belonging and mutual responsibility to each other depends on trust, and trust reposes in turn on the idea that beneath difference there is identity.

It is easy enough to perceive such a bonding with our known kith and kin, but more difficult to extend it into the infinite world of people we shall never meet. Yet what has prompted theorists of human behavior to persist with the idea of such an otherwise absurd connection of obligation and identity is its observable reality in everyday life. What remains elusive after centuries of analysis is a watertight formulation that applies to all situations and cultures. Even Rawls's commanding construction of solidarity as the foundation of social justice, using the mythical device of "the veil of ignorance" which ensures "fairness," is criticized because it is inescapably rooted in the author's defining notion of liberty within a liberal framework.

So the main issues are: If there is a contract between people and generations at large, is it a strong version (one where the conditions, duties, and reciprocal benefits are clearly known to all parties), or is it a weak version in which there is a broadly defined commitment for each generation to reward the preceding cohort for their lifetime contribution to the social good? If it is of this weaker sort, what latitude is there for redefinition in the light of current economic circumstances and prevailing ideas of solidarity? In short, is it acceptable for the quantity and quality of intergenerational transfers to be modified (reduced) in the light of new variables like the demographic revolution or the arrival of large-scale unemployment necessitating many people who are not old and not disabled to draw on the communal resource?

Laslett argues that it is the weaker form of contract which prevails in the modern world and that it is inevitably subject to renegotiation as cohort succeeds cohort and as their social, economic, and political circumstances change. Some, like Epstein (59), would argue that the only tenable response is to allow the market mechanism to determine what the generational contract can deliver, while others would share Baybrooke's (60) criticism that such an abandonment to market forces risks consigning some of our successors to effective slavery. In consequence those who hold the authority of government are beholden to sustain the essence of the obligation to provide an adequate level of social and economic well-being for their older citizens. It is this very challenge that preoccupies governments across the world—not as a philosophical notion, but as an operational reality.

At this point I wish to re-engage with Selbourne and his preoccupation with duty as the binding agent of civil order. He reminds us of the importance of citizenship, but insists that propinquity is not sufficient to bind us together; society cannot simply be a randomly associated mass. For him "civic order cannot be founded upon relations between individuals who are moral strangers to each other" (3, p. 18). His own distinctive words elaborate the fundamentals of his argument (3, p. 19):

> I therefore place as an axiom at the heart of this body of ideas the notion that a constellation of moral and practical duties, some embodied in law and others the preserve of conscience alone, is owed by the individual to himself, his fellows, and to the civic order to which he belongs. I do so in the conviction that egoistic *Homo Sapiens,* increasing as if inexorably in numbers, as well as in the insatiable impatience of his desires, is a present danger to himself, to others, to the civic order and to the natural world itself; that a settled condition of *dutiless- ness* makes him more dangerous still.

Here Callahan's pessimism is matched by Selbourne's arch authoritarianism, moderated by notions of free citizenship. In the same way it is valuable to take the metaphor and not the ideology. He refashions key concepts of the social good by signaling the need to counter liberal and individualistic tendencies (coming as they do from quite different ideological sources) to undermine the quintessential fabric of society. His preoccupation with duty has too little by way of countervailing account- ability and social justice—but it is a rapidly dissolving reality in the developed world. So if generational equity is to be preserved and enhanced, it will be important to reinforce the fragile superstructure of societies and states. To pursue only the challenging middle-order questions of contractarianism, distributive justice (61), and communitarianism will be to fulfill Callahan's fears for the living and Laslett's for the world to come.

Gerontologists have largely selected their agendas—quite reasonably—from the empirical world around them, in which old age and aging are still misunderstood. So the emergence of a political economy of aging brought a new fusion of theoretical and policy issues which linked with but, until Callahan, did not fully embrace the issues raised in this section.

THE POLITICAL ECONOMY PERSPECTIVE

The political economy of aging made its first significant mark in 1981 when Peter Townsend published his seminal paper "The Structured Dependency of the Elderly: A Creation of Social Policy in the Twentieth Century" (62). In it he drew attention, not simply to the socially and economically submerged position of elderly people as a group, but to the way society contrived to make and keep it so. In his own words: "I wish to put forward the thesis that the dependency of the elderly in the twentieth century is being manufactured socially and that its severity is unnecessary." Almost a decade later, the vigorous debate which Townsend provoked took another decisive turn, but one which asserted that the old are taking too large a part of the national incomes of developed societies.

Gerontologists in general, led initially by Alan Walker (63) (who had foreshadowed these ideas), welcomed the political statement Townsend had made and a number went on to offer their own elaborations of it. In Britain, Chris Phillipson's research on U.K pension policies over the past hundred years led to the publication of his influential book *Capitalism and the Construction of Old Age* (64). In the United States, Carroll Estes (65) wrote convincingly and trenchantly about the oppression of older people in America and their labeling as a social problem in a way which purported to provide munificently for its workers. Inevitably others joined in, John Myles (66) among others in the United States. In Europe, Martin Kohli's (67) studies of enforced retirement in the German tobacco industry and Xavier Gaullier's (68) of the same phenomena in France led an emerging consensus that employers, trade unions, and governments were co-conspirators against older citizens.

Early critics of Townsend's thesis were hardly visible. The new orthodoxy gained a self-evident status. It took another new perspective on aging which emerged fully in the mid-eighties—the history of aging and old age—to supply evidence that weakened some of the empirical support for "structured dependency." From France there already existed the influential, if flawed, earlier work of Peter Stearns (69), which by showing the great variety of experience of older people in France both supported and challenged the Townsend view. In North America, Andrew Achenbaum's (70) concern with historical analysis of what constituted a "young" society cast further doubts on claims that the retired population in the past was ill-treated and deprived.

The concerted work of the Cambridge Group for the History and Structure of Population under the Leadership of Peter Laslett brought the weight of scholarship to the history of aging. Laslett's work has made its own global impact. But it was probably the work of his colleague, the New Zealander David Thomson (71), that created the greatest controversy. In a paper on the decline of the welfare state, he both undermined the myth of the Victorian golden age in Britain and raised serious questions about the comparative economic treatment given to different generations and age groups.

Questions about the relative share of the national economic cake given to old people and to the young started to come to the fore in the United States during Ronald Reagan's presidency. They arose from the reaction of commentators on the political right to the growing "burden" of health and Social Security payments to the expanding retired population. They saw the public cost of maintaining elderly people escalating at the same time as an observed growth in the discretionary income of people over 55 amounting to one-third of the national total. A view emerged in what Meredith Minkler (72) calls "corporate America" that the old constituted a group of developing wealth while children and young people were suffering as a consequence of social programs for their elders.

In 1985 a new organization formed in America under the leadership of Senator David Durenberger and Representative James Jones. They called it Americans for Generational Equity (AGE). It defined itself as a nonpartisan coalition whose mission was to build an intellectual and mass membership movement to promote the interests of the younger and future generations in the national political process. Its main targets were to increase the political power of young people and to reduce government expenditure on Social Security and Medicare—a form of federal hospital and medical insurance for those aged 65 and over.

AGE claimed that as the elderly population grows bigger it becomes richer. It is also more demanding of costly public services with the result that it is taking "more than its fair share." Children and young people are losing out. AGE points out that although constituting only 11.5 percent of the U.S. population, those over 65 consume 28 percent of the national budget and 51 percent of all government expenditure on social services. However, the objectives are not simply fiscal. Senator Durenberger is reported as saying: "The assumption that each working generation will take care of the one that proceeded it is finished" (72).

Perhaps prompted by a public relations visit to Britain by AGE representatives, David Lovibond wrote a piece in *The Daily Telegraph* entitled, "Why Should We Pamper the Whingeing Pensioners?" (73):

> Contrary to the popular understanding and arguably as a result of filial guilt, perhaps too much sympathy is offered to the old rather than too little. After all, is the prospect of an expensively maintained, ever multiplying hoary headed horde any less dispiriting than the present hegemony of the yobs and the yahoos.

This kind of verbal face-pulling may not match the public relations cleverness of AGE, but it espouses the same purposes—to undermine social support for the old to relieve the young. Moreover, it seeks to challenge the social contract between the generations, that a life of hard labor, which includes supporting the young, is repaid with income and care in retirement. Instead it is everyone for themselves from birth to death.

Those of us who contribute to the literature of gerontology are well aware that across Europe, one in three of the retired population are officially below the poverty line. On the other hand, we recognize that there is a growing subgroup of retired people who continue to be prosperous into old age (74). This latter group includes not only those with accumulated wealth but also those with inflation-proof pensions and lump-sum retirement bonuses. The elderly population is far from homogeneous (75).

So, however distasteful its motives and publicity-seeking its pronouncements, it is not possible to dismiss AGE (now defunct as an organization) and its imitators as having no case. As David Thomson's (76) research on historical patterns of welfare spending in New Zealand points out, there are accumulated benefits to the elderly which leave young age groups gravely disadvantaged. The most obvious examples are the relative difficulty for younger people to enter the housing market as expenditure on public housing has been withdrawn. Similarly, the greatest burden of unemployment has fallen on those under 25, while health care costs for the old have escalated. State pension levels have, in real terms, fallen in recent years, but the total cost continues to rise steeply.

Johnson and Falkingham (15), observing the measurable disparities in generational shares in the United States, have conducted an analysis of public expenditure in the United Kingdom. Their conclusions are that the British welfare state has been remarkably neutral in its allocation of resources between the generations. They go on to show that any discussion of intergenerational conflict for welfare resources in the United Kingdom would establish a false division. In their view the inequalities lie along class lines in all age groups. Many other writers would see gender, at all ages, as a major variable which, combined with class and ethnic origin, overshadows generation and cohort as the defining division (77–81).

The publication of a collection of papers by an international selection of authors under the provocative title *Workers v. Pensioners: Intergenerational Justice in an Aging World* (82) attracted attention well beyond academic gerontology. The overt espousal of an intergenerational struggle for primacy and resources attracted the mass media, and Paul Johnson, the principal editor, presented the statistical evidence as he saw it. Not all were persuaded. In a spirited review of the book, Eric Midwinter (83) wrote of it as a lynching party, relishing the prospect of mistrust and lack of cooperation between the generations. He goes on to challenge the authors' interpretation of state welfare transfers, their misunderstanding of the reality of the so-called dependency ratios (see Chapter 4) and the ability of developed societies to sustain those no longer in paid employment.

The political economy discourse now continues at two levels: one concerned with distributive justice and the other with mechanisms and constraints of state institutions and economic systems. In particular it focuses on changing concepts of welfare (84) and the impact of the mixed economy of welfare which has now invaded all the post Second World War welfare states. But even where pluralistic systems are long established, as in North America, the energy thrust and policy-making attention is with the economists concerned with pensions and social security. In the United Kingdom, Andrew Dilnot and colleagues' (85) detailed economic projections and models of age-related income patterns over time, alongside alternative pension policies, represent the center ground. Their work and that of others in the field were heavily drawn on by the Social Justice Commission (86) initiated by the Labor Party.

Parallel activity in the United States is exemplified by the work of Williamson and Pampel (87), whose concerns mirror Dilnot's. From their review of the policy alternatives studied in the United States, United Kingdom, Germany, and Sweden, they recommend the new German and Swedish indexing formulas, both of which, they claim, emphasize generational burden sharing. But their consideration of burden sharing makes no reference to the ethical debate, only to that of contemporary politics.

The economist Yung-Ping Chen (88) addresses the long-term care component of the aging population "problem" by proposing that a "three legged stool" of social insurance, private insurance, and social security should meet the costs which are now estimated to total $108 billion a year (89). This approach is based on technical criteria that will ensure a spread of responsibility for paying. It adds the novelty of proposing "tradeable benefits" to allow holdings in one benefit (e.g., pension) to be transferred to another (e.g., long-term care).

Thus the dialogue about relations between the old and the young has become a new industry for financial institutions and their advisers. Townsend's original concerns have lost salience, and the ethical discussion only occasionally coincides with the other two. Yet only if the three levels of analysis are integrated can we as citizens, growing older, hope to see generational equity as opposed to political fixes.

CONCLUSIONS

The object of this chapter has been to bring together several streams of research analysis and conceptualizing, which continue to develop along largely parallel paths. In reviewing each body of literature and ideas my concern has been to draw out the main themes, evidence, and opinion, rather than to make a comprehensive interdisciplinary assessment (a task in progress). In doing so I am conscious of leaving many important associated themes unattended to. There is no assessment here of the disputes about what constitutes a cohort or a generation, communitarianism is given no more than a passing reference, and there is no detailed scrutiny of the economics of social security. Feminist critiques of social welfare and pension systems are underrepresented as are references to experiences beyond Europe, Australasia, and North America. Nonetheless I offer this selective scrutiny of generational relations as a contribution that might stimulate others to join me in a larger debate.

What prompted this new direction, for me, was a growing concern that the increasing acceptance in academic circles of a world view that sees only disintegration and disorder serves society ill. Moreover, the more I read the less persuaded I am that it represents the lived reality for people at large. Like R. D. Laing's eloquently corrosive views of the family in the sixties, it has beguiling qualities. Not the least of these attractions is the prospect of constructing and revealing a new reality. However, apart from the ideological vacuum and the temporary sovereignty of a post-Thatcherite individualism, reinforced by marketization (all likely to diminish in importance before the decade is out), I observe no radical changes in the fundamentals of human societies—only in the clothes they wear.

So I find myself in unexpected company and coming to conclusions which stretch my imagination. With David Selbourne, I see the need for a renewal of citizenship, moral considerations, and a new disposition of freedom and duty. His anxiety about civic order is not one I can share in its entirety; but any involvement with justice between generations must pay regard to the robustness of the society which promises to provide for those who follow. Which means that I also join in Laslett's procession, recognizing that the generational contract cannot be fixed for all time, but must be open to re-negotiation. Yet the parameters of that new deal need to be set within a framework of secure knowledge that the central promise of the contract—adequate income and care of the old—is an enduring right.

A greater recognition of finitude in old age and the need to talk about and plan for the dependency the fourth age might bring is one prerequisite for the new contract. But it will serve also as a necessary prologue to the continuing but largely silent dialogue between generations—at the personal and the societal levels. It is about the giving and receiving of nurture and dignity in old age and the ways in which these processes are transformed into a right through reciprocal giving in life and after its end. In this way the necessary re-negotiation of the details can proceed without crises and major generational conflicts.

The large literature on family formations and family caring leads me to believe that this most central agency in human society is not in terminal decline. On the contrary, its modification and diversification provide more options and more strengths. It is clear that single-parent family formats can succeed, but usually only where there are other adult long-term helpers for the single parent. Similarly, inter-generational helping transfers are still empirically well evidenced. As Janet Finch puts it, these forms of help are taken for granted, they are seen as unremarkable.

While philosophers trade their abstractions based on intuition, they observe a continued willingness to recognize a contract of sorts (a compact) between the age cohorts and generations. And these observations fit well with the more data-based accounts which shape the political economy debate. There are already indications that the American right-wing backlash against the old is losing prominence. This does not mean the end of the concern for intergenerational equity, but it may herald a less ideological and more pragmatic phase in which fit older people are expected to be active socioeconomic contributors for longer, but where the gains of the modern welfare state are not wholly replaced by market mechanisms.

As for older people themselves, there may be less evidence of the new indi-vidualism which prompts some of them to neglect traditional inheritance patterns in order to sustain their own life styles.

Undoubtedly the state will seek to constrain the costs of long-term health care and income support by introducing more charges to lay claim to accumulated wealth, where it exists. But families may choose to become more overt about the reciprocity involved in inheritance as the state siphons off more. In all of this the changing circumstances of women, of all ages, are likely to be the single most powerful influence on intergenerational solidarity.

Like the sculptor who sees an angel in the marble, I see, in the vast debate about the family and its willing capacity to provide social and economic support to its members, a remarkable continuity. Changes in form and the range of configurations are self-evident; but as this planet's central nuclear grouping it remains paramount and the single most powerful source of human well-being. Moreover, the empirical as opposed to the theoretical evidence also indicates a sustained willingness to express solidarity with strangers—both contemporaries and those born before and after. This latter orientation is being strained by an unprecedented and permanent change in population structure. I have long believed we have the global capacity to support all the earth's people, but to do so will require a revolution in economic and political action that re-establishes human solidarity and reciprocity as central features of our social order. As has been argued, these transformations are essentially moral; but failure to address them puts at risk not only the contract between young and old, but society itself.

Note — This chapter is an extensively revised and extended version of "Genera-tional Relations Under Review," published in *Uniting Generations: Studies in*

Conflict and Cooperation, edited by David Hobman, Age Concern Publications, London, 1993.

REFERENCES

1. Rawls, J. *A Theory of Justice.* Harvard University Press, Cambridge, Mass., 1971.
2. Selbourne, D. *The Spirit of the Age.* Sinclair Stevenson, London, 1993.
3. Selbourne, D. *The Principle of Duty: An Essay on the Foundation of Civic Order.* Sinclair Stevenson, London, 1994.
4. Titmuss, R. *The Gift Relationship: From Human Blood to Social Policy.* Allen and Unwin, London, 1970.
5. Nozick, R. *Anarchy, State and Utopia.* Basic Books, New York, 1974.
6. MacIntyre, A. *After Virtue: A Study in Moral Theory,* Ed. 2. Duckworth, London, 1985.
7. Taylor, F. W. *Principles of Scientific Management.* Harper, New York, 1914.
8. Doray, B. *From Taylorism to Fordism: A Rational Madness.* Free Association Books, London, 1988 [1981].
9. Bell, D. *The Coming of Post-Industrial Society.* Basic Books, New York, 1973.
10. Baudrillard, J. *Simulations.* Semiotext, New York, 1983.
11. Turner, B. S. (ed.). *Theories of Modernity and Postmodernity.* Sage, London, 1990.
12. Williams, F. Social relations, welfare and the post-Fordism debate. In *Towards a Post-Fordist Welfare State,* edited by Burrows and Louder. Routledge, London, 1994.
13. Daniels, N. *Am I My Parents' Keeper: An Essay on Justice between the Young and the Old.* Oxford University Press, New York, 1988.
14. Walker, A. The economic burden of ageing and the prospect of intergenerational conflict. *Ageing Soc.* 10(4): 377–396, 1990.
15. Johnson, P., and Falkingham, J. Intergenerational transfers and public expenditure on the elderly. *Ageing Soc.* 8(2): 129–146, 1988.
16. Murdock, P. *Social Structure.* Macmillan, New York, 1949.
17. Parsons, T., and Bales, R. F. *Family, Socialization and Interaction Process.* The Free Press, New York, 1955.
18. Bell, N. W., and Vogel, E. F. (eds.). *A Modern Introduction to the Family.* Collier, Macmillan, London, 1968.
19. Gough, K. Is the family universal? The Nayor case. In *A Modern Introduction to the Family,* edited by N. W. Bell and E. F. Vogel. Collier, Macmillan, London, 1959.
20. Bettelheim, B. *Children of the Dream.* Thames and Hudson, London, 1969.
21. Spiro, M. E. Is the family universal? In *A Modern Introduction to the Family,* edited by N. W. Bell and E. F. Collier, Macmillan, London, 1968.
22. Gonzalez, N. L. Towards a definition of matrifocality. In *Afro-American Anthropology,* edited by N. W. Whitten and J. F. Szwed. The Free Press, New York, 1970.
23. Hannerz, U. *Soulside: Inquiries into Ghetto Culture and Community.* Columbia University Press, New York, 1969.
24. Leach, E. *A Runaway World.* BBC Publications, London, 1968.
25. Laing, R. D., and Esterson, A. *Sanity, Madness and the Family.* Penguin, Harmondsworth, 1970.
26. Toffler, A. *Future Shock.* Pan, London, 1971.
27. Greer, G. *The Female Eunuch.* Paladin, London, 1970.
28. Oakley, A. *Housewife.* Martin Robertson, Oxford, 1974.
29. Finch, J. *Family Obligations and Social Charge.* Polity, London, 1989.

30. Cunningham Burley, S. Constructing grandparenthood—Anticipating appropriate action. *Sociology* 19: 3, 1985.
31. Arber, S., and Ginn, J. *Gender and Later Life: A Sociological Analysis of Resources and Constraints.* Sage, London, 1991.
32. Bengtson, V., and Mangen, D. Generations, families and interactions. In *Measurement of Intergenerational Relations,* edited by D. Mangen, V. Bengtson, and P. Landry. Sage, Newbury Park, 1988.
33. Cain, L. D. Age, status and generational phenomena: The new old people in contemporary America. *Gerontologist* 7: 83–92, 1967.
34. Bengtson, V., and Cutler, N. Generations and intergenerational relations. In *Handbook of Aging and the Social Sciences,* edited by E. H. Binstock and E. Shanas. Van Nostrand Reinhold, New York, 1976.
35. Mannheim, K. The problem of generations. In *Essays on the Sociology of Knowledge,* edited by P. Kecskemeti. Routledge and Kegan Paul, London, 1952 [1928].
36. Townsend, P. *The Family Life of Old People.* Routledge and Kegan Paul, London, 1957.
37. Shanas, E. *The Health of Older People.* Harvard University Press, Cambridge, 1962.
38. Shanas, E., et al. *Old People in Three Industrial Societies.* Routledge and Kegan Paul, London, 1968.
39. Bengtson, V., et al. (eds.). *Measurement of Intergenerational Relations.* Sage, Newbury Park, 1988.
40. Chatters, L., and Taylor, R. Intergenerational support: The provision of assistance to parents by adult children. In *Aging in Black America,* edited by J. S. Jackson, L. M. Chatters, and R. J. Taylor. Sage, Newbury Park, 1993.
41. Wellman, B., and Wortley, S. Brothers' keepers: Situating kinship relations in broader networks of social support. *Sociol. Perspect.* 32(3): 273–306, 1989.
42. Wellman, B. The Place of kinfolk in personal community networks. *Marriage Fam. Rev.* 15(1/2): 195–228, 1990.
43. Wellman, B. Which types of ties and networks provide what kinds of social support? *Adv. Group Processes* 9: 207–235, 1992.
44. Finch, J., and Mason, H. *Negotiating Family Responsibilities.* Tavistock/Routledge, London, 1992.
45. Nardi, P. (ed.). *Men's Friendships.* Sage, Newbury Park, 1992.
46. Laslett, P. *Locke's Two Treatises of Government.* Cambridge University Press, Cambridge, England, 1960.
47. Plamenatz, J. *Man and Society.* Longman, London, 1963.
48. Laslett, P., and Fishkin, J. (eds.). *Justice Between Age Groups and Generations.* Yale University Press, New Haven, Conn., 1992.
49. Moody, H. R. *Ethics in an Aging Society.* Johns Hopkins University Press, Baltimore, 1992.
50. Crystal, S. *America's Old Age Crisis.* Basic Books, New York, 1982.
51. Callahan, D. *Setting Limits: Medical Goals in an Aging Society.* Simon and Schuster, New York, 1987.
52. Binstock, R. H., and Post, S. G. (eds.). *Too Old for Health Care: Controversies in Medicine, Law, Economics and Ethics.* Johns Hopkins University Press, Baltimore, 1991.
53. Moody, H. R. Allocation, yes; age-based rationing, no. In *Too Old for Health Care: Controversies in Medicine, Law, Economics and Ethics,* edited by R. H. Binstock and S. G. Post. Johns Hopkins University Press, Baltimore, 1991.
54. Aries, P. *The Hour of Our Death.* Editions du Seuil, Paris, 1977.
55. Jecker, N., and Pearlman, R. A. Ethical constraints on rationing medical care by age. *J. Am. Geriatr. Soc.* 37: 1067–1075, 1989.

56. Winslow, G. R., and Walters, J. W. (eds.). *Facing Limits: Ethics and Health Care for the Elderly.* Westview Press, Boulder, Colo., 1993.
57. Callahan, D. Setting Limits: A response. *Gerontologist* 34(3): 393–398, 1994.
58. Ignatieff, M. *The Needs of Strangers.* Chatto and Windus, London, 1984.
59. Epstein, R. Justice across generations. In *Justice Between Age Groups and Generations,* edited by P. Laslett and J. Fishkin. Yale University Press, New Haven, Conn., 1992.
60. Baybrooke, D. The social contract and property rights across generations. In *Justice Between Age Groups and Generations,* edited by P. Laslett and J. Fishkin. Yale University Press, New Haven, Conn., 1992.
61. Miller, D. *Market, State and Community.* Cambridge University Press, Cambridge, England, 1989.
62. Townsend, P. The structured dependency of the elderly: A creation of social policy in the twentieth century. *Ageing Soc.* I: 5–28, 1981.
63. Walker, A. The social creation of poverty and dependency in old age. *J. Soc. Policy* 9: 49–75, 1980.
64. Phillipson, C. *Capitalism and the Construction of Old Age.* Macmillan, London, 1982.
65. Estes, C. L. et al. *Political Economy, Health and Aging.* Little, Brown, New York, 1984.
66. Myles, J. Income inequality and status maintenance. *Res. Aging* 2: 123–141, 1981.
67. Kohli, M., Rosenow, J., and Wolf, J. The social construction of aging through work: Economic structure and life world. *Ageing Soc.* 3: 23–42, 1983.
68. Gaullier, X. Economic crisis and old age: Old policies in France. *Ageing Soc.* 2: 165–182, 1982.
69. Stearns, P. *Old Age in European Society.* Croom Helm, London, 1977.
70. Achenbaum, A. Aging of the first new nation. In *Our Aging Society,* edited by A. Pifer and L. Bronte. W. W. Norton, New York, 1986.
71. Thomson, D. The decline of social welfare: Failing support for the elderly since early Victorian times. *Ageing Soc.* 4: 451–482, 1984.
72. Minkler, M. The politics of generational equity. *Soc. Policy,* Winter 1987.
73. Lovibond, D. Why should we pamper the whingeing pensioners? *Daily Telegraph,* January 15, 1989.
74. Victor, C. Income inequality in later life. In *Growing Old in the Twentieth Century,* edited by M. Jefferys. Routledge, London, 1987.
75. Midwinter, E. *The Wage of Retirement: The Case for a New Pensions Policy.* Centre for Policy on Aging, London, 1985.
76. Thomson, D. The Welfare State and Generational Conflict: Winners and Losers. Paper presented at the Conference on Work, Retirement and Intergenerational Equity, St. John's College, Cambridge, England, 1988.
77. Miller, J., and Glendinning, C. Gender and poverty. *J. Soc. Policy* 18(3), 1989.
78. Falkingham, J., and Victor, C. *The Myth of the Woopie?: Incomes, the Elderly and Targeting Welfare.* Suntory Toyota International Centre for Economics and Related Disciplines, London School of Economics, London, 1991.
79. Family Law Committee. *Maintenance and Capital Provision on Divorce.* The Law Society, London, 1991.
80. Fennell, G. Housing or income: A review of recent housing research. *Ageing Soc.* 10(1): 95–104, 1990.
81. Parker, H. *Citizen Income and Women.* Basic Income Research Group, London, 1993.
82. Johnson, P., Conrad, C., and Thomson, D. (eds.). *Workers v. Pensioners: Intergenerational Justice in an Aging World.* Manchester University Press, Manchester, 1989.
83. Midwinter, E. Book review of Johnson, P., Conrad, C., Thomson, D. (eds.). *Workers v. Pensioners: Intergenerational Justice in an Aging World. Ageing Soc.* 9: 446–448, 1989.

84. Hills, J. *The Future of Welfare.* Joseph Rowntree Foundation, York, 1993.
85. Dilnot, A., et al. *Pensions Policy in the UK: An Economic Analysis.* Institute for Fiscal Studies, London, 1994.
86. Social Justice Commission. *Social Justice: Strategies for National Renewal.* Vintage, London, 1994.
87. Williamson, J. B., and Pampel, F. C. Paying for the baby boom generation's social security pensions: United States, United Kingdom, Germany and Sweden. *J. Aging Stud.* 7(1): 41–54, 1993.
88. Chen, Y. P. A three legged stool: A new way to fund long term care. In *Care in the Long Term: In Search of Community Security.* Institute of Medicine. National Academy Press, Washington, D.C., 1993.
89. Vladeck, B. C., Miller, N. A., and Clauser, S. B. The changing face of long term care. *Health Care Financ. Rev.* 14(4): 5–23, 1993.

CHAPTER 4

Beyond Apocalyptic Demography:
Toward a Moral Economy of Interdependence

Ann Robertson

Without the light of language, we risk becoming strangers to our better selves.

Ignatieff (1, p. 142)

In the preceding chapter, Malcolm Johnson explored the nature and basis of intergenerational patterns of obligation and concluded with a call for transformations in economic and political action that are "essentially moral" (page 69). This chapter represents a contribution to those transformations by offering a moral language for social policy in general, and aging policy in particular, a language that seeks to "[re-establish] human solidarity and reciprocity as central features of our social order" (page 69).

By examining a number of assumptions that underlie the prevailing notions of population aging in terms of "apocalyptic demography," this chapter explores the politics of need as it relates to aging policy in the context of the modern welfare state. More specifically, it is about how we define ourselves as a human community, in terms of how we discuss and arbitrate issues of human need. And, finally, it is about how we might replace the therapeutic language of need and the "rights talk," which characterize the prevailing discourse on human need in the modern welfare state, with the language of a moral economy of interdependence.

APOCALYPSE REVISITED

Catastrophic projections of the burden to society of an increasing aging population abound (2–4). The prevailing belief is that an increasing aging population inevitably means increasing demands on the resources of society, including health care resources, in the face of competing interests and diminishing, or at best finite, resources. According to this scenario, people will live longer but sicker (5). The greater morbidity of increasing numbers of elders, so the argument goes, will drive

This chapter is reprinted with permission from *Ageing and Society,* 1997, in press. © 1997, Cambridge University Press.

up health care costs. In addition, public pension plans will collapse under the sheer weight of the numbers of older people. This "bankruptcy hypothesis of aging" in which "oncoming hordes of elderly" (6) deplete societal resources constitutes apocalyptic demography.

It is not so much the increase in the absolute size of the older age groups that is seen to be the problem as it is the size of the older age groups relative to younger age groups. With the obvious demographic shift toward older age groups, the traditional demographic model, represented by a pyramid, is undergoing a phenomenon known as the "squaring of the pyramid" (7). The compellingness of the apocalyptic demography argument appears to rest, in part, on the assumption that the population pyramid represents the "natural" or "normal" and, therefore, "proper" demographic structure for a society. The squaring of the pyramid is presented in hyperbolic language as being "unprecedented" and having "profound implications"; the notion that the square might become an inverted pyramid is seen by some as being "tantamount to national suicide" (7).

Increases in the relative size of the over-65 population, together with the evidence for higher morbidity rates in older age groups, means that younger, working people will bear an increased burden of support. In other words, there exists—so the argument goes—an ever increasing net transfer of resources from relatively healthy, younger, working people to older, sicker, retired people. This notion of the burden of support is traditionally expressed in terms of *dependency ratios,* defined as "a numerical relationship between the 'productive' and 'non-productive' or 'dependent' components of a population" (80). Despite attempts to critique the use of dependency ratios in constructing demographic apocalypse (4, 9), they nevertheless remain central to the apocalyptic demography argument.

By invoking the symbolic rhetoric of the notion of the "squaring of the pyramid" and increasing dependency ratios, all in the context of a cost-containment agenda, the question that is framed by the proponents of apocalyptic demography is: Will the elderly really bankrupt us? (10). In the shadow of such a framing of the question, older people have been blamed, not only for the rising costs of health care and income security programs, but also for the poverty of children, the national deficit, and the increase in real estate prices (11). In other words, the proponents of apocalyptic demography have constructed a potential battleground for intergenerational competition for resources (3), finding expression in, among other things, the notion of age-based rationing of health care (12, 13). Although the apocalyptic demography scenario found its earliest expression in the United States, a similar rhetoric is emerging in the United Kingdom (14) and to a lesser extent in Canada (15).

Underlying the apocalyptic demography argument are more fundamental notions of "dependency" versus "independency" which require closer examination.

THE SOCIAL CONSTRUCTION OF DEPENDENCY

Many investigators in the critical gerontology field (16) have argued that much of the dependency of older adults is encouraged and fostered—wittingly or unwittingly—by service professionals, service agencies and institutions, and certain policies which shape the daily lives of older adults (see Chapter 7). It could be argued that the currently prevalent "biomedicalization" (17) and "gerontologization" of old age has resulted in old age being reconceptualized as a new "medical space" (18).

New medical spaces require supporting ideologies in the form of theories, practitioners, institutions, and social policies, policies which in turn can reproduce and entrench them. The creation of new medical spaces, with the potential to encompass more of their lives, may lead to an "overservicing" of older people in a more fundamental way than simply manipulating utilization patterns, an explanation offered by many for the rise in health care costs of the elderly (e.g., 19).

New medical spaces require new customers. Elsewhere, using Alzheimer's disease as a recent example of a new medical space (4), I have explored the extent to which "need" and "morbidity"—and hence, dependency in old age—may be, in part, socially constructed. But what interests or purpose does the dependency of older adults serve? As Estes (20) has argued, it serves, in part, the interests of the entire "aging enterprise"—all those professionals, agencies, facilities, bureaucracies, and academic and research institutions established to "serve" older people (see Chapter 7).

At a more macro level, many writers have analyzed retirement and old age pensions (public and occupational) as major vehicles for the modern capitalist state to control the wage labor market, noting that, from this perspective, old age itself can be regarded as a social construction (14, 16, 21, 22). In analyses such as these, the socially constructed dependency of older adults is seen to serve structural interests. Retirement illustrates a case where, as a matter of public policy, a whole population group, on the basis of chronological age, is excluded from the work-based distribution system, the primary distributive mechanism of the modern capitalist state.

In her book *The Disabled State,* political scientist Deborah Stone (23) argues that the failure of the work-distribution system to provide adequately or equitably for the needs of those who, for various reasons, are excluded from it or are marginal to it invokes the other major distributive mechanism—namely, the need-based system. The nature and extent of these two distributive systems and the boundaries between them constitute major dilemmas for the modern welfare state, and are the subject of much social policy deliberation. A major policy issue is the control of entry into the need-based system; hence, the necessity to distinguish between the "deserving" and "nondeserving," most often framed in terms of "eligibility." The inevitable tension between these two distributive systems leads to questions such as: Who gets what and on what basis?

Evoking the concept of need raises further questions about how we define need, and the related concepts of fairness and just exchange, and how those concepts—always historically contingent—are reflected in our thinking and in social policy. This requires us to consider the politics of need.

THE POLITICS OF NEED

Discussions of need in the last few decades have been dominated by two related discourses: a therapeutic language of need and rights talk.

A Therapeutic Language of Need

> There are few presumptions in human relations more dangerous than the idea
> that one knows what another human being needs better than they do themselves
> (1, p. 11).

It is precisely this presumption by service providers to define need that has led
social critics like Ivan Illich (24) and John McKnight (25) to talk about "disabling
professions," and others to characterize the modern welfare state as a "therapeutic
state" (26, 27).

Illich characterizes "the age of disabling professions" as "an age when people had
'problems,' experts had 'solutions,' and scientists measured imponderables such as
'abilities' and 'needs'" (24, p. 11). In the therapeutic encounter, an ontological
transformation occurs in which persons are reproduced as clients or patients (25),
and thus become "experts in the art of learning to need" (24, p. 24). For example, as
discussed earlier, the social construction of dependency in older adults, by connecting them to and embedding them within a multiplicity of institutional and
community services and agencies, as well as within particular retirement and pension policies, constitutes such a transformation (16, 20, 28, 29).

But, why this propensity on the part of dominant professions to transform persons
into clients? According to McKnight, the answer lies in the shift in the economies of
late 20th century post-industrial societies from a commodity base to a service base
(27, p. 74; emphasis added):

> In a modernized society where the major business is service . . . the client is less
> a person in need than a person who is needed. . . . *The central political issue
> becomes the servicers' capacity to manufacture needs in order to expand the
> economy of the servicing system.*

It could be argued that in the modern welfare state we have witnessed the commodification of need itself and the emergence of a "services fetishism." In terms of
the elderly, the commodification of need has been manifested in what has been
called an "aging enterprise" (20). This, in turn, has fostered a therapeutic language of
need. By locating need in individual "clients," a therapeutic language of need effectively depoliticizes the problem of human need and renders us all potential clients of
the therapeutic state.

In their book *Habits of the Heart*, sociologist Robert Bellah and his colleagues
(30) argue that the "therapeutic mode" is not simply a clinical technique, but has
become a cultural phenomenon. The therapeutic mode is characterized, in part, by an
attitude that all relationships and all activities are merely means to the end of
self-realization, the goal of life. Manifested in the notion of a social contract in
which commitments are made by freely choosing individuals, "the therapeutic attitude distances us from particular social roles, relationships, and practices" (30,
p. 127), thereby resulting in the erosion of public and civic life.

An individualized therapeutic language of need also has spawned an accompanying discourse on individual rights.

Rights Talk

In *Rights Talk: The Impoverishment of Political Discourse,* Harvard law professor Mary Ann Glendon critically examines current American political discourse in terms of the "tendency to speak of what is most important to us in terms of rights, and to frame nearly every social controversy as a clash of rights" (31, p. 4).

Glendon characterizes rights talk in terms of the following: an absoluteness which heightens social conflict and precludes even the possibility of finding common ground; a resounding silence concerning responsibilities—both personal and civic; a "relentless individualism" which conceives of the individual as a lone rights-bearer, and which, as a result, "fosters a climate that is inhospitable to society's losers, and that systematically disadvantages caretakers and dependents, both young and old" (31, p. 14); a neglect of civil society—families, neighborhoods, ethnic and religious associations, and the like—which Glendon believes to be "the principal seedbeds of civic and personal virtue" (31, p. 14) where "human character, competence, and capacity for citizenship are formed" (31, p. 109); and finally, an insularity from moral and political discussion. The social and political result of this emphasis on rights talk, Glendon claims, is the "atrophy of vital local governments and political parties, and the disdain for politics that is now so prevalent" (31, p. 5). As she wryly observes: "the language of rights is the language of no compromise. The winner takes all and the loser has to get out of town. The conversation is over" (31, p. 9).

The dominance of rights talk not only has led to the diminishment of the public conversation about need, it also tends to move whatever discussion there is from the domain of public discourse to the courts. Rights talk finds expression in claims of entitlement, often made on the basis of special status. The rhetoric behind public old age pensions is comprised, in part, of the notion of entitlement: that is, if you live a life of "hard work, diligence to the best of your ability, not idling or squandering your resources—you *deserve* to live decently for the entire span of your life" (32, p. 148; emphasis added). The failure of the U.S. 1988 Catastrophic Health Insurance Act, which expanded health care benefits beyond the 1965 Medicare bill, has been explained, in part, by the " 'senior backlash' against the legislation and its unpopular self-financing mechanism," which violated entrenched notions about the claims of elderly Americans (33).

Rights-based language represents an individualized, ultimately depoliticized, discourse on human need, for it acknowledges only persons who make a claim against the collectivity. Rarely does it consider those against whom the claim is made. Rights talk is not a language of community, for although "rights language offers a rich vernacular for the claims an individual may make on or against the collectivity, . . . it is relatively impoverished as a means of expressing individuals' needs *for* the collectivity" (1, p. 13).

This takes us to a consideration of the way in which a language of need is bound up, in part, with the language of community.

Needs and the Life of the Community

Much of politics is . . . an effort to define need collectively. (34, p. 81)

Politics is the collective activity in which any group or community engages when it seeks to arbitrate competing claims of need. According to political scientist Michael Walzer, "the social contract is an agreement to reach decisions together about what goods are necessary to our common life, and then to provide those goods for one another" (35, p. 65).

Politics is not only about the definition and discussion of need; it is also about how a community defines and recognizes itself as a community: "Political community for the sake of provision, provision for the sake of community: the process works both ways and that is perhaps its crucial feature" (35, p. 64). In other words, there is no collective provision of needs without community; nor is there any community without the collective provision of needs.

The nature of a community is characterized, in part, by the kinds of needs it collectively provides for, and the extent to which it provides for those needs. It is the definition and collective provision of human needs which determines the cohesiveness—or lack thereof—of any group or community. Stone contends that "communal provision . . . may be the most important force holding communities together" (34, p. 82). In a similar spirit, and in opposition to the prevailing economic view of human motivation and behavior, Ignatieff says that "the deepest motivational springs of political involvement are to be located in this human capacity to feel needs for others" (1, p. 17).

Walzer (35) argues that it is through the collective provision of needs that the community recognizes membership in the community. Which needs come to be recognized as legitimate for collective provision is determined by who participates in the discussion about need, and says much about who is considered to be a member of the community. Indeed, as Walzer says, "When all the members share in the business of interpreting the social contract, the result will be a more or less extensive system of communal provision" (35, p. 83).

In *The Needs of Strangers* (1), a contemporary meditation on the nature of human need, historian Michael Ignatieff says that "a decent and humane society requires a shared language of the good" (1, p. 14) and, further, that it is in "needs language" that a particular language of the human good can be found.

The remainder of this chapter represents a response to Ignatieff's challenge to create a new language of need "adequate to the times we live in" (1, p. 141).

AN ALTERNATIVE LANGUAGE OF NEED

In an attempt to construct an alternative to the prevailing therapeutic and rights-based language of need discussed above, and in order to go beyond the apocalyptic demography scenario, I now turn to a consideration of the related notions of "moral economy" and "interdependence."

Moral Economy: The Notion of Reciprocity

The moral issue at the heart of the modern welfare society is: when does need give people the right to make a claim against the collective? Any given society's answer to this question is embodied in its "moral economy." Deborah Stone characterizes the concept of moral economy thus (23, p. 19):

> The moral economy of a society is its set of beliefs about what constitutes just exchange: not only about how economic exchange is to be conducted in normal times but also . . . when poor individuals are entitled to social aid, when better-off people are obligated to provide aid, and what kinds of claims anyone— landowners, employer, governments—can legitimately make on the surplus product of anyone else.

Moral economy is grounded in "the collectively shared basic moral assumptions constituting a system of reciprocal relations" (21, p. 275). As noted in Chapter 2, this analytical framework, originating in the work of E. P. Thompson (36), can complement and extend political economic analyses in the field of critical gerontology. The notion of moral economy thus has proven a useful conceptual tool for analyzing issues of generational equity at the familial and societal levels (see Chapter 2) (11, 34), macro aging policy, such as retirement and pension policies (21), and health care policy (33).

What distinguishes the concept of moral economy from more narrowly based concepts of rights and entitlements—which characterize most contemporary discussions of need—is that it is as much about our obligations to one another as it is about the claims we are entitled to make against each other. The language of moral economy—as a language of needs—acknowledges both sides of the reciprocity equation (1, p. 27; emphasis added):

> Need is a vernacular of justification, specifying the claims of necessity that those who lack may rightfully address to those who have. . . . The pathos of need, like the pathos of all purely verbal claims to the justice or mercy of another, is that need is powerless to enforce its right. It justifies an entitlement *only if the powerful understand themselves to be obliged by it.*

What binds the powerful—those who have—and the powerless—those who have not—is "a matter of custom, habit and historical inheritance as much as a matter of explicit moral commitment" (1, p. 27).

One of the best articulations of what shared assumptions of reciprocity might look like is found in Richard Titmuss's book *The Gift Relationship* (37), a discussion of blood donation practices in the United Kingdom and the United States. Implicit in the voluntary donation of blood *to* a "stranger" is a sense of reciprocity, the sense that some day one—or a loved one—might be dependent on the gift of blood *from* a "stranger." Titmuss eloquently summed up the moral economy underlying this one area of social life thus (37, p. 269; emphasis added):

> In not asking for or expecting any payment of money these donors signified their belief in the willingness of other men to act altruistically in the future, and to combine together to make a gift freely available should they have a need for it. *By expressing confidence in the behavior of future unknown strangers they were*

thus denying the Hobbesian thesis that men are devoid of any distinctively moral sense.

In the preceding chapter, Malcolm Johnson makes the observation: "Were Titmuss writing today he would be as exercised about justice between age groups and the inescapable need to retain gift relationships between generations as he was about the commercialization of the giving and receiving of blood (page 56).

Moral economy notions of reciprocity are in marked contrast to what Bellah and colleagues (30) call "giving/getting" notions of reciprocity, which characterize therapeutic and rights-based notions of reciprocity. Thinking in terms of moral economy thus leads us to a deeper understanding of the nature of the relationship between the individual and the community. Philosopher Mark Sandel characterizes this as (38, p. 143; emphasis added):

> an enlarged self-understanding . . . [such] that when 'my' assets or life prospects are enlisted in the service of a common endeavor, I am likely to experience this less as a case of being used for others' ends and more as *a way of contributing to the purposes of the community . . . with which my identity is bound.*

This formulation of reciprocity differs significantly from marketplace notions of reciprocity, for, by placing community at the center, it acknowledges our fundamental interdependence.

Interdependence: Beyond the Dependency/Independency Dichotomy

The issue of "dependency" underlies the majority of social policy debate in the modern welfare state. Most welfare policy is made on the basis that to be "dependent" is bad and to be "independent" is good. Older people often end up in a Catch-22, caught between a social ethic of independence on the one hand, and a service ethic which constructs them as dependent on the other. Ideas about "giving" and "taking"—that is, ideas about reciprocity—lie at the heart of this dichotomy between dependency and independency, and have to do with our ideas about the proper relationship between the individual and the community.

One of the more significant sociopolitical legacies from the European Enlightenment which informs most contemporary liberal debate is a radical individualism in which the individual is regarded both as a "lone-rights bearer" (31) and as an autonomous moral agent (38, 39). Deriving from Locke's and Rousseau's notion of "natural man" as a solitary self-sufficient creature, and Kant's notion of man as a freely choosing, rational actor, the contemporary version of this kind of individualism pays "extraordinary homage to independence and self-sufficiency, based on an image of the rights-bearer as a self-determining, unencumbered individual, a being connected to others only by choice" (31, p. 48).

This libertarian, contractual individual resembles a therapeutic version of the self. Because this therapeutic self is "defined by its own wants and satisfactions, coordinated by cost-benefit calculation" (30, p. 127) and regards interpersonal interactions in terms of the liberal notion of the social contract—entered into by freely

[handwritten margin notes: "one individual not real", "we are located"]

choosing autonomous individuals—it can pretend that it lives a life of self-reliance and self-sufficiency. But, for all the symbolic power of the rhetoric of independence, this mythic lone individual "possesses little resemblance to any living man, and even less to most women" (31, p. 48). On the contrary, as Bellah and coworkers argue: "our individualism, our sense of the dignity, worth, and moral autonomy of the individual, is dependent in a thousand ways on a social, cultural, and institutional context that keeps us afloat even when we cannot describe it" (30, p. 84). In other words, our very individuality exists only as a result of our embeddedness in a network of relationships both private and public. None of us is totally independent of our context—social, political, and economic; rather, we are located and live within complex webs of mutual dependence, that is, webs of "interdependence."

The concept of interdependence lies at the heart of discussions of generational equity (3, 32) (see also Chapter 3). While a fuller discussion of the issues surrounding generational equity is beyond the scope of the present discussion, several points are worth noting. At the level of the family, there is considerable evidence for the transfer of care and money across generations (see Chapter 3) and that "families are flexible, adaptable and keen to meet their obligations" (32, p. 146). Moreover, in spite of the arguments of those who claim a high degree of intergenerational *ine*quity (3), considerable evidence exists at the societal level that, in the United States, there is still strong support among the young for universal health care and pension programs for the elderly (11).

Generational equity represents a paradigmatic study in notions of reciprocity. In a recent book entitled *Inequality and Old Age,* John Vincent (32) distinguishes between three ways of thinking about reciprocity between the generations: (*a*) a narrow restricted view which sees reciprocity as delayed exchange—what is given is returned (e.g., caregiving from parents to children and back to parents at the family level; contributory old age pensions at the societal level); (*b*) a more inclusive view, similar to Daniels's (40) prudential life span view of reciprocity, which includes indirect exchange in that what is received from the preceding generation is returned to the following one (e.g., funding public education and universal old age pensions from the income tax of working people); and (*c*) a generalized reciprocity in which there is "a generalized expectation of generosity and a right to receive but no specific counting of who gives or receives" (32, p. 149). Reflecting this last view of reciprocity, Johnson notes in Chapter 3, with specific reference to generational equity, that "The compact between the generations is not only between unknown parties, it is between the dead and living and the unborn" (page 63).

In addition to embodying particular notions of reciprocity, the concept of interdependence embraces the notion that our good or bad fortune, our achievements or failures, are never entirely "ours." In *Liberalism and the Limits of Justice,* philosopher Mark Sandel (38) writes of our indebtedness—and, therefore, reciprocal obligation—to others in the larger context within which we live. Sandel eloquently and succinctly captures this notion of our fundamental interdependence in the following (38, p. 143):

> . . . it seems reasonable to suppose that what at first glance appears as 'my' assets
> are more properly described as common assets in some sense. Since others made

> me, and in various ways continue to make me, the person I am, it seems appropriate to regard them . . . as participants in 'my' achievements and common beneficiaries of the rewards they bring. [Thus] . . . we may come to regard ourselves . . . less as individuated subjects with certain things in common, and more as members of a wider (but still determinate) subjectivity, less as 'others' and more as participants in a common identity, be it a family or community or class or people or nation.

In other words, the fact that we live in communities means that we are ipso facto interdependent. The modern welfare state—inasmuch as it institutionalizes particular shared assumptions of reciprocity, that is, a particular moral economy—represents an administrative attempt to extend this concept of interdependence to "the strangers at my door" (1, p. 16). However, as Ignatieff says, "in many Western welfare states . . . to be in receipt of welfare, is still understood as a source of shame" (1, p. 16).

A very different moral position was taken by Richard Titmuss (41), one of the more eloquent and persuasive articulators of the moral economy underlying the modern welfare state. As part of his justification for the principle of universality—that is, the universal provision of and access to a wide range of social, health, and income security programs—Titmuss invoked and developed the concept of "diswelfare." Diswelfare finds the causes of misfortune in the social structure and thus recasts the disenfranchised and disadvantaged as "the social pathologies of other people's progress" (41, p. 134). Says Titmuss (41, p. 119; emphasis added):

> The emphasis today on "welfare" and the "benefits of welfare" often tends to obscure the fundamental fact that for many consumers the services are not essentially benefits or increments to welfare at all; they represent partial compensation for disservices, for social costs and social insecurities which are the product of a rapidly changing industrial-urban society. *They are part of the price we pay to some people for bearing part of the costs of other people's progress.*

This view of welfare—based on the notion of interdependence—represents a radically different view from the one which currently presides over the near global dismantling of the welfare state. At the same time, as the case of generational equity demonstrates, interdependence is consistently—and persistently—woven throughout our social interactions at all levels. With the concept of interdependence, we cut to the essence of what it means to live in a community, for underlying the notion of interdependence is a particular moral economy.

TOWARD A MORAL ECONOMY OF INTERDEPENDENCE

> . . . individual freedom and the general welfare alike depend on the condition of the fine texture of civil society—on a fragile ecology for which we have no name. (31, pp. 109–110)

I suggest that what Glendon calls that "for which we have no name" be named a "moral economy of interdependence." This chapter concludes with a brief discussion of what a moral economy of interdependence might look like, and how it might allow us to go beyond the rhetoric of apocalyptic demography.

As a fundamental and first step, a moral economy of interdependence admits the language of moral reasoning into discussion of need. Contemporary discussions of need are notable for their lack of moral reasoning, and there appears to be a number of reasons for this. As discussed earlier, in the context of the modern welfare state as a "therapeutic state," moral and political language has been replaced, in part, by a therapeutic language of need. Because the therapeutic self defines situations in terms of its own wishes and wants, the question is not "Is this right or wrong?" but rather "Does this work for me?" As Bellah and colleagues observe: "In asserting a radical pluralism and the uniqueness of each individual, [the therapeutically inclined] conclude that there is no moral common ground and therefore no public relevance of morality outside the sphere of minimal procedural rules and obligations not to injure" (30, p. 141). For its part, rights talk tends to frame the question in terms of "To what am I entitled?"—a perspective which reduces our public life to a contest of claims. This kind of thinking represents, at best, a kind of moral relativism, or, at worst, a kind of moral nihilism.

Many on the left have displayed an uneasiness with philosophy in general and moral reasoning in particular. The roots of some of this uneasiness in Marx's notion of morality as "a form of ideology" are discussed in Chapter 2. As noted in that chapter, however, Marx himself argued for "a morality of *emancipation*, based on an imagined harmony of social unity and individual self-development" (page 39).

Recent attempts by communitarians, feminists, and others to revitalize political discourse with moral reasoning (1, 30, 31, 38, 39, 42–46) all dismiss the liberal notion of the individual as an autonomous moral agent, and seek to place the individual back into the moral context of the community. Philosopher Alasdair MacIntyre argues for a social morality in the following way (39, p. 258):

> . . . good, and with [it] the only grounds for the authority of laws and virtues, can only be discovered by entering into those relationships which constitute communities whose central bond is a shared vision of and understanding of [the good]. To cut oneself off from shared activity . . . to isolate oneself from the communities which find their point and purpose in such activities, will be to debar oneself from finding any good outside of oneself. It will be to condemn oneself to [a] moral solipsism.

The question from this place becomes "What kind of society do we want to live in?"

A moral economy of interdependence also decommodifies reciprocity, for it acknowledges that "what people do or make but will not or cannot put up for sale is as immeasurable and as invaluable as the oxygen they breathe" (24, p. 29). Our embeddedness in a market economy leads us to view reciprocity in particularly materialist and instrumental commodified terms: we know when an object or money or work is exchanged. But, how do we count or measure love, time, energy, kindness, commitment, shared memories, care—all the things that constellate human relationships and create community? A commodified notion of reciprocity has significant consequences for older people (14, p. 385):

Since the commodified form of social relations implicit in neo-classical economics undervalues both the role of older people and the unpaid work of carers (more important in the life worlds of older people than formal care), there is an antagonistic relationship between the needs of older people and their families and the assumptions underlying macroeconomic policy. In other words, raw neo-classical macroeconomics is unlikely to produce an equitable outcome in resource distribution for older people (or anyone else for that matter).

A moral economy of interdependence decommodifies reciprocity—and, thereby, decommodifies need—by recognizing that not all human exchanges can be entered into cost-benefit analyses. For example, consider the innumerable number of volunteer hours donated to various social and civic causes, without which many community institutions like hospitals, or services like Meals on Wheels, could not function. Much of this volunteer time is given by older people, whom apocalyptic demography tends to cast as "takers."

A moral economy of interdependence not only takes the discourse on need out of the marketplace where needs are commodified, it also takes it out of the courts where needs are framed as rights. Bellah and colleagues describe the ultimate inadequacy of the courts to talk in terms of a moral economy of interdependence (43, p. 130):

. . . they adjudicate only particular cases rather than formulating general social policy; and they respond to the adversaries in cases brought before them rather than framing a debate about what is best for the common good . . . [which] inadequately addresses the kind of interdependence that is crucial in modern society.

Arguing that "our rights-laden public discourse easily accommodates the economic, the immediate, and the personal dimensions of a problem, while it regularly neglects the moral, the long-term, and the social implications" (31, p. 171), Glendon advocates tempering the rhetoric of rights with the language of responsibility and reciprocity. Many contemporary writers on need (1, 31, 34, 43, 47) argue for a politicization of need by placing the discussion and arbitration of issues of need back into the public discourse.

To politicize need means, in part, to curb the power of the "experts" and the growth of the "therapeutic state." This means that people and communities must be involved in determining their own needs and the most appropriate ways to meet them. Health educators and community organizers like John McKnight (48), Paolo Freire (49), Saul Alinsky (50), and Meredith Minkler (51) demonstrate ways in which this can be accomplished. To politicize need is to support and strengthen those community structures which intervene between the person and the state, and which have been called "mediating structures." These include families, local service organizations, neighborhood associations, churches, various ethnic communities, and "communities of memory" (30, p. 152), all of which Glendon calls "the seedbeds of civic virtue" (31, p. 109).

Aging policies that take decision-making out of the hands of experts and place it back into the community, thereby supporting and strengthening these mediating structures, might include: supporting the development of community health centers run by community boards; providing funds to families who care for a dependent family member rather than to institutions or professionals; integrating community centers and community activities through existing neighborhood centers like schools and community centers, rather than segregating people by age groups into day care centers, seniors' activity centers, teen centers, and so forth; and reversing the ghetto-ization of old people by encouraging the development of smaller residential care facilities like group homes in local neighborhoods.

Whatever the form such actions take, *"what matters at this stage is the con-struction of local forms of community* within which civility and the intellectual and moral life can be sustained" (39, p. 263; emphasis added). The awful irony of these kinds of community initiatives is that they are often co-opted as justification for the dismantling of the welfare state. Just as the integrity of the individual is sustained by being embedded in webs of mutual dependence, so too the integrity and effective-ness of civil society is sustained by being embedded within a welfare state based on a moral economy of interdependence.

CONCLUSION: ON THE POWER OF LANGUAGE

By engaging in an analysis of the politics of need in the context of the modern welfare state, this chapter represents a challenge to the apocalyptic demography scenario. In the course of the discussion, we have seen how "some individuals and groups have much greater power than others to influence the definition of social problems and to specify the policy interventions that address these problems" (52, p. 241). It is hoped that the perspective developed in this chapter will help shift future policy initiatives away from older people themselves and toward the context within which people grow old. We need not believe ourselves to be at the mercy of blind forces, such as demographic and economic imperatives, as if these existed outside the realm of public discussion and debate. As John Myles has said, "we must acknowledge that it is "politics, not demography, [which] now determines the size of the elderly population and the material conditions of its existence" (53, p. 175).

A fundamental conviction behind this work is that words and ideas matter! Words matter because they give birth to ideas. It matters that we speak a language of moral economy and interdependence, rather than a language of moral nihilism and radical individualism. Words matter because "what we cannot imagine and express in lan-guage has little chance of becoming a sociological reality" (43, p. 15).

Ideas matter, for without them our actions in the world have no foundation, no grounding. As Stone says (34, p. 7; emphasis added):

> . . . the essence of policy making in political communities [is] the struggle over ideas. *Ideas are a medium of exchange and a mode of influence even more powerful than money and votes and guns.* Shared meanings motivate people to action and meld individual striving into collective action. Ideas are at the center of all political conflict.

In the current context of marketplace approaches to need, ideas of community, reciprocity, and interdependence must be revitalized and legitimized, for "our strongest bulwark against demagoguery is the habit of critical discussion about and self-conscious awareness of the public ideas that envelop us" (47, p. 10). We live in an age characterized, in part, by the rapid retreat of the welfare state, fueled largely by public ideas like "fiscal crisis," which, in turn, spawn ideas like "apocalyptic demography." In these mean-spirited times, the idea of a moral economy of interdependence is offered as an alternative to the prevailing public discourse on aging.

Questions of language and ideas and meaning often do not intrude into aging policy discussions on the assumption that these kinds of questions are abstract, have little to do with the "real world" of practical policymaking, and, thus, are better left to philosophers. But, as philosopher and gerontologist Harry Moody has said: "questions of meaning are of the utmost importance for practical decisions in ethics and public policy. Without reflection on these metaphysical questions we will inevitably lose our direction when we try to think about very specific matters in gerontology" (54). In other words, we cannot know where we are going if we do not know where we are coming from.

REFERENCES

1. Ignatieff, M. *The Needs of Strangers*. Penguin Books, Harmondsworth, 1984.
2. Quadagno, J. Social security and the myth of the entitlement "crisis." *Gerontologist* 36(3): 391–399, 1996.
3. Minkler, M., and Robertson, A. The ideology of "age/race wars": Deconstructing a social problem. *Ageing Soc.* 11: 1–22, 1991.
4. Robertson, A. The politics of Alzheimer's disease: A case study in apocalyptic demography. *Int. J. Health Serv.* 20(3): 429–442, 1990.
5. Verbrugge, L. Longer life but worsening health? Trends in health and mortality of middle-aged and older persons. *Milbank Mem. Fund Q.* 62: 475–519, 1984.
6. Barer, M. L., et al. Aging and health care utilization: New evidence on old fallacies. *Soc. Sci. Med.* 24(10): 851–862, 1987.
7. Pifer, A., and Bronte, L. Introduction: Squaring the pyramid. In *Our Aging Society,* edited by A. Pifer and L. Bronte. W. W. Norton, New York, 1986.
8. Friedmann, E. A., and Adamchak, D. J. Societal aging and intergenerational support systems. In *Old Age and the Welfare State,* edited by A. M. Guillemard, pp. 53–73. Sage, Beverly Hills, 1983.
9. Calasanti, T. M., and Bonanno, A. The social creation of dependence, dependency ratios, and the elderly in the United States: A critical analysis. *Soc. Sci. Med.* 23(12): 1229–1236, 1986.
10. Hertzman, C., and Hayes, M. Will the elderly really bankrupt us with increased health care costs? *Can. J. Public Health* 76: 373–377, 1985.
11. Minkler, M. Scapegoating the elderly: New voices, old theme. *J. Public Health Policy,* 1997, in press.
12. Binney, E. A., and Estes, C. L. Setting the wrong limits: Class biases and the biographical standard. In *A Good Old Age? The Paradox of Setting Limits,* edited by P. Homer and M. Holstein. Simon and Schuster, New York, 1990.
13. Callahan, D. *Setting Limits: Medical Goals in an Aging Society.* Simon and Schuster, New York, 1987.
14. Walker, A. The economic 'burden' of ageing and the prospect of intergenerational conflict. *Ageing Soc.* 10: 377–396, 1990.

15. Star, T. T. Apocalypse soon? Ominous forecasts about our graying population and the next recession. *Toronto Star,* Business Section, p. 1, Jan. 1, 1995.

16. Estes, C. L. The new political economy of aging: Introduction and critique. In *Critical Perspectives on Aging: The Political and Moral Economy of Growing Old,* edited by M. Minkler and C. L. Estes. Baywood, Amityville, N.Y., 1991.

17. Estes, C. L., and Binney, E. A. The biomedicalization of aging: Dangers and dilemmas. *Gerontologist* 29(5): 587–596, 1989.

18. Armstrong, D. *The Political Anatomy of the Body: Medical Knowledge in the Twentieth Century.* Cambridge University Press, Cambridge, England, 1983.

19. Evans, R. G., et al. The long good-bye: The great transformation of the British Columbia hospital system. *Health Serv. Res.* 24: 435–459, 1989.

20. Estes, C. L. *The Aging Enterprise.* Jossey-Bass, San Francisco, 1979.

21. Kohli, M. Retirement and the moral economy: An historical interpretation of the German case. In *Critical Perspectives on Aging: The Political and Moral Economy of Growing Old,* edited by M. Minkler and C. L. Estes. Baywood, Amityville, N.Y., 1991.

22. Myles, J. Postwar capitalism and the extension of social security into a retirement wage. In *Critical Perspectives on Aging: The Political and Moral Economy of Growing Old,* edited by M. Minkler and C. L. Estes. Baywood, Amityville, N.Y., 1991.

23. Stone, D. A. *The Disabled State.* Temple University Press, Philadelphia, 1984.

24. Illich, I. Disabling professions. In *Disabling Professions,* edited by I. Illich et al. Marion Boyars, London, 1977.

25. McKnight, J. Professionalized service and disabling help. In *Disabling Professions,* edited by I. Illich et al. Marion Boyars, London, 1977.

26. Lasch, C. Life in the therapeutic state. In *New York Review of Books,* pp. 24–32, June 12, 1980.

27. O'Neill, J. *Five Bodies: The Human Shape of Modern Society.* Cornell University Press, Ithaca, N.Y., 1985.

28. Walker, A. Social policy and elderly people in Great Britain: The construction of dependent social and economic status in old age. In *Old Age and the Welfare State,* edited by A. M. Guillemard, pp. 143–167. Sage, Beverly Hills, 1983.

29. Townsend, P. The structured dependency of the elderly: Creation of social policy in the twentieth century. *J. Ageing Soc.* 1(1): 5–28, 1981.

30. Bellah, R., et al. *Habits of the Heart: Individualism and Commitment in American Life.* Harper and Row, New York, 1985.

31. Glendon, M. A. *Rights Talk: The Impoverishment of Political Discourse.* The Free Press, New York, 1991.

32. Vincent, J. A. *Inequality and Old Age.* UCL Press, Exeter, England, 1995.

33. Holstein, M., and Minkler, M. The short life and painful death of the Medicare Catastrophic Coverage Act. In *Critical Perspectives on Aging: The Political and Moral Economy of Growing Old,* edited by M. Minkler and C. L. Estes. Baywood, Amityville, N.Y., 1991.

34. Stone, D. A. *Policy Paradox and Political Reason.* Scott, Foresman/Little, Brown College Division, Glenview, Ill., 1988.

35. Walzer, M. *Spheres of Justice.* Basic Books, New York, 1983.

36. Thompson, E. P. *The Making of the English Working Classes.* Vintage, New York, 1966.

37. Titmuss, R. M. *The Gift Relationship.* Penguin Books, Harmondsworth, 1973.

38. Sandel, M. J. *Liberalism and the Limits of Justice.* Cambridge University Press, Cambridge, England, 1982.

39. MacIntyre, A. *After Virtue: A Study in Moral Theory,* Ed. 2. University of Notre Dame Press, Notre Dame, Ind., 1984.

40. Daniels, N. *Am I My Parents' Keeper: An Essay on Justice between the Young and the Old.* Oxford University Press, Oxford, 1988.
41. Titmuss, R. M. *Commitment to Welfare.* George Allen and Unwin, London, 1968.
42. Fraser, N. Talking about needs: Interpretive contests as political conflicts in welfare-state societies. In *Feminism and Political Theory,* edited by C. R. Sunstein. University of Chicago Press, Chicago, 1990.
43. Bellah, R. N., et al. *The Good Society.* Alfred A. Knopf, New York, 1991.
44. Frazer, E., and Lacey, N. *The Politics of Community: A Feminist Critique of the Liberal-Communitarian Debate.* University of Toronto Press, Toronto, 1993.
45. Friedman, M. Beyond care: The de-moralization of gender. In *An Ethic of Care: Feminist and Interdisciplinary Perspectives,* edited by M. J. Larrabee. Routledge, New York, 1993.
46. Tronto, J. C. *Moral Boundaries: A Political Argument for an Ethic of Care.* Routledge, New York, 1993.
47. Reich, R. B. (ed.). *The Power of Public Ideas.* Ballinger, Cambridge, Mass., 1988.
48. McKnight, J. Regenerating community. *Soc. Policy,* Winter 1987, pp. 54–58.
49. Freire, P. *Pedagogy of the Oppressed.* Continuum, New York, 1988.
50. Alinsky, S. *Rules for Radicals.* Random House, New York, 1972.
51. Minkler, M. Improving health through community organization. In *Health Behavior and Health Education: Theory, Research and Practice,* edited by K. Glanz, F. Lewis, and B. Rimer, pp. 253–287. Jossey-Bass, San Francisco, 1990.
52. Estes, C. L. Austerity and aging: 1980 and beyond. In *Readings in the Political Economy of Aging,* edited by M. Minkler and C. L. Estes, pp. 241–253. Baywood, Amityville, N.Y., 1984.
53. Myles, J. F. Conflict, crisis, and the future of old age security. In *Readings in the Political Economy of Aging,* edited by M. Minkler and C. L. Estes, pp. 168–176. Baywood, Amityville, N.Y., 1984.
54. Moody, H. R. *Abundance of Life: Human Development Policies for an Aging Society,* Columbia Studies of Social Gerontology and Aging, edited by A. Monk. Columbia University Press, New York, 1988.

CHAPTER 5

Disability Theory and Public Policy:
Implications for Critical Gerontology

Jae Kennedy and Meredith Minkler

The concentration of disability in older age groups is an epidemiological fact so widely recognized by researchers, policy analysts, and service providers that it is often seen as truistic. Indeed, this relationship is the empirical basis of the "decline and loss" paradigms of aging (1) and, when combined with current population trends, leads to the sort of "apocalyptic demography" described by Robertson in Chapter 4. In the public service sector, "the aged and disabled" are frequently treated as a single target population, and with good reason—recent census data indicate that although less than 16 percent of the total adult non-institutionalized population is over age 65, this subgroup accounts for over 60 percent of all adults who report need for assistance with the most basic activities of daily living (2).

Yet there has been an ongoing effort on the part of aging advocates and analysts to distinguish disability from aging, stressing that covariance is not equivalence (e.g., 3). They point out that much of the "normal" functional decline associated with aging is due to poor health behaviors (4) and statistical aggregation of internally heterogeneous age groups (5). This has led some researchers to distinguish between "successful aging" (i.e., avoiding functional limitation through exercise, diet, and appropriate medical care) and "usual aging" (6). Although this distinction is a useful one—for example, in underscoring the importance of health promotion over the life course—a problematic consequence of this sort of dichotomy involves the potential for further stigmatization of older persons with disabilities (7).

In the area of disability studies, there has likewise been a tendency to distinguish disability from aging. This is due primarily to the centrality of workforce participation in both disability theory and policy. Disability is seen as a discrete categorical workforce exemption for groups otherwise expected to participate in the labor market—that is, young and middle-aged adults. A large and multifaceted rehabilitation industry has grown around the provision of various private and public disability services to this group, and benefit eligibility is typically related to employment status (8). Crucial "non-wage-earning" populations—children, homemakers, and the elderly—are therefore acknowledged only in passing in most prominent critical analyses of disability policy (9, 10), despite the fact that they make up the bulk of the disabled population, at least in industrial and postindustrial societies.

This lack of conceptual crossover is unfortunate, particularly for those working in critical gerontology. Perhaps because advocates have played such a vocal and consistent role in the development of disability studies, the field as a whole is considerably more familiar with, and willing to employ, the general theoretical frameworks of political and moral economy. Indeed, one might argue that the Independent Living Movement was in large part a backlash against traditional biomedical conceptions of disability. Much of the current theoretical work in this area explicitly recognizes the role that economic systems and social values play in the construction and reproduction of disability.

Toward the end of applying a critical gerontology framework to aging and disability, we begin by examining different definitions and models of disability, stressing the contribution of newer approaches that give prominence to the role of broader environmental factors in the disablement process. We then turn to the social production and distribution of disability, using both epidemiology and political economy as conceptual frameworks. The linkage of disability and work impedance is then examined, and the consequences in disability programming explored, with special consideration to inherent age, gender, and racial biases. Some of the historical antecedents of disability stigma in aging populations are also identified. We conclude by suggesting that analysts develop the principles put forth by the Independent Living Movement, as well as recent work on the moral economy of interdependency over the life course, to broaden our ways of thinking about and addressing disability and aging.

DEFINING DISABILITY

Disability, or more accurately, the disablement process, is a dynamic social phenomenon that has as much to do with cultural norms and socioeconomic status as it does with individual physiological conditions (11, 12). While disease (particularly chronic disease) and injury are often related to disability, they are neither sufficient nor necessary causes. Perhaps the most influential theorist in this area, sociologist Saad Nagi, defines disability as "an inability or limitation in performing roles and tasks expected within a social environment" (13). This is an explicitly relational perspective, dependent on the social environment that defines the parameters of normal activity.

This relational perspective is evident in current typologies of disablement such as the World Health Organization's International Classification of Impairments, Disabilities, and Handicaps (ICIDH), a supplement to the International Classification of Diseases (ICD) (14). The ICIDH defines specific classes of disease, impairment, disability, and handicap (note that the latter term is controversial in North America, for reasons that we will discuss later in this section). Disablement, according to this model, starts within the individual's body and ends in her sociocultural environment. There is a recognition that disease or injury can lead to a loss of individual physiological function (impairment), which may in turn affect capacity or performance on a number of levels. Yet there is an important distinction between difficulty in performing basic tasks (disability) and the social, economic, and interpersonal consequences of that deficit (handicap). Despite the fact that aging increases the likelihood of disease, impairment, disability, and handicap, age per se plays no direct part in the disablement process.

A crucial feature of stage typologies such as the ICIDH is that the progression between stages is not viewed as inevitable, allowing a more precise discussion of cause and effect, and therefore a more coherent analysis of potential interventions. Thus, it is observed that medical treatment may prevent active pathologies from causing impairments, and effective rehabilitation may reduce or eliminate disabilities resulting from impairments. Assistive devices can moderate the effects of impairments and disabilities. Environmental modifications such as the reduction of physical barriers can reduce or prevent handicap, and so can anti-discrimination laws such as the 1990 Americans with Disabilities Act (ADA).[1] Indeed, an individual may actually skip steps in the disablement process. For example, a disfiguring impairment may not lead to any disability, but if it negatively affects a person's social interactions or opportunities, it constitutes a handicap. Likewise, various "hidden" conditions such as diabetes or epilepsy may have few social or economic consequences, although they can cause significant disability.

Models like the ICIDH have been criticized on various grounds. As noted earlier, the use of the term "handicap" (the etiology of which is explicitly linked to dependency, i.e., beggars with hand-in-cap) is so offensive to many North American disability activists as to render the whole exercise suspect (16). Other critics detect a clinical bias. Zola (17) observes that, because stage frameworks originate disablement process within the individual, they invariably downplay the pivotal role of the sociopolitical environment. Such models are thus sociological extensions of a standard biomedical model (which views disability as an individual deficit to be ameliorated by professional intervention). Analysts such as Hahn, in contrast, describe disability as an oppressed minority group status (18, pp. 46–47):

> All facets of the environment are molded by public policy and government policies reflect widespread social attitudes and values; as a result, existing features of architectural design, job requirements, and daily life that have a discriminatory impact on disabled citizens cannot be viewed merely as happenstance or coincidence. On the contrary, they seem to signify conscious or unconscious sentiments supporting a hierarchy of dominance and subordination between nondisabled and disabled segments of the population that is fundamentally incompatible with the legal principles of freedom and equality.

In defense of the ICIDH, authors have noted that the framework in no way posits the primacy of disease, impairment, disability, or handicap (19), and indeed that the acknowledged discontinuities between these stages allow emphasis of different parts

---

[1] The ADA prohibits discriminatory treatment of persons with disabilities in employment, transportation, and public accommodation. In the employment area, for example, organizations making hiring and promotion decisions are required to consider the qualifications of employees or potential employees independent of their disability status. Federal enforcement of the ADA has been uneven to date, as private businesses and public agencies struggle with implementation issues (15).

of the disablement process, including sociopolitical critiques of handicap status (20, 21). By integrating the clinical and social aspects of disability, the ICIDH and similar disability typologies offer analysts the opportunity to refine discussion of individual and environmental factors affecting the production and distribution of disability within a population. As suggested in the next section, one possible extension of this approach, and one that complements a political economy perspective, explicitly incorporates the population focus of social epidemiology in the study of disability across age groups.

THE SOCIAL PRODUCTION AND DISTRIBUTION OF DISABILITY

The fundamental premise of social epidemiology is that illness is generated by the interaction of the physical and cultural environment with the biophysiological properties of individuals within a population (22, 23). Consider the example of chronic respiratory disease. The prevalence of such disease in a community is determined not only by individual factors (e.g., age, sex, hereditary predisposition, smoking behavior, diet, and exercise) but by a host of interrelated factors in the physical and biological environment (e.g., climate, air pollution, and prevalence of viral and bacterial agents) and the sociocultural environment (e.g., general socioeconomic level of the community and distribution of resources within the community, availability of medical and social services, lifestyle norms, and workplace conditions) (24–26).

A similar, but not identical, approach can be taken to describe the production of disability. A higher prevalence of conditions such as respiratory disease thus would lead to a higher rate of disability within a community. The production of disability is also mediated by various environmental factors, but these are not necessarily the same factors as those which produce disease and impairment. As Albrecht observes (8, p. 35):

> Diseases and impairments are organically based, whereas disability is more strongly influenced by the environment. For many persons with disabilities, public attitudes, emotions, stigma, stereotypes, lack of access to rehabilitation, and occupational barriers are more limiting than the physical impairment. Hence we speak of the disabling environment. This concept places the locus of disability not solely within individuals who have impairments but also in the social, economic, and political environment. By this argument, people are impaired but the environment is disabling. In truth, disability is constituted both by impairments and the disabling environment. The concept of disabling environment, however, forces us to acknowledge that disabilities are physically based but socially constructed. Societies, then, produce disabilities differently from impairments.

Disabling environments vary among and within cultures and communities, and the production of disability appears to be closely linked to the dominant means of production and distribution of resources. This is, of course, the axiomatic premise of the political economy framework. A nomadic hunter-gatherer society, for example, would presumably deem a modest mobility impairment as considerably more disabling than would a stable agrarian society with greater role division and food surplus. In industrial and postindustrial societies, disability is constructed primarily as an impedance to wage labor. We will return to the policy consequences of this employment-based construction of disability; but the point here is that a condition is truly disabling only if the individual's community perceives it as such.

The fact that disability is unequally distributed within cultures also indicates a distinct sociogenic component to disability. There is compelling evidence that the prevalence of disability, like morbidity (27–30) and mortality (31–33), varies inversely with socioeconomic factors such as income, employment status, and education (34–36).

Again, the causal linkage of socioeconomic status and disability is different from the linkage of socioeconomic status and disease. Aside from exposure to various health risks leading to higher levels of physical and/or cognitive impairment, persons of low socioeconomic status presumably lack both the external and internal resources to prevent or minimize the transformation of impairment to disability and disability to handicap. There are, of course, the obvious financial barriers to medical, rehabilitative, and support services and technologies which disproportionately affect persons of low socioeconomic status (i.e., the uninsured and underinsured), but there are multiple human capital constraints that may also limit the ability to cope with changes in functional capacity. Indeed, the experience of poverty itself could be described as disabling or, to use the more precise ICIDH terminology, *handicapping,* in the general sense of imposing grave social disadvantage. In any case, descriptive analyses indicate that disability, like age, race, and gender, is a cumulative marker of social stratification (37).

An environmental perspective is useful for describing another important phenomenon: the steady rise in the total incidence and prevalence of disability in developed nations (38–43). Zola (17) attributes this rise to three general factors: (a) the development and widespread application of life-prolonging treatments and technologies, which may increase morbidity while decreasing mortality; (b) the relative and absolute growth of elderly populations; and (c) political, economic, and social pressures to expand the categorization of people as disabled. In other words, technological and demographic transformations affect the production of impairment and disability, while changes in definitions affect the construction of disability. Industrialized countries share not only a rise in disability rates, but a rise in the level of publicly voiced concern among policymakers and social critics about this growth (9). A rhetoric of crisis pervades policy discussions of disability and disability programming which mirrors the Cassandraesque vision of aging described by Robertson (see Chapter 4) and suggests a common ontology.

In most public policy discourse, the "problem of disability" is described in terms of economic costs. These include direct expenditures for acute medical care, institution-based long-term care, and various rehabilitative and support services and technologies. They may also include indirect economic costs such as diminished labor force participation on the part of persons with disabilities and the family and friends who support them. So defined, disability is indeed a staggering expense: LaPlante and his colleagues (44), updating Chirikos's (45) assay, estimate total social costs of disability in the United States (including work and productivity loss) at roughly $150 billion per year. But these superficial economic descriptions do not address the underlying symbolic and structural role of disability status within the modern welfare state. The next section will review the theoretical work linking disability to labor market participation, and the problems this approach presents for our thinking about aging and disability.

THE CONSTRUCTION OF DISABILITY CATEGORIES

The ICIDH and similar theoretical models define disability as a disruption or violation of "normal" roles, but define those roles fairly broadly. However, not all roles are equally important to the larger social system. Using Mills's (46) distinction, role discontinuities become public problems rather than private troubles only when they are seen as directly or indirectly incurring public costs (monetary or otherwise). Disability is deemed a problem when it causes persons to consume rather than produce economic surplus. This can occur directly, via consumption of publicly funded services, and indirectly, via failure to participate in the wage labor market. The latter problem is the typical focus of most disability theorists working within a political economy framework.

Persons with disabilities, insofar as their impairments limit or preclude workforce participation, present a challenge to the standard exchange relationships within the capitalist economic system. They are unable to sell their labor, and therefore unable to access the goods and services they need to survive. The modern state has traditionally responded to disability in the so-called "working-aged" population in one of two ways. It either compensates those deemed unable to participate in the workforce, or provides training and rehabilitation to prepare persons with disabilities to enter or re-enter the labor market. A third option, regulating the workplace directly by defining the rights of persons with disabilities as employees, is a relatively recent policy development typified by the 1990 Americans with Disabilities Act.

Underlying all government disability programs is an elaborate control apparatus, setting multiple barriers to accessing benefits and defining narrow eligibility categories. From a political economy perspective, the state has a great stake in containing the total proportion of persons deemed unable to work. The challenge for the state is to ensure that only the most desperate take advantage of nonwork allocations—simultaneously maintaining a needs-based distributional system and an array of institutional and structural barriers designed to discourage its use.

The main ways to contain the utilization of the state's welfare systems involve making the resources unappealing or unattainable. This may include subjecting needs-based claims to various social sanctions and a host of legal and administrative requirements that make accessing resources difficult and demeaning. Perhaps the most common and straightforward approach is to narrowly define categories of legitimate need, thereby making the resources unattainable to the majority of the population (9). As Stone suggests, old age, youth, widowhood, and sickness have evolved as categories "granted social exemption from participation in the work-based distributive system." It is these *categories,* rather than older or disabled *individuals,* which "have a legitimate claim on social aid. . . . the categories thus act as boundaries between the primary, work-based distributive system and the secondary, needs-based system."

For categories to fulfill this boundary function, they must: (*a*) coincide with widely accepted norms of control and responsibility with regard to workforce participation; (*b*) be readily identifiable; and (*c*) be relatively stable conditions that are not easily feigned. Old age (arbitrarily designated as 65 or older in U.S. policy) and youth have become the primary categories for workforce exemption, in part because they are stable and easily measured states. In contrast, the category of disability (the modern policy formulation of illness), like that of single motherhood (the modern policy formulation of widowhood), is the subject of constant debate and regular reformulation by policymakers.

There are clearly intertwined moral and economic dimensions to the public definition of disability categories. The moral issues have to do with individual volition— are people "really" unable to participate in the labor market or do they simply choose not to? The work-based distribution system is buttressed by a powerful set of public attitudes about the social obligation to work. Persons who opt out of the labor force to seek public benefits may therefore be subject to considerable stigma. The legitimacy of needs-based claims is imputed on the basis of the perceived capacity for work and on the degree to which life choices influence this capacity.

The economic issues focus mainly on public expenditure containment. The crafting of the ill-fated U.S. Health Security Act in 1993, for example, included a heated debate over whether limitations in two or in three or more activities of daily living (ADLs) constituted grounds for covered services. Cost considerations appeared to be most persuasive in this debate, since use of the more liberal definition of disability (difficulty with two ADLs) would have added more than 900,000 disabled people to the rolls of those eligible for services (47).

We will now explore the consequences of the programmatic linkage of disability to workforce participation, focusing particularly on those groups already marginalized by the wage labor market.

GENDER, RACE, CLASS, AND AGE BIASES IN DISABILITY PROGRAMS

The primacy of work can be readily observed in U.S. disability programs, which can be broken down into two major classes: social insurance (e.g., Social Security Disability Insurance or SSDI, worker's compensation, and state disability), and social assistance or welfare (e.g., Supplemental Security Income or SSI). Eligibility for both types of programs is explicitly linked with the work-based distributional system. This linkage is positive for social insurance programs, in that benefit eligibility is dependent on current employment or prior work history, and negative for social assistance programs, for which benefit eligibility is dependent on nonparticipation in the workforce. As we will discuss below, gender, race, age, and class considerations play an important role in influencing program eligibility and the nature of the assistance received.

Social insurance disability programs such as SSDI are modeled after private insurance, and are subject to some of the same shortcomings. They are intended to be self-financing, so they usually cover only those workers who are currently contributing or have contributed to the program fund. Benefit levels are often tied to contribution level (i.e., salary) instead of severity of disability. The bio-medical eligibility criteria employed by these programs tend to favor acute conditions and injuries rather than the chronic conditions that are more prevalent in older workers.

While social insurance programs help program workers from impoverishment resulting from the sudden onset of disability, they also function as a stop-loss mechanism for industry. Worker's compensation programs, for example, were developed during the middle of the industrial revolution (after rudimentary worker protection laws were enacted) to help shield manufacturers from unpredictable and potentially costly lawsuits from employees injured or the kin of employees killed on the job. Social insurance programs also function to reproduce and reinforce the economic and social disparities among workers after withdrawal from the workforce by linking benefit levels to work history and contribution level. For example, Social Security is effective at maintaining income levels after retirement, but because of the enormous wage inequities in the United States, the program helps perpetuate social class differences and high levels of relative economic vulnerability among large subgroups of the elderly (48).

In contrast, social assistance programs such as SSI, Medicaid, and food stamps are supported by general government funds, and eligibility is not directly tied to employment. They offer significantly less generous benefits than their social insurance counterparts (lest they serve as disincentives to workforce participation), and eligibility criteria assess family income and assets as well as long-term impairment. Benefits are usually targeted to those at or below the federal poverty line, and often consist of direct services rather than cash transfers. The needs that are addressed are defined in the most basic survival terms. Resources are the targeted for subsistence—direct provision or indirect payments for food, housing, or medical care. Because programs are funded directly by the federal or state government, caseloads and costs are closely monitored and controlled. For most people with disabilities, public assistance is limited to this latter class of programs.

An analysis of modern welfare policy suggests that disability, defined as inability to participate in the workforce due to a physical or mental impairment, is only one of a series of complex and nondiscrete social categories bounding the labor market. These categories segment the population into wage-payers, wage-earners, and dependents, thereby facilitating the concentration of political and economic power.

One of the primary ways that the state (and the dominant economic institutions it supports) enforces the boundaries of the wage labor market is by defining a huge class of important social maintenance activities, and the persons who perform them, as outside the sphere of paid work. Gender has historically been the main criterion used to separate these spheres of public and private responsibility. The social roles of wife, mother, and daughter carry overt and significant expectations for unpaid labor—the care of children, spouses, and elderly or disabled parents (49).

Leaving aside the broader critique of the social inequity inherent in such a system, it is important to stress the consequence of these gender expectations for disability policy. Impairment or disability among family members can and does dramatically increase the time and effort required to fulfill the caregiving responsibilities "normally" assigned to women as wives, mothers, and daughters (50). Since these support activities are devalued to begin with, the additional caregiving demands (and concomitant stress and impedance to workforce participation) are typically not recognized, at least as a public problem worthy of policy remediation or compensation.

Disability within non-wage-earning groups including, importantly, the elderly, is thus generally construed as a family problem rather than an individual problem. The physical support and maintenance of family members with disabilities becomes a public rather than private concern only when caregivers are unable or unwilling to provide adequate unpaid assistance. The institutional and community-based long-term care services in the United States therefore function as a secondary support system. Because this system is conceptually and programmatically linked to failures of family supports, it also tends to be devalued and therefore chronically underfunded.

Consider the case of a typical Medicaid-funded program, providing older disabled clients with a modest level of personal assistance and household chores on a daily basis. Eligibility for such a program would be based not only on medically verifiable impairment, but on availability of unpaid family support and on family income. Only in rare cases would family members or other "informal caregivers" be paid by such a program to assist their disabled relatives.

Although women are more likely to become disabled and require assistance, their unpaid caregiving activities limit their access to public supports. Insofar as family care responsibilities constrain workforce participation, they serve as a barrier to accessing the benefits of the wage market. If a woman designated as an unpaid caregiver becomes disabled herself, she will not be eligible for work-based social insurance.

Social assistance programs for non-wage-earning groups are embedded in the needs-based distributional system, with all of its accompanying barriers discouraging utilization of benefits (i.e., social stigma, access hurdles, and limited direct services rather than cash benefits). Such programs are directly targeted to the poor, and indirectly targeted to women. In the absence of any individual earned income, means-testing shifts the unit of analysis from the person with a disability to her family. Fraser notes that there is an overt gender subtext to such program eligibility requirements (51, p. 149):

> The system as a whole is a two-tiered one. . . . One set of programs is oriented to individuals and tied to participation in the paid work force . . . [and] is designed to supplement and compensate for the primary market in paid labor power. A second set of programs is oriented to households and tied to combined household income . . . [and] is designed to compensate for what are considered family failures, in particular the absence of a male breadwinner. What integrates the two sets of programs is a common core set of assumptions regarding the sexual division of labor, domestic and nondomestic. It is assumed that families do or

should contain one primary breadwinner who is male and one unpaid domestic worker (homemaker and mother) who is female.

This institutional gender bias is carried into old age via contribution-based retirement programs such as Social Security and means-tested health and long-term care programs such as Medicaid. Moreover, because of differences in the demography of aging, morbidity, and mortality (52), women are more likely to rely on such programs for longer periods of time (53).

Race, like gender, also has profound implications for the definition and experience of disability in old age. People of color are at elevated risk both for experiencing disability and for having their impairments "treated" and managed for long periods of time, often through public programs. Although most of the research on race differences in disability among the elderly tends to be limited to comparisons of whites and African Americans, even this narrow literature is revealing.

While African American adults have a lower mean adult age than whites, they report significantly higher rates of activity limitation: 5.1 percent of the African American population, as opposed to 3.7 percent of the white population (2). Moreover, as Gibson (54) notes, many African Americans aged 55 and over appear to constitute a new type of retiree—the "unretired retired." She suggests that a significant portion of this population opts out of the workforce before the Social Security retirement threshold of 65, choosing to rely on modest federal disability benefits such as SSI rather than equally modest wages. According to this argument, the status of disabled worker is economically and psychologically preferable to that of marginal worker, particularly in communities where employment opportunities are extremely limited. Further research is needed to explicate the degree to which race may be, in part, a proxy for social class in relation to the phenomenon of the "unretired retired," but the latter's importance as a descriptively accurate category for many older African Americans underscores the value of taking it into account in retirement planning and policy development.

Although the emphasis on employment in disability programs differentially affects populations already facing social and structural barriers to workforce participation (i.e., women and people of color), it also creates some distinct age biases. Because the primary objective of most disability support services and cash transfers is to establish or restore independence, typically defined in a narrow financial sense of economic self-sufficiency, older persons already given a permanent exemption from the workforce are often excluded, even if they could benefit from those services.

The limited social insurance benefits available to disabled seniors focus almost entirely on the avoidance or postponement of costly institution-based services. As Estes (55) has noted, the primary beneficiaries of programs for the elderly (and we would add, the disabled elderly in particular) have often tended to be service providers, rather than elders themselves. These programs embody the "decline and loss" paradigm of disability and aging which pervades much of geriatrics and gerontology. In the following section we briefly discuss the evolution of this perspective on aging and disability.

AGE, DISABILITY, AND STIGMA:
CONTEMPORARY AND HISTORICAL PERSPECTIVES

A decline and loss paradigm often ignores the broader needs and aspirations of older people with disabilities, reinforcing the biomedicalization of aging (56) and the marginalization of disabled seniors. In the latter regard, as noted earlier, recent attempts to stress "healthy" and "successful" aging have sometimes had the effect of reinforcing negative attitudes toward those elders who are in fact disabled. Arguing that it is "ageist" to equate old age with disability, gerontologists and aging advocates sometimes wittingly or unwittingly help transfer fears about aging to fears of disability. Cohen observes that the accompanying prejudice against disabled elders, which he called "the elderly mystique,"[2] is not infrequently shared by older people: "the elderly themselves have concluded that when disability arrives, hope about continued growth, self realization and full participation in family and society must be abandoned so that all energy can be directed toward the ultimate defeat, which is not death but institutionalization" (58, p. 25).

There is a growing appreciation of the potential for reaching goals of autonomy, growth, participation, and high life satisfaction on the part of the non-disabled elderly, but these goals tend to be recalibrated dramatically downward for those elders who become disabled. Whereas "access" and "full participation" have become key concepts for the younger disabled population, for disabled elders, the sights of families and professionals, and of the disabled elders themselves, tend to be far more circumscribed. In this way, aging professionals, elders, and society in general appear to have traded earlier, limited views of aging for an even more limited view of what it means to be old and disabled (1).

Although a thorough discussion of this phenomenon is beyond the scope of this chapter, it is interesting to speculate about the roots of our current tendency to "split" old age into healthy or successful on the one hand, and unhealthy or unsuccessful—with little chance of autonomy and participation—on the other. Historian Thomas Cole, for example, has suggested that this tendency may be part of an historical pattern based on splitting or dichotomizing the 'negative' from the 'positive' aspects of aging and old age" (59, p. 18):

> The primary virtues of Victorian morality—independence, health, success—required constant control over one's body and physical energies. The decay of the body in old age, a constant reminder of the limits of self control, came to signify precisely what bourgeois culture hoped to avoid: dependence, disease, failure and sin.

The view of a dichotomized old age, and of the virtuous and benevolent execution of one life stage as heavily influencing one's happiness in the next, was further

---

[2] The term "elderly mystique" was coined by Rosenfelt in 1965 (57) in reference to a more general negative view of aging and the elderly held by young and old alike. While Cohen resurrected and used the same term more than 20 years later, he has defined it more specifically as prejudice against the disabled elderly—the conceptualization employed in the current discussion.

reinforced in the spheres of health and medicine. Since many prescriptions for a moral life were also the maxims for good health, physicians of the early 1800s often stressed a life of righteousness as a means of achieving a good and healthy/non-disabled old age (60).

Beginning in the late 1800s, a variety of political, economic, and other social forces resulted in a gradual movement away from a dichotomized view of old age and toward a general devaluation and medicalization of this life stage. As Cole notes, for example, in both the United Kingdom and the United States, "the word 'senile' itself was transformed . . . from a general term signifying old age to a medical term signifying the inevitably debilitated condition of the aged" (61). By equating old age with disability, reformers in many European countries provided additional momentum in the movement to enact old age pension schemes. While their motives were often laudable, the effect of this "compassionate ageism" (62) was much the same as its earlier, less compassionate version: the elderly were systematically devalued and aging became increasingly synonymous with disease, disability, and decline.

Missing from both the earlier, Victorian-era notions of a dichotomized old age and later emphasis on a decline and loss paradigm is, of course, a dialectical vision of aging—one that truly respects its diversity and its place as part of a natural and unified lifetime. A dialectical vision of aging would acknowledge both able-bodiedness and disability as valid parts of the aging experience. By holding both visions simultaneously, moreover, it would enable a more thoughtful approach to meeting the needs of those elders who are or become disabled (1). A useful framework for moving in this direction may be found in the disability literature, in the latter's concept of independent living.

INDEPENDENT LIVING AND INTERDEPENDENCE— AN ALTERNATIVE VIEW OF THE DISABILITY EXPERIENCE

The Independent Living Movement is a loose coalition of persons with disabilities and their allies (advocates and analysts sympathetic to the aims of the Movement) who pursue public policies that minimize segregation and maximize autonomy. The Movement has proven remarkably effective in advancing its political agendas, and the philosophy of independent living is increasingly influential in disability theory and research. According to Ratzka, the principles of independent living assert (63):

> The right of all persons, regardless of age, type or extent of disability, to live in the community, as opposed to living in an institution; have the same range of choices as everyone else in housing, transportation, education, and employment; participate in the social, economic, and political life of their communities; have a family; live as responsible, respected members of their communities, with all the duties and privileges that entails; and unfold their potential.

The independent living perspective suggests that the condition of the body is, or rather should be, irrelevant to the economic, social, and family life of the individual. This does not deny the need for support services and technologies; indeed, it implies that considerable resources should be directed toward the full integration of persons with disabilities. But these services and technologies must be, to the fullest extent possible, under the direct control of the recipient. In the words of Judy Heumann, director of the U.S. Department of Education's Office of Special Education and Rehabilitation, "Independent living is not doing things by yourself, it is being in control of how things are done (quoted in 64).

Such a philosophy has important implications for our consideration of the aging and disabled. First, as noted earlier, it provides an important counterpoint to conceptual and programmatic approaches to disability in old age which stress avoidance of institutionalization as a necessary and sufficient goal of maintenance or rehabilitation efforts. Second, and relatedly, it reminds us that even in advanced old age, "Life is more than simply the sum of a list of activities of daily living. There must be room for experiencing a fluid, unpredictable story line unfolding over time" (65, p. 278).

Finally, the philosophy of the Independent Living Movement extends gerontology's concerns with "aging in place" by underscoring the importance of minimizing not only geographical disruptions, but also social and economic ones, as well as disruptions in the sense of control that we now know to be an important component of well-being across the life course (66–69).

Despite its emphasis on the language of independence, the Independent Living Movement is philosophically very much in tune with the notion of a "moral economy of interdependence" described in Chapter 4. As Robertson points out, the elderly (and, we would add, people with disabilities), are often "caught between a social ethic of independence on the one hand, and a service ethic which constructs them as dependent on the other" (page 82). Getting beyond this dilemma means embracing a deeper sense of the relationship between individuals with disabilities and the larger community, stressing reciprocity, but a reciprocity far removed from narrow marketplace conceptualizations of giving and getting in return.

Applied to people with disabilities and the broader community, a moral economy of interdependence would stress creating conditions within which the former exercise control over their lives and participate equally in the larger society. It would stress that people with disabilities and people without disabilities are intimately tied to one another and that the needs of the disabled are, in a real sense, shared by all of us. The Independent Living Movement philosophy and related conceptualizations of interdependence, in short, have a great deal to offer those concerned with developing broader and more empowering approaches to aging and disability.

IMPLICATIONS OF DISABILITY THEORY AND RESEARCH FOR CRITICAL GERONTOLOGY

Although substantial portions of the older population are free of disability at any given time, disability is a typical part of the individual aging process. As Zola (17) points out, "the issue of disability for individuals . . . is not whether but when, not so much which one, but how many and in what combination." Most of the theoretical work to date in both gerontology and disability studies has failed to adequately acknowledge this fact. By creating artificial distinctions based on chronological age and government retirement policies, we risk overlooking common service needs and desires for personal autonomy which bridge age groups.

We have proposed several directions for researching policy and practice to help break down these artificial walls and promote a common ground. First, there is continued need for the development of models of disability and aging that underscore the broader environmental contexts within which the disablement process takes place. By stressing that disabilities are indeed physically based but socially constructed, we can better understand the political and moral economic forces that help explain the distribution and meaning of disability within and across diverse groups and society.

Second, in the light of the disproportionate representation of disability among the old, the definitional and programmatic linking of disability to workforce participation merits careful reconsideration. We have argued that such a linkage not only reinforces the valuing of people primarily in economic terms, but further marginalizes groups such as caregivers and the elderly, who are already excluded from the labor force.

Third, and relatedly, the gender, race, class, and age biases inherent in existing programs serving the elderly and disabled are in need of further research and policy attention. The two-tier system of financial assistance works to the systematic disadvantage of elders who are low-income, women, people of color, and/or disabled. Such populations are disproportionally represented in second-tier programs such as SSI. These social insurance programs tend to have "a low compassion index" (70), providing miserly benefits and stigmatizing beneficiaries.

Recent policy proposals that would tighten program eligibility would further disadvantage these groups. Likewise, proposals to increase normal retirement age to 67 or 70 would penalize those groups most likely to leave the workforce early due to disability and/or caregiving responsibilities (i.e., women, low-income elders, and elders of color). Research and policy efforts must recognize and address the differential impacts of such "reforms." The current biases against caregivers merit particular scrutiny, as the aging of the population and the rapid spread of managed care and other cost-containment approaches promise to increase reliance on informal family support for the elderly and disabled in the years ahead.

Finally, as noted earlier, concepts such as healthy and successful aging, while useful in pointing up the importance of health promotion and disease prevention across the life course, need to be used with considerable caution for the many elders who are or will become disabled. Idealized "one hoss shay" notions of old age in which the elderly, like the master's horse in Oliver Wendell Holmes's (71) poem, live out a full and long life with little or no impairment and then simply die, are both unrealistic and potentially victim blaming. A dialectical vision of old age, which appreciates the diversity of the aging experience and makes room for both able-bodied and disabled elders, is an important one to bear in mind as we plan for unprecedented numbers of elders in the decades ahead.

The spirit and philosophy of the Independent Living Movement, which stresses choice, participation, and minimization of the economic and social disruptions associated with the onset or aggravation of disability, provides an important framework for analysis and action. Yet as Robertson suggests in Chapter 4, of at least equal importance is movement toward a moral economy of interdependence, which moves beyond narrow conceptualizations of needs, rights, and entitlements to focus instead on a broad vision of reciprocity. Instead of segmenting the needs of the elderly and disabled, we should acknowledge as a society the "webs of interdependence" in which all members of the national community live. Aging and disability are facts of life that ultimately confront most human beings, and recognition of this fact may help form the basis of a more caring and civilized society.

REFERENCES

1. Minkler, M. Aging and disability: Behind and beyond the stereotypes. *J. Aging Stud.* 4(3): 245–260, 1990.
2. Kennedy, J., and LaPlante, M. A profile of adults needing assistance with activities of daily living. *Disabil. Stat. Rep.* 9, 1977, in press.
3. Riley, M., and Bond, K. Beyond ageism: Postponing the onset of disability. In *Aging in Society: Selected Reviews of Recent Research,* edited by M. Riley, B. Hess, and K. Bond. Lawrence Erlbaum, Hillsdale, N.J., 1983.
4. Gorman, K., and Posner, J. Benefits of exercise in old age. *Clin. Geriatr. Med.* 4: 181–192, 1988.
5. Bortz, W. Disuse and aging. *JAMA* 248: 1203–1208, 1982.
6. Rowe, J., and Kahn, R. Human aging: Usual and successful. *Science* 237: 143–149, 1987.
7. Minkler, M. Critical perspectives on aging: New challenges for gerontology. *Ageing Soc.* 16: 467–487, 1996.
8. Albrecht, G. *The Disability Business: Rehabilitation in America.* Sage Library of Social Research, Newbury Park, 1992.
9. Stone, D. *The Disabled State.* Temple University Press, Philadelphia, 1984.
10. Bickenbach, J. *Physical Disability and Social Policy.* University of Toronto Press, Toronto, 1993.
11. Haber, L. Identifying the disabled: Concepts and methods in the measurement of disability. *Soc. Sec. Bull.* 12: 17–34, 1967.
12. Nagi, S. Some conceptual issues in disability and rehabilitation. In *Sociology and Rehabilitation,* edited by M. Sussman. American Sociological Association, Washington, D.C., 1965.
13. Nagi, S. An epidemiology of disability among adults in the United States. *Milbank Q.* 54: 439–467, 1976.
14. World Health Organization. *International Classification of Impairments, Disabilities, and Handicaps.* Geneva, Switzerland, 1980.
15. West, J. *Federal Implementation of the Americans with Disabilities Act, 1991–1994.* Milbank Memorial Fund, New York, 1994.
16. Pfeiffer, D. The problem of disability definition. *J. Disabil. Policy Stud.* 4(2): 23–28, 1993.
17. Zola, I. Disability statistics, what we count and what it tells us: A personal and political analysis. *J. Disabil. Policy Stud.* 4(2): 10–39, 1993.
18. Hahn, H. The political implications of disability definitions and data. *J. Disabil. Policy Stud.* 4(2): 11–17, 1993.
19. Wood, P. The language of disablement: A glossary relating to disease and its consequences. *Int. Rehabil. Med.* 2(2): 86–92, 1980.
20. Wood, P. Maladies imaginaires: Some common misconceptions about the ICIDH. *Int. Disabil. Stud.* 9(3): 125–128, 1987.

21. Brown, S. *Defining Persons with Disabilities: A Lack of Science.* Society for Disability Studies Annual Conference, Seattle, Wash., 1992.
22. Kleinbaum, D., Kupper, L., and Morgenstern, H. *Epidemiologic Research: Principles and Quantitative Methods.* Lifetime Learning Publishers, Belmont, Calif., 1982.
23. Gordis, L. *Epidemiology.* W. B. Saunders, Philadelphia, 1996.
24. Stehr, D., Klein, B., and Murata, G. Emergency department return visits in chronic obstructive pulmonary disease—the importance of psychosocial factors. *Ann. Emerg. Med.* 20(10): 1113–1116, 1991.
25. Weinberger, S. *Principles of Pulmonary Medicine,* Ed. 2. Saunders, Philadelphia, 1992.
26. Baum, G. L. (ed.). *Textbook of Pulmonary Disease.* Little, Brown, Boston, 1994.
27. Adler, N., et al. Socioeconomic status and health: The challenge of the gradient. *Am. Psychol.* 49(1): 15–24, 1994.
28. National Center for Health Statistics. Health characteristics by occupation and industry. *Vital Health Stat.* 10(170), 1989.
29. Syme, S., and Berkman, L. Social class, susceptibility and sickness. *Am. J. Epidemiol.* 104(1): 1–8, 1976.
30. Syme, S., Hyman, M., and Enterline, P. Some social and cultural factors associated with the occurrence of coronary heart disease. *J. Chron. Dis.* 17: 277–289, 1964.
31. Antonovsky, A. Social class, life expectancy, and overall mortality. *Milbank Mem. Fund Q.* 45: 31–73, 1967.
32. Frey, R. The socioeconomic distribution of mortality rates in Des Moines, Iowa. *Public Health Rep.* 97: 545–549, 1982.
33. Kitigawa, E., and Hauser, P. *Differential Mortality in the United States: A Study in Socioeconomic Epidemiology.* Harvard University Press, Cambridge, Mass., 1973.
34. Chirikos, T., and Nickel, J. Socioeconomic determinants of continuing functional disablement from chronic disease episodes. *Soc. Sci. Med.* 22(12): 1329–1335, 1986.
35. Ficke, R. *Digest of Data on Persons with Disabilities.* NIDRR, Washington, D.C., 1992.
36. Rice, D., and LaPlante, M. Chronic illness, disability, and increasing longevity. In *The Economics and Ethics of Long-Term Care and Disability,* edited by S. Sullivan and M. Lewin. American Enterprise Institute, Washington, D.C., 1988.
37. LaPlante, M. The demographics of disability. *Milbank Q.* 2: 55–77, 1991.
38. Colvez, A., and Blanchet, M. Disability trends in the United States population 1966–76: Analysis of reported causes. *Am. J. Public Health* 71(5): 454–471, 1981.
39. LaPlante, M. *Trends in Survival of Persons with Severe Disability, U.S. 1970–85, and Implications for the Future.* Paper presented at the 21st National Meeting of the Public Health Conference on Records and Statistics, Hyattsville, Md., 1987.
40. Manton, K. The dynamics of population aging: Demography and policy analysis. *Milbank Q.* 69(2): 309–338, 1991.
41. Verbrugge, L. Recent, present, and future health of American adults. *Annu. Rev. Public Health* 10: 333–361, 1989.
42. Ycas, M. Trends in the incidence and prevalence of work disability. In *Disability in the United States: A Portrait From National Data,* edited by S. Thompson-Hoffman and I. Storck. Springer, New York, 1991.
43. Zedlewski, S., and McBride, T. The changing profile of the elderly: Effects on future long-term care needs and financing. *Milbank Q.* 70(2): 247–275, 1992.
44. LaPlante, M., et al. *Briefing on Employment and Disability.* Disability Statistics Rehabilitation Research and Training Center, San Francisco, 1994.
45. Chirikos, T. Aggregate economic losses from disability in the United States: A preliminary assay. *Milbank Q.* 67: 59–91, 1989.

46. Mills, C. *The Power Elite.* Oxford University Press, New York, 1956.
47. Kennedy, J. Americans Needing Assistance with Activities of Daily Living: Current Estimates and Policy Implications. Doctoral dissertation, University of California, Berkeley, 1996.
48. Myles, J. Postwar capitalism and the extension of social security into a retirement wage. In *Critical Perspectives on Aging: The Political and Moral Economy of Growing Old,* edited by M. Minkler and C. Estes. Baywood, Amityville, N.Y. 1991.
49. Abel, E. Man, woman, chore boy: Transformations in the antagonistic demands of work and care on women in the 19th and 20th centuries. *Milbank Q.* 73(2): 187–211, 1995.
50. Abel, E. *Who Cares for the Elderly? Public Policy and the Experience of Adult Daughters.* Temple University Press, Philadelphia, 1991.
51. Fraser, N. *Unruly Practices: Power, Discourse, and Gender in Contemporary Social Theory.* University of Minnesota Press, Minneapolis, 1989.
52. Seigel, J. *A Generation of Change: A Profile of America's Older Population.* Russel Sage Foundation, New York, 1993.
53. Butler, R. On behalf of older women: Another reason to protect Medicare and Medicaid. *N. Engl. J. Med.* 334(12): 794–796, 1996.
54. Gibson, R. The subjective retirement of black Americans. *J. Gerontol.* 46: S204–S209, 1991.
55. Estes, C. *The Aging Enterprise.* Jossey-Bass, San Francisco, 1979.
56. Estes, C., and Binney, L. The biomedicalization of aging: Dangers and dilemmas. *Gerontologist* 29: 587–596, 1989.
57. Rosenfelt, R. The elderly mystique. *J. Soc. Issues* 21: 37–43, 1965.
58. Cohen, E. The elderly mystique: Constraints on the autonomy of the elderly with disabilities. *Gerontologist* 28: 24–31, 1988.
59. Cole, T. The specter of old age: History, politics and culture in an aging America. *Tikkun* 3: 14–18, 93–95, 1988.
60. Achenbaum, W. *Images of Old Age in America, 1790 to the Present.* Institute of Gerontology, University of Michigan/Wayne State University, Ann Arbor/Detroit, 1978.
61. Cole, T. Aging, history and health: Progress and paradox. In *Health and Aging,* edited by J. J. F. Schroots, J. Birren, and A. Svanborg. Springer, New York, 1988.
62. Binstock, R. The oldest old: A fresh perspective or compassionate ageism revisited? *Milbank Mem. Fund Q.* 63: 420–541, 1983.
63. Ratzka, A. The user cooperative model in personal assistance: The example of STIL, the Stockholm Cooperative for Independent Living. In *PAS in Europe and America: Report of an International Symposium,* edited by B. Duncan and S. Brown. Rehabilitation International, New York, 1994.
64. Kennedy, J., Litvak, S., and Zukas, H. Independent living and personal assistance services: The research, training and technical assistance programs at the World Institute on Disability. *OSERS* 3: 43–49, 1994.
65. White, H. Disabled elderly: You can't run, but you can hide. *Gerontologist* 31(2): 278, 1991.
66. Langer, E. Old age: An artifact? In *Aging: Biology and Behavior,* edited by J. McGough and S. Kiesler. Academic Press, New York, 1981.
67. Schulz, R. Aging and control. In *Human Helplessness: Theory and Applications,* edited by J. Garber and M. Seligman. Academic Press, New York, 1980.
68. Seeman, T. Personal control and coronary artery disease: How generalized expectancies about control may influence disease risk. *J. Psychosom. Res.* 35: 661–669, 1991.

69. Syme, S. Control and health: An epidemiological perspective. In *Stress, Personal Control and Health,* edited by A. Steptoe and A. Appels. Wiley, New York, 1989.
70. Margolis, A. *Risking Old Age in America.* Westview, San Francisco, 1990.
71. Holmes, O. *The Deacon's Masterpiece on the Wonderful "One Hoss Shay."* Houghton Mifflin, Cambridge, Mass., 1881.

CHAPTER 6

Special Interests or Citizens' Rights?
"Senior Power," Social Security, and Medicare

Debra Street

The two most successful social welfare programs in the United States, Social Security and Medicare, are under political attack. Critics of public health insurance and pensions that provide income security in old age argue that we must retrench these programs, claiming that what John Myles called the "welfare state for the elderly" (1, p. 2) is unaffordable (2–4). An anti-statist political climate (5) has reigned over the politics of the U.S. welfare state for more than 15 years, with means-tested programs particularly hard hit by retrenchment and budget cuts (6, 7). Over the same period, however, cuts to Social Security and Medicare have been made at the margins, leaving both programs structurally intact.

What accounts for the durability of these two social insurance programs? Social Security and Medicare are political creations of the federal government, and most analysts offer political explanations for their continued endurance. However, researchers who do so offer political explanations from two decidedly different perspectives.

Many conventional academic analysts, critics of the welfare state, and the media argue that these programs survive because of the effective exercise of *senior power* within the "politics of aging" (8–14). They view elderly Americans as a homogeneous *special interest* of almost mythic proportions, capable of routinely winning political contests that further their own interests at the expense of Americans of other ages. Political economists and critical gerontologists reject this uncritical attribution of senior power as simplistic. They focus instead on how historically specific institutional and policy contexts differentially empower or constrain different subgroups of political actors (15–21). This critical perspective underscores heterogeneity among elderly Americans and calls into question the utility of thinking about Social Security and Medicare in terms of a "politics of aging." Instead, the political economy perspective emphasizes how Social Security and Medicare reflect "middle class incorporation"—cross-class and intergenerational political support—for social insurance programs (22, 23). Further, political economists and critical gerontologists argue that political identities, cleavages, and meanings are historically specific social

109

constructions transformed at the intersection of social, political, and economic institutions, and not merely or even especially conditioned by age or aging.

These conflicting political models beg several questions: What is the political relationship between age and the state? Do older citizens, either as an aggregate of individual voters or as interest group members, display senior power in the politics of Social Security and Medicare? To what extent does age interact with other statuses, such as class, gender, and race/ethnicity, to structure political power resources and income security for elderly citizens? Which institutional and political structures empower elderly citizens?

In this chapter I reflect on the way age becomes politicized in welfare state policymaking. The conventional view that Social Security and Medicare politics arise as the result of *special interest* politics is contrasted with the political economy perspective that these programs represent *citizens' rights*. I argue that these two contrasting models of politics are characterized by different political relations of interest, different levels of analysis, and different moral economy assumptions implicit in their models. By contrasting conventional political analyses that focus on age-based electoral bloc voting or interest group power models with the political economy perspective that emphasizes the stratification of interests embedded in welfare state social programs, we show that the latter offers a more adequate explanation of Social Security and Medicare politics.

AGE AND THE STATE

Because governments have invested special significance in the age of individuals, age has an undeniably political aspect. Governments use age as a regulatory mechanism to establish eligibility for particular statuses and benefits that, in part, shape the life course of individuals. *Chronological* age is an ascribed characteristic that changes in predictable ways as individuals age through time. What attaining a particular *political* age signifies is not as predictable. Political age is a historically specific, socially constructed variable that differs in its significance and effects over time (24–26). Political age's meaning is shaped and reformulated through interaction between governments and citizens, as prescribed and proscribed activities and statuses change through political actions and legislative initiatives.

In capitalist democracies like the United States, the state shapes the life course of individuals in myriad ways through its use of age as a criterion for specific state-regulated statuses. For instance, age criteria establish when a child must begin attending school and a minimum age for school leaving, when individuals are old enough to begin paid work and when they become eligible to claim Social Security and Medicare benefits, when full adult citizenship rights and responsibilities attain to individuals through enfranchisement as eligible voters, to name just a few.

What political age means is contested terrain and varies over time with respect to individual responsibilities, status, and entitlement to state benefits. Historically, age combined with other criteria has determined whether individuals are eligible to receive Social Security and Medicare benefits (27). Consequently, age may have special political significance to individuals who, by virtue of their age status, qualify for age-based state benefits like Social Security and Medicare. To the extent that political age is either a unifying or discriminating factor, or both, it matters in the policymaking arena and may be a mobilizing influence in political contests.

SPECIAL INTERESTS OR CITIZENS' RIGHTS?

The contrasting views of conventional and political economy models of the politics surrounding Social Security and Medicare reflect differences in the political relations of interest to each model, the level—situational, institutional, or systemic—of analysis held to be central to understanding political outcomes (19, 28) and differing assumptions about the moral economy (29–31) (see Chapter 2) undergirding Social Security and Medicare. Conventional accounts focus on citizens as individual voters or voluntary interest group members at situational or institutional levels of analysis. Political economy models emphasize how structural features of democratic capitalism shape political relationships and the capacity for effective political action among subgroups within U.S. society from institutional or systemic levels of analysis.

Besides these differences in the levels of analysis and political relations of interest, contrasting traditions of moral economy are implicit in most conventional and political economy models. Moral economy models reflect "collectively shared moral assumptions defining the rules of reciprocity on which the market economy is grounded (30, p. 125). Conventional *special interest* constructions often depend upon assumptions of what we call the *individualist* moral economy tradition, defined by Hendricks and Leedham (31) as the "exchange value" form of moral economy. The individualist moral economy model holds that reciprocity is appropriately bounded within kin relations and grounded in market exchange "for advantage or profit in individual transactions" (31, p. 56). Most individualists believe that market provision of pensions and health benefit is superior to state provision, arguing that coercive elements of taxation required to support state provision for anything more than subsistence poverty relief undermine individual freedom, work effort, and family values (32). Rather than collective provision of health and retirement benefits through the welfare state, adherents to the individualist moral economy perspective favor individual thrift and voluntary arrangements to finance health insurance and pensions in old age (33–35).

Political economists and critical gerontologists challenge both the adequacy of conventional explanations for the continuity of social insurance programs and the moral economy assumptions that are foundational to the special interest perspective. Political economists argue that Social Security and Medicare arise from much broader political compromises than just age-based ones, based in the need for labor market management (36–38) and intergenerational risk-sharing (17, 18, 39) in capitalist economies. Historically, Social Security pensions and health insurance coverage under Medicare have contributed to the institutionalization of retirement by guaranteeing workers a measure of income security in old age—what John Myles called a *citizen's right* to "cease work before wearing out" (40, p. 280).

Citizens' rights embedded in entitlement programs like Social Security and Medicare reflect the assumptions of a *collectivist* moral economy—what Hendricks and Leedham (31) call the "use value" form. This moral economy construct is grounded in meeting human needs by creating "social arrangements that maximize lifechances for all members of society over time, given resource constraints" (31, p. 56). The collectivist moral economy tradition has been an explicit part of social insurance programs like Social Security and Medicare from their inception. By instituting an earnings-related social insurance program, the architects of Social Security sought to convey a contribution-linked "right" for citizens to receive public pensions. As Franklin Roosevelt characterized his rationale for the structure of the Social Security program: "We put those payroll contributions there so as to give the contributors a legal, moral and political right to collect their pensions and employment benefits. With those taxes in there, no damn politician can ever scrap my social security program" (quoted in 41, p. 55). From the beginning, its architects intended Social Security to foster a sense of entitlement, both from the individual beneficiary's perspective and from a budgetary/political perspective. The Medicare program, implemented in 1965, built upon similar social insurance principles of entitlement. It was always intended that individuals would not have to feel guilty about accepting Social Security and Medicare benefits, and that governments would be loath to tamper with the programs (42). Through their payroll tax contributions, individuals earned the right to claim Social Security pensions and Medicare benefits free from the stigma of means-testing. From budgetary and political perspectives, Social Security and Medicare entitlement arose from the fact that the programs were exempt from the regular, contingent appropriations process, since their growth over time depended on eligibility criteria and benefits defined by law. This budgetary/political feature guaranteed both stability of coverage and predictability of benefits (43, p. 2).

Thus, conventional and political economy perspectives offer competing explanations for the politics surrounding Social Security and Medicare. Conventional analyses emphasize senior power within the domain of the politics of aging. Political economists argue that the only way to understand the durability of Social Security and Medicare is to critically examine the way political institutions, economic relations, elite and citizen political actors of all ages interact to shape political outcomes affecting those programs.

IS THERE A POLITICS OF AGING?

A complete exploration of any political issue has situational, organizational (institutional), and systemic (structural) components—each having a functionalist and political aspect (28). The point of a complete analysis within a policy domain such as age-based public policy is to make explicit the connections between these different levels of analysis (44). Wallace and colleagues (19) argue that we have addressed these three levels of analysis when age-based political analyses provide explanations of how older citizens demonstrate situational power through the senior vote and their influence on "normal" politics; institutional power through their capacity to work together through organizations or interest groups run for their own benefit; and, structural power when political and economic systems automatically consider age-based interests. Yet traditional welfare state theories of politics are at odds when trying to explain the potential role that elderly citizens might play in political contests and policymaking processes.

The Special Interest Perspective

Neo-pluralist and institutional theories, consistent with the construction of the special interest model of the politics of Social Security and Medicare, dominate academic political analyses in the United States. In neo-pluralist models, entitlement to age-specific benefits creates age as an important cleavage that contributes to political interest formation and serves as an incentive to activism (44). Similarly, in institutional models, feedback effects of age-based policies shape age interests that may then be expressed through age-based political activity (7). They assume that interest formation is straightforward: Social Security and Medicare benefits create material and political reasons for elderly people to act in self-interested ways to maintain their claim on benefits. The *specialness* of old-age interests, presumably, arises from assumptions in most conventional political analysis of zero-sum political contests over divisible benefits or privileges, where all participants in the process, even broadly based aggregates of voters or citizens' groups, risk definition as "special interests." The combination of "special" interest formation and mobilization in these models could operate in two somewhat different ways.

In the first variant, age would determine political identity, implying homogeneous age interests consistent with the idea of a welfare state for the elderly largely determined by the elderly. It assumes that individuals vote to benefit themselves, by rewarding or punishing parties in elections. In this formulation, the aged electorate would exercise political power by prospectively voting for political candidates who appeal to their interests by pledging to continue or expand Social Security and Medicare benefits or by retrospectively withholding their vote from political candidates who harm their interests by retrenching age-based public programs (46). Systematic prospective or retrospective voting hypotheses would be supported if analysis of voting patterns showed the electoral influence of aggregates of elderly voters who rewarded or punished politicians based on voters' perceived self-interest.

A more nuanced variant of age as a special interest would be its expression through interest group politics. In this formulation, age need only occasionally be a unifying force, superseding interests accruing from, for example, one's role as a worker or a woman, as the salient characteristic around which individuals organize their political activity. Again, several hypotheses can be derived: Age-based interest groups exercise political power (*a*) by vetoing policy decisions they dislike, (*b*) by framing the parameters of age-based policy debates, (*c*) by setting the policymaking agenda. These three hypotheses reflect different levels of political power (47) elderly citizens might exert. Support for the first hypothesis would require evidence that age-based interest groups effectively blocked legislation inimical to their interests. The second hypothesis would be supported by evidence that age-based interest groups effectively shaped the parameters of policymaking debates. The third hypothesis would be supported by evidence that age-based interest groups were successful in placing policy issues important to them on the political agenda and seeing them to fruition.

The Citizens' Rights Perspective

But perhaps age-based political activity has scant or merely episodic influence on the politics of Social Security and Medicare. This is the perspective of political economists who emphasize how the dualism inherent in social policy regimes in liberal welfare states like the United States mediates capacities for citizens to be effective political actors (22, 48). Means- or income-tested benefits go to the poor aged, consistent with the neo-Marxist designation of pensioners as part of the surplus army of labor (33, 49). Social insurance benefits such as Social Security and Medicare constitute an emancipatory guarantee—a citizen's right—that aged Americans need no longer depend exclusively on the "cash nexus" and can choose to retire with a measure of income security (1, 22, 40).

Political economists argue that policy rules and outcomes shape potential age-based interests in a variety of cross-cutting ways. The age basis for Social Security and Medicare entitlement creates an "age" interest. Age status interacts with a variety of other statuses such as race/ethnicity, gender, and income to condition citizens' political mobilization. This conception of age interests incorporates the insights suggested by neo-Marxist models that social marginalization and limited political potential may condition age interests (16, 33, 49) and power resource theorists' emphasis on how the U.S. welfare state establishes systems of stratification that differentially constrain or empower subgroups of elderly Americans (6, 18, 48, 50). The political economy perspective takes the potential political influence of citizens through democratic processes seriously. It presupposes that elderly citizens' political interests do not derive activities from class, race/ethnicities, gender, or age in isolation. Overlapping statuses within a variety of categories shape political identities and interests within the American political culture. Further, historically specific institutions pattern elderly citizens' ability to participate in and influence the politics of Social Security and Medicare.

AGE AND ELECTORAL POLITICS

Do elderly Americans constitute a powerful voting bloc? If "age interests" were homogeneous and were the sole basis for voting that elderly people used, their power in the electoral process would increase with their numbers. Elderly citizens represent large and growing proportions of the U.S. population and they are increasing as a proportion of eligible voters as well. If Census projections are correct, by 2020 just over 20 percent of the population in the United States will be age 65 or older (51). Obviously, the elderly electorate is growing, a fact that politicians do not overlook.

Political Parties and Older Voters

Political parties seeking votes seldom deliberately alienate potential blocs of voters. Instead, political parties usually make broad policy statements addressing a variety of issues in hopes of "being all things to all people." In national electoral politics, the major parties often attempt to address the concerns of elderly citizens in their party platforms by making promises to expand or protect Social Security and Medicare during the run-up to elections. Nevertheless, specific party intentions for Social Security and Medicare policy may be difficult for voters to identify, particularly since they are only one aspect of national party platforms and are often vaguely defined. Still, if campaigns are short on specifics, the growth of the aged electorate and the proportion of the federal budget allocated to their needs have made Social Security and Medicare prominent features of recent party campaign platforms.

Elderly Voters in Recent Presidential Elections

In 1972, the Nixon Administration sought to insulate Social Security from electoral politics by introducing automatic indexing provisions intended to end the traditional "bidding war" of benefit increases between the Democrats and Republicans in the run up to elections (52). But the politicized nature of the Social Security program was highlighted early in President Reagan's first term. His suggested Social Security cutbacks evoked a storm of protest, and Reagan backed down from his proposed reforms. Elderly citizens, identified by Medicare and Social Security critics as one of the most powerful special interest electoral blocs in the United States (3, 10), were often characterized as the catalyst to Reagan's reversal on Social Security issues. The press fostered the impression of a vengeful elderly voting bloc, suggesting that Reagan's Social Security agenda so angered older voters that they turned control of the Senate back to the Democrats in the 1982 midterm elections.

While that explanation may, on its surface, appear plausible, substantial evidence contradicts the view that an angered elderly electorate was principally responsible either for Reagan's policy retreat or for the reversal of Republican party fortunes. There is really no way to know whether aged voters exacted revenge when incumbent Republican senators were defeated in 1982; Republican policy initiatives other than Social Security cuts may as plausibly have been the primary motives for individuals' voting decisions (21). The allegation that elderly voters exacted retribution, costing Republicans control of the Senate, is not supported by empirical evidence. In fact, the 1981 Social Security cuts were opposed by Americans in all age groups—who were willing to pay higher taxes to maintain benefit levels—and not just the elderly (53), undermining the thesis that Social Security is politically supported mainly, or even dominantly, by the aged. And despite Reagan's personal advocacy of Social Security cuts in his first term, older voters were more likely than any other age group to have voted for Reagan in the 1984 presidential election, undermining a voter "punishment" hypothesis.

In his analysis of the 1980, 1984, and 1988 presidential elections in the United States, political scientist Robert Binstock found no discernible pattern that differentiated the distributions of ballots by age categories (21, p. 602), and thus no directly observable age-based electoral behavior. Analysis of age group voting patterns in the past two elections also belies the myth of age-based bloc voting. Table 1 shows a breakdown of votes by selected demographic characteristics of the U.S. electorate in the past two presidential elections. Clearly, the difference in voting patterns among

Table 1

Voting patterns in the 1992 and 1996 U.S. presidential elections[a]

Voter characteristic	1992			1996		
	Clinton	Bush	Perot	Clinton	Dole	Perot
Gender						
Men	41	38	21	43	44	10
Women	45	37	17	54	38	7
Race/ethnicity						
White	39	40	20	43	46	9
Black	83	10	7	84	12	4
Hispanic	61	25	14	72	21	6
Asian	31	55	15	43	48	8
Age group						
18–29 yrs	43	34	22	53	34	10
30-44 yrs	41	38	21	48	41	9
45–59 yrs	41	40	19	48	41	9
60 yrs and over	50	38	12	48	44	7
Family income						
Under $15,000	58	23	19	59	28	11
$15,000–29,999	45	35	20	53	36	9
$30,000–49,999	41	38	21	48	40	10
Over $50,000	39	44	17	44	48	7
Over $75,000	36	48	16	41	51	7
Over $100,000	—	—	—	38	54	6

[a]Source: *New York Times National Edition,* November 10, 1996, p. 16.

age groups in the past two election cycles has been slight. The 1996 Medicare issue—dubbed by Republicans the "Mediscare" campaign (54)—touted widely in the media as a sure vote-getter for Democrats who claimed Republicans would cut Medicare benefits, failed to produce gains for Clinton among older voters. In 1992, Clinton won the over-60 vote by 12 percentage points; in 1996 he beat Dole among this age group by only four percentage points (55). Voting differences by gender and race/ethnicity dwarf age-based differences; a direct linear relationship exists between income and voting, with a propensity to vote for Republican candidates increasing systematically with income. What we can accurately observe about the voting behavior of elderly Americans is that they do vote at higher rates than their younger counterparts. Young voters (age 18 to 29) have the lowest rate of participation among Americans of voting age, with participation climbing for every other age group, peaking at 70 to 79. But no empirical evidence supports an age-based voting bloc thesis (21).

What accounts for the discrepancy between assertions that elderly Americans are a powerful voting bloc and their actual voting behavior? There are several potential explanations. First, rational self-interest models used to predict and interpret voting behavior lead conventional analysts to characterize the political situation "not as it appears *subjectively* to the voter but as it appears *objectively* to the analyst" (21, p. 602). As Robert Binstock points out, even if voters share analysts' concepts of self-interest (which is by no means certain), other factors including beliefs and values affect voting behavior. He cautions that this problem is compounded when older voters are singled out as an electoral constituency, through a focus on old-age characteristics to the exclusion of other characteristics. This can result in old-age interests being treated as somehow separable from interest that flow from family status, gender, race/ethnicity, religion, education, economic condition, and so on (21, p. 603). But these are the very characteristics that predict the political attitudes of older persons (56, 57) and create distinctions in policy preferences and interests among elderly Americans. In the United States, the *perception* that the elderly operate as a formidable voting bloc—a belief fostered by the generational equity rhetoric (see Chapter 4)—is contradicted by the evidence. Political attitudes and orientations among elderly Americans are about as diverse as in the population at large (21, 58), undermining the very notion of bloc voting. This does not mean, however, that an age-based voting bloc will not materialize in the future, nor that age-based electoral influence is necessarily trivial. As Robert Binstock observes, the perception that older Americans vote as a bloc—wielding what he calls the "electoral bluff"—may have an indirect influence on U.S. politics and policymaking (21). I only assert that there is no credible evidence in the United States that age-based voting blocs are a feature of national election landscapes. Consequently, there is no evidence to support a hypothesis that the politics of Social Security and Medicare is an age-based electoral politics. Only in the face of contradictory evidence between the fact of voting patterns and the perception of a powerful aged voting bloc could an electoral politics of aging hypothesis be supported.

INTEREST GROUPS AND THE ELDERLY

Most researchers conclude that it is not as individual voters, but rather through the collective actions of old-age interest/pressure groups that elderly citizens can influence the political process (9, 23, 56, 59, 60). A common assumption about liberal democracies like the United States is that citizens can join voluntary organizations to pursue common views and interests in the policymaking process. The growth, both in number and size of membership, of age-based interest groups in recent decades has been dramatic (9, 56, 61–63). What role, then, have age-based interest groups played in recent policy debates, and how effective have they been? To answer this question, we examine the role of age-based interest groups in three specific Social Security/Medicare policy contests.

Sacred Cows

The Social Security "crisis" started before Ronald Reagan took office. In the late 1970s, several age-based interest groups formed an umbrella group, Save Our Security (SOS), to coordinate efforts to preserve benefits in the face of an impending Social Security trust fund shortfall. Age-based interest groups heightened their political efforts to stave off immediate Social Security cuts that the Carter administration recommended to deal with the Social Security "crisis." Despite Congressional legislation passed in 1977, with the support of most age-based interest groups, to "save" Social Security from the funding crisis, the legislation solved the problem only in the short term. By the early 1980s, the crisis perception of Social Security funding escalated, accompanied by Ronald Reagan's election as President (64).

Ronald Reagan had little taste for the welfare state. Armed with the knowledge that the Social Security reserve fund was nearing imbalance because of pressures from high unemployment and inflation, Reagan moved early in his term of office to make substantial cuts in Social Security (23). His attack on middle-class entitlements included suggestions for a 10 percent cut in future benefits to all American retirees, a 31 percent cut in early-retirement benefits, and stricter rules regulating disability eligibility. These actions evoked immediate reaction from the old-age lobby.

As middle-class entitlements came under attack in Reagan's budget proposal, old-age interest groups such as the American Association of Retired Persons (AARP) and the National Council of Senior Citizens (NCSC) mobilized for action. The umbrella group SOS stepped up its lobbying efforts. New groups, such as the National Committee to Preserve Social Security and Medicare (NCPSSM), were founded to defend Social Security against threatened cuts.

With his public popularity plummeting, Reagan backed away from his 1981 proposals, and it was not until 1983 that reforms finally addressed the financing of the Social Security reserve fund. This time, the Bipartisan Social Security Commission provided political cover for both major political parties as a widely acceptable strategy to restore Social Security's fiscal health was worked out (65). The Commission consulted the old-age interest groups, soliciting their views and political support for Social Security reforms. The 1983 Social Security amendments included a six-month COLA (cost-of-living adjustment) delay, increased payroll contributions, included newly hired federal workers in the program, taxed benefits of upper-income retirees, and gradually increased the retirement age from 65 years to 67 years. In the short term, Social Security—the so-called "sacred cow" of American politics—was safe (66).

Notch Babies

Mobilization over Reagan's proposed Social Security cuts indicated cohesion within the community of U.S. age-based interest groups; the "notch" issue highlights cleavages. The 1972 Social Security amendments that provided automatic indexing also introduced a flawed benefit calculation formula. The flaw interacted with unexpected economic changes—high inflation and low wage increases—to "over-index" benefits for individuals retiring in 1972 or later (67). Consequently, new retirees began receiving benefits much higher than the Social Security Administration intended, creating long-term financing problems. To address the issue, the 1977 Social Security amendments implemented a new benefit formula that "notched down" and lowered benefits for workers born from 1917 to 1921, and maintained the lower benefit levels at these more realistic levels for all workers born after 1921.

Fixing the flaw, however, created a perception of unfairness in the Social Security program. While "notch babies" (68, p. 225) born between 1917 and 1921 had their anticipated Social Security benefits cut by the fix, American pensioners born between 1910 and 1916 received an unexpected windfall. The net result of the 1977 benefit formula fix was to create an anomaly in Social Security benefits, such that individuals with roughly identical work histories received substantially different benefit amounts. An individual "lucky" enough to be born in 1916 received windfall benefits, while his or her "unlucky" notch counterpart born a year later had benefits cut (67).

Most mainstream age-based interest groups shared the government's view that the 1977 Social Security fix was the fairest and most prudent response to the benefit calculation problem (69, 70), but the National Committee to Preserve Social Security and Medicare disagreed. It spent more than ten years lobbying Congress to improve benefits for the unfortunate notch babies. NCPSSM's tenacious pursuit of redress on the notch issue, according to interviews with NCPSSM staff and representatives of other age-based interest groups, created substantial dissension among the ranks of national age-based interest groups (48).

Catastrophic Politics

A departure from the universal cost-sharing in the Medicare program resulted in the most prolonged—and divisive—action by American old-age interest groups in the 1980s. Because Medicare benefits are distributed as a right and not as a means-tested privilege, Medicare enjoys broad-based legitimacy and political support—another instance of "middle class incorporation." No stigma attaches to individuals receiving Medicare benefits; Medicare coverage has traditionally been considered an appropriate sharing of the burden of health care costs for elderly Americans (71).

In 1987 President Reagan surprised nearly everyone when, in his State of the Union Address, he announced an initiative to relieve Medicare recipients of the expenses of catastrophic illness. The Medicare Catastrophic Coverage Act of 1988 (MCCA) was the only social policy expansion advocated by the Reagan administration, intended to fill gaps in the safety net of health care for elderly Americans. Reagan stipulated that the bill could not add to the federal deficit and that its cost had to be borne entirely by the elderly. Congressional representatives from both political parties jumped on the bandwagon, and in 1988 passed MCCA by an overwhelming margin.

Problems soon arose as implementation of MCCA became a reality. Problems centered on what was not offered—long-term care benefits—and who was going to pay the bill. Under the provisions of the legislation, Medicare premiums increased and a new income tax surcharge on the elderly was instituted. This was a substantial departure from the social insurance principle that had prevailed in earlier Medicare funding. Medicare beneficiaries bore the entire burden of paying for the expansion of services, with higher-income elderly people footing a larger share of the bill. Under mounting pressure from certain old-age interest groups, most parts of MCCA were repealed in 1989 (19, 20, 50, 72, 73).

Initially, the Medicare Catastrophic Coverage Act received substantial lobbying support from some prominent age-based interest groups, such as the American Association of Retired Persons and the National Council of Senior Citizens. Other age-based lobby groups withheld support, claiming that MCCA was fundamentally flawed. The Gray Panthers, for instance, opposed MCCA from the beginning because it neither structurally reformed health care financing nor guaranteed health insurance to Americans of all ages (74). The Gray Panthers were not alone. The National Association of Retired Public Employees opposed the bill; because their members had guaranteed health insurance in retirement, MCCA meant that they would be paying twice for catastrophic care (74). The National Committee to Preserve Social Security and Medicare lobbied against MCCA because it represented a radical departure from the intergenerational sharing of the costs of the Medicare program. NCPSSM objected not to MCCA's new provisions, but to the funding mechanism, claiming it would hurt its members. Once MCCA was passed, NCPSSM lobbied even more aggressively for repeal of the law (50).

AARP held the line by opposing repeal of MCCA after its enactment, despite the organization's reservations about the surtax; on the other hand, NCSC revised its original position of support because of the uproar over the funding issue. These two groups' initial support reflected a pragmatic attitude toward the possibilities of health care reform, although both organizations preferred funding based on social insurance principles. Both AARP and NCSC were influential in their roles supporting the initial legislation. However, grassroots mobilization of many senior citizens and the stepped-up efforts of organizations such as NCPSSM turned the tide of support away from MCCA and toward its repeal.

The new surtax that funded MCCA stratified older Americans into payer and non-payer categories. Upper-income elderly people had little to gain and much to lose financially should MCCA be fully implemented. High- and middle-income elderly people with sufficient resources could purchase private Medigap insurance that covered medical costs more comprehensively and inexpensively than the government program. Many of them were unwilling to support what for them was a bad deal—publicly provided catastrophic insurance that only they, and not low-income elderly people, would have to pay for. It was this threat to its financial interests that catalyzed the mobilization of the "payer" group to sustained interest group action calling for repeal of MCCA (50).

Although some groups within the old-age lobby were decisive actors in the repeal of the Medicare Catastrophic Coverage Act, it was only within a very limited context that they exercised their political power. Old-age interest groups demonstrated apparent power in health policy formation during the activities surrounding MCCA only to the extent that their agenda did not conflict with vested elite interests in health policy—particularly employers who provided health coverage for retirees, physicians', and hospital organizations. Segments of the old-age lobby rallied against the MCCA funding mechanism and exercised veto power over legislation that would have provided catastrophic health insurance to all elderly Americans, rich and poor alike. However, the subgroups among the elderly that could have benefited most from MCCA—low-income elderly people (who would have received acute care coverage under MCCA that they could not afford to buy in the private Medigap market) were not effectively represented by grassroots organizations lobbying on their behalf.

The Special Interest Perspective and the Politics of Aging

I have argued that one way political interests may be shaped is through age-based entitlement to social benefits like Social Security and Medicare, which gives age salience as a potential political cleavage. At the situational level of individual voting, presumption of homogeneous age-based interests is necessary for the concept of an age-based voting bloc to be meaningful. In its simplest form, the special interest perspective suggests that since elderly individuals qualify for Social Security and Medicare, they have identical interests in voting for politicians who promise to protect or increase these benefits. Yet the absence of evidence for age-based voting blocs refutes the neo-pluralist thesis that numbers alone translate into political power. The potential for elderly people to vote in blocs is unexpressed (75, 76). Older Americans are good citizens—they exhibit high levels of electoral participation—but their diversity precludes bloc voting. The elderly appear to base their voting decisions upon the same complex criteria as do other age groups, influenced by factors such as family political socialization in childhood, socioeconomic status, party identification, the state of the economy, concerns about law and order, and candidate appeal, to name just a few.

A more sophisticated formulation of the potential for a politics of aging focuses on the organizational level of analysis through the activities of interest groups and offers more nuanced analytical possibilities than a mere "numbers count" approach. Age-based interest groups in the United States have tools for influence other than threats of electoral punishment. Most age-based groups, including prominent groups such as AARP, NCSC, and NCPSSM, are widely perceived by U.S. politicians as legitimate representatives of positions reflecting the needs and interests of elderly people who belong to their organizations. Representatives of these groups are invited to participate in the hundreds of committee hearings that shape policy in the United States (9, 56). The relative openness of the U.S. political system, the legitimacy accorded age-based interest groups, the campaign needs of U.S. politicians, the perceived political power of the elderly, and multiple points of entry within the United States federal system of government—all provide a hospitable climate for a measure of age-based interest group influence. But do age-based interest groups represent homogeneous age interests?

A historically based examination of age-based interest group participation demonstrates that the social organizational effects of policy structures contribute to differences in the political stances of various old-age interest groups and condition opportunities for effective political influence (77). However, it is not just that policy structures create political constituencies; mobilized interest groups can, in turn, contribute to the process of policy formation by influencing policy debates. In specific contexts, interest groups can exert some influence over policy outcomes, most notably by exercising veto power over policy positions they oppose, such as immediate benefit cuts to Social Security in 1981. Yet the Social Security notch issue and Medicare Catastrophic Coverage Act demonstrate clearly that an interest group politics of aging offers, at best, only partial explanation for policy interests and outcomes. Despite substantial agreement among age-based interest groups on many issues, there are obvious cleavages among the constituencies represented by these groups. Also apparent is the inadequate representation of the interests of vulnerable, low-income elders—citizens who are most likely to be women, ethnic or racial minorities, and the very old—within the realm of interest group politics.

In fact, the special interest perspective of the politics of aging hides more than it reveals. By construing the legitimate income and health security needs of elderly citizens as a "special interest," age-based accounts of electoral or interest group politics conceal the cross-class and intergenerational nature of the politics of Social Security and Medicare.

THE CITIZENS' RIGHTS PERSPECTIVE

Most researchers conclude that major policy victories benefiting the elderly in the 1960s and 1970s, including the enactment of Medicare, the Employee Retirement Security Act, Supplemental Security Income (SSI), and improvements to Social Security benefits, resulted from the efforts of elite state actors with the support of organizations such as organized labor, social welfare groups, and consumer groups, and not old-age interest groups (6, 78, 70). "The old age lobby didn't create the policies; rather the policies created the lobby" (6), demonstrating the capacity of universal programs to unify the middle class behind the welfare state—what power resource theorists call, as noted earlier, "middle class incorporation" (22, 23). This suggests that the so-called politics of aging may look quite different when viewed from the perspective of a different level of analysis.

Universalist programs such as Social Security and Medicare create solidaristic political interests among elderly citizens who depend upon them for the shared experience of retirement income security and access to health care. They also create solidarity between elderly and younger citizens who recognize the need for collective risk-sharing in a rapidly changing capitalist economy. Despite nearly two decades of "crisis" mongering (64, 80–82), Social Security and Medicare remain the most popular components of the U.S. welfare state among citizens of all ages (71, 83).

But the U.S. welfare state consists of more than just social insurance programs like Social Security and Medicare. It also features two distinctive types of targeted social welfare programs. The better known of these targets means-tested subsistence benefits to the poor—such as AFDC (Aid to Families with Dependent Children), SSI, and Medicaid. The less well-known welfare state program targets benefits to the well-off, through tax subsidies for private pensions and health insurance, available only to those whose incomes are high enough to purchase these benefits in the first place. Targeted programs, whether in the form of social assistance or tax subsidies, undermine political solidarity by fragmenting citizens' interests in pension and health insurance policies (17, 48, 84). Elderly Americans near the poverty line who depend exclusively on Social Security and Medicare benefits, and those below the poverty line who depend on means-tested Medicaid and SSI benefits for income security in old age, have scant organizational, material, or political resources to defend the value of those benefits. Low-middle- and middle-income Americans bear the largest tax burdens for all welfare state programs, whether Social Security and Medicare, means-tested assistance, or tax subsidies for private provision.

Middle-income groups are caught between an interest in maintaining the value of Social Security and Medicare and the realization that income security in old age—particularly in the context of recent reform efforts that suggest major cutbacks to Medicare and the partial privatization of Social Security (85, 86) (see Chapter 19)—depends on capturing access to tax-subsidized private pensions and health insurance. High income earners receive sufficient incomes from their generously tax-subsidized private pensions to purchase private health insurance to fill the gaps between Medicare benefits and actual medical costs; protecting that tax perquisite is far more important to their future income security than defending state programs (48). Interest formation is strongly embedded in the structure of the U.S. welfare state and class relations in its capitalist economy. Conventional accounts that focus on the politics of aging conceal this fundamental reality.

A more plausible explanation than the special interest perspective is that some older Americans have organizational resources that permit a measure of political influence due to a variety of conditions arising from welfare state policy legacies and unique aspects of U.S. economic and political institutions (7, 77). Political process structures, economic resources, and age-based policies create different constituencies and trajectories for political participation among subgroups of elderly American citizens.

Policy Legacies and Age-Based Interests

Recent research in other social policy domains has focused on the impact of policy structures on shaping both actors' interests and the contexts within which the politics of policy formation take place (44). Walter Korpi (87) has argued that whether social policy formation takes place within marginal systems that seek to limit assistance to the poor, or within institutional systems that emphasize universality, is important for understanding both distributional processes and interest constituencies. Once implemented, social policies "change public agendas and the patterns of group conflict through which subsequent policy changes occur" (88, p. 149). Policy legacies shape both political actions and the interests of collectivities involved in the political processes of policy formation and implementation (7, 48, 77, 88). Popular support for needs-based benefits is scant; universal benefits, on the other hand, are widely viewed as social rights, and receive broad political support across classes and age groups within U.S. society (22, 23, 82, 83). Policy legacies, therefore, shape interest formation and political activism. Elderly people have material reasons for actively supporting or opposing public policies that either benefit or harm them, particularly when the policies depart from the principle of universalism. Groups with the resources to do so often form interest groups to promote, preserve, or protect their interests.

THE MYTHS AND REALITIES OF SENIOR POWER

Older citizens in the United States participate in the national political process in several ways. They vote in elections to select new governments that pursue particular policy initiatives. They participate as interest group members trying to influence policy decisions. Yet the evidence presented in this chapter contradicts an undifferentiated electoral politics of aging. The evidence for an interest group politics of aging, while more ambiguous, leads us to conclude that this perspective, too, inadequately captures the complexities of Medicare and Social Security politics.

Age as a political organizational principle, in isolation, shapes neither the situational nor the institutional politics of Social Security and Medicare. Rather, the critical intersection of age and other statuses shapes the politics of these programs. These multiple statuses *in combination* reveal the policy cleavages around which age-based constituencies have mobilized (or failed to mobilize) politically. Sometimes, when universalism prevails, old-age policies attract broad-based support among diverse subgroups of elderly citizens. Yet many age-based policies reproduce and even exacerbate the inequalities of earlier life. At a structural level, the politics of Social Security and Medicare assumes another aspect. To the extent that age-based policies intensify stratification, structural conditions render invisible an important political reality: the exclusion from effective political participation of many disadvantaged subgroups of elderly citizens, especially among the poor working class, racial/ethnic minorities, women, and the oldest old.

What this analysis reveals is that age interests are neither insignificant, nor undifferentiated, but neither are they necessarily central to the politics of age-based public policies. Age-based political interests are historically contingent, conditioned by a variety of other statuses and constrained by policy legacies, political culture, and changing socioeconomic conditions. It is apparent, as Myles and Quadagno note, that political contests differ "not only in the tones in which debates are conducted, but also in the groups mobilized, the cleavages invoked, and the alliances created in the course of these debates" (77). The combination of age, gender, race/ethnicity, and class interests differentially empowers subgroups of elderly citizens in specific ways.

On occasion, broad age-based interest groups can mobilize (often in alliance with other groups) and defend policies they favor, as was the case in the proposed cuts to U.S. Social Security benefits in 1981. The distinctive feature of that political episode was the threat of immediate cuts to current beneficiaries. American politicians probably learned a valuable political lesson from this case—pensioners will mobilize to protect their current pension benefits. The Social Security reforms in 1983 left current pensioners' benefits mainly intact, with the main policy effects concentrated in the outyears, affecting a diffuse and unmobilizable constituency (7).

More often, however, even when they are influential, age-based interest groups must accept compromises that undermine universalism and hence the basis for solidarity. This was the case with increased taxation (which disadvantaged the well-to-do) and increased retirement age (which disproportionately disadvantaged low-wage manual workers) under the 1983 Social Security amendments. In fact, most recent Social Security and Medicare reforms have been implemented in opposition to the policy preferences of age-based interest groups, policy outcomes at odds with senior power arguments (79). Perceptions of unfairness, which occurred both in the Social Security notch issue and the Medicare Catastrophic Coverage Act, undermine solidarity among older Americans and contradict a homogeneous special interest politics of aging.

Age-based interest groups have only limited capacity to achieve political ends, usually restricted to exercising veto influence over policy reforms they oppose. Even under the comparatively "ideal" conditions present for interest group politics in the United States—access to organizational resources, universalist policy structures, high levels of legitimacy as political actors, intense electoral competition, and relatively open policymaking processes—"victories" by age-based interest groups, unless expressed as contributing to policy vetoes, are difficult to identify. It is true that age-based groups are routinely consulted on policy issues that affect elderly Americans. What is not certain, however, is whether that consultation translates directly into influence. Age-based groups are helpful for politicians seeking to identify potentially harmful or unexpectedly beneficial consequences of a variety of policy options. However, age-based groups respond to initiatives already on the policy table—they do not put them there (48, 57, 78, 79). Age-based interest groups do not demonstrate the more elusive aspects of political power—framing the parameters of policy debates, or setting the policy agenda. Even organizational insiders concede that U.S. age-based interest groups' "power" is severely constrained (48, Chapt. 5).

CONCLUSION

The most likely outcome for old-age interests is that "the elderly" will be losers rather than gainers in terms of power and influence over future Social Security and Medicare policy. Budget constraints and a well-funded and deliberate campaign to cast elderly citizens as "greedy geezers" and a drain on the national treasury have taken their toll on the legitimacy of aged political actors and the prospects of citizens' claims on the social wage for dignified income security in old age (48, 64, 82). Recent trends in the United States signal an increasing reliance on market-conforming pensions and health insurance, with the state's role increasingly limited to social assistance models. These trajectories, combined with the likelihood that the eligibility age for Social Security and Medicare benefits will be increased, may mean that the importance of age as a political cleavage—already limited—will diminish. There is little evidence that the push toward less universal social provision and government preferences for needs-targeted social programs in the United States, with their attendant political and economic divisiveness, are on the wane. Departures from universalism and increased reliance on means- or income-tested state programs for poor Americans and private pensions and health insurance for the rest will undermine the bases of broad support for Social Security and Medicare among Americans of all ages. And as the case of the Medicare Catastrophic Coverage Act illustrates and the notch issue underscores, there is precious little space for solidaristic maneuver among old-age interest groups when universalism is under attack (6).

As principles of universalism, "age versus need," market versus state provision, and the fairness of generational claims to social benefits are debated in the future, adequate explanations of the politics of "the welfare state for the elderly" will depend upon adopting a critical perspective at odds with conventional accounts. Socioeconomic conditions, political institutions, effective mobilization of ideological resources, policy structures, the actions of both elite and non-elite political actors, and explicit attention to the moral economy assumptions undergirding social programs—are all necessary components for understanding the politics of Social Security and Medicare. In the future, cleavages among elderly Americans arising from socioeconomic status, race/ethnicity, gender, and family status may become far deeper than any currently perceived between the elderly and other age groups in the U.S. population, particularly if the gaps between state–dependent and private pension and health insurance–dependent pensioners increase. While the percentage of politically enfranchised elderly American voters will increase in the future, the "politics of aging" is likely to become even less, and not more, descriptive of policy processes than any functionalist "strength in aged numbers" thesis would suggest.

Future political debates surrounding Social Security and Medicare may result in increased mobilization among segments of the elderly population. Nevertheless, the political and policy legacies of recent years make it difficult to imagine fertile soil for future "triumphs" arising exclusively from either the electoral influence of elderly voters or the activities of age-based interest groups. Arrayed against exclusively age-based interests of citizens are seminal differences rooted in class, gender, and race/ethnicity. Diversity among elderly citizens in the United States—already a very heterogeneous population—will increase if their shared experience as recipients of universal Social Security and Medicare benefits declines.

Acknowledgments — I appreciate the helpful comments on earlier drafts of this chapter by Charles Shipan and Jill Quadagno.

REFERENCES

1. Myles, J. *Old Age in the Welfare State: The Political Economy of Public Pensions.* University of Kansas Press, Lawrence, 1989.
2. World Bank. *Averting the Old Age Crisis: Policies to Protect the Old and Promote Growth.* Oxford University Press, New York, 1994.
3. Longman, P. *Born to Pay: The New Politics of Aging in America.* Houghton Mifflin, Boston, 1987.
4. Peterson, P. *Facing Up: How to Rescue the Economy from Crushing Debt and Restore the American Dream.* Simon and Schuster, New York, 1993.
5. Block F. *The Vampire State and Other Myths and Fallacies about the U.S. Economy.* The New Press, New York, 1996.
6. Quadagno, J. *The Color of Welfare: How Racism Undermined the War on Poverty.* Oxford University Press, New York, 1994.
7. Pierson, P. *Dismantling the Welfare State? Reagan, Thatcher, and the Politics of Retrenchment.* Cambridge University Press, Cambridge, England, 1994.
8. Pratt, H. *Gray Agendas: Interest Groups and Public Pensions in Canada, Britain and the United States.* University of Michigan Press, Ann Arbor, 1993.
9. Callahan, D. *Setting Limits: Medical Goals in an Aging Society.* Simon and Schuster, New York, 1987.
10. Boskin, M. J. *Too Many Promises: The Uncertain Future of Social Security.* Dow Jones-Irwin, Homewood, Ill., 1986.

11. Committee for Economic Development. *Who Will Pay For Your Retirement? The Looming Crisis.* New York, 1995.

12. Peterson, P. G., and Howe, N. *On Borrowed Time: How the Growth in Entitlement Spending Threatens America's Future.* Institute for Contemporary Studies, San Francisco, 1988.

13. Becker, G. S. Social Security should benefit only the elderly poor. *Business Week,* January 16, 1989.

14. Smith, L. The tyranny of America's old. *Fortune,* January 13, 1992.

15. Estes, C. L., Linkins, K. W., and Binney, E. A. The political economy of aging. In *Handbook of Aging and the Social Sciences,* edited by R. H. Binstock and L. K. George, pp. 346–361. Academic Press, New York, 1995.

16. Hardy, M. A. Vulnerability in old age: The issue of dependency in American society. *J. Aging Stud.* 9(1): 43–63, 1988.

17. Myles, J., and Street, D. Should the economic life course be redesigned? Old age security in a time of transition. *Can. J. Aging* 14(2): 335–359, 1995.

18. Street, D., and Quadagno, J. The state, the elderly and the intergenerational contract: Toward a new political economy of aging. In *Societal Impact on Aging: Historical Perspectives,* edited by K. W. Schaie and W. A. Achenbaum, pp. 130–150. Springer, New York, 1993.

19. Wallace, S. P., et al. A lamb in wolf's clothing? The reality of senior power and social policy. In *Critical Perspectives on Aging: The Political and Moral Economy of Growing Old,* edited by M. Minkler and C. L. Estes, pp. 95–116. Baywood, Amityville, N.Y., 1991.

20. Holstein, M., and Minkler, M. The short life and painful death of the Medicare Catastrophic Coverage Act. *Int. J. Health Serv.* 21(1): 1–16, 1991.

21. Binstock, R. H. Older voters and the 1992 presidential election. *Gerontologist* 32(5): 601–606, 1992.

22. Esping Andersen, G. *The Three Worlds of Welfare Capitalism.* Polity Press, Cambridge, England, 1990.

23. Quadagno, J. Interest group politics and the future of old age security. In *States, Labor Markets, and the Future of Old Age Policy,* edited by J. Myles and J. Quadagno, pp. 36–58. Temple University Press, Philadelphia, 1991.

24. Jacobs, K., and Rein, M. The future of early retirement. In *States, Labor Markets and the Future of Old Age Policy,* edited by J. Myles and J. Quadagno, pp. 250–261. Temple University Press, Philadelphia, 1991.

25. Ginn, J., and Arber, S. "Only connect:" Gender relations and ageing. In *Connecting Gender and Ageing: A Sociological Approach,* edited by S. Arber and J. Ginn. Open University Press, Buckingham, 1995.

26. Cornman, J. M., and Kingson, E. R. Trends, issues, perspectives and values for the aging of the baby boom cohorts. *Gerontologist* 36(1): 15–26, 1996.

27. Harrington-Meyer, M., Street, D., and Quadagno, J. The impact of family status on income security and health care in old age: A comparison of western nations. *Int. J. Sociol. Soc. Policy* 14(1/2): 54–83, 1994.

28. Alford, R. R., and Friedland, R. *The Powers of Theory.* Cambridge University Press, New York, 1985.

29. Minkler, M., and Cole, T. R. Political and moral economy: Not such strange bedfellows. In *Critical Perspectives on Aging: The Political and Moral Economy of Growing Old,* edited by M. Minkler and C. L. Estes, pp. 37–49. Baywood, Amityville, N.Y., 1991.

30. Kohli, M. Retirement and the moral economy. *J. Aging Stud.* 1(2): 125–144, 1987.

31. Hendricks, J., and Leedham, C. A. Dependency or empowerment? Toward a moral and political economy of aging. In *Critical Perspectives on Aging: The Political and Moral*

Economy of Growing Old, edited by M. Minkler and C. L. Estes, pp. 51–64. Baywood, Amityville, N.Y., 1991.

32. Murray, C. *Losing Ground: American Social Policy 1950–1980.* Basic Books, New York, 1984.
33. Feldstein, M. Social Security and private saving. *J. Polit. Econ.* 90(4): 630–642, 1982.
34. Ferrara, P. Social Security and the Super IRA: A populist proposal. In *Social Security: Prospects for Real Reform,* edited by P. Ferrara, pp. 193–220. Cato Institute, Washington, D.C., 1985.
35. Roberts, P. C. How Social Security and Medicare rip off Americans. *Business Week,* May 27, 1996.
36. Graebner, W. *History of Retirement: The Meaning and Function of an American Institution.* Yale University Press, New Haven, Conn., 1980.
37. Phillipson, C. The state, the economy, and retirement. In *Old Age and the Welfare State,* edited by A. M. Guillemard, pp. 127–139. Sage Studies in International Sociology, 28, Sage, London, 1986.
38. Schulz, J. H. *The Economics of Aging.* Wadsworth Publishing, Belmont, Calif., 1995.
39. Kingson, E., Hirshorn, B. A., and Cornman, J. M. *Ties that Bind: The Interdependence of Generations.* Seven Locks Press, Washington, D.C., 1986.
40. Myles, J. Postwar capitalism and the extension of Social Security into a retirement wage. In *The Politics of Social Policy in the United States,* edited by M. Weir, A. S. Orloff, and T. Skocpol, pp. 265–284. Princeton University Press, Princeton, N.J., 1988.
41. Rose, R. *Understanding Big Government: The Programme Approach.* Sage, London, 1984.
42. Banting, K. Visions of the welfare state. In *The Future of Social Welfare Systems in Canada and the United Kingdom,* edited by S. B. Seward, pp. 147–163. Institute for Research on Public Policy, Halifax, 1986.
43. Moon, M., and Mulvey, J. *Entitlement and the Elderly: Protecting Promises, Recognizing Realities.* Urban Institute Press, Washington, D.C., 1995.
44. Burstein, P. Policy domains: Organization, culture and policy outcomes. *Annu. Rev. Sociol.* 17: 327–350, 1991.
45. Williamson, J. B., and Pampel, F. *Old Age Security in Comparative Perspective.* Oxford University Press, New York, 1993.
46. Rose, R., and McAllister, I. *The Loyalties of Voters: A Lifetime Learning Model.* Sage, London, 1990.
47. Lukes, S. *Power: A Radical View.* Macmillan, New York, 1974.
48. Street, D. The Politics of Pensions in Canada, Great Britain and the United States: 1975–1995. Ph.D. dissertation, Florida State University, Tallahassee, Fla., 1996.
49. Walker, A. The politics of ageing in Britain. In *Dependency and Inter-dependency in Old Age,* edited by C. Phillipson, M. Bernard, and P. Strang, pp. 30–45. Croom Helm, London, 1986.
50. Street, D. Maintaining the status quo: The impact of old age interest groups on the Medicare Catastrophic Act of 1988. *Soc. Probl.* 40(4): 431–444, 1993.
51. Day, J. C. Population projections of the United States, by age, sex, race, and Hispanic origin: 1992–2050. *Curr. Popul. Rep.,* Ser. P25, No. 1092. Government Printing Office, Washington, D.C., 1992.
52. Tufte, E. R. *Political Control of the Economy.* Princeton University Press, Princeton, N.J., 1978.
53. Employee Benefit Research Institute. *Louis Harris Survey of the Aged.* Washington, D.C., 1981.

54. Calmes, J. Angry GOP isn't in the mood to talk Medicare deal. *Wall Street Journal,* November 11, 1996.
55. Edsall, T. B., and Morin, R. Winning over the women. *Washington Post National Weekly Edition,* November 11–17, 1996, p. 12.
56. Day, C. *What Older Americans Think: Interest Groups and Aging Policy.* Princeton University Press, Princeton, N.J., 1990.
57. Hudson, R. B., and Strate, J. Aging and political systems. In *Handbook of Aging and the Social Sciences,* Ed. 2, edited by R. H. Binstock and E. Shanas, pp. 554–585. Van Nostrand Reinhold, New York, 1985.
58. Dobson, D. The aging as a political force. In *Aging and Public Policy: The Politics of Growing Old in America,* edited by W. P. Browne and L. K. Olson, pp. 123–144. Greenwood Press, Westport, Conn., 1983.
59. Binstock, R. Reframing the agenda on policies on aging. In *Readings in the Political Economy of Aging,* edited by M. Minkler and C. L. Estes, pp. 157–167. Baywood, Amityville, N.Y., 1984.
60. Quadagno, J. Generational equity and the politics of the welfare state. *Polit. Soc.* 17: 353–376, 1989.
61. Walker, J. L. *Mobilizing Interest Groups in America: Patrons, Professions, and Social Movements.* University of Michigan Press, Ann Arbor, 1991.
62. Van Tassel, D. D., and Meyer, J. E. W. *U.S. Aging Policy Interest Groups: Institutional Profiles.* Greenwood, New York, 1992.
63. Wallace, S. P., and Williamson, J. B. *The Senior Movement: References and Resources.* G. K. Hall, New York, 1992.
64. Quadagno, J. Social Security and the myth of the entitlement "crisis." *Gerontologist* 36: 391–399, 1996.
65. Light, P. *Artful Work: The Politics of Social Security Reform.* Random House, New York, 1985.
66. Sacred cow. *Time,* November 9, 1987.
67. Kingson, E. R., and Berkowitz, E. D. *Social Security and Medicare: A Policy Primer.* Auburn House, Westport, Conn., 1993.
68. Chakravarty, S., and Weisman, K. Consuming our children: The intergenerational transfer of wealth. *Forbes,* November 14, 1988.
69. General Accounting Office. *Social Security: The Notch Issue.* Washington, D.C., 1988.
70. National Academy of Social Insurance. *The Social Security Benefit Notch: A Study.* Washington, D.C., 1988.
71. American Association of Retired Persons. *Anniversary Research: Public Attitudes Toward Social Security and Medicare.* Washington, D.C., 1995.
72. Himelfarb, R. *Catastrophic Politics: The Rise and Fall of the Medicare Catastrophic Coverage Act of 1988.* Pennsylvania State University Press, University Park, 1995.
73. Torres-Gil, F. Seniors react to the Medicare Catastrophic Bill: Equity or selfishness? *J. Aging Soc. Policy* 2: 1–8, 1990.
74. United States Senate. Hearing before the Committee on Finance, Catastrophic Health Insurance, S.Hrg.100-169, Part 1, January 28, 1987.
75. Jacobs, B. Aging and politics. In *Handbook of Aging and the Social Sciences,* Ed. 3, edited by R. Binstock and L. K. George, pp. 349–359. Academic Press, San Diego, 1990.
76. Peterson, S. A., and Somit, A. *The Political Behavior of Older Americans.* Garland Reference Library of the Social Sciences, Issues in Aging, 4, Garland, New York, 1994.
77. Myles, J., and Quadagno, J. The politics of income security for the elderly in North America: Founding cleavages and unresolved conflicts. In *Economic Security and*

Intergenerational Justice: A Look at North America, edited by T. R. Marmor, T. M. Smeeding, and V. L. Greene, pp. 61–90. Urban Institute, Washington, D.C., 1994.

78. Derthick, M. *Policymaking for Social Security.* Brookings Institution, Washington, D.C., 1979.

79. Binstock, R. H., and Day, C. L. Aging and politics. In *Handbook of Aging and the Social Sciences,* Ed. 4, pp. 362–387. Academic Press, San Diego, 1990.

80. Marmor, T. R., Cook, F. L., and Scher, S. Social Security politics and the conflict between the generations. In *Social Security in the 21st Century,* edited by E. R. Kingson and J. H. Schulz, pp. 195–207. Oxford University Press, New York, 1997.

81. Hess, B. Aging policies and old women: The hidden agenda. In *Gender and the Life Course,* edited by A. S. Rossi, pp. 319–322. Aldine, New York, 1986.

82. Powell, L. A., Branco, K., and Williamson, J. B. *The Senior Rights Movement: Framing the Policy Debate in America.* Twayne Publishers, New York, 1996.

83. Cook, F. L., and Barrett, E. J. *Support for the American Welfare State: The Views of Congress and the Public.* Columbia University Press, New York, 1992.

84. Esping Andersen, G. Welfare states and the economy. In *Handbook of Economic Sociology,* edited by N. Smelser and R. Swedberg, pp. 711–732. Russell Sage Foundation, New York, 1994.

85. Krauthammer, C. Finding the political courage to cut Medicare entitlements. *Chicago Tribune,* November 11, 1996.

86. Calmes, J. Wall Street quietly promotes Social Security overhaul. *Wall Street Journal,* December 3, 1996.

87. Korpi, W. *The Democratic Struggle.* Routledge and Kegan Paul, London, 1983.

88. Skocpol, T., and Amenta, E. States and social policies. *Annu. Rev. Sociol.* 12: 131–157, 1986

PART III: DEVOLUTION, CRISIS MENTALITY, AND THE TRANSFORMATION OF HEALTH AND SOCIAL PROGRAMS FOR THE OLD

The utility of political and moral economy perspectives for understanding the development and evolution of aging policy is perhaps nowhere better illustrated than in the areas of health and health care access. In Part III we look in detail at contemporary efforts to transform health and social policies for the old, primarily in the name of cost containment.

Carroll Estes begins in Chapter 7 by revisiting the concept of the "aging enterprise" which she developed over 20 years ago in reference to the huge array of interest groups, providers, government bureaucracies, and other stakeholders that has heavily influenced the construction and treatment of aging as a social problem. Themes such as the biomedicalization of aging and the treatment of the old as separate and different from the rest of society are set forth, and Estes uses both the shift to managed care and the devolution of community care to illustrate contemporary developments that may have problematic consequences for the elderly.

Most of this part of the book focuses exclusively on the rapidly changing health care system as it affects elders in the United States. In Chapter 8, however, Phillip Clark broadens our horizons by comparing health care for the old in the United States with care provision in Canada. Using moral economy as a conceptual framework, Clark also draws upon the related notion of public ethics, or the hidden values underlying and implicitly guiding the policymaking process. As Clark points out, both countries are concerned with rising health care costs, and both are undergoing major reassessments in their assumptions about the "legitimate and necessary" roles of government vis-à-vis care provision. Yet the greater accent on collectivism and the sense of community in Canada bode well for a continuing (albeit modified) commitment to universal access to health care in that country. In contrast, the ethos of individualism predominant in the United States continues to have substantial implications for the formulation of public policy, making the development of a more universal health care coverage extremely unlikely. Clark concludes that in the emerging drama of health care policy for the old in the United States and Canada, "aging can be seen both as a lens to magnify and scrutinize social institutions . . . and as a prism to separate underlying fundamental moral assumptions that make living in a society possible and enriching" (page 162).

Clark's notion of aging as a lens through which to better see and study social institutions is well documented in Chapter 9, as Carroll Estes and Karen Linkins examine "the race to the bottom" in long-term care. They see dramatic reductions in the legitimization role of the federal government in the area of health and social services over the past two decades as amounting to a "devolution revolution," in which national policy commitments and goals in long-term care are replaced by an ever greater emphasis on state and local freedom in decision-making—often at the expense of the elderly and disabled. Arguing that "devolution raises crucial questions about . . . the future of aging and long term care policy," Estes and Linkins describe how states that have historically been more generous in terms of benefits and eligibility for long-term care are effectively penalized for this generosity under devolution. They further examine the growing gap between health and social services, the potential reconstruction of the elderly as less "deserving" of support, and the public and private costs of managed care as these may converge to accelerate the race to the bottom in long-term care.

The proposed restructuring of Medicare and Medicaid that forms a crucial part of this race to the bottom is described in greater details in Chapter 10. Marty Lynch and Meredith Minkler begin by presenting a broad conceptual framework that combines precepts from political and moral economy. They then describe several of the key proposals for transforming Medicare and Medicaid, with special attention to how these changes would be likely to affect such vulnerable groups as the elderly poor and disabled, older women, and elders of color. Although the specific proposals for restructuring described in Chapter 10 continue to be revised and fine-tuned at this writing, the common threads identified are likely to remain, with potentially deleterious effects for the most vulnerable segments of the elderly population.

Among the Medicare reform options currently being discussed is the proposal to change this federal health insurance program into a voucher system, through which elders would receive a fixed monetary contribution from the government for the purchase of health insurance. In Chapter 11, Jonathan Oberlander describes how the notion of vouchers for Medicare has moved from being a marginal right-wing proposal to a seriously discussed option whose backers include the American Medical Association. Touted as enhancing consumer choice, using market competition to control costs, and decreasing the need for government regulation, vouchers in reality may have a far different set of outcomes. As Oberlander suggests, the introduction of vouchers would penalize those who chose to stay in more expensive fee-for-service plans (including many of the chronically ill and disabled elderly) and would further exacerbate inequalities in access to health care.

Although Chapter 11, like the two preceding chapters, focuses exclusively on the current debates around the transforming of health care in the United States, its implications for other nations are significant. As Oberlander notes, with many European nations grappling with rising health care costs, interest in "managed competition" principles and practices has grown considerably. "Such interest," Oberlander concludes, "should be accompanied by a healthy dose of skepticism," since both the framework and such specific applications as the proposed voucher system for Medicare may well create more problems than they solve.

We end Part III with Charlene Harrington's critical examination of the nursing home industry, and the nursing home reality for elderly Americans who live in these environments (Chapter 12). The growing demand for nursing home services, the increasing complexity of care, and the constrained supply of nursing homes (particularly for those with the greatest need) combine with high costs and increasing chain ownership to set the stage for continued problems with quality of care. Harrington describes key elements of the landmark Nursing Home Reform Act of 1987 which endeavored to improve the quality of care in these institutions by requiring additional staffing and staff training, banning physical and chemical restraints, and so on. As Harrington suggests, however, although some improvements have been documented, inadequate staffing, "scandalously low" wages and benefits, and the continued power of special interest groups with a stake in maintaining the status quo have resulted in the Act's having had little overall effect in the decade since its passage. While stepped up regulatory efforts are needed, these must be accompanied, Harrington argues, by structural reforms, including efforts to reduce consolidation and for-profit ownership, if real improvements in quality of care are to be achieved.

CHAPTER 7

The Aging Enterprise Revisited

Carroll L. Estes

The Aging Enterprise (1) examined the relationship between social policy and the condition and needs of the elderly. The conclusion of that analysis was that the individual experience of aging is shaped by (*a*) the perceptions, myths, and messages about aging that are communicated to old and young alike by media and opinion leaders, including gerontological researchers, and (*b*) the way a society treats its elders (directly or indirectly) via social policies on employment, retirement, health care, income, and the family.

The socially constructed "problem," and the remedies invoked on the policy level, are related, first, to the capacity of powerful and strategically located interests and classes to define "the problem" and to press their views into public consciousness and law and, second, to the objective facts of the situation. Note the order of influence: power and class, first; facts, second. Phenomena associated with chronological aging and intrinsic biological conditions may be said to be objectively real, *regardless* of how they are perceived. The key point is, however, that social action is indivisible from the *socially constructed* ideas that define and provide images of the phenomena of old age and aging—whether or not these images are empirically demonstrated.

THE SOCIAL CONSTRUCTION OF REALITY

Although competing perspectives exist, the dominant view, or social construction of reality, reflected in public policy is that the aged are a *problem* to society. Old age is a problem that is defined as treatable by the provision of services on the *individual* level. With the Older Americans Act in the mid-1960s, the problem of age also was conceptualized as being *special and different,* justifying the provision of *age-segregated* categorical services. Medicare, as a program of health insurance for older persons, has reinforced and institutionalized this age-segregated approach in public policy—although Medicare was designed to address the lack of health insurance for

This chapter is reprinted with permission from *The Gerontologist,* Volume 33, Number 3, Pages 292–298, 1993. © 1993, The Gerontological Society of America.

older retirees in a health system operating on employer-based health insurance. Only recently has there been an explicit recognition by gerontologists of the intergenerational stake and attention to the commonalities in the problems of and solutions for older persons and those of other generations and groups in society.

Another important construction of reality is that the aging process is one of biological, physiological, and cognitive decline and decay (2). In this view, old age is portrayed as a medical problem that can be alleviated, if not eradicated, through the "magic bullets" of medical science. Focused on individual organic pathology and medical interventions, physicians are placed in charge of the definition and treatment of old age as a disease. This view is consistent with public policy to provide individual acute care services within the dominant medical model of aging, as Medicare presently does.

Probably the most disturbing construction of aging in the past decade is the contention that the nation's economic problems are caused by the elderly. The fruits of this and other crisis constructions are another set of constructions—the inevitability of rationing and "the intergenerational war" (3).

These constructions of aging and the social policies that result not only *reflect,* but also *reproduce* existing social class, gender, and racial and ethnic disparities among the old. That is, social policy on aging presently does little to alter or disturb the relations of power or the distribution of economic and other resources in the society.

THE AGING ENTERPRISE

One major product of these constructions of aging is the *aging enterprise*—the "programs, organizations, bureaucracies, interest groups, trade associations, providers, industries, and professionals that serve the aged in one capacity or another" (1). The aging enterprise, which includes a large segment of the $900 billion medical-industrial complex, assures that the needs of the aged will be processed and treated as a commodity. Many of the resulting commodities, especially medical services, are sold for a profit.

Revisiting the aging enterprise in 1993, it is apparent that public policy and the cost containment philosophy of the 1980s have promoted a growing commitment to "indirect" services such as case management, assessment, and managed care systems. This "rationalization" of care has occurred simultaneously with virtually no growth (an absolute decline) in social service funding and a tripling of expenditures for the medical-industrial complex.[1] The promotion of indirect services provides a symbolic solution to the problem of needed services, while being packaged as a cost

---

[1] Older Americans Act funding declined 36 percent in real terms between 1980 and 1991. Among expenditures for the medical-industrial complex are Medicaid dollars, including funding for home and community-based care. Although these Medicaid expenditures rose from $1.2 billion to $13.4 billion between 1982 and 1992 (4), these funds are usually targeted to extremely frail elders at risk of institutionalization or post-acute patients in need of skilled care. They also have supported multiple demonstrations in care management and managed care. While this "back door" funding for home and community-based care provides some social services (5), these services are medically driven and responsive. The resources devoted to community and social supportive services are dwarfed by those in the medical-industrial complex for acute care and related services, equipment, and technology.

containment mechanism. This raises a potential problem of goal displacement, where there is an inversion of the means and ends to solving a problem, and the emphasis on the means actually displaces the ability to reach the ends. To the extent that there is support of indirect rather than direct services, there is a fundamental *goal displacement* in which the *means* (e.g., care management) and the *ends* (e.g., direct long-term care services) are inverted. None of these developments in indirect services will alter either the status or condition of the aged. In fact, if the development of "services" continues along such lines, they will remain frustratingly elusive and marginal in their capacity to touch or improve the lives of the aged (1). Far from draining the economy, the national policy approach has actually supported the sustained development of a huge and highly profitable, largely private (but substantially publicly funded) enterprise of largely medical or medically related facilities and services, and a growing industry of care management products.

SOCIAL CREATION OF DEPENDENCY

As the 21st century approaches with its demographic changes, the issues of individual and population dependency are paramount. Dependency is not a "given" but is a product of both *intrinsic* and *extrinsic* aging—that is, an as yet undetermined (but significant) amount of dependency is modifiable, preventable, or reversible (6).

The environmental and social origins of dependency (1, 7–9) can be easily understood in terms of the effects of public policy. For example, without Social Security, nearly one-half of older persons would be impoverished—not because of lack of foresight, but because the economy is organized according to differential rewards for productive labor, from which elders are generally and systematically excluded via retirement (10). Similarly, without Medicare, a much larger segment of the older population would be more economically and/or physically dependent due to their full exposure to the unaffordability of medical care.

As a social product, dependency is the result of a multitude of social forces:

* Social policies and practices that permit age discrimination and, until recently, mandatory retirement;
* Lower incomes of retired persons that decline with age;
* High and growing out-of-pocket health costs that are not offset by Medicare or Social Security;
* The treatment of functional debility and chronic illness with acute medical care rather than rehabilitative and personal support;
* The discrimination and exclusion of elders from multiple arenas of social life precipitated by loss of social contact through retirement, widowhood, and the death of friends;
* The low self-esteem and lack of confidence resulting from the stigmatized status of older persons (11); and
* The asymmetrical power relations between older persons and the professional caregivers who provide them services (1, 12).

There is also an important link between socially produced dependency and community care. The community long-term care "system" is more than a *system for distributing services;* it is a *system of social relationships* that reflects and bolsters the power inequities between experts and lay persons. This system of care may be deleterious, especially where the emphasis is on social management or control of older persons rather than on opportunities for participation, rehabilitation, and self-determination.

FISCAL CRISIS AND THE RESTRUCTURING OF COMMUNITY CARE

Serious considerations of public policy and community care must take into account the state of the existing system of service provision in view of the dramatic and rapid changes of the 1980s and 1990s. Policy changes, budget cuts, cost containment, and deepening fiscal austerity in the states and localities have challenged and compromised the capacity of both formal and informal caregivers to address the community care needs of elders.

As a result of changes occurring during the prior decade, the 1990s opened with a challenged, weakened, and transformed system of community care. The inadequacy of the existing system has created problems for elders living in the community, their families, the public, employers, and government. These problems are exacerbated by policy approaches to the elderly—approaches that have simultaneously financed and institutionalized the medicalization of care, challenged the charitable impulse in nonprofit service delivery, and fostered the dependency of elders.

Research on the effects of public policy on local services for elders from 1981 to the present [1993] (13, 14) has documented a series of deleterious processes in the ongoing restructuring of community care, including the privatization of profitable services (growth of for-profits); bureaucratization (industry consolidation and rationalization); service fragmentation; and deepening class divisions in access. These trends in the restructuring of care are widespread and affect other age groups and populations as well. One result for the elderly is the widening gap between the available services and services that are appropriate to elders, called a no-care zone (14).

PROBLEMS IN THE NONPROFIT SECTOR

Overall changes in local service delivery include the weeding out of the weaker, less competitive nonprofit community-based agencies; restructuring and concentration within and across provider industries, with independent free-standing agencies facing especially tough survival questions; dramatic growth in the number and influence of for-profit providers; and blurred boundaries between nonprofit and proprietary service sectors.

The cultural revolution in nonprofit service delivery has imposed a new set of values on community services: winning in price competition; quick turnover of clientele; policies and strategies to provide the greatest number of service units at the lowest cost; the unbundling or selling of single services to increase reimbursement;

eliminating unprofitable services regardless of need; attracting private-pay clients; and avoiding the "adverse selection" of no-pay and low-pay clients. These values initially were more familiar to the medical care industry than to traditional voluntary social service providers.

Ideological and political attacks have been advanced against nonprofit service providers on several fronts (15), including (a) questions concerning the right of nonprofits to their special tax status and government tax subsidies; (b) accusations that nonprofits evade their charitable missions; and (c) contentions that nonprofits "unfairly" compete with for-profits in health and social services.

Free-market advocates have even called nonprofit provider organizations "illegitimate" in a capitalist system. Political attacks include challenges to the right of particular entities (e.g., hospitals) to tax-exempt status, charitable deductions, property tax exemptions, unrelated business income, and postal subsidies. The unfortunate predicament of nonprofits represents a contradiction during the Reagan–Bush years, given the ideology and rhetoric that the private voluntary sector must assume more responsibility and government less, while at the same time systematic attacks against the nonprofit sector were being mounted by the federal government through the Small Business Administration and others.

The majority of community care workers (paid and unpaid) who provide long-term care are in the voluntary sector. Nonprofits comprise more than half of all social services delivered and about half of all community health services (16, 17). Because of the degree of nonprofit involvement in local care, the difficulties and changes in the behavior of these service providers affect older service recipients.

SOCIAL POLICY AND COMMUNITY CARE:
THE EMPOWERMENT IMPERATIVE

Formidable challenges confront efforts to develop community care policy. These include the sociodemographics, the biomedicalization of aging, the deepening problems of access to and affordability of health services and long-term care, and the realization that our present approach to aging may *produce,* rather than ameliorate, dependency.

The *empowerment imperative* is proposed as an alternative to the present approach. This alternative involves a commitment to the design and evaluation of social interventions that enhance the capacity of the old and chronically ill for self-esteem, personal control, individual and social involvement, and social action. The commitment also is to the development and implementation of interventions that modify the structural conditions (e.g., inadequacies in health or housing policy) that contribute to or generate dependency problems in old age.

Levels of Intervention

Three levels of intervention have been identified: everyday life, professional practice and service delivery, and social structure (18). Empowerment or disempowerment may be facilitated at each level.

Everyday Life. Interventions designed to improve personal control by the elderly in everyday life situations include the creation of alternative care services, establishment of self-help support systems, and formation of organizations and advocacy groups that serve the self-defined needs of elders (19). Independent living centers developed by younger disabled people provide an excellent example of this type of intervention if modified for the special needs of the elderly. In this context, empowerment and self-care are adjuncts to, rather than replacements for, professional services and community care.

Another area of intervention to empower older persons is rehabilitation (20). The neglect of rehabilitation reflects the emphasis of the field of gerontology on accommodative rather than restorative approaches (21). The dominant accommodative approach views improvement as unlikely, indirectly discouraging elders from becoming independent. The alternative restorative approach builds on the excellent potential of well-designed interventions to improve functioning in old age (e.g., for stroke, hip fracture, and urinary incontinence) (20).

Professional Practice and Organization. Interventions are needed to promote the ability of institutions and professionals to enhance the personal control of older persons. The most immediate tasks are to expand access to needed community-based care that meets *nonmedical* needs, and to renegotiate the boundaries separating the expert from the elder (22, 23) by qualitatively changing the relationship between elders and professionals.

Community gerontology teams, working on a neighborhood or block basis, are a potential vehicle for reshaping the power imbalance between elders and professionals who try to serve them (12). Another example is the development of coordinated systems of care (e.g., social health maintenance organizations or S/HMOs), but built around models of self-management and patient empowerment by elderly users. To promote the empowerment of older persons, explicit programs of training are needed for professional caregivers and the resocialization of those who are already trained in order to counter the dependency-generating approaches resulting from their professional training and the medicalization of aging (2, 12).

Social Structure. Interventions are needed to address the deep structural conditions that generate and institutionalize discriminatory and deleterious practices toward the old in society. Paradoxically and perversely, age-specific benefits and politics may even contribute to such practices through a backlash against age or other groups that are perceived as receiving more than their fair share. Examples of interventions at the socio-structural or macro level include policies designed to improve the economic status of the disadvantaged, to promote job and economic security for all Americans who want to work, to provide decent housing with integrated social and health services, and to entitle persons to long-term care as part of citizenship. Universal health coverage for people of all ages with comprehensive long-term care would eliminate the need for an age-specific health insurance program such as Medicare, which covers only part of the costs of care and contributes to elder dependency by excluding needed chronic illness, rehabilitative, and social supportive care.

Contradictions and Problems in Community Care

Although community care is an increasingly salient concern for the public and policymakers, little effort has been devoted to developing policy models from a critical perspective, and even less attention has been accorded the issues of empowerment. The literature reflects substantial skepticism about the cost-effectiveness of community-based care (24), although research shows that quality-of-life improvements may be the "result." Research also documents the significant sacrifices that caregivers, particularly women, make in providing the majority of the nation's long-term care without financial compensation (25, 26).

Not surprisingly, the research reflects the dominant value standard (ideology) of the day; the benefits of community care are investigated according to efficiency rather than equity measures. The latter would calculate gender, ethnic, or other forms of equity or inequity that particular policies produce. Two serious problems plague community care today: the rationing of care and the unequal access that results from differences in the ability to pay, and the absence of countervailing power by care recipients (27). Both represent profound policy dilemmas for the design of community care interventions.

Because the client and the professional "belong to two basically different worlds . . . the asymmetry is not only of feelings and attitudes, it is also an asymmetry of power" (28). The deleterious effects of such power inequities on the weaker party are well-documented (29, 30) since that "power resides implicitly in the other's dependency" (31). This fact explains research findings that older persons resent unpaid charitable help and that those "who are unable to reciprocate may themselves avoid establishing relations with others" (29), even to the point that they are willing to become destitute, if that is the price. The essential question with regard to community care policies is whether they will become a vehicle for the *production* of more, rather than less dependency; or "Will community care become a euphemism for a somewhat more benign but still dependency-creating paternalism?" (32).

THE MANAGED CARE REVOLUTION

The 1990s are the age of managed care, as the truly remarkable market penetration of managed care illustrates. Ninety-five percent of employees insured for health care are in some kind of managed care, the proportion rising from 60 percent as recently as 1987 (33). Cost containment and President Clinton's health reform[2] are likely to further extend the proportion of providers and consumers covered by some form of managed care.

Austin and O'Connor (34) note that there are different models of case management—gatekeeper and advocacy. Within managed care, others have described the range of interventions—from utilization review and second opinion to capitated staff

[2] *Editors' note* This was written in 1993, while the President's health care reform task force was still debating potential reforms. Although the reform effort failed, the central arguments in this chapter remain salient in its aftermath.

model group practice pre-paid programs. In long-term care, case management has come to mean anything from a gatekeeper to a social/health maintenance organization (S/HMO) (35).

Indeed, managed care has come to mean so many things that it is questionable what it means at all (36). As a mixed bag of organizations, procedures, and goals, case management promises an easy "solution" to the multiple problems plaguing health care: inadequate access, skyrocketing costs, service fragmentation, and the lack of a long-term care policy. The Congressional Budget Office notes that the intended purpose of managed care is "to eliminate unnecessary and inappropriate care and to reduce costs" (33).

There are two competing and potentially contradictory elements of the attractiveness of managed care—altruism and cost containment. Geriatric assessment and case management and managed care systems theoretically each provide a means of improving the quality and appropriateness of care, undoubtedly accounting for their popularity among some professionals. In the present fiscal and policy content, however, the popularity of managed care among insurers, government, and other payers is motivated more by cost containment than client advocacy goals.

Through the 1980s rhetoric of the market and "consumer choice," the concept of client, patient, and older person has been reconstituted as a conscious, informed actor capable of rational choice (37). Yet care management decision-making is organized in ways that constrain both consumer participation and choice. The structurally inherent tensions between the preferences of consumers and gatekeepers are real, and mechanisms are not readily available for their resolution given the informational and power deficits on the consumer side and the pressures for cost containment on the gatekeeper and payer side.

By definition, case management requires professionals to coordinate efforts in the provision of care. The daily lives of those needing assistance require continual negotiations with others—family members, voluntary workers, and formal care providers—all of which involve struggles and conflicting interests, but with the greatest personal stakes and consequences for the care recipient. Significantly, the present constructs of managed care contain virtually no provisions or mechanisms for elders or their informal caregivers to participate in or challenge the decisions of case managers, should there be serious or consequential disagreements with the assessments and decisions made by the case managers (38).

Thus, in the present environment, a legitimate concern is that managed care not only will be the blunt instrument of rationing, but also will institutionalize mechanisms that deprive consumers, including the disabled and dependent, of the last remnants of their personal control. These worries are compounded by the problem that the research on the effectiveness of managed care is both limited and equivocal. For example, Callahan notes that "15 years of research on community-based care management fails to support most of the claims of its effectiveness in solving the problems for which it was intended" (39). A recent Congressional Budget Office study (1992) also concludes that there is little evidence of the cost effectiveness of managed care. An even bigger concern is that managed care does not address the problem of access to care at all. This may explain the wariness, even cynicism, expressed about it, as well as about managed competition—the proposal to rationalize the purchase and delivery of care—on Clinton's agenda for health care reform. Although as many definitions and forms of managed competition exist as of managed care, there is little reason to believe that this approach is the panacea that its proponents contend. Vladeck has described managed competition as "this decade's intellectual and moral equivalent of the Laffer Curve"—a form of "voodoo economics" since it provides "a grand design for the complete reorganization of the American health care system, but it speaks only tangentially to the most important problem of health care in the U.S. . . . [that is,] access" (40).

ENTITLEMENT TO COMMUNITY CARE

Entitlement to community care is absolutely essential to the empowerment of elders. Under conservative regimes, the "ethos of community care" will likely reinforce, but only minimally supplement, the already existing "networks" of family, friends, and neighbors. Policies to promote care *by* the community rather than care *in* the community (41) require an ever widening circle of willing and largely unpaid members of the personal network or social world of the person needing help. However, as Collins (29) notes, these policies are predicated on assumptions that overstate the forms and extent to which personal networks truly exist and ignore how they operate. People have "supportive strands" but these are not interrelated, coherent, predictable, or stable.

Recent opinion studies and attitude surveys challenge the rhetoric of informal care and necessitate a reassessment of the nature (and certainty) of family obligations in the light of recent and provocative findings on the caregiving preferences of elders (38, 42–45). Findings that family informal care is one of "the least preferred options" among community-dwelling elders and that care by providers in the formal sector is strongly preferred are understandable in view of the public's expressed unwillingness "to place the major burden of care on informal carers . . . the family and women in particular" (43).

Collins's research demonstrates that, where social relationships are not reciprocal, older persons prefer to "rely on paid agents of the state rather than on volunteers, even kin . . . [in part] because the recipients of care are then exonerated from liability for direct and personal reciprocation" (29). The ultimate dilemma and contradiction is that the volatile and sensitive nature of personal relationships "undermines another cornerstone argument advanced in support of community care . . . that it will enable people in need to exercise power in their own affairs to a greater extent than previously" (29). Collins persuasively argues that social policy that provides the right (entitlement) to both payment and choice is requisite to the preservation of a person's personal control.

Universal entitlement offers the advantage of assured predictability in the supply of, and equity in access to, the community-based services for which it exists (1, 38, 46). The variations in resources and access to care across the states under Medicaid and other discretionary state and local programs are well documented in terms of both eligibility and benefits (47). Without the uniform provisions assured by entitlement, wide disparities will remain and grow in the availability of and access to community care. Without entitlement, not only will there be continuing inequity in access to care from community to community, but also discrimination in that access according to race, class, and gender.

CONCLUSION

Empowerment to the fullest extent possible must be the goal of public policy, and scholars must give as much research attention to questions of empowerment and equity (class, gender, and race) as to those of cost and efficiency. Because our definitions, our "reality" about what old age and aging are, are socially constructed, as are the policy interventions that flow from them, they also are modifiable. There is "plasticity" not only in the physiological and cognitive processes of aging. We can deconstruct and reconstruct our ideas (and experience) of old age and the direction of public policy, but not easily.

The Aging Enterprise concluded with the statement: "It is time that America became dedicated to the task of transforming old age itself and, in the process, to dismantling the aging enterprise" (1). That conclusion is as true in 1993 as it was in 1979. Scholars must challenge and reframe the questions that have defined the mainstream. In Robert Lynd's (48) words, we must not be satisfied with "short run statements of long term problems." Questions of empowerment and the promotion of gender and ethnic justice need to be on the research agenda. The goal of national policy must be nothing less than a reconstruction of old age to promote the empowerment of elders in concert with other generations and social groups, as well as the empowerment of professionals and service providers in the service of this goal.

REFERENCES

1. Estes, C. L. *The Aging Enterprise.* Jossey-Bass, San Francisco, 1979.
2. Estes, C. L., and Binney, E. A. The biomedicalization of aging: Dangers and dilemmas. *Gerontologist* 29(5): 587–596, 1989.
3. Binney, E. A., and Estes, C. L. The retreat of the state and its transfer of responsibility: The intergenerational War. *Int. J. Health Serv.* 18: 83–96, 1988.
4. Miller, N. A. Medicaid, 2176 home and community based case waivers: The first 10 years. *Health Aff.,* 1993.
5. Kane, R. personal communication, 1993.
6. Rowe, J. W., and Kahn, R. L. Human aging: Usual and successful. *Science* 237(4811): 143–149, 1987.
7. Walker, A. The social creation of poverty and dependency in old age. *J. Soc. Policy* 9(1): 49–75, 1980.
8. Walker, A. (ed.). *Community Care: The Family, the State and Social Policy.* Basil Blackwell and Martin Robertson, Oxford, 1982.
9. Townsend, P. The structured dependency of the elderly: A creation of social policy in the twentieth century. *Aging Soc.* 1(6), 1981.
10. Estes, C. L. et al. *Political Economy, Health, and Aging.* Little Brown, Boston, 1984.
11. Rodin, J. Sense of control: Potentials for intervention. *Ann. Am. Acad. Polit. Soc. Sci.* 503: 29–41, 1989.

12. Phillipson, C., and Walker, A. *Ageing and Social Policy.* Gower, Aldershot, England, 1986.
13. Estes, C. L. The politics of ageing in America. *Ageing Soc.* 6(2): 121–134, 1986.
14. Estes, C. L., et al. *The Long Term Care Crisis: Elders Trapped in the No-Care Zone.* Sage, Newbury Park, Calif., 1993.
15. Estes, C. L., Binney, E. A., and Bergthold, L. A. The delegitimation of the nonprofit sector: The role of ideology and public policy. In *The Nonprofit Sector,* edited by V. Hodgkinson and R. Lyman, pp. 21–40. Jossey-Bass, San Francisco, 1988.
16. Salamon, L. M. Partners in public service: The scope and theory of government-nonprofit relations. In *The Nonprofit Sector: A Research Handbook,* edited by W. W. Powell, pp. 99–117. Yale University Press, New Haven, Conn., 1987.
17. Hodgkinson, V. A., and Weitzman, M. S. *Dimensions of the Independent Sector,* Ed. 3. Independent Sector, Washington, D.C., 1989.
18. Riley, M. W., and Riley, J. W. The lives of older people and changing social roles. *Ann. Am. Acad. Polit. Soc. Sci.* 503: 14–28, 1989.
19. Bernard, M., and Phillipson, C. Self-care and health in old age. In *Nursing Elderly People,* Ed. 2, edited by S. Redfern, pp. 405–415. Churchill Livingstone, Edinburgh, 1991.
20. Ory, M. G., and Williams, F. T. Rehabilitation: Small goals, sustained interventions. *Ann. Am. Acad. Polit. Soc. Sci.* 503: 60–71, 1989.
21. Estes, C. L. Construction of reality: Problems of aging. *J. Soc. Issues* 39(2): 117–132, 1980.
22. Savo, C. *Self-Care and Self Help Programmes for Older Adults in the U.S.* Working Papers on the Health of Older People, No. 1. Health Education Council and Department of Public Education, University of Keele, Keele, England, 1984.
23. Glendenning, F. (ed.). *Educational Gerontology: International Perspectives.* Croom Helm, London, 1985.
24. Weissert, W. G., Cready, C. M., and Pawelak, J. E. The past and future of home and community-based long-term care. *Milbank Q.* 66: 309–388, 1988.
25. Stone, R., Cafferata, G. L., and Sangl, J. Caregivers of the frail elderly: A national profile. *Gerontologist* 27(5): 616–626, 1986.
26. U.S. House Select Committee on Aging, Subcommittee on Human Services. *Exploding the Myths: Caregiving in America.* Government Printing Office, Washington, D.C., 1988.
27. Phillipson, C. Personal community, January 25, 1992.
28. Coser, L. The sociology of poverty. *Soc. Prob.* 13: 140–148, 1963.
29. Collins, J. Power and local community activity. *J. Aging Stud.* 5(2): 209–218, 1991.
30. Blau, P. M. *Exchange and Power in Social Life.* Wiley, New York, 1964.
31. Emerson, R. M. Power dependence relations. *Am. Sociol. Rev.* 27(1): 31–41, 1962.
32. Lloyd, P. C. The empowerment of elderly people. *J. Aging Stud.* 5(2): 125–135, 1991.
33. Congressional Budget Office. The Effects of Managed Care on the Use and Costs of Health Services. CBO Staff Memorandum. Washington, D.C., June, 1992.
34. Austin, C., and O'Connor, M. Case management: Components and program contexts. In *Health Care of the Elderly,* edited by M. Petersen and D. White. Sage, London, 1989.
35. Harrington, C., and Newcomer, R. J. Social/health maintenance organization's service use and costs, 1985–89. *Health Care Financ. Rev.* 12(3), 1991.
36. Hunter, H. Unpublished manuscript. Health Care Administration Program, California State University, Long Beach, 1991.
37. Enthoven, A. C. Health care costs: Why regulation fails, why competition works, how to get there from here. In *The Nation's Health,* edited by P. R. Lee and C. L. Estes, pp. 286–293. Jones and Bartlett, Boston, 1990.

38. Phillipson, C. Challenging the spectre of old age: Community care for older people in the 1990s. In *Social Policy Yearbook,* edited by R. Page and N. Manning. Social Policy Association, London, 1992.

39. Callahan, J. J. Case management for the elderly: A panacea? *J. Aging Soc. Policy* 1(1/2): 181–195, 1989.

40. Vladeck, B. *President's Letter.* United Hospital Fund of New York, New York, 1992.

41. Phillipson, C. *Capitalism and the Construction of Old Age.* Macmillan, London, 1982.

42. Salvage, A. V., Vetter, N. J., and Jones, D. A. Opinions concerning residential care. *Age Ageing* 18: 380–386, 1989.

43. West, P., Illsley, R., and Kelman, H. Public preferences for the care of dependency groups. *Soc. Sci. Med.* 18: 417–446, 1984.

44. Daatland, S. What are families for? On family solidarity and preference for help. *Ageing Soc.* 10: 1–17, 1990.

45. Waerness, K. Informal and formal care in old age: What is wrong with the new ideology in Scandinavia today? In *Gender and Caring,* edited by C. Ungerson, Harvester Wheatsheaf, London, 1990.

46. Phillipson, C. Inter-generational relations: Conflict or consensus in the twenty-first century. *Policy and Polit.* 19: 27–36, 1990.

47. Holohan, J., and Cohen, J. W. *Medicaid: The Trade-off between Cost Containment and Access.* Urban Institute Press, Washington, D.C., 1986.

48. Lynd, R. *Knowledge for What?* Princeton University Press, Princeton, N.J., 1939.

CHAPTER 8

Moral Economy and the Social Construction of the Crisis of Aging and Health Care: Differing Canadian and U.S. Perspectives

Phillip G. Clark

Strikingly similar images have recently taken center stage in both the media and the public consciousness of Canada and the United States. Canadian seniors, who remember what it was like before Medicare existed in their country, mobilize to preserve and protect it in the face of perceived waning federal support for the program. The elderly in the United States and such powerful lobby groups as the American Association of Retired Persons brace for Congressional battles on the fate of Medicare south of the border. These public demonstrations make apparent the increasingly important connections between aging and health care in social awareness and policy.

The fate of the Medicare programs in both countries is an issue of growing importance socially, politically, and economically. The ways Canada and the United States grapple with the interconnected issues of the graying of their populations and the escalating cost of health care reveal much about the social institutions, public policies, and guiding principles of these North American neighbors. This is so because aging in a social context is both a lens and a prism (1). It is a lens because an examination of the experience of growing older enables us to study the detailed relationships among societal, political, and economic institutions that together create the collective environment in which individual aging occurs. However, aging is also a prism, splitting up the shaded tones of moral obligations, collective and individual responsibilities, and principles of social justice that affect how the elderly are treated in a particular social setting—such as the health care system.

The comparative study of these relationships, obligations, responsibilities, and principles is the subject of this chapter. The conceptual framework to be used throughout this discussion has been characterized by Minkler and Cole as the "moral economy of aging." This approach "helps to surface and make explicit the often

This chapter is reprinted from *The Moral Economy of Health and Aging in Canada and the United States,* published by the Canadian-American Center, 1995. With permission from the Canadian-American Center and Canadian-American Public Policy.

implicit cultural beliefs and values underlying societal policies and practices affecting the old" (2, p. 4). This exploration of the interrelationships among moral principles, aging, and public policy has also been proposed in the concept of "public ethics," which deals with uncovering and examining the principal values underlying and guiding the social policy process (3). In particular, the approach of public ethics helps to examine the assumptions implicit in definitions of policy "problems" and to evaluate the range of their proposed "solutions."

As Susan McDaniel reminds us, the "ideas, research and policy thinking about aging can never be divorced from the socioeconomic context in which the phenomenon occurs" (4, p. 330). The emergence of population aging as a "problem paradigm," a model of shared social reality, can be traced to the interaction among researchers, policymakers, and program developers and funders. In this view, demographic change becomes the engine driving a number of emerging crises, all of which are tied in some way to the growing numbers of the elderly—not to the underlying social and economic relationships that characterize a society. The development of this mind-set prevents us from seeing the "problem" of an aging society differently, and therefore limits the range of potential "solutions" that might be considered (5–7).

The moral economy approach encourages—indeed, requires—us to look beyond the "appearance of things" at the underlying foundational assumptions, facts, loyalties, and values that undergird and shape the "superstructure" of public policy (8). For example, in the context of defining a "problem" and seeking "solutions" to it, we need to keep in mind both facts and values. In spite of what policymakers would like to believe, there is no purely quantitative, objective approach sufficient to an understanding of a social "problem." Empirical data can be used, shaped, and wielded by special interest groups guided by a particular ideology based on a set of social values formed from political, economic, and historical experience.

It is this "hidden" dimension of values that the moral economy approach uncovers and analyzes. For example, defining population aging as a "problem" is a process shaped by the conflicting social values of individualism and collectivism, as will become apparent in the comparative analysis of the experiences of Canada and the United States to follow. Assumptions about the differing roles and responsibilities of individuals, families, and government can shape how solutions to this "problem" are defined and implemented. The existence of the political will to seek creative and appropriate responses is shaped by unique historical and cultural experiences that influence how fragmented or cohesive a particular society is as it deals with compelling issues and challenges. All these factors fall within the purview of the moral economy perspective.

This chapter develops a framework for considering these issues as they emerge from an historical backdrop of social institutions and health care policies in both Canada and the United States. The emphasis in this discussion, however, will be on the Canadian experience and how it can help to inform the development of the moral economy perspective on aging and health care. This analysis is divided into four major sections. First, emerging issues in the current concerns of both countries about the effects of aging on health care policy considerations—particularly cost— are explored. Second, the backdrop to these current discussions is examined, particularly in the context of previous studies, reports, and projections that sketched out the assumed linkages between aging and health care service needs. The third section highlights differences in the changing moral underpinnings of health and social service policy between the two societies, including reflection on the shifting balance between the competing values of individual and collective responsibility. Finally, the conclusion explores the significance of the moral economy approach for predicting the future of health care policies for the elderly in both countries.

EMERGING ISSUES IN AGING AND
HEALTH CARE POLICY

The growth in health care costs and the aging of the population are frequently linked in the popular press, government reports, academic studies, and public consciousness. After all, the elderly are the heaviest users of health care, and their numbers are increasing (particularly the "old old"—those 85 and older—who are the greatest consumers of health care services). This assessment leads to the obvious conclusion that health care costs will continue to skyrocket in the future, fueled by the volatile mixture of aging baby boomers and high health care demands. Whatever the validity of this presumed connection, it is apparent that seniors in Canada and the United States are playing an active role in current debates over the future of health care policy in both countries. They are concerned about the level of continued health care program benefits, access to needed services, and costs to the consumer.

The Struggle to Preserve Medicare in Canada

Persons 65 and older currently constitute 12.3 percent of the Canadian population, and their numbers are expected to exceed 20 percent by around the year 2025. With regard to the costs of care, health expenditures in Canada represented 9.9 percent of gross domestic product (GDP) in 1991, a figure that is the highest among countries with national health insurance. In contrast, during the 1960s total spending on health care ranged from 5.5 to 7.0 percent of GDP (9).

While the linkage between aging and increasing health care costs is recognized in Canada, there are other—more powerful—forces at work as well that contribute to the popular perception of a looming crisis. The following summary describes the current key issues and players in this unfolding drama, organized around the following themes: (a) preserving Medicare, (b) national debate and dialogue, (c) concerns of seniors, and (d) emergent new directions for health care in Canada.

Preserving Medicare. Primary among current issues is the Canadian tradition of universal access to medical services, available nationally as Medicare in every province by 1971, based initially on a model of physician availability and acute hospital care funded by matching federal dollars to the provinces on a one-to-one basis. Hallmarks of the system include universality, accessibility, comprehensiveness, portability, and public funding. Not long after the original program was put into place, however, changes were beginning to be made. In 1977, the Established Programs Financing Act replaced the original hospital and medical insurance legislation with block grants to the provinces tied to rates of population and economic growth. Subsequent continuing legislation has further cut the amount of federal transfer payments to the provinces, reducing the original "50 cent dollars" to about "30 cent dollars" currently. Recent legislation provides the basis for the eventual reduction of federal support for health care to the provinces to zero. In spite of the federal government's reassertion in 1984, in the Canada Health Act, of the importance of universal access to services by its attempt to eliminate user fees and "extra-billing" by providers, recent legislation has undercut this policy by simultaneously increasing provincial taxing authority to make up for the federal reduction and weakening the federal government's ability to prevent extra-billing and ensure comparable services across provinces (10). The burden of health care costs has now effectively been shifted to the provinces, which are in turn being pressured to pass it on to both providers and consumers (11). *Shift to provinces.*

National Debate and Dialogue. Based on the belief that "Canada's health system is changing and there needs to be a national dialogue with Canadians to chart the future, building on the fundamental values that are embedded in the Canada Health Act," in 1994 the federal government created the National Forum on Health as a citizens' advisory group to make sure that (12):

> national priorities are identified and that Canadians are involved and informed about the issues and options. . . . The Forum will examine specific issues, help focus discussion, and assist in developing solutions and strategies to improve the health of Canadians and ensure that the health system is equipped to deal with the challenges of the future.

As stated in public announcements about its work, the Forum "sees its mandate as improving the health of Canadians as well as the efficiency and effectiveness of health services" and is guided by three major principles: (*a*) supporting a national, universally accessible health system, (*b*) strengthening public understanding of health and health care and developing support for change, and (*c*) providing government with recommendations for action, reflecting Canadian values (13). The Forum considers its primary responsibility as investigating issues, examining assumptions, and asking questions about health care, its delivery and funding (14).

However, public pronouncements by key members of the National Forum provide some insight into its orientation. First, in a 1995 conference address, Marie Fortier, the Forum's Executive Director, underscored the central importance of maintaining a single-tier system of health care, based in no small part on fundamental concerns about cost control and Canadian values. With regard to the latter, she emphasized the "fundamental values of Canadian society: our compassion, fairness, and community spirit. Canadians don't want a society where the poor cannot get quality health care. We are proud of a system that provides quality service for everyone" (15). Second, in a 1995 meeting of the National Forum, members confirmed their support for the principles articulated in the Canada Health Act and for public funding of the system. Importantly, they stated that what the health care system needs now is not more money, but better management (16). This theme has been reiterated in more recent reports of the Forum (17).

Concerns of Seniors. The unique issues relevant to the elderly in the debate over the future of Medicare are represented by two national organizations: the National Advisory Council on Aging (NACA) and One Voice: The Canadian Seniors Network. The National Advisory Council on Aging, created in 1980 and receiving operational support from the federal government, consists of 18 members from across Canada, who assist and advise the Minister of Health on issues related to the aging of the Canadian population and the quality of life of seniors. In its recently published monograph, *The NACA Position on Determining Priorities in Health Care: The Seniors' Perspective* (18), NACA offers specific principles and recommendations for establishing priorities in health care, based on consultation with major Canadian seniors' organizations and experts in the field. While recognizing that choices among health care services will have to be made if the health care system is to remain affordable as well as universal, the position paper also reaffirms the belief that "Canada's health care system is a source of pride for Canadians and a cherished symbol of the values of equity and compassion that are intrinsic to our national identity" (18, p. 11).

A second organization that speaks on behalf of seniors is One Voice: The Canadian Seniors Network. It is a national seniors' organization that lobbies, educates, and raises consciousness among legislators and the public at large on issues affecting the elderly. In September 1994, nearly 250 delegates from across Canada met in Montreal to answer the question, "How can we help save Medicare?" and developed a report, entitled *Health Aging: A Canadian Commitment?* (19), that embodied their concerns and recommendations. Many conference participants remembered the days before Medicare and were committed to its maintenance as an essential strand in the social safety net not only for seniors, but for all Canadians. Indeed, participants felt the need to maintain and revitalize the political will needed to keep Medicare intact as an expression of collective responsibility for health care in Canada—especially in the face of the growing threats of deinsuring, privatization, and user fees raised by the specter of shrinking federal involvement and growing provincial responsibility, driven by the apparent need to control costs, restrict access, and reduce benefits.

Emergent Directions for Health Care in Canada. The current debate over the future of Medicare has triggered a reassessment and reconsideration of how health care services should be defined (broadly or narrowly) and what model (medical, social, or some combination) should structure the system. In addition to major general concerns about the efficiency, organization, and effectiveness of the services delivered by the health care system, there are two areas in particular where discussion has been driven by issues relevant to the care of the elderly: long-term care, and health promotion and healthy public policy.

Long-term care in Canada exhibits great variation among the provinces with regard to organization, payment, and dominant models. While there may be consensus on the human values underlying the system—for example, dignity, security,

Consensus are values

self-determination, and independence—there seems to be substantial variability in other areas (20). Although Medicare established an essential foundation of medical services upon which a long-term care system could be built (21), it simultaneously sharply narrowed the view of what constitutes health and how to structure services to achieve it. Long-term care to manage chronic illness and provide support to improve quality of life of the frail elderly falls considerably outside the biomedical model associated with the acute care system. While long-term services in chronic hospitals and nursing homes may be covered under Medicare and the Canada Assistance Plan in some provinces, non-institutional home and community-based services are covered only by a crazy-quilt payment system of public and private programs, including nonprofit agencies and user fees for consumers. Thus, long-term care is increasingly discussed and debated across the Canadian provinces, particularly the need to enhance public support for home and community-based services outside an institutional context (10).

In addition to concerns about long-term care, observers also emphasize the importance of expanding the model of care to embody a more holistic emphasis on health promotion and healthy public policy. Rather than relying on a health care system that is reactive—"fixing" problems after they have arisen—they are calling for a greater emphasis (along with increased resources) on health promotion and disease prevention. This is especially the case within the gerontological community, where authors have emphasized the importance of preventing or postponing health problems in designing a strategy for maximizing well-being and quality of life for the elderly (5, 22). More broadly interpreted, this approach also includes greater recognition of the need for "healthy public policy," supported by the belief that the scope for thinking about health and aging must be broadened well beyond a model based simply on demography, economic costs, and disease and operating within a system characterized by organizational boundary disputes, lack of adequate data, and few mechanisms to coordinate decision-making across the system.

Saving the Medicare Program in the United States

In the United States, elderly persons currently make up about 12.6 percent of the population, with projected increases due to the aging of the "baby boom" generation to approximately 21.8 percent in the year 2030 and 22.6 percent in 2040 (23). As in Canada, concerns are also directed on the southern side of the border toward the skyrocketing cost of health care services, which in 1990 constituted 12.4 percent of the GDP in the United States (11). In particular, the U.S. Medicare program has grown rapidly since its inception in 1965, averaging 16 percent annual growth rate in its first 25 years of existence (24). In spite of efforts over the past few years to stem the rate of growth—such as the development of diagnostic related groups (DRGs) to establish limits on hospital care for the elderly—current projections indicate that the trust fund for hospital insurance will be depleted by 2002 (25).

Two recent developments in the United States have highlighted the interrelationships between health and aging policy: (a) the central importance of health care issues at the 1995 White House Conference on Aging, and (b) the Congressional debate over the future of Medicare.

Health Care Issues at the 1995 White House Conference on Aging. Observers prior to the 1995 White House Conference on Aging suggested the conference was particularly important because the country was about to enter a new phase in national history when the challenges of aging would become more critical (26). Of the 50 resolutions adopted by conference participants, approximately half dealt in some way, directly or indirectly, with health care and long-term care. The preservation of Medicare benefits and coverage, the development of a universal health care system, better support for a unified home and community-based long-term care system, and more emphasis on health promotion and disease prevention for the elderly were recurrent themes. Although White House conferences are advisory in nature, the past successes of such events (e.g., the addition of much-needed support in 1961 for the then-proposed Medicare program) suggest that they may indeed help to shape and influence the development of public policy.

Congressional Debate over the Future of Medicare. Recent budgetary debates in the U.S. Congress have thrust Medicare cost projections into the public consciousness, with resultant concerns raised about the impending insolvency, particularly of the Hospital Insurance trust fund. Televised images of Members of Congress brandishing copies of the Medicare Trustees' Report as evidence that something must be done about "runaway" health care costs for the elderly have contributed to the public perception of a looming disaster. Under "intermediate" cost assumptions, projections of the solvency of the Health Insurance trust fund indicate that it will be exhausted by the year 2002 (27). In concluding their report to Congress, the trustees urged the government to take action, based on their summary assessment that there has been (25, p. 11):

> deterioration in the long-range financial condition of the Social Security and Medicare programs and an acceleration in the projected dates of exhaustion in the related trust funds. . . . These adverse trends can be expected to continue and indicate the possibility of a future retirement crisis as the U.S. population begins to age rapidly.

Comparative Summary

A comparison of current issues in geriatric health care policy on both sides of the U.S.-Canadian border gives evidence that mounting concerns over the cost of health care—emerging from the lengthening shadow cast by demographic aging—are increasingly driving public discourse on the future of health care service delivery systems, payment mechanisms, and appropriate care models. Whether or not the two countries' systems are converging from past histories representing very different assumptions about the role of government in health care (11), what is clear is that the elderly and their health care concerns are taking a prominent place in the unfolding drama or debate and discussion over the future of the health care system in both the United States and Canada. In order to understand how these two countries arrived at their current situations, however, we must examine their recent pasts in the context of studies, reports, and forces shaping the nexus between aging and health care policy—and, in particular, the development of a perceived "problem."

IS POPULATION AGING A "PROBLEM PARADIGM"?

The current debates over aging and health care in Canada and the United States have an interesting and important historical backdrop, an understanding of which can enrich our insights into the emerging trends currently shaping health care policy in both countries. An analysis of the patterns and themes in previous studies on the relationships between population aging and health care can capture the trends and forces shaping the issues facing a society and its government—and thereby provide a firm foundation for informing our thinking about the future.

In particular, the development of the concept of aging as a "problem paradigm" helps to provide a basis for this approach. For example, studies of population aging may lead to forecasts of demographic doom based on projections of age composition, dependency ratios, disability rates, and the economic impact of population structure into the future—an activity characterized as "alarmist. or apocalyptic demography" (28). In this approach there is an implicit faith that an emphasis on quantitative data will free policymakers from the difficult (and ultimately value-based) decisions implicit in making choices and establishing priorities. It is important that we recognize, however, that numbers may simply be used to mask a call for more money to respond to an imminent "health care crisis," obscure important facts, or veil alternative options that should be considered by policymakers. Numbers can be manipulated and "massaged" to generate quite different conclusions and interpretations (29). Indeed, demographic research itself suggests that the projected negative impact of population aging on rates of economic growth may have been greatly exaggerated (30).

Seen from a critical and comparative perspective, Canada and the United States have different histories and emerging patterns, which will now be reviewed.

Canadian Demographic Projections: Looking Beyond the Numbers

The mid-1970s saw the beginning of published reports based on the empirical study of population aging in Canada. Importantly, Canadian observers have usually been more reluctant than their U.S. counterparts to embrace a one-dimensional quantitative approach to the aging "problem." Some of the earliest studies focused on general issues and trends dealing with a changing age structure or, more specifically, with concerns about its impacts on health care services (31–33). Although alarmist themes could be detected in some of these studies, most tended to downplay the "problem" of demographic aging and to avoid the more apocalyptic tones that were beginning to emerge in the United States. For example, in their 1978 study on health care impact, Boulet and Grenier (34) used utilization and cost data on hospital and medical care services to project the effects of an aging Canadian population to the year 2031. Although the graying of Canada would have a significant impact, the authors determined that it would not be unmanageable in its effects on per capita growth of medical and hospital costs. Similarly, at about the same time Ridler (35) accurately captured the growing Canadian concern with questions about the country's ability to continue supporting pension programs and health care services in the face of an aging population, but he concluded that these anxieties were overstated. These early studies are significant because they set the theme that the "problems" potentially associated with an aging population were overblown and could be addressed through appropriately chosen, proactive governmental policies.

Skepticism with data-driven decrees of doom continued into the decade of the 1980s. In 1984 the Canadian Medical Association released its report by the Task Force on the Allocation of Health Care Resources, *Health: A Need for Redirection* (36). A separate report projected the impacts of population aging on health care costs over a 40-year period (37). The report concluded that the effect of resource redirection (e.g., substituting less costly community-based services for institutional ones) would be considerable savings to the health care system, and it observed that the overall impact of the graying of Canadian society could be greatly reduced by appropriately designed policies.

This same theme has been sounded in 20 years of studies by Frank Denton, Byron Spencer, and their colleagues at McMaster University. For example, based on a series of earlier analyses (38, 39), they concluded in 1987 that a significant proportion of elderly Canadians need not pose a crisis, for two reasons: (a) rising health care costs in the future will at least be partially offset by increases in gross national product, and (b) important reductions may occur in the cost of health care services— for example, advancements in technology and the use of less expensive forms and settings of care and health care professionals (40). Such policy choices may not be easy ones, however, because population aging's greatest challenge is to deal with shifting dependency ratios—not simply insufficient levels of social resources to support the increased impact of the elderly. Government will have to decide whether and how to redirect social resources and public spending for education, pension, and health care programs (41). Most recently, these researchers suggest that although their projections of population aging do have major implications for the future costs of health care services, overall more attention must be paid to developing an integrated systems approach to health care policy (9). The consistent theme remains one of the necessity of making choices, based on a firm working knowledge of the system and what expenses are really necessary.

Finally, Robert Evans, Morris Barer, and their colleagues at the University of British Columbia have for several years studied the "risks" associated with an aging Canadian population, and they have consistently defused the apocalyptic rhetoric associated with the looming "crisis" created by the perceived impact of the elderly on health care service utilization. For example, they have drawn attention to the important distinction between simple population aging and the ways in which the health care system responds to the needs of the elderly and how these needs may be changing (42). They have also suggested that challenges to the Canadian universal health care system based on the pressures of an aging population are factually and analytically wrong. Rather, these are simply thinly veiled professional or political agendas intended to create a demographic smokescreen to hide other objectives. The real challenge for an aging society is to develop a collective decision-making context to determine new intellectual and conceptual frameworks for thinking about health in a broader social context, and about the nature of the interrelationships and obligations among the individual, the family, and the wider society (43).

Most recently, Barer, Evans, and their colleagues attempt once more to lay the demographic apocalyptic rhetoric to rest (44). Using the metaphor of aging as a glacier—not an avalanche—they explain the persistent grip of the image of demographic doom as part of the "problem paradigm" explored earlier by Canadians McDaniel (4) and Northcott (5, 6). Their suggestion for an antidote to this poisoned projection is the realization that the forces driving health care cost increases are the product of a struggle over social priorities—an outcome that can be altered, if the social and political will exists. Patterns of health care for the elderly need to be changed—which is a management issue, not one dealing with absolute levels of social resources. In other words, choices will have to be made, and government will have to make better decisions about how it spends its money on health care in general and on the elderly in particular.

Apocalyptic Aging in the United States

Studies and projections of the effects of aging on health care costs can be found on both sides of the border. Unlike the predominant numerical skepticism north of the border, however, policy analysts in the United States seem, on the whole, to have a mind-set that embraces quantitative studies of population aging as an objective validation of "worst case" fears about the looming geriatric "crisis." Some U.S. observers suggest that this unquestioned reliance on numerical interpretations of the gerontological "population problem" is tied to the emergence of the biomedical paradigm of aging (45). The overall characterization of this "culture of crisis" has four distinct but interrelated aspects: demographic, epidemiologic, economic, and technologic.

Demographic Forces. Simple numerical projections are often used to create a sense of the helpless inevitability of the future aging "crisis" in the United States. One study found that "middle series projections" predict that the number of persons over age 65 will increase to 52 million by the year 2020 and to 68 million by 2040 (46). By 2030 the elderly will constitute roughly 21 percent of the U.S. population. Projections of the "aged dependency ratio," the number of aged persons per working population aged 19 to 64 and a crude measure of "dependency," show similar supposedly alarming trends: set at 20 percent in the mid-1980s, it is expected to increase to 33 percent by 2025 and to 38 percent by 2050 (47). Moreover, persons 85 and older—those most likely to use health care services—are the fastest growing population group; by 2020 there will be 7 million individuals in this group, or approximately 2.5 percent of the total population, up from roughly 1.4 percent at present (48).

Epidemiological Trends. Closely related in popular consciousness to the demographic "facts" are epidemiological trends, especially projections of the disease

Burden on Health Care.

burden which the skyrocketing numbers of the elderly represent. Based on the concept of the "failures of success" explaining the growing prevalence of chronic illness due to the successful treatment of acute diseases (49), epidemiologists point to the growing specter of a "pandemic of chronic diseases and associated disabling conditions" (50). Although more optimistic projections of a declining duration of chronic illness—the "compression of morbidity" at the end of life—have been made by such observers as James Fries (51), many of his critics have suggested that there is little, if any, evidence for this trend as yet (52, 53).

This increased burden of chronic illness will affect most directly the institutional long-term care system, with a recent U.S. General Accounting Office report projecting that costs will almost triple in the next 27 years and then nearly triple again by the middle of the next century (54). In constant 1987 dollars, costs are expected to rise from $42 billion in 1988 to $120 billion in 2018 and $350 billion by 2048. The number of elderly persons using a nursing home during the course of a year is projected to increase 76 percent over the next 30 years, from roughly 2.3 million in 1988 to about 4 million in 2018. The report also suggests that shifting dependency ratios will place a greater burden on the working population in paying for these increased costs.

Costs

Economic Forces. Concerns about costs—especially those for medical care—arise naturally from projections of the growing numbers of elderly with chronic illness. Although the elderly currently represent over 12 percent of the American population, they use roughly a third of the total U.S. expenditures on health care. A study of future Medicare expenses concluded that "the projected total cost . . . rises impressively during the upcoming decades, nearly doubling by the year 2020. . . . By 2040, the average age of a baby boomer will be 85 years, and the level of Medicare spending . . . could range from $147 to $212 billion" (46, p. 2337). In 1991, the Medicare Board of Trustees projected that the Medicare Hospital Insurance fund would be exhausted by 2005 (55), and the more recent 1995 alarmist projections of insolvency by 2002 have already been discussed.

Technology. Advancement in medical technology tends to be seen by many observers as inevitable. Such progress, however, raises concerns over whether society will be able to continue funding unlimited access to this technology. As ever more sophisticated and expensive diagnostic procedures and interventions become available to treat the symptoms and causes of chronic illness, and as more and more members of the nation's aging society have at least one chronic illness, it is clear that the United States will be increasingly likely to be caught in a medical Malthusian dilemma: the demographic-epidemiological demand will far outstrip the economic "carrying capacity" of our society to meet it. This widening gap will inevitably result in the need for explicit rationing of health care services (56). The best known of the age-based rationing suggestions are those of Daniel Callahan, based on his argument about the natural human lifespan and the necessity for "setting limits" (57, 58). This suggestion has created controversy among its reviewers, drawing fire based on philosophical, clinical, and policy-related grounds (59–65).

Capitalism

Ageism?

MORAL DIMENSIONS OF THE "CRISIS" OF
AGING AND HEALTH CARE

Differences in approaches between Canada and the United States with regard to the interpretation of population aging and its impact on health and social programs and resources suggest that there may be underlying forces at work beyond simply different numbers. Indeed, how data are defined and how information is collected, analyzed, and presented reveal the presence of other social, economic, political, and moral agendas. As Carroll Estes and her colleagues suggest, "each of the crises making their way into the public consciousness is socially 'produced,' or constructed by what politicians, economists, experts, and the media have to say about or impute to the issues they address" (66, p. 92). In this regard, a Canadian-U.S. comparison reveals moral dimensions of the "crisis of aging," of how the "problem" of the elderly and their impact on the public purse is defined.

In a fundamental way, the resolution of geriatric health care policy debates in Canada and the United States will depend on the outcome of a shifting balance between the values of collectivism and individualism as they are interpreted within the political ideologies and social histories of these two countries. The elderly in Canada are concerned about the unraveling of the welfare net that many of them can remember being woven: Will government retreat from its more recent historical commitment to social programs that were built on a strong collectivistic ethos and replace it instead with a growing emphasis on individual responsibility? Similarly, in the United States the elderly are lobbying to preserve their Medicare benefits in the face of a Congress threatening to dismantle or at least restrict or reduce them. Importantly, though, in the United States there is no history of a strong role for government in supporting universal health care for all Americans.

Collectivism versus individualism: this fundamental tension lies at the core of the emerging social and political debate in both countries over the future of health care policy in general and, in particular, health care for the elderly. An examination of these two value themes—as suggested by the moral economy approach—can reveal underlying trends in the two countries and help further an understanding of what may happen in the future.

Universal Health Care in Canada: Eroding Consensus or Solid Bedrock?

It is striking that many observers of differences between Canada and the United States have commented on a more collectivistic ethos north of the border, in both "popular" Canadian publications and presentations in the United States (67, 68) and in the more "academic" literature (69). A fundamental issue at stake in this debate is the origin and presumed permanence of this difference. Some observers—such as Seymour Martin Lipset (70, 71), Gad Horowitz (72), and Louis Hartz (73)—argue that out of the American Revolution emerged a relatively unchanging value system for the United States and Canada: the United States more individualistic, Canada more collectivistic. Others have vigorously questioned the extent to which such events were deterministic in shaping national character differences and have suggested that this earlier thesis has now been virtually discredited among most sociologists and historians (74–77). This debate does not mean that there are no value differences between the two societies; it simply suggests that far from being determined by some historical event in the distant past, these values have evolved (and will continue to evolve) under the influence of changing social, political, and economic forces.

John Conway (78) contends, for example, that the Canadian sense of community draws on a political and religious history different from that of the United States, extending across generations to unite the society through time. In addition, he observes that there is a less marked separation between church and state in Canada. Historian John Herd Thompson (77) sees the real roots of social democratic institutions in Canada as arising after 1945 and during the Cold War, when the United States invested its resources in the military-industrial complex and Canada into social welfare programs, such as universal health care insurance.

In health care in particular, the universal system in effect in Canada certainly embodies the collectivistic principle that the community has responsibility for the welfare of its members (79–81). Robert Evans (43), for example, has argued that the different structures of the health care systems in the United States and Canada may act as a mirror or a lens through which their different value systems may be revealed. Other observers have noted that collectivistic ideals have in the past differentiated Canada from the United States in defining the very nature of the problems in geriatric health care and in quality-of-life considerations for the elderly (82, 83). Moreover, this universalistic approach to social welfare policy has effectively short-circuited any development of polarizing "intergenerational equity" rhetoric in Canada by meeting the health care needs of all persons across the entire family life cycle (76).

Another expression of the value of collectivism is found in the openness and vigor of public debate and dialogue over major social issues in Canada and in differences in the political systems between the two countries. For example, Canada has a Parliamentary form of government, greater citizen participation, and less domination of politics by special interests (such as business)—what one set of observers has called the greater likelihood that "public opinion will be more easily translated into public policy" north of the border (69). In addition, there has traditionally been a sense of reliance on government to deal with pressing social issues, though there are signs that this value is declining as the average citizen's trust in government's ability to confront major economic and political problems has been eroded.

In spite of this, historically the universal health care system has forced discussion of important issues and priorities out into the open. As Robert Evans and his colleagues (84) have suggested, a hallmark of the Canadian health care system is continuing debate over health care expenditures—for example, annual fee negotiations between provincial medical societies and governments, and the establishment of global hospital budgets. There is some faith that this open discussion will serve to reveal the underlying social values necessary to guide the health care system through difficult times (85). This belief is embodied in the National Forum on Health process discussed earlier.

However, it is also clear that major changes in thinking are occurring in Canada that portend a reassessment of the traditional assumptions about government. For example, Susan Fletcher, the Executive Director of the Division of Aging and Seniors of Health Canada, spoke in October 1995 at the annual meeting of the Canadian Association on Gerontology. Her message was that new "ways of doing business" will characterize the federal government in the future, including an assessment of what are legitimate and necessary roles for government and how programs and policies can be realigned to be made more efficient and sustainable. Government will increasingly become more of a "partner" than a "parent," emphasizing the development of interdepartmental, multisectoral, and horizontal collaboration and partnerships. The federal government is still committed to a universal health care system, but it is clear that the meaning of this commitment will be influenced by major shifts in the ideology about government's role in health and health care.

Thus, changing economic and sociopolitical contingencies may once again influence the role of universalism in shaping health care policies in Canada. Pressures exist that may cause change, but the development of a health care system similar to that in the United States seems to be opposed by everyone. Growing emphasis on population health, the determinants of health, health promotion, and groups at risk for health problems will expand the definition of health and health care in Canada. Though the future is uncertain, it is clear that major changes will, in fact, force a redirection of the relative roles of federal, provincial, and local governments in promoting the health of Canadians in general and that of the elderly in particular.

Social Values in Health Care in the United States

In considering the social value base of current political ideology south of the border, it can be argued that the individual in the United States serves both as the unit of need or service and as the core organizing principle around which government policy is formulated and developed. This perspective has achieved new prominence in the recent ascendancy of the Republic Party agenda in Congress—emphasizing the value of smaller and weaker central government and of increased personal and local control over social problems. This ideology is evident in the tendency to define problems as individual rather than as social, political, or economic—thereby making it more difficult to achieve far-reaching social reforms (86). Social researchers such as Robert Bellah and his colleagues (87) have found that individualism is a major characteristic defining how persons in the United States view themselves and organize their relationships and lives . Indeed, the preeminence of the individual is enshrined in the notion of individual rights, which are reinforced in the U.S. legal system and in ethical guidelines in such areas as health care.

This individualistic ethos has profound implications for how public policy is formulated. First, the individual is seen as bearing the main responsibility for meeting his or her primary needs. Only when the individual fails in doing this will the government step in as a last resort to guarantee some minimal level of social assistance. Within the domain of health care, for example, services have traditionally been allocated based on individual need and the ability to pay—in other words, by a market-based mechanism.

At a social level, the growing perceived public policy polarization between the young and the old, "kids versus canes," in the generational equity debate further exemplifies the growing fragmentation and group-based nature of U.S. politics. Originally presented as a demographic and economic argument (88, 89), the inter-generational "war" has been correctly unmasked as an ideological struggle between competing forces over the future of the welfare state (90, 91), the nature of social inequities (92), and differing interpretations of the relationship between the state and families (93). Unlike many other nations, the United States particularizes and com-partmentalizes social policies along lines of individual or static group-based need, rather than seeing public programs as responding to changing life course needs across the entire society (94). In this view, the United States has spawned the generational equity debate *precisely because* it does not have adequate social programs to meet the needs of families over the entire life course. In spite of calls for recognizing the inextricably related needs of individuals and families across the generations (95) and for a new intergenerational politics to forge a common agenda uniting people of all ages in expanding social welfare policies (96, 97), it remains unclear how successful such efforts will be.

As a consequence, emphasis on individualism makes the development of more universalistic policies difficult, if not impossible. If concern is directed mainly toward the self, rather than to the welfare of others, then there is little chance that a sense of community responsibility will evolve to underwrite a significantly broadened social policy base, such as universal health insurance. Indeed, little sense of identification with the broader societal interest precludes the kind of social discus-sion and debate that is needed to forge a moral consensus on new social priorities, especially in the health care field. Increasing emphasis on cost-cutting measures, for example, cannot substitute for social discussion to reach agreement on health care policies and priorities (98).

CONCLUSIONS

Aging is a universal process affecting all individuals and, inevitably, societies and governments as they deal with the development of policies and programs to respond to the unique challenges represented by the experience of growing older. This chapter has presented an argument for why a moral economy framework is essential if we are to understand fully the similarities and differences both in the definition of the "problem" of aging and in the development of "solutions" to it. In this process, we must consider both the facts and the values implicit in any policy debate (8). In spite of what policymakers like to believe, purely quantitative or factual approaches are insufficient for a complete understanding of a social "problem." Empirical data can be manipulated as an instrument to advance agendas based on social ideology and embodying values rooted in historical social and political assumptions about the nature of the state and the responsibilities and obligations of individuals and families. Thus, aging may be seen as a "problem" to be "solved," rather than as a modern triumph of the maintenance and extension of life on a scale unparalleled in human history. Instead of seeing the elderly as the "enemy" and a burden, we must come to see them as embodying needs like any other social group—a group that we are all becoming. As the cartoon character, Pogo, observed: "We have met the enemy, and he is us."

The moral economy perspective permits observers to uncover and study the prevailing social values underlying current public policy discussions and debates, allowing insight into questions about our relative priorities as a society and whether these are the right priorities. That this is a dynamic process has been made evident in the preceding description of the shifting balance between individualism and collectivism in the United States and Canada. Whether the two countries are actually converging from very different recent histories remains to be seen.

What is apparent in both countries is that the elderly and their advocates are moving health care policy toward embracing a broader vision of health than has traditionally been evident in either nation. Growing recognition of the importance of disease and disability prevention, as well as long-term care for the chronically ill, has emerged from the realization that the prevailing acute care, medical model is not adequate to deal with the unique health problems of the elderly. What is yet to be seen, however, is whether and how this new and expanded interpretation of health will actually be translated into real policy shifts and new programs. Canada's traditional reliance on an open process to involve all elements of society in determining new policy directions, as well as its current commitment to changing the ways in which the health care system is managed, seem to offer a brighter future for this possibility in Canada than in the United States. However, some observers remain skeptical and emphasize the sometimes large gap between rhetoric and reality. On the U.S. side of the border, gridlock in any attempts to bring about major changes in health care policy seems to be the norm, particularly in the absence of any tradition of collective responsibility for ensuring universal access to health care and in the light of current efforts to turn back the clock on several welfare policies in general. The current rush to managed care seems to be more policymaking by default—in the name of cost containment—than by carefully developed and agreed upon social consensus-building.

In sum, the fundamental conflict evident in health care concerns driven by the recognition of an aging society is between collectivistic and individualistic responsibility. It is this balance of competing values along a continuum constructed by historical social and political forces on which the emerging drama of geriatric health care policy will be acted out. In this play, however, we need to be aware not only of the stage, but also of what is going on behind the scenes with regard to assumptions about the nature of the aging "problem." Reality may go beyond appearances, and in fact be obscured by the social construction of the "stage set"—social "problems" in the service of other agendas. In reviewing how this play is performed in both Canada and the United States, we can gain much insight into why aging can be seen both as a lens to magnify and scrutinize social institutions in the two countries, and as a prism to separate the underlying fundamental moral assumptions that make living in society possible and enriching. Taken together, more light will be shed in this process both on aging as an individual and social experience, and on the underlying nature of the public policies that respond to it.

REFERENCES

1. Clark, P. G. [Review of *Critical Perspectives on Aging: The Political and Moral Economy of Growing Old,* edited by M. Minkler and C. L. Estes]. *Can. J. Aging* 14: 800–803, 1995.
2. Minkler, M., and Estes, C. L. (eds.). *Critical Perspectives on Aging: The Political and Moral Economy of Growing Old.* Baywood, Amityville, N.Y., 1991.
3. Jonsen, A. R., and Butler, L. H. Public ethics and policy making. *Hastings Center Rep.* 5(4): 19–31, 1975.
4. McDaniel, S. A. Demographic aging as a guiding paradigm in Canada's welfare state. *Can. Public Policy* 13: 330-336, 1987.
5. Northcott, H. C. *Aging in Alberta: Rhetoric and Reality.* Detselig Enterprises, Calgary, Alberta, 1992.
6. Northcott, H. C. Public perceptions of the population aging "crisis." *Canadian Public Policy—Analyse de Politiques* XX(1): 66–77, 1994.
7. Robertson, A. The politics of Alzheimer's disease: A case study in apocalyptic demography. In *Critical Perspectives on Aging,* edited by M. Minkler and C. L. Estes, pp. 135–150. Baywood, Amityville, N.Y., 1991.
8. Potter, R. B. *War and Moral Discourse.* John Knox Press, Richmond, Va., 1969.
9. Denton, F. T., and Spencer, B. G. Demographic change and the cost of publicly funded health care. *Can. J. Aging* 14: 174–192, 1995.
10. Chappell, N. L. The future of health care in Canada. *J. Soc. Policy* 22: 487–505, 1993.
11. Maioni, A. Divergent pasts, converging futures? The politics of health care reform in Canada and the United States. *Canadian-American Public Policy,* No. 18, August 1994.
12. National Forum on Health. *Background Information.* Ottawa, no date.
13. National Forum on Health. *Activities Update.* Ottawa, no date.
14. National Forum on Health. *The Public and Private Financing of Canada's Health System: A Discussion Paper.* Ottawa, September 1995.
15. National Forum on Health. *Remarks for the Financial Post Conference by the Executive Director of the National Forum on Health.* Ottawa, May 2, 1995.
16. National Forum on Health. *The Members of the National Forum on Health Support Public Funding for Health Care.* Ottawa, April 4, 1995.
17. National Forum on Health. *Advancing the Dialogue on Health and Health Care: A Consultative Document.* Cat. No. H21-126/4-1966. Minister of Public Works and Government Services, Ottawa, October 21, 1996.
18. National Advisory Council on Aging. *The NACA Position on Determining Priorities in Health Care: The Seniors' Perspective.* Cat. No. H-71-2/2-17-1995. Minister of Supply and Services Canada, Ottawa, 1995.
19. One Voice: The Canadian Seniors Network. *Healthy Aging: A Canadian Commitment? A National Conference on Protecting and Improving Canada's Health Care System.* Ottawa, 1995.
20. Beland, F., and Shapiro, E. Ten provinces in search of a long term care policy. In *Aging: Canadian Perspectives,* edited by V. Marshal and B. McPherson, pp. 154–255. Broadview Press, Peterborough, Ont., 1994.
21. Kane, R. L., and Kane, R. A. *A Will and a Way: What the United States Can Learn from Canada about Caring for the Elderly.* Columbia University Press, New York, 1985.
22. Marshall, V. A critique of Canadian aging and health policy. In *Aging: Canadian Perspectives,* edited by V. Marshall and B. McPherson, pp. 232–244. Broadview Press, Peterborough, Ont., 1994.

23. Kart, C. S. *The Realities of Aging,* Ed. 4. Allyn and Bacon, Boston, 1994.
24. Rubenstein, L. Z., et al. Medicare: Challenges and future directions in a changing health environment. *Gerontologist* 34: 620–627, 1994.
25. Social Security and Medicare Boards of Trustees. *Status of the Social Security and Medicare Programs: A Summary of the 1995 Annual Reports.* Washington, D.C., 1995.
26. Pillemer, K., et al. Setting the White House Conference on Aging Agenda: Recommendations from an expert panel. *Gerontologist* 35: 258–261, 1995.
27. Board of Trustees of the Federal Hospital Insurance Trust Fund. *Annual Report.* Washington, D.C., 1995.
28. Katz, S. Alarmist demography: Power, knowledge, and the elderly population. *J. Aging Stud.* 6: 203–225, 1992.
29. Evans, R. G. Illusions of necessity: Evading responsibility for choice in health care. *J. Health Polit. Policy Law* 10: 439–467, 1985.
30. Easterlin, R. A. The economic impact of prospective population changes in advanced industrial countries: An historical perspective. *J. Gerontol. Soc. Sci.* 46: S299–S309, 1991.
31. Auerbach, L., and Gerber, A. *Implications of the Changing Age Structure of the Canadian Population.* Science Council of Canada Pub. No. SS21-3/2-1976. Ministry of Supply and Services, Ottawa, 1976.
32. Rombout, M. K. *Hospitals and the Elderly: Present and Future Trends.* Long Range Health Planning Staff Paper 75-2. Health and Welfare Canada, Ottawa, 1975.
33. Rombout, M. K. *Health Care Institutions and Canada's Elderly.* Supplement to Long Range Health Planning Staff Paper 75-2. Health and Welfare Canada, Ottawa, 1975.
34. Boulet, J.-A., and Grenier, G. *Health Expenditures in Canada and the Impact of Demographic Changes on Future Government Health Insurance Program Expenditures.* Discussion Paper No. 123. Economic Council of Canada, Ottawa, 1978.
35. Ridler, N. B. Some economic implications of the projected age structure of Canada. *Canadian Public Policy—Analyse de Politiques* V: 533–548, 1979.
36. Canadian Medical Association. *Health: A Need for Redirection.* Report of the Task Force on the Allocation of Health Care Resources. Ottawa, 1984.
37. Canadian Medical Association. *Investigation of the Impact of Demographic Change on the Health Care System in Canada.* Report of the Task Force on the Allocation of Health Care Resources, prepared by Woods Gordon Management Consultants. Ottawa, 1984.
38. Denton, F. T., and Spencer, B. G. Health-care costs when the population changes. *Can. J. Econ.* 13: 34–48, 1975.
39. Denton, F. T., and Spencer, B. G. Some economic and demographic implications of future population change. *J. Can. Stud.* 14: 81–93, 1979.
40. Denton, F. T., Li, S. N., and Spencer, B. G. How will population aging affect the future costs of maintaining health-care standards? In *Aging in Canada: Social Perspectives,* Ed. 2, edited by V. W. Marshall, pp. 553–568. Fitzhenry and Whiteside, Markham, Ont., 1987.
41. Denton, F. T., and Spencer, B. G. Population aging and the economy: Some issues in resource allocation. In *Ethics and Aging: The Right to Live, the Right to Die,* edited by J. E. Thornton and E. R. Winkler, pp. 98–123. University of British Columbia Press, Vancouver, 1988.
42. Barer, M. L., Evans, R. B., and Lomas, J. Aging and health care utilization: New evidence on old fallacies. *Soc. Sci. Med.* 24: 851–862, 1987.
43. Evans, R. G. "We'll take care of it for you": Health care in the Canadian community. *Daedalus: Proc. Am. Acad. Arts Sci.* 117(4): 155–189, 1988.

44. Barer, M. L., Evans, R. G., and Hertzman, C. Avalanche or glacier?: Health care and the demographic rhetoric. *Can. J. Aging* 14: 193–224, 1995.
45. Estes, C. L., and Binney, E. A. The biomedicalization of aging: Dangers and dilemmas. In *Critical Perspectives on Aging,* edited by M. Minkler and C. L. Estes, pp. 117–134. Baywood, Amityville, N.Y., 1991.
46. Schneider, E. L., and Guralnick, J. M. The aging of America: Impact on health care costs. *JAMA* 263: 2335–2340, 1990.
47. Etheredge, L. An aging society and the federal deficit. *Milbank Mem. Fund Q.* 62: 521–543, 1984.
48. Rabin, D. L., and Stockton, P. *Long-Term Care for the Elderly: A Factbook.* Oxford University Press, New York, 1987.
49. Gruenberg, E. M. The failures of success. *Milbank Mem. Fund Q.* 55: 3–24, 1977.
50. Kramer, M. The Increasing Prevalence of Mental Disorders: Implications for the Future. Paper presented at the National Conference on the Elderly Deinstitutionalized Patient in the Community, Arlington, Va., May, 1981.
51. Fries, J. F. The compression of morbidity. *Milbank Mem. Fund Q.* 61: 397–419, 1983.
52. Meyers, G. C., and Manton, K. G. Compression of mortality: Myth or reality? *Gerontologist* 24: 346–353, 1984.
53. Schneider, E. L., and Brody, J. A. Aging, natural death, and the compression of morbidity: Another view. *N. Engl. J. Med.* 309: 854–855, 1983.
54. U.S. General Accounting Office. *Long-Term Care: Projected Needs of the Aging Baby Boom Generation.* Report No. HRD-91-86. Washington, D.C., 1991.
55. Ross, S. G. The Financial Status of the Social Security and Medicare Programs. Presentation at the Annual Meeting of the Gerontological Society of America, San Francisco, November 22–26, 1991.
56. Evans, R. W. Health care technology and the inevitability of resource allocation and rationing decisions. *JAMA* 249: 2047–2052, 2208–2219, 1983.
57. Callahan, D. *Setting Limits: Medical Goals in an Aging Society.* Simon and Schuster, New York, 1987.
58. Callahan, D. *What Kind of Life.* Simon and Schuster, New York, 1990.
59. Binstock, R. H., and Kahana, J. [Review of D. Callahan, *Setting Limits: Medical Goals in an Aging Society*]. *Gerontologist* 28: 424–426, 1988.
60. Binstock, R. H., and Post, S. G. Old age and the rationing of health care. In *Too Old for Health Care? Controversies in Medicine, Law, Economics, and Ethics,* edited by R. H. Binstock and S. G. Post, pp. 1–12. Johns Hopkins University Press, Baltimore, Md., 1991.
61. Brock, D. W. Justice, health care, and the elderly. *Philos. Public Aff.* 18: 297–312, 1989.
62. Churchill, L. R. Should we ration health care by age? *J. Am. Geriatr. Soc.* 36: 644–647, 1988.
63. Jecker, N. S. Excluding the elderly: A reply to Callahan [Review of D. Callahan, *Setting Limits: Medical Goals in an Aging Society*]. *Philos. Public Policy* 7(4): 12–15, 1987.
64. Jecker, N. S. Disenfranchising the elderly from life-extending medical care. *Public Aff. Q.* 2(3): 51–68, 1988.
65. Singer, P. [Review of D. Callahan, *Setting Limits: Medical Goals in an Aging Society*]. *Bioethics* 2: 151–169, 1988.
66. Estes, C. L., et al. *Political Economy, Health, and Aging.* Little, Brown, Boston, 1984.
67. Fulford, R. The Canadian difference. *Canada Today* 20(1): 2–4, 1989.
68. McNeil, R. Looking for my country. *Am. Rev. Can. Stud.* 21: 409–421, 1991.
69. Dreier, P., and Bertrand, E. Canada: A kinder, gentler nation. *Soc. Policy* 23(1): 6–19, 1992.

70. Lipset, S. M. *The First New Nation: The United States in Historical and Comparative Perspective*. Basic Books, New York, 1963.
71. Lipset, S. M. *Continental Divide: The Values and Institutions of the United States and Canada*. Routledge, Chapman, and Hall, New York, 1990.
72. Horowitz, G. Conservatism, Liberalism, and Socialism in Canada: An interpretation. *Can. J. Econ. Polit. Sci.* 32(2): 143–171, 1966.
73. Hartz, L. *The Liberal Tradition in America*. Longman's, Toronto, 1955.
74. Babcock, R. [Review of S. M. Lipset, *Continental Divide: The Values and Institutions of the United States and Canada*]. *Histoire Sociale—Social History* 48: 408–410, 1991.
75. Brym, R. J., and Fox, B. J. *From Culture to Power: The Sociology of English Canada*. Oxford University Press, Toronto, 1989.
76. Cook, F. L., et al. Intergenerational Equity and the Politics of Income Security for the Old. Paper presented at the Donner Conference on A North American Look at Economic Security for the Elderly, Yale University, New Haven, Conn., May 17–18, 1991.
77. Thompson, J. H. "National Character" and United States-Canadian Differences: An Exploration of [Seymour Martin] Lipset's Explanation of the Continental Divide. Paper presented at the Learned Societies Conference, Calgary, Manitoba, June, 1994.
78. Conway, J. An "adapted organic tradition." *Daedalus: Proc. Am. Acad. Arts Sci.* 117: 381–396, 1988.
79. Taylor, M. G. *Health Insurance and Canadian Public Policy: The Seven Decisions That Created the Canadian Health Insurance System*. McGill–Queen's University Press, Montreal, 1978.
80. Tuohy, C. Conflict and accommodation in the Canadian health care system. In *Medicare at Maturity: Achievements, Lessons, and Challenges,* edited by R. G. Evans and G. L. Stoddart, pp. 393–434. University of Calgary Press, Calgary, Alberta, 1986.
81. Weller, G. R., and Manga, P. The development of health policy in Canada. In *The Politics of Canadian Public Policy,* edited by M. M. Atkinson and M. A. Chandler, pp. 223–246. University of Toronto Press, Toronto, 1983.
82. Clark, P. G. Geriatric health care policy in the United States and Canada: A comparison of facts and values in defining the problems. *J. Aging Stud.* 5: 265–281, 1991.
83. Clark, P. G. Ethical dimensions of quality of life in aging: Autonomy vs. collectivism in the United States and Canada. *Gerontologist* 31: 631–639, 1991.
84. Evans, R. G., et al. Controlling health expenditures: The Canadian reality. *N. Engl. J. Med.* 320: 571–577, 1989.
85. Manga, P. Medicare: Ethics versus economics. *Can. Med. Assoc. J.* 136: 113–116, 1987.
86. Estes, C. L. The new political economy of aging: Introduction and critique. In *Critical Perspectives on Aging,* edited by M. Minkler and C. L. Estes, pp. 19–36. Baywood, Amityville, N.Y., 1991.
87. Bellah, R. N., et al. *Habits of the Heart: Individualism and Commitment in American Life*. University of California Press, Berkeley, 1985.
88. Preston, S. H. Children and the elderly: Divergent paths for America's dependents. *Demography* 21: 435–457, 1984.
89. Preston, S. H. Children and the elderly in the U.S. *Sci. Am.* 251(6): 44–49, 1984.
90. Quadagno, J. Generational equity and the politics of the welfare state. *Polit. Soc.* 17: 353–376, 1989.
91. Walker, A. The economic "burden" of ageing and the prospect of intergenerational conflict. *Ageing Soc.* 10: 377–396, 1990.
92. Minkler, M. "Generational equity" and the new victim-blaming. In *Critical Perspectives on Aging,* edited by M. Minkler and C. L. Estes, pp. 67–80. Baywood, Amityville, N.Y., 1991.

93. Binney, E. A., and Estes, C. L. The retreat of the state and its transfer of responsibility: The intergenerational war. *Int. J. Health Serv.* 18(1): 83–96, 1988.
94. Heclo, H. Generational politics. In *The Vulnerable,* edited by J. L. Palmer, T. Smeeding, and B. B. Torrey, pp. 381–411. Urban Institute Press, Washington, D.C., 1988.
95. Kingson, E. R., Hirshorn, B. A., and Cornman, J. M. *Ties That Bind: The Interdependence of Generations.* Seven Locks Press, Washington, D.C., 1986.
96. Kingson, E. R. Generational equity: An unexpected opportunity to broaden the politics of aging. *Gerontologist* 28: 765–772, 1988.
97. Wisensale, S. K. Generational equity and intergenerational policies. *Gerontologist* 28: 773–778, 1988.
98. Daniels, N. Why saying no to patients in the United States is so hard: Cost containment, justice, and provider autonomy. *N. Engl. J. Med.* 314: 1380–1383, 1986.

CHAPTER 9

Devolution and Aging Policy:
Racing to the Bottom in Long-Term Care

Carroll L. Estes and Karen W. Linkins

During the past two decades, decentralization, devolution, and other challenges to the federal role in domestic health and human services policy have been fundamental processes shaping the structure and delivery of long-term care (LTC) in the United States. The devolution of policy evokes crucial questions concerning the future of entitlement programs such as Social Security and Medicare and, with them, the future of aging and LTC policy. "Long-term care" refers to the continuum of institutional and noninstitutional services from nursing to in-home and adult day care.

Following the failed health care reform efforts of President Clinton in the early 1990s, health reform has been driven by the private sector rather than active government policy. In the absence of a uniform national policy commitment to universal health insurance and in the presence of increasing devolution of federal responsibility for social programs to states and localities, uncertainty about the fate of LTC policy has risen.

Major questions concern how governors, mayors, and other state and local officials will deal with the federal retrenchment and their increased discretion and responsibilities, especially when confronted by difficult social and economic choices both within and outside their respective locations. States and their politicians compete with one another (1–3) to attract and retain business and investment capital to enhance their economy, as well as the votes to augment their political fortunes. Competition among different geopolitical units can manifest itself in a "race among the states"—sometimes referred to as a "race to the bottom" (1)—in which states compete with one another by decelerating their levels of commitment to safety-net programs in attempts to achieve their economic and political goals.

The 1996 Welfare Reform legislation signed by President Clinton exemplifies the trend toward devolution of responsibility for policymaking from the federal to the state level. It gives states much greater control in determining eligibility and benefit levels for welfare and decouples the program from automatic eligibility for

This research was supported by the AARP/Andrus, Frost, McCune, and Public Welfare Foundations.

Medicaid, the federal–state program of health insurance for the poor. With Welfare Reform, entitlement to Aid to Families with Dependent Children (AFDC) is abolished as a right of all citizens who qualify.

At the same time that political trends press for the diminution if not abolition of social programs, demographic trends signal the urgent need for an LTC policy solution. The population 65 and older grew 22 percent in the 1980s, more than double the growth of the U.S. population as a whole, and the older population will at least double again in the next 40 years. Those 85 years and older are the fastest growing group, projected to increase more than fivefold (from 3 to 15 million) between 1990 and 2050 (4). Even these startling figures may be a gross under-estimate, given Manton and Stallard's (5) recent data on mortality declines of 8.6 percent for those 85 and older between 1988 and 1991 alone. The 78 million members of the baby boom generation born between 1946 and 1964 are expected to create significant demand for LTC services throughout the first half of the 21st century and beyond. By 2050, nearly one-fourth of the population (80 million) will be 65 and older. Given that 90 million Americans today (all ages) live with chronic health conditions, 60 percent of whom are working-aged adults (6), the need for LTC is an important intergenerational issue. The demand for different types of LTC including home and community-based care will double or triple, as total expenditures for personal care for the elderly are projected to rise by nearly 170 percent between 1991 and 2050 (7, Table 15, p. 39).

DEVOLUTION AND THE ROLE OF GOVERNMENT

The notion of federalism that underlies the decentralization and devolution debate dates back to the nation's beginning. Five consistent and important themes have emerged concerning the role of government: (a) the delineation of national, state, and local responsibilities; (b) the capacity and structural incentives of different governmental levels; (c) equity; (d) accountability; and (e) democratic participation and the distribution of power (8).

The intensity of the current debate about the appropriate role of the government and of the private sector underscores the fundamental questions of national purpose and goals, and the means by which these goals will be achieved. There is continuing dispute about whether devolution reform can in fact achieve national goals other than those related to a reduced federal role in domestic health and social policy. Reagan and Sanzone argue that the "belief that national goals can be achieved by decentralizing subnational choice and policy priorities within the broad federal parameters" is the "myth of decentralization" (9, p. 148).

Today's federal system is a result of "three waves of centralization, launched respectively by Presidents Lincoln, Roosevelt, and Johnson" (10, p. 20). Each wave was born of societal crises: Lincoln's from the crisis of sectionalism; Roosevelt's from the crisis of industrialism; and Johnson's from the crisis of racism. Each gave rise to a distinctive public philosophy shared by a broad coalition, and each shaped intergovernmental roles in a different fashion. Between 1861 and 1930, the dominance or role of the federal government was primarily in the military, foreign policy, monetary, and banking (11). The federal government regulated the economic system while the responsibility for public services was the domain of state governments. This pattern of "dual federalism" was altered over the next four decades as federal income support and other entitlement programs were legislated, with a high degree of public support for such safety-net programs (8, 12). The system that developed shares responsibility for financing and program design between the federal and state governments.

Historically, the justification for the evolving federal role has been that federal grants (a) provide for a necessary equalization in the level of public services among states and localities; (b) provide for a level of services that the national interest requires; (c) reflect the capacity of the national government to collect taxes; and (d) involve national administrators, ensuring performance and competence.

THE DEVOLUTION REVOLUTION

President Nixon introduced revenue sharing and block grants in the early 1970s, commencing the first wave of New Federalism designed to reduce both the federal role and federal funding and to mark the end to the Great Society. The Community Action Program of President Johnson's War on Poverty was replaced by a much more distant form of political participation—opportunities to testify at public hearings. President Reagan reintroduced New Federalism to reduce categorical federal programs through budget cuts and block grants in the 1981 Omnibus Budget Reconciliation Act. Called by some "fend for yourself" federalism (13), devolution in this period was accompanied by declining federal grant-in-aid money to states and localities. As David Stockman, director of the Office of Management and Budget, stated, New Federalism would put an end to the idea that citizens have "any right to legal services or any other kinds of services" (14).

The present wave of decentralization, which one observer has called, "Newt Federalism" (15), reflects a core element of the Contract for America forwarded with the 1994 Republican Congressional and gubernatorial sweep. Welfare reform and other proposals are designed to transfer, and in some cases abolish, the federal role in redistributional outlays across entitlement programs as responsibility is devolved to the states. The impact of the power shift from the nation's capitol to statehouses through welfare reform is augmented by Medicaid cuts, managed care, and the massive restructuring of health care by the private market. The combination of these forces significantly raises the stakes in how the states will exercise their discretion, and explains why the changes afoot are appropriately called the "devolution revolution" (15). Concerns are the extent to which this delegation of authority will result in more versus less responsive programs for the disadvantaged, and in better versus worse planned programs and expenditures (16).

Deregulation is one instrument of devolution that is being used selectively, both legislatively and administratively, to further the goals of devolution. An example is the Unfunded Mandates Reform Act of 1995 that limits federal power to set out future mandates for states, localities, and tribal governments without paying for them. Given that, historically, such Congressionally mandated actions have served as an important mechanism of federal control over state policy without incurring fiscal costs (15, p. 48), the prohibition of unfunded mandates is a highly significant change in federal state relations. Privatization, in the form of shifting responsibility for health care from a right or merit good to a market good, can be seen as another instrument of devolution—although an indirect instrument.

With regard to LTC and other safety-net programs, the devolution or diminution of federal responsibility has six potentially negative effects that are particularly relevant to disadvantaged groups including the elderly (17, pp. 255–260; 18):

1. Decentralization supplants national policy goals and commitments with the more autonomous and variable state and local policy choices, particularly in essential programs for the aging, blunting the more progressive changes that could be more easily generated at the national level rather than across 50 state jurisdictions.

2. With decentralization, the dominant structural economic and political interests operating at the federal level are not likely to be challenged by the fragmented and diverse interest groups for the poor operating at the state and local levels.

3. To the extent that federal (and public sector) responsibility is divested through deregulation and decentralization of policy goal-setting, the influence in policy-making of private sector interests in contrast to public interests is likely to increase. Public policy, especially for the chronically ill and disadvantaged elderly, is mediated in largely invisible ways by business and provider interests.

4. With decentralized policymaking, those who are well-off, best funded and best organized, have the most influence through their ability to mobilize across multiple and dispersed geopolitical jurisdictions.

5. Increased state and local responsibility for programs places human services demands on the most fiscally vulnerable and politically sensitive levels of decision-making, given that states and localities have more variable and limited taxing capacity and fiscal resources than the federal government. Thus, decisions about services for the elderly and low-income, including LTC services, are located precisely where pressures to control social expenses are greatest and necessarily the most conservative. Problems of access to care are likely to increase.

6. Decentralization raises important accountability issues, given that federal oversight and uniform requirements for data give way to highly variable state and local information on programs and the distributional impacts of policy decisions across multiple jurisdictions.

DEVOLUTION AND LONG-TERM CARE

State discretionary policies are a key element in determining LTC services for elders and the younger disabled. States have "potent" levers to affect delivery of LTC services (19), through discretion in their legislative, allocative, administrative, and program functions. The discretionary options in Medicaid and Social Service Block Grants have been augmented by welfare reform in 1996. Policy choices under the domain of the states pose a challenge and dilemma for LTC for two reasons. First, the wide areas of policy discretion and attendant uncertainty permitted under decentralized policies such as welfare, Medicaid, and block grants for social services and mental health produce considerable variability and demonstrably large inequities between the states; and second, issues of accountability arise under conditions of enhanced autonomy, reduced and fragmented data collection, and program variability (17, pp. 17–39).

Political scientists attribute these accountability problems to a "leaking of authority" (20). Related accountability issues are associated with the now-traditional and increasingly used state contracting-out of services once performed by government (21). The concept of "hollow state" describes this separation between government and the services it funds. At the extreme, it "refers to a government that as a matter of public policy . . . contract[s] out all of its production capability to third parties, perhaps retaining only a systems integration function responsible for negotiating, monitoring, and evaluating contracts." The hollow state has a "central task . . . to arrange networks, whereas the traditional task of government is to manage hierarchies" (20). This problem of accountability is the core issue in the recent successful lawsuit against the Health Care Financing Administration concerning its failure to monitor the quality and access to care for Medicare beneficiaries under managed care contracts. The Health Care Financing Administration argued unsuccessfully that, once it had contracted to third-party health maintenance organizations (HMOs), the government had no responsibility for consumer oversight of the contracted programs! A federal judge disagreed and argued that government has a responsibility for assuring that Medicare patients are protected even in the case of HMO contracting.

At the heart of the devolution debate "is a disagreement about which level of government in the federal system should be responsible for designing, implementing, and funding the nation's safety net" (1, p. 3). The increases in decentralized authority for priority-setting and resource allocation resulting from devolution and decategorization may have positive or negative effects for particular target groups or populations such as those needing LTC. The potential exists for increased resources in community-based LTC as states are released from unfunded mandates and other federal requirements. Concurrently, power struggles are escalating among competing groups, with conflicts, trade-offs, and resource losses. This process is particularly hazardous for those repressed interests (22) that are less organized, less powerful, and considered "undeserving."

Under devolution, more "generous" states are penalized, particularly those whose costs of providing higher levels of state-determined benefits are not matched or otherwise shared by the federal government. State generosity (defined as providing benefits or eligibility above the minimum level) is a liability under programs that are federally capped such as block grants, in contrast to those with open-ended federal matching as formerly provided under Medicaid. The eradication of entitlements such as the AFDC program and their replacement by a cash block grant provides a clear financial incentive to states to reduce or restrain their eligibility and costs. Stated another way, block grants and financially capped programs create an economic disincentive for the states to offer anything more than the minimum level of benefits that can be politically accommodated. As Peterson and his colleagues note, "The more control states have over policy choices, and the more they bear the costs of providing welfare or obtain savings from restricting it, the greater the incentives to race" (1, p. 4).

What is known about devolution and aging services? Studies of the effects of Reagan's New Federalism (23) give relatively sparse attention to aging services, with a few exceptions (24–26). Estes and colleagues (27) found that in the 1980s, New Federalism, block grants, and fiscal crises resulted in state-level budget cuts, with the largest proportion of cuts occurring in the human services—including social services, community health services, aging services, and income maintenance programs—rather than other state programs. Services to the elderly, children, and disabled did not receive any preferential treatment in decisions to make cutbacks. State-level cuts were associated with cuts at the local level; thus, problems at one geopolitical level exacerbate problems at another. Social services and health departments responded to budget cuts by decreasing service volume, tightening eligibility, increasing client copayments, and eliminating certain services, each of which affected access to services. State-level fiscal constraints were passed on to service providers. However, political mobilization and organized advocacy made a difference. Programs with strong community grassroots support and active advocacy efforts at the local and state levels lost less funding (were more protected) than did programs without the clout of advocates.

THE RACE TO THE BOTTOM AND LONG-TERM CARE

Given this prior research on devolution and aging services during the 1980s (28) and research on the propensity for states to "race to the bottom" in welfare policy (1, 29), we can summarize the central issues as:

1. The extent to which state-level discretionary policy options alter priorities, services, and other policy outcomes for community-based LTC.
2. The existence and extent of a race to the bottom in LTC in the states.
3. Whether LTC programs and populations are as vulnerable as or more or less vulnerable than other health or welfare programs and populations to cuts and entitlement reforms.
4. The factors that influence the nature and direction of such changes.
5. The trade-offs in and consequences of shifting policy and funding for LTC and its recipients along generational, gender, racial and ethnic, and social class lines (8, 28, 30).
6. The role of managed care and its effects on LTC, including the effects on the "rest" of the nonprofit community-based LTC system (e.g., adult day care, nutrition, and personal assistance).
7. The effects of devolution on the health of communities (population health).
8. The extent and effects of political mobilization of LTC advocates and other advocates on state and local choices (27).

Fiscal Condition of the States

The recent joint report of the National Governors' Association and the National Association of State Budget Officers shows that in 1995, state government year-end balances as a percentage of total expenditures improved from a 25-year low of

1.1 percent in 1991 to the highest level since 1980 (5.7 percent). In 1996, 26 states enacted tax reductions, while only eight enacted tax increases. "Overall, welfare reform in the middle-1990s finds the states in relatively good fiscal condition but with demands for those resources increasing on all fronts" (31, p. 87).

In the face of this good news, the states are pressing forward with a new wave of tax revolt—this time spearheaded by the nation's statehouses. A 1996 survey by the National Governors' Association reports decreases in state support and "losers" among the health and human services, even in states with substantial budgetary surpluses (e.g., California). The present conservative political context, together with the skittishness about the disappearance of work, supports state decisions to provide costly subsidies (tax cuts, infrastructure costs) to business while cutting welfare benefits to pay for them (32). Corporate mergers and downsizing threaten individual workers and state economies, as well as the state politicians. Legitimated by an increasingly strong market ideology, pressures on the states to make fiscal concessions—costing taxpayers millions of dollars—to attract new and retain old businesses are often accepted without question. It is important to note that the research shows little evidence that such concessions produce their desired economic effects; however, they do reduce states' need standards for welfare below levels of minimum adequacy.

Devolution and Nonprofit Sector Services

The partnership between the nonprofit sector (NPS) and government expanded and flourished during the Great Society. By the 1970s, nonprofits were the primary providers of both government and privately financed health and human services. In concert with budget cuts imposed in its early days, the Reagan administration's promotion of voluntarism, paradoxically, was used to initiate the dismantling of what had been a historic partnership between government and nonprofits in the provision of health and human services (33). Thus, Ronald Reagan's legacy was to discipline (34) and to initiate the unraveling of the NPS in the services (35).

Salamon and Abramson note that the Contract with America "threatened to plunge the NPS into fiscal crisis for the rest of the 1990s" (33, p. vii). With Congressional action proposed in 1995, nonprofits were targeted to absorb 55 percent of all budget cuts, which would have amounted to $355 billion lost (and a 28 percent revenue reduction for education and social services) in federal support from 1996 to 2002. A study by Independent Sector showed that services for the aging were to be among the most severely affected. Although these proposals were not adopted in toto, the 1996 appropriations did reduce discretionary spending on programs of interest to nonprofits to 12 percent below 1995 levels (33). Private giving would have had to increase by 15 to 30 percent a year to make up for the direct losses, which is five to ten times the growth rate in private giving. Salamon and Abramson (33) attribute current battles of the sector to a "significant deterioration" in public understanding of the NPS, and lament that support for the NPS is "in danger of eroding."

With regard to the effects of devolution and the NPS response, Julian Wolpert asks: "How should responsibility for maintaining safety nets, amenities, and quality of life be shared between government and charitable institutions?" (36, p. 2).

Wolpert's research on private giving patterns and public support illustrates the inter-actions between NPS health and social services, state and local wealth and fiscal resources, and local values and social preferences (36, p. 2). He reports important variations across states and localities in both government and NPS generosity and "highly uneven support . . . for transfer payments and social services" (36, p. 7). However, he also finds decreasing disparities between metropolitan statistical areas (MSAs) such that the historically more generous places are *reducing* their generosity and becoming more like less generous MSAs in terms of private giving for social services. Such "smoothing" in generosity across places supports the plausibility of the "race to the bottom" for localities as well as states. Because differences in resource capacity and levels of community distress do not predict generosity, serious questions exist about the likely consequences of devolution and decentralized policymaking for populations most in need of community health and human ser-vices. Significantly, also, Wolpert (36) points out the disparity between individual private giving for amenity (leisure and cultural) services (services located in or of benefit to the suburban middle class, which comprises the majority of givers) and individual giving to social services for inner city disadvantaged residents (services for which the need is rising out of proportion to the increase in private and public generosity). Private giving for amenity services for the middle class is rising while that for social services for the inner city disadvantaged is declining.

Nonprofits, Devolution, and Aging Services

A study of the impact of devolution on aging services in the 1980s under Presi-dent Reagan identified seven processes of market and service restructuring of community-based nonprofit health and human services comprising the LTC con-tinuum (37, 38): privatization (decline of public and growth of for-profit providers); competition; rationalization (organizational restructuring and bureaucratization); fragmentation; informalization; medicalization; and stratification of care. As a result of a decade of policy changes, nonprofit LTC services entered the 1990s as a weakened and overburdened delivery system (39). Community nonprofit resources have already undergone almost two decades of cuts and reorganization that have profoundly altered the culture of caring. Nonprofits have been required to initiate and raise fees, tighten eligibility, adopt means to limit charity care, and develop business and other income sources. Some of these actions have challenged public sensibility about nonprofits' charity character and thus entitlement to tax subsidies (40).

Additional criticism of the NPS emanates from the blurring of the boundaries (and differences) between nonprofit and for-profit entities and the diminishing differences between nonprofit and for-profit providers (41, 42). Hansmann's (43) and Salamon's (44) distinction between the two independent sectors, the philanthropic versus the commercial NPS, points to a major source of legitimacy problems for the NPS in health care—the wealth and influence of large nonprofit health and hospital entities contrasted with their levels of charity care, and increasing competition with for-profit medical corporations that pushed the nonprofits into isomorphic behavior more like that of their for-profit medical corporate competitors (42). The rising number of conversions of nonprofit to for-profit medical corporations has fanned the flames of concern about both for-profit and nonprofit medical care companies, and has heightened the need for accountability regarding the accurate determination and disposition of assets developed with the assistance of tax subsidies for nonprofit medical entities such as Blue Cross (45, 46). Attacks on the legitimacy of the NPS have quickened, especially in arenas of greatest proprietary interest and profits—medical care and managed care. Home care is another major growth industry for proprietary corporations in which the power and influence of both nonprofit and public agencies have been eclipsed by for-profits (47).

The attack on nonprofits, and the debilitating effects of 15 years of policy directed at diluting the federal role and constraining the funding of social services, has contributed to a sense of crisis in LTC (39). McCormack (48) aptly describes the present "storm clouds over nonprofits": nonprofits are increasingly financially pressed and the incentives have changed. This is occurring at a time when, according to McCormack, "Needs will explode" with the demographics of aging. McCormack notes that "There is no credible example of state or federal recognition of this demographic reality." Further, he observes, "The middle class will be restless" with the result that middle-class entitlements, and the traditional favorites of tax cuts, property tax reversions, and higher education funding, "will be expanded only at a direct cost to programs aimed at the poor" (48, pp. 5–6).

Change has been accelerating, and for nonprofits operating in health and LTC, these changes are more profound than ever. The attacks on nonprofits that initiated delegitimation crisis tendencies early in the 1980s (40) reached a new intensity in the form of the Istook Amendment proposed in the 104th Congress. It would have prohibited organizations from educating and advocating for their constituencies if they received any federal funding. The commitment of the Republican Congress to this form of repression of nonprofit voices was so strong that Congress risked two separate episodes of the closing of government and continuing resolutions in an attempt to force the President to sign a budget bill containing this amendment. Renewed efforts in the 105th and future Congressional sessions will attempt to defund nonprofits that speak out. Whether or not such initiatives become law, they have already had a "chilling effect" on the voices of nonprofits, and most likely the resources available to them.

LONG-TERM CARE IN THE CONTEXT OF MANAGED CARE

Medicalization and Managed Care

The rapid growth of managed care raises larger questions about long-term care. Among the most salient for the elderly and disabled are whether all or particular elements of the LTC continuum will be more or less accessible under managed care; how those needing LTC will fare; and what the health outcomes, cost, and quality of LTC will be under managed care compared with the fee-for-service system or other alternatives. Another issue concerns whether capitation will freeze out social services. Will managed care bring the hypothetically promised service integration, including LTC and other social supportive services?

Given the newness and rapidity of the development of managed care and its use by an increasing number of states and localities to cut Medicaid and other public sector costs (e.g., mental health), there is a growing need for knowledge about the role of managed care organizations and their effects on the health and human services that make up the LTC continuum of services. Among the significant questions are the effects of managed care organizations on the traditional nonprofit community-based social supportive services and their potential to medicalize social services (30).

Because of Medicaid state contracting with managed care and other block grant decisions, social services may be reduced or lost all together. Managed care entities, although organized differently from fee-for-service medicine, are culturally committed to the same acute care medical model. Managed care organizations will redefine the social support needs of older patients in medical terms (if they are defined as service eligible at all) in order for such services to be provided under their plans. Services will have to be justified in terms of the bottom line—the acute-care costs saved or profits. Social services are not likely to "save" acute care dollars; they have historically been justified as serving other purposes, such as improving the quality of life or easing the burden on other family members. Social services have not been the subject of much research in general; thus, most such services have not been demonstrated as profitable or beneficial in the rather narrow cost-benefit "metric" of medical outcomes research.

The growth of managed care and HMOs will increase the utilization control over various elements of the LTC system, particularly for those services that are brought into the managed care system. The power shifts from government and fee-for- service to insurers and the managed care industry will be extremely consequential for all services that come under the managed care umbrella, including LTC. Post-acute, subacute, and acute care services will continue to move from hospital to home. Medicare and Medicaid cuts, welfare reform, and increased state discretion and power will exert downward pressure on what little reimbursement there is for home and community-based services unless their cost savings for insurers and managed care are proven.

Managed Care, the Free Rider Problem, and Long-Term Care

The free rider problem has been described as a situation in which people "free ride" (49) or "mooch" on the system (50) without paying their way. Here, the question is whether managed care is "free riding" on community-based services. At issue are the new "uses" and support that managed care organizations are extracting from home and community-based LTC services in their drive to further reduce costly lengths of stay in hospitals and in their use of outpatient surgical procedures. How many community-based social supportive service resources and what increases in the informal (family and friends) care burden (work) will result from the drive by managed care organizations to improve the bottom line? How much, if any, of the profits or "saved" resources generated by managed care will be transferred to compensate or pay for the increased home and community-based LTC services drawn upon to maximize the cost savings of individual managed care corporations?

The situation may be appropriately described using O'Connor's (51) concepts of the "socialization of the costs" and "privatization of the profits" of business. The costs being socialized and passed on to the public include the government's funding of medical care (about 40 percent of expenditures), tax subsidies for health insurance (exceeding $30 billion), the public costs for the uninsured that are not paid for through the private market, and managed care corporations "mooching" off the increasingly stressed community delivery system—a public resource largely funded by public monies and operated through the nonprofit sector. Examples of the privatization of the profits of business include managed care companies raking in the profits extracted from their operations and not plowing them back into the health care sector, but instead paying them out in stockholder dividends and extravagant CEO salaries and stock options. In other words, managed care entities pass on significant public costs both to the public and to individual patients and families through their decisions, such as "drive by" or "drive through" deliveries and mastectomies that "dump" patients out of medical facilities when they still require considerable health and supportive care—caring work extracted from the family and community that is not paid for by the managed care entities.

Today's question is whether there is a deleterious process of "dumping" and "bumping down" of older persons out of managed care settings and onto the community-based LTC system and the unpaid work of women and families. A related question is whether the changes under managed care will create their own social "iatrogenic" effects through the production of increased forms of dependency among patients and, more broadly, within the population. Such dependency may result from inadequate social and rehabilitative support for elders to enable them to achieve reasonable functional levels and self-esteem (52). Recent research on the poorer outcomes of HMOs than of fee-for-service for home health care (53), and research by Ware and colleagues (54) showing that older and disabled patients experience worse outcomes in managed care (HMOs) than in fee-for-service, heighten the salience of concerns about the outcomes of managed care for the elderly. Will access to LTC become an even greater problem under managed care? And what interventions do policymakers need to adopt to address this problem?

THE FUTURE OF LONG-TERM CARE

A key question in the area of aging and long-term care is whether those traditionally seen as more deserving—older persons in general and the aged, blind, and disabled under Supplemental Security Income (SSI)—are being reconstructed as less deserving as larger political and economic interests promote the social construction of the "intergenerational war." This, too, is an empirical question. Will the "center" hold on entitlements for groups other than the welfare population? Or does the same fate await programs for the elderly as for welfare recipients, whether on SSI, Social Security, or Medicare?

With regard to devolution, questions are whether and how states will use their policy discretion to rebalance the growing gap between funds available to support the social services and funds for acute care services in order to assure an LTC continuum. Block grants and budget stringencies at different governmental levels have decreased available funds for social supportive services to address the new needs created by three forces operating simultaneously: (*a*) shorter and shorter hospital lengths of stay, now projected to decline another 50 percent in the next few years; (*b*) increased pressures from technological advances and managed care corporations for more home and community-based care; and (*c*) the socio-demographics of the aging and disabled populations. In 1996 welfare reform imposed cuts on Title XX Social Services Block Grant funds. These were added to cuts carried out in the early 1980s under President Reagan. Older Americans Act funding has remained fairly constant in absolute dollars, but inflation-adjusted funding for this line of social service has declined about 30 percent since the 1980s. Over time, much of the social service funding has been shifted to Medicaid waiver programs. As described earlier, the potential new free rider problem in community-based LTC under managed care also raises significant questions. The fate of the social services under managed care, increased state discretion, and Medicaid policy changes yet to come is unclear.

With politically and economically motivated attacks on entitlement, the fates of Medicare and Medicaid entitlements, and health reform more broadly, are inextricably entwined with the future of LTC. The challenge to the LTC population, workers, and advocates is profound. The larger goal of LTC policy must address the social as well as the economic objectives, including an approach that is empowering to consumers rather than dependency generating and does not exploit families or the largely nonprofit community-based social service system that is a core element of the safety net. Our approach to LTC recipients and LTC workers (informal and formal) alike must be one that is socially just, one that promotes gender, ethnic, intergenerational, and class justice through a system that offers long-term care that is accessible, affordable, and universal.

REFERENCES

1. Peterson, P., Rom, M., and Scheve, K. The Race Among the States: Welfare Benefits, 1976–1989. Paper presented at the meeting of the American Political Science Association, San Francisco, August 1996.
2. Dye, T. *Competitive Federalism: Competition Among Governments*. D. C. Heath, Lexington, Mass., 1990.
3. Eisinger, R. *The Rise of the Entrepreneurial State: State and Local Economic Policy in the US*. University of Wisconsin Press, Madison, 1988.
4. Taeuber, C. *Sixty-five Plus in America*. Current Population Reports, pp. 23–178. U.S. Department of Commerce, Economics and Statistics Administration, Washington, D.C., 1992.
5. Manton, K., and Stallard, E. Changes in Health, Mortality, and Disability and Their Impact on Long-Term Care Needs. Paper presented at the Florida State University Conference on Long-Term Care, Tallahassee, 1994.
6. Hoffman, C., Rice, D., and Sung, H. Persons with chronic conditions: Their prevalence and costs. *JAMA* 276(18): 1473–1479, 1996.
7. Rice, D. P. Beneficiary Profile. Paper presented at 30th Anniversary of Medicare Symposium, Lyndon B. Johnson Library, Austin, Texas, May 6, 1996.

8. Estes, C., and Gerard, L. Governmental responsibility: Issues of reform and federalism. In *Fiscal Austerity and Aging*, edited by C. Estes et al., pp. 17–40. Sage, Beverly Hills, 1983.

9. Reagan, M., and Sanzone, J. *The New Federalism*. Oxford University Press, New York, 1981.

10. Beer, S. *Federalism: Lessons of the Past, Choices for the Future*. Center for National Policy, Washington, D.C., 1982.

11. Walker, A. Towards a political economy of old age. *Ageing Soc.* 1(1): 73–94, 1981.

12. Lee, P., and Benjamin, A. Health policy and the politics of health care. In *The Nation's Health*, Ed. 4, edited by P. Lee and C. Estes, pp. 121–136. Jones and Bartlett, Sudbury, Mass., 1994.

13. Shannon, J. Fend for yourself (new) federalism. In *Perspectives on Federalism*, edited by H. Sheiber. Institute for Governmental Studies, University of California, Berkeley, 1987.

14. Stockman, D. Testimony in U.S. Senate Hearings, 1983, p. 363.

15. Nathan, R., et al. The "nonprofitization movement" as a form of devolution. In *Capacity for Change? The Nonprofit World in the Age of Devolution*, edited by D. Burlingame et al., pp. 23–56. New Partnership Conferences, Indiana University Center on Philanthropy, Indianapolis, 1996.

16. Estes, C. *The Aging Enterprise*. Jossey-Bass, San Francisco, 1979.

17. Estes, C. The future of aging and public policy: The perspective of a political economist. In *Fiscal Austerity and Aging*, edited by C. Estes et al. Sage, Beverly Hills, 1983.

18. Estes, C. The Reagan legacy: Privatization, the welfare state and aging in the 1990s. In *States, Labor Markets, and the Future of Old-Age Policy*, edited by J. Myles and J. Quadagno, pp. 59–83. Temple University Press, Philadelphia, 1991.

19. Beer, S. Federalism, nationalism, and democracy in America. *Am. Polit. Sci. Rev.* 71(1): 9–21, 1978.

20. Bardach, E., and Lesser, C. Accountability in human services collaborative—for what? And to whom? *J. Public Admin. Res. Theory* 6(2): 193–194, 1996.

21. Smith, S., and Lipsky, M. *Nonprofits for Hire: The Welfare State in the Age of Contracting*. Harvard University Press, Cambridge, Mass., 1993.

22. Alford, R. The political economy of health care: Dynamics without change. *Polit. Soc.* 2: 127–164, 1972.

23. Palmer, J. (ed.). *Perspectives on the Reagan Years*. Urban Institute Press, Washington, D.C., 1986.

24. Storey, J. *Older Americans in the Reagan Era*. Urban Institute Press, Washington, D.C., 1983.

25. Estes, C., et al. *Fiscal Austerity and Aging: Shifting Government Responsibility for the Elderly*. Sage, Beverly Hills, 1983.

26. Swan, J., and Estes, C. Fiscal crisis and aging services. In *Fiscal Austerity and Aging*, edited by C. Estes et al. Sage, Beverly Hills, 1983.

27. Estes, C., et al. *Fiscal Crisis: Impact on Aging Services. Final Report*. Aging Health Policy Center, San Francisco, 1982.

28. Estes, C. Austerity and aging in the United States: 1980 and beyond. In *Old Age and the Welfare State*, edited by A. M. Guillemard, pp. 169–185. Sage, Beverly Hills, 1983.

29. Peterson, P., and Rom, M. *Welfare Magnets: A New Case for a National Standard*. Brookings Institute, Washington, D.C., 1990.

30. Polivka, L., Dunlop, B., and Rothman, M. *Long-Term Care for the Frail Elderly in Florida: Expanding Choices, Containing Costs*. Long-Term Care Policy Series. Florida Policy Exchange Center on Aging, University of South Florida, Tampa, 1996.

31. Luce, T. Jr. The capacity of state and local governments to respond to reductions in federal support for welfare. In *Capacity for Change? The Nonprofit World in the Age of Devolution*, edited by D. Burlingame et al., pp. 81–93. New Partnership Conferences. Indiana University Center on Philanthropy, Indianapolis, 1996.

32. Hartman, J., and Hanson, R. The New Federalism and the Mean Season: Modeling the Business Climate/Welfare Trade-off. Paper presented at the annual meetings of the American Sociological Association, Washington, D.C., 1995.

33. Salamon, L., and Abramson, A. The federal budget and the nonprofit sector: Implications of the Contract with America. In *Capacity for Change? The Nonprofit World in the Age of Devolution*, edited by D. Burlingame et al., pp. 1–22. New Partnership Conferences. Indiana University Center on Philanthropy, Indianapolis, 1996.

34. Estes, C. The aging enterprise revisited. *Gerontologist* 3(3): 292–298, 1993.

35. Estes, C., and Bergthold, C. The unraveling of the nonprofit sector in the U.S. *Int. J. Sociol. Soc. Policy* 9(213): 18–33, 1989.

36. Wolpert, J. *Patterns of Generosity in America: Who's Holding the Safety Net?* Twentieth Century Fund, New York, 1993.

37. Estes, C. The politics of ageing in America. *Ageing Soc.* 6: 121–134, 1986.

38. Estes, C., and Binney, E. Restructuring of the nonprofit sector. In *The Long Term Care Crisis: Elders Trapped in the No-Care Zone*, pp. 22–42. Sage, Newbury Park, Calif., 1993.

39. Estes, C., et al. *The Long Term Care Crisis: Elders Trapped in the No-Care Zone.* Sage, Newbury Park, Calif., 1993.

40. Estes, C., Binney, E., and Bergthold, L. How the legitimacy of the sector has eroded. In *The Future of the Nonprofit Sector*, edited by V. A. Hodgkinson et al., pp. 21–40. Jossey-Bass, San Francisco, 1989.

41. Estes, C., and Alford, R. Systemic crisis and the nonprofit sector: Toward a political economy of the nonprofit health and social services sector. *Theory Soc.* 19: 173–198, 1990.

42. Estes, C., and Swan, J. Privatization and access to home health care. *Milbank Q.* 72: 2, 1994.

43. Hansmann, H. The two independent sectors. In *Looking Forward to the Year 2000: Public Policy and Philanthropy*, pp. 15–24. Spring Research Forum Working Papers. Independent Sector, Washington, D.C., 1988.

44. Salamon, L. The Voluntary Sector and the Future of the Welfare State: Some Initial Thoughts. Paper presented at the Spring Research Forum, Independent Sector, San Francisco, 1988.

45. Families USA Foundation. *States of Health*, Vol. 6. Boston, September 1996.

46. Managed care: Buyout fever, merger mania. *Health Lett.* 11(12), December 1995.

47. Estes, C. The Future of Home Health Care. Paper presented at the University of Florida, 1996.

48. McCormack, P. Nonprofits at the brink: Lean budgets, growing needs, and the fate of nonprofits. *Northwest Report 20*, pp. 1–6. Northwest Area Foundations, St. Paul, Minn., 1996.

49. Enthoven, A., and Kronick, R. Universal health insurance through incentive reform. In *The Nation's Health*, Ed. 5, edited by P. Lee and C. Estes. Jones and Bartlett, Sudbury, Mass., 1997.

50. Reinhardt, U. The rise and fall of health care reform: A dialogue between Mark Pauly and Uwe Reinhardt. In *Looking Backward, Looking Forward: "Staying Power" Issues in Health Care Reform*. The Richard and Hinda Rosenthal Lectures 1994–1995. National Academy Press, Washington, D.C., 1996.

51. O'Connor, J. *The Fiscal Crisis of the State*. St. Martin's, New York, 1973.
52. Estes, C. Long-term care is mainstream. Why isolate it from acute care? In *Perspective on Aging*, pp. 4–8. National Council on Aging, Washington, D.C., 1990.
53. Shaughnessey, P., et al. Home health care outcomes under capitated and fee for service payment. *Health Care Financ. Rev.* 16(1): 187–221, 1994.
54. Ware, J., et al. Differences in 4-year health outcomes for the elderly and poor, chronically ill patients treated in HMO and fee-for-service systems. Results from the Medical Outcomes Survey. *JAMA* 276(13): 1039–1047, 1996.

CHAPTER 10

Impacts of the Proposed Restructuring of Medicare and Medicaid on the Elderly: A Conceptual Framework and Analysis

Marty Lynch and Meredith Minkler

Among the groups likely to be hardest hit by the proposed restructuring of the U.S. welfare state are the elderly. Although initial discussion of deep cuts in Social Security proved politically unfeasible, proposals for major cutbacks in other vital health and welfare programs did not. As a consequence, and couched in the language of presenting a bold and fresh approach to America's health and social problems, the Republican Congress was able to propose, and gain a serious hearing for, measures that would have culminated in the most dramatic transformations in the U.S. health and welfare landscape in half a century. The Congressional proposals catalyzed a number of countermeasures which, while not as extreme as the Republican originals, also would have the effect of significantly altering key welfare state programs.

This chapter examines the principal competing proposals for transforming two major programs, Medicare and Medicaid, as these will have a great effect on the nation's 33 million elders. We begin, however, by presenting a broad conceptual framework within which to better understand the current upheavals. For in the last analysis, it is this broader contextual understanding that offers us a deeper grasp of the significance of what is being attempted and the political and economic climate that has both reflected and reinforced it. Following the development of a theoretical framework and a discussion of the major competing Medicare and Medicaid proposals, we examine the proposals' likely differential impacts on the elderly. We address in particular the effects these measures would be likely to have on vulnerable subgroups within the elderly population, including the low-income elderly and those who bear the greatest burden of illness and disability.

This chapter is reprinted from *International Journal of Health Services*, Volume 27, Number 1, Pages 57–75, 1997.

186 / Critical Gerontology

CONCEPTUAL FRAMEWORK

Central to an understanding of the proposed restructuring of Medicare and Medicaid are a number of key tenets of the political economy of aging. As Estes has pointed out (1):

> the political economy of aging offers a theoretical and empirical perspective on the socioeconomic determinants of the experience of aging and old age and on the policy interventions that emerge in the context of capitalist society. . . . A major contribution of this work is its illumination of how social policy for the aged mirrors the structural arrangements of U.S. society and the distribution of material, political, and ideological resources within it.

Because older people are, as a group, more dependent on state policy than are younger people, the role and functions of the state, and particularly its legitimation functions with respect to resource and benefit allocation, play a pivotal role in the political economy of aging (1). In this regard, O'Connor's (2) perspective on the shifting of government away from a major emphasis on its legitimation functions and toward its functions in the realm of capital accumulation is helpful in better illuminating the meaning and significance of the proposed restructuring of Medicare and Medicaid, and its impacts on the elderly. Briefly, O'Connor has argued that government budget decisions can be examined in terms of the political-economic interests they serve. Growing demands for government to meet the needs of important business interests while also attempting to maintain social programs lead to expenditures outstripping tax revenues with resulting deficits and government fiscal crises. There is a tension between government expenditures that primarily promote profitable accumulation and those that are required to promote social harmony in the society (2). Expenditures for the elderly tend to fall into this latter category and, although they may provide business opportunities for the for-profit medical and service industry, are not aimed primarily at improving the economic climate. Of course, Republican leaders such as House Speaker Newt Gingrich and presidential contender Bob Dole did not pose the public debate in terms of these interests directly competing over limited government resources. Rather, they spoke in terms of the common-sense need to have a balanced budget that would not saddle our children and grandchildren with debt. This is consistent with O'Connor's premise that direct and obvious support for corporate and wealthy interest groups is not politically acceptable to most of the population and must be couched in other terms (2).

Miller's (3) notions concerning the expansion and contracting of social problems in accordance with the needs of the national economy also have relevance for our analysis of the proposed restructuring of Medicare and Medicaid. Whereas in economically "fat times" health and social problems are defined broadly, with correspondingly broad-based "solutions" such as Medicare and Medicaid attempted, in times of real or perceived scarcity such problems are redefined in ways that permit contracted and less costly approaches. By defining "the problem" in terms not of lack of equity and access to health care but rather of "too much government" and the need for fostering decentralization, privatization, and individual responsibility, the

Republican Congress has made the case for major policy shifts in this direction. As Kingson and Quadagno have argued, the strategy of tying programs like Medicare and Medicaid "to the rhetoric of an 'entitlement crisis' is a carefully conceived and executed strategy to shrink federal government and advance the idea that radical reforms are needed" (4).

Helping to undergird these ideological arguments were, of course, claims by the right that the 1994 elections, which brought a majority of Republicans to the House and Senate for the first time in 40 years, constituted an historic mandate in support of the Party's "Contract with America." Although the latter referred specifically to ten legislative measures which the Republicans hoped to pass in their first 100 days in office, "the Contract" quickly became shorthand for an overall philosophy and approach that stressed the radical restructuring of many entitlement and safety-net programs for the poor, a harsher penal system, and tax cuts for the wealthy. The claim of an historic mandate for the right's Contract with America posited a shift in basic moral economy notions of what is "due" the elderly, the poor, the disabled, and other subgroups on the part of the American public at large. The concept of moral economy indeed enriches our understanding of the current reforms, in having us look more deeply at the collectively shared moral assumptions underlying norms of reciprocity in which a society is grounded (5, 6). In Deborah Stone's words (7):

> the moral economy of a society is its set of beliefs about what constitutes just exchange: not only about how economic exchange is to be conducted in normal times, but also . . . when poor individuals are entitled to social aid, when better off people are obligated to provide care, and what kinds of claims anyone—landowners, employers, government—can legitimately make on the surplus product of anyone else.

In relation to the current politics of retrenchment, a moral economy perspective would have us reflect on the degree to which these politics do or do not reflect changes in some of the most basic value premises underlying U.S. health and welfare policy.

Finally, and drawing on both moral and political economy, attention to notions of the "deserving" versus the "undeserving" poor, elderly, and so forth (8, 9) enhances our theoretical framework for examining the proposed restructuring of Medicare and Medicaid and its impacts on the elderly. As Katz (8) has argued, a long tradition in U.S. health and welfare policy has involved carefully distinguishing between deserving and undeserving subgroups in the population and developing different programs or policies for people on the basis of whether they are seen as fitting within one or the other of these categories. Like the British before us, Americans have had a preoccupation with worthiness that has often made it a primary consideration in policy deliberations.

As we suggest below, proposed policy shifts with regard to Medicare and Medicaid represent a bifurcation in care (10), with a new system of often attractive options developed for the deserving elderly (in this case, those who have saved and are financially better off) and further reductions in care and care options for the less deserving or low-income elderly. In examining the alternative proposals for transforming Medicare and Medicaid and their differential impacts on elders, special attention should be devoted to examining how perceptions of "deservingness" are implicitly or explicitly embedded in who benefits and who pays.

THE "CONTRACT WITH AMERICA" 'S ATTEMPT TO RECREATE MEDICARE AND MEDICAID IN ITS IMAGE

In the battle to shift public resources to the profit-making accumulation functions of the economy (2), the Republican agenda has made Medicare and Medicaid primary targets. These programs control billions of dollars and they also symbolize a much earlier and different contract with America, the social contract initiated during the New Deal and continued in the War on Poverty. The 30-year-old Medicare program largely has eliminated racial differences in care of the elderly. And despite continuing inadequacies in coverage, Medicare and Medicaid have dramatically improved access to health care and health care financing for the programs' 70 million current elderly and low-income beneficiaries (11).

Attacks on Medicare and Medicaid are in some ways the signal effort of the Gingrich Congress. Social insurance programs that were heretofor sacrosanct are now fair game (4). The social contract with working America can and will be broken at the same time as the health industry is handed billions in privatized public dollars (12). Successfully questioning basic tenets of the Medicare program paves the way for attacks on the other major program (and icon) of the U.S. social contract, Social Security. Indeed, recent proposals to partially privatize Social Security represent the greatest potential change in this social insurance program since its inception in 1935.

Parallel attempts to gut Medicaid protections in the Republican and the National Governors' Association proposals signal that basic services for a group widely regarded as being among the "deserving" poor—elders who have become impoverished by nursing home costs—will not be guaranteed by the federal government. Together the attacks on Medicare and Medicaid indicate that the U.S. budget struggle is being lost by those interested in the service/legitimation function of government in favor of promoting the increased profitability of certain sectors of the economy. Wall Street, and especially health maintenance organizations (HMOs) and the pharmaceutical industry, do well, while low-income elders will pay more for their health care (13).

The Proposals

Although Medicare and Medicaid legislation has not been enacted as this chapter is being written, general trends are apparent in legislation proposed by Republicans and Democrats alike. We will review these proposals for Medicare and Medicaid and then draw out the common threads and the potential impacts on the most vulnerable segments of the elderly population.

Medicare. The two competing proposals come from the Gingrich- and Dole-led Republicans and from President Clinton (Table 1). They both propose major cuts in the Medicare program over the next seven years. These cuts range from $100 billion

Table 1

Medicare restructuring proposals

	Congressional proposal	Clinton proposal
Amount cut over 7 years	$270 billion	$100 billion
HMO enrollment	Encourage	Encourage
Medical Savings Accounts	Yes	No
Part B premiums	Increase to 33%	Stay at 25%
Copays and deductibles in traditional Medicare	Increase	Increase, but less than Congress
Provider payments	Ratchet down hospital and M.D. payments	Control hospital and M.D. payments
Graduate medical education	Decrease payments	Decrease payments
Provider flexibility	Ease requirements to set up managed care networks; allow referral to M.D.-owned businesses	Current standards
New disease prevention and management benefits	No new benefits	Several new disease prevention and management benefits including limited respite care

in the president's proposal to $158 billion in the Republicans' modified proposal (May 1996) and $270 billion in the latter's initial proposal. Although the Republicans argued early on that cuts at the high end of this range would be needed to save Medicare, less than half of the $270 billion in savings would have reached the Medicare trust fund under their original proposal, with much of it going to help finance large tax cuts. An analysis by the consumer group Families USA thus demonstrated that 54 percent of the tax cuts in the Contract with America, which include most prominently deep cuts in Medicare and Medicaid, would have gone to those earning more than $100,000 per year (14).

Both Republican and White House proposals rely heavily on a shift of Medicare beneficiaries from traditional fee-for-service Medicare to at-risk HMOs with the hope that these HMOs will save money by reducing inappropriate use of services. Republican proposals also called for the introduction of medical savings accounts (MSAs) that would allow healthy beneficiaries to buy high-deductible catastrophic care insurance policies and bank the savings. The approval of the Kassebaum–Kennedy health insurance bill, which enables 750,000 Americans to purchase such policies on an experimental basis, increases the likelihood of this option being further extended in the future.

Dramatically increased beneficiary cost-sharing through higher Medicare premiums, copayments, and deductibles also were proposed. Under the original Republican plan, for example, an estimated $55 billion of the Medicare "savings" would come from the elderly, whose share of premiums would nearly double to over $1,000 per person annually by 2002. Although an eleventh hour change would have resulted in the wealthier elderly paying more, and in some cases all of their Part B premiums (for outpatient care), the overall impact of the proposed cut would be disproportionately borne by the less "deserving" low-income elderly.

Other important features of the Republican proposal included providing physicians with added flexibility to form their own HMO-type networks, and reducing controls on self-referral to physician-owned businesses. Although details of reduced payments to hospitals and doctors were not specified, these measures were designed to mitigate the deleterious effects of prospective cuts in physicians' incomes.

Another critical aspect of the Republican plan involves its proposed reductions in disproportionate share hospital payments to hospitals that serve a large number of poor people. As discussed below, this feature of the plan would have a particularly deleterious impact on public hospitals in inner city and rural areas. Similarly, proposed reductions in graduate medical education payments represent yet another part of the plan for overhauling Medicare that also would harm the low-income elderly by adversely affecting teaching hospitals, which often serve the poor (Table 1).

As noted above, the Clinton plan for Medicare as it appears in the March 1996 balanced budget plan is similar to the Congressional proposal in several ways, including, most importantly, the heavy emphasis it places on managed care. The White House plan would also reduce payments to hospitals, M.D.s, and other providers, though without going as far as the Republicans in actually ratcheting down such payments (Table 1). And like the Congressional proposal, the Clinton plan would "reform" financing for graduate medical education and training provided by the nation's academic health centers and teaching hospitals. At the same time, however, important differences exist between the two proposals. The Clinton plan thus strongly opposed MSAs and would maintain rather than relax current regulations on physician self-referral and the setting up of managed care networks. Under the White House plan, Medicare premiums would remain at 25 percent of program costs, rather than being raised. New, albeit only modestly increased preventive care would be covered under Clinton's plan, including annual mammograms for beneficiaries aged 50 and over; a waiver of cost sharing for mammography; several procedures for early detection of colorectal cancer; glucose monitors and associated supplies and professional assistance for managing diabetes; and increased payments for preventive injections. The White House proposal also includes a new respite care benefit for beneficiaries with Alzheimer's disease or other irreversible dementias, amounting to 32 hours per year of nonmedical respite for their family caregivers.

Despite these added benefits, the White House plan insists that it will impose "no new cost increases on Medicare beneficiares." As noted below, however, many analysts remain highly skeptical of this claim.

The proposals to transform Medicare have been critiqued on numerous grounds, key among them what many see as a misguided overemphasis on managed care. As

Oberlander has pointed out, "enrollment in Medicare at risk plans has grown rapidly in recent years, averaging 22% annually from 1992–1995" (15). But as Commonwealth Fund President Karen Davis (11) has noted, the wide variation in per capita Medicare expenditures—from $28,120 in outlays for the sickest 10 percent in 1993 to just $1,340 for the healthiest 90 percent—gives HMOs and other managed care plans a strong incentive to enroll only the healthiest beneficiaries. As a consequence, taxpayers will likely end up paying more rather than less money if the proposals are enacted. The possibility of increased rather than decreased costs was further underscored by Johns Hopkins professor Vicente Navarro (16), who has noted that "managed care is simply a different name for the reforms adopted in the early 1970's by the Nixon Administration as the Republican alternative to a single payer proposal." As Navarro went on to note, although two-thirds of Americans were enrolled in managed care plans by the early 1990s, costs during this period have risen faster than ever, while coverage has decreased.

In a strongly worded critique of the original Republican Medicare proposal, Harvard professor Steffie Woolhandler (17) predicted that the plan would "unleash a frenzy of risk selection by insurers/HMOs," whose "cherry picking" of the healthiest seniors would leave sicker patients, who are less willing to change physicians, concentrated in the traditional Medicare program. She added that (17):

> Medical savings accounts will further shrink the funds available for care of the frail elderly, as they will attract only the healthiest seniors, and end up costing Medicare funds that would not otherwise have been spent. As provider reimbursement is ratcheted down by the Republicans to meet the budgetary "fail safe," traditional Medicare will be left looking a lot like Medicaid, where measures of access to care are no better than for the uninsured.

As will be discussed later, real and potential problems of underregulation and underprovision of care for elderly patients with chronic illnesses have been cited (15).

Finally, an important criticism of both the Republican and the president's proposals for Medicare is that neither addresses the effects these measures are likely to have on the costs to the elderly who wish to remain in traditional Medicare of the supplemental insurance or "Medi-gap" policies that the vast majority of seniors now own. Yet in 1996 alone, in anticipation of significant changes in Medicare, major supplemental insurance companies announced premium increases amounting to 30 percent (18).

In sum, and whether one examines the original Republican proposal or the more modest Clinton counterproposal, dramatic changes are in store for Medicare which, as noted below, will affect most harshly the less "deserving" low-income elderly and other vulnerable groups.

Medicaid. In the Medicaid arena the Republicans and the National Governors' Association have put forth similar proposals, which although differing slightly in approach would have a similar effect (Table 2).

These proposals would change the Medicaid program from a federal entitlement program to either a block grant or a lump sum payment program to the states. The

Table 2

Competing Medicaid restructuring proposals

	Congressional reconciliation proposal	Clinton proposal	National Governors' proposal
Approach	Block grant to states	Capped entitlement	Lump sum payment to states
Amount cut over 7 years	$163 billion	$54 billion	Undetermined
Federal entitlement	Pregnant women, children under 13, disabled (as defined by states); eliminates for others	Maintains current entitlements	Pregnant women, children to 12, frail elders, disabled (as defined by states)
State flexibility	Eliminates mandated services, free choice of providers, provider rate standards; allows higher copays	Allows mandated managed care enrollment, more flexibility for HMOs; maintains restrictions on state match	Reduces mandatory services; allows mandated HMO enrollment; eliminates provider rate standards; no restrictions on how match is met
State match and maintenance of effort	85% of 1992–94 expenditures	Same match, but federal spending growth capped	Reduces maximum match to 40%
Nursing home standards	Allows more state flexibility	Maintains existing standards	Maintains standards but allows state discretion on enforcement
Immigrants	State option to provide emergency services to undocumented and full services to legal; new funds for states' costs	Maintains existing standards; new funds for states with most immigrants	No provisions

federal contribution would be allowed to rise more slowly than recent expenditure increases. Under the National Governors' Association proposal the amount of state match required would be reduced to a maximum of 40 percent from the current 50–50 level, potentially reducing available dollars in the program. Although agreement on welfare reform legislation seems to indicate that an individual Medicaid entitlement will remain in place, albeit for fewer people, it is quite possible that block grant proposals will once again surface after the 1996 election.

These proposals also would allow states to define eligibility and benefits, with potentially devastating impacts on users. For example, the National Long Term Care

Campaign estimates that only 15 percent of the current long-term care dollars spent by Medicaid would be guaranteed if the governors' proposal was to be adopted (19). This is because definitions of disability set by the state would likely be more restrictive than current federal definitions. Also, older people above the poverty level who now spend all of their income on nursing home share-of-cost payments would no longer be guaranteed coverage. This group uses 85 percent of current Medicaid long-term care expenditures (19). Finally, as Riley has pointed out, "Medicaid today makes Medicare work, paying the cost-sharing for one in ten elderly and disabled who receive Medicare" (20). If states slash these cost-sharing payments, particularly at a time when Medicare's premiums and deductibles are expected to increase significantly, access to health care for the low-income elderly and disabled will be further cut back. Subgroups with lower incomes and greater functional limitations, among them women, elders of color, and the "oldest old" (85 and over), would be particularly disadvantaged. Finally, passage of a "welfare reform" bill promises to remove even legal immigrants from Medicaid and other "welfare" programs. This bill will have a particularly devastating effect on the health and welfare of this large population subgroup. It would curtail SSI payments for legal immigrants and remove entitlement to Medicaid, including coverage for nursing home as well as home and community care benefits. In California fully one-third of aged and disabled SSI recipients fit this category of legal immigrants (21). Trying to patch this hole in the safety net will be next to impossible. Although Clinton has vowed to "fix" the harshest components of the welfare reform bill he signed, it is unclear whether this fixing will include restoration of Medicaid benefits for elderly and other legal immigrants (22).

States may, of course, continue to cover the groups formerly covered with the same benefit package. But there is great fear that as state budget crises occur, dollars might be shifted to more politically conservative programs, such as prisons, which typically are important to many Republican governors and legislators.

All current proposals would give the states more flexibility, allowing them, for example, to shift recipients into mandatory managed care programs. Most states already have begun this process by mandating that women and children on Aid to Families with Dependent Children (AFDC) join HMOs. At least ten states are now exploring moving their aged and disabled populations into mandatory HMO enrollment (23), creating problems we will discuss below.

All of the current Medicaid proposals also call for the reduction or elimination of certain programs that now serve low-income elders. These include the Federally Qualified Health Center program, which supports community health centers in inner city and rural areas, and the earlier mentioned disproportionate-share hospital monies, which are critical in supporting public and community hospitals in low-income and medically underserved areas of the country.

Despite similar trends in all of the proposals, there is still a significant difference between the Republican and the Governors' (a majority of whom are Republican) proposals and the Clinton proposal, as indicated in Table 2. Clinton would maintain a federal entitlement to Medicaid-covered services with set definitions of eligibility and some required services. The entitlement would be capped in the sense that the Medicaid federal contribution growth rate would be capped at a lower level than the current one. The Clinton plan would maintain existing nursing home standards and enforcement requirements. Although the Nursing Home Reform Act of 1987 has been only partially implemented, its results have been sizable: the number of nursing home patients who are physically restrained dropped in half, from about 40 percent to about 20 percent; the use of chemical restraints went down by a third; and improvements in nurse and paraprofessional staffing and training have taken place (24). There remains much room for improvement, but relaxing the minimal regulations now in place on this industry in which ten firms control 70 percent of the profits (25) is certainly not going to help.

The proposals would cut amounts ranging from $50 billion to $182 billion from Medicaid over the next seven years. The difference in levels of cuts as well as the continued guarantee of entitlement under the President's plan caused advocates for the elderly, disabled, and low-income people of all ages (26) to strongly support the Clinton proposal as the better of bad options.

Common Threads

There are several common themes in the whole range of Medicare and Medicaid proposals.

1. The major political parties are in agreement that economic belt-tightening is necessary and will come at the expense of health programs for the elderly and the poor. The budgetary struggle between corporations interested in increased profitability and labor and advocacy groups promoting increased government responsibility for health and social services is once again being won by the corporate side. Medicare and Medicaid continue to be treated as fair game in return for tax breaks for the wealthy.

2. There will be restricted spending in both the Medicare and Medicaid programs in the next few years. Political debate concerns how large the cuts will be and the specifics of how they will occur, rather than *if* they will occur.

3. Both Medicare and Medicaid will rely heavily on HMOs as a way to slow the growth in costs. Shifting publicly funded health care to the for-profit HMO arena also opens up the opportunity for corporate health providers and insurers to make billions of dollars (12). The original Republican Medicare proposal, for example, would have funneled anywhere from $84 billion to $189 billion into private insurance companies and for-profit HMOs over the next seven years. This is consistent with the privatization and corporatization of the U.S. health care system (27).

4. Both Medicare and Medicaid will reduce their support for community health centers and inner city hospitals which serve low-income populations and have made up a critical part of the so-called safety net.

HMOs and Low-Income and Disabled Elders. One of the key ways that elders will be affected by the proposed changes in Medicare and Medicaid will involve their enrollment in HMOs. Those elders put most at risk by this change also are those subgroups of the elderly who are most economically vulnerable. Both additional disability and high rates of poverty are associated with very old age (28, 29). Women also tend to be poorer than men, and elders of color poorer than whites (30). For several reasons discussed below, disabled elders and those who are low-income—including disproportionate numbers of women and elders of color—are threatened by the move to managed care.

For the low-income older person, the appearance of choice presented by the development of Medicare HMOs tends to be illusory. Although the Clinton plan argues to the contrary, under all of the legislative proposals, out-of-pocket costs are likely to rise rapidly for those who stay in traditional Medicare. There will therefore be a strong incentive for low-income elders to give up their choice of providers and join an HMO, which they hope will lower their out-of-pocket costs. This is particularly true in some of the large urban markets where Medicare rates paid to HMOs are high and plans are offering $0 premium options which include additional covered services such as limited pharmaceutical benefits (31). Because there is an overlap between those who are most likely to be disabled and to be low-income (i.e., older beneficiaries), giving up choice of specialists or the ability to go to special diagnostic or treatment centers, such as those for Alzheimer's disease, is especially painful. Financially well-off elders with the ability to cover the increased payments in traditional Medicare will not be forced into this choice. This creates a basic inequity problem within the Medicare program, which will only compound existing inequalities in health care due to social class. In 1994, for example, low-income elders paid 34 percent of their incomes on out-of-pocket medical costs, compared with 15 percent for elders in the highest income quartile (32). Such already sizable class differentials in personal expenditures on health costs cast into sharp relief the added problems that further increasing costs for the most economically vulnerable elders would pose.

Elders with complex medical problems and disabilities face additional problems caused by the shift of Medicare and (eventually) Medicaid to an HMO-based system. The Health Care Financing Administration–sponsored evaluation of the early Medicare risk HMO program showed that HMOs were enrolling the healthy elders who would have cost the program 89 percent of the average beneficiary cost in their rate category. The HMOs were then being paid 95 percent of the average cost by Medicare and thus making money even before they reduced utilization (33). As market penetration grows and as Medicaid enrollment in HMOs becomes mandatory, the plans also will enroll those with more difficult health and disability problems. In California, where over 40 percent of Medicare recipients are enrolled in HMOs, compared with 10 percent nationally (34), Medicare HMOs simply take a cut off the top of 15 to 20 percent and pass on all of the risk to the physicians and hospitals. This profit and overhead cost is consistent across the country (35), but the shift of risk also takes away the plan's incentive to cream the healthiest Medicare members, especially as Medicare HMOs struggle to gain dominance in market share. Growth of market share, Medicaid policy, and shifting where the risk resides all make it likely that many more disabled elders will soon be enrolled in HMOs. HMOs have promised more preventive care, but with plans seeking short-term economic gains, it is questionable whether disabled elders will receive any long-term preventive care.

Finally, as an HCFA-sponsored study suggested, even legitimate emergency care coverage may be refused. The study revealed a 40 percent denial rate of claims for emergency care sought by elderly Medicare HMO enrollees. Fully half of these denials were reversed upon further review (36).

The disabled of all ages face a number of special problems in the HMO arena. They are the ones most likely to need broad access to specialists, second opinions, and focused services. As high service users, they are also the members likely to be most affected by HMOs' incentive to control utilization. In addition, most HMO quality standards are focused on minimal medical issues, not on the interplay between chronic disease and physical disability. Even special demonstration programs such as the Social HMO have been shown to have difficulty integrating services for disabled members (37). How much more difficult will it be, then, for traditional for-profit HMOs feeling the pressure of the bottom line? Unfortunately there is little research to date on how the disabled, in general, fare in HMOs, and thus on what standards should be. We do know that Medicare HMOs provide only half as much home health care as traditional Medicare (33) and have poorer health outcomes related to home care (38, 39). Elderly arthritic HMO patients with per-sistent joint pain also showed less improvement in symptoms than Medicare fee-for-service patients (40). When HMOs provide chronic disability care, the specific plan to which a Medicare beneficiary belongs and the geographic area where it is located are at least as important as individual needs in determining the amount and type of care received (41). Given these early findings, it is worrisome to leave the develop-ment of needed standards to corporate health care executives. This is an area where consumers and their families (who are responsible for the great bulk of chronic disability care) should have oversight and involvement in designing services. Yet with the exception of the co-op model Group Health in Seattle, there are few models for consumer involvement among large HMOs. This is certainly a problem in the rapidly growing for-profit HMO sector, where stockholders may have more say about care than patients or their families.

PUTTING THE PROPOSED TRANSFORMATIONS IN PERSPECTIVE

The current restructuring of Medicare and Medicaid does provide opportunity for policy reform advocates to have input at the state level. The increased flexibility offered to states means that more decisions will be made at that level. While there is justified fear about the negative effect of removing federal guarantees and protec-tions on low-income elders, there also may be possibilities for activists to promote long-term policy reform at the state level. The area of long-term care provides a good case in point. Currently over 80 percent of U.S. long-term care dollars are spent on nursing home care (42). Advocates have long sought the reallocation of dollars to home and community care. Although the nursing home lobby is a for-midable one, advocates in some states may be able to use changes in Medicaid as an opening to promote more humane long-term care policies.

Overall, however, the direction of Medicare and Medicaid restructuring is consis-tent with the Republican Contract with America's attack on government-supported human services programs and the reduction of expenditures on its legitimation functions. The balance between government support to profitable corporations and their shareholders and support for the meeting of human needs has taken a hard right turn in favor of profitability. The Republican Medicare proposal, for example, would have funneled anywhere from $84 billion to $189 billion into private insurance companies and for-profit HMOs over a seven-year period. Even under the more moderate proposal they subsequently put forward, some of the big losers are low-income and disabled elders. Eighty-three percent of Medicare beneficiaries have incomes under $25,000 and more than half of beneficiaries are disabled or over age 75 (43)—this casts the true impact of the proposed cuts in sharp relief.

Miller's (3) notions concerning the expansion and contracting of social problems in accordance with national economic needs, and O'Connor's (2) concept of a modern class struggle being waged through government budget battles over legitimation and accumulation functions, appear to be particularly applicable to the current attempt to implement the Republican contract. Attacks on Medicare and Medicaid as well as attempts to privatize these programs are supported by an ideology of individual responsibility and distrust of government. Further, as noted earlier, notions of fiscal crisis increasingly have been invoked to justify proposals and cutbacks that would previously have been unthinkable. And the argument that the 1994 elections represented a major ideological shift to the right has been used to justify the severity of the proposed cutbacks by giving them the aura of an "historic mandate." America's moral economy notions of what is "due" the elderly, the poor, and other vulnerable groups are undergoing radical transformation, according to this perspective, with more attention to responsibilities and less to unearned rights and entitlements.

Yet despite the popularity of such rhetoric on the right, the data do not bear out either an historic mandate or a significant shift in our moral economy. First, as Navarro (44) has pointed out, claims of a popular mandate for the right's harsh new policies (claims that also occurred with Ronald Reagan's election to the presidency in 1980) ignore the fact that well under half of eligible voters go to the polls in U.S. elections, and that those who do often are disillusioned by what they perceive as a lack of real choice between parties and candidates. Second, while opinion poll data continue to reveal Americans' dissatisfaction with "welfare," they at the same time demonstrate a consistently high level of support for welfare and social insurance programs for single mothers and their children, the elderly, and other vulnerable groups (45). A recent (May 1994) Yankelovich Partners poll for *Time*/CNN thus found that almost identical proportions of young people aged 18–34 (81 percent) and people 65 and over (80 percent) agreed with the statement that it was more important "to prevent significant cuts in Medicare" than to balance the budget by 2002. Further, as Navarro (16) has noted, at least 70 percent of the American people continue to desire a national health program that would cover all Americans regardless of income or other "deservingness" criteria.

CONCLUSION

Our critique is not intended to deny the need for substantial changes in Medicare and Medicaid programs. These two programs are expected to grow by over 10 percent annually over the next five years, giving them a faster growth rate than any other part of the federal budget (11). Together they will constitute an estimated one-third of the federal budget by 2002, with Medicare alone approaching 20 percent of the budget by that year. At the state level, Medicaid's projected growth remains almost three times the rate of growth of states' overall budgets, with no change in sight (20). Despite these high costs, moreover, Medicare continues to cover only about 45 percent of the health care costs of the elderly, and Medicaid still fails to reach millions of those who are deemed medically indigent (46, 47).

As noted above, however, although serious inadequacies continue to plague both of these programs, these deficiencies have been more than counterbalanced by the programs' successes in reducing inequities in health care access and providing a vital safety net for many of the nation's most vulnerable populations. Additionally, the administrative costs of Medicare and Medicaid, at under 5 percent, compare very favorably with those of the for-profit managed care plans, which typically are in the range of 15 to 20 percent (12).

The idea that "business can do it better" has not received a critical assessment. What evidence is in, furthermore, is disturbing. As Woolhandler and Himmelstein have noted, "Many big employers and state Medicaid programs have already adopted . . . hard bargaining and restrictions on patient choices . . . without noticeable effect on health spending" (12). And while much further research is needed, some preliminary studies suggest that sick and low-income patients may do poorly in even the best HMOs (48). In the area of Medicare privatization through HMOs, we know already that business can certainly do well at greater cost to the taxpayer. And in the area of Medicaid, the high costs of cutbacks far less severe than those currently proposed are painfully in evidence. The Republican Congress's originally proposed $182 billion spending reductions in Medicaid over seven years, for example, are more than 15 times the size of any Medicaid spending cuts Congress has ever approved in the past. Cuts of this magnitude, it has been calculated, are the equivalent of completely closing down this program for two of the seven years (49)! Yet even under the far more modest Medicaid reductions that previously have been enacted, the costs to patients in terms of access to care, even in life-threatening emergencies, and to the adequacy of states' medical care infrastructures have been profound (49).

For the elderly, who increasingly are scapegoated as the cause of the nation's fiscal problems (50), the proposed transformations in Medicare and Medicaid may be particularly harmful. As we have suggested, such transformations reflect an accelerated movement of government away from its legitimation functions and toward an increasing emphasis on capital accumulation. They reflect, too, the reframing of our perceptions of the state of the economy so that more radical cutbacks and austerity measures can be justified. Finally, the "Republican revolution" of 1994 has been hailed and used by the right as a "popular mandate" for the proposed reforms, many of which would culminate in an increasing bifurcation of care along lines of perceived deservingness. As Friedland has noted, "these proposals say that as a nation, we are no longer willing or able to assure people that they will have assistance if they become destitute" (51).

As we have argued, however, public opinion does not appear to support the political rhetoric suggesting a basic shift in American attitudes or in the moral economy notions that underlie programs like Medicare and Medicaid. Both young and old remain opposed to deep cuts in Medicare, and the great majority remain in favor of a national health program that would cover all Americans (16). As the debate over Medicare and Medicaid once again moves into high gear, we must keep these contextual factors in mind so as to better tease apart myths and realities and to more accurately gauge the effects of what is being proposed on vulnerable groups, including the low-income and disabled elderly.

EPILOGUE

After the reelection of President Clinton and a Republican majority Congress in 1996, a budget debate over the future of Medicare and Medicaid, not unlike the one described in this chapter, was waged in 1997. As of this writing, the President and Republican Congressional leaders have announced agreement on a series of Medicare and Medicaid cuts similar to those described above. Although no final legislation has passed, the announced agreement included cuts that would reduce the growth in Medicare by $115 billion over the next five years while reducing the growth in Medicaid by $24 billion.

Although final details were not available, the cuts in Medicare would include increased beneficiary premiums, increased reliance on HMOs, and cuts in reimbursement to hospitals and physicians. Medicaid cuts would continue to increase states' flexibility to determine benefits and eligibility. Part of the announced new budget deal also included increased capital gains tax cuts targeted primarily to the wealthy and a reduction in the cost of living allowance for Social Security of 0.3 percent.

Despite the reelection of a Democratic president and the loss of popularity of House Speaker Newt Gingrich, the restructuring of Medicare and Medicaid has continued to proceed, with potentially devastating effects on the low-income and disabled elderly.

REFERENCES

1. Estes, C. L. The new political economy of aging: Introduction and critique. In *Critical Perspectives on Aging*, edited by M. Minkler and C. L. Estes, pp. 19–36. Baywood, Amityville, N.Y., 1991.
2. O'Connor, J. *The Fiscal Crisis of the State*. St. Martin's Press, New York, 1973.
3. Miller, S. M. Themes for the 1976 SSSP Meetings. In *Official Program*, 26th Annual Meeting of the Society for the Study of Social Problems, 1976.
4. Kingson, E., and Quadagno, J. Social Security: Marketing radical reform. *Generations* 19(3): 43–49, 1995.
5. Kohli, M. Retirement and the moral economy: An historical interpretation of the German case. *J. Aging Stud.* 1(2): 125–144, 1987.
6. Thomspon, E. P. *The Making of the English Working Class*. Vintage Books, New York, 1966.
7. Stone, D. A. *The Disabled State*. Temple University Press, Philadelphia, 1984.
8. Katz, M. *The Undeserving Poor: From the War on Poverty to the War on Welfare*. Pantheon, New York, 1990.

9. Katz, M. *Improving Poor People*. Princeton University Press, Princeton, N.J., 1995.
10. Hudson, R. Newt Federalism: The Contract with America, Aging Policy and the Fraying Safety Net. Symposium comments at the Annual Meeting of the Gerontological Society of America, Los Angeles, November 15, 1995.
11. Davis, K. Health and Society, 1965–2000. *The Commonwealth Fund Annual Report*, pp. 3–13. The Commonwealth Fund, New York, 1996.
12. Woolhandler, S., and Himmelstein, D. U. Clinton's health plan: Prudential's choice. *Int. J. Health Serv.* 24(4): 583–592, 1994.
13. Anders, G. HMO's pile up billions in cash, try to decide what to do with it. *Wall Street Journal*, December 21, 1994, p. 1.
14. Families USA. Middle Class to Pay for Tax Breaks for Rich and Balanced Budget Amendment. Press release, Washington, D.C., January 10, 1995.
15. Oberlander, J. Managed care and Medicare reform. *J. Health Polit. Policy Law,* 1997, in press.
16. Navarro, V. Wrong medicine. *The Nation* 256(4): 113, 1993.
17. Woolhandler, S. *Statement of Dr. Steffie Woolhandler on the House Republican Proposal on Medicare*. Physicians for a National Health Program, Cambridge, Mass., 1995.
18. Diamond, L. M. The Medicare debate: Dollars, cents and sensibility. *Aging Today* 17(1): 1, 4, 1996.
19. Long Term Care Campaign. *A Hollow Guarantee: Less than 15 Cents on the Dollar*. Washington, D.C., 1996.
20. Riley, P. Long term care: The silent target of the federal and state budget debate. *Public Policy and Aging Report* 7(1): 4–5, 7, 1995.
21. California State Assembly Democratic Human Services Staff. *Federal Welfare Reform Bill*. Sacramento, Calif., 1996.
22. Chronicle News Service. Clinton signs landmark welfare bill. *San Francisco Chronicle*, August 23, 1996, pp. A1 and A21.
23. Saucier, P. *Public Managed Care for Older Persons and Persons with Disabilities: Major Issues and Selected Initiatives*. National Academy for State Health Policy, Portland, Me., 1995.
24. Kane, R. L., et al. Restraining restraints: Changes in a standard of care. *Annu. Rev. Public Health* 14: 545–584, 1993.
25. Dow, M. M. *Managed Care Digest: HMO Edition*. Kansas City, Mo., 1993.
26. Families USA. Medicaid and Medicare: Saved by the (veto) pen? *A.S.A.P. Update* 12(1): 1, 1996.
27. Estes, C. The Reagan legacy: Privatization, the welfare state, and aging in the 1990s. In *States, Labor Markets, and the Future of Old-Age Policy*, edited by J. Myles and J. Quadagno. Temple University, Philadelphia, 1991.
28. Rice, D., and LaPlante, M. Chronic illness, disability, and increasing longevity. In *The Economics and Ethics of Long Term Care and Disability*, edited by S. Sullivan and M. Lewin. Brookings Institute, Washington, D.C., 1988.
29. U.S. Bureau of the Census. *Curr. Popul. Rep.*, March 1990.
30. U.S. Bureau of the Census. Money income and poverty status in the United States, 1989. *Curr. Popul. Rep.*, Ser. P-60, No. 168, September 1990.
31. McMillan, A. Trends in Medicare health maintenance organization enrollment: 1986–93. *Health Care Financing Rev.* 15(1): 135–146, 1993.
32. American Association of Retired Persons, Public Policy Institute, and Urban Institute. *Coming Up Short: Increasing Out of Pocket Health Spending by Older Americans*. Washington, D.C., April, 1995.

33. Brown, R., et al. Do health maintenance organizations work for Medicare? *Health Care Financing Rev.* 15(1): 7–24, 1993.
34. U.S. General Accounting Office. *Long Term Care: Current Issues & Future Directions.* Washington, D.C., 1995.
35. Physicians for a National Health Program. U.S. Health Reform: Unkind Cuts. Unpublished paper, 1995.
36. Richardson, D. A., Phillips, J., and Conley, D., Jr. Study of coverage denial disputes between Medicare beneficiaries & HMO's. HCFA Cooperative Agreement #17-C-979/2-01. Health Care Financing Administration, 1993.
37. Harrington, C., Lynch, M., and Newcomer, R. Medical services in the Social Health Maintenance Organizations. *Gerontologist* 14(2): 790–800, 1993.
38. Shaughnessy, P., Schlenker, R., and Hittle, D. Home health care outcomes under capitated and fee-for-service payment. *Health Care Financing Rev.* 16(1): 187–221, 1994.
39. Schlenker, R., Shaughnessy, P., and Hittle, D. Patient-level cost of home health care under capitated and fee-for-service payment. *Inquiry* 32: 252–270, 1995.
40. Schlesinger, M., and Mechanic, D. Challenges for managed competition from chronic illness. *Health Aff. (Suppl.),* 1993, pp. 123–137.
41. Lynch, M., Harrington, C., and Newcomer, R. Predictors of use of chronic care services by impaired members in the Social Health Maintenance Organization Demonstration. 1996, in press.
42. Levit, K., et al. National health expenditures, 1990. *Health Care Financing Rev.* 13(1): 29–54, 1991.
43. Commonwealth Fund. Sick and poor at greatest risk under proposed Medicare changes. *Commonwealth Fund Q.* 1(3): 1–2, 1995.
44. Navarro, V. *Dangerous to Your Health: Capitalism in Health Care.* Monthly Review Press, New York, 1993.
45. Sidel, R. *Keeping Women and Children Last: America's War on the Poor.* Penguin Books, New York, 1996.
46. Chairman, Select Committee on Aging, House of Representatives. *Emptying the Elderly's Pocketbook—Growing Impact of Rising Health Care Costs.* U.S. Government Printing Office, Washington, D.C., 1990.
47. Rowland, D. *Fewer Resources, Greater Burdens: Medical Care Coverage for Low-Income Elderly People.* Bipartisan Commission on Comprehensive Health Care, May 1990.
48. Ware, J. E., et al. Comparison of health outcomes at a health maintenance organization with those of fee-for-service care. *Lancet* 1: 1017–1022, 1986.
49. Fineberg, J., and Dorn, S. *Unraveling the Mysteries of Medicaid Block Grants.* Consumers Union of the U.S. and the National Health Law Program, San Francisco, July 1995.
50. Minkler, M., and Robertson, A. The ideology of age/race wars: Deconstructing a social problem. *Ageing Soc.* 11: 1–22, 1991.
51. Friedland, R. B. Medicare, Medicaid and the budget. *Public Policy and Aging Report* 7(1): 1–2, 14–16, 1995.

CHAPTER 11

Vouchers for Medicare: A Critical Reappraisal

Jonathan Oberlander

An increasingly prominent option for Medicare reform is to transform the federal health insurance program for the aged and disabled into a voucher system (1). Under such a system, Medicare beneficiaries would receive a fixed-dollar contribution from the government to purchase health insurance. It is anticipated that the introduction of vouchers would trigger a large-scale movement of program beneficiaries from the present Medicare system into private health insurance plans. Vouchers would thus represent a privatization of federal health insurance and a radical change in the philosophy and operation of Medicare.

Once promoted by only a small coterie of conservative health economists, during the 1980s vouchers for Medicare were thought to be an "impossible dream" by even their own advocates (1). Now, however, vouchers have been endorsed by a growing number of health policymakers and analysts, as well as by the American Medical Association and *The New York Times* (2, 3). The political ascendance of Medicare voucher plans is due in large part to the election of a Republican Congressional majority in 1994. The Republican leadership's ideology of reducing the welfare state and privatization has created a receptive climate for long-term voucher proponents, while Washington-based policy analysts have simply followed the political winds in putting forward their own voucher proposals, a bandwagon that has been joined by the Congressional Budget Office (4–8).

Interest in vouchers is also being driven by well-publicized alarm over financial problems in Medicare. In the short-term, Medicare faces a trust fund "crisis" and pressures from deficit reduction. Medicare's hospitalization insurance trust fund is projected to be insufficient to pay out all benefit costs (commonly, but incorrectly, referred to as "bankruptcy") by as soon as 2001. Moreover, Medicare is one of the fastest growing components of the federal budget, and most balanced budget plans consequently call for substantial reductions in the rate of growth in program expenditures. In the long run, Medicare's financial problems are expected to worsen with the retirement of the baby-boom generation beginning in the second decade of the 21st century and the accompanying decline in the number of active workers per retiree. At the program's current rate of growth, it is feared that the working population will not be able to support the growing population of Medicare beneficiaries. These demographic pressures have led some observers to claim that Medicare is "unsustainable in its current form" (4).

There is reason to believe, however, that both Medicare's current financing problems and the longer-term "crisis" of the retirement of the baby boomers are exaggerated. The short-run problem of Medicare's trust fund shortfall can be redressed through modest adjustments in program policies (9). The retirement of the baby boomers will exert substantial financial pressures on the program, but other countries have successfully dealt with similar demographic pressures without the dire consequences now being predicted for the United States. Furthermore, as international experience suggests, vouchers hardly represent the only (or best) alternative for a health insurance system to manage the costs of an aging population.

In large part, as suggested in earlier chapters, the warnings of impending "bankruptcy" and "crisis" represent emotionally loaded images that are intended by program critics to conjure up public anxiety in order to permit radical restructuring of Medicare (10, 11). Indeed, voucher advocates have taken advantage of, and intentionally fueled, the current climate of crisis surrounding Medicare to promote vouchers as a solution to Medicare's financial problems. Vouchers, though, are touted by their supporters for more than fiscal prowess. Advocates also claim that vouchers would benefit Medicare enrollees by increasing the range of choices available to program beneficiaries and by decentralizing power over health coverage decisions from federal bureaucracies to individual consumers (12). In addition, vouchers are believed to promote fair market competition by rewarding cost-conscious behavior from medical providers, health plans, and beneficiaries (13). Vouchers, then, combine the assurance of fiscal control with the symbolism of individual empowerment and market efficiency.

Given the powerful appeal of these claims, the recent enthusiasm for transforming Medicare into a voucher system is not surprising. I argue here, however, that such enthusiasm is misplaced and that many of the claims made for vouchers are false. Vouchers would not work as advertised by their advocates, and their adoption would pose substantial risks for both beneficiaries and the Medicare program. In particular, I show why the elderly and disabled Medicare population is ill-suited for a voucher system and how vouchers would exacerbate patterns of inequality in access to medical care. I also emphasize the serious problems that would arise in a voucher system due to the absence of working risk-adjustment technology.

The first section of this chapter summarizes the claims that are made for vouchers and reviews how they might operate in Medicare. The second section examines potential problems with a Medicare voucher system and explains why these problems are sufficiently serious to warrant rejection of vouchers as program policy. I conclude by examining the implications of this analysis for other public policy issues and outlining an alternative for Medicare reform.

A MEDICARE VOUCHER SYSTEM

How Vouchers Would Work

A Medicare voucher system would embody the principles of "managed competition" developed by Alain Enthoven and resemble the health insurance system currently used by federal employees (the Federal Employees Health Benefits Plan, FEHBP) (4, 5, 13).[1] Rather than providing federal insurance for a defined package of medical services, as Medicare currently does, the federal government would give program beneficiaries a voucher ("defined-contribution") to purchase health insurance. The government, through the Department of Health and Human Services or the Health Care Financing Administration, would then contract with private insurance companies that wished to compete for Medicare enrollees, potentially encompassing health maintenance organizations (HMOs), preferred provider organizations, point of service plans, and indemnity insurers. Health plans could be required to offer a standard minimum benefit package, while being permitted to vary coverage above that minimum as well as their cost-sharing arrangements and organization of medical services. The current Medicare program would compete with private plans for enrollees.

Health plan marketing would be centralized through an annual enrollment process, or "open season," supervised by the federal government. During open season, beneficiaries would select the health plan they wanted from those participating in the Medicare insurance system. Medicare enrollees would receive comparative information on health plans from the government sponsor, or private intermediaries and consumer groups, to assist them in making informed choices. This information might include comparisons of premium costs, covered benefits, and cost-sharing arrangements in different plans, as well as quality indicators such as member satisfaction and disenrollment rates. Participating plans would have to accept any beneficiary during open season, and beneficiaries would have to remain in health plans for the entire year. In addition to organizing annual enrollment and operating a public Medicare plan, the federal government would monitor the behavior of private insurers to assure that they did not violate prohibitions on selective marketing or enrollment of healthier beneficiaries ("cherry-picking"), and would pay health plans the voucher amount once they had been selected for the upcoming year by a Medicare beneficiary. The voucher payments to health plans could be adjusted for enrollee characteristics such as age and disability status ("risk adjustment") to pay elevated rates for beneficiaries who were expected to incur higher than average medical expenses.

Beneficiaries would receive the same fixed-dollar voucher regardless of the plan they enrolled in and would therefore bear the financial consequences of their health insurance choices. If the premium of the plan they selected cost less than the value of the voucher, they could receive a cash rebate or premium give-back. If, however, they chose a plan that charged premiums exceeding the dollar amount of the voucher, they—not Medicare—would pay the difference, creating strong incentives for beneficiaries to select low-cost health plans.

The Case for Vouchers

Consumer Choice. Vouchers are claimed by their proponents to have four major advantages over traditional Medicare. First, it is argued that vouchers would enhance

[1] For critiques of managed competition as a model for national health reform, see references 14–16.

consumer choice in health care. Ninety percent of Medicare beneficiaries are currently enrolled in the federally operated indemnity insurance plan. While Medicare permits beneficiaries to join HMOs, the program has been slow to contract with other types of managed care plans, such as preferred provider organizations and point of service plans. Nor can Medicare beneficiaries use their coverage to enroll in private indemnity insurance. Voucher advocates contend that, as presently organized, Medicare constitutes a public monopoly on health insurance for program beneficiaries (1, p. 25).

A Medicare voucher system would seek to end that monopoly by expanding the range of health insurance choices available to beneficiaries and opening up the program to private insurers. Medicare enrollees could choose plans that matched their preferences for premium cost, benefit coverage, and cost-sharing. Beneficiaries who were comfortable with managed care organizations could join them, while those who preferred fee-for-service insurance would be free to choose that type of plan. It is argued that a voucher system would decentralize authority over Medicare coverage; individuals, rather than the government, would make decisions about what type of health coverage was best for them (1, p. 33).

In addition to increasing the range of consumer choice, vouchers would also, according to their advocates, improve the quality of choice. Medicare beneficiaries currently have little access to data on the hospitals and physicians they use. In a voucher system, beneficiaries would be provided with detailed information on health plan characteristics and performance. This information would enable beneficiaries to compare health insurance products on a variety of dimensions in order to select an appropriate plan.

Fiscal Control A second advantage claimed for vouchers is that they would introduce firm fiscal controls on federal Medicare expenditures. Medicare spending is currently open-ended; program expenditures in any given year depend on the quantity and cost of services provided to Medicare beneficiaries. In large part, this is because Medicare is an entitlement (17). By virtue of their eligibility for the program, beneficiaries are entitled to (and Medicare obligated to pay for) any medical services delivered by licensed medical practitioners. Although there are regulatory controls on federal payments in some parts of the program (the Prospective Payment System for hospitals and the Medicare Fee Schedule for physicians), there is no prospective budget that sets a hard limit on federal Medicare spending (18).

A voucher system would dramatically alter Medicare's budgetary and entitlement status. In contrast to the present open-ended system, vouchers would establish a prospective limit on federal Medicare spending that would simply be the product of the number of Medicare beneficiaries and the value of the federal voucher. Federal Medicare expenditures could consequently be made predictable and controllable. The rate of growth in Medicare expenditures would be controlled by adjusting the dollar amount of the voucher, and federal spending on any individual beneficiary would be limited to that amount. If Medicare enrollees wished to spend more than the government contribution on their health insurance, they would have to pay for it themselves. Vouchers, then, would impose a budget on both the federal government and beneficiaries. As noted earlier, the fiscal control offered by vouchers is thought to make the specter of the retirement of the baby-boom generation less threatening. In fact, some analysts claim that vouchers represent the only feasible option for restructuring Medicare to absorb the baby boomers (4).

Competition. Third, vouchers are believed to produce the benefits of market competition: reduced costs, enhanced quality, and greater efficiency. A voucher system would introduce incentives to engage in cost-conscious behavior for health plans, medical providers, and beneficiaries. Health plans would compete against each other to gain shares of the Medicare market. Competition for beneficiaries could take place on quality, cost, and satisfaction, with plans lowering premiums, expanding benefit coverage, and improving services to attract enrollees. In such a competitive environment, health plans are assumed to have incentives to innovate in the organization and delivery of medical care services; inefficient plans that failed to maximize benefits per cost or had poor quality would be driven out of business (13). These competitive pressures would shift down to physicians, who would come under pressure from health plans to deliver cost-effective and high-quality care to their patients or risk losing contracts.

Since they would receive fixed-sum vouchers, beneficiaries would also have incentives for cost-conscious behavior. A central tenet of voucher plans is that consumers "should bear the financial costs of their [health insurance] choices" (4). Beneficiaries who chose low-cost health plans could receive cash rebates, while those who enrolled in plans that cost more than the Medicare voucher would pay the balance. A beneficiary who wanted the right, for instance, to self-refer to see a specialist, and consequently wanted to enroll in an indemnity insurance plan, could do so, but would have to pay for this "extra" option. Medicare beneficiaries in a voucher system would thus face trade-offs in cost, convenience, and benefits when choosing insurance plans. Voucher proponents believe that this system rightly rewards those who enroll in cost-effective health plans while penalizing those who select less efficient providers.

Regulatory Relief. A fourth argument that is made for vouchers hinges on their presumed ability to reduce the regulatory burden on the federal government and to avoid the political pathologies associated with regulation. Vouchers are claimed to assign government a simpler, less intrusive role than it currently plays in Medicare. No longer would the primary role of the federal government be to offer a defined-benefit package or to regulate payments to hospitals and physicians. Instead, its main task in a Medicare voucher system would be to monitor the competition by private insurance plans; government would move from regulator to referee. Federal policy-makers, rather than micro-managing Medicare policy, would let private plans decide on their own how to pay providers, what benefits to cover, and how to organize medical care delivery (5, 12).

According to voucher advocates, by redirecting federal payments from a price schedule to a flat per beneficiary voucher, the incidence of "gaming"—where affected actors attempt to get around government regulations—would be lessened (11; 13, pp. 93–95). Hospitals currently operate sophisticated computer programs to determine which diagnostic categories earn them the most money, so that patients can be assigned profitable diagnoses ("upcoding"), and physicians often unnecessarily break a single office visit into multiple visits and services ("unbundling") in order to protect their incomes. Medical providers also react to price controls by increasing the volume and complexity of the services they deliver ("behavioral offset"), weakening the effectiveness of regulation. Since a voucher system would not contain any government price regulation other than the basic voucher amount, it is assumed that providers would have little opportunity or incentive to engage in regulatory gaming.

Proponents also contend that vouchers would avoid the bias in regulatory politics toward an imbalanced political market dominated by the concentrated interests of regulated industries. Since regulated industries are greatly affected by regulatory decisions, they exert considerable efforts to "capture" government agencies and shape regulation to their benefit (13, pp. 110–114). They may be aided in this enterprise by their ability to offer policymakers financial resources and political support, as well as their willingness—in contrast to the general public or consumers—to pay the information costs necessary to monitor regulatory developments. It is argued that a voucher system would temper these dynamics by focusing attention on a single decision—the setting of the voucher amount—thus lowering information costs and offsetting some of the medical industry's political advantage. Because regulation in a voucher system would not involve price controls, and would modify the behavior of health plans only at the margin, it is also believed that regulated entities would make fewer attempts to engage in pressure politics, since they would "derive little financial benefit from changing or evading the rules" (13, p. 94).

REASSESSING VOUCHERS

At first glance, vouchers appear to offer an attractive option for Medicare reform. As presented by their supporters, vouchers promise to control Medicare costs, enhance beneficiaries' choice of medical care, substitute market efficiency for ineffective government regulation, and make the program "safe" for the retirement of the baby boomers. As this section demonstrates, however, the actual performance of a Medicare voucher system is likely to fall considerably short of this promise. Rather than being a panacea for Medicare's problems, a voucher system would undermine many of the program's existing strengths.

The Illusion of Choice

While vouchers are commonly promoted as expansions of consumer choice, in reality they would significantly reduce the medical care choices available to Medicare beneficiaries. In fact, voucher systems are explicitly designed to force individuals to leave indemnity and fee-for-service insurance for managed care plans such as HMOs, though this goal is shrouded in the rhetoric of choice (19). Under current arrangements, Medicare beneficiaries are free to choose any physician they want. A voucher system would take that freedom away; beneficiaries who wished to enroll in insurance plans that guaranteed free choice of physicians would have to pay financial penalties if the premiums of those plans cost more than the voucher. In private health insurance markets, indemnity plans—those that allow free choice of provider on a fee-for-service basis—tend to be more expensive than managed care organizations that limit selection of medical providers. It is virtually certain that this pattern would hold as well in a Medicare voucher system. Beneficiaries who wished to remain in the present Medicare program would thus be forced to pay a supplemental premium and consequently, the "choice" offered by vouchers would be loaded against indemnity insurance. This choice would be particularly illusory for poorer beneficiaries who lacked the money to select more expensive plans. And if voucher payments did not keep pace with the costs of medical care, or if competition did not produce the savings anticipated by its advocates, a growing proportion of Medicare enrollees would be forced over time either into low-cost (and potentially low-quality) health plans or to pay a greater share of their income toward health insurance. In this sense, vouchers represent an attempt to shift the costs of medical care onto the elderly and the disabled.

Moreover, if the premium differentials between indemnity insurance and lower-cost managed care plans became extreme, beneficiaries might not have any choice at all as fee-for-service plans were priced out of reach for all but the wealthiest Medicare enrollees. This is precisely what has happened in some private and public sector insurance plans that have adopted voucher frameworks. Indemnity plans are at particular risk in voucher systems because sicker individuals are less likely than healthier enrollees to leave these plans for managed care organizations. This adverse selection can induce a "death spiral" in which indemnity plans are left with sicker, and thus more expensive, insurance pools and therefore must charge higher and higher premiums to cover their costs.[2] Eventually, these selection dynamics may boost indemnity premiums so high as to drive the plans out of business.[3] The introduction of vouchers, then, may cause Medicare beneficiaries to lose their ability to choose the one type of health plan that guarantees them free choice of medical provider.

Finally, many Medicare beneficiaries would not enjoy the almost unlimited choice of health insurance that voucher advocates envision because much of the United States does not have the population density or health care infrastructure to support a local Medicare market of competing health plans. And even in those areas that had sufficient populations and resources to support competing plans, choice of private options could turn out to be less diverse than expected if the current trend of health insurance mergers continues and creates monopolies or oligopolies in Medicare markets (23, 24).

[2] The effects of this "death spiral" have been apparent in the University of California health insurance system, where the high-option indemnity plan (Prudential) lost 80 percent of its enrollment within 5 years after the implementation of a defined-contribution system, while its premiums increased tenfold during the same period (20).

[3] In 1989, selection effects forced Aetna to withdraw its high-option plan from the FEHBP (21, pp. 5–6; 22).

Managed Care and the Chronically Ill

It is, of course, no accident that the financial incentives introduced by a voucher system encourage consumers to exit indemnity/fee-for-service insurance. Voucher proponents regard indemnity insurance as inefficient, rewarding of wasteful care, costly, and inimical to competition in health care markets (13). Moving Medicare enrollees into managed care, especially prepaid insurance plans such as HMOs, is thus a primary goal of voucher proposals and is viewed as potentially beneficial for both the federal government and beneficiaries. It is argued that HMOs, often depicted as the epitome of cost-effective medical care, could reduce federal Medicare expenditures, offer health coverage broader than traditional Medicare, and improve the quality of medical care services (25–27).

HMOs do have features—such as coordination of health services—that may benefit Medicare enrollees. And for many beneficiaries, HMOs can provide medical care that costs less than that delivered in fee-for-service settings without harming quality. However, there is significant evidence that HMOs are not appropriate for all segments of Medicare beneficiaries, particularly those with chronic conditions (28, 29). A recent report from the Medical Outcomes Study concluded that over a four-year period, chronically ill elders in HMOs were twice as likely to experience a decline in their health status as were chronically ill elders in fee-for-service Medicare, and that low-income elderly fared particularly poorly in prepaid settings (30). These findings corroborate other studies that have found worse outcomes in HMOs for home health care and for patients with persistent joint pain (31–33). In part, the worse outcomes may be due to the reliance of HMOs on primary care gatekeepers, which may adversely affect the care of elders who have multiple conditions that can be better diagnosed and treated by specialists.

In extolling the virtues of HMOs, voucher advocates often fail to note these problems. Managed care does not work equally well for all patients, and it would therefore pose risks to the health of some Medicare beneficiaries. Vouchers, then, would effectively create financial pressures for some segments of the Medicare population to join insurance plans that would provide them with inadequate health care. Moreover, the burden of such pressures would fall disproportionately on the most vulnerable of Medicare beneficiaries, the chronically ill and the poor, making these incentives particularly troubling.

The Limits of Consumerism

Voucher advocates envision that in a competitive health system, Medicare beneficiaries would become effective consumers of medical care. When confronted with financial incentives, it is expected that beneficiaries would respond by shopping for the "best buy" in health insurance. Beneficiaries would carefully calculate their preferences for cost, quality, and convenience; weigh the differences between health plans on these dimensions; and seek out information to make more informed choices. This consumer role, which requires patients to be cost-conscious, well-informed, and aggressive, would represent a substantial transformation from the traditionally passive role of medical care patients (34).

The problem is that the Medicare population is ill-suited to assume the consumer role that a voucher system would assign to them. Studies have found that the elderly are less likely to be effective consumers of medical care than the general population (34, 35). Program beneficiaries have consistently demonstrated widespread confusion about Medicare coverage and cost-sharing arrangements (35–37). And the one area where Medicare beneficiaries presently select private insurance—the Medigap market—provides little optimism for turning the elderly into rational consumers. Medicare beneficiaries, confused about their existing coverage and the benefits of Medigap, and sometimes duped by the marketing practices of insurance companies, have purchased overlapping policies that they did not need or that did not cover what they expected (24, 38, 39). Similar patterns of "irrational" consumer behavior by the elderly have been found in the health plan choices of retirees in the Federal Employees Health Benefit Plan.[4]

If elders cannot navigate the Medigap market, there is little reason to believe they would fare better in a voucher system that increases the range, complexity, and consequences of their medical care choices. For elderly who are long retired and accustomed only to indemnity insurance, the panoply of new insurance options, including point of service plans and preferred provider networks, would seem bewildering. Beneficiaries who are seriously ill and those who are lower-income and less educated would similarly be in a poor position to judge alternative health plans or to engage in consumer behavior. The wide choice of health plans offered by a voucher system would thus be rendered meaningless for much of the Medicare population.

The Risk-Adjustment Dilemma

A properly functioning voucher system depends on effective risk adjustment: that is, the ability to predict individuals' expected medical costs and adjust payments to health plans accordingly. Risk adjustment would help ensure access to medical care for sicker enrollees that insurers might otherwise shun by paying elevated rates on their behalf. It would also be critical to promoting fair market competition between health plans. Without risk adjustment, plans could gain a competitive advantage by attracting healthier risks, rather than innovating or providing cost-effective care. In a risk-adjusted world, healthier enrollees would bring lower payments, taking away the financial benefits of "cherry-picking." Risk adjustment is thus a fundamental requirement of an efficient and fair voucher-based health insurance system (12).

The problem is that a working risk-adjustment system does not currently exist. It is extremely difficult to define actuarial categories that accurately predict individual medical expenses. Medicare's troubled experience with risk adjustment is indicative of the general problem. The present Medicare risk-adjustment system has managed to explain less than 1 percent of the variance between beneficiaries' medical expenses (40). As a consequence, Medicare substantially overpays the HMOs

---

[4] Many retirees in the FEHBP select high premium plans even though these plans offer them little extra benefit for the additional cost (21, p. 5).

that contract with the program for treating beneficiaries who are healthier than the program average, causing the federal government to lose money on Medicare HMO patients (25). While alternative risk-adjustment models have been proposed, none has yet to work in practice or to predict accurately the huge variation in individual medical expenses. Even when researchers refined the Medicare risk-adjustment formula by incorporating additional variables to reflect beneficiary health status and prior utilization of medical services, a paltry maximum of only 10 percent of the variance in individual expenditures could be explained (41–43). Some of the health insurance systems cited as exemplars by voucher proponents—including the FEHBP—do not even attempt risk adjustment. Given the enormity of the task and the technological limitations inherent in actuarial science, there is little chance that an ideal individual-level risk-adjustment system will emerge anytime soon, if ever.

The dilemma of risk adjustment, then, is that voucher systems depend crucially on a technology that does not exist. As a result, a Medicare voucher system would likely be implemented *without* effective risk adjustment. Voucher advocates frequently downplay this omission by claiming that it can be dealt with in implementation and arguing that it does not pose a serious problem for their model (4, p. 21; 5, p. 57; 12). There is strong reason to doubt these claims: the limitations of risk adjustment will not somehow magically disappear during implementation and they would pose a significant threat to the successful operation of a voucher system.

Four problems can emerge in a voucher system without effective risk adjustment. First, efficient and socially desirable health insurance plans could go out of business because of adverse selection. In the idealized world of voucher advocates, the market works with Darwinian efficiency: plans that deliver poor quality, are unable to maximize productivity or control costs, or do not offer products demanded by consumers will fail economically. Health plans that "lose" in a voucher system, in other words, deserve to lose because they are inefficient. However, without workable risk adjustment, plans may lose simply because of their risk pool. If a health plan attracts disproportionately sick enrollees, and is not compensated through risk adjustment, its premiums will rise and it may suffer the "death spiral" described previously. Similarly, plans may succeed by attracting healthier risks that enable them to offer low premiums, thus forgoing the pursuit of organizational innovation and cost-effective medical care that voucher advocates expect. Under these conditions of risk-based competition, the market will not fairly reward efficiency and punish inefficiency as it is supposed to in a voucher system, but will instead reward those insurers who are the most clever at enrolling good risks while punishing those who provide coverage to sicker individuals (44).

A second, closely related problem is that without working risk adjustment, a voucher system may produce considerable instability as health insurers that are subject to adverse selection go out of business. Health plans that are caught in "death spirals" of increasingly sick insurance pools and rising premiums can go bankrupt in relatively short periods of time. Moreover, if, for example, an indemnity plan fails because of adverse selection, those selection effects may simply be transferred to the next plan likely to attract sicker enrollees, such as a preferred provider organization. Consumers in a voucher system could therefore find themselves forced to change plans and doctors as their previous choice disappears, while administrators would have to devise efforts to stabilize the system.

A third problem is that in the absence of effective risk adjustment, one of the central rationales for vouchers—making people pay more for choosing expensive health plan—unravels. Proponents believe that in a voucher system it is fair to charge enrollees higher amounts for more expensive plans because these plans are presumed to be less efficient than lower-cost medical care organizations. Why should the government, voucher advocates ask, subsidize Medicare beneficiaries for inefficient and "cost-unconscious" behavior? This argument is central to the justification for transforming Medicare from a defined-benefit into a defined-contribution program. Yet without good risk adjustment, there is no way to know whether the higher premium amounts paid by enrollees who choose more expensive plans are due to differences between plans in their efficiency or, rather, in the health status of their insurance pools. Nor is this only a theoretical possibility. In the FEHBP, there are differences of 100 percent in premiums between health plans that differ only 5 percent in their covered benefits; the wide disparity is predominantly due to differential risk selection (45).[5] Under a voucher system, Medicare beneficiaries would consequently pay the price not for selecting inefficient health plans, but simply for being in the wrong risk pool. In the absence of effective risk adjustment, then, there seems to be no compelling normative justification for imposing financial penalties on enrollees in more expensive plans.

A fourth and final problem is that access for sicker Medicare beneficiaries could suffer if risk-adjusted payments proved insufficient to cover their actual costs. In this circumstance, plans would have a strong incentive to shun sicker enrollees because they would be revenue losers and would potentially threaten the competitive position of their insurers. A voucher system would formally prohibit selective marketing and other techniques used by health plans to discourage beneficiaries from selecting that plan or renewing their coverage. However, plans have used a variety of tactics to induce disenrollment of costly beneficiaries, including creating barriers to care for particular services, and it is by no means clear that regulators could consistently deter plans from this behavior.

In sum, the absence of working risk-adjustment technology is not merely another implementation matter. Rather, it is a crucial flaw in voucher systems that undermines both their stable operation and normative justification.

The Challenge of Regulating Vouchers

It is unlikely that vouchers will, as claimed by their proponents, significantly reduce the regulatory burden on the federal government. The primary argument for vouchers as a source of regulatory relief is that the government would get out of the business of setting price schedules and controlling the volume of services delivered

---

[5] In 1989, the Congressional Research Service estimated that the most generous plan in the FEHBP was worth 42 percent more than the least generous plan. However, its premium were 264 percent higher, suggesting that health plan premium prices are "more affected by the plan enrollees than by differences in the value of benefit packages" (21, p. 6).

by medical providers, and instead settle into a simpler role of paying health plans their voucher amounts, as well as monitoring the enrollment process. However, most voucher plans assume that the government would continue to operate a public Medicare program, meaning that the type of federal regulation currently in use would continue, with the added responsibilities (and administrative costs) of regulating the voucher system.

Those responsibilities, contrary to the image of the federal government as a mere "referee" that must only intermittently intervene in the "game," would be formidable. Two of the regulatory challenges in a voucher system have already been mentioned: operating an effective risk-adjustment system and preventing plans from selectively enrolling healthier beneficiaries and disenrolling the seriously ill. Neither of these tasks would be easily accomplished and both would require considerable resources to monitor individuals' experiences with health plans, risk selection among plans, marketing behavior, and the internal operations of medical care organizations. It is by no means clear that the costs of this type of regulation would be less than those in Medicare's current regulatory regimen (44, 46).

Voucher advocates commonly argue that government regulation of medical care prices and volume is doomed to fail because it works against the natural economic incentives (i.e., increasing income or maximizing profits) of health providers (13, pp. 110–114). Yet prohibitions on "cherry-picking" raise exactly the same issue, with no greater likelihood of success. The costs of medical care in the Medicare population are highly concentrated, with 10 percent of beneficiaries accounting for 70 percent of program spending in 1995, at a per person average expenditure of $28,120, compared with $4,020 for the average Medicare beneficiary (47). The payoff for health plans to avoid this group is extremely high; regulations requiring health plans to accept all-comers thus run directly counter to the economic interests of insurers. Vouchers would not eliminate the tensions between financial incentives and regulation.

Similarly, vouchers are unlikely to reduce significantly the incidence of "gaming" in Medicare. Voucher advocates rightly note that hospitals and physicians presently respond to federal payment regulations by delivering more services, unbundling one service into multiple visits, and "upcoding" diagnoses to correspond with higher payment categories. However, a voucher system would generate its own set of regulatory games. For example, health plans could be expected to devote considerable effort to identifying categories of beneficiaries whose risk-adjusted voucher payments, due to actuarial imperfections, exceeded their actual medical care costs (44, p. 241). Computer programs that now detect profitable diagnosis categories would simply be reprogrammed to detect profitable risk-adjustment categories.

Nor will a voucher system take the politics out of regulation. Voucher advocates claim that the political activities of the regulated would be reduced because there would be only one major regulatory decision—the setting of the basic voucher amount—to influence, and rules in a voucher system would affect the behavior of medical plans only at the margin. This story seems highly improbable. As already noted, medical plans would have a strong financial stake in the formulation and implementation of rules governing enrollment, marketing, benefit coverage, and risk adjustment. Their financial performance would also be substantially determined by the amount of the federal voucher, and they could be expected to lobby aggressively to shape its outcome. Private insurance companies would become the prime stakeholders in Medicare policy and could be expected to exert their considerable political influence on federal policymakers (48). Finally, the introduction of risk adjustment would engender its own politics, with various groups of patients and medical lobbies vying to get their illness a higher risk-adjustment category so as to make patients more attractive to health insurers (46).

In sum, a voucher system would move the focus of regulation from hospitals and physicians to health insurers and medical plans. Regulatory gaming would change from upcoding and unbundling to locating profitable risk-adjustment categories. And regulatory politics would center on marketing regulations and the voucher amount rather than on price schedules. Vouchers, then, would not reduce regulation in Medicare, only change its character.

Political Fragmentation

Medicare is a universal social insurance program; all workers who pay into the system through mandatory payroll taxes are eligible—regardless of their income—for program benefits, and virtually all beneficiaries are enrolled in a single insurance program. As a result, Medicare has a cross-class program constituency, with program beneficiaries encompassing the middle class and the wealthy, as well as lower-income persons. The universal model of social program that Medicare embodies contrasts with means-tested welfare programs—such as Aid to Families with Dependent Children—that serve only the poor. That contrast is by design; Medicare's programmatic architects believed that universal social insurance was politically stronger than welfare programs (49). Programs targeted exclusively to the poor often turned out to be poor programs, in terms of both administration and inadequate benefits, because the poor lacked political clout. Social insurance sought to protect the poor by putting them in the same program with middle-class and wealthier beneficiaries, thereby giving these politically more powerful classes a stake in maintaining the program.[6] During Medicare's three decades of operation, the universal scope of its constituency has made it difficult for policymakers to cut back program benefits or to impose substantial new costs on program beneficiaries.

A voucher system would unravel the universal fabric of Medicare politics. Instead of all beneficiaries joining the same program, enrollment would fragment as many elderly and disabled enrollees left public Medicare to join private health insurance plans. This fragmentation could prove especially hazardous for the traditional Medicare program if it disproportionately lost wealthier beneficiaries to private insurance. Without these beneficiaries, the constituency for maintaining and improving program benefits would weaken considerably (1, pp. 42–44; 50). Moreover, if current enrollment trends in managed care were to hold in the future, the public Medicare program would be left with a sicker insurance pool. A public program of

---

[6] The recent repeal of the Aid to Families with Dependent Children (AFDC) program would appear to confirm the political logic of social insurance advocates.

the poor and sick not only would be politically weak, it would also more than likely incur high costs because of the health care needs of its clientele, triggering political pressure as the program appeared (unfairly) to be less efficient than its private sector counterparts.

Vouchers would also exacerbate inequality in the health care experiences of Medicare beneficiaries. There is, of course, inequality in the present Medicare system, in large part due to the limited scope of benefits and differential access to Medigap and supplemental insurance policies. A voucher system would significantly worsen this pattern. Wealthier beneficiaries would have a wider choice of insurance plans than they now have, while poorer beneficiaries could be forced to join only those plans whose premiums were covered by the government voucher. Discrepancies in benefit coverage would also grow; some voucher proposals would permit insurance plans to offer less than the current Medicare benefit package. In this case, Medicare could quickly deteriorate into a tiered system of medical insurance with excellent coverage for those who could afford to supplement the voucher and mediocre coverage for those who could not.

Finally, the political effects of converting a defined-benefit of health insurance into a voucher are uncertain. The experience of Social Security indicates that the political resilience of cash-benefit programs might not be any less than that of in-kind benefits. However, some observers have suggested that a voucher system would make it easier to impose cuts on Medicare enrollees because it is politically easier to hold down the growth of vouchers than to curtail defined benefits (1, pp. 42–44). It is also possible that the fragmentation of medical care experiences would weaken the constituency for increasing the annual value of the voucher. Affluent beneficiaries might have little reason to support voucher increases designed to enable lower-income enrollees to purchase bottom-end insurance with improved benefit packages.

CONCLUSION

This chapter raises serious doubts about the desirability of transforming Medicare into a voucher system. The Medicare population, because of the high number of elderly and disabled persons who are seriously or chronically ill and their limited consumer sophistication, is ill-suited to succeed in a competitive insurance environment. The attraction of broader choice that is offered by vouchers would therefore prove illusory for many Medicare beneficiaries. Furthermore, the highly concentrated distribution of medical care costs among the Medicare population, and the absence of effective risk adjustment to control for the effects of this concentration on health plan premiums, pose formidable, and perhaps insurmountable, barriers to implementing a workable voucher system in the program. Under these circumstances, introducing vouchers into Medicare would unfairly penalize beneficiaries who enrolled in more expensive health plans; threaten the availability of fee-for-service insurance guaranteeing free choice of provider; and create an unstable system of risk-based competition in which health plans were rewarded for attracting healthier enrollees rather than pursuing efficiency or innovation. Finally, a voucher system would have adverse distributional consequences, exacerbating existing inequalities in access to medical care and undermining the universal and cross-class political coalition that has supported Medicare. In sum, vouchers for Medicare are neither feasible nor desirable (44).

These arguments have implications beyond the Medicare case. Some European countries, in efforts to strengthen cost containment and enhance efficiency and accountability, are interested in applying the principles of Alain Enthoven's "managed competition" scheme to their own health systems. The analysis in this chapter suggests that such interest should be accompanied by a healthy dose of skepticism about the benefits of such a framework. In the United States, the current Medicare reform debate is part of a broader political argument over the adoption of vouchers in a variety of public policies, including education and housing. Many of the arguments developed here might also apply to these other policy areas. For example, the illusion of choice in a voucher-based health insurance system probably has parallels in "school choice" systems. Finally, the harmful effects of transforming public Medicare into private health insurance are analogous to the perils inherent in current proposals to privatize Social Security (51). In both cases, proposed market-based reforms would subject retirees to substantial risk while exacerbating inequality and fragmenting the universal political coalition of social insurance that protects lower-income elderly.

That vouchers are undesirable for Medicare should not be taken to mean that fiscal control of Medicare expenditures is an undesirable goal. On the contrary, reducing the rate of growth in Medicare is important to maintaining the program, absorbing the coming demographic bulge in beneficiaries, and pursuing other social priorities and government programs. Restraining the growth of Medicare expenditures is particularly vital in order to prevent burdensome increases for beneficiaries in program premiums and cost-sharing payments.[7] In one crucial respect, I believe that voucher advocates are correct: long-term control of Medicare expenditures is unlikely without the introduction of a prospective budget on program spending. However, vouchers are not, as their advocates often suggest, the only option for budgeting Medicare. One alternative would be to impose a global budget on Medicare expenditures in much the same manner that the single-payer and all-payer health systems in Canada and European countries control their health spending. (I have described elsewhere (52) how such a system might operate in Medicare.) This approach would rely on regulating payments to medical providers—rather than shifting costs to elderly and disabled patients as voucher advocates propose—as the means of stabilizing Medicare expenditures.[8] By adopting a single-payer-style budget,

[7] Since premiums for Medicare part B and cost-sharing arrangements for both part A and part B—such as the inpatient hospital deductible—are tied to overall program spending, restraining the growth of program expenditures will moderate the financial burden of medical care costs experienced by elderly and disabled enrollees.
[8] The spread of managed care in the private sector has created an opportunity for Medicare to reduce payments to hospitals and physicians. Whereas during the 1980s, Medicare payment rates were substantially lower than those in the private sector, in many markets Medicare is now the high-payer as a consequence of the low payment rates attained by managed care organizations. Medicare can therefore lower its payment rates without adversely affecting beneficiary access to care.

Medicare could thus achieve fiscal control while avoiding the risks to beneficiaries inherent in a voucher system.

Acknowledgments — I gratefully acknowledge the help of Mark Schlesinger in thinking about this project. I have also benefited from numerous conversations with Theodore Marmor on this subject. My thanks to Timothy Prinz, Michael Schoenbaum, Harold Wilensky, and the editors of the volume—Meredith Minkler and Carroll Estes—for their insightful comments on this essay. Preparation of the chapter was assisted by a grant from the Robert Wood Johnson Foundation, Princeton, New Jersey.

REFERENCES

1. Bovbjerg, R. R. Vouchers for Medicare: The impossible dream. In *Lessons from the First Twenty Years of Medicare,* edited by M. V. Pauly and W. L. Kissick. University of Pennsylvania Press, Philadelphia, 1988.
2. Rich, S. AMA's Medicare plan borrows from G.O.P. *Washington Post,* December 5, 1996, p. A11.
3. Rich, S. The new consensus. *New York Times,* December 11, 1996, p. A26.
4. Aaron, H. J., and Reischauer, R. D. The Medicare reform debate: What is the next step? *Health Aff.* 14(4): 8–30, 1995.
5. Butler, S. M., and Moffit, R. E. The FEHBP as a model for a new Medicare program. *Health Aff.* 14(4): 47–61, 1995.
6. Wilensky, G. The score on Medicare reform—minus the hype and hyperole. *N. Engl. J. Med.* 333(26): 1174–1177, 1995.
7. Congressional Budget Office. *Reducing the Deficit: Spending and Revenue Options.* Government Printing Office, Washington, D.C., 1996.
8. Fraley, C. Using vouchers for Medicare may help GOP cut costs. *Congressional Q.,* July 22, 1995, pp. 2189–2190.
9. Moon, M., and Mulvey, J. *Entitlements and the Elderly.* Urban Institute, Washington, D.C., 1996.
10. Estes, C. L. Social Security: The social construction of a crisis. *Milbank Mem. Fund Q.* 61: 445–461, 1983.
11. Marmor, T. R., Mashaw, J. L., and Harvey, P. L. The attack on Social Security. *Domestic Aff.* 1: 115–145, Summer 1991.
12. Elhauge, E. Vouchers: Medicare's only hope. *New Republic,* November 13, 1995, pp. 24–27.
13. Enthoven, A. C. *Health Plan: The Only Practical Solution to the Soaring Cost of Medical Care.* Addison-Wesley, Reading, Mass., 1980.
14. White, J. *Competing Solutions: American Health Care Proposals and International Experience,* Chaps 7, 8. Brookings Institution, Washington, D.C., 1995.
15. Navarro, V. *The Politics of Health Policy,* pp. 205–210. Blackwell, Cambridge, Mass., 1994.
16. Marmor, T. *Understanding Health Care Reform.* Yale University Press, New Haven, Conn., 1994.
17. Wildavsky, A. *The New Politics of the Budgetary Process,* Ed. 2. Harper Collins, New York, 1992.
18. Moon, M. *Medicare: Now and in the Future.* Urban Institute, Washington, D.C., 1993.

19. Light, D. W. Homo Economicus: Escaping the traps of managed competition. *Eur. J. Public Health* 5(3): 151, 1993.
20. Buchmueller, T. C., and Feldstein, P. J. The Effect of Price on Switching among Health Plans. Unpublished paper. University of California, Irvine, August 1995.
21. Evans, A. *The Federal Health Benefits Program, Managed Competition, and Considerations for Medicare.* National Academy on Aging, September 1995.
22. Congressional Research Service. *The Federal Employees Health Benefits Program: Possible Strategies for Reform.* Washington, D.C., 1995.
23. Kronick, R., et al. The marketplace in health care reform: The demographic limitation of managed competition. *N. Engl. J. Med.* 328: 148–152, 1993.
24. Light, D. W. The traps of managed competition. *N. Engl. J. Med.* 328: 147–148, 1993.
25. Brown, R. S., et al. Do health maintenance organizations work for Medicare? *Health Care Financ. Rev.* 15(1): 7–23, 1993.
26. Luft, H. S. (ed.). *HMOs and the Elderly.* Health Administration Press, Ann Arbor, Mich., 1994.
27. Iglehart, J. K. Medicare turns to HMOs. *N. Engl. J. Med.* 312(2): 132–136, 1985.
28. Schlesinger, M. On the limits of expanding health care reform: Chronic care in prepaid settings. *Milbank Q.* 64(2): 189–215, 1986.
29. Schlesinger, M., and Mechanic, D. Challenges for managed competition from chronic illness. *Health Aff.,* Suppl. 1993, pp. 123–137.
30. Ware, J. E., et al. Differences in 4-year health outcomes for elderly and poor, chronically ill patients treated in HMO and fee-for-services systems. *JAMA* 276(13): 1039–1047, 1996.
31. Shaughnessy, P. W., et al. Home health outcomes under capitated and fee-for-services payment. *Health Care Financ. Rev.* 16(1): 187–221, 1994.
32. Clement, D. G., et al. Access and outcomes of elderly patients enrolled in managed care. *N. Engl. J. Med.* 271(19): 1487–1492, 1994.
33. Oberlander, J. Managed care and Medicare reform. *J. Health Polit. Policy Law* 22(2): 593–629, 1997.
34. Hibbard, J. H., and Weeks, E. C. Consumerism in health care. *Med. Care* 25(11): 1019–1032, 1987.
35. Davidson, B. Designing health insurance information for the Medicare beneficiary: A policy synthesis. *Health Serv. Res.* 23(5): 685–720, 1988.
36. Cafferata, G. L. Knowledge of their health insurance coverage by the elderly. *Med. Care* 22(9): 835–847, 1984.
37. McCall, N., et al. Consumer knowledge of Medicare and supplemental insurance benefits. *Health Serv. Res.* 20(6): 633–657, 1986.
38. U.S. House of Representatives Select Committee on Aging. *Abuses in the Sale of Health Insurance to the Elderly in Supplementation of Medicare: A National Scandal.* Government Printing Office, Washington, D.C., 1978.
39. McCall, N., et al. The effect of state regulations on the quality and sale of insurance policies to Medicare beneficiaries. *J. Health Polit. Policy Law* 12: 53–76, 1987.
40. Newhouse, J. P. Rate adjusters for Medicare under capitation. *Health Care Financ. Rev.,* Suppl. 1986, pp. 45–55.
41. Newhouse, J. P., et al. *Objective Measure of Health and Prior Utilization as Adjusters for Capitation Rates.* Rand Publication WD-3479-2-HCFA. Rand Corporation, Santa Monica, Calif., 1987.
42. Davidson, B., et al. Consumer information and biased selection in the demand for coverage supplementing Medicare. *Soc. Sci. Med.* 34(9): 1031–1032, 1992.

43. Newhouse, J. P. Reimbursing health plans and health providers: Efficacy in production versus selection. *J. Econ. Lit.* 34: 1236–1263, September 1996.

44. Luft, H. S. On the use of vouchers for Medicare. *Milbank Mem. Fund Q.* 62(2): 240–242, 1984.

45. Jones, S. et al. The risks of ignoring insurance risk management. *Health Aff.* 13(2): 121, 1994.

46. Morone, J. A. The ironic flaw in health competition. In *Competitive Approaches to Health Care Reform,* edited by R. J. Arnould et al. Urban Institute, Washington, D.C., 1993.

47. Kaiser Family Foundation. *Medicare Chart Book.* Menlo Park, Calif., 1995.

48. Navarro, V. *Dangerous to your Health: Capitalism in Health Care,* pp. 31–37. Monthly Review Press, New York, 1993.

49. Marmor, T. R. *The Politics of Medicare.* Aldine, Chicago, 1973.

50. Schlesinger, M., and Drumheller, P. B. Medicare and innovative insurance plans. In *Renewing the Promise: Medicare and Its Reform,* edited by D. Blumenthal, M. Schlesinger, and P. B. Drumheller. Oxford University Press, New York, 1988.

51. Marmor, T., and Mashaw, J. The great Social Security scare. *Am. Prospect* 29: 30–37, November–December 1996.

52. Oberlander, J., and Marmor, T. Rethinking Medicare Reform. Unpublished paper. Yale University, School of Management, New Haven, Conn., January 1997.

CHAPTER 12

The Nursing Home Industry:
The Failure of Reform Efforts

Charlene Harrington

The poor quality of care provided in U.S. nursing homes has long been a matter of concern to consumers, professionals, and policymakers. In the 1970s, a number of exposés were written about the poor conditions in nursing homes. The roots and the intractability of these problems were carefully documented by Vladeck in 1980 (1). In 1986, the Institute of Medicine's Study on Nursing Home Regulation reported widespread quality-of-care problems and recommended the strengthening of federal regulations for nursing homes (2). The next year, the General Accounting Office reported that over one-third of the nation's nursing homes were operating at a substandard level, below minimum federal standards during three consecutive inspections (3). Among the findings were evidence of untrained staff, inadequate provision of health care, unsanitary conditions, poor food, unenforced safety regulations, and many other problems (3). No other segment of the health care industry has been documented to have such poor quality of care. Despite a large infusion of public funds into the nursing home industry over the past 25 years, investigations and exposés continue to find inadequate care and patient abuse.

The Institute of Medicine recommendations, as well as the active efforts of many consumer advocacy and professional organizations, resulted in the U.S. Congress passing a major reform of nursing home regulation in 1987, the first significant changes since Medicare and Medicaid were adopted in 1965 (4). Congress made enhanced regulatory efforts a priority, in spite of the costs associated with regulation, in an effort to improve quality of care and to protect residents from abuse.

This chapter examines the structural features of the nursing home market and the industry itself in an effort to identify factors related to poor quality of care. It will argue that regulatory efforts, while essential, have not been sufficient to improve the overall quality of nursing home care ten years after Congress passed the Nursing Home Reform Act of 1987 (Omnibus Budget Reconciliation Act, OBRA 1987). Rather, new reform efforts to regulate the economics of the industry will be necessary to provide safe nursing home care, to ensure high quality of care, to preserve basic resident's rights, and to promote quality of life for residents.

THE NURSING HOME MARKET

Increased Demand

The quality of nursing homes has become important as the demand for nursing home services enlarges with the increasing numbers of aged and chronically ill individuals. In 1987, there were about 30 million Americans aged 65 and older, and this number is projected to increase to 51 million in 2020 (5). As the population ages and develops chronic illnesses, the need for long-term care services, including nursing home services, increases. The total risk for becoming a nursing home resident after age 65 is 43 percent and peaks at age 75 to 80 (6). The number of elderly who need nursing home care is expected to increase from 1.8 million in 1990 to 4.3–5.3 million in 2030 (7, 8).

The adoption of Medicare prospective payment systems for hospitals in 1983 resulted in shortened hospital stays and increased demand for nursing home care. This policy change has led to greater numbers of referrals and admissions to nursing homes from hospitals, as well as increased levels of acute illness of nursing home residents (9). At the same time, the 1988 Health Care Financing Administration Medicare guidelines to fiscal intermediaries liberalized Medicare coverage for nursing homes (10). These changes have encouraged the demand for and use of nursing home and other long-term care services.

Increased Complexity of Care

The demand for increasingly complex services in nursing homes is growing with the aging and disability of the residents. While only 4 percent of the nation's elderly are currently in nursing homes, 88 percent of nursing home residents are aged 65 and older (10). Moreover, the average age of residents is increasing.

The disability levels of nursing home residents are high. On a three-point scale (where 1 is the lowest need for assistance and 3 is the greatest), the average nursing home resident in 1995 had a score of 1.7 for assistance with eating, 2.1 for toileting, and 2.0 for transferring from bed to a chair. About 8 percent of all nursing home residents were bedfast and 48 percent were chairbound, showing a slight increase over 1991 statistics (11).

As the level of acute illness of nursing home residents increases, medical technology formerly used only in hospitals is now being used in nursing homes. Thus, the "performance of duties" has become an even more complex task for personnel. The use of intravenous feedings and medication, ventilators, oxygen, special prosthetic devices, and other high-technology equipment has made patient care management more difficult and challenging (12). The appropriate use of technology, the training and skill levels needed by nursing home personnel, and the need for emergency back-up procedures have all become problems deriving from the use of advanced technology. Thus, changes in the characteristics of residents are placing greater demands on nursing home providers—demands that are frequently beyond the capacity of the current financing and delivery system.

Constrained Supply

As the demand for increasingly complex nursing home care is growing, the supply of nursing home beds is not keeping pace with demand by the oldest old. In 1995, the United States had 17,422 licensed nursing home facilities with 1.78 million beds. The average number of beds per 1000 persons aged 85 and over declined from 610 in 1978 to 491 in 1995 (13). The paradox is that even though the supply of beds has been somewhat constrained relative to the aging of the population, nursing home occupancy rates declined from 93 percent in 1984 to 90 percent in 1995 (although occupancy rates are higher in the north central and northeastern regions than the average). The declining occupancy rates are probably the result of an increasing number of home care and community care alternatives to nursing homes, because many older individuals strongly prefer to remain at home if at all possible.

Even though occupancy rates are declining, nursing homes continue to screen and select the residents they admit. Because they can obtain private-paying residents who can be charged higher daily rates than public-paying residents, nursing homes prefer private clients and frequently discriminate against those on Medicaid (14, 15). Nursing homes also tend to "cream" or select those clients that are the least sick or for whom they can provide the most cost-efficient care. This, in some situations, reduces access for those individuals with the greatest need and certainly limits consumer choice and the competitive market for services.

High Costs

The costs of nursing home services are growing rapidly. The nation spent $80 billion on nursing home services in 1995 (8 percent of its total health dollars) and expects to spend $121 billion in 2000, making this segment of the health industry third only to hospitals and physicians. While the growth in nursing home costs has slowed somewhat, the increase in 1995 was 8 percent over the previous year, well beyond the rate of inflation (16).

These growing costs have negative consequences for consumers and public payers. In 1995, Medicaid paid for one-half of the total nursing home expenditures. Medicare paid for about 12 percent, and other government sources paid 2 percent. Consumers paid directly for 32 percent of the costs, and only 2.5 percent were paid from private insurance and 2 percent from other private sources (16). Because of these costs, most public policy efforts, particularly by the state Medicaid programs, are focused on controlling or reducing spending in this area.

Since private insurance for nursing home services is virtually unavailable and currently pays for less than 3 percent of the costs, most individuals who require these services for any extended period of time are forced to spend their life savings before they become poor enough to qualify for Medicaid services, which will then pay for such care. In 1995, the average Medicaid rate was $84 per day (13, 17), for an average annual cost of $31,000. Private pay rates are generally higher than Medicaid rates. These high costs result in many individuals spending their assets within weeks of admission to a nursing home and becoming eligible for the Medicaid program (18, 19). The high costs of care produce inequities in access, with the greatest access for those with the greatest income and limited access for the poor (19). This situation has fueled the demand for a public national long-term care insurance program, but no progress has been made in this area legislatively.

THE NURSING HOME INDUSTRY: OWNERSHIP AND STAFFING

Nursing Home Ownership

With the exception of the pharmaceutical industry, the nursing home industry has more proprietary ownership and chain ownership than any other segment of the U.S. health care industry. In 1995, 67 percent of all nursing homes were profit-making, 26 percent were nonprofit, and 7 percent were government facilities (11). A growing number of nursing homes are chain-owned or operated, and they have increased their control of the total market dramatically. In 1985, chains owned 41 percent of U.S. nursing home facilities and 49 percent of the nation's nursing home beds (7). In 1995, chains owned 52 percent of the facilities (11), and the largest 20 chains operated 18 percent of the total beds (20).

The nursing home industry continues to consolidate into larger corporations, like other components of the health care industry. The merger and acquisition activity has been high, with 23 of the largest 25 nursing home chains involved in acquisitions during 1993 (20). In 1994, the merger and acquisition activity was reported at $60 billion (21). In addition, 16 nursing home companies have become public in the past two years, giving these companies new sources of capital for growth and acquisitions (21).

Proprietary facilities generally are oriented toward maximizing profits, and an increasing number are publicly traded corporations: these facilities make profits by reducing operating costs. *Forbes* reported that nursing homes exceeded the all-industry medians for return on equity in 1994 (22). Manor Care had an 18 percent return on equity for the latest 12 months and a sales growth of 14 percent on $1.2 billion in revenue in 1994. The earnings per share increased by 16.5 percent, and the profit margin was 6.9 percent (23). Manor Care, Health Trust, and Hillhaven exceeded the all-industry medians in earnings per share, while Beverly Enterprises was slightly lower. Manor Care, Health Care and Retirement, and Health Trust exceeded the all-industry medians for profit margins, while Hillhaven was similar to the national industry medians and Beverly Enterprises fell below (23). The health care industry, including the nursing home corporations, ranked first of 21 industry groups for its five-year return on equity.

The total profit margin for the free-standing nursing home industry (calculated as the difference between total net revenue and total expenses divided by total net revenues reported from facility cost reports) was reported at 4 percent for 1993. Profit margins were higher in investor-owned and system-affiliated facilities (4.11 percent in 1993) than in other types, and higher in medium-sized than in small facilities (20).

Administrative costs were reported at 28 percent of operating expenses (20). Only 35 percent of total nursing home expenditures go into providing direct care (nursing staff and other direct care staff) and another 18 percent into indirect care (food, housekeeping, and other such activities). The nursing home industry retains its high profits by limiting its expenditures on care-related activities. It is unlikely that the industry will increase the proportion of its expenditures on nurses and direct resident care.

Several factors have contributed to the growth in chain operations. As Hawes and Phillips (24) have noted, capital reimbursement policies encourage the sale and resale of facilities and other real estate manipulations favor more sophisticated operators. The increased demand for services, constrained bed supply, high profitability, and increased complexity required to meet federal certification standards and to obtain public reimbursement have also encouraged growth.

One of the major debates in research, policy, and consumer advocacy circles is whether the proprietary nature of the nursing home industry negatively affects access, costs, and quality of care. Access to services is limited to those who can pay privately because proprietary facilities provide little uncompensated care. Costs of care are driven up by the increasing demand for short-term profits (24). The effects on quality of care have been disputed (25). A review of the research studies on ownership and quality, however, suggests that the preponderance of the evidence supports the superiority of nonprofits, particularly church-related nonprofits (24).

Staffing and Labor Issues

The federal nursing home legislation (OBRA 1987) required additional registered nurses (RNs), but facilities are still not required to have 24-hour registered nursing coverage. Beyond the minimum levels, facilities are expected to ensure adequate staffing to meet the needs of the residents (4).

In spite of the federal requirements, the staffing levels in nursing homes are low and have remained so for the past five years. The federal On-Line Survey Certification and Reporting System (OSCAR) shows that in 1995 the average ratio of hours per resident day for RNs was 0.5 hours (30 minutes), for LPN/LVNs was 0.7 hours (42 minutes), and for nursing assistants was 2.0 hours (120 minutes), with a total of 3.1 nursing hours per resident day for all nursing facilities in the United States (11). (This is calculated by dividing the total average nursing hours per day by the total average number of nursing residents per day.) This translates to about 10 minutes of registered nursing time per resident on each shift—but most of this time is allocated to administration and delivering medications to patients. Staffing levels for the subset of Medicare-only certified facilities were substantially higher, but these represented only about 10 percent of all nursing home facilities. Overall, there was no increase in nursing staff hours over the five-year period of 1991 through 1995 (11).

Nursing experts consider the staff ratios to be entirely too low to provide adequate nursing care. Moreover, nursing staff are not evenly distributed over 24 hours. Most health facilities have fewer staff on evening and night shifts because there are somewhat fewer care activities than during the day. Staffing is usually lower on holidays and weekends, in terms of both licensed personnel ratios and total numbers of staff.

It was the inadequate level of RN staffing in nursing facilities that prompted a recent committee at the Institute of Medicine (1996) to recommend increases in staffing in its report *Nursing Staff in Hospitals and Nursing Homes: Is It Adequate?* (26). Specifically, the report recommended beginning by requiring facilities to have 24-hour (rather than 8-hour) RN staffing as a minimum in all nursing facilities. The major barrier to improved staffing is the cost to nursing homes, which must be paid through Medicaid nursing home reimbursement.

Not surprisingly, higher staffing levels in nursing homes are associated with better nursing home care. Spector and Takada (27), in a study of 2,500 nursing home residents in 80 nursing homes in Rhode Island, found that low levels of staffing in homes with very dependent residents were associated with a reduced likelihood of residents' functional improvement. High catheter use, a low percentage of residents receiving skin care, and low participation rates in organized activities were also associated with reduced outcomes, in terms of functional decline and death. Low RN turnover was associated with an increased likelihood of functional improvement for residents. Cohen and Spector (28) also found that staffing ratios have a significant impact on resident outcomes, and these impacts vary by professional category of staff. A higher RN intensity was associated with a lower rate of mortality; a higher intensity of LPN staffing significantly improved functional outcomes.

Higher staffing levels not only could improve quality of care but could reduce the costs of hospitalization. A study of nursing home residents found that 48 percent of the hospitalizations could have been avoided. Factors such as an insufficient number of adequately trained nursing staff, the inability of nursing staff to administer and monitor intravenous therapy, lack of diagnostic services, and pressure for transfer to hospital exerted by the staff and family contributed to hospitalization (29). The authors estimated that nursing home residents who are hospitalized might be treated in the nursing home itself, for a cost savings of $0.9 billion in 1989 dollars.

Wages and Benefits

Wages and benefits for nursing home employees are scandalously low. The average annual income of RNs employed full-time in nursing facilities was $33,846 in 1992. Overall RN nursing home salaries were 14 percent below the levels for comparable positions in hospitals (30). Nursing aides or attendants, who make up 65 percent of all nursing home direct care personnel, generally work for minimum wage, and few have benefits.

Low wages and benefits are directly reflected in the high turnover rates for nursing home personnel—overall, frequently as high as 53 to 100 percent per year (31). A number of studies have identified poor working conditions combined with heavy resident workloads, inadequate training and orientation, and few opportunities for advancement as other factors contributing to high turnover rates in some facilities (26, 32). While high turnover rates are considered undesirable for quality of care, nursing homes, like other health facilities, have some economic incentives to encourage such rates to keep wages low (33). Higher turnover rates are associated with proprietary institutions (32).

Education and Specialty Training of Staff

Nurses working in nursing homes have less education than hospital nurses. In 1992, the majority of all nursing home RNs were diploma-prepared nurses and less than 3 percent had a master's degree (30). Diploma-prepared nurses have had little educational training in the care of geriatric patients. Many nursing homes are unwilling to pay the higher wages required to attract better prepared nurses, and yet evidence suggests that geriatric nursing specialists may be cost effective.

Several geriatric nurse practitioner (GNP) demonstration projects examined the effect of GNPs in the practice setting. One evaluation, which compared 30 nursing homes employing GNPs with 30 matched control homes, found that the use of GNPs produced favorable changes in two of eight activity of daily living measures, five of 18 nursing therapies, two of six drug therapies, and six of eight tracer diseases or conditions (34). The study also reported some reduction in hospital admissions and total days in GNP homes.

The Robert Wood Johnson Teaching Nursing Home demonstration project was designed to bring nursing schools together with nursing homes to improve nursing education and patient care. In these projects, nurse clinicians and faculty provided direct care to patients and worked as consultants and advisors to staff. The preliminary results showed improvements in both the process of care and the outcomes of care (35).

At one demonstration project, the presence of master's degree nurses resulted in decreases in pressure sores, incontinence, and dependency, and in the use of physical restraints, catheters, psychotropic drugs, enemas, and laxatives (36). However, there was a reversal in some of these outcomes in subsequent years. Another study reported a gradual decline in emergency room visits, hospital admissions, infections, and falls (37). Another reported a decrease in use of pharmacological agents and in nosocomial infections from the use of clinical specialists (38). Although the results of the demonstration projects appear to be positive, foundation support for the teaching nursing homes cannot fund such programs indefinitely. It is hoped that nursing homes will use the findings from the research to make changes in the types of nursing personnel they use.

Because of the inadequate education and training levels of nurses in nursing homes, the recent Institute of Medicine Committee on the Adequacy of Nurse Staffing in Hospitals and Nursing Homes recommended that nursing facilities should use geriatric nurse specialists and GNPs in both leadership and direct care positions (26). It also recommended that the training for nursing assistants be structured and enriched with "appropriate clinical care of the aged and disabled; occupational health and safety measures; culturally sensitive care; and appropriate management of conflict."

PUBLIC INFORMATION

Public information about the quality of nursing home care, such as guides or rating systems, would also be helpful in improving quality. Consumers needing nursing home services are vulnerable and lack the type of information they need to make informed choices about what facilities they should use. Many individuals rely on hospital discharge planners, physicians, and other health professionals for assistance in making plans and decisions about nursing home services. Evidence suggests that the discharge planning process is complex and not always operating effectively (39). Discharge planners and other health professionals frequently have inadequate information on nursing homes and other long-term care provider options, particularly on the quality of providers. Public disclosure of administrative information, consumer guides, and rating systems are methods for assisting consumers and health professionals in making more informed decisions in the marketplace.

Expanding public information about nursing home quality may also be valuable in stimulating nursing homes to improve their services. While hospitals compete, to some extent, on the basis of the quality of their nursing services, nursing homes have generally not done so. The 1986 Institute of Medicine Committee to Study Nursing Home Regulation recommended the development of nursing home rating systems based on quality indicators as one method of creating pressure on facilities to improve services (3). Such approaches, aimed at giving consumers and professionals greater choice in making more informed decisions, are attractive but difficult to develop.

REGULATORY APPROACHES

The OBRA 1987 Nursing Home Reform legislation made the first major legislative improvements in federal regulation of nursing homes since 1965 (4). The legislation mandated comprehensive assessments of all nursing home residents after admission and periodically, so that nursing homes can define clients' functional, cognitive, and affective levels initially and over time. The legislation required the development of quality indicators that are more outcome-oriented than process-oriented. Such outcome measures would include resident behavior, functional and mental status, and conditions such as incontinence, immobility, and pressure sores. Regulations implemented the 1987 legislation in 1990 and 1994. For example, the regulations established criteria for and prohibited the use of "unnecessary drugs." The legislation also required changes in the federal survey procedures to orient them more toward the residents and toward enforcement of the law.

The new regulation and enforcement effort was expected to bring about substantial improvements in quality of care. The new regulations do not allow the inappropriate use of restraints (used to tie nursing home residents in beds or chairs), and may have had some beneficial effects in this area. A number of nursing homes are now reporting new efforts to train staff not to use such restraints and to move toward restraint-free nursing homes.

Unfortunately, the latest statistics show that nursing homes continue to have the same problems that predominated over the past 20 years. The top ten most frequently cited deficiencies in U.S. nursing homes in 1995 were for failure to: conduct comprehensive resident assessment (27 percent), ensure sanitary food (26 percent), prepare comprehensive resident care plans (24 percent), provide care that protects the dignity of residents (20 percent), remove accident hazards (19 percent), prevent the inappropriate use of physical restraints (19 percent), prevent pressure sores (17 percent), provide adequate housekeeping (17 percent), accommodate the needs of residents (14 percent), and ensure infection control (13 percent) (11). These problems have not improved substantially over the past five-year period.

The Health Care Financing Administration began new enforcement efforts (mandated in 1987) in 1995 with the authority to impose civil money penalties, denial of payment for new admissions, temporary management, immediate termination, and other actions. In spite of the new enforcement measures, the federal government has not used its authority. The average number of citations per facility decreased from nine in 1991 to only six citations in 1995 (11). Only a small minority of the citations have resulted in penalty actions by the federal government.

SPECIAL INTEREST GROUP POLITICS

Three key special interest groups are involved with nursing home issues: (a) the industry, represented by the American Health Care Association and the American Association of Homes for the Aging; (b) government, whose interests are split between those of the quality regulators and those of the fiscal agents who pay for services; and (c) the consumer, primarily represented by the National Citizens Coalition for Nursing Home Reform (NCCNHR). While both the American Medical Association and the American Nurses' Association have interests in nursing homes, neither organization has given these issues priority in relation to their other professional concerns. Nursing organizations have advocated for improving nursing staff levels and wages and benefits in nursing homes, but few nurses working in nursing homes are active members of major nursing organizations. This low membership translates into a lower organizational priority on nursing home lobbying efforts when organizational resources are limited.

Unfortunately, the special interests of the three major group are often conflicting and frequently lead to stalemate. The industry is primarily interested in minimizing government regulation of quality and access, while obtaining high government reimbursement rates with minimal strings attached. The industry wants to increase reimbursement rates substantially, but generally opposes efforts to guarantee that rate increases would be passed on to employees. Government monitoring systems, such as improved financial reporting and increased numbers of audits, could be developed to ensure greater financial accountability, but the industry would fight such efforts. Because substantial amounts of public funds to nursing homes have traditionally been used to finance excessive administrative costs, high profit rates, and the expansion of chain operations, there is a legitimate distrust of the industry and an unwillingness to spend more government money.

Government is struggling to balance its interests in ensuring minimum levels of quality while controlling costs and operating under severe fiscal constraints. Consumer representatives primarily want to ensure quality and access to appropriate services through greater governmental regulation of the industry and improved enforcement efforts.

At the same time there is an unequal distribution of power. The nursing home industry is well represented by highly paid professionals with extensive organizational resources for lobbying government. Consumer groups have little funding and resources, and must operate primarily through commitment and volunteer efforts, even though they do have a strong presence in Washington through NCCNHR. If professional groups (particularly those of nurses and physicians) were to form a coalition with consumer groups and were willing to allocate resources to representing the public interests, their added efforts could shift the power base to favor consumer interests.

Consumer representative groups, particularly NCCNHR, have worked extremely hard to have the legislation passed and to develop the regulations and the new survey procedures (40, 41). Nursing home industry representatives, although cooperating with the new legislation generally, have made efforts to weaken its implementation and to use it as a means of increasing Medicaid reimbursement rates.

The current struggles between the industry and consumers are focused on the development of new regulations and on enforcement efforts to improve the quality of regulation. Efforts by consumer groups should receive stronger support from nursing and other professional organizations to give the groups greater weight in their efforts to prevent the watering down of regulations by industry officials. In addition, consumers and professionals should be supporting greater allocations of federal funds by Congress and the administration for implementing state survey procedures to protect the public interest.

SUMMARY

The nursing home industry is growing in size and importance as a provider of long-term care. The major problems in quality and access are likely to grow as demand increases and supply remains relatively inelastic. Highest priorities should be placed on supporting regulatory efforts to improve quality of care. At the same time, renewed efforts should go into improving the wages, benefits, and staffing levels for professional staff in nursing homes. This will cost substantially more in terms of public funds but is essential for improving the system. Methods are needed to ensure financial accountability by nursing homes, with maximum limits on administrative costs, profits, and capital expenditures. Finally, efforts should center on reducing the trend toward consolidation of the industry and proprietary ownership so as to stimulate ownership and management by government and nonprofit corporations.

REFERENCES

1. Vladeck, B. C. *Unloving Care: The Nursing Home Tragedy.* Basic Books, New York, 1980.
2. Institute of Medicine, Staff and National Research Council Staff. *Improving the Quality of Care in Nursing Homes.* National Academy Press, Washington, D.C., 1986.
3. U.S. General Accounting Office. *Medicare and Medicaid: Stronger Enforcement of Nursing Home Requirements Needed.* Report to the Chairman, Subcommittee on Health and Long-Term Care, Select Committee on Aging, House of Representatives. Washington, D.C., 1987.

4. Omnibus Budget Reconciliation Act of 1987. Public Law 100-203. Subtitle C: Nursing Home Reform. Signed by the President, Washington, D. C., December 22, 1987.

5. U.S. General Accounting Office. *Long-Term Care for the Elderly: Issues of Need, Access, and Cost.* Report to the Chairman, Subcommittee on Health and Long-Term Care, Select Committee on Aging, House of Representatives. HRD-89-4. Washington, D.C., November 1988.

6. Murtaugh, C. M.. Kemper, P., and Spillman, B. C. The risk of nursing home use in later life. *Med. Care* 28(10): 952–962, 1990.

7. Zedlewski, S. R., and McBride, T. D. The changing profile of the elderly: Effects on future long-term care needs and financing. *Milbank Q.* 70(2): 247–275, 1992.

8. Mendelson, D. N., and Schwartz, W. B. The effects of aging and population growth on health care costs. *Health Aff.* 12(1): 119–125, 1993.

9. Guterman, S., et al. The first 3 years of Medicare prospective payment: An overview. *Health Care Financ. Rev.* 9(3): 67–77, 1988.

10. National Center for Health Statistics, Hing, E., Sekscenski, E., and Strahan, G. *National Nursing Home Survey: 1985 Summary for the United States.* Vital and Health Statistics, Ser. 13, No. 97. DHHS Pub. No. (PHS) 89-1758. Public Health Service. Government Printing Office, Washington, D.C., 1989.

11. Harrington, C., et al. *Nursing Facilities, Staffing, Residents, and Facility Deficiencies, 1991 through 1995* Report prepared for the Health Care Financing Administration. University of California, San Francisco, 1996.

12. Shaughnessy, P. W., and Kramer, A. M. The increased needs of patients in nursing homes and patients receiving home health care. *N. Engl. J. Med.* 322(1): 21–27, 1990.

13. Bedney, B., et al. *Long Term Care Program and Market Characteristics.* Report prepared for the Department of Housing and Urban Development and the Health Care Financing Administration. University of California, San Francisco, 1996.

14. Phillips, C. D., and Hawes, C. *Discrimination by Nursing Homes Against Medicaid Recipients: The Potential Impact of Equal Access on the Industry's Profitability.* Research Triangle Institute, Research Triangle Park, N.C., 1988.

15. Wallace, S. Racial Segregation in Health Care: The Continuing Problem in Nursing Homes. Paper presented at the meeting of the Society for the Study of Social Problems, Miami Beach, Fla., 1993.

16. Burner, S. T., and Waldo, D. R. National health expenditure projections, 1994–2005. *Health Care Financ. Rev.* 16(4): 221–242, 1995.

17. Swan, J. H., Dewit, S., and Harrington, C. *State Medicaid Reimbursement Methods and Rates for Nursing Homes, 1995.* Paper prepared for the Department of Housing and Urban Development and the Health Care Financing Administration. Wichita State University, Wichita, Kan., 1996.

18. Short, P. F., et al. Public and private responsibility for financing nursing-home care: The effect of Medicaid asset spend-down. *Milbank Q.* 70(2): 277–298, 1992.

19. Snow, K. I. *How States Determine Nursing Facility Eligibility for the Elderly: A National Survey.* American Association of Retired Persons, Washington, D.C., 1995.

20. HCIA and Arthur Andersen. *The Guide to the Nursing Home Industry.* Baltimore, Md., 1994.

21. HCIA and Arthur Andersen. *The Guide to the Nursing Home Industry.* Baltimore, Md., 1995.

22. Kichen, S. Annual report on American industry. *Forbes* 155(1): 122–125, 1995.

23. Walsh, M. Health. *Forbes* 155(1): 180–182, 1995.

24. Hawes, C., and Phillips, C. D. The changing structure of the nursing home industry and the impact of ownership on quality, cost, and access. In *For-Profit Enterprise in Health Care,*

edited by B. H. Gray, pp. 492–538. National Academy Press, Institute of Medicine, Washington, D.C., 1986.

25. Davis, M. A. Nursing home quality: A review and analysis. *Med. Care Rev.* 48: 129, 1991.

26. Institute of Medicine, Committee on the Adequacy of Nurse Staffing in Hospitals and Nursing Homes. *Nursing Staff in Hospitals and Nursing Homes: Is It Adequate?* National Academy Press, Washington, D.C., 1996.

27. Spector, W. D., and Takada, H. A. Characteristics of nursing homes that affect resident outcomes. *J. Aging Health* 3(4): 427–454, 1991.

28. Cohen, J. W., and Spector, W. D. The effect of Medicaid reimbursement on quality of care in nursing homes. *J. Health Econ.* 15: 23–48, 1996.

29. Kayser-Jones, J., Wiener, C., and Barbaccia, J. Factors contributing to the hospitalization of nursing home residents. *Gerontologist* 29(4): 502–510, 1989.

30. Moses, E. B. *The Registered Nurse Population: Findings from the National Sample Survey of Registered Nurses, March 1992.* Division of Nursing, Bureau of Health Professions, Health Resources and Services Administration, Washington, D.C., 1994.

31. American Health Care Association. *Facts and Trends 1995: The Nursing Facility Sourcebook.* Washington, D.C., 1995.

32. Jones, D., et al. *Analysis of the Environment for the Recruitment and Retention of Registered Nurses in Nursing Homes.* U.S. Department of Health and Human Services, Washington, D.C., 1987.

33. Harrington, C. Nursing home reform: Addressing critical staffing issues. *Nurs. Outlook* 35(5): 208–209, 1987.

34. Kane, R., et al. Effects of a geriatric nurse practitioner on process and outcome of nursing home care. *Am. J. Public Health* 79(9): 1271–1277, 1989.

35. Mezey, M., Lynaugh, J., and Cartier, M. Reordering values: The teaching nursing home program. In *Nursing Homes and Nursing Care: Lessons from the Teaching Nursing Homes,* pp. 1–12. Springer, New York, 1989.

36. Joel, L., and Johnson, J. The teaching nursing home experiences, Rutgers—The State University of New Jersey and Bergen Pines County Hospital. In *Teaching Nursing Homes, the Nursing Perspective,* edited by N. Small and M. Walsh. National Health Publishers, Owings, Mill, Md., 1988.

37. Dimond, M., Johnson, M., and Hull, D. The teaching nursing home experiences, University of Utah College of Nursing and Hillhaven Convalescent Center. In *Teaching Nursing Homes, the Nursing Perspective,* edited by N. Small and M. Walsh. National Health Publishers, Owings Mill, Md., 1988.

38. Wykle, M., and Kaufmann, M. The teaching nursing home experiences, Case Western Reserve University, Frances Payne Bolton School of Nursing and Margaret Wagner House of the Benjamin Rose Institute. In *Teaching Nursing Homes, the Nursing Perspective,* edited by N. Small and M. Walsh. National Health Publishing, Owings Mill, Md., 1988.

39. Wollock, I., et al. The posthospital needs and care of patients: Implications for discharge planning. *Soc. Work Health Care* 12(4): 61–76, 1987.

40. National Citizens Coalition for Nursing Home Reform. *Consumer Statement of Principles for the Nursing Home Regulatory System—State Licensure and Federal Certification Programs.* Washington, D.C., 1983.

41. Burger, S. G., et al. *Consumer Statement of Principles for the Nursing Home Regulatory System—State Licensure and Federal Certification Programs.* Report prepared by National Citizens Coalition for Nursing Home Reform, Washington, D.C. American Source Books, San Luis Obispo, Calif., 1996.

PART IV: RACE, CLASS, GENDER, AND AGING

The often profound impacts of race, class, and gender on aging and aging policy constitute a major theme running throughout this volume. In Part IV, we look in more detail at some of these impacts and at the ways in which "interlocking systems of inequality" help shape and determine the aging experience of diverse groups.

We begin in Chapter 13 with Steven Wallace and Valentine Villa's review of public policy and minority elderly in the United States at the end of the 20th century. These authors see the "relative invisibility" of minority elders in the political arena as reflecting, in part, the small (albeit growing) numbers of elders of color, their low voting rates, expectations of familial support, and the greater primacy accorded social problems (e.g., unemployment, gangs, and violence) affecting youth. Yet alongside this relative invisibility is the increasing visibility of minorities in general reflected in anti-immigrant laws and measures, key among them the Welfare Reform Bill which was "sold" in part through the promotion of negative stereotypes of the "Black Welfare Mom." Although the recent legislation is not directed specifically at minority elders, the latter are indeed "caught in the cross-fire" as legal immigrants face the loss of Supplemental Security Income, food stamps, and other benefits, and as low-income grandparents raising grandchildren are threatened with the imposition of harsh new restrictions on their ability to access government assistance. In the health policy arena, increasing out-of-pocket costs, the shift of the low-income elderly to managed care, and contemporary efforts to reduce the use of nursing homes are seen by Wallace and Villa as disproportionately hurting minority elders for whom a generally poorer health status and such potential barriers as language limitations may combine to increase the deleterious effects of these changes.

Although most of Chapter 13 emphasizes the *problems* being faced by the minority elderly, some encouraging notes are sounded as well. The rapid increase in the proportion of elders of color early in the new century, for example, is likely to contribute to the growing visibility of this population group in the years ahead. Wallace and Villa conclude by calling upon minority elected officials and national aging organizations that represent elders of color to "make health and long-term care parts of their national agendas," adding their voices to what ideally might be a renewed and powerful demand for a national health insurance program.

While Chapter 13 examines a variety of changing public policies as they affect minority elders, Chapter 14 focuses more specifically on one particular area: caregiving for (and often by) the elderly, and principally older women. Joanna

Weinberg begins by examining the paradox of caregiving within the context of the rapidly eroding welfare state and the continued ambivalence over this role, which has been simultaneously "minimized or ignored," expected, romanticized, and devalued at each step in the evolution of welfare state policies. Weinberg traces the history of such policies from Biblical times to the dramatic policy shifts of the 1980s and 1990s, culminating in the abolition of the 60-year-old Aid to Families with Dependent Children (AFDC) program in 1996. At each of these stages of policy development, the centrality of the notion of deservingness is highlighted, with caregivers frequently seen as unworthy of assistance in the conduct of this expected part of their unpaid labor in the private world of the home.

Weinberg highlights the skewing of caregiving responsibilities by gender, race, and class, with particular attention to the fact that despite the dramatic increase in female labor force participation, caregiving remains in large measure "a women's issue." Recent Congressional proposals to cut health care costs by reducing already inadequate support for in-home and community-based care of the elderly penalize not only the caregivers and care recipients who depend on these services but also the low-income women who constitute the vast majority of formal home and community care providers. Chapter 14 concludes by calling for an "alternative interpretation" of the activities of family caregivers—one that explicitly recognizes "the essentially political nature of the public/private spheres of caregiving roles." By legitimating and articulating the actual caregiving tasks of women, viewing such care as part of a "vertical continuum of the life course," and expanding rather than shrinking our notions of entitlement and community, such an alternative interpretation could appreciably increase the caring capacity of our society.

Although issues of race, class, and gender often are viewed separately within the context of aging and aging policy, the interlocking nature of oppressions based on these constructs is clear from each of the preceding chapters. In the final chapter of Part IV, Paula Dressel, Meredith Minkler, and Irene Yen underscore the need for gerontology to more critically address the challenges of inclusiveness and of interlocking oppressions and intersectionality in the study of aging.

Chapter 15 begins with a critique of the traditional methods employed in the study of marginalized groups, including between-group comparisons and what Margaret Andersen (1) has referred to as "the add and stir approach." Although such approaches are often well intentioned, they are problematic on multiple grounds, such as their tendency to answer inappropriate questions, to measure marginalized groups against the dominant group's standards, and to further perceptions of the subordinate groups as being on the periphery, rather than a part of the whole. The authors describe the concepts of interlocking oppressions/intersectionality as macro- and micro-level phenomena, respectively, that involve the interactions between systems of inequality that help shape human experience—in this case, in relation to aging. Together with such sociological concepts as Omi and Winant's (2) "racial projects" and "racial formations," these theoretical notions are promising new tools for better understanding the dynamic interplay of gender, race, class, and age.

Despite some recent and fruitful developments in the application of concepts such as the "persistent inequality" hypothesis of aging and race/ethnicity, Chapter 15 portrays the field of gerontology as a whole as relatively impoverished in its theoretical development in the area of race, class, gender, and aging. Dressel and her colleagues therefore conclude by looking beyond gerontology to recent and promising developments in fields such as epidemiology, geography, and sociology for new approaches that may also hold promise for the more inclusive study of aging in the years ahead.

REFERENCES

1. Andersen, M. L. *Thinking about Women: Sociological and Feminist Perspectives.* Macmillan, New York, 1983.
2. Omi, M., and Winant, H. *Racial Formations in the United States.* Routledge, New York, 1994.

CHAPTER 13

Caught in Hostile Cross-Fire: Public Policy and Minority Elderly in the United States

Steven P. Wallace and Valentine M. Villa

Minority elderly[1] in the United States at the end of the 20th century find themselves in a hostile cross-fire of social policy. Historically, racial and ethnic minorities have been exploited for cheap labor and scape-goated during periods of economic downturns. Public policy has alternatively encouraged immigration and the economic improvement of minority groups, only to later marginalize and penalize some of them. The 1990s is witnessing an anti-minority policy space that blames non-European immigrants and minorities for the social and economic problems generated by multinational corporations and the globalization of the economy. Added to the punitive policies aimed at minorities and non-European immigrants is a historic attack on the legitimacy of the elderly in the public policy arena. Beginning in the late 1970s and accelerating in the 1980s there has been a growing effort to counter the image of the elderly as a deserving group. The increasingly accepted public image of the elderly as generally healthy and well-off further marginalizes minority elderly who are disproportionately low-income and in poor health. Thus, policies that are punitive for minorities and immigrants are compounded by those that weaken public programs for the elderly.

In this context of hostility to immigrants and minorities, and the shrinking legitimacy of the elderly, federal policy has become dominated by budget issues. The

---

[1] We use the "minority" rather than "ethnic" elderly to emphasize the element of socially imposed stratification and inequality experienced by older African Americans, Asian Americans, Latinos, and Native Americans. The concept is based on power relationships rather than numerical size. The term "ethnic elderly" is broader and encompasses the variation in cultural practices and heritages of different groups of older persons. Thus, Irish American elderly may be an ethnic group to the extent that they hold distinct beliefs, family patterns, and behaviors, but are not a minority (during the 1990s) because they face no institutional barriers to their full participation in society based on their heritage.

This chapter is reprinted from *Aging, Health, and Ethnicity,* edited by K. Markides and M. Miranda, published by Sage Publications, Inc., in press with permission.

rising cost of health care has combined with a primary emphasis on reducing government spending to create pressures to reduce health care costs, resulting in policies that may decrease access to the health care services needed by minority elderly. The chapter concludes with an overview of likely policy and other trends into the 21st century that may influence access to care and the appropriateness of care for minority elderly.

THE INVISIBILITY OF MINORITY ELDERLY IN PUBLIC POLICY

Throughout most policy discussions minority elderly remain invisible in the United States, even though the elderly are a central focus of public policy, as are racial and ethnic minorities. This invisibility is a consequence, in part, of demography, the role of race and immigration in labor market policies, and the role of older persons in minority communities.

Much of this volume has correctly emphasized the *growing* numbers of minority elderly. But, historically, the proportions of older persons in minority populations has been comparatively small. Table 1 shows that the non-Latino white population has the largest proportion of elderly, while minority populations have the highest proportions of children and youth. For politicians whose motivations are partly based on the reactions of voters, the relatively small numbers of minority elderly (4.9 million versus 28.6 million older non-Latino whites in 1995) and their lower voting rates make minority elderly a marginal constituency. Minority communities as a whole are similarly less likely to push the needs of the elderly in policy arenas. While the non-Latino white population has about one and one-half youths for each elder, most of the minority groups have about four youths per elder (Table 1). The Latino population is the youngest, with about six youths per elder. The needs of youth—education, employment, reproductive health services—are therefore more prominently experienced in minority communities. In addition, the social problems experienced by the young are more likely to be visible to the entire community. Unemployment, gang violence, and drug abuse are more likely to involve the young, and in turn affect many others in the community. In contrast, when older persons

Table 1

Demographic composition of the U.S. population, 1995[a]

	Total population, thousands	Percent age 65 and over	Percent age 17 and under	Ratio of youth to elderly
Non-Latino white	193,566	14.8%	23.6%	1.60
African American	31,598	8.4	32.2	3.85
Latino	26,936	5.6	35.6	6.38
Asian American	8,788	6.8	29.1	4.27
Native America	1,931	6.7	34.9	5.21

[a]Source: U.S. Bureau of the Census, 1996.

experience poverty, chronic illnesses, or inadequate housing they are unlikely to be disruptive to those around them. Their problems become a liability for families, but not for the wider community in the same way as the problems of the young. While the problems encountered by the young and old in minority communities often share a common *source,* the *symptoms* of those problems appear more in the private sphere among the old and more in the public sphere among the young.

To the extent that minority communities have limited resources to advocate for public policies, it is logical that prominent organizations such as the Urban League and the National Council of La Raza have not prioritized their policy efforts toward proportionally small numbers of elderly. The organizations that represent minority elderly policy interests, such as the National Center for Black Aged, the National Hispanic Council on Aging, and other minority-group-specific national senior organizations, grew out of federal funding designed to foster such centers rather than from grass-roots organizing. On the other hand, the growing proportion of elderly in minority communities, combined with the aging of community activists who developed advocacy skills in the 1950s and 1960s, will likely increase the amount of minority-community policy activity on aging policy in the coming years.

A second factor making minority elderly invisible in much social policy is their low labor force participation rates. Policymakers are interested in labor force issues of racial and ethnic minorities because high unemployment rates in many minority communities generate a number of social problems (1). Similarly, the *employment* of recent immigrants is periodically viewed as a threat to native-born laborers, generating policy activity around issues of immigration (2, 3). This contributes to research and policy attention to issues including the causes of unemployment, limited economic opportunity, and welfare dependency in immigrant and racial/ ethnic minority communities. Once an individual reaches older ages, however, separation from the labor force is seen as normal and desirable. When absent from the labor force due to age, immigrant and minority elderly are no longer considered either problems or threats, and they fall out of consideration in the frequent policy activity focused on economic and labor policy.

Finally, the status of the elderly in most minority families likely contributes to the limited policy attention paid to minority elderly. The elderly in minority communities generally have higher levels of family support than non-Latino white older persons (4, 5), indicating that the families are assuming the duty of providing for the care of disabled older relatives. While this provides the potential for family advocacy on policy issues, in practice family care is experienced as a private obligation. Expectations of family support by minority elders are also likely to lead elders to focus their efforts on securing family relationships rather than moving to political action.

POLITICAL AND ECONOMIC CHANGE DRIVES
PUBLIC POLICY

This situation of invisible minority elders in the public policy arena occurs within a context that is increasingly hostile to minorities and older persons. Aging advocates often focus on the immediate threats to public programs for older persons—battling a cut in home-delivered meals here, increased Medicare premiums there, and all the while trying to decrease negative perceptions of aging that contribute to age discrimination (6). It is useful to take a step back, however, and look at some of the basic economic and political forces that frame these changes in public policy. In particular, we summarize some of the changes in the U.S. economy and the consequences of those changes on the public perception of immigrants and minorities. We then look at how the politics of health and aging policy shifted when the primary focus of federal policymaking became dominated by budget debates. This will provide a better understanding of why aging policies that negatively affect minority elderly are being proposed, as well as the timing of their political popularity.

Changes in the economy and the growing importance of economics in public policy decisions are major factors driving aging and health policies. Much has been written about the economic restructuring in the United States during the 1980s and 1990s. During this time period the United States has shifted away from manufacturing toward a service economy. The result has been an increasing bifurcation of the workforce into well paid and poorly paid positions. Leading the decline in jobs that provided middle-class earnings were manufacturing positions (7). It has become increasingly easy for manufacturing industries to move their production out of the United States to developing countries where wages are low, benefits nonexistent, and environmental and safety regulations lax. Some manufacturing jobs that have remained in the United States have relocated from the higher waged upper midwest and northeast to the lower waged south and southeast. The new jobs being created are disproportionately upper and lower wage positions. Between 1983 and 1993, 21 percent of job growth occurred in the service sector in industries such as retail sales and food service. Similarly, the number of clerical and other administrative support positions grew rapidly during this period and had median earnings below the average for all occupations (7). In addition, these positions are less likely to include health insurance, employer-paid pensions, or union protections. At the higher end of the wage scale, administrative specialty jobs increased rapidly, led by teachers and registered nurses (7). In addition, the competition from international competitors and pressures to increase profits have pushed U.S. companies to become increasingly "lean," resulting in restructurings and reorganizations involving layoffs of previously secure white-collar middle managers (8). Even companies such as IBM, which for decades had a "no layoff" policy, fired thousands of workers during the 1990s to reduce expenses (9). These, and other pressures, have resulted in an overall stagnation or decline of the purchasing power of family wages for over ten years, and increased insecurity among many about the long-term future of their jobs, health insurance, and pensions.

Historically, when the general public faces increased economic insecurity there is increased public concern about threats to jobs and the standard of living. These are the historical periods in which immigrants and people of color are most vulnerable to punitive public policies. During the Great Depression, for example, thousands of persons of Mexican ancestry were rounded up and deported to Mexico, often without concern for whether they were permanent residents or even U.S. citizens, because of a publicized belief that they were taking jobs from (non-Latino white) citizens (10). In the 1990s the public debate has shifted from jobs, where it has become less convincing that low-skilled immigrants compete for well-paying jobs, to the costs of public benefits used by immigrants. Federal legislation passed in 1996 gives states the option of cutting off most public assistance benefits to noncitizen immigrants who have worked for less than 10 years in the United States. Depending on how taxes paid and public programs used are counted, research can show that immigrants provide a net *contribution* or a net *drain* on public resources (11). But the *politics* of immigration has emphasized only the use of health, education, and welfare programs by immigrants, with no attention to the taxes paid and other contributions of immigrants. As a result, nearly 55 percent of Americans believe that immigrants cause economic crisis by increasing the demand on government services (12). Anti-immigrant sentiment has been expressed in a number of public votes, such as Proposition 187 in California that would have made undocumented immigrants ineligible for almost all public services and required public services to identify and report possible undocumented immigrant users (13). It is no accident that the anti-immigrant movement is strongest in the west: workers in the west during the early 1990s were more likely than average to lose their jobs and not find another one (8), and also lived in the region with the highest rates of immigration (14).

Anti-immigrant policies are not directed specifically at the elderly, but the elderly are often caught up in the effects of the broader policy changes. Limiting public benefits received by *legal* immigrants would penalize numerous older persons who depend on Supplemental Security Income (SSI) and Medicaid. About one-quarter of SSI recipients nationally are noncitizen, legal immigrants (15). Some proposals aimed at reducing public assistance spending would prohibit most immigrant elderly from receiving any health or income support (16). The undercurrent of anti-immigrant sentiment indirectly affects older persons with family and other relatives who may be affected by proposed legislation. Some elderly are reluctant to use services that they are eligible for because they fear bringing government attention to others in their family, putting them at risk.

At the same time that immigrants are being scape-goated for problems with government finances and other economic problems, people of color in general are the subject of negative policy actions, as exemplified by attacks on affirmative action. Some politicians have used affirmative action as a "wedge issue" to attract white voters who perceive minority workers as unfairly competing for jobs, as seen in the recent California proposition banning affirmative action in government programs (17). Efforts to overcome centuries of race-based discrimination began in the 1960s with programs designed to give minorities and women a chance to obtain jobs and education in areas from which they had been traditionally excluded. Public opinion polls in the 1990s document the public perception by whites that race-based discrimination no longer exists (contrary to the findings in the academic literature (e.g., 18)), while African Americans continue to perceive an impact of race on the opportunity structure (19). Whites focus on how affirmative action may make it harder for them to obtain desirable jobs, while overlooking the problem of the decreasing pool of desirable jobs resulting from economic processes. This reflects the fact that it is easier to blame social problems on persons than on social institutions or historical processes. This trend in public opinion serves to delegitimate programs that are believed to disproportionately serve racial and ethnic minority populations.

Similar attempts at scape-goating have occurred with the elderly. Since the 1980s there has been an organized effort to portray the elderly as uniformly wealthy and taking an unfair share of public resources. These groups worked to make the government role in pensions and health care for the elderly (via Social Security and Medicare) appear unnecessary (20), and have tried to frame policy debates within a context of intergenerational conflict (21). High levels of poverty and lack of access to health care for children and low-income adults are erroneously attributed to the successes of Social Security and Medicare in preventing those problems among older persons. Minority children are portrayed as particularly disadvantaged by the spending on older persons. Yet, programs for the elderly are especially important in minority communities because of the interdependence of family units, and the causes of poverty among racial and ethnic minority communities (unemployment, single-headed households, etc.) are unrelated to spending on programs for older persons (22).

There have also been significant political changes that have shifted the *context* of aging and health policy. One of the most significant public policies that affects minority elderly is the federal budget process. During the 1980s a series of taxing and spending changes occurred that has severely limited the ability of policymakers to respond creatively to social needs. First, President Reagan led the fight for the largest tax cut in history. Cutting income taxes (which become progressively higher as income from all sources, including investments, rises) while raising Social Security taxes (a regressive flat tax on only wages) provided tax relief primarily to those with the highest incomes while substantially reducing government revenues (23). Second, this era saw an enormous peace-time military buildup that increased spending during a time of falling tax revenues. The result was that the federal deficit ballooned, making the deficit *the* central policy issue at the federal level (24). Laws passed to reduce the deficit required that any new spending be offset by spending cuts elsewhere or by new taxes. These changes have resulted in federal planning being driven by budgetary rather than programmatic considerations (25).

The economic uncertainties of the 1990s have contributed to the continued concern over the size of the budget deficit. In attempts to reduce the deficit, the politics of economic crisis has led most political discussions to involve cuts in programs (although tax hikes were also approved during the early 1990s). The largest federally funded programs are Social Security (22 percent of federal spending), Medicare and Medicaid (17 percent), the military (16 percent), and interest on the national debt (16 percent). Despite the large amount of public attention paid to them, all means-tested (welfare) programs account for only 6.0 percent and foreign aid 1.4 percent of the federal budget (26). Even though Social Security and most of Medicare are self-funded (i.e., special, dedicated taxes support them and cannot be used for any other purpose), these two programs have been the special targets of many budget cutters. Cuts in these programs would, by and large, only postpone the deficit because the savings could only be loaned to reduce the deficit rather than actually pay off some of the accumulated debt. But the cuts would be "real" for those low- and moderate-income elderly who rely on Social Security for most of their monthly income and have Medicare as their only form of health insurance. In the next section we identify the key actors in health policy and discuss how these constraints result in specific types of health policies for minority elderly.

ELITE INTERESTS IN THE HEALTH POLICY PROCESS

To understand the politics of health policy, it is essential to briefly review the key players in the health policy arena. While minority elderly are largely invisible in public policy as both targets of policies and influences on policy, a set of powerful groups are clearly visible as central players in shaping and benefiting from health policy changes. Historically, elites such as the American Medical Association (AMA), the American Hospital Association, the insurance industry, and the pharmaceutical industry have held sway over U.S. health policy (27). More recently, employers who pay for the health insurance of their employees have become a major player in health policy (28). Unfortunately, the interests of none of these groups overlap with the health needs of minority elderly.

The corporate health sector's primary interests are maximizing profits and minimizing government regulation of their business, although the drug companies, insurance companies, and hospitals often differ on the particulars of specific legislation. The other powerful private interest is organized medicine, which tries to support high physician incomes and professional autonomy. These medical interests were particularly visible in the 1993 battles over President Clinton's proposed national health care reform. One estimate is that over $100 million was spent by over 650 groups on campaign contributions and advertising in attempts to influence the outcome of health care reform. Campaign donations in 1993 and 1994 by the AMA to members of Congress totaled $772,042; the American Hospital Association contributed $459,741, and the American Healthcare Association $215,025. In addition, the health insurance industry ran a $10 million television campaign designed to undermine public support for any changes that would decrease the role of private insurance (29).

Business has been a key actor in health policy debates over the past 15 years. Both locally and nationally, businesses have formed "business coalitions on health" in response to the rising proportion of total compensation spent on medical benefits (30). Employers have a stake in health policy for the elderly both because they pay half of Medicare taxes (the other half being paid by the employee) and because many large employers offer retirees insurance that supplements Medicare (Medi-Gap insurance). Most business efforts have been aimed at limiting their exposure to the rising costs of medical care, with no attention to the special needs of low-income or minority elderly. With health care policy regulating, subsidizing, and otherwise affecting the health care sector, which comprises as much as one-seventh of the U.S. economy (31), health policy is also caught up in the broader ideological and economic conflicts over the extent and direction of government involvement in the economy and society.

The federal bureaucracy has also been the site of a moderate amount of policy influence and initiative, though the federal health bureaucracy has not been as active in health issues as the Pentagon has in military issues. The Social Security

Administration was instrumental in shaping the design and implementation of Medicare in the 1960s, the initial push to encourage health maintenance organizations (HMOs) in the 1970s came from the executive branch, and the hospital and physician reimbursement changes of the 1980s were the result of administrative initiatives. The organizational tendency to enhance one's own department is evident in the multiple and overlapping programs focusing on long-term care for the elderly which are jealously guarded at the local level by the Area Agencies on Aging, Medicaid agencies, and state-funded (through federal Social Service Block Grant money, for example) programs (32). Since no government office focuses specifically on minority elderly (as the Department of Veteran's Affairs focuses on vets, or the Administration on Aging focuses on all elderly), there is no institutional voice at the federal level that can advocate for minority elderly policies.

None of the central interests in health care policy are particularly responsive to minority community needs, especially not among the elderly. The sector least interested in minority elderly is the corporate medical sector. Since the first concern of this sector is profits, and minority elderly are more likely to have lower incomes, the minority market is not a major concern. The history of the growth of for-profit hospitals, for example, has found them concentrating in growing, middle-class, white, suburban areas, where there are the highest concentrations of privately insured (i.e., most profitable) individuals. In contrast, inner cities have been losing hospitals because of the economics of serving inner city residents, not because of a lack of need for medical care (33, 34).

The high level of social and economic segregation of most minorities, on the other hand, could make it possible for them to become an attractive "niche" market for some providers if the minority community has sufficient purchasing power. Enhancing purchasing power in a market system was the goal of Medicare, for example. It provided the equivalent of private insurance to all persons aged 65 and over. The result was an increase in the use of the covered hospital and doctor services, reducing or eliminating earlier differences by race and income in the overall use of those services (35). Medicare also helped increase access to medical services for African American elderly by strictly enforcing antisegregation provisions against hospitals that accepted any Medicare. With Medicare's hospital reimbursement policies being exceptionally lucrative in the 1960s, and the elderly being the highest users of medical care services, hospitals that had been segregated had a powerful incentive to open their doors equally to blacks and whites.

The situation in the 1990s, however, has changed substantially. Medicare has reduced reimbursements to hospitals and doctors as a way to slow rising costs, making Medicare patients less attractive (36). Even less desirable are Medicaid patients. Comparatively low payments by Medicaid lead many physicians and nursing homes to avoid Medicaid patients (37), and many hospitals view treating Medicaid patients as a cost rather than a revenue. To the extent that minority elderly are disproportionately concentrated in low-income and racially homogeneous areas (4), the trends affecting the entire health care system hit them the hardest.

Without any institutional interests that have a vested interest in the needs of minority elderly, health policy takes shape with limited attention to their needs. The dominant issue in health policy at the end of the 20th century has been containing health care costs. The next section focuses on the strategies likely to be followed in that effort, and their consequences for minority elderly.

COST-CONTAINMENT POLICIES AND MINORITY ELDERLY

Most health policies that affect the elderly fail to take into account the differential impact of those policies on subgroups of elders. Cost-containment policy is a particularly important area that is receiving extensive policy attention, but with limited consideration of racial and ethnic populations. Several areas of cost containment have particularly severe effects on minority elderly, including changing the out-of-pocket costs for health care, shifting toward managed care, and trying to discourage the use of nursing homes. In each of these areas, the impact on minority elderly is likely to be different than for the elderly population in aggregate.

Increasing Out-of-Pocket Costs

One common approach to reducing health care spending has been to increase out-of-pocket costs. Using classical economic models, it is assumed that the higher the cost of an item (medical care), the more judiciously an individual will make use of it. Medicare includes copayments and deductibles that are designed, in theory, to reduce the unnecessary use of services.

The deductibles paid under Medicare are amounts that the individual has to pay out of pocket (or with private insurance) before Medicare begins to pay for services. These are the equivalent of one day's hospital charge for inpatient care (in 1996 it was $736) and $100 for physician services (38). In addition, there is a copayment of 20 percent of physician charges. Finally, there is a premium charge for Medicare Part B (which covers physician care), $42.50 in 1996 (38), up from $14.50 in 1984 (39). These costs, along with the costs for services not covered by Medicare such as prescription drugs, dental care, and long-term care, can add up to quite high costs for an older person with a chronic illness. Excluding nursing home expenses, the average out-of-pocket costs (including insurance premiums) for older persons *living in poverty* were $1,860 in 1994, equivalent to over one-third of their income (40).

These high costs motivate the majority of older persons to obtain private supplemental insurance in addition to Medicare. About 75 percent of the total population aged 65 and over has private supplemental insurance, while only 15 percent rely exclusively on Medicare (Table 2). There are great disparities by race and ethnicity, however. African American and Hispanic elderly are two to three times more likely than whites to have no insurance except Medicare (Table 2). Since minority elderly are also more likely to have low and middle incomes, changes in the financing of Medicare that increase out-of-pocket costs will disproportionately hurt minority elderly.

Proposals to dramatically increase the out-of-pocket costs for the elderly have been discussed for a number of years (41), but have been most clearly articulated by

Table 2

Health insurance of older persons in the United States, 1994[a]

	Medicare and private	Medicare and Medicaid	Medicare only
All older persons	75.1%	5.3%	14.8%
White	80.3	3.7	12.3
African American	44.9	14.4	34.6
Hispanic	49.2	19.5	23.2

[a]Source: National Center for Health Statistics, 1996.

the 1994 Republican Congressional election platform that promised to roll back the role of government in the health and welfare of the country. Republican Congressional candidates ran on a platform of policy proposals they called the "Contract with America," based on the assumption that government had too large a role in the health and welfare of the population and that individuals should instead assume a greater "responsibility" for their own health and well-being. Under this Contract, premiums and out-of-pocket costs and deductibles under Medicare would have doubled. Cost-sharing for Medicaid would also have increased, and states would have been given the option to limit the amount and scope of assistance provided to recipients, such as eliminating existing protections against spousal impoverishment when one spouse requires nursing home care (42). Because of the increased spending by older persons for health care required under these proposals, they have the potential to increase economic vulnerability among minority elders and to decrease their access to health and long-term care.

Limited access to health and long-term care services for older minorities means that greater responsibility for their well-being would be shifted to minority families who, like their elderly members, are disproportionately economically and socially vulnerable. According to the Center on Budget and Policy Priorities (43), about one in four Latino workers paid by the hour does not earn enough to keep a family of three out of poverty. In addition, African Americans and Latinos are more often in female-headed households, resulting in more families dependent on a single wage earner and more living in poverty (44). Moreover, increases in teen pregnancy and increases in the prevalence of AIDS, HIV, and drug dependence among younger members of minority populations have resulted in an increase in four-generation households where, for the most part, middle-aged women are caring for parents, adult children, and grandchildren (45–47). Thus there is an increasing number of minority women age 55 and over who must quit their jobs to care for family members, while at the same time receiving no income from Social Security or private pensions (44, 48). Clearly, minority families have accepted the "responsibility" of caring for family members, and indeed express a preference for caring for relatives in the home (46, 49). However, given the challenges of increased financial burdens for medical care, caring for family members without assistance from government programs is unrealistic.

Managed Care

The most significant trend in the health care system during the 1990s is the growth of managed care systems. Medicare, a relative latecomer to the managed care revolution, has over 10 percent of its insured in managed care plans. Medicare HMO plans grew at a rate of 30 percent in 1995, and Congressional proposals would greatly increase that growth (50). In California well over 40 percent of all Medicare recipients are in HMOs, accounting for over one-quarter of all Medicare HMO enrollees nationally (50). This rapid change in the organization of health care financing and delivery is occurring with only limited government involvement and oversight, despite the potential consequences of the shift in access to care and quality of care for older persons.

Managed care takes a wide variety of different forms, all of which focus on containing costs. The type of managed care currently being used by most Medicare is prepaid, at-risk HMOs. The archetypal HMO is the staff model in which the plan receives a fixed payment per enrollee regardless of the enrollee's actual health care use (called capitation), the health care providers are on salary, and all health care facilities (hospitals, labs, offices) are owned by the organization. Other HMO models contract out for physician services to physician groups or individuals, usually capitating the physician care and often putting the physicians at some risk for hospitalization costs. These models generally limit patient choice to a limited number of physicians and hospitals chosen by the plan. It is this "closed panel" feature that older persons most often find objectionable because of the importance they place on their relationship with their current care providers (51).

At an organizational level, managed care moves medicine from a guild or craft model to more of an industrial or bureaucratic model. This new organizational model has the *potential* to increase accountability, continuity, and efficiency. The wide gulf between providers and patients in knowledge about disease and its treatment means that under the traditional individual practitioner model, the patient was at the mercy of the abilities and prejudices of each individual provider. Under a more bureaucratic system it is possible to have more comprehensive checks and balances to prevent inappropriate care, lack of follow through, and other problems. In addition, most managed care plans require lower copayments and few or no deductibles compared with fee-for-service insurance, reducing the out-of-pocket costs for older persons and improving their financial access to care.

On the other hand, as organized systems, managed care organizations introduce a new set of systemic incentives. The most widely discussed incentive under capitated systems is to undertreat patients in order to maximize profits since the plan receives a fixed premium payment per enrollee. Some HMOs make physicians personally at-risk for above-average hospital costs (regardless of whether the costs are justified or not), providing the greatest incentive to undertreat (52). Other characteristics of some managed care organizations that patients are particularly sensitive to include a weaker commitment to a particular practice site by physicians that increases provider turnover, reduced patient autonomy, and increasingly bureaucratized systems that can be hard to negotiate (51). Less visible to individual patients, but particularly important for access to care for minority elders, are incentives that exist in some large capitated systems to preferentially recruit or "skim" the healthiest patients who will be the lowest users of services, to avoid the chronically ill and disabled, and to enroll patients with little attention to whether the location and service mix are most appropriate for the enrollee (36). Press accounts of marketing problems are common, including marketers who split their commission with new enrollees, high pressure tactics, and misinformation (53). These and other problems have led to an average of 20 percent of new enrollees dropping out of HMOs within one year (54).

One potentially worrisome trend in the managed care field is the rapid growth of for-profit HMOs in the market. Generating profits to pay to shareholders and to pay the excessive salaries of some top executives (e.g., $6.1 million per year to the CEO of one HMO in 1995 (55)) exaggerates the incentives to undertreat patients. While nonprofit HMOs can be pressured to provide extra services such as medical education or uncompensated care in exchange for their tax-exempt status, for-profit businesses have profits as their foremost goal. On the other hand, the behavior of nonprofit chains in other sectors of the health care industry has been little different from that of the for-profits because both operate under similar market conditions (56).

As large organizations, it is reasonable to expect managed care systems to operate similarly to other large organizations in U.S. society. Discrimination based on both race and age is common in many key institutions. Research has shown how the educational system reinforces racial inequality, how the labor market perpetuates the disadvantaged positions of minorities and older workers (57), and how housing markets and the mortgage system perpetuate discrimination based on race (18). Each of these sectors—education, employment, and housing—is dominated by large institutions that rationalize and direct the operation of each sector, and in each sector there has been a continuing concern with access and equity. While older persons may have faced racial barriers in education, employment, and housing earlier in their lives, the health care system is the most important public social institution with which they *currently* interact.

The quality of life of minority elderly is largely dependent on the *past* dynamics of social systems that have resulted in their current levels of knowledge, income, health status, and housing. Those conditions are combined with the *current* dynamics of the medical care system that influences their medical care use and outcomes of health care. There is ample evidence that minority elderly receive different patterns of care under the fee-for-service system (e.g., 58). The bureaucratic organization of managed care could serve to equalize the care received by different groups of older persons, or it could accentuate those differences in ways that have a substantial impact on the quality of life of minority elders. As long as the primary driving force of health care policy is cost containment, however, issues such as access to care, quality, and equity for racial and ethnic minority elderly will remain on the back burner (59), and the managed-care-based health care system will evolve with little attention to minority elders.

Reducing the Use of Nursing Homes

While Medicare pays for very little nursing home care, Medicaid pays for almost half of all nursing home expenses (31). Paying for all this nursing home care consumed about 20 percent of *all* Medicaid spending in 1993 (31). As these costs continue to rise, there have been a variety of policy approaches to reducing the high costs of care. On the supply side, changes were made starting in the 1970s in the way nursing homes were paid, effectively reducing the reimbursement rates. Many states have also placed restrictions on the construction of new nursing homes to reduce the supply of beds. On the demand side, beginning in the 1980s the federal government allowed states to expand home and community services (such as homemakers and adult day care) under their Medicaid programs as a way of helping older persons remain in their own homes. In addition, there have been a number of demonstration projects designed to make it more attractive for individuals to purchase private insurance that covers long-term care.

The primary motive in all of these policy changes has been to reduce the costs to the government of nursing home care (59). On one level, the change in emphasis from institutional to community long-term care is beneficial to minority elderly since they are less likely than non-Hispanic whites to use nursing homes. In 1990, about 26 percent of non-Hispanic whites aged 85 and over lived in nursing homes, compared with 17 percent of African Americans, 11 percent of Hispanics, and 12 percent of Asian Americans (60). These high rates of the oldest-old minorities *outside* nursing homes create a special need for community-based services in minority communities. The extra funding and expanded programs for community care under Medicaid in all states are likely to especially benefit minority elderly, since they are also more likely than non-Hispanic whites to receive Medicaid (see Table 2). Thus, the effort on reducing nursing home spending may have a positive (if unintended) benefit to minority elders.

On the other hand, the growing restrictions on nursing home availability will make it increasingly difficulty for minority elderly who need nursing home care to obtain it. Nursing homes are an appropriate source of care for some. Their residents are most commonly persons with high levels of physical and cognitive disabilities and low levels of available family support. When Medicaid reduces reimbursements and makes it ever less financially attractive to admit Medicaid patients, minority elderly are the most likely to face discrimination based on their source of payment. While about 40 percent of older persons overall enter nursing homes on Medicaid, over 70 percent of African American elderly enter nursing homes with Medicaid as their primary source of payment (61). The effort to increase the proportion of the population with private long-term care insurance for nursing homes will only exacerbate this problem. The high costs of private long-term care insurance result in no more than 20 percent of persons being able to afford it (62). The high incomes needed to make long-term care insurance affordable will result in a lower proportion of racial and ethnic minorities being able to afford it, and the higher payment rates of private insurance than Medicaid will further disadvantage minority elderly when they compete for a nursing home bed.

For minority elders to benefit from expanded in-home and community-based services, their access to these programs must be improved. Studies of community-based long-term care use among minorities have found lower participation rates than needs would indicate (63). Barriers to utilization include money, a lack of knowledge about services, language barriers, the complexity of the application process, location of providers outside minority communities, and lack of bilingual staff (64–66). Improving access would require a commitment on the part of policymakers to develop legislation that mandates providers to create culturally appropriate and sensitive programs and develop information and outreach strategies targeted to minority communities.

HEALTH POLICY
FOR THE TWENTY-FIRST CENTURY

It has been said that individuals make their own history, but not under the conditions of their own choosing. Minority elderly have not chosen to be surrounded by an anti-immigrant and anti-minority policy space, attacks on programs for the elderly, and powerful interests in the health care system that do not prioritize their needs. But minority elderly and their communities are *not* passive objects of health policy, either. Most take active roles in maintaining their physical and spiritual health, and in managing their medical care needs. But the forces that shape health policy for the elderly take little notice of this group. The health problems and concerns of older minorities are mainly invisible in the larger health policy context. And the interests of the most influential players in the health policy arena—medical providers and businesses that pay for employee health insurance—rarely include special attention to the elderly in racial and ethnic minority groups.

Even while health policy largely overlooks minority elderly, they are caught in the cross-fire of social trends that are separately attacking public policies for immigrants and minorities as well as older persons. Large, impersonal changes in the structure of the U.S. economy have increased income inequality and heightened racial, ethnic, and generational conflict. And the changing nature of the federal policy process has made budgetary issues the cornerstone of all other public policy. These trends can be seen in the health care cost-containment policies embodied in increased Medicare out-of-pocket costs, an increased reliance on managed care, and continuing efforts to reduce nursing home use.

If older minorities are being buffeted by policy changes that do not take them into account, is there any hope that policy in the 21st century may be more appropriate for minority elderly? Some changes are likely to increase the awareness of health policy on issues of minority aging, especially demographic changes, while other social changes such as continuing increases in the cost of health care may provide counterpressures on public policy to ignore the health care needs of minority elderly.

Perhaps the most significant change that will occur in the 21st century is the increasing diversity of the older population. Torres-Gil (67) identifies three trends that will reshape aging policy in the future, one of which is growing diversity (race/ethnicity, family structure, income distribution, etc.). As the proportion of the older population that is minority grows from 14 percent of those aged 65 and over in

1990 to 32 percent by 2050, it will be increasingly difficult to simply ignore that segment of the older population. And as the older population becomes increasingly diverse, the working-age adult population will become more diverse as well. In California, for example, non-Latino whites will comprise less than half of the total population before the year 2000 (68). This historic demographic shift could increase attention to the needs of minority populations at all ages, or it could be used to increase the racial and ethnic tensions of the 1990s.

Demography alone will not influence public policy, however, as is shown by the political activity required by women (who comprise a majority of the population) in the early 1900s to obtain the right to vote (69). Ensuring that health policy and long-term care policy are responsive to minority elderly populations, therefore, will require increased advocacy as the population grows. Minority elected officials and national aging organizations representing minority populations, in particular, need to make health and long-term care parts of their larger agendas and to move toward developing proposals and platforms that are informed, visible, and best suited for the populations they represent. The development of proposals for the financing, development, and delivery of health and long-term care will also require minority scholars and service providers to play a key role in educating policymakers about the needs and experiences of aging among minority elders. In addition, it is critical that communities, service providers, and advocacy groups work to empower older minorities to move toward self-advocacy. These kinds of activities can ultimately lead to policy agendas that not only better dovetail with needs, but are more proactive than reactive.

The other trend that could bode either ill or well for minority elderly is the continued growth of medical care costs. The ever growing share of the national economy devoted to medical services guarantees that efforts to rein in medical inflation will continue. The emphasis on managed care as a way to contain costs is helping change the structure of the U.S. medical care system, although pressures continue to increase the out-of-pocket costs of the elderly and to restrict access to some services. If current dominant interests in health care policy reform continue to shape public policy in the coming years, changes in the medical care system are likely to protect corporate profits and existing medical care enterprises at the expense of adequate access to care for minority elderly. It is possible, however, that minority communities and organizations representing the interests of minority elderly will be able to form effective coalitions with mainstream aging organizations, citizens' lobby groups, and organized labor to push for policy changes that prioritize the human needs of diverse populations (21, 24). One major step in that direction would be to bring the United States into step with the rest of the industrialized world and establish some form of national health insurance that provides equal financial access to health care for all older Americans and nondiscriminatory forms of cost control over the entire medical care system (70, 71). Such a system of health insurance could be structured in such a way as to minimize many of the problems facing minority elderly in access to care, the growing financial burdens of health services, and institutional barriers to appropriate care. As demonstrated in the efforts to reform health insurance in the early 1990s, powerful interests with a stake in the currently inequitable system will oppose many of the needed changes. Only a concerted effort by a broad coalition has a chance of enacting the types of health policy changes needed by minority elderly.

REFERENCES

1. Wilson, W. J. *When Work Disappears.* University of Chicago Press, Chicago, 1996.
2. Portes, A., and Bach, R. L. *Latin Journey: Cuban and Mexican Immigrants in the United States.* University of California Press, Berkeley, 1986.
3. Rothstein, R. Immigrant dilemmas. *Dissent* 40: 455–463, 1993.
4. Wallace, S. P. The political economy of health care for elderly blacks. *Int. J. Health Serv.* 20(4): 665–680, 1990.
5. Wallace, S. P., and Lew-Ting, C. Y. Getting by at home: Community based long-term care of Latino elderly. *West. J. Med.* 157(3): 337–344, 1992.
6. Wallace, S. P., and Williamson, J. B. The senior movement in historical perspective. In *The Senior Movement: References and Resources,* edited by S. P. Wallace and J. B. Williamson, pp. vii–xxxvi. G. K. Hall, New York, 1992.
7. Rosenthal, N. H. The nature of occupational employment growth: 1983–93. *Monthly Labor Rev.* 118(6): 45–55, 1995.
8. Gardner, J. M. Worker displacement: A decade of change. *Monthly Labor Rev.* 118(4): 45–58, 1995.
9. Langberg, M. IBM cuts first S.J. workers. *San Jose Mercury News,* October 29, 1993, p. 1E.
10. McWilliams, C. *North from Mexico: The Spanish-Speaking People of the United States.* Greenwood Press, New York, 1948.
11. Fix, M. E., and Passel, J. S. Setting the record straight: What are the costs to the public? *Public Welfare* 52(2): 6–15, 1994.
12. Moore, D. W. Americans feel threatened by new immigrants. *Gallup Poll Monthly* 334: 2–17, 1993.
13. Armbruster, R., Geron, K., and Bonacich, E. The assault on California's Latino immigrants: The politics of Proposition 187. *Int. J. Urban Regional Res.* 19(4): 655–663, 1995.
14. Smith, M. P., and Tarallo, B. Proposition 187: Global trend or local narrative? Explaining anti-immigrant politics in California, Arizona, and Texas. *Int. J. Urban Regional Res.* 19(4): 664–676, 1995.
15. U.S. Social Security Administration. *Aliens Who Receive SSI Payments.* Office of Supplemental Security Income, Baltimore, Md., March 1994.
16. Wallace, S. P., and Manuel-Barkin, C. Older Immigrants in California: Health Care Needs and the Policy Context. Final Report. November 1995.
17. Pear, R. In California, voters bar preferences based on race. *New York Times,* November 7, 1996, p. B7.
18. Massey, D. S., and Denton, N. A. *American Apartheid: Segregation and the Making of the Underclass.* Harvard University Press, Cambridge, Mass., 1993.
19. Stall, B. Prop. 209's fate may hinge in two words. *Los Angeles Times,* October 31, 1996, p. A1.
20. Quadagno, J. Generational equity and the politics of the welfare state. *Polit. Soc.* 17(3): 353–376, 1989.
21. Binstock, R. H. A new era in the politics of aging: How will old-age interest groups respond? *Generations* 19(3): 68–74, 1995.

22. Minkler, M. Generational equity or interdependence. In *Diversity: New Approaches of Ethnic Minority Aging,* edited by E. P. Stanford and F. M. Torres-Gil, pp. 65–72. Baywood, Amityville, N.Y., 1992.

23. U.S. House of Representatives, Committee on the Budget. *President Reagan's Fiscal Year 1988 Budget.* Government Printing Office, Washington, D.C., 1987.

24. Wallace, S. P., and Estes, C. L. Health policy for the elderly: Federal policy and institutional change. In *Policy Issues for the 1990's,* pp. 591–613. Policy Studies Review Annual, No. 9. Transaction Publishers, New Brunswick, N.J., 1989.

25. Waldivsky, A. B. *The New Politics of the Budgetary Process,* Ed. 2. Harper Collins, New York, 1992.

26. U.S. Office of Management and Budget. *The Budget of the United States, 1996.* Executive Office of the President, Washington, D.C., 1995.

27. Starr, P. *The Social Transformation of American Medicine.* Basic Books, New York, 1982.

28. Bergthold, L. The fat kid on the seesaw: American business and health care cost containment, 1970–1990. *Annu. Rev. Public Health* 12: 157–175, 1991.

29. Center for Public Integrity. *Well-Healed: Inside Lobbying for Health Care Reform.* Washington, D.C., 1994.

30. Bergthold, L. *Purchasing Power in Health.* Rutgers University Press, New Brunswick, N.J., 1990.

31. Levitt, K. R., et al. National health expenditures, 1993. *Health Care Financ. Rev.* 16: 247–294, 1994.

32. Estes, C. L. *The Aging Enterprise.* Jossey-Bass, San Francisco, 1979.

33. Rice, M. F. Inner city hospital closures/relocations: Race, income status, and legal issues. *Soc. Sci. Med.* 24(11): 889–896, 1987.

34. Witeis, D. G. Hospital and community characteristics in closures or urban hospitals: 1980–1987. *Public Health Rep.* 107(4): 409–416, 1992.

35. Feder, J. M. Medicare implementation and the policy process. *J. Health Polit. Policy Law* 2: 173–189, 1977.

36. Moon, M., and Davis, K. Preserving and strengthening Medicare. *Health Aff.* 14(4): 31–46, 1995.

37. Institute of Medicine. *Improving the Quality of Care in Nursing Homes.* National Academy Press, Washington, D.C., 1986.

38. U.S. Health Care Financing Administration. *Medicare Fact Sheet.* U.S. Department of Health and Human Services, Baltimore, Md., 1996.

39. U.S. Congressional Budget Office. *Changing the Structure of Medicare Benefits: Issues and Options.* Government Printing Office, Washington, D.C., 1993.

40. American Association of Retired Persons. *Coming Up Short: Increasing Out-of-Pocket Health Spending by Older Americans.* AARP Public Policy Institute, Washington, D.C., 1994.

41. Villers Foundation. *On the Other Side of Easy Street: Myths and Facts About the Economics of Old Age.* Washington, D.C., 1987.

42. Administration on Aging. Medicaid block grants and OAA performance partnerships: Potential impacts on LTC for diverse communities. *Diversity and Long Term Care Newsletter.* Washington, D.C., 1995.

43. Center on Budget and Policy Priorities. Minimum wage veto hurts Latinos and blacks. *Hispanic Link Wkly Rep.,* June 26, 1989, pp. 2–4.

44. Garcia, A. Income security and elderly Latinos. In *Elderly Latinos: Issues and Solutions for the 21 Century,* edited by M. Sotomayor and A. Garcia. National Hispanic Council on Aging, Washington, D.C., 1993.

45. National Council of La Raza. *The State of Hispanic America 1991: An Overview.* Washington, D.C., 1992.
46. Antonucci, T. C., and Cantor, M. H. Strengthening the family support system for older minority persons. In *Minority Elders: Five Goals Toward Building a Public Policy Base.* Gerontological Society of America, Washington, D.C., 1994.
47. Sotomayor, M. The Latino elderly: A policy agenda. In *Elderly Latinos: Issues and Solutions for the 21st Century,* edited by M. Sotomayor and A. Garcia. National Hispanic Council on Aging, Washington, D.C., 1993.
48. Minkler, M., and Roe, K. *Grandmothers and Caregivers: Raising Children of the Crack Cocaine Epidemic.* Sage, Newbury Park, Calif., 1993.
49. Kiyak, H. A., and Hooyman, N. R. Minority and socioeconomic status: Impact on quality of life in aging. In *Aging and the Quality of Life,* edited by R. P. Ables, H. C. Gift, and M. G. Ory. Springer, New York, 1994.
50. U.S. General Accounting Office. *Medicare HMOs: Rapid Enrollment Growth Concentrated in Selected States.* Washington, D.C., 1996.
51. Frederick/Schneiders, Inc. *Analysis of Focus Groups Concerning Managed Care and Medicare.* Report prepared for the Kaiser Family Foundation. Washington, D.C., 1995.
52. Pauly, M. V., Hillman, A. L., and Kerstein, J. Managing physician incentives in managed care. *Med. Care* 28: 1013–1024, 1990.
53. Olmos, D. R. HMO accused of marketing fraud, other improprieties. *Los Angeles Times,* June 25, 1996, p. D2.
54. Brown, R., et al. *The Medicare Risk Program for HMOs—Final Summary Report on Findings from the Evaluation.* Mathematica Policy Research, Princeton, N.J., 1993.
55. Mathews, J. $6.1 million a year to run an HMO. *Washington Post,* December 27, 1995, p. B1.
56. Clarke, L., and Estes, C. L. Sociological and economic theories of markets and nonprofits: Evidence from home health organizations. *Am. J. Sociol.* 97: 945–969, 1992.
57. Farley, R., and Allen, W. R. *The Color Line and the Quality of Life in America.* Oxford University Press, New York, 1989.
58. McBean, A. M., and Gornick, M. Differences by race in the rates of procedures performed in hospitals for Medicare beneficiaries. *Health Care Financ. Rev.* 15(4): 77–90, 1994.
59. Wallace, S. P., Abel, E. K., and Stefanowicz, P. Long-term care and the elderly. In *Beyond Health Care Reform: Key Issues in Policy and Management,* edited by R. Andersen, T. Rice, and G. Kominski, pp. 180–201. Jossey-Bass, San Francisco, 1996.
60. Damron-Rodriguez, J., Wallace, S. P., and Kington, R. Service utilization and minority elderly: Appropriateness, accessibility and acceptability. *Gerontol. Geriatr. Educ.* 15(1): 45–64, 1994.
61. Hing, E. *Use of Nursing Homes by the Elderly: Preliminary Data from the 1985 National Nursing Home Survey.* NCHS Advance Data, 135. National Center for Health Statistics, Hyattsville, Md., 1987.
62. Wiener, J. M., Illston, L. H., and Hanley, R. J. *Sharing the Burden: Strategies for Public and Private Long-Term Care Insurance.* Brookings Institution, Washington, D.C., 1994.
63. Hyde, J. C., and Torres-Gil, F. Ethnic minority elders and the Older Americans Act: How have they fared? *Generations* 15(3): 57–62, 1991.
64. Moon, A., Lubben, J., and Villa, V. M. Awareness and utilization of community long term care services by elderly Korean and non-Hispanic white Americans. *Gerontologist* 1997, in press.
65. National Council of La Raza. *On the Sidelines: Hispanic Elderly and the Continuum of Care.* Washington, D.C., 1991.

66. Wallace, S. P., Levy-Storms, L., and Ferguson, L. R. Access to paid in-home assistance among disabled elderly people: Do Latinos differ from non-Latino whites? *Am. J. Public Health* 85(7): 970–975, 1995.

67. Torres-Gil, F. M. *The New Aging: Politics and Change in America.* Auburn House, New York, 1992.

68. Hayes-Bautista, D. E. Young Latinos, older Anglos, and public policy: Lessons from California. *Generations* 15(4): 37–42, 1991.

69. Skocpol, T. *Protecting Soldiers and Mothers: The Political Origins of Social Policy in the United States.* Harvard University Press, Cambridge, Mass., 1992.

70. Pepper Commission. *A Call for Action.* U.S. Bipartisan Commission on Comprehensive Health Care. Government Printing Office, Washington, D.C., 1990.

71. Brown, E. R. Should single-payer advocates support President Clinton's proposal for health care reform? *Am. J. Public Health* 84(2): 182–187, 1994.

CHAPTER 14

Caregiving, Age, and Class
in the Skeleton of the Welfare State:
"And Jill Came Tumbling After . . ."

Joanna K. Weinberg

"Still," she thought, "it had seemed like a good idea once upon a time: spare children, like spare tires, or those extra lisle stockings they used to package free with each pair." "You should have arranged for a second-string mother, Ezra," she said. Or she meant to say.

Anne Tyler, *Dinner at the Homesick Restaurant* (1)

One of the fundamental debates in U.S. social policy has centered on whether individuals should be free to accumulate wealth for distribution as they individually choose, or whether there is some underlying community value that recognizes the importance of redistribution of wealth—ultimately, asking the question: What kind of legacy or debt is appropriate to pass on to future generations? Over the years, social policy has puzzled over the concept of what kinds of policy decisions are least likely to burden future generations, and whether to support communitarian goals for society as a whole, as a way of not "obligating" future generations, or whether individuals must have the freedom (and the responsibility) to make their own decisions. In the 20th century alone, the pendulum has swung toward individual obligations, then toward broad community responsibilities, then back toward what is now termed "individual responsibility." Feminists have characterized public (male and in the forefront) and private (female and invisible) domains as a way of explaining public society's inattention to the work of women. It is not always recognized, however, that both domains embody community as well as individual values; the private domain too often is considered to exist exclusive of the community. In this context, even the public role of caregiving may become invisible. As the nation's commitment to community values gives way to mandates of personal responsibility, the loss of public consensus for entitlements was caused in part by the failure of U.S. social policy to recognize the community elements of the caregiving role. Ultimately, this failure doomed the idea of redistribution of wealth through a benevolent welfare state, and resulted in elimination of the 60-year-old federal government promise of an economic safety net (2).

This chapter looks at the historical and contemporary marginalization of caregiving, and questions the ways in which social policies have treated people who provide caregiving services. Further, it examines the reasons why caregiving historically has been an easy scapegoat for the problems of the welfare state, and why this scapegoating undermines rather than supports the social and economic security of families. The first section examines the underlying principles of welfare state organization and structure that have made caregiving an easy target. It then looks at the practical and theoretical underpinnings of caregiving policies, with respect to care for children and care for the elderly, examining how the historical policies have contributed to the marginalization of caregiving. Finally, it presents the argument that the policies limiting the autonomy of female caregivers are the current practical formulation of the policy of marginalization.

THE PARADOX OF PUBLIC BENEFITS

The relationship between the obligations of caregiving and receipt of public benefits is one of the continuing paradoxes of the welfare state. The paradox of policy stems from the fact that while both the private employment sector and the public social safety nets depend on caregiving work, as both paid and uncompensated employment, caregiving is not seen as a legitimate activity of the welfare state, and caregivers (as well as recipients of care) are increasingly seen as undeserving of public funds or benefits. The paradox has deep roots in U.S. social policy and common law, which have combined a generalized reluctance to codify the value of caregiving in concrete policy with the imposition of moral, social, and sometimes legal mandates to provide those services (3, 4).

Three conceptual dichotomies provide insight into the paradox: the need of U.S. policy to make distinctions between "deserving" and "undeserving" recipients of public benefits; the ongoing dichotomy between formal (paid) caregiving work and informal (unpaid) caregiving work; and the distinction between recipients of care services and providers of these services. Certain common features mark these dichotomies: all are elemental social constructions, without solid evidentiary support; all are artificial and perhaps inaccurate constructions; and all incorporate ambivalent perspectives about caregiving.

Ultimately, ambivalence about caregiving may have unforeseen costs for the broader economy. As the safety net is removed from recipients of caregiving services, it is also removed from the providers of those services, and from paid as well as unpaid workers. Moreover, the idea of what constitutes full employment has changed with the expansion of a global economy and a restructured workplace, and the increasing difficulty of balancing caregiving and work responsibilities (5). The dilemma of the baby boom "sandwich" generation and the changing demographic and social milieu of the workplace underscore the increasingly important role played by caregiving; women of all social classes, having raised their own children, find themselves caring for their own (or their spouse's) aging parents, or for their own grandchildren (6).

Historically, it is clear that at each stage of the development of welfare state policies, the importance of caregiving as a role has been minimized or ignored. The social policies that circumscribe caregiving have developed in a piecemeal manner, without a unifying rationale and without addressing the various dimensions of caregiving (7–9). The fact that welfare policies have ignored the mechanics of what it means to be a caregiver suggests why policymakers seem to be unable to provide both resources and alternatives to the obligations of caregiving, although they condemn as dysfunctional members of society those who do the work of caregiving. Popularly, especially in fiction, caregiving has been romanticized to the point that it is easy to forget its crucial role in pre-industrial society (4).

Folklore tells us that when infant mortality was high and families needed to be self-sufficient, people had many children, "extra" children, so that there would be children to carry on even if one or more children died. There were also "extra mothers," grandmothers, unmarried aunts and other relatives, and older siblings, to care for children. (For the same reason, when clothing was made to last a lifetime, clothing manufacturers often included a second pair of pants or a third stocking—as the opening quotation notes (1).) While these "extra mothers" no longer exist, women with means can afford to hire "extra mothers," poor or immigrant women who then have no one to provide for their own caregiving needs. The underlying inequity of this was part of the Zoe Baird "story": the undocumented worker who leaves her own children in a foreign country in order to earn more money taking care of a wealthy family's children (10).

While politicians look for family values from the 1950's sitcom moms, waiting at home with milk and cookies, the pioneer or dust-bowl mother enduring her fate in stony, silent suffering may be a more accurate reality. Several years before the Zoe Baird debacle, the movie "Baby Boom" presented the humorous side of the caregiver's dilemma (11). Diane Keaton plays a super-career woman who acquires a child as a legacy from a deceased relative. As a single mom, the Keaton character gives up her career for her child and moves to the Vermont woods, where, amazingly, she becomes the ultimate boomer entrepreneur. As she confronts her uncertainty about motherhood, she seeks counsel, and turns to, not her own mother (who is completely absent from the movie), or her daughter (who is, in any event, too young), or her friends, but those fifties' sitcom moms, of course—Jane Wyatt, mother of Bud, Princess, and Kitten in "Father Knows Best"; and Beaver's mom, "June, dear" (Barbara Billingsley) of "Leave it to Beaver." And do they pat her on the head and tell her that she can be a great mom just like them? Not at all. They tell her that they were "just actresses playing parts," that in their real lives "we reported to work and they tied aprons on us . . . we were working mothers putting in a twelve-hour day. . . . Except that we weren't called 'working mothers' back then." In the movie, we are permitted to have sympathy for the character played by Diane Keaton—she is an unwed mother, but the baby is not illegitimate. And in the end, morality (and Hollywood) triumph—the Keaton character sells her start-up baby food business to a major company and finds a man to "legitimize" her adopted child. And of course, in the film we leave Keaton at the height of her productive baby boomer years; she seems not to have parents who may need her services as a caregiver, and we have no way of knowing whether Baby Keaton will care for her mom in later life.

Both stories highlight the lesson: the work of caregiving has traditionally, although not exclusively, been a woman's role—as an unpaid role, caring for children, for aging or ill parents or relatives, motivated by moral, and sometimes legal, mandates; as a poorly paid role, caring for other people's children (in schools and day care centers) and aging or ill relatives (in hospitals and nursing homes) (12).

CHARACTERISTICS OF CAREGIVING ROLES IN THE WELFARE STATE

Caregiving is fraught with complex and conflicting meanings, with respect to duty, choice, right, and benefit. Early Judeo-Christian-Moslem doctrine placed caregiving at the center of the deed of charity, both for the "caregiver" (as a *duty*) and for the recipient (as *a right to receive*) (13). The construction of care as a right (or entitlement) with a corresponding duty stands in counterpoint to Carol Gilligan's (14) placement of the ethic of care as a separate sphere in apposition to the ethic of rights. According to Gilligan, responsibility for care exists within a context or web of relationship, whereas the theory of rights embodies obligation and a hierarchy of moral imperatives. One might see the ethic of care and the ethic of rights as part of a single system because the activity of caring is perceived as "superogatory" for men, but as obligatory for women; and because the ethic of care is the underlying basis for an ethic of rights (15). This latter analysis fits more clearly within the earlier notions about caring as a universal moral obligation.

Caregiving by definition is task-oriented and is about relationships, defined by the caregiver's relationship to the specific needs of recipients of care. Unlike other tasks, such as factory work or the practice of law or medicine, caregiving is not recognized as a "skill" that stands alone. As long as society is reluctant to ascribe specific skills to the task of providing care, it is easier to discount the inherent value of caregiving, and hence to perpetuate the notion that caregiving is something that requires no particular skill, and that anyone can do. Moreover, what constitutes a "task" and how the attributes of the task are defined are not necessarily consistent. Designating caregivers as either formal or informal, for example, says little about what tasks the caregivers actually perform (16). Formal caregivers have been described as people performing tasks that are instrumental and "are undertaken by specified individuals within a framework of professional or occupational hierarchical" relationships; informal caregivers, in contrast, are categorized by "the attachment of caregivers to recipients of care and not a commitment to tasks" (17). As suggested above, the irony of juxtaposing the presumption that a significant portion of most women's lives will be spent as a caregiver with the disregard given to the mechanics of being a caregiver suggests why policymakers are unable to provide both resources and alternatives to the obligations of caregiving, although they condemn those who do the work of caregiving as dysfunctional members of society.

As noted earlier, caregiving roles are also defined by a relationship to the needs of specific recipients of care. Since caregiving is not seen as a skill in and of itself, it has been more difficult to attach credibility to relationships of care than to other task-oriented skills. A lawyer, however much she needs a client to represent, can represent any client; a surgeon can operate on anyone. The character and nature of the recipient are unimportant.

Caregiving is romanticized in literature and in everyday social life—which probably accounts for the continuing resonance of the "family values" theme as a political issue. But despite the romanticization, concrete benefits for caregivers are few. When caregiving roles are uncompensated in dollars, they are idealized and given a high value in the moral economy, especially for middle-class (white) women. When the same roles are compensated in dollars, they tend to be valued at the low end of compensation scheme, justified by the choices of "the market" (18, 19). And for the poor women and women of color who either choose to or of necessity devote their lives to the care of family members, little monetary compensation is provided (20, 21).

Current and Historical Policy Perspectives:
Caregiving "As We Knew It"

Caregiving in formal social welfare policy can be documented at least as far back as Biblical times. According to the Old Testament, "one might break off [one's] iniquities by showing mercy to the poor," poverty was not to be considered a crime, and the duty (of charity of almsgiving) existed regardless of the character of the recipient. Moreover, these early social policies specified that need arose as a result of misfortune, for which society was required to assume responsibility, as an act of justice, not charity (22). Commentary on the Biblical story of Sodom and Gomorrah is particularly enlightening. While modern society associates the "sins of Sodom" with sexual depravity, commentary on the text has always described Sodom not as a center of wild depravity, but as corrupt because its laws forbade giving alms, or otherwise aiding the poor, and made it a crime for a stranger to take up residence within the city. One legend suggests that Lot's daughter was stoned to death because she took water to a stranger who came within the city's gates (23).

Sometime around the Middle Ages, however, caregiving and charity were institutionalized through formal civil government structures that created distinctions among recipients based upon moral categories (24). Beginning in 1532, the English Parliament passed a series of laws intended to regulate the poor, culminating in the now famous Poor Laws of 1601. These laws codified the religious and secular policies on support for the needy that had emerged through the Middle Ages, and institutionalized the distinction between "deserving" and "undeserving" poor. The laws forbade giving charity to "sturdy" alms seekers, and required that such people be punished or placed in workhouses and put to work. However, in keeping with the Biblical tradition, mayors and city officials were directed to "make diligent search and iniquity of all aged poor and impotent persons which live or of necessity be compelled to live by alms of the charity of the people" (21).

The Poor Laws classified the poor by defining three major categories of dependents and formulating policies for each: apprenticeship for needy children; work for the able-bodied; and home relief ("outdoor") or institutional relief ("indoor") for the incapacitated, helpless, or "worthy" poor. There is also a long tradition of children in almshouses (with or without their mothers) and later, in orphanages; we also know that adoption in a formal sense did not exist in English common law, and emerged in the United States in the late 19th century. Young children and the infirm elderly were clearly placed in this last helpless or "worthy" category; there probably were very few "able-bodied" elderly because "elderly" was defined more by physical condition than age (24). (The placement of "able-bodied" women was less clear. Since children as young as seven or eight could be apprenticed, their able-bodied mothers would be put to work as well.) Later, mothers of very young children were considered "worthy" poor, as the concept of childhood expanded in the late 19th and 20th centuries (25). There are no studies as to the status of the caregivers for disabled or elderly adults, or whether the provision of charitable relief to the elderly or infirm included support for their caregivers (25).

What is clear is that there has been a sharp differentiation between societal attitudes toward the moral obligations of caring for one's immediate family, neighbors, and friends, and the perception of public or state obligations to care for these same people. That differentiation is behind the still popular theory that private charity is appropriate, but, as President Herbert Hoover said in opposing federal benefit programs, that public charity would "demoralize and enslave its recipients" (21). Hoover believed that public aid was wrong because it was contrary to the ethic of self-help: "You cannot extend the mastery of government over the daily lives of the people without at the same time making it the master of their souls and thoughts." The most graphic manifestation of this approach came in 1930, when President Hoover approved an emergency appropriation of $45 million to feed starving livestock of bankrupt Arkansas farmers, but vetoed an additional $25 million to feed the farmers and their families (21).

The passage of the Social Security Act in 1935 was both a logical extension of developing policy and the most profound change in public social welfare policy since the Poor Laws. Both the Social Security Act and the Poor Laws were designed to control social unrest as much as to provide for the welfare of benefit recipients (4). However, the Social Security Act implemented for the first time in the United States an acceptance of community responsibility for the welfare of members of the community, in direct contrast to, as Franklin D. Roosevelt noted, continued "unbridled accumulation of personal wealth" (26).

Conceptually, the Social Security Act added an employment link to the concept of entitlement; where the Poor Laws had classified the poor into two categories— "deserving" and "undeserving"—the Social Security Act implemented the "shared responsibility" concept by commodifying the value of present waged work for a future entitlement, and by tying the guarantee of entitlement to individual or spousal participation in the waged workforce, through unemployment insurance, retirement pensions, health care (after 1965), and assistance for the disabled (27). Thus the entitlement programs for the "deserving poor"—Social Security Retirement Income and Medicare—were premised upon employee and employer contributions during work years, even though it is now clear that most people ultimately collect far more in entitlement benefits than they pay in contributions. The rage with which any attempts to revise or means-test Social Security and Medicare have been met makes clear that, to the public at least, these attempts are tantamount to a parent cutting a child out of a promised legacy.

The one major exception to the waged work connection was the program providing aid to single mothers with children under 18, Aid to Dependent Children (ADC, later AFDC), which codified into the emerging legislative policies the flexibility for government to set and modify eligibility standards (28). The deserving/undeserving characterization created a strange anomaly with respect to waged work. AFDC in its original characterization was the only public benefit program that recognized caregiving for one's family as a legitimate quasi-employment, albeit one which could only receive compensation if the recipient complied with statutory and regulatory requirements (28). The differentiation between "deserving" and "undeserving" poor was cemented into the emerging legislative policies through a skillful application of eligibility standards. Unemployment, Social Security Retirement, and, later, Social Security Disability programs were created to mirror private insurance plans, with individuals paying into the trust funds in order to ensure eligibility for the benefit, regardless of need, as long as they met the categorical requirements (such as age or physical condition) (29). In contrast, the AFDC program had rigid eligibility standards relative to income and assets (as does TANF, its successor). It has relied on various forms of social control to exert control over recipients' behavior, as a way to ensure the validity of eligibility information and as a reflection of the social work ideology inherent in the Social Security Act from its outset. The differentiation in status and scope of the AFDC program, with respect to both the rigid eligibility standards and the absolute exclusion of two-parent working families from eligibility, ultimately formed the basis for the erosion of the social consensus about welfare.

The distinction between the AFDC program and the Social Security programs (both retirement and needs-based) is instructive. The programs were implemented at the same time, both as part of the 1935 Social Security Act (28), and initially the only distinction between them was the classification of the retirement benefit of the Social Security program as a benefit based on work experience (of an individual) rather than on need. Mothers of young children, the elderly without a work history, and later the disabled could be eligible to receive benefits under the program.

The disadvantage of this structure has been well-documented. Widows of eligible workers originally were ineligible for the Social Security retirement benefit, a more generous benefit than the Supplemental Security Income (SSI) benefit (4). In part to correct this disparity, widows of qualified workers were made eligible for the Social Security retirement benefit, and the SSI benefit was divided into two segments: what we now know as SSI, for low-income elderly and later for disabled individuals without the requisite work history; and ADC, later AFDC, intended as a benefit for mothers of small children. The distinction between the work-based program and the needs-based programs was thus cemented into policy; and because mothers of young children had their own separate classification, seen as temporary (until the children reached maturity when, presumably, they would be able to support their parents), it was relatively easier to stigmatize this group (28).

Another effect of the bifurcation of Social Security Act policy is that the only specific benefit for caregivers was limited to custodial parents of minor children (through AFDC). The Social Security Act contains no provision for adult caregivers, other than the spousal eligibility for retirement income for caregivers married to eligible beneficiaries. In fairness to history, the popular view of the social climate in

1935 was such that most women who were caregivers were thought to be supported by husbands or fathers and, in their later years, to be cared for themselves by adult children (or the wives of children).

Caregiving in the New Ideal

The reality was different, as Gordon (9) and Abel (18) have pointed out. While the popular view (and that of the President and Congress) may have been true for upper-class and some middle-class women, women from poor families, especially women of color and immigrant women, rarely had such supports, for several reasons. For many, income from two or more family members was often needed to support a family. Moreover, as is true today, single parenthood, family violence, and unmarried status made life for poor women difficult (30). Finally, even after the Social Security Act provisions were available, many of these women were ineligible for the retirement benefit, which was the most generous benefit and the only benefit that was not needs-based (and therefore least stigmatized the recipient) (28). Not only was eligibility predicated on a connection to the workforce, but originally, only the worker himself or herself was eligible. Moreover, a large number of poor workers and occupations were entirely excluded from the original Social Security Act categories. Housekeeping and janitorial work, most part-time work, and farm work were not covered by Social Security until the 1970s, and workers in the marginal or underground economy, which employs many of the poor, by definition still do not qualify (28).

There was public consensus in the 1930s for a benefit system that enabled certain caregivers to receive some income while providing in-home care, even though (or perhaps because) the population was limited to a sympathetic group, single mothers of young children, through AFDC (28). The consensus began to erode following the shift in public perception during the 1960s and 1970s. When the public began to see AFDC recipients not as white widows, but as African American teenagers, public consensus and then public policies shifted away from a guarantee of support for children whose mothers were supposed to spend their time caring for them (31, 32). Other factors contributed to the erosion of the consensus. In the 1960s, many middle-class women began to work outside the home; working poor women had done so for a long time (19, 33). These constituencies had been logical supporters of the benefit, since most women could envision themselves in such a situation. However, the movement of younger middle-class women into the paid workforce altered this support. Because the AFDC program by limiting earnings from waged work, limited the ability of its recipients to move meaningfully to the private work economy, there could not be a gradual shift from welfare to work (31). Even after 1988, when work requirement received formal encouragement and child care, education, and job training assistance programs were given statutory recognition, the move from welfare to work was slow, and welfare recipients were competing with counterparts not substantially different from themselves, in a shrinking pool of less skilled jobs (29). Moreover, working women were not receiving assistance in child care, transportation, and education. Older women, meanwhile, not in direct competition with welfare recipients, nevertheless no longer saw the commonalities of status, and considered themselves to be more deserving of the increasingly scarce resources (12).

As was true throughout the 1980s, the 1996 round of welfare restructuring paid little attention to the relationship of the work of caregiving to public benefit programs. Instead, the goal of work (in the paid economy) completely replaced the dual goals of balancing paid economy work and unpaid economy work (caregiving), which had been the foundation of the New Deal's public benefit programs. The restructuring redefined who should and should not be eligible to receive benefits. The passage of the Family Responsibility Act of 1996 (34) underscored this paradox—poor mothers were unilaterally declared to be responsible for their own plight. The accompanying rhetoric was particularly troubling because of the power of the "family values" theme and because of the barely subdued class, race, gender, and immigrant antipathy (35).

The 1996 Act eliminated the federal entitlement to welfare for qualified applicants, Aid to Families with Dependent Children. While never a guarantee of a specific welfare benefit, much less a guarantee or right to a benefit sufficient to move an individual out of poverty, AFDC had been a safety net providing a minimal benefit for qualified applicants, with federal oversight to ensure consistency of application and fairness in process, recognized by the Supreme Court under the due process clause. The new legislation removed the federal guarantee of per-beneficiary reimbursement to the states, in favor of annual block grants, with broad discretion on benefit eligibility given to the states through a program renamed Temporary Assistance to Needy Families (TANF) (34).

Under TANF, poor (single) mothers with children are eligible to receive benefits only for a short period of time (two years), with states free to impose more stringent work requirements. Unmarried custodial parents, regardless of caregiving obligations, were singled out for the most stringent restrictions, despite the fact that, as has been pointed out, the fathers may be unsuitable as husbands because of unemployment or unemployability, poor education, substance abuse problems, or histories of violence (30). Imposition of the work requirement and benefit time restrictions are mandatory for all but women who were documented victims of domestic abuse. And because eligibility for AFDC was also used to determine eligibility for Medicaid, bifurcation of the programs left Medicaid eligibility entirely to state discretion (34).

Invisible in the restructuring was the subtle tightening of restrictions on older needy women. For the first time, the anti-welfare rhetoric was expanded to poor older women. In recent years, AFDC policies had focused many of the program's resources on the older AFDC recipient, about to lose benefits as children turned 18. In addition, AFDC waiver policies had begun to recognize the needs of older caregivers, such as grandmothers caring for children. The new work requirements under TANF are unclear as to the work mandate for either of these populations.

Legal immigrants who do not have a work history that would make them eligible for Social Security retirement income are excluded from all federal benefit programs. These include SSI, the needs-based benefit for the elderly and disabled; Medicare and Medicaid; food stamps; housing assistance, including Title 8 housing for the elderly; and long-term care under Medicaid. Individuals with substance abuse convictions are also excluded from the programs, and substance abuse is no longer a category for disability under SSI. Of more than 800,000 legal immigrants no longer eligible for benefits, almost three-quarters are elderly or disabled women (35, 36).

COMMUNITY AND RESPONSIBILITY

Caregiving in an Age of Aging

Recognition that someone needs to provide caregiving has been a necessary but invisible component of public benefit programs; only AFDC (and to a lesser degree the foster parent programs) codified a role for caregivers. The constituency for the welfare entitlement evaporated in part because the success of its limited benefit divided the caregiver population. Caregiving was recognized as a legitimate activity *only* for poor custodial parents with minor children; the working poor, with one or both parents as waged workers, were not eligible for any of the benefits, and unemployed two-parent families became eligible for AFDC much later, more or less as an afterthought.

Neither the legal nor the legislative structures of the remaining programs addressed the economic and social autonomy of providers of care, even though the public benefit structure was predicated on the presumption that informal caregiving would always be available. A survey of the non-AFDC Social Security Act and its revisions over the years suggests a statutory fiction of a beneficiary who, although elderly or disabled, is socially autonomous, needing only economic support (37). Only recently have Medicare and Medicaid recognized a need for caregivers, with provision for some paid home care, a minimal amount of paid care by relatives, and attendant care for the disabled (38). And even these statutory provisions focus on providing means by which the beneficiary can pay for these services; they do not provide support for the caregiver who provides so-called unskilled caregiving in activities of daily living. Moreover, this recognition has come about primarily as an adjunct to the cost-savings trend in health care (39, 40).

With more women entering the paid workforce, and the elderly living longer, policymakers have belatedly come to recognize the expansion in the demand for paid and unpaid caregiving for non-minors (41). The original premise that the only non-working recipients of subsidies should be caregivers of children may have changed, but as the caregiving demands on women have increased (and the pool of unpaid caregivers has decreased), the systems have not consistently addressed the issues of who should provide what kinds of care; what kinds of caregiving are to be compensated; whether there should be a public structure for care needs; or when this should be entirely a matter for individual personal responsibility. Disparities of race, class, and economic status among recipients of care, day-to-day direct caregivers, and the corporate providers of care (e.g., hospitals, nursing homes, health plans, and home care agencies) have pushed the interests of providers, recipients, and payors far apart (12).

This should not be surprising. Traditional legal policies about caregiving are similarly ambivalent. For example, the legal system sometimes provides compensation for people who are deprived of caregivers—such as, in tort law, a husband receiving compensation for the loss of his wife's services as homemaker and caregiver (42, 43). The trend toward gender equality in the law has permitted a woman to be similarity compensated, if she can prove that her husband provided the services. Formerly, a wife's performance of the "services" of homemaking, child care, and sex were considered part of the marriage contract (on her side, only). Moreover, the only common-law caregiving mandates in U.S. law are that parents care for children and husbands for wives (in modern times, wives for husbands, as well). The law has never required that adult children care for parents; wills from the 18th and 19th centuries indicate that it was a common practice for a father to write into his will a provision that an inheriting son provide a home for his (the son's) mother, even detailing the bed and furnishings she was to retain (43).

Gender and the Entitlement of Care

Caregiving responsibilities are skewed by gender, as well as by race and ethnicity. Thirty-five percent of all caregivers (formal and informal) are women over 65, and most family (informal) caregivers provide care for more than five years, with 80 percent of these caregivers providing care seven days a week without respite (44). Despite the increased numbers of women entering the workforce in the 1970s, and the fact that most working women continue to do the bulk of family chores, the corollary has not been true: society has not valued, economically or in theory, the work of caregiving (33, 45).

Caregivers for the ill or the elderly have added these tasks to their ongoing responsibilities for child care, household chores, and "outside" work, with only occasional consultation with medical professionals. Had there been a system of income support for all caregivers, as suggested earlier in this chapter, there might have been a broader public consensus for the entitlement for non-working AFDC recipients. When health care became more widely available, through the growth of hospitals for the ill and, to a lesser degree, nursing homes for the elderly and infirm, the character of women's caregiving changed, but did not necessarily diminish, because hospitals were primarily for those who were both destitute and alone (46, 47). The burdens were mediated in the area of health care after the establishment of Medicare and Medicaid in the 1960s; but benefits in those programs have primarily covered formal professional and acute care and services. Women continued to provide the informal care (39, 48). The increase in compensation for community-based care and care in the home corrected some of the inequities, providing some compensation for caregivers to provide less skilled care, but these services require an illness or condition specifically covered by Medicare and Medicaid (48).

The growth in home and community-based care has been praised by health care reformers as a cost-saving measure, and this has given rise to an expansion in home and community-based care for elderly people living at home, with the necessary attendant services. In 1974, Medicare paid for home care services for about 393 thousand persons, costing about $360 per person; in 1989, Medicare reimbursed 1,565 thousand persons for home care, at an average cost of $1,145 per person. The Medicare contribution to home care rose from $46 million in 1967 to $366 million in 1977, and over $2 billion in 1985, and the number of Medicare home care recipients rose from 948 thousand in 1981 to 2,065 thousand in 1990 (49). Medicaid has more generous home care and long-term care benefits than Medicare; however, individuals must "spend down" most of their assets in order to qualify for Medicaid, with limited provisions for protecting spousal or family assets (50, 51). Some of the Medicare and Medicaid reforms urged by Congress in order to "save" these programs would reduce payments for these services and return the burden to informal family caregivers (41, 52).

While women who provide informal care for their own relatives are disadvantaged by the existing system, health care workers are increasingly mistreated by the same system (39). Many home care agencies consider their workers to be "independent contractors," meaning that the employer does not have to provide health care or retirement benefits, vacations, or Social Security contributions. The differences in race, ethnicity, and class between employee and employer/recipient exacerbate the problem (53). These caregiving jobs tend to be low-skill, poorly paid jobs that are often part-time, without medical benefits or Social Security contributions (54, 55). Home care workers often receive lower pay than hospital workers. In many urban areas, home care salaries were 30 to 60 percent lower than those of hospital-employed workers with the same skill level, with poorer benefit packages (54, 55). A Senate Special Committee on Aging reported in 1987 that most nursing home patients are institutionalized only because they are so sick and frail that there is no alternative, but that most such people typically receive months or even years of unpaid in-home care from relatives, usually women, before entering a nursing home. The Committee noted that in comparison with other industrialized nations, the United States relies far more heavily on informal unpaid caregivers, largely middle-aged or elderly themselves (7).

Limits on Caregiver Autonomy

The policy community has, of course, been highly concerned with issues of cost containment. For example, it is commonly believed to be less expensive for elderly people to live in the community, rather than in institutions, where that is physically and logistically possible. This is not necessarily true, although living in the community with appropriate services is desirable for social and psychological reason (56). However, it turns out that autonomy in the context of care is a double-edged issue. On the one hand, formal or informal care in the community can provide the care-receiver with increased autonomy; on the other hand, the caregiver gives up substantial autonomy by providing the care (41).

CONCLUSION:
CAREGIVING AS A LEGACY OF PUBLIC RESPONSIBILITY

The inequitable division of care for and by older people can be viewed through several lenses. First, as suggested earlier, the social structure of relationships, as well as the legislative structure of the welfare state, presumes the unpaid labor of female relatives: relevant social policies are structured in such a way as to incorporate that labor. Second, older women have health care needs substantially different from those of men; they are more likely to suffer from long-term chronic illnesses and less likely to suffer from acute illnesses, but the structure of Medicare and Medicaid reimbursements are weighted toward standards based upon the needs of men. Women may not be able to afford the medical services they need in order to maintain physical or psychological autonomy. Third, women occupying the caregiving role is both a cause and a consequence of the division of labor that confines women to the private sphere and constrains access to resources and to independence.

Caregiving is inherently a private activity, not in the sense that caregivers are closed off from public view, but in the sense that the activity tends to be both isolating and invisible. The activity of family caregiving, for example, is simply not counted, for the most part, as an activity different from homemaking. While the interpretations presented above describe similar consequences, they suggest different solutions. The first interpretation suggests that social policies may need to be restructured to provide for compensation for caregiving. The second interpretation suggests that the caregiving role itself might need to be restructured, so that men and women participate more equitably in the tasks, and so that the role becomes visible and more a part of the public domain. Other roles that involve the ethic of care focus more on legislative formulation or political development, "public" spheres of care. In this manner, what women do to care for their children is ordinarily confined to the private sphere, except when politicians or policymakers decide that the government should not subsidize this role (for poor women) (57).

A third interpretation would incorporate the reciprocity inherent in the caregiving relationship. This interpretation would agree with the principles for reform underlying the other interpretations—that is, that social policies relating to the compensation of caregiving should be restructured; that alternatives to the woman-as-caregiver construction be explored as a means of altering the underlying obligation; and that the essentially political nature of the public/private spheres of caregiving roles be recognized—but it would also recognize the essentially subjective nature of the character of care. Even where a formal relative caregiver and care-receiver relationship is identified, the person theoretically receiving the care often perceives herself as a caregiver for a son or daughter (57, 58). An ethic of reciprocity and continuity prevails. The alternative perspective alters the axis on which the ideology of caregiving is considered, by delimiting the dichotomy between caregiver/care-provider and care-receiver and placing the constructions inherent in the ethic of care on a vertical continuum of the life course, rather than situating them as an isolated collection of disparate roles. It also legitimizes and gives voice to the actual caregiving tasks that many women play throughout their life course.

The concept of caregiving as obligation, while it fits within the Biblical analysis described earlier, has been criticized as a distortion of "the meaning and content of the ethic of care," because it fails to take into account, for example, the nature and quality of the caring that mothers do for children. While women have often maintained homes and have worked outside as well as inside the home, they have recently entered the "public" working world in greater numbers, and this requires a re-characterization of the ideas about compensation and allocation of caregiving responsibilities. This analysis is correct as far as it goes, but it is only middle- and upper-class women who have recently entered the "public" world of work outside the home; poor women have always had these dual responsibilities. They have not been "public" because poor women have no public visibility; the current "public" nature of women's work is a direct result of the public and political vindication of women who work outside the home. The separation of the ethic of care from the ethic of rights generally advantages rights that are quantifiable, such as political rights, and affirmative rights to participate in the public economy (education, professional work, etc.). For poor women, the failure to perform traditional functions that include both caregiving and other work inside the home as well as work outside the home, would seriously disadvantage the dominant group. This dominant group includes not only men (middle- and upper-class), but also middle- and upper-class women—both those who work outside the home and can afford to replace their own caregiving responsibilities, and those who choose not to work outside the home and can afford to live without that source of income.

The marginalization of caregiving, and its absence from the vision of what individuals ought to expect from their government, heightens the artificiality of any public/private distinction in social policy. It is equally feasible to view many of the entitlements that we receive from the government as legacies held in a kind of public trust until such time as we are entitled to receive them, and distributed according to statutory instructions that parallel instructions in a will. A more equitable characterization of public benefits or entitlements would recognize that while Americans retain the ability to dispose of most of their property as they wish, some property is reserved as property that is owned and distributed collectively, which is the way the estate taxes are viewed. Unlike estate taxes, however, which simply become part of the general public coffers, entitlements characterized as a form of public legacy could also facilitate a mechanism for converting into "currency" activities such as caregiving that otherwise have no marketable value (59). This form of legacy is based on an expanded concept of entitlement, founded on an American concept of community, mediated by social norms and legal policies that traditionally have relied on community expectations and obligations. It may be true that it "takes a village to raise a child" (60), but if children, the poor, and the elderly are not to be confined to the ghettoes of that village, the community as a unit needs to recognize the value of caregiving (61).

REFERENCES

1. Tyler, A. *Dinner at the Homesick Restaurant.* Random House, New York, 1982.
2. Cline, F. Clinton signs bill cutting welfare; states in new role. *New York Times,* August 23, 1996, p. A-1.
3. Ellwood, D. *Poor Support: Poverty in the American Family.* Basic Books, New York, 1991.
4. Abramowitz, M. *Regulating the Lives of Women: Social Welfare Policy from Colonial Times to the Present,* Ed. 2. South End Press, Boston, 1996.
5. Abramowitz, M. The Reagan legacy: Undoing class, race and gender accords. *Soc. Soc. Welfare* 3: 91, 92, 1992.
6. Minkler, M., and Roe, K. *Grandmothers as Caregivers.* Sage, Newbury Park, Calif., 1993.
7. Kingson, E. The graying of the baby boom in the United States: Framing the policy debate. *Int. Soc. Sec. Rev.* 44, January/February 1991.

8. Ikenberry, J. G., and Skocpol, T. Expanding social benefits: The Roe of Social Security. *Polit. Sci. Q.* 102(3), 1987.
9. Gordon, L. *Women, The State and Welfare.* University of Wisconsin Press, Madison, 1991.
10. Segal, T. Zoe Baird is not alone. *Business Week,* 3303: 29–30, February 1, 1993.
11. Gerard, J. TV generation ages into 'baby boom.' *Detroit Free Press,* November 2, 1988, p. 1B.
12. Chafetz, J. S. The gender division of labor and the reproduction of female disadvantage. *Fam. Labor* 9: 108, 131, 1981.
13. Niebuhr, R. *The Contribution of Religion to Social Work.* The Forbes Lectures of the New York School of Social Work. Columbia University Press, New York, 1932.
14. Gilligan, C. *In a Different Voice: Psychological Theory and Women's Development.* Harvard University Press, Cambridge, Mass., 1982.
15. Kroeger-Mappes, J. The ethic of care vis-a-vis the ethic of rights: A problem for contemporary moral theory. *Hypatia* 9(3): 108, 1994.
16. Brabeck, M. M. (ed.). *Who Cares?: Theory, Research, and Educational Implications of the Ethic of Care.* Praeger, New York, 1989.
17. Bond, J. The politics of caregiving: The professionalization of informal care. *Ageing Soc.* 12(5): 21, 1992.
18. Abel, E. K. Man, woman and chore boy: Transformations in the antagonistic demands of work and care on women in the nineteenth and twentieth centuries. *Milbank Q.* 73(2): 187, 1995.
19. Huber, J., and Spitze, G. *Sex Stratification: Children, Housework and Jobs.* Academic Press, New York, 1983.
20. Stone, R., Cafferata, G. L., and Sangl, J. Caregivers of the frail elderly: A national profile. *Gerontologist* 27(5): 616–626, 1987.
21. Trattner, W. *From Poor Law to Welfare State.* Free Press, New York, 1976.
22. Steinsaltz, A. *The Essential Talmud.* Weidenfeld and Nicolson, London, 1976.
23. Hertz, J. H. (ed.). *The Pentateuch and Haftorahs: Hebrew Text, English Translation and Commentary.* Oxford University Press, London, 1929–1936.
24. Webb, S., and Webb, B. *English Local Government (1927–29)* (English Poor Law History). Archon Books, Hamden, Conn., 1963.
25. Folks, H. *The Care of Destitute, Neglected and Delinquent Children.* Macmillan, New York, 1902.
26. Roosevelt, F. D. Message to Congress (June 19, 1935). H.R. Rep. No. 1681, 74th Cong., 1st Sess. Reprinted in 1939-1 C.B. (Pt. 2) 642, 642–43. Washington, D.C., 1935.
27. Danziger, S., and Weinberger, D. The historical record: Trends in family income, inequality and poverty. In *Confronting Poverty: Prescriptions for Change,* edited by S. J. Danziger, G. D. Sandefur, and D. H. Weinberger. Harvard University Press, Cambridge, Mass., 1994.
28. Handler, J. F., and Hasenfeld, Y. *The Moral Construction of Poverty: Welfare Reform in America.* Sage, Newbury Park, Calif., 1991.
29. Bane, M. J., and Ellwood, D. T. *Welfare Realities: From Rhetoric to Reform.* Harvard University Press, Cambridge, Mass., 1994.
30. Kurz, D. *For Richer, For Poorer: Mothers Confront Divorce.* Routledge, New York, 1995.
31. Thurston, H. W. *The Dependent Child.* Columbia University Press, New York, 1930.
32. Handler, J. Constraining the political spectrum: The interpretation of entitlements, legalization and obligation in social welfare history. *Brooklyn Law Rev.* 56: 899, 1990.
33. Hochschild, A. *The Second Shift.* Viking Press, New York, 1989.

34. The Personal Responsibility and Work Opportunity Reconciliation Act. U.S. Congress, Washington, D.C., August 1996.
35. Edelman, P. The worst thing Bill Clinton has done. *Atlantic Monthly* 279(3): 43–58, March 1997.
36. Families USA. *Hurting Real People: The Human Impact of Medicaid Cuts.* Washington, D.C., 1997.
37. Weinberg, J. Unpublished statutory analysis. Institute for Health and Aging, University of California, San Francisco, November 1996.
38. Lyons, B., Rowland, D., and Hanson, K. Another look at Medicaid (Where is healthcare headed?) *Generations* 20(2): 24, 1996.
39. Gornick, M., et al. Twenty years of Medicare and Medicaid covered populations: Use of benefits and program expenditures. *Health Care Financ. Rev.,* Suppl. 1985, pp. 13–59.
40. Levit, M., et al. National health expenditures, 1990. *Health Care Financ. Rev.* 13: 29–54, 1991.
41. Abel, E. K. *Who Cares for the Elderly?: Public Policy and the Experiences of Adult Daughters.* Temple University Press, Philadelphia, 1991.
42. Abel, R. A critique of torts. *UCLA Law Rev.* 37: 785, 1990.
43. Estin, A. L. Love and obligation: Family law and the romance of economics. *William and Mary Law Rev.* 36: 989, 1995.
44. Charny, D. Symposium: The changing workplace: The employee welfare state in transition. *Texas Law Rev.* 74: 1601, 1991.
45. Fineman, M. A. Images of mothers in poverty discourses. *Duke Law J.* 274: 289–293, 1991.
46. DeVault, M. *Feeding the Family: The Social Organization of "Caring" as Gendered Work.* University of Chicago Press, Chicago, 1991.
47. Oday, L. Medicare and Medicaid update. In *Legal and Ethical Aspects of Health Care for the Elderly,* edited by M. Knapp, H. Pies, Jr., and A. Doudera, pp. 65–72. Health Administration Press, Ann Arbor, Mich., 1985.
48. Gueron, J., and Pauley, E. Manpower Demonstration Research Corporation. *From Welfare to Work.* Russell Sage Foundation, New York, 1991.
49. Torres-Gil, F. *The New Aging.* Auburn House, New York, 1992.
50. U.S. Senate Special Committee on Aging. *Aging America: Trends and Projections.* Department of Health and Human Services, Washington, D.C., 1987.
51. Crystal, S. *America's Old Age Crisis: Public Policy and the Two Worlds of Aging.* Basic Books, New York, 1983.
52. American Public Health Association. Latest Medicaid reform plans would jeopardize health of poor. *The Nation's Health,* March 1996, pp. 1, 4.
53. Feldman, P. H. Work life improvements for home care workers: Impact and feasibility. *Gerontologist* 33(1): 47–54, 1993.
54. Piven, F. F., and Cloward, R. A. *Regulating the Poor: The Function of Public Welfare.* Pantheon Books, New York, 1971.
55. Collopy, B., Dubler, N., and Zuckerman, C. The ethics of home care: Autonomy and accommodation. *Hastings Center Rep.,* Suppl. March/April 1990, p. 4.
56. Halamandaris, V. The future of home health care in America. *Generations* 10: 48–51, 1986.
57. Skocpol, T. *Protecting Soldiers and Mothers: The Political Origins of Social Policy in the United States.* Harvard University Press, Cambridge, Mass., 1992.
58. Montgomery, R., and Datwyler, M. M. Women and men in the caregiving role. *Generations* 34, Suppl., Summer 1990, p. 38.

59. Aronson, J. Women's sense of responsibility for the care of old people: 'But who else is going to do it?' *Gender Soc.* 6(1): 8, 1992.
60. Clinton, H. R. *It Takes a Village: And Other Lessons Children Teach Us.* Simon and Schuster, New York, 1996.
61. Weinberg, J. K. Reconstructing legacy: Public and private contexts. *Generations* 20: 3, November 1996.

CHAPTER 15

Gender, Race, Class, and Aging:
Advances and Opportunities

Paula Dressel, Meredith Minkler, and Irene Yen

Gerontologists, along with other social scientists, have been challenged to move our field away from questions, theories, and methods that prioritize and privilege dominant group experience and ignore, obscure, or distort the realities of subordinate groups. As a profession we have taken the challenge seriously and made some important strides toward more inclusive and thus more accurate and useful research. At the same time, much remains to be done. This chapter seeks to move that agenda further.

We begin the chapter by defining the challenges of inclusiveness and interlocking oppressions/intersectionality for social science. Next we borrow perspectives from new social scientific thinking about race to identify avenues gerontologists might pursue in order to advance our own work. We then provide a brief synopsis of earlier gerontological work's attention—or inattention—to issues of gender, race, and class. Following this setting out of historical context, we highlight some recent gerontological work that is at least partially responsive to the foregoing challenges, paving the way for further progress. We conclude by delineating some issues adapted from other social science and health settings and applied to compelling questions of aging which can frame a more inclusive and critical gerontological agenda.

THE CHALLENGES OF INCLUSIVENESS AND
INTERLOCKING OPPRESSIONS/INTERSECTIONALITY

The emergence in academia of women's studies and ethnic studies, which paralleled and benefited from activism around gender, race, and class issues in more overtly political arenas, challenged social science to become more representative of the experiences and perspectives of previously marginalized or overlooked groups (1). Once this legitimate need was articulated, the question became one of method. Key debates have centered on how to make social science research more representative and how to apprehend the complexities of peoples' lives when it comes to issues of gender, race, and class.

Inclusiveness

In the 1970s, researchers began to address the lack of inquiry into marginalized groups, expanding their protocols to include or "target" additional groups. The results of such research efforts typically were analyzed as comparisons—for example, of whites versus blacks. Although generally well intentioned, such research failed to understand or address the goal of truly inclusive research, which, as bell hooks (2) argues, is to bring those at the margins of discourse to the center. That is, researchers must seek to understand social realities through the eyes of variously positioned groups rather than imposing the frameworks of dominant groups onto the others. Further, truly inclusive research recognizes that group membership cuts across categories such as race, class, and gender and explores the interconnections of these, rather than reducing an individual or group's reality to a single factor (1).

Traditional approaches to addressing the issue of inclusion have been roundly critiqued for their perpetuation of problems inherent in research by, and typically on, member of dominant groups. One such criticism has centered on the tendency of such research to employ what has been referred to as the "add-and-stir" approach (3). As Andersen (3) notes, researchers in this tradition simply add heretofore overlooked samples or groups to their data collection or analysis without appreciating that the questions which frame their research may not be responsive to the realities of these new groups. Writings on the feminization of poverty in later life, for example, while not overlooking women of color, have tended to take an add-and-stir approach that has led to "race blind theoretical formulations" (4, 5). As Dressel notes (5, p. 178):

> what are meant to be general statements about gender and poverty are made and then, as an afterthought or elaboration, specialized statements about black (or Hispanic or Native American) women are made. . . . The point here is subtle but critical. In the . . . add-and-stir approach . . . it is implied that similar outcomes in women's lives are produced by the one and only factor of patriarchy. Acknowledged, but not accounted for, are the worse (and sometimes different) conditions faced by racial-ethnic women . . . [whose] experiences are forced into the model rather than being utilized to refine or critique the model itself.

Research in the add-and-stir tradition often proceeds from the assumption that race, gender, class, or age are properties that differentiate individuals, the consequences of which can be ascertained merely be examining between-group comparisons. The comparison approach frequently used in such research has several serious shortcomings.

1. Most fundamentally and most problematically, the project of comparison assumes a group essentialism; that is, the assumption that characteristics such as gender, race, and (old) age are fixed, immutable, biologically based individual properties with predictable (if as yet undetermined) behavioral and social consequences.

2. Comparisons then tend to be made between dominant and subordinated groups along dimensions whose questions derive from dominant group paradigms.

3. If data derived from these paradigms indicate that subordinated groups do not measure "up" to dominant groups, the stigma of social deficit at the least, or inherent inferiority at the worst, becomes implicit, if not overt; this in turn fuels the essentialist assumption.

4. Relatedly, even though the comparison approach used in add-and-stir research may enable marginalized groups to become a focus for research attention, such attention frequently reproduces the problem of marginalization, albeit now through findings rather than oversight. By answering to inappropriate questions and concentrating on how marginalized groups may not meet the dominant group's standards, such research may further perceptions of the subordinate groups as being on the periphery or fringe rather than a part of the whole.

5. Finally, as Collins (6, p. 494) notes, insofar as such work produces only notions of difference and deficit, power relations and material inequalities that constitute oppression remain obfuscated. That is, the concentration of research in this tradition on how subordinate groups differ diverts necessary attention from the power dynamics that produce such differences. Further, this emphasis shifts questions of agency and responsibility away from social and political structures that shape inequities. Social structural analyses, which would reveal "the race, class and gender patterns and processes that form the very framework of society" (1, p. 5) implicitly are ignored.

Another misguided quest for inclusiveness involves the continuing practice of tokenism (7). In this approach, journal editors may choose to focus a special issue on an under-researched group, or conference organizers may seek panelists from previously under-represented groups to create diversity for an otherwise homogeneous collection of scholars. These efforts are not without some merit. However, to the extent that they substitute for encouraging inclusive research for *all* journal issues or challenging *all* researchers to become conversant with more inclusive work, they achieve limited results. As a consequence, the burden for scholarly advance falls disproportionately on the shoulders of scholars from marginalized groups. In Audre Lorde's (8, p. 114) words, "it is members of the oppressed, objectified groups who are expected to stretch out and bridge the gaps." In this case, between the realities of their lives and the consciousness of researchers and academics from dominant groups. Furthermore, all too often on these occasions, the issues or topics are already framed from the vantage point of the dominant group, thereby injecting the add-and-stir problem into the situation of tokenism. Here again, scholars from marginalized groups are burdened disproportionately with attempting to reframe an already-set discourse which may be fundamentally ignorant of or unwittingly disrespectful to the groups from which they come or for which they advocate.

As noted earlier, by attempting to bring to the center of discourse those groups that are traditionally kept at the margins, researchers concerned with increasing inclusivity attempt to apprehend social realities from the latter's perspectives and vantage points. A conscious effort is made to avoid imposing the frameworks of dominant groups onto the others. In so doing, researchers can achieve an appropriate contextualized and centered understanding of the groups that are repositioned or brought to the center. Through this process the research can uncover alternative paradigms and conceptualizations through which to perceive and understand the world. Finally, the process enables the development of further grounded and thus relevant questions for investigation, and the identification of intervention strategies for applied research whose efficacy is more likely. For example, when Dressel and Barnhill (9) move the lives of African American grandmothers raising grandchildren under harsh economic conditions to the center of focus, they reveal that age is not a master or primary status for their sample. That is, issues that have oppressed these women all their lives—poverty, racism, and sexism—have greater salience than age-based issues for their well-being and the welfare of their families. As a consequence, age-focused service interventions are less useful to them than are financial assistance, legal aid, and improved educational services for their grandchildren.

Research that brings to the center those who have historically been at the margins also offers the opportunity for an enriched understanding of dominant groups. The latter claim derives from acknowledgment of the relational character of power. It is impossible to fully understand the dynamics of oppression without understanding the dynamics of domination (10). One cannot fully understand the social construction of black without understanding its counterpart construction, white, or the construction woman without critically examining the construction man. We cannot know what it means to be poor without understanding what it means to be rich, or how "the aged" get to be set off from other age groups without realizing the forms of advantage of those other age groups. In short, movement of marginalized groups to the center of investigation enhances the research effort in relation to those groups— an effort worthy in and of itself—as well as in relation to dominant groups, for whom taken-for-granted constructions will thus become revealed and problematized. Calasanti ably summarizes the approach of inclusiveness with regard to race (11, pp. 148–149):

> Incorporating diversity . . . first requires that we investigate various racial/ethnic groups from their standpoint, privileging their knowledge. . . . The second step, using the knowledge of racial/ethnic groups derived in this manner to compare to whites, exposes the racial/ethnic dynamics which shape aging experiences, including previously invisible aspects of the privileged group's experiences. . . . Incorporating diversity, then, ultimately means broadening our knowledge of *all* groups.

Extrapolating beyond race, the principles reflected in Calasanti's approach challenge us to be gender-, race-, class-, and age-conscious without being essentialist. These categories are socially constructed classifications rather than static, essential, or immutable properties of individuals. As suggested throughout this volume, such classifications are shaped by, and in turn shape, not only individual actions and interactions but also institutional arrangements and processes. They are phenomena that arise through the course of political and social interaction so that people come to be gendered, racialized, classed, and aged, with significant political and social consequences accompanying such categorization. As we discuss shortly, in addition to being individuals' socially constructed sociopolitical locations, the categories are also designations of group power relations, foundations for social organization, and features of social policy.

Interlocking Oppressions and Intersectionality

Gender, race, class, and age represent interlocking systems of inequality (12), "different, but interrelated, axes of social structure" (1, p. i), and "not just . . . separate features of experience" (1, p. xiv). Collins makes a conceptual distinction between interlocking oppressions and intersectionality as follows (6, p. 492):

> First, the notion of interlocking oppressions refers to the macro level connections linking systems of oppression such as race, class, and gender. This is the model describing the social structures that create social positions. Second, the notion of intersectionality describes micro level processes—namely, how each individual and group occupies a social position with interlocking structures of oppression described by the metaphor of intersectionality. Together they shape oppression.

The domain of caregiving for (and frequently by) the elderly is illustrative of the separate but interrelated roles of interlocking oppressions and intersectionality. On the macro level, as Abel (13) notes, public policies around caregiving tend to both "sentimentalize and devalue" this activity, which is implicitly regarded as "women's work." The failure of public or private pension schemes in the United States to recognize caregiving as legitimate work, and the consequent penalizing of those who must leave the paid workforce to become full time caregivers, disproportionately disadvantage women, who comprise about 70 percent of the nation's caregivers for the old (see Chapter 14). For women of color, who are heavily concentrated in the lowest paying jobs with few or no fringe benefits (14), early exit from the labor force in order to provide care may exact a particularly high toll, by diminishing still further the adequacy of an already inadequate income base. Finally, on the micro level, the caregiver who is a woman, and who is poor or working class, is far more likely than a man or a middle- or upper-class woman to be a hands-on caregiver, rather than a care manager, for her disabled elderly parent or partner (15). In short, both interlocking oppressions on the macro or policy level and intersectionality on the level of the individual woman's lived experience critically help to shape the ways in which caregiving is experienced.

Literature of the past decade, especially that produced by women of color, has repeatedly revealed the inadequacy of focusing on issues of gender or race or class alone (1, 8). Class dynamics have come to be understood as simultaneously gendered and racialized phenomena; gender dynamics are understood to vary because of the racialized and classed nature of relationships; and race dynamics are both gendered and classed in their various manifestations. As a consequence, studies that examine either gender or race or class or age will be unable to understand individuals, groups, or social life in appropriately complex ways. Indeed, their conclusions may even by misleading because of the failure to appreciate variation among individuals and within group experience.

Furthermore, interlocking oppressions and the intersection of multiple subordinate statuses cannot be presumed to be additive in their impact. As Andersen and Collins point out (1, p. xii):

> [while] the effect of race, class, and gender does "add up" both over time and in intensity of impact, . . . seeing race, class and gender only in additive terms misses the social structural connections between them and the particular ways that different configurations of race, class, and gender affect group experience.

Indeed, interlocking oppressions and intersectionality often produce qualitatively different experiences and consequences as well as quantitatively different ones. For example, concepts such as "adjustment to old age" may have little relevance among groups such as older African Americans for whom aging may be experienced not as a series of adjustments but as a process of survival (16), and for some of whom, as Dressel and Barnhill (9) maintain, age is not a master or primary status. As Burton and her colleagues (16) point out, although concepts such as positive adjustment to old age have been studied among diverse racial/ethnic groups, the derivation of such concepts from the study of middle-class European American samples often has resulted in their failure to capture the meaning of adjustment for African Americans, Mexican Americans, Asian Pacific Islanders, and other groups.

The need for rethinking some of our most cherished concepts and research foci within a conceptual frame emphasizing interlocking oppressions and intersectionality also is illustrated with respect to the phenomenon of retirement. As Gibson (17) notes, for example, the concept of "retirement" may have little meaning within the cultural context of low-income African Americans who frequently become redundant or permanently unemployed in their 40s or 50s. Similarly, the sharp gender distinctions drawn in most retirement research within the dominant culture appear to blur to the level of unimportance when low-income African Americans' experiences are brought to center stage. In this group, the realization that one must work periodically well into old age; the lack of private pensions as a source of income; indistinct lines between work in youth and in old age; and the greater psychological and economic benefits of defining one's self as disabled rather than retired, all have combined to result in a new status—that of the "unretired retired" (17). Rather than excluding African Americans from retirement research because they do not meet narrowly defined retirement criteria, our research should make room to include "the unretired retired" and other conceptualizations that better capture the qualitative experience of different subgroups within the heterogeneous aging population.

GENDER, RACE, AND CLASS AS SOCIAL FORMATIONS AND SOCIAL PROJECTS

As a result of extensive and sometimes acrimonious critique, for foregoing challenges to social science have produced some meaningful change in approaches to gender, race, and class. Additional change is underway thanks to the growing adoption of the conceptualization, implicitly or explicitly, of the perspectives of gender, race, and class as social formations and social projects.

The formation and project perspectives are presented more explicitly by Omi and Winant (18), who write in terms of racial formation and racial projects. While we borrow here—at some length—from their specific application, we maintain its broader utility as an approach to questions of gender, class, and age as well. Omi and Winant define racial formation as "the sociohistorical process by which racial categories are created, inhabited, transformed, and destroyed. . . . [It] is a process of historically situated projects in which human bodies and social structures are represented and organized (18, pp. 55–56).

The racial formation perspective reminds us that race is a socially constructed phenomenon rather than an essential property of individuals. Racial formation is well illustrated in the changing composition of racial categories over time. In the United States, for example, the Irish were not considered white in the 19th century. Similarly, East Indians were originally classified as Hindus (although most were in fact Sikhs), later classified as non-whites, then reclassified as whites as a "reward" for their service in World War II. In the post–Civil Rights era, still another reclassification occurred as East Indians fought for official designation as Asians for affirmative action purposes (19). As the racial formation perspective illustrated here suggests, "the fact that we know at all which race we belong to says more about our society than about our biology" (20, p. 85).

In contrast to a racial formation, Omi and Winant note that (18, p. 56):

> *A racial project is simultaneously an interpretation, representation, or explanation of racial dynamics, and an effort to reorganize and redistribute resources along particular racial lines.* Racial projects connect what race *means* in a particular discursive practice and the ways in which both social structures and everyday experiences are racially *organized,* based upon that meaning.

The racial project perspective reminds us that race is a contested phenomenon in political life, with different historical moments reflecting different racial formations and varying racial projects. Racial projects are political (i.e., power-informed) projects in a given historical moment, such as the creation of discriminatory Jim Crow laws and practices after Reconstruction, which "provided new official and unofficial vehicles for violence against blacks" (21, p. 125). More recently, the creation of the notion of Asian Americans as "model minorities" and the mobilization of sentiment regarding alleged "reverse discrimination" as a frame for truncating and even reversing the quest for equal economic opportunities for all women and for women and men of color provide telling examples of contemporary racial projects.

The dual conceptualizations—formations and projects—also enable the linkage and simultaneous appreciation of material relations and ideological forces. As such, they are fully compatible with the ideas of critical race theorists (22), who maintain that domination is largely constituted through economic power, but is legitimated through race (and, we would add, gender) power. Omi and Winant's (18) discussion of the changing nature of racial projects from the Civil Rights movement of the

1960s to the present illustrates the dynamic process of racial formation through racial projects. Similarly, the move from the concept of equal pay for the same work to that of equal pay for work of comparable worth is illustrative of a subtle but important gender project at work. A further utility of these perspectives is to remind social scientists that apart from whatever overt rhetoric surrounds political debate, political decisions must be critically examined for the extent to which they may indeed be racialized or gendered.

As suggested above, we believe that the perspectives of formations and projects can fruitfully be applied to gender, class, and age dynamics as well as to race, and to their intersectionality. Indeed, we document shortly the ways in which gerontologists implicitly use these perspectives without employing Omi and Winant's terminology.

GERONTOLOGY'S TRAJECTORY ON GENDER, RACE, AND CLASS

Early Theory and Research

Markides and Black (23) argue that the early theoretical development within social gerontology, which dates back to the 1950s and 1960s, included little or no attention to racial or ethnic diversity. While this appears to be accurate, it cannot be said that race itself was not a feature of early theory and research. Instead, it was a feature normalized by the development of theories based on samples comprised almost exclusively of European Americans (23). Similarly, to the extent that workforce and retirement issues were conceptualized on the basis of middle-class European American male experience, this gerontological research was a racialized and a gendered undertaking, as well. While inclusiveness was not a feature of early gerontology, race, gender, and class were present, albeit usually as unexamined issues reflecting the privileged status of most subjects and most researchers.

Competing Hypotheses about Inequalities

When conceptual development did begin to occur in the specialties known as "minority aging" and "gender and aging," it tended to be built around the notion of inequality, reflecting, as Burton and her colleagues (16) note, "ways of thinking" that were prevalent in the 1970s, when issues of social inequality, racism, and sexism were becoming an increasing focus of concern among researchers. Both specialties stressed the notion of "double jeopardy"—a phrase coined by the National Urban League in 1964 to capture the dual disadvantage faced by aged African Americans as a consequence of being both old and members of an oppressed racial minority group (24). Subsequent formulations discussed triple or multiple jeopardies to reflect the intersection of more than two subordinate statuses.

The double or multiple jeopardy thesis played an important research and advocacy role in bringing attention to some of the problems faced by elders of color and, in subsequent applications, to the problems faced by older women, older gays and lesbians, disabled elders, and other oppressed groups. But the thesis has been heavily critiqued in recent years, on both philosophical and methodological grounds.

The heavy focus on social disadvantage in this conceptualization has thus been seen by Jackson (25) and others (12, 16, 26) as inadvertently contributing to a deficit thinking mentality that disempowers elders of color by ignoring their strengths and the strengths of their communities. Further, as Burton and colleagues (16, p. 131) argue, the double jeopardy thesis places disproportionate emphasis on between-group differences, paying little attention to the cultural meaning and dynamics of aging within groups.

Competing with the double jeopardy hypothesis is the "age-as-leveler" hypothesis which posits that inequalities experienced by race or class earlier in the life course will diminish or level out over time, since many of the declines associated with old age cut across racial/ethnic group lines (16, 27). For example, with regard to health, Dowd and Bengtson (27) hypothesized that age may have the effect of decreasing racial differences as challenges to functional ability begin to overshadow racial inequality and/or as a result of oppressed groups' development of coping strategies earlier in life that could be applied to later-life health issues. In relation to income issues, the age-as-leveler hypothesis, or the "rising tide model" (28), suggests that public benefit programs in later life disproportionately benefit lower-income persons, thereby narrowing income distribution (29).

A third hypothesis on inequalities is that of status maintenance as it relates to income questions (29), or "persistent inequality," as it has been phrased for health questions (30). That is, racial ethnic inequalities of earlier years are simply carried over into later years. From this perspective, old age as a social formation has a negligible impact on other forms of inequalities. A final hypothesis, and one that has been applied to income issues in particular, is that of cumulative advantage/disadvantage (28, 29). This thesis posits that "some effects of early head starts and handicaps may cumulate over the life span" (29, p. S308), thereby increasing disparities in later life.

How do empirical data speak to these competing hypotheses? Although some initial support was found for the double jeopardy hypothesis with respect to health and income, other studies contradicted these findings, with contradictory findings also emerging in the area of family supports (23). In a longitudinal study of men, Crystal and Waehrer (29) confirmed earlier evidence (28) of the dynamic of cumulative advantage/disadvantage. At the same time that they found increasing inequality within an aging cohort, however, they also found a considerable degree of turnover in relative status position among individuals.

In the health domain, a recent national longitudinal study (30) testing the double jeopardy hypothesis among whites and African Americans concluded that most evidence supports the alternative hypothesis of persistent inequality. Some support for the double jeopardy hypothesis was found, with African Americans who had heart failure, for example, being more likely than whites to be disabled by the condition and more likely to have been treated later. However, evidence of an age-as-lever effect was eliminated when selective mortality during the study was taken into account, leading the authors to conclude that "the hypothesis specified by aging as leveler should be recast as selective survival as leveler among populations" (30, p. S327).

The foregoing research efforts revolve around attempts to understand how age interacts with other forms of inequalities to affect peoples' lives. The most notable shortcomings of studies using the delineated hypotheses is that they typically examine only one category of analysis in addition to age. As noted earlier, Dressel's (5) and Burnham's (4) critiques of the feminization of poverty argument as it applies to later life—an implicit double jeopardy thesis—center on its failure simultaneously to take into account how race structures inequality. To the extent that studies using the foregoing hypotheses neglect the question of interlocking oppressions, they are subject to a similar criticism.

RECOGNITION OF THE NEED FOR INCLUSIVENESS

Gerontological research has increasingly recognized the need for inclusiveness. How this is evidenced, however, varies widely. At the most basic level, scholars whose samples are not inclusive note in their discussion that research is needed on the groups left out (e.g., 31–33), and those who use models generated from one group to test another discuss the inadequacies of such an approach (e.g., 34). Somewhat more helpful are studies that conduct descriptive between-group comparisons, without falling into the deficit interpretations that can fuel the tendency toward essentialism. Many of these studies recognize that explanations of the dynamics of any established differences are either post hoc or unavailable through the current project (e.g., 35, 36). A growing number of researchers are investigating issues among historically under-studied ethnic populations (37–41). Others are moving the lives of marginalized groups to the center of discourse and investigating how such shifts challenge existing paradigms (e.g., 9, 11). At an especially useful critical level, still other scholars are interrogating gendered processes (e.g., 42) and examining race and gender as contexts for action (e.g., 43).

Social Formations and Social Projects

Gerontologists have long recognized that age is a social formation, whether their focus was on changing meanings of old, changing age-based norms, or changing social policies. Lynott and Lynott succinctly describe the contributions of the phenomenological approach to this enterprise (44, p. 754):

> phenomenologists . . . ask how persons (professional and lay alike) make use of age-related explanations and justifications in their treatment and interaction with one another. . . . Facts virtually come to life in their assertion, invocation, realization, and utility. From this point of view, language is not just a vehicle for symbolically representing realities; its usage, in the practical activities of everyday life, is concretely productive of the realities. Accordingly, to the extent a form of discourse becomes institutionalized (becomes the organizing principle of a variety of formal activities), objects become systematic productions and reproductions of their applications to human affairs.

Political economists also have demonstrated long-standing interest in age projects, especially in how the meanings of old age and strategies for the distribution of resources are interconnected and shift over time (e.g., 45–49). Attention is given to the role gerontologists have played in such age projects (e.g., 46, 50), with Estes (46) taking the lead in raising critical questions about the witting and unwitting contributions of gerontologists to the whole "aging enterprise" (see Chapter 7).

The ongoing debate about the allocation of resources on the basis of age versus need reflects competing age- and class-focused projects. Often embedded within the latter is the understanding that class is both gendered and racialized. However, because gender and race representations seem to have less political capital than need-based claims, especially for the older population, political projects are more likely to get constructed as need-focused undertakings. It should be noted here that while in Canada, Europe, and elsewhere, such need-based claims are often explicitly phrased in terms of class, continuing reluctance to speak or explicitly formulate policy in terms of class in the United States (or, as Navarro (51) notes, to routinely collect health statistics by class) has led to an obscuring of the class basis of need in this country. In the latter regard, as Krieger and Moss point out, "the absence, and not just the presence, of particular social categories speaks volumes about how those afforded responsibility for collecting and disseminating data construe—and circumscribe consciousness about—the public's health" (52, p. 384). The tendency of researchers in aging and other fields to control for social class, either through sampling or through analytic techniques, rather than studying its effects, may contribute to this problematic obfuscation.

Some gerontologists, of course, have well articulated the role of class and its intersections with gender and age formations. Critical examinations of women's disadvantage with regard to Social Security policy provide a case in point. As Quadagno and Harrington Meyer (53) demonstrate, for example, the linking of Social Security benefits to wages, which remain substantially higher for men than for women, and the program's complete disregard for household labor and caregiving, results in a public pension structure that penalizes women in profound but "invisible" ways. Similarly, private pensions, which accent "lengthy, continuous employment," are least likely to be available in industries such as retail and service where women are heavily over-represented. As a result, and without making overt gender distinctions, pension policies in both public and private sectors differentially affect men and women by virtue of their different resources and life trajectories (54).

The intersections of gender and class in age formations also have been explored with respect to health policy for older persons. Studies of reimbursement patterns under Medicare have demonstrated how the acute care bias in coverage corresponds to a male pattern of illness, and particularly disadvantages older low-income and minority women, who bear a disproportionate share of chronic illnesses. Although architects of the Medicare program did not intentionally discriminate against women, the structure of coverage is such that the program is far from "gender neutral" in its effects (54).

The intersections of gender, class, race, age, and it should be added, sexual orientation, in terms of their public policy effects are perhaps best illustrated by the Supplemental Security Income (SSI) program. Designed to provide a minimum

guaranteed income for poor elderly and disabled people, SSI benefits have historically brought a married couple to 90 percent of the poverty line, while bringing a
single person to just 75 percent of the federal poverty threshold. Since older women,
many older people of color, and gays and lesbians are far less likely to be married
than are white men, the program works to the systematic disadvantage of these more
marginalized groups (54).

As the above examples illustrate, class, race, gender, and age formations and the
interactions between them have had a profound effect on health and social policies in
the United States and hence on the ways in which aging is experienced, managed,
and treated in this country.

TOWARD A MORE INCLUSIVE, INTERSECTIONAL, AND CRITICAL GERONTOLOGY

In this concluding section we offer suggestions that may help the field of gerontology become more inclusive, critically focused, and attentive to questions of
interlocking oppressions/intersectionality. In particular, we underscore the advantages of life course over cross-sectional perspectives, and the utility for gerontology
of the renewed interest in conceptualizing social class, the introduction of spatial
location into the conversation on social location, and the recognition and study of
subjective aspects of gender, race, age, and class experiences.

In an effort to push the field forward, we suggest that taking a step back will bring
clarity to our tasks. With a more distant perspective, we can take in a wider view.
Geriatricians and epidemiologists, for example, have long recognized that as cohorts
get chronologically older, the range of observed physical functioning, cognitive
status, and social health becomes wider, with less clustering around the mean than is
found in younger cohorts (55, 56). That is, knowing a person's age does little to
inform us of his or her physical, mental, or social circumstances. A wider view of
aging, which combines political economy analyses with life course perspectives and
also considers the strengths of different groups and the commonalities they may
share, as well as their unique attributes and the barriers and problems they confront,
will greatly enrich our understanding of the complexity of the aging experience.

Our understanding of interlocking oppressions throughout life also may be
enhanced through further conceptual attention to social class. When Max Weber (57)
described social class originally, an important part of the definition was life chances.
This core concept has been lost in much mainstream research, with social class
measurements typically reduced to income, education, or occupation. Acker (58,
p. 488) argues persuasively that classes are structured through relations of (resource)
distribution as well as relations of production. Gerontologists have given considerable attention to relations of production with regard to work and retirement, and to
relations of distribution with regard to Social Security, aging services, and formal
and informal caregiving. They have also begun to examine how relations of production and distribution play out across the life course. These efforts would benefit,
however, from a more thorough integration of questions of life chances across the
life course, especially as they are informed by race and gender (cf. 12, 46, 59, 60).
Increased attention to analyses of how cohort and period effects—which may have

racialized and gendered impacts—shape the possibilities and constraints experienced by individuals and groups as they age (e.g., 12, 61) is also needed to enhance the relevance and the richness of our research in this area.

Finally, as noted earlier in this chapter and elsewhere in this book, such taken-for-granted concepts as retirement, adjustment to old age, and healthy, productive or successful aging need to be carefully reconsidered within a broad critical gerontology perspective. Such a perspective would challenge us to consider, among other things, the sociohistorical origins of such concepts, their roles and functions, and the degree to which they capture—or fail to capture—the experience of diverse groups of elders.

The multidisciplinary nature of gerontology enables and encourages us to borrow and adapt, from a diversity of fields, exciting new theoretical frameworks and methodological approaches which make possible a more inclusive, intersectional gerontology. In rethinking our approaches to aging and social class, for example, we may look to the work of social epidemiologists and medical sociologists (62–64) who have been conducting investigations into place or neighborhood as a means of better understanding how social class functions in the etiology of nearly all diseases. They have documented that neighborhood or place is an important contributor to social class and that understanding place will contribute to understanding experiences that put people at risk for poor health. Similarly, neighborhood racial/ethnic composition has been found to be an important contextual factor related to mortality (65). Such work holds special relevance for gerontological research, since the decreased mobility of the elderly means that many older people are more influenced by their immediate physical and social environments than are their younger counterparts. An investigation into the environments in which people age, particularly if it is both inclusive and intersectional, can greatly enrich our understanding of aging on the individual through the broader societal levels.

Gerontologists also can benefit from the interesting work being undertaken by geographers on the role of space and place in decision-making about various life circumstances. For example, Gilbert (66) demonstrates how space and questions of travel are important considerations in job-seeking and child care for working-class women. Her approach to space, when adapted to questions of aging, recommends that we carefully explore the role of spatial location and distance in decisions of later life, including those surrounding the search for medical care, housing, part-time work, and companionship.

The foregoing issues about location could be fruitfully articulated with work about neighborhoods and poverty (cf. 67). For example, in declining neighborhoods where work is disappearing, what is the role of elders in terms of their contribution to the socialization of children and adolescents into normative work roles? Do such roles vary by ethnicity, gender, or other factors? Addressing such research questions has the potential to link issues of individual, group, and community well-being in ways that could shape more effective social policies and community development activities.

The work of epidemiologists who are looking in some new ways at the role of race/ethnicity in disease etiology and health status also has relevance for critical gerontology. Jones (68), for example, has developed questions to help gauge how often a person thinks about his or her own race or ethnicity. She finds that while African Americans report high frequencies of thinking of their own race (on the order of every hour or many times a day), European Americans report thinking about it once a week or once a month. Other epidemiologists have developed and used survey questions to address perceived discrimination and to investigate the role of discrimination in explaining black-white differences in blood pressure levels (20, 69, 70). Recent research by Krieger and Sidney (69), for example, revealed that working-class African Americans who reported no racial discrimination had significantly higher blood pressure than those who reported one or more instances of such discrimination. The investigators suggest that those who report no racial discrimination may be hiding their anger, protecting against recrimination, and playing into derogatory stereotypes (71)—with adverse health consequences. The high rates of hypertension among older African Americans, and the potential cumulative effects of a lifetime of subtle and overt discrimination (which many were taught to respond to passively rather than assertively) (71), suggest the special relevance of such research for critical gerontology.

The general issue of identity salience is an important subjective dimension of intersectionality for gerontologists to tap. As we have noted, gender, race, class, and age are not essential properties of individuals but rather political and social constructions. As such, they have official, social, and subjective dimensions. In the former case, researchers and policymakers may locate individuals within particular categories, with certain consequences flowing from such placement. The decennial debate over what categories to use for race/ethnicity in census enumeration, including the current contentious debate over whether to add a "mixed race" category, illustrates efforts at official categorization and the heat which they often engender.

Social definitions also arise in social interactions in which individuals make (often immediate) categorical assessments about others. Such assessments typically have interactional consequences. A number of authors have described the effects of being seen as old, noting that such perceptions may influence not only how one is treated in daily social encounters (12, 72–74) but even the type of medical care prescribed (74, 75). In the latter regard, numerous studies have shown psychiatrists to prescribe more passive drug therapies for older patients while recommending psychotherapy and other active treatments for younger patients with identical symptoms and conditions (74). Not infrequently, such ageism intersects with racism and sexism. Not only are women and African Americans more likely to receive passive drug therapies for mental health problems, but several recent studies (75–78) suggest that they also are less likely to receive a thorough diagnostic work up for conditions such as heart disease. In the latter case, moreover, a significant race and gender gap in such treatments as cardiac bypass surgery and angioplasty remains, even when such medically relevant variables as types of angina, age, symptoms, and previous myocardial infarction are controlled for (76–78).

An individual's subjective self-definition, and the salience of each of the categories of intersectionality, are important features of being gendered, raced, classed, and aged, and constitute another important domain for gerontological research. For example, Yearwood and Dressel (79) describe the high salience of race for African American but not for European American participants in a southern rural senior center, precisely because the center was organized and administered in ways that reinforced historical patterns of dominance and subordination in the local community.

Finally, gerontologists must be increasingly concerned with questions of identity salience which derive from the intersection of the official, social, and subjective dimensions of the phenomenon. For example, if aging services are offered in a single location for broad categories of elders (e.g., Asian Americans), to what extent will specific groups (e.g., second-generation Korean Americans or recent Laotian immigrants) identify with and use such services, or even find the services responsive to their particular needs? How will gender and class issues inform these questions? And how will those who do use such services be perceived by their counterparts (e.g., as not fulfilling group expectations and thus not really being a member of "the in-group")?

Looking to anthropology, we find value in new ethnographic investigations in which the social and cultural aspects of aging are explored through participant observation, richly textured in-depth interviews, and other means (80). Barbara Myerhoff's classic look at definitional ceremonies among the old as "strategies that provide opportunities for being seen and in one's own terms, garnering witness to one's worth, vitality and being" (81, p. 266) thus deepens and extends our understanding of "the problems of invisibility and marginality" in late life and how some elders deal with these problems.

Finally, literature provides a largely untapped source of rich expression (82), and one with particular salience as we seek to better understand the lived experience of racial/ethnic groups with a rich oral tradition. Characters such as Baby Suggs in Toni Morrison's novel *Beloved* (83) may provide insights into the historical role of older African American women as caregivers across generations that are difficult to capture through traditional social science research. Identifying and interpreting what is important in understanding elders from diverse backgrounds may indeed mean "going outside one's traditional value orientation and training" and viewing often overlooked venues, such as the art, music, and literature of a people, "as appropriate means through which one creates and develops conceptual ways of thinking" (16, p. 135).

SUMMARY

As Linda Burton and her colleagues note (16, p. 129):

> Current and future generations of the elderly are a part of a quiet revolution—a revolution of older individuals representing the broadest range of ethnic, racial . . . regional and [class] diversity ever witnessed. . . . This diversity challenges us to evaluate the applicability of existing research, policy and programs to emerging elderly populations. And more important, it prods us to reassess the relevance of gerontological theories and perspectives.

Responding to Burton and colleagues' challenge, this chapter has offered a critique of traditional research questions, theories, and methods that distort or simply fail to take into account the realities of those groups of elders who are disadvantaged by virtue of their race, ethnicity, class, and/or gender. It has underscored the need to look beyond "add-and-stir" and other simplistic approaches to inclusivity and interlocking oppressions/intersectionality which, while often well intentioned, may have the effect of furthering the marginalization of already subordinate groups while obfuscating the structural dynamics that shape inequities.

We have highlighted the relevance for critical gerontology of recent promising theoretical and methodological developments in fields such as sociology and epidemiology, and the need for looking to previously neglected areas such as the humanities to increase the relevance and the adequacy of our research efforts.

As John Bond and Peter Coleman point out, aging into the 21st century ideally will see gerontology "growing into a more liberating subject, less concerned with charting decline and predicting outcomes and more with outlining possibilities (84, p. 339). For gerontology to reach its full potential, however, the important work that continues to take place in the biological and psychological aspects of aging must be complemented by a far greater accent on critical perspectives from political economy and feminist scholarship, coupled with newer, culturally relevant ways of thinking about aging in our increasingly diverse societies (16, 85).

As we have argued in this chapter, the role of interlocking systems of inequality in shaping how aging is experienced on both the macro and the micro levels must be a central focus of this research. For only by incorporating such a perspective can we move the field beyond established and limited "ways of thinking" to construct new analyses that capture the intimate interdependence of race, class, and gender in individual, group, and societal aging.

REFERENCES

1. Andersen, M. L., and Collins, P. *Race, Class, and Gender: An Anthology,* Ed. 2. Wadsworth, Belmont, Calif., 1995.
2. hooks, b. *From Margin to Center.* South End Press, Boston, 1984.
3. Andersen, M. L. *Thinking About Women: Sociological and Feminist Perspectives.* Macmillan, New York, 1983.
4. Burnham, L. Has poverty been feminized in black America? *Black Scholar* 16: 14–24, 1985.
5. Dressel, P. L. Gender, race and class: Beyond the feminization of poverty in later life. *Gerontologist* 28(2): 177–180, 1988.
6. Collins, P. H. Symposium on West and Fenstermaker's 'doing difference.' *Gender Soc.* 9(4): 491–494, 1995.
7. Kantor, R. M. *Men and Women of the Corporation.* Basic Books, New York, 1977.
8. Lorde, A. Age, race, class, and sex: Women redefining difference. In *Race, Class, and Gender: An Anthology,* Ed. 2, edited by M. L. Andersen and P. H. Collins. Wadsworth, Belmont, Calif., 1995.
9. Dressel, P. L., and Barnhill, S. K. Reframing gerontological thought and practice: The case of grandmothers with daughters in prison. *Gerontologist* 34(5): 685–691, 1994.
10. Freire, P. *Pedagogy of the Oppressed.* Herder and Herder, New York, 1970.
11. Calasanti, T. M. Incorporating diversity: Meaning, levels of research, and implications for theory. *Gerontologist* 36(2): 147–156, 1996.

12. Stoller, E. P., and Gibson, R. C. *Worlds of Difference: Inequality in the Aging Experience,* Ed. 2. Pine Forge, Thousand Oaks, Calif., 1997.

13. Abel, E. *Who Cares for the Elderly? Public Policy and the Experience of Adult Daughters.* Temple University Press, Philadelphia, 1991.

14. Sidel, R. *Keeping Women and Children Last: American's War on the Poor.* Penguin Books, New York, 1996.

15. Archibold, P. G. An impact of parent-caring on women. *Fam. Relations* 32: 39–45, 1983.

16. Burton, L. Dilworth-Anderson, P., and Bengston, V. Creating culturally relevant ways of thinking about aging and diversity: Theoretical challenges for the 21st century. In *Diversity: New Approaches to Ethnic Minority Aging,* edited by E. P. Stanford and F. M. Torres-Gil. Baywood, Amityville, N.Y., 1992.

17. Gibson, R. C. The subjective retirement of black Americans. *J. Gerontol. Soc. Sci.* 46: S204–S209, 1991.

18. Omi, M., and Winant, H. *Racial Formation in the United States.* Routledge, New York, 1994.

19. Hinsen, P. Theories of Race and Ethnicity. Paper presented to the American Cultures Faculty Seminar, University of California, Berkeley, June 2, 1994.

20. Krieger, N., et al. Racism, sexism, and social class: Implications for studies of health, disease, and well-being. *Am. J. Prev. Med.* 9(Suppl.): 82–122, 1993.

21. Gordon, D. R. Equal protection and unequal justice. In *Minority Report: What Has Happened to Blacks, Hispanics, American Indians and Other Minorities in the Eighties,* edited by L. W. Dunbar, pp. 118–151. Pantheon Books, New York, 1984.

22. Crenshaw, K., et al. (eds.). *Critical Race Theory: The Key Writings that Formed the Movement.* W. W. Norton, New York, 1995.

23. Markides, K. S., and Black, S. A. Race, ethnicity, and aging: The impact of inequality. In *Handbook of Aging and the Social Sciences,* Ed. 4, edited by R. H. Binstock and L. K. George. Academic Books, New York, 1995.

24. National Urban League. *Double Jeopardy: The Older Negro in America Today.* New York, 1964.

25. Jackson, J. J. The Current Status of Ethnogerontology and Its Complementary and Conflicting Social and Cultural Concerns for American Minority and Ethnic Elders. Paper presented at the annual meeting of the American Society on Aging, New Orleans, 1991.

26. Blakemore, K., and Boneham, M. *Age, Race and Ethnicity: A Comparative Approach.* Open University, Philadelphia, 1994.

27. Dowd, J. J., and Bengtson, V. L. Aging in minority populations: An examination of the double jeopardy hypothesis. *J. Gerontol.* 33: 338–355, 1978.

28. Crystal, S., and Shea, D. Cumulative advantage, cumulative disadvantage, and inequality among elderly people. *Gerontologist* 30(4): 437–443, 1990.

29. Crystal, S., and Waehrer, K. Later-life economic inequality in longitudinal perspective. *J. Gerontol.* 51B(6): S307–S318, 1996.

30. Ferraro, K. F., and Farmer, M. M. Double jeopardy, aging as leveler, or persistent health inequality? A longitudinal analysis of white and black Americans. *J. Gerontol.* 51B(6): S319–S328, 1996.

31. Ekerdt, D. J., and Deviney, S. Evidence for a preretirement process among older male workers. *J. Gerontol.* 48: S35–S43, 1993.

32. Robinson, J., Moen, P., and Dempster-McClain, D. Women's caregiving: Changing profiles and pathways. *J. Gerontol.* 50B(6): S362–S373, 1995.

33. Kramer, B. J., and Kipnis, S. Eldercare and work-role conflict: Toward an understanding of gender differences in caregiver burden. *Gerontologist* 35(3): 340–348, 1995.

34. Richardson, V., and Kilty, K. M. Retirement intentions among black professionals: Implications for practice with older black adults. *Gerontologist* 32(1): 7–16, 1992.
35. Himes, C. L., Hogan, D. P., and Eggebeen, D. J. Living arrangements of minority elders. *J. Gerontol.* 51B(1): S42–S48, 1996.
36. McLaughlin, D. K., and Jensen, L. Poverty among older Americans: The plight of nonmetropolitan elders. *J. Gerontol.* 48(2): S44–S54, 1993.
57. Levin, J. S., and Cole, T. R. 'Songs of Ourselves': A quantitative history of American biographies. *Gerontologist* 36(4): 448–453, 1996.
38. Angel, J. L., et al. Nativity, declining health, and preferences in living arrangements among elderly Mexican Americans: Implications for long-term care. *Gerontologist* 36(4): 464–473, 1996.
39. Tanjaseri, S. P., Wallace, S. P., and Shibata, K. Picture imperfect: Hidden problems among Asian Pacific Islander elderly. *Gerontologist* 35(6): 753–760, 1995.
40. Burr, J. A., and Mutchler, J. E. Nativity, acculturation, and economic status: Explanations of Asian American living arrangements in later life. *J. Gerontol.* 48(2): S55–S63, 1993.
41. Moon, A., and Williams, O. Perceptions of elder abuse and help-seeking patterns among African-American, Caucasian American, and Korean-American elderly women. *Gerontol. Soc. Am.* 33(3): 386–395, 1993.
42. Hardy, M. A. The gender of poverty in an aging population. *Res. Aging* 15(3): 243–278, 1993.
43. Danigelis, N., and McIntosh, B. Resources and productive activity of elders: Race and gender as contexts. *J. Gerontol.* 48(4): S192–S203, 1993.
44. Lynott, R. J., and Lynott, P. P. Tracing the course of theoretical development in the sociology of aging. *Gerontologist* 36: 749–760, 1996.
45. Binstock, R. H. The aged as scapegoat. *Gerontologist* 23: 136–143, 1983.
46. Estes, C. L. *The Aging Enterprise.* Jossey-Bass, San Francisco, 1979.
47. Binstock, R. H. Changing criteria for old age programs: The introduction of economic status and need for services. *Gerontologist* 34(6): 726–730, 1994.
48. Hudson, R. B. The changing face of aging politics. *Gerontologist* 36(1): 33–35, 1996.
49. Minkler, M., and Robertson, A. The ideology of age/race wars: Deconstructing a social problem. *Ageing Soc.* 11: 1–22, 1991.
50. Cole, T. R. What have we 'made' of aging? *J. Gerontol.* 50B(6): S341–S343, 1995.
51. Navarro, V. Race v. class or race and class? *Lancet* 336: 1238–1240, 1990.
52. Krieger, N., and Moss, N. Accounting for the public's health: An introduction to selected papers from a U.S. conference on "Measuring Social Inequalities in Health." *Int. J. Health Serv.* 26: 383–390, 1996.
53. Quadagno, J., and Harrington Meyer, M. Gender and public policy. In *Gender and Aging,* edited by L. Glasse and J. Hendricks, pp. 121–128. Baywood, Amityville, N.Y., 1992.
54. Moon, M. Public policies: Are they gender neutral? In *Gender and Aging,* edited by L. Glasse and J. Hendricks, pp. 111–120. Baywood, Amityville, N.Y., 1992.
55. Rowe, J. W., and Kahn, R. Human aging: Usual and successful. *Science* 237: 143–149, 1987.
56. Seeman, T. E., et al. Behavioral and psychosocial predictors of physical performance: MacArthur Studies of Successful Aging. *J. Gerontol.* 50A: M177–M183, 1995.
57. Weber, M. *Economy and Society: An Outline of Interpretive Sociology,* edited by G. Roth and C. Wittich, translated by E. Fischoff et al. University of California Press, Berkeley, 1978.
58. Acker, J. Class, gender, and the relations of distribution. *Signs* 13(3): 473–497, 1988.

59. Quadagno, J., and Hardy, M. Work and retirement. In *Handbook of Aging and Social Sciences,* Ed. 4, edited by R. H. Binstock and L. K. George, pp. 326–345. Academic Press, San Diego, 1996.

60. Bernard, M., et al. Gendered work, gendered retirement. In *Connecting Gender and Ageing: A Sociological Approach,* edited by S. Arber and J. Ginn, pp. 56–68. Open University Press, Buckingham, England, 1995.

61. Kutza, E. A. A policy analyst's response. *Gerontologist* 26(2): 147–149, 1986.

62. Macintyre, S., Maciver, S., and Sooman, A. Area, class and health: Should we be focusing on places or people? *J. Soc. Policy* 22: 213–234, 1993.

63. Kaplan, G. A. People and places: Contrasting perspectives on the association between social class and health. *Int. J. Health Serv.* 26: 507–519, 1996.

64. O'Campo, P., et al. Neighborhood risk factors for low birth weight in Baltimore City: A multi-level analysis. *Am. J. Public Health* 1997, in press.

65. LeClere, F. B., Rogers, R. G., and Peters, K. Socioeconomic Status and Mortality in the U.S.: Individual and Community Correlates. Paper presented at the annual meeting of the Population Association of America, San Francisco, April 6–8, 1995.

66. Gilbert, M. Ties to People, Bonds to Place: The Urban Geography of Low Income Women's Survival Strategies. Unpublished dissertation, Clark University, Worcester, Mass., 1993.

67. Wilson, W. J. *The Truly Disadvantaged: The Inner City, the Underclass, and Public Policy.* University of Chicago Press, Chicago, 1987.

68. Jones, C. P. The Racism in "Race." Paper presented at the annual meeting of the American Public Health Association, San Diego, November 1995.

69. Krieger, N., and Sidney, S. Racial discrimination and blood pressure: The CARDIA Study of young black and white adults. *Am. J. Public Health* 86: 1370–1378, 1996.

70. Krieger, N. Racial and gender discrimination: Risk factors for high blood pressure? *Soc. Sci. Med.* 30: 1273–1281, 1990.

71. Feagin, J., and Sikes, M. P. *Living with Racism: The Black Middle-Class Experience.* Beacon Press, Boston, 1994.

72. Featherstone, M., and Hepworth, M. Images of aging. In *Ageing in Society: An Introduction to Social Gerontology,* edited by J. Bond, P. Coleman, and S. Peace, pp. 304–332. Sage, London, 1993.

73. MacDonald, B., with Rich, C. *Look Me in the Eye: Old Women, Aging and Ageism.* Spinsters Ink, San Francisco, 1983.

74. Butler, R. N., and Lewis, M. I. *Aging and Mental Health,* Ed. 4. C. V. Mosby, St. Louis, 1991.

75. Belgrave, L. Discrimination against older women in health care. *J. Women Aging* 5(3/4): 181–199, 1993.

76. Tobin, J., et al. Sex bias in considering coronary bypass surgery. *Ann. Intern. Med.* 107: 19–27, 1987.

77. Ford, R. E., et al. Coronary artiography and coronary bypass surgery among white and other racial groups relative to hospital based incidence rates for coronary artery disease: Findings from the NHDS. *Am. J. Public Health* 79: 437–440, 1989.

78. Steingart, R. M., et al. Sex differences in the management of coronary artery disease. *N. Engl. J. Med.* 325: 226–230, 1991.

79. Yearwood, A., and Dressel, P. Interracial dynamics in a Southern rural senior center. *Gerontologist* 23: 512–517, 1983.

80. Kaufman, S. R. *The Ageless Self: Sources of Meaning in Late Life.* University of Wisconsin Press, Madison, 1986.

81. Myerhoff, B. "Life, not death, in Venice:" Its second life. In *The Anthropology of Experience,* edited by V. Turner and E. M. Bruner, pp. 261–286. University of Chicago Press, Chicago, 1986.
82. Holstein, M. Taking next steps: Gerontological education, research and the literary imagination. *Gerontologist* 34: 822–827, 1994.
83. Morrison, T. *Beloved.* New American Library, New York, 1987.
84. Bond, J., Coleman, P., and Peace, S. (eds.). *Ageing in Society.* Sage, London, 1993.
85. Minkler, M. Critical perspectives on ageing: New challenges for gerontology. *Ageing Soc.* 16: 467–487, 1996.

PART V. WORK, RETIREMENT, SOCIAL SECURITY, AND "PRODUCTIVE AGING"

"One of the worst failings of mainstream gerontology," write Chris Phillipson and Alan Walker is that "in its gender blindness, it has failed to provide a rigorous assessment of the crisis that awaits women—particularly those in the working class—as they approach and enter old age" (1, p. 9). Although Part V deals broadly with issues of retirement, Social Security, and "productive aging," we respond to Phillipson and Walker's concern by beginning with a sobering look at the retirement prospects of older women in the United States. The ideal of the "three-legged stool" of retirement income, supported by the legs of Social Security, employer-paid pensions, and savings and investment, is seen as poorly approximating the retirement reality of many older American women, for whom two of the legs may be weak or missing altogether.

The Older Women's League's analysis of women's retirement income presented in Chapter 16 vividly demonstrates the continuing gender and marital-status-based inequities in the U.S. Social Security system and the Supplemental Security Income (SSI) program for low-income elderly, blind, or disabled persons. The implicit gender bias in private pension plans is examined also, as are the vast differences by race, class, and gender in the degree to which people are able to save and invest for their retirement years. As noted in the Introduction to this volume, Chapter 16 departs from the other chapters by offering no explicit conceptual framework for the stark facts and statistics presented. Yet a political economy perspective is implicit in this report, which dramatically illustrates how inequities based on gender, and on the interactions of gender, race, class, and age, place many women in a financially precarious position as they enter their "golden years."

In Chapter 17, Chris Phillipson draws upon both critical theory and political economy to review and interpret the retirement experience of the last half century, as well as possible scenarios for the future. As he notes, while the institutionalization of retirement reached a peak in the 1950s, by the 1970s and 1980s high unemployment and growing perceptions of fiscal crisis raised questions about the location and stability of retirement within the life course. Phillipson sees the transformations that have occurred in the domains of work and retirement as reflecting broad social dynamics, including, importantly, the emergence of postindustrial and postmodern societies. Whereas in simple modernity "retirement is characterized by the struggle to secure an identity that transcends the tendency of the state to 'welfarize' the old," with advanced or post modernity," a new social construction of later life" is taking hold. Phillipson describes the latter as opening far more possibilities, stemming in part from growing self-awareness and the loosening of the "contours" of earlier notions of what it meant to be retired. At the same time, he stresses that social inequalities based on class, gender, and the like may take new forms and definition in post modernity, as retirement "reverts to being a social risk rather than a social right." Phillipson concludes by sounding both a note of caution and a note of cautious optimism as we move into the next phase of the history of retirement in a new decade and a new century.

From Phillipson's highly theoretical examination of the social construction of retirement, we move in Chapter 18 to a cross-national examination of recent trends in the evolution of the welfare state as these are affecting the retired. Robert Hudson begins by reviewing the warning bells that have been sounded by those concerned with the potential threats to universalism and other welfare state principles and by those who see costly government programs for the old as threatening the well-being of younger and future generations. Both value shifts and sector shifts characterize the current debates over welfare policy, with overall improvements in the status of the old, rapidly rising health care and pension costs, and privatization and other market pressures converging to alter the accepted place of the old in welfare policy. To make sense of these various trends and to better address the questions they raise, Hudson proposes a "social contingency framework" within which the different risks of old age can be weighed and reassessed. Although values such as universalism, adequacy, and solidarity are taken as "bedrock concerns," questions of how and where to apply these principles are ripe for rethinking.

Hudson's broad cross-national analysis of welfare state policy for the old provides a helpful backdrop for the more detailed examination of the changes now taking place in the United States in its once sacred Social Security system. In Chapter 19, Eric Kingson and Jill Quadagno note that the rhetoric of an "entitlement crisis" has reached new heights, "crafting a message of fear" that makes radical reform appear not only permissible but indeed the only responsible course of action for the fore-seeable future. While acknowledging that Social Security does have a financing problem, the authors suggest that the tendency to lump Social Security with other entitlement programs (e.g., Medicare and Medicaid), together with the failure to consider the human costs of radically restructuring the nation's largest social insurance program, has led to proposals far more severe than is prudent or necessary. After criticizing such radical solutions as means-testing or privatizing Social Security, Kingson and Quadagno go on to discuss a variety of far more modest adjustments that could restore the Social Security trust fund to long-range solvency, without destroying in the process the essence of the program and the moral commitments on which it is based.

In the final chapter, Martha Holstein broadens the scope of our thinking beyond retirement and Social Security to the very meaning of a "good" old age. In particular, she critically examines the notion of a "productive aging society," which in the United States has become a "cultural ideal" in the dominant culture, with potentially negative consequences. In contrast to "enriched" notions of productive aging, which place a high value on volunteer work, caregiving, and the like, Holstein sees narrow interpretations focused solely on paid work as limiting and problematic, particularly for older women. Advocates of a productive aging society thus may unwittingly support work situations that reinforce "patterns of inequality and allow the continued exploitation of women." Further, Holstein argues, the emphasis on paid work may prevent us as a society from paying greater attention to norms of caring and responsibility toward others, personal as opposed to merely functional relationships for life fulfillment, and other themes that older women might enable us to more fully develop.

In many ways, this final chapter of the text brings us back to the piercing questions and challenges posed by Malcolm Johnson and Ann Robertson in Chapters 3 and 4. Holstein thus advocates for an intergenerational dialogue about the meanings of old age, rather than a premature embracing of narrow notions of a "productive aging society." Without such a dialogue, she cautions, we are likely both to reinforce earlier perceptions that devalue women, people of color, and low-income elders, and to miss the opportunity to embrace "a rich and feminist" appreciation of old age and its gifts.

REFERENCE

1. Phillipson, C., and Walker, A. The case for a critical gerontology. In *Social Gerontology: New Directions,* edited by S. DeGregorio, pp. 1–15. Croom Helm, London, 1987.

CHAPTER 16

The Path to Poverty:
An Analysis of Women's Retirement Income

Older Women's League

For many women, the path to poverty in old age begins the first day they go to work. Women in 1996 earned 75 percent of what men earned (1). As women age, this gap widens and continues into retirement. Even with Social Security benefits, one in four women today aged 65 and older lives near or below the poverty line (2).

The foundation of a woman's economic security in retirement is Social Security. Ninety-two percent of older women (more than 18 million) receive Social Security retirement benefits of some kind. Private pensions are the second major source of income for retirees. However, by the mid-1990s only 18 percent of women aged 65 and over were receiving a pension (3).

Growing old in the United States is very different for women than for men. Race and ethnicity, family, and economic resources are primary influences in the quality of older women's lives. The economic status of older women reflects their past lives, their education, employment history, and marital status. The financial problems faced in old age are often extensions of the problems and choices women dealt with earlier in their lives (4). For most women, decades of Social Security contributions will translate into virtually the same retirement benefits as those paid to their mothers and grandmothers, who may never have earned wages or paid Social Security taxes. These benefits alone are inadequate for all generations.

The work patterns of today's young women will likely follow the same course as those of their mothers in the baby boom generation: periods of paid work, interspersed with time taken off to have and raise a family and/or care for older relatives. If these patterns hold, younger women will continue to predominate in the same low-paying, non-benefits occupations as older women; 58 percent of younger women and 59 percent of older women work in sales, service, and clerical jobs (1). When these women retire, they will not only receive low Social Security benefits, they will have little or no pension income (5). Data from the Survey of Income and

This is an adapted and updated version of the 1995 Mother's Day Report *The Path to Poverty,* and is reprinted here with permission from the Older Women's League.

Program Participation showed that for all men only 1.6 percent of all potential work-years were spent away from work; for women workers, 14.7 percent of all potential work-years were spent away from paid work. Thus women spend far more time away from work and are unable to build the seniority that men may achieve (6).

What will the future hold for women in retirement? Today a woman's race/ ethnicity and marital status largely determine whether she will be poor. By 2020, 21 percent of the female population aged 65 and older will be comprised of women of color, compared with 10 percent now. Unless there are societal changes, these older minority women of the future will face the same hardships as today's older women of color.

Whether a woman is married or widowed, divorced, separated, or single makes a big difference in her economic situation in retirement today. Older married women are generally the most economically secure. Conversely, 4 of 10 older women living alone are poor or near poor. Because of later marriages, more divorces, and greater longevity, older women of the future will have spent a greater proportion of their lives unmarried. A higher proportion of younger women will remain single all of their lives. Trends suggest that more older women will live alone and enter their later years without a husband. Today, 3 in 10 households are married couples without children under 18. This raises serious questions for baby boomers and younger people who will retire in the 21st century. Who will care for this retired population? Without their own financial resources, how will they fare? The Social Security retirement trust funds are projected to be depleted by 2029 unless modest changes of the type described in Chapter 19 are enacted. Long-range planning for retirement is essential.

The legacy of poverty in older age does not need to be passed from mothers to daughters and granddaughters born in the 1990s and beyond. We know the faults and biases in the structure of the U.S. retirement system. That gives women the power to make changes to that structure. Further, women know that the decisions they make during their work lives can alter the cycle of poverty among older women.

OLDER WOMEN AND POVERTY

Although most older people are more economically secure than their predecessors, many women and minorities aged 65 and over live in poverty (4). Forty-two percent of women aged 65 and over are living below 125 percent of the poverty level (3). Poverty in late life begins with lower wages during the working years. As noted earlier, overall, year-round, full-time female workers earned 75 percent of what men earned in 1995 (1). The wage gap widens with age; women aged 55 and older employed full time in 1994 earned $391 a week compared with $591 a week for men, or 66 percent of men's wages. Women 25 to 54 years old earned 74 percent of the wages of men in the same age range: $425 a week for women versus $575 a week for men (1).

The economic chasm that is evident between women and men during their work lives continues to widen then they retire. Women 65 and over in 1995 had a median income of $9,335—62 percent of the $14,983 annual median income of older men (3). In 1995, older women were over twice as likely to be living below the poverty line as older men (13.6 percent versus 6.2 percent). Another 8.5 percent of older women were near poor, compared with 5.2 percent of men (7). Ninety-two percent of women aged 65 and over in 1994 got some form of income from Social Security, while 77 percent received income from their assets (3). Among unmarried women 65 and older in 1994, without Social Security 64 percent of those getting these monthly checks would have been poor, and 20 percent of those receiving Social Security were poor in spite of their coverage. Ninety percent of all unmarried 65-year-old and older recipients depend on Social Security for 90 percent or more of their income; 22 percent of these people have no other income (3). Income obtained from Social Security varies by race, with 92 percent of white women receiving benefits compared with 86 percent of African American women and 77 percent of Hispanic-origin women. African American women and women of Hispanic origin also have significantly less retirement income from assets than do white women: 33 percent for African American women and 31 percent for women of Hispanic origin, compared with 69 percent for white women. Further, 19 percent of African American and 26 percent of Hispanic-origin women aged 65 and over received some form of public assistance, compared with only 5 percent of white women (3).

Almost three-fourths of the 4 million older poor people in the United States are women. In 1995, only 10.5 percent of all people aged 65 and over were poor (3), but 75 percent of this group were women (7). Further since the threshold used to establish poverty status for older persons is about 10 percent lower than for other groups, these poverty estimates understate the degree of economic hardship actually experienced.

Older African American and Hispanic-origin women are especially vulnerable to a life of poverty. In 1995, 31 percent of African American women aged 65 and over and 28.9 percent of older women of Hispanic origin were living in poverty, compared with 14 percent of white women and 13.6 percent of all older women (4).

Marital Status Often Determines Whether Women Are Poor

Separated and divorced older women are substantially poorer than widows, and all are poorer than wives. Approximately 37 percent of women over 61 years old who were separated from their husbands in 1994 lived below the poverty line. Thirty-three percent of divorced women over 65 lived in poverty, compared with 27 percent of widowed women (3).

The net worth of married couples is far greater than that of single male and female householders. In 1993, women aged 65 and over had a median net worth of $9,560 compared with $12,927 for men and $44,410 for married couples. These data exclude the equity in home ownership, which for most people is the largest share of their net worth (8). Many women are only a man away from poverty. Half of all poor widows were not poor before the death of their husbands. Almost four times more widows live in poverty than do wives of the same age.

By some projections, Social Security and pension systems will have practically ended poverty among older men by 2020 (see Chapter 15). But poverty will remain widespread among older women living alone, those who are separated, divorced, widowed, or never married (9).

THE U.S. RETIREMENT SYSTEM DOES NOT WORK
FOR MANY WOMEN

Retirement plans, both Social Security and private pensions, benefit male work patterns. First enacted in 1935 when lifestyles were very different, Social Security retirement benefits best served the traditional family: a paid worker (usually the husband), an unpaid homemaker (usually the wife), and children. But most American families do not fit that profile today, and even fewer will fit it in the future (10). Today, women are in the workforce in greater numbers than ever. According to the Social Security Administration, nearly 60 percent of women work outside the home.

Many factors leave older women at severe economic disadvantage:

- Women's labor force participation often includes gaps for raising a young family and providing care for older relatives that make it difficult (if not impossible) for many older women to qualify for high Social Security retirement and private pension benefits.
- As noted earlier, almost two-thirds of women work in traditionally lower-paying jobs, such as sales, service, and clerical work.
- Women's work patterns (e.g., taking part-time or contingent jobs, moving in and out of the labor force, choosing lower-paying employment because of caregiving responsibilities) will continue to keep women's wages considerably below men's, and therefore women's retirement benefits low.
- The types of jobs (such as temporary and part-time work) that give women the flexibility to move in and out of the job market do not usually provide pension coverage. As a result, Social Security is often the only income they have in retirement.
- Women live longer than men.
- Women have to pay more out-of-pocket health care costs because they live longer and have more disabilities (11, 12).
- The money that married women in the workforce pay into Social Security may not be counted when benefits are calculated.

Many of these factors are beyond most women's power to control. However, female workers should be aware that the choices they make about work and family in their earlier lives will have serious consequences when they enter retirement. An examination of the three primary sources of retirement income sheds some light on why many older women live in or near poverty.

THE THREE-LEGGED STOOL OF THE
U.S. RETIREMENT SYSTEM

The basis for U.S. retirement policy has been the concept of the three-legged stool. The three legs of the stool are Social Security, employer-paid pensions, and savings and investment income. But this stool has never worked for women. Social Security, of course, is paid for by the employer and the employee in equal amounts during the working years. The traditional pension in the private sector is paid by the employer. Each individual is responsible for the savings and investment leg of her stool (13).

Thus, theoretically, one leg is shared equally by the employer and employee, one leg is paid by the employer, and one leg by the employee. In reality, many employers either have never offered pensions or have been eliminating the employer-paid pension plans, thereby removing or shortening their leg of the stool. Too often, women have no money left after the expenses of daily living to put toward an Individual Retirement Account (IRA) or other savings.

Social Security remains the most reliable leg of the stool. But the 1994 Old Age, Survivors and Disability Insurance (OASDI) Trustees Report projects that by 2013, some of the interest earned by the Social Security trust funds will need to be spent along with tax revenue to cover benefit payments. By 2019, it will be necessary to redeem some trust fund securities because income (including contributions and interest) will be less than expenditures. OASDI trust funds will be depleted by 2029 according to projections of the trustees' report, unless components of the system are modified (14). (See Chapter 19 for a good discussion of some of these modifications.)

Social Security

Almost 19 million women aged 65 and over received Social Security benefits in December 1996, and $11.3 million in monthly benefits were paid by the federal government at that time for all persons covered by OASDI, totaling $29.4 billion in that one year (15). In 1996, 11.3 million women had enough earnings in covered employment to qualify for retired worker benefits; of these, about 6.5 million were entitled to benefits solely as workers. Nearly 5 million women were entitled to both a spousal benefit and a retired worker benefit; their earnings as wives and widows were greater than if they chose a benefit based on their own earnings (15). Approximately 7.1 million women were entitled to spousal benefits only (15); 49.2 million people received monthly OASDI benefits, 58.3 percent of whom were women; and 137.8 million people worked in jobs covered by Social Security (1).

Fundamental biases persist in the Social Security retirement program. Social Security penalizes dual-earner families and discriminates against caregivers, divorced spouses, and people who retire early and live long (16). Generally, women are entitled to Social Security retirement benefits in one of three ways: solely as retired or disabled workers, solely as wives or widows, or, ideally, on the basis of their own earnings and those of their husbands (10).

Retired Workers. Among retired workers receiving Social Security benefits on their own work records, the average Primary Insurance Amount (PIA) a man receives in his check is 29 percent more than the average PIA of a woman ($817 versus $634) (17). Because Social Security benefits are wage-based, women's continuing lower earnings translate into lower retirement benefits. The wage gap ensures that the average woman will have consistently lower benefits than the average man (11).

Although more women have joined the paid workforce, their Social Security retirement income does not reflect their growing contributions. In 1970, women received 70 percent of the Social Security benefits men received. In 1995, as noted earlier, that proportion was 75 percent.

Twenty-seven percent of all older women, and 37 percent of unmarried older women, rely on Social Security retirement benefits for at least 90 percent of their income. Further, 20 percent of older unmarried women have no other source of income (9). When Social Security is their principal source of retirement income, older women are more likely to be poor. Only 11 percent of older women with 50 to 75 percent of their income from Social Security are poor, whereas 56 percent of older women with 100 percent of their income from Social Security are poor (13).

Dual Entitlement. Dually entitled women who are both married and wage earners receive higher benefits primarily based on their husband's records. Since 1960, the percentage of women drawing benefits based on their own work records has remained virtually constant at 36 percent, even though the percentage of women dually entitled to benefits on both their own work records and those of their husbands jumped from 5 percent in 1960 to 25 percent in 1993. Those years during which a working woman paid into the system through payroll taxes do not yield higher benefits but do decrease the liability to the Social Security system. She will receive exactly the same spousal benefit that she would have received had she never worked outside the home.

In 1994, only 64 percent of married women born in the early Depression years were eligible for their own Social Security retired worker benefits. Projections indicate that increasing numbers of married women will be eligible for Social Security benefits on their own work records. These include:

• 76 percent of married women in 1999 born in the late Depression;
• 79 percent of married women in 2004 born during World War II; and
• 85 percent of married women in 2009 born in the early baby boom generation.

In 1994, approximately two-thirds (64 percent) of older women received spousal benefits, including 26 percent who were dually entitled. Benefits for dually entitled women averaged $617 per month, including $408 for wives and $758 for widows. Another 39 percent received spousal benefits only, which averaged $533 per month, $373 for wives and $636 for widows. These were still higher than 100 percent of what the average married woman would have received based on her own low-earnings record. The other 36 percent of older women received higher benefits as retired workers in 1994, an average monthly benefit of $623 (17).

Spousal Benefits. A life-long homemaker has no Social Security protection in her own right. Even though she has worked for decades in the home and has contributed substantially to her family's economic well-being, a homemaker will receive only a spousal benefit equal to half of the benefit her husband receives if she has no earnings (11).

For the homemaker who is divorced, half a benefit can be far too little to live on. A divorced woman is eligible to receive a spousal benefit if she was married for at least 10 years. However, half of her ex-husband's benefit is just one-third of what they would receive as a couple. Together, they were receiving 150 percent of his Social Security, 100 percent for him and 50 percent for her. As an individual, she receives only the 50 percent. This provides many divorced, life-long homemakers with benefits that leave them living in poverty. The average monthly spousal benefit in 1994 was $361 for divorced women aged 62 or older (17).

A newly divorced woman aged 62 and over must wait two years to receive Social Security benefits if her former husband is still working, but she can receive benefits immediately if her ex-husband is already drawing Social Security. This two-year waiting period can be a time of great deprivation with no other source of income. It can also be regarded as imposing a penalty on divorce. Sixty times more women than men are dependent on their divorced spouse's earnings for Social Security benefits (18).

A divorced woman is financially better off after her ex-husband dies, because even a divorced widow receives 100 percent of her deceased husband's benefit. However, a widow may not draw any benefits until age 60, unless she has a child under 16 or a disabled child. A widow's gap is created for widows under age 60 who have no children under age 16 and who, therefore, cannot yet draw benefits. Once a widow has reached age 60 (or 50 if she is disabled), should she draw her benefits early rather than wait until age 65, her benefits are actuarially reduced to around 70 percent of her normal widow's benefit (11). Social Security is the sole source of income for 21 percent of all widows who receive benefits. Without Social Security, 62 percent of widows would be poor. Further, 1.6 million widowed beneficiaries live below the poverty line (9).

Lower wages prompt single and divorced women to draw their benefits early, and thereby have their benefits actuarially reduced. Benefits are reduced to 80 percent of their normal amount for workers who retire early at age 62, yet 72 percent of retired female workers draw their benefits early (11).

For a woman drawing an early spousal benefit, as opposed to a worker's benefit, the shortfall is even worse. The spousal benefit is reduced to 75 percent of the full benefit for a spouse electing to draw benefits at age 62. Eighty-two percent of spouses draw early benefits. Many are separated or divorced and in need of immediate income and cannot consider the consequences down the road (12). Projections indicate that Social Security retired worker spousal benefits will decrease by 18 percent by 2009. Twenty-nine percent of married women born in the early Depression years who retired in 1994 received no retired worker spousal benefits. By the time they retire in 2009, that percentage will be 47 percent for women born in the early baby boom years.

Supplemental Security Income

The Supplemental Security Income (SSI) program was established as a joint federal-state program in 1972 to help poor elderly Americans, and the blind and disabled of all ages, to meet their most basic needs. SSI is administered by the Social Security Administration and financed by general revenues and the states. The program is designed to guarantee a minimum level of income to help those who do not qualify for Social Security benefits or whose benefits are not adequate for subsistence by providing cash payments for the very poor. Benefits are means-tested; that is, if recipients have too many assets, they are required to "spend down" or impoverish themselves in order to qualify. Although the process of qualifying for SSI is difficult, those who qualify are also eligible for Medicaid, food stamps, and rehabilitation and home health care assistance.

Even with SSI, however, many women are still poor. The maximum federal SSI benefit of $458 per month in 1995 brings an individual up to only 75 percent of poverty, and the maximum benefit of $687 for a couple reaches only 90 percent of the poverty line. Half of the states provide additional supplements to persons living independently, but even these add-ons are inadequate in terms of raising recipients' income above the poverty level.

Who receives SSI? In 1995, 6.5 million poor elderly, disabled, and blind Americans received SSI. Thirty-three percent of these were aged 65 and over, and almost 60 percent were women. Older women constitute one-fourth of older persons receiving SSI (17). More than 1 million older women eligible for SSI benefits are not receiving them. Of Americans who qualify for SSI benefits because of age and poverty status, 79 percent are 70 or older, 54 percent are 75 or older, and 35 percent are 80 or older. Finally, women are more likely to rely on SSI at an earlier age. Starting at age 50, more women than men receive SSI benefits based on disability.

SSI is vulnerable to budget cuts at both the federal and state levels. The traditional immunity that programs for older Americans have enjoyed at the federal level is no longer assured. Some Congressional leaders want to reform welfare by eliminating the entitlement status of SSI and imposing a spending cap on the program. If entitlement status is eliminated and a federal spending cap becomes law, eligible recipients will no longer have a right to receive SSI. In an amended program, SSI would become a discretionary (rather than entitlement) program, and Congress could appropriate a set amount of money each year. This could result in:

• Serious funding reductions, given expected cuts in domestic discretionary spending;
• Not appropriating sufficient funds in a given year; and
• Appropriated funds that would fail to address the factors causing increased applications, such as economic downturns or higher numbers of elderly persons.

If there is no right to receive SSI, and appropriated funds fall short in a given year:

• New applications would not be taken from eligible persons;
• Waiting lists would develop for elderly and disabled individuals who would have been eligible previously;
• Benefits to current recipients could be reduced;
• Cost-of-living adjustments (COLAs) could be lowered or eliminated; and
• More persons could become homeless or remain in institutions due to the loss or unavailability of cash assistance.

Finally as discussed in Chapters 10 and 14, provisions in the welfare reform bill signed by President Clinton in 1996 also bode ill for many elderly women. Of the

800,000 legal immigrants slated to lose SSI under this measure, for example, almost 75 percent are elderly or disabled women (19).

The Employment Retirement Income Security Act

Prior to the enactment of the Employee Retirement Income Security Act (ERISA) in 1974, there was very little regulation of pensions. ERISA provided a number of rights to individual participants for the first time, establishing minimum participation and vesting requirements, and setting standards for the number and percentage of employees to be covered by a pension plan. A pension with survivor benefits was established as the standard for married participants, and vested workers could opt for a survivor benefit once they reached the planned early retirement age.

Over the years, there have been frequent amendments to ERISA, including expanded protections for workers and beneficiaries. The Tax Equity and Fiscal Responsibility Act of 1982 (TEFRA) sought to establish equity in coverage; plans that paid a disproportionate amount of pension benefits to high-paid employees were required to provide a minimum benefit to moderate- and lower-paid employees (13).

Passage of the Retirement Equity Act (REA) in 1984 increased survivor benefit protection. A retiring worker must now obtain a spouse's written consent before electing a pension without survivor benefits. The REA also lowered the participation and vesting ages. Qualified Domestic Relations Order (QDRO) provisions made it easier to get a share of a company pension as marital property at divorce, with payment coming directly from the company (13).

The Tax Reform Act of 1986 (TRA) reduced the vesting rules such that, now, most plans have a five-year vesting schedule. The Omnibus Budget Reconciliation Act of 1986 (OBRA) prohibits employers from excluding workers close to retirement age from participating in a pension plan, and requires plans to continue accruing benefits for participating workers who stay on the job past age 65 (13).

Private Pension Plans

Social Security was never intended to be the sole source of retirement income for older Americans. An employer-paid pension should form the second solid leg of the retirement stool, accompanying Social Security benefits and savings and investment income for workers in the private sector. Unfortunately, for many women the pension leg may be missing entirely, producing a shaky future. The addition of pension income would allow many women on the edge of or in poverty to move into economic security.

There are thousands of different state and local government pension systems and several federal plans, which make it difficult to generalize about all public employee pension plans. Workers with private pensions have traditionally been covered under defined benefit plans, which guarantee a specific benefit amount based on factors such as the employee's salary and years of service. The employer funds this type of plan and the federal Pension Benefit Guaranty Corporation (PBGC) guarantees the payment of benefits. The defined benefit plan is being replaced more often with a defined contribution plan, which does not guarantee a specific benefit amount and is based on how much money the company and/or worker contributes and the interest earned on the investments in the plan. The risk under these plans has shifted from the employer to the employee.

One form of retirement plan is a tax-sheltered savings plan called the 401(k) in which workers choose their own investments. These do-it-yourself plans are less costly for the employer than traditional pension plans because the workers themselves must contribute and bear the risk that the investments will do well. The company is not obligated to add additional money but may pay into the plan only after an employee makes a contribution. These plans are not federally guaranteed and are not considered pensions (13).

Those favoring 401(k) plans see them as the wave of the future, benefiting people who frequently change jobs because they do not lose their savings upon leaving a company (that is, the plans are portable). Opponents of 401(k) plans predict danger as baby boomers reach retirement age because fewer employees are participating in pension plans.

For too long, pensions have been the invisible benefit in the employment package (13). Many people do not consider pensions when they plan careers or choose jobs. In theory, if more women were aware of the impact that pensions can make on their economic security in retirement, and were to factor this into their work and retirement decisions, tomorrow's older women would attain greater financial security than their struggling mothers and grandmothers have achieved (20). In practice, however, few women have the option for a pension, and those who do may face situations in which the choice is more money for survival now or less money today in order to save for the future. In this scenario, present economic hardship will win out.

Which Women Receive Pension Coverage? Employer-sponsored pension plans are increasingly being replaced by 401(k) plans. In 1992 there were over 708,000 employer-sponsored pension plans, approximately 100,000 were defined benefit and 600,000 were defined contribution. Pension trusts held $2.1 billion in assets, which paid for annuities (16). More than 30 million active workers are now covered by 401(k) plans (21).

Private pension plans favor employees following typical male work patterns: long, continuous years of service in higher-paid specific types of jobs. The same factors that contribute to women's receiving lower Social Security retirement benefits— changing jobs, receiving low wages, limiting hours, or moving in and out of the labor force in primarily nonunion service jobs—make it difficult for women workers to qualify for private pensions. Women are half as likely as men to receive a pension, and those who do get have as much. Twenty percent of women and 47 percent of men over 65 receive pensions. Only 18 percent of women aged 65 and over receive pension income, compared with 34 percent of men. The mean pension income for older women who do receive private pensions is $2,682 annually, compared with $5,731 for men (3). The mean government pension is $7,569 for women compared with $14,722 for men (3). Many women work for small businesses that do not provide pension plans (4). Forty-five percent of women in the paid labor force work for firms with less than 100 employees, and only 24 percent of companies this size offer pensions (4).

Women in the contingent labor force often do not qualify for pension coverage. Requirements for purposes of participation such as the number of hours worked virtually freeze out many women who work part-time, seasonal, or temporary jobs. One-fourth of all female workers are employed part time, compared with only 11 percent of men. Women make up about two-thirds of the part-time labor force (1).

Vesting, Portability, and Integration. As examined shortly, requirements of the type noted above make it more difficult for the typical female worker to obtain a pension and to get the maximum income possible when she retires.

Because of female work patterns, many women who qualify for pensions leave before their pensions vest. The vesting period is the years of working in a company required to earn a legal right to a pension. Most plans require five years on the job before pension rights vest. Half of all men have been on their current job more than 5.1 years, compared with 3.8 years for women. Only 36 percent of female workers in the private sector who have pensions are vested (21).

Unlike Social Security, most traditional pensions are not portable; that is, most cannot be moved from job to job, which especially hurts women who change jobs frequently. Only 7 percent of full-time workers with defined benefit plans had portability provisions in 1993 (22). Pension integration, in which a pension is reduced by taking Social Security into account when figuring pension benefits, more commonly occurs with women. Integration is most common for lower-paid workers, where women are over-represented (11). Sixty percent of clerical and sales employees with defined benefit plans had their pensions integrated with Social Security in 1993. Only 4 percent of retirees with defined benefit plans got cost-of-living adjustments in 1993. Ninety percent received no post-retirement pension increases of any kind (21).

The Move to 401(k) Plans. Eighty-seven percent of private sector pension plans are defined contribution plans; 52 percent of all participants in private plans are in defined contribution plans (16). An increasing number of businesses that discontinue defined benefit plans either establish less generous 401(k) plans or leave workers without an employer-provided pension (4). Largely because of 401(k) plans, full-time worker participation in traditional employer-paid pension plans declined from 48 percent in 1979 to 26 percent by the early 1990s (16). Middle- and upper-income retirees are more likely to prosper with 401(k) plans.

Because workers are required to make their own investment decisions with 401(k) plans, many employees (especially service and blue-collar workers) invest more conservatively than professional plan managers. These employees are cautious because they are worried about losing their money. The result is that their investments do not prosper sufficiently.

Pensions and the Family. Women who leave jobs to assume family obligations pay a heavy pension penalty. Because pension benefits are typically calculated on the worker's final earnings, leaving a job significantly before normal retirement age means that the pension will be based on wages that may be 10 or 20 years out of date, with no indexing for inflation. A man and a woman can each work 40 years, with both working under the same type of pension plan at all times. However, the man remains in the same job and the woman works in four different jobs. The result is that the man's pension could be twice the woman's (1).

More flexible job arrangements made to accommodate working women's family responsibilities will greatly diminish women's retirement income. Consultancies, part-time jobs, shared jobs, seasonal employment, and home-based self-employment are all increasingly popular alternatives for women. All are virtually unprotected by pension coverage. More than 44 percent of employers now use part-time help of some kind; three out of four began the practice within the last 12 years. Under federal law, employers who do choose to offer a pension plan may exclude from coverage employees working less than 20 hours a week (1,000 hours a year) (11).

Spousal Benefits for Women Who are Wives, Widowed, or Divorced. Women are more likely to receive pension benefits as a wife, divorced spouse, or widow—usually 50 percent or less than a worker's benefit—than they are from their own work years (20). The primary factors in determining an employee's benefit level are salary and total years of service, areas where working women often fall short and thus do not qualify for pensions on their own work records.

Many divorced women lose out on their former husband's pension benefits. Only 27 percent of divorced women collect pensions in relation to their spouse (13). Women of all ages need to know that if they get divorced, a portion of their husband's pension can become part of the divorce settlement (20). Federal law includes provisions for a divorced woman to receive a retiree's pension and survivor benefits on the death of a former husband. However, it does not require pension-sharing upon divorce. More important are state divorce laws that specify whether pensions are considered property and how they are dealt with at the time of divorce (20). To collect an ex-husband's pension benefits, a woman must obtain a court order dividing the pension benefit, called a Qualified Domestic Relations Order (QDRO). She will most likely be awarded less than half of the pension, based on the value of the pension at the time of the divorce and the length of the marriage. Pension plans are only required to offer widow's benefits of half the amount received while the husband was alive. If the worker is the survivor, however, the worker's pension is not decreased. The survivor is most often the wife, leaving widows as a group with a much lower pension income than widowers (11). Many couples continue to waive survivor's benefits in order to receive higher benefits while both are living or because they do not understand the waiver they are signing.

IRAs and Savings

The third leg of the retirement stool is personal savings, which include Individual Retirement Accounts (IRAs) and investments. More than $200 billion in U.S. retirement savings are in private pension plans (16). However, many women living from paycheck to paycheck are unable to put anything in savings, and find this leg of the stool more of a theory than a realistic option. After home ownership, interest-earning assets accounted for the next largest share of net worth in 1991, at 14 percent. These included savings accounts and money market accounts. IRA or Keogh accounts made up only 5 percent of most people's assets (23).

Although 67 percent of retirees have some income from assets, more than 20 percent have less than $250 in annual asset income. This comes mostly from savings, certificates of deposit, and interest on checking accounts. The median amount of asset income is only $1,720 a year (8).

Fewer women than men participate in IRAs. Among full-time workers, 20 percent more men than women have IRAs. However, among part-time workers, twice as many women as men contribute to an IRA. Women are less able to accumulate savings than men because they earn less, and because the money they earn during their work lives has gone to the expenses of daily living (11).

Married women in the paid workforce are substantially penalized by IRA laws. Married couples are disqualified from tax-deductible IRA contributions above a certain income level if either spouse has pension coverage at work. Since men are more likely than women to have this coverage, women are more likely to be disqualified from a deductible IRA, even though they may have no pension benefit in their own right and would need an IRA if they were divorced or widowed (11).

Homemakers are also penalized. Normally, each wage earner may deduct an IRA contribution of up to $2,000 a year for income tax purposes. Under federal law, if only one spouse works in paid employment, the couple can contribute a maximum of $2,250 per year to IRAs for both of them. This contribution may be split between them in any way, as long as no more than $2,000 per year is invested in any one IRA account. Therefore, in effect, the value of a homemaker's work is set at $250 (11).

CONCLUSION

This chapter has presented a sobering account of women's prospects for economic security in retirement. For despite dramatic increases in female labor force participation, a host of factors continue to leave many women—including those who have worked for long periods of time—economically vulnerable in late life.

The already significant economic divide between men and women widens still further in retirement, with women continuing to comprise nearly three-quarters of the elderly poor. For older women who live alone, or who are African American or of Hispanic origin, poverty rates are particularly troubling.

The concept of retirement income as a three-legged stool supported by Social Security, employer-paid pensions, and savings and investments is more ideal than real for many older women. Heavy reliance on Social Security as the sole or primary source of income; continuing poor access to pensions, especially in the private sector; and the inability to save due to the necessity for many of living from paycheck to paycheck—all leave many older women at risk for a shaky economic future.

Based on these realities, the Older Women's League has called upon the U.S. Congress to reform the nation's retirement income systems to ensure that women are rewarded for their contributions both to their employers and to their families.

Acknowledgments — The 1995 Mother's Day Report on which this chapter is based was researched and written by Allison Porter with contributions from Dianna Porter, Emily Cornell, Carol Downs, Vicki O'Reilly, and Amy Shannon of the Older Women's League, and was edited by Lisa Lederer of PR Solutions. Additional assistance was provided by the following reviewers: Vicki Gottlich, National Senior Citizens Law Center; Cindy Hounsell, Pension Rights Center; Sara Rix, American Association of Retired Persons; and Mary Jane Yarrington, National Committee to Preserve Social Security and Medicare. The report was made possible in part through funding from the Retirement Research Foundation. The Older Women's League gratefully acknowledges Patsy Wakimoto, Meredith Minkler, John Woods, and Arline Easley for their help in updating a number of the facts and statistics in this chapter.

REFERENCES

1. U.S. Bureau of the Census, U.S. Bureau of Labor and Employment Statistics. *Employment and Earnings.* BLS Bull. 2340 and unpublished tables. Washington, D.C., February 1997.
2. U.S. Bureau of the Census, U.S. Department of Commerce. *Consumer Income.* Current Population Reports, P60-194. Washington, D.C., September 1996.
3. Grad, S. *Income of the Population 55 or Older, 1994.* U.S. Department of Health and Human Services, Social Security Administration, Office of Research and Statistics. SSA 13-11871. Government Printing Office, Washington, D.C., 1996.
4. Malveaux, J. *The Economic Predicament of Low-Income Elderly Women, Southport, CT: Project on Women and Population Aging.* In series: Impact of Population Aging on Women. Southport Institute for Policy Analysis, Southport, Conn., 1992.
5. U.S. Bureau of Labor Statistics. *Employment and Earnings* 42(1), January 1995.
6. U.S. Department of Labor, Women's Bureau. *Facts on Working Women,* No. 93-5. Washington, D.C., December 1993.
7. U.S. Bureau of the Census, U.S. Department of Commerce, Economic and Statistics Administration. Poverty in the United States: In *Consumer Income.* Current Population Reports, P60-194. Washington, D.C., September 1996.
8. U.S. Bureau of the Census. *Household Wealth and Asset Ownership: 1993.* Current Population Reports, P70-34. Washington, D.C., 1995.
9. Grad, S. *Income of the Population 55 or Older, 1992.* U.S. Department of Health and Human Services, Social Security Administration, Office of Research and Statistics. SSA 13-11871. Government Printing Office, Washington, D.C., 1994.
10. Social Security Administration. *Social Security: What Every Woman Should Know.* SSA 05-10127. Washington, D.C., September 1996.
11. Older Women's League. *Heading for Hardship: Retirement Income for American Women in the Next Century.* Washington, D.C., 1990.
12. U.S. Department of Health and Human Services, Administration on Aging. *HHS Fact Sheet: Aging America: Priority Initiatives of the Administration on Aging.* Washington, D.C., May 1994.
13. Older Women's League. *Women and Pensions.* Washington, D.C., 1994.
14. American Association of Retired Persons. *Public Policy Institute Fact Sheet: Social Security Trust Funds: Some Basics.* Washington, D.C., December 1994.
15. Social Security Administration. *Highlights of Social Security Data, January 1997.* Office of Research and Statistics, Washington, D.C., 1997.

16. U.S. Department of Labor. *Private Pension Plan Bulletin,* No. 5. Washington, D.C., 1996 [data for 1992].

17. Social Security Administration. *Annual Statistical Supplement to the Social Security Bulletin.* Office of Research Evaluation and Statistics. Washington, D.C., 1996.

18. Social Security Administration. *Annual Statistical Supplement to the Social Security Bulletin.* Office of Research Evaluation and Statistics. Washington, D.C., 1994.

19. Families USA. *Hurting Real People: The Human Impact of Medicaid Cuts.* Washington, D.C., 1997.

20. Center on Aging, University of Maryland. *Income Security and Retirement Decisions: Informing Older Women About Private Pension Programs.* Baltimore, October 1993.

21. U.S. Bureau of the Census. *Pension and Health Benefits of American Workers: New Findings from the April 1993 Current Population Survey.* Washington, D.C., 1994.

22. U.S. Department of Labor, Bureau of Labor Statistics. *Employee Benefits in Medium and Large Private Establishments, 1993.* Washington, D.C., November 1994.

23. U.S. Bureau of the Census. *Household Wealth and Asset Ownership: 1991.* Washington, D.C., 1994.

CHAPTER 17

The Social Construction of Retirement: Perspectives from Critical Theory and Political Economy

Chris Phillipson

Understanding the emergence and development of retirement is rapidly becoming a central topic of concern within and beyond the discipline of gerontology. Explaining the factors behind the creation of retirement has generated debate and controversy among groups such as economic historians, cultural historians, sociologists, and social policy analysts (1–7). The range of contributions reflects the fact that this institution is at the intersection of key social changes in the 20th century, most notably the rise of social security and the welfare state; the growth of industrialization and mass production; and the increased importance of leisure and consumption in daily life.

Attempts, therefore, to develop a fresh approach to retirement must take into account its changing relationship to a range of economic and social relationships. The aim of this chapter is to use the perspective of critical gerontology to reexamine and reinterpret the postwar history of retirement. The focus of a critical perspective is taken to be one that explores the way in which retirement is shaped by the social structure and by those social and economic factors which affect the individual's place in that structure. This perspective shifts the focus of investigation from one of individual adjustment, to examining the sociopolitical factors which influence and control retirement outcomes (8).

An additional aim of this chapter is to use arguments from critical social theory to analyze the social dynamics underpinning retirement. Here, the work of Giddens, Beck, and other social theorists will be used to chart the way in which retirement has been affected by the move into a period of advanced or late modernity (9–12). A central argument will be that the changes affecting the transition from work provide a clear illustration of developments associated with what have come to be described as post-traditional or postmodern societies.

The main elements of this chapter comprise a review of postwar trends in the field of retirement; an interpretation of these, drawing on perspectives from within critical theory; and a review of possible futures for the development of retirement as we move into the 21st century.

THE EMERGENCE OF RETIREMENT:
POSTWAR DEVELOPMENTS

Instit. of retirement .

In 1960, Donahue, Orbach, and Pollak published a wide-ranging essay charting the rise of retirement, noting that it had now come to "occupy a place of central concern in Western society" (13, p. 330). The publication of this essay (in the *Handbook of Social Gerontology,* edited by Clark Tibbitts) came at the midpoint of the institutionalization of retirement between 1950 and 1970. Historians and sociologists have argued that this period may be seen as the "triumph of retirement" (14), with the growth of the institution taking place on three different dimensions: first, the increase in the proportion of people reaching retirement age; second, the decreasing significance of paid work after retirement; third, the importance of income derived from the state and from occupational pensions (15).

For Donahue and her colleagues there could be little doubt that these changes were deep-rooted, leading to major claims on the priorities of social institutions. In this context, government and the state would, it was argued, be drawn upon to provide a framework for supporting people after the cessation of work. Writing from the perspective of the late 1950s, Donahue and colleagues concluded that "the long-range development of our retirement system will undoubtedly tend more and more to assume entirely the character of a government function as it moves in the direction of providing an adequate economic basis for the years in retirement" (13, p. 353).

By the 1970s, however, the role of government began to be questioned. Graebner, for example, sees retirement's triumph as "short-lived" (3). He argues that by the late 1970s, two decades after the institution had reached its peak of influence and acceptance, a period of retreat had begun. This had followed a gradual evolution from the late 19th century onward. From its tentative beginnings, retirement had begun by the late 1950s and 1960s to enter popular consciousness. People began to "expect" something; wanted to be "prepared" for the event; and certainly wanted income security independent of their families. This development—at the level of ideology at least—was in many respects very new, especially for working-class retirees. Peter Stearns, for example, describing attitudes among the French working class in the 1920s and 1930s, notes the absence of "an active concept of what retirement should be" (16, pp. 65–66):

> it represented stopping something, work, but did it represent starting or con-
> tinuing anything of interest? Without pretending to fathom the fate of retirees as
> a whole, for even in old age, and perhaps particularly then, individual variations
> are immense, we can suggest that a rapidly changing behavior pattern found no
> correspondence in public policy or collective activities.

Forty years on, however, Francois Cribier (17) described a significant change among French retirees. For the younger cohorts in her study there was a marked increase in the proportion of people viewing retirement as a desirable goal, and early retirement as especially desirable. Findings showing more positive attitudes have been regularly reported in the U.S. literature, from the work of Corson and McConnell (18) in the 1950s, to that of Atchley (19) and Palmore and colleagues

(20) in the 1970s and 1980s. Even in Britain, where the findings on attitudes have tended to be more negative, a shift toward accepting retirement, and early retirement in particular, began to emerge from the 1970s (15).

All of this may be said to reflect the way in which (for men at least) retirement became "a normal feature of the life course," from the 1960s onward. Kohli and Rein describe this change as follows (21, p. 21):

> The modern tripartition of the life course into a period of preparation, one of 'active' work, and one of retirement had become firmly established. Old age had become synonymous with the period of retirement: a life phase structurally set apart from 'active' work life and with a relatively uniform beginning defined by the retirement age limit as set by the public old-age pension system. With the increasing labor force participation of women, they too have increasingly been incorporated into this life course regime.

By the 1970s and 1980s, however, the development of a stable life course was brought to an abrupt halt by two interrelated trends: first, the spread of mass unemployment; second, the fiscal crisis affecting the welfare states of industrialized countries (22). The former, while initially strengthening the spread of early retirement, reinforced trends that were undermining the idea of stable periods of "preparation," "activity," and "retirement." The latter began to call into question the idea of reciprocity across generations, with governments "talking-up" the potential economic burden associated with aging populations (23, 24). Taken together, both developments raised questions about the location and stability of retirement within the life course.

CHANGING WORK AND RETIREMENT

The above changes have provoked a number of important debates at the level of research. Kohli and Rein (21), for example, focus on the emergence of a gap between retirement and exit from work, with a variety of pathways (institutional arrangements or supports) being used to manage the transition from the workplace. In this approach, the move into retirement is seen to have become more complex, with a range of different pathways which people take before they describe themselves, or are defined within the social security system, as "wholly retired."

The implication of this model, however, is that while the transition from work is more diverse, retirement as an institution remains in place. Kohli and Rein (21) point out that most people at age 55 and below still work, while most above the age of 65 are neither employed nor seeking employment. There is little evidence, they suggest, that what Best (25) described as the "education-work-retirement-lockstep" is breaking up.

In contrast, Anne-Marie Guillemard (26) holds that the changes affecting retirement represent a "deinstitutionalization" of the life course. She argues that the threefold model described by Best will fall apart as retirement loses its role of regulating the withdrawal of older workers. Moreover, Guillemard argues that retirement no longer provides a homogeneous meaning to the third phase of life, this following a period of stable occupation. Accordingly (26, pp. 177–178):

> The elderly no longer have a clearly defined social status. Definitive withdrawal, old age and retirement no longer concur with each other: occupational old age begins with definitive withdrawal, well before retirement and physical old age. The life course as an institution is coming undone. Retirement is no longer a central means of socialization that determines the identities and symbolic universes of individuals. There is less and less of a definite order to the last phase of life. The life course is being de-institutionalized.

Guillemard goes on to argue that this deinstitutionalization undermines the idea of continuity and a predictable lifespan (crucial elements in the development of the modern life course). Moreover, the break-up of retirement also has implications for the reciprocal ties formed between generations. Such commitments, Guillemard suggests, become less reliable in a society where time is accelerating, and where the lifespan is no longer marked by standardized chronological milestones.

Both these perspectives indicate the strength of the changes affecting work and retirement. But the scale of these also suggests that broader social forces need to be acknowledged. The argument of this chapter is that changes to work and retirement reflect wider social dynamics, most notably the trends associated with the emergence of postindustrial and postmodern societies. The changes identified with these societies raise vital issues for the debate on the political economy of aging, introduced by Estes (27), Townsend (28), Myles (29), and others from the late 1970s (30, 31). The remainder of this chapter reviews the implications of a postmodernization of the political economy of retirement, and some issues for research in this area.

SOCIAL CHANGE IN THE PERIOD OF LATE MODERNITY

The argument of this chapter is that changes to the institution of retirement are bound up with what Giddens (9) defines as a period of "high modernity," or what has been more generally called the move toward a "postmodern" society (11). Despite the different points of emphasis between these terms, areas of agreement are also apparent: First, significant changes within industry, with flexible forms of work organization increasingly displacing mass production (broadly conceived as the shift from an industrial to a postindustrial society). Second, the globalization of social life, viewed by Giddens as "the interlacing of social events and social relations 'at distance' with local contextualities" (9, p. 21). Third, a weakening in the institutions and practices of the nation state. Here, according to Kumar (11), the "collective identities" associated with social class dissolve into more pluralized forms. Social identity becomes more fluid, fed by multiple sources and taking a variety of forms (most notably, perhaps, in the case of older people as retirees).

The issue of identity is fundamental to much of the literature in this area. Anthony Giddens, in his book *Modernity and Self-Identity* (9), is concerned with the emergence of what he sees as new mechanisms of self-identity, these both shaping and shaped by the institutions of modernity. In the late modern age, self-identity becomes a "reflexively organized endeavor." Giddens presents a picture of the self as a "reflexive project," built around the development of "coherent, yet continuously revised, biographical narratives" (9, p. 5). Furthermore, these are seen to operate on the basis of choice and flexibility, this replacing the rigidity of the traditional life cycle with its predetermined rites of passage.

The idea of reflexivity is also central to the work of Ulrich Beck, as developed in his book *The Risk Society* (10). Here, Beck presents a dystopian vision of a rampant industrialism, generating risks and hazards on a scale surpassing all other historical periods. Such risks—illustrated by the threat of toxins and pollutants on the environment—exert a global reach, albeit affecting some communities and social groups more than others. For Beck, challenging such threats will only be achieved at the point when society becomes truly reflexive—the period of reflexive modernization. This may be conceived in terms of individuals and the lay public exerting control and influence over the shape and character of modernity. Reflexive modernity thus challenges the insecurities introduced by the process of modernization. At the core of the theory is the thesis that "the more societies are modernized, the more agents (subjects) acquire the ability to reflect on the social conditions of their existence and to change them in that way" (10, p. 22).

Beck's approach is based upon a three-stage periodization of social change, comprising: first, premodernity; second, simple modernity; third, reflexive modernity. Scott Lash notes that with this model, simply modern societies are not yet fully modern. He argues (32, p. 114):

> In this context reflexive modernity comes after simple modernity. Put another way, traditional society here corresponds to Gemeinschaft; simple modernity to Gesellschaft; and its successor to a Gesellschaft that has become fully reflexive. The motor of social change in this process is individualization. In this context Gesellshaft or simple modernity is modern in the sense that individualization has largely broken down the old traditional structures—extended family, church, village community—of the Gemeinschaft. Yet it is not fully modern because the individualization process has only gone part way and a new set of gesellschaftlisch structures—trade unions, welfare state, government bureaucracy, formalized Taylorist shopfloor rules, class itself as a structure—has taken the place of traditional structures. Full modernization takes place only when further individualization also sets agency free from even these (simply) modern social structures.

The implication of this argument, then, is that reflexive modernization involves a separation of individuals from the collective structures that had formed in the period of simple modernity. This arises, according to Lash, through such factors as the crisis in the nuclear family, changes in the influence of class structures, deindustrialization, ecological concerns, and the critique of institutionalized science.

These developments raise important issues for institutions such as retirement. Atchley (4) notes here that current retirement policies were built around a society based on mass production and mass institutions. The changes affecting both elements raise significant questions for self-identity and social relationships after the

[handwritten marginalia: forms of modernity / 3 retirement forms.]

cessation of work. The nature of these will now be analyzed, with a particular focus on the implications for debates within critical gerontology.

[handwritten marginalia: social + econ base of retirement]

RETIREMENT AND THE MOVE FROM STRUCTURED DEPENDENCY

The model outlined in the preceding section suggests some useful pointers to changes in the social and economic base of retirement. Taking the period of simple modernity, we can see this associated with a specific kind of retirement, formed within the context of full employment and expanding welfare states. The emergence of retirement coincided, in fact, with the period known as "organized capitalism," with the development of mass production along Fordist and Taylorist lines (7). The latter provided the foundation for the spread of retirement, notably through age-based discrimination within industry, and the growth of occupational pensions (3).

The period of simple modernity also fostered a particular kind of social relationship as regards the position of older people and the state. Researchers such as Estes (27), Townsend (28), and Phillipson and Walker (30) point to the social creation of dependency in old age, this reflecting factors such as low income, the exclusion of elders from key social and economic arenas, and inequalities of power between professionals and lay persons. Townsend, in his development of the theory of structured dependency, gave particular emphasis to the impact of mandatory retirement (28). This was seen to promote alienation for groups such as working-class retirees, forced as they were into a period of "enforced leisure." Retirement also exacerbated social inequalities, with the middle class able to benefit to a greater extent from occupational benefits and income from savings and investments. *[handwritten marginalia: greater inequality / injustice]*

A counterargument to the above was developed by those such as Johnson (33), who challenged the idea of a necessary link between state support and dependency. He noted that (33, p. 67):

[handwritten marginalia: Mandatory retirement]

> There is no theoretical reason to suppose that a transition from labor market income to state benefit income induces the onset of dependency: indeed, logically the reverse should happen as individuals shift from being dependent on finding employment in the labor market, to being in receipt of an independent income guaranteed by the taxable capacity of the state.

[handwritten marginalia: politics of retirement]

In a similar vein, Haber and Gratton, in their history of old age in America, note the influence of Social Security in redefining the relationship between work and retirement (34, pp. 114–115):

> Since the preindustrial period, elderly men and women have struggled to find security in their last years. For most of that history, independence could be attained only by controlling children, land, or assets. Most older workers achieved a measure of success in occupational status or in accumulating savings to buffer income declines in old age. Nonetheless, even the industrial era's economic vitality provided only a minority with enough confidence to stop work altogether. Social Security removed the last constraint and brought to an end the

expectation that work was the natural condition of life for the elderly. Since its enactment, the history of the older worker has given way to the history of retirement.

The difficulty with this position, however, is that it involves a structural as well as ideological separation between work on the one hand and retirement on the other. In the period of simple modernity, this was never really sustained, with retirement being always subordinate to the social and economic relationships associated with work. Martin Rein (35), arguing from the case of Germany (although his view is applicable to countries such as Britain and the United States), notes the extent to which the institutionalization of the life course was shaped around the social organization of work. This was especially the case with respect to benefits such as social security, which were linked to participation in the labor market, with citizenship denied to those not continually engaged in salaried work.

More fundamentally, however, it may be argued that strict regulations are applied to the conditions under which non-participation in the labor market is possible. Offe (36) makes the point that the choice between a life of wage labor and subsistence outside the labor market is not left to the discretion of labor power. When, and for how long, people can remain outside the labor market, or the decision whether someone is too old or too sick or too disabled, is not left to the individual to decide. Rather (36, p. 95):

> These choices must be positively regulated through politically defined criteria, for otherwise there would be incalculable tendencies for wage laborers to evade their function by slipping into the flanking subsystems. This is why a precondition of the constitution of a class of wage-laborers is the political institutionalization—and not merely the de facto maintenance—of categories of non-wage-laborers.

This argument leads to a more general point about the position of retirement in the period of simple modernity: in system terms it has no particular status outside occupation on the one hand and the welfare state on the other. This is not to say that individuals are unable to derive meaning and satisfaction from the experience of retirement; rather, it is to say that this is in contradistinction to the dominant relationships associated with work and welfare. In the period of simple modernity, retirement is characterized by the struggle to secure an identity that transcends the tendency of the state to "welfarize" the old. In some cases (and especially for those from economically secure high-status occupations) this may certainly be achieved. For many, however, being a retired person remains beset with contradictions, chief among these being the desire to avoid welfare dependency, but also to move from the restrictions of the workplace. These pressures underwent a significant degree of change from the late 1960s onward. This marks the beginning of the second phase in the history of retirement in the postwar period, one that both challenged and reinforced the experience of structured dependency. The implications for retirement of what has been termed "the postmodernization of contemporary political economies" will now be assessed.

RETIREMENT IN A PERIOD OF REFLEXIVE MODERNIZATION

A key argument in the preceding section is that retirement both developed and was constrained within the framework of an industrial society. By the late 1960s, however, the "contours" of this society had begun to dissolve (37). Lash and Urry (38) view this in terms of the move from "organized" to "disorganized capitalism," with the growth of pluralism and fragmentation in all spheres of society. The phenomenon of early exit from the workplace itself reflects the changes associated with flexible and discontinuous work careers. In particular, there is the growth of different work categories and statuses in between full-time work and complete retirement; the ending of lifetime employment—especially within a single organization; and the growing convergence of patterns of male and female employment (7).

The argument here is that just as the period of simple modernity generated a specific retirement experience, one located within the context of structured dependency, the transition toward advanced modernity is itself leading to a new social construction of later life. The loosening of the contours of industrial society is helping to generate new definitions (and new visions) about the nature of retirement and growing old. Three examples will illustrate this point: first, the question of self-identity in retirement; second, the issue of inequality; third, the issue of diversity.

First, the experience of retirement is likely to undergo significant change within the context of the shift toward a high degree of "reflexivity or self-consciousness" of populations within late or postmodern societies. Giddens and others see this as creating significant possibilities for new forms of intimacy and friendship, both within and beyond traditional work, family, and leisure relationships (9–12). This argument suggests a different approach from that currently developed in critical gerontology. For example, within the context of structured dependency theory, the self is viewed as locked into the structures and ideologies associated with work and the welfare state. The transition to retirement is seen as a process through which a "working" or an "occupational self" is replaced by a retired self, but with many elements of the former being retained. Against this, the view of the self as a reflexive project provides a different perspective on the move from work to retirement. The possibilities become more open and subject to individual as well as social construction. For working-class retirees it may involve supplanting aspects of the self formed within particular types of work and occupational cultures. In certain cases these may have been built around a core of oppression, a challenge to which becomes important in the second half of life (39–41).

This perspective is similar to that developed in analytic psychology, with its focus on individuation and acceptance of the self, as products of the process of aging. Biggs (42) describes the idea of individuation in terms of the gradual withdrawal of the various constraints and contradictions placed upon the personality, this resulting in a more complete sense of self. In the second half of life the individual can take on board a radical critique of work, family, and gendered identities (the experience of Maggie Kuhn (43) may be taken as a paradigmatic example in this regard). Freed from the pressures of traditional structures, this process is seen to lead to enhanced awareness of the self in comparison to the first half of life.

This process may be reinforced by the developments associated with the shift to a new kind of modernity, and the emergence of what Beck and Giddens view as "reflexive biographies." According to Giddens (9, p. 14):

> Each of us not only 'has' but *lives* a biography reflexively organized in terms of flows of social and psychological information about possible ways of life. Modernity is a post-traditional order, in which the question, How shall I live? has to be answered in day-to-day decisions about how to behave, what to wear and what to eat—and many other things—as well as interpreted within the temporal unfolding of self-identity.

The institution of retirement offers significant opportunities for social actors to explore and reshape biographies. Moreover, the absence of specific rites of passage itself assists this process of self-determination. Indeed, rather than a negative feature (as was originally conceived in the retirement literature), the absence of formal rituals can be seen as a positive element in allowing individuals greater freedom in this new phase of the life course.

The second feature of retirement in a period of reflexive modernization suggests less positive developments than those discussed thus far: namely, the growth of new inequalities alongside the continuation of traditional social divisions. Overall, the argument here is not that class, gender, and other types of inequality become less important, rather they become (re)defined and experienced in different ways in comparison to early periods of modernity. Giddens argues here that "Modernity, one should not forget, produces *difference, exclusion* and *marginalization.* Holding out the possibility of emancipation, modern institutions at the same time create mechanisms of suppression, rather than actualization, of self" (9, p. 6).

In one sense, retirement offers a vivid illustration of the above argument: namely, the way in which, for working-class retirees especially, the emancipation from work that comes with retirement actually reveals very clearly the injustices associated with wage labor—notably with the experience of poverty, degrading forms of health and social care, and various forms of discrimination. Moreover, in the conditions of advanced modernity, these experiences become commonplace as retirement reverts to being a social risk rather than a social right. This process develops as (in many cases) long-established income and welfare supports are withdrawn, with the emphasis placed increasingly upon individual rather than collective support for retirees.

This withdrawal of collective structures is without question the negative side of the process of reflexive modernization. On the one hand, it may enhance the experience of retirement for some, especially with the loosening of the pressures and constraints associated with the work ethic. On the other hand, for a much larger number, experiencing retirement as a risk (one which may extend for more than 20 or 30 years) threatens new types of insecurities. Beck (10) notes that the individual is indeed removed from traditional commitments and supports, but exchanges these for the constraints of existence in the labor market and, as a consumer, with the associated standardizations and controls that these contain. For many retired people, however, they are denied opportunities either in the labor market or as consumers. In this context, the basis for sustaining biographies—or as Giddens would put it, "to keep a particular narrative going" (9, p. 54)—may be especially difficult. The narrative of the retired person as a recipient of the welfare state has thus been challenged, but with the alternatives raising significant contradictions for the lives of many groups of retirees.

Finally, it follows from the above analysis that retirement is more accurately seen as a mode of existence with a variety of orientations by different groups. The idea of a modal type of retirement is challenged under conditions of advanced or reflexive modernity. Social groups, as Calasanti (44) observes, construct retirement in many different ways. She cites research in the United States by Gibson showing that working-class black men do not identify themselves as retired as readily as their white counterparts. In particular, the lifelong labor force instability experienced by working-class African American men blurs the work/retirement dichotomy. Noting other such differences (for example between Mexican American men and women), Calasanti concludes that such divergent identities in retirement raises a number of issues (44, p. 150):

> First, they challenge the utility of trying to measure "retirement" along the "usual" dimensions. Second, they point to the exclusivity of the concept itself, as it assumes white, middle-class men's experiences: a stable work history, one that has a clear beginning and end, and is followed by retirement income. Overall, then, these discrepant identities question the notion of retirement itself.

This point is even more valid given the unraveling of lifetime employment and the growth of what Quadagno and Hardy (45) and others call the "contingent workforce." The growth of contingent labor has meant more part-time employees, short-term contracts, temporary consultancies, and employment subcontracting. These developments undermine attempts to develop a shared or common retirement ideology. On the contrary, the effect of changes in the workplace has been to pull apart any consensus (fragile at best in the postwar years) as to the meaning of retirement. In this context, the history of retirement is one that may have ended by the 1970s. After that, we have the beginning of a history of different types of withdrawals from the labor market, a diminishing number of which took place within the context of an environment of mutual agreement after a lifetime of secure work.

CONCLUSION:
DEVELOPING A NEW POLITICAL ECONOMY OF RETIREMENT

A concluding argument of this chapter is that new directions are needed in the political economy of retirement. The context for this has been analyzed in terms of some of the changes associated with the development of postmodern societies, or the process of reflexive modernization. Much of the analysis remains somewhat contentious: for example, it is unclear that the influence of social class has receded quite to the extent argued by many theorists. Moreover, the growth of new types of structural inequality raises complex issues for social theories emphasizing the possibilities for personal and biographical development.

At the same time, the theories discussed in this chapter do have radical implications for approaches to retirement. Traditionally, retirement has been viewed from the perspective of lifetime employment on the one side, together with an expanding welfare state on the other. Both were seen to contribute to the emerging identity associated with old age. Retirement had begun to provide a secure status for (in the United States) "senior citizens" and (in France) those entering the "third age." Alternatively, for those entering or inside what Featherstone and Hepworth (46) were to term "deep old age," the welfare state offered its own set of values and justification for being a "very elderly person."

In the 1990s, however, the unraveling of the system of retirement, combined with the crisis in the welfare state, has posed significant threats to the identities of older persons. Both institutions have, it might be argued, suffered a crisis in their meaning and status within society. Retirement is no longer central—for increasing numbers of men and women—as a system organizing exit from the workplace. Added to this, the welfare state is increasingly undermined or "residualized" as a system for providing support and care in old age. At one level, these changes have resulted in the language and ideology that scapegoat the old, defining them as a burden and cost for society. At a more individual level, however, they raise important existential issues about the nature and meaning of old age.

Despite the pressures and crises affecting the lives of many older people, some positive conclusions are still possible. It may be that new "voices and visions" of retirement begin to emerge as traditional retirement and welfare systems are challenged. Atchley (4) writes of the need to develop an emancipatory vision of future employment and retirement systems, and to consider the type of economic and social policies needed to promote effective change. The key question, however, will be who has ownership and control over the institution of retirement. Historically, older workers have rarely been able to control the pace and timing of their own retirement: corporate time has taken priority over individual time (notably for women, for black people, and for those from the working class). Whether a different type of retirement will emerge in a period of advanced modernity remains to be seen. Retirement can still hold out the promise of emancipation, but it needs appropriate resources in terms of both ideas and financial support to make this a reality. The next decade of debate and social action should see crucial developments in the next phase of retirement's new social history.

REFERENCES

1. Engerman, S. Economic history and old age. *J. Econ. Hist.* 56(1): 1–4, 1996.
2. Conrad, C. Old age in the modern and postmodern world. In *Handbook of Aging and the Humanities,* edited by T. Cole, D. Van Tassel, and R. Kastenbaum. Springer, New York, 1992.
3. Graebner, W. *A History of Retirement.* Yale University Press, New Haven, Conn., 1980.
4. Atchley, R. Critical perspectives on retirement. In *Voices and Visions of Aging,* edited by T. Cole et al. Springer, New York, 1993.
5. Atkinson, A. B., and Rein, M. *Age, Work and Social Security.* Macmillan, New York, 1993.

6. Kohli, M., et al. (eds.). *Time for Retirement: Comparative Studies of Early Exit from the Labour Force.* Cambridge University Press, Cambridge, England, 1991.
7. Laczko, F., and Phillipson, C. *Changing Work and Retirement.* Open University Press, Milton Keynes, England, 1991.
8. Stone, L., and Minkler, M. The socio-political context of women's retirement. In *Political Economy of Aging,* edited by M. Minkler and C. Estes. Baywood, Amityville, N.Y., 1984.
9. Giddens, A. *Modernity and Self-Identity.* Polity Press, Cambridge, England, 1991.
10. Beck, U. *The Risk Society.* Sage, London, 1992.
11. Kumar, K. *From Post-Industrial to Post-Modern Societies.* Blackwell, Oxford, 1995.
12. Beck, U. Giddens, A., and Lash, S. *Reflexive Modernisation.* Polity Press, Cambridge, England, 1994.
13. Donahue, W., Orbach, H., and Pollak, O. Retirement: The emerging social pattern. In *Handbook of Social Gerontology: Societal Aspects of Aging,* edited by C. Tibbitts. University of Chicago Press, Chicago, 1960.
14. Freter, H. J., Kohli, M., and Wolf, J. *Early Retirement and Work after Retirement.* Freie Universitat Berlin, Berlin, 1987.
15. Phillipson, C. The sociology of retirement. In *Ageing in Society,* edited by J. Bond, P. Coleman, and S. Peace. Sage, London, 1993.
16. Stearns, P. *Old Age in European Society: The Case of France.* Croom Helm, London, 1977.
17. Cribier, F. Changing retirement patterns of the seventies: The example of a generation of Parisian salaried workers. *Ageing Soc.* 1(1): 51–73, 1981.
18. Corson, J., and McConnell, J. *Economic Needs of Older People.* Twentieth Century Fund, New York, 1956.
19. Atchley, R. Retirement and leisure participation. *Gerontologist* 11: 13–17, 1971.
20. Palmore, E., et al. *Retirement: Causes and Consequences.* Springer, New York, 1985.
21. Kohli, M., and Rein, M. The changing balance of work and retirement. In *Time for Retirement: Comparative Studies of Early Exit from the Labour Force,* edited by M. Kohli et al. Cambridge University Press, Cambridge, England, 1991.
22. Estes, C. The aging enterprise revisited. *Gerontologist* 33(3): 292–298, 1993.
23. Bengston, V., and Achenbaum, W. (eds.). *The Changing Contract Across Generation.* Aldine de Gruyter, New York, 1993.
24. Walker, A. (ed.). *The New Generational Contract.* UCL Press, London, 1986.
25. Best, F. *Flexible Life Scheduling.* Praeger, New York, 1980.
26. Guillemard, A.-M. The trend towards early labour force withdrawal and the reorganization of the life course. In *Workers versus Pensioners: Intergenerational Justice in an Aging World,* edited by P. Johnson, C. Conrad, and D. Thomson. Manchester University Press, Manchester, 1989.
27. Estes, C. *The Aging Enterprise.* Jossey-Bass, San Francisco, 1979.
28. Townsend, P. The structured dependency of the elderly. *Ageing Soc.* 1(1): 5–28, 1981.
29. Myles, J. *Old Age and the Welfare State: The Political Economy of Public Pensions.* University Press of Kansas, Lawrence, 1989.
30. Phillipson, C., and Walker, A. (eds.). *Ageing and Social Policy.* Gower, Aldershot, 1986.
31. Guillemard, A.-M. *Old Age and the Welfare State.* Sage, New York, 1983.
32. Lash, S. Reflexivity and its doubles: Structure, aesthetics, community. In *Reflexive Modernisation,* edited by U. Beck, A. Giddens, and S. Lash. Polity Press, Cambridge, England, 1994.
33. Johnson, P. The structured dependency of the elderly: A research note. In *Growing Old in the Twentieth Century,* edited by M. Jeffries. Routledge, London, 1989.

34. Haber, C., and Graton, B. *Old Age and the Search for Security.* Indiana University Press, Indianapolis, 1993.
35. Kohli, M. Retirement and the moral economy: An historical interpretation of the German case. In *Critical Perspectives on Aging,* edited by M. Minkler and C. Estes. Baywood, Amityville, N.Y., 1991.
36. Offe, C. *Contradictions of the Welfare State.* Hutchinson, London, 1984.
37. Beck, U. The reinvention of politics. In *Reflexive Modernisation,* edited by U. Beck, A. Giddens, and S. Lash. Polity Press, Cambridge, England, 1994.
38. Lash, S., and Urry, J. *The End of Organised Capitalism.* Polity Press, Cambridge, England, 1987.
39. Sennett, R., and Cobb, J. *The Hidden Injuries of Class.* Cambridge University Press, Cambridge, England, 1972.
40. Beynon, H. *Working for Ford.* E. P. Publishing, Wakefield, 1975.
41. Nichols, T., and Beynon, H. *Living with Capitalism.* Routledge and Kegan Paul, London, 1977.
42. Biggs, S. *Understanding Ageing.* Open University Press, Buckingham, England, 1993.
43. Kuhn, M. *No Stone Unturned: The Life and Times of Maggie Kuhn.* Ballantine Books, New York, 1991.
44. Calasanti, T. Incorporating diversity: Meanings, levels of research and implications for theory. *Gerontologist* 36(2): 147–156, 1996.
45. Quadagno, J., and Hardy, M. Work and retirement. In *Handbook of Aging and the Social Sciences,* Ed. 4, edited by R. Binstock and L. George. Academic Press, New York, 1995.
46. Featherstone, M., and Hepworth, M. Ageing and old age. In *Becoming and Being Old,* edited by B. Bytheway et al. Sage, London, 1989.

CHAPTER 18

The Evolution of the Welfare State: Shifting Rights and Responsibilities for the Old

Robert B. Hudson

Two interrelated trends have marked the assaults on welfare state programming over the past 20 years: a value shift (rising concern with work-related incentives and behaviors) and a sector shift (away from national, formal, and public programs). Policy and policy rationales affecting the old have not been exempt from these new concerns. Questions about who should be responsible for the well-being of the old and what role the old themselves should play in assuring their own well-being are very much part of these larger developments.

Understandably, those who have built or witnessed the successes of contemporary social welfare programs throughout the industrial West are alarmed at the threats posed to core welfare state tenets of universalism, adequacy, and solidarity. Yet it has not only been hard core conservatives (neoliberals) calling for retrenchment. A broad spectrum of policymakers—much more than among the public at large—argue that such programming is no longer affordable at its current scale and that the programs themselves have grown to the point where they are overindulging populations previously warranting substantial coverage.

After briefly reviewing the arguments on both sides of this question, this chapter proposes a strategy for cutting into arguments such as these. It suggests that different "negative events" or contingencies may be amenable to greater or lesser intervention than is now the case and, as well, that various sectors may be relatively advantaged in addressing the properties associated with different contingent events. The application here is confined to aging-related policy, but the scheme itself could be applied more broadly. By analyzing social welfare programming in this manner, I hope to demonstrate that core welfare state principles—universalism, adequacy, and progressivity—can and should be maintained. What circumstances may require, however, is a careful reexamination of the *application* of these principles.

This chapter is reprinted with permission from *International Social Security Review,* Volume 48, pages 3–17, 1995.

THE NATURE OF THE CHALLENGE

In both "market-based" and "citizen-based" welfare states, macro-economic events dating to the early 1970s—slow economic growth, inflation, unemployment—have placed enormous pressures on welfare state growth and stability. But more has been at work here than the question of affordability. Were that the only matter in question, it might be possible to devise formulas to restrain future growth, level funding, or even cut current benefits. The more fundamental consequence of economic concerns has been in providing a platform for attacks much more basic than those centered on cost alone. Most especially, questions about values and responsibilities, long indelibly part of the modern welfare state, have come under intense security. These pose a much more central challenge to public social welfare than do expenditures alone.

The Question of Values

In public discussion of social welfare, the past 15 years have seen a marked shift in the balance between concerns with "self-sufficiency" and "mutual support" (1), between "social discipline and social rights" (2). Quadagno (3) has characterized efforts involving these values in the United States as nothing less than attempting to "desocialize" social welfare programming. In fact, it is the normative base of social welfare programming that has been struck harder than actual benefit levels, which in many instances continue to grow. Strains on the values of solidarity and universality are such, however, that welfare reforms in many parts of Europe are now mimicking American practice after years in which the United States moved, however, haltingly, in a European direction.

In Myles's (4) words, a pendulum shift is well under way in the direction of "economic liberalism" and away from "political democracy." As a matter of values, it is a function of both renewed faith in market principles and lowered faith and trust in government. Hibbs and Madsen (5) see the assault on the welfare state being more about concern with government inefficiency and unresponsive public bureaucracies than against social welfare benefits themselves. In the United Kingdom, electoral utilitarianism (maintenance of benefits in many areas) has been successfully combined with programmatic delegitimization (attacking the ideology of the welfare state): in Krieger's words, "government provision of social services within an anti-welfarist ideology" (6, p. 156).

As an alternative, market-driven social welfare—whether as a matter of actual responsibility or merely administration—is viewed as dynamic and rewarding. Market incentives generate both individual effort and economic growth. Perhaps best capturing the move to the right has been the prominence of concerns about so-called "moral hazard" in skewing incentives and promoting wasteful growth in public programs. Barr captures the appeal of moral hazard concerns to those who would tear down the public welfare edifice: "the more complete the [insurance] cover . . . the less the individuals have to bear the consequences of their actions and the less, therefore, the incentive to behave as they would if they had to bear the loss themselves" (7, p. 753).

Moral hazard is featured in critiques of virtually all coverage areas of contemporary social welfare: the poor and unemployed have insufficient incentives to work; clients and providers in health care have good reason to overutilize and to overserve; and those providing social services fare well while, wittingly or not, inducing their clients into "dependency relationships." Barr and Coulter speak to British reforms of the 1980s as designed, in part, to "reduce replacement rates for those groups for whom labor supply incentives are relevant" (8). Greve observes that in many European countries, there has been "a move towards systems which put more emphasis on the individual's responsibility—thereby changing the system in a way so that only basic support, and to very few people, may be handed out by the public sector" (9, p. 8). Marmor and colleagues note the intent of the United States' Family Support Act of 1988: "Entitlements to cash income are to be replaced by entitlements to job training and job placement, and cash relief is to be conditional on work effort (10, p. 83).

Programming for the old has not gone unmentioned in these discussions, but neither has it been subject to so much scrutiny. Primarily, this is because the old continue to be the largest of the so-called "deserving" recipient populations, a designation which vastly reduces concern about moral hazard. If the old are not to be expected to work, there is no need to be concerned about the labor force consequences of pension policy. There appears to be less agreement on this point in the United States than elsewhere, as reflected in a school of thought holding that at least some of the old could or should be working as one means of better taking care of their own needs. Certainly, as the cross-national work of Kohli and colleagues (11) makes abundantly clear, neither the public nor the private sector in the United States makes available any of the "pathways" to retirement used in European nations— special unemployment and disability benefits, to name two. In fact, characteristically, the United States has chosen to protect older persons through a civil rights approach—barring age-based discrimination in the workplace—rather than using the substantive rights approach widely employed in Europe, which provides compensation to older workers (while mandating their exit from the labor force). Public opinion in opposition to mandatory retirement is also much further advanced in the United States than in Europe (12). Raising the eligibility age for Social Security benefits is one consequence of this willingness to allow or insist on greater work effort among the old.

In the case of the old, moral hazard and overutilization worries are focused more in the area of health and long-term care. Talk and actions in several countries centered on increases in insurance deductibles, and copayments are direct attempts to lessen service utilization. Long-term care may present even more formidable moral hazard barriers because, as noted subsequently, the "insurable event" is often hard to define, measure, and predict. As a result, in the United States, conservative critics of public long-term care insurance raise the specter of a "woodwork effect," that is, people coming out of the walls to take advantage of the new benefits whether they need them or not.

Shifting Sectors of Responsibility

Three interwoven trends—decentralization, "informalization" (i.e., reliance on social networks), and privatization—capture the principal ingredients of the "sector shift" associated with the assault on contemporary welfare state programming.

Of these, decentralization is seemingly the least threatening to the public sector as guarantor of social benefits. Nonetheless, it represents a frontal assault on a core principle of social insurance: the presence of national coverage which brings with it a maximally broad risk pool and clear and uniform statutory benefits. Much of decentralization's appeal lies in the presumed weakening of rigid bureaucratic controls "bringing government closer to the people." But with discretion can come discrimination, and with subnational decision-making can arise major questions around adequacy and equity (13). There is, as well, an interesting literature developed in the United States on the theory that "have-not" groups can expect to be systematically denied in smaller rather than larger jurisdictions (14).

Decentralization efforts have been more at work in the personal social services than in income maintenance transfers, and there are stronger arguments for favoring enhanced discretion and flexibility in the first arena than in the second. Where, however, the matter is more one of transferring programmatic and budgetary responsibility from the national to the local level (15) than providing subnational decision-makers with greater latitude in allocating their share of nationally generated revenues, decentralizing efforts can be seen as evidence of pressure on national budgets and a desire to reassign responsibilities, even if only elsewhere in the public sector.

Greater reliance on social networks of family, friends, and neighbors—that is, on informal supports—has also gained new prominence in social welfare discussion. Arguments favoring greater family involvement in care provision are both politically and ethically sensitive, being about saving public funds and encouraging families to fulfill their "natural" obligations. Underlying arguments for greater "social network" involvement in caregiving are both the rising level of governmental expenditures related to caregiving of the old—especially in institutional settings (16, 17)—and findings suggesting that families and elders favor caregiving provided by family members. Yet the societal-level (demographic) and individual-level (psychological) strains on informal caregiving raise fundamental questions about how much, if any, expansion can realistically be expected in the family caregiving role. Moreover, government may neither know what to do to enhance family caregiving (18, 19) nor be able to develop, in Andersen's (20) words, a governmentally based "culture of the social networks" whereby it could take over from family-based provision in a manner consistent with the affective values associated with informal provision.

Privatization is the third and most profound sectoral shift taking place among contemporary welfare states. Privatization represents the structural format through which normative concerns with choice, self-sufficiency, effort, merit, and incentives can be realized. Individual decision-making and nominally free markets in which those decisions play out are at the heart of private systems. In the case of social welfare, unbridled privatization means the normative ascendancy of equity over adequacy, autonomy over solidarity, selectivity over universalism, and obligation over entitlement.

Privatization threatens two key structural features in the design of social welfare policy: universal coverage and progressive financing mechanisms. Universal public social insurance is able to eliminate the problem of adverse selection wherein high-risk individuals cannot be excluded from coverage nor can low risks opt out of the pool altogether. Regarding financing, social insurance is able to break the "link between premium and individual risk" (7). Privatization sacrifices inclusiveness and redistribution in the name of choice and fairness. In its overt repudiation of "structural" and stratifying understandings of social insecurity, privatization also undermines tenets of solidarity, leaving individuals largely to their own devices.

THE CHANGING PLACE OF THE OLD
IN WELFARE POLICY

As with other populations, the old have been subject to these value and sector shifts marking the current welfare policy debate. Yet a developing clash between long-standing assumptions about the needs of the aged and current population dynamics among the old lends a particular cast to aging debates. Coming to grips with reforming old-age policy requires melding these new realities with the ongoing debate about overall welfare state policy.

Old Age as Risk

Coverage against the "risk" of growing old dates to the beginning of social insurance. Old age was long seen as one of the "common misfortunes" (21) or "ordinary contingencies" (22) that faced individuals in industrial society. As such, along with accident insurance and workmen's compensation, protection against the vicissitudes of aging was among the earliest areas of social insurance protection. In Heclo's words, "indeed, it was the quiet desperation of economic insecurity in old age that gave rise to one of the first and largest forms of public income support—old age pensions" (23).

Among the risks historically covered by insurance, aging was especially problematic. As argued by Rubinow (24), in other areas preventive measures might lessen risks; however, in the case of aging, such interventions "aggravated" risk. Moreover, aging appears as "the final emergency," coming at a time when one can only ask: "How many vicissitudes may not [the workingman's] savings have to face through all these long years?" (24, p. 250). The physical and psychological declines long associated with aging meant, as well, that it was long viewed as an illness. The ability of the old to work was devalued (25), and, in fact, legislation was proposed in the United States in 1906 equating old age—turning 62—with disability (26). Historically, old age was seen as a risk in and of itself, and thus a status automatically deserving recognition. That life expectancies were short— 43 in Great Britain in the 1880s; 49 in the United States in 1900—meant that old age was also an insurable and affordable risk. Constructing aging as illness may have been as misguided then as it would be now, but the fact remained that impoverishment, illness, and loneliness were long held to be virtually definitional properties of the old.

The Old as Social Institution

This singular and marginalizing characterization of the aged no longer holds today. Thanks largely to the growth and evolution of social insurance programs in the period after the Second World War, destitution is no longer the dominant economic status of the old. Cross-nationally, income security for the old represents perhaps the greatest success of modern social welfare policy. Between 1930 and 1980, the proportion of workers across 18 industrial nations covered by old-age pension insurance increased from just under 20 percent to nearly 80 percent, and over the same period the income replacement rate for the standard worker increased from 14 to 55 percent (27). In Heclo's (23) words, in less than half a century the objective of economic security among the old evolved "from relief to income maintenance."

Improved well-being and longer life expectancy have generated new social constructions of aging, such as Neugarten's (28) "young-old" and Laslett's (29) "Third Age." The latter's "Third Age Indicator" (a 0.5 or greater probability that persons, having attained age 20, will live to age 70, and that at least 10 percent of a country's population is age 65 or above) finds the presence of a "third age" population throughout the industrial nations; yet nowhere was it a "majoritarian reality" prior to the 20th century.

The emergence of more diverse and, in aggregate, better-off older populations has important ramifications. First, there is now a large number of older persons who have been removed from the labor force and for whom neither work nor illness is a defining feature but for whom new social roles are yet to be developed (30).

By reasons of choice and politics, their return to work is unlikely; the vast majority of elders do not wish to work, and a nearly equal proportion of younger workers concerned about their own economic prospects do not want them to work. Thus, the third age represents the emergence of a prolonged period of good health and well-being in old age but one where roles, obligations, and responsibilities are yet to be worked out. The transition of old age from a residual to an institutional stage of life is one of the most profound demographic transformations of the 20th century.

The arrival of a third age group represents only the first element of what might be termed "the new aging." The second element has been brought about by the increased life expectancy that has created growing numbers of "old-old" individuals or, to extend Laslett's terminology, persons who have entered a fourth age. Because improvements in morbidity have not kept pace with improvements in mortality, persons of very advanced years are growing in numbers and are increasingly afflicted with impairing chronic conditions and functional incapacities. Whereas policy has been a major contributing factor behind the creation of a third age, it has been, virtually everywhere, inadequate or misdirected in addressing the problems associated with a fourth age (17, 31). Meeting the needs of this growing population—in the face of fiscal pressures to do less and ideological pressures to shift responsibilities for social care—is the special age-related problem confronting contemporary social welfare.

CHALLENGES TO AGING POLICY

Threats to long-standing welfare state assumptions and changes in the aggregate well-being of the old have created an important set of challenges to aging-related welfare policy.

Fiscal Pressures

Aging-related costs for pensions and health care are among the fastest rising elements of welfare programming. Organization for Economic Cooperation and Development (OECD) estimates show pension expenditures as a proportion of national income rising from 10.3 percent in 1984 and 11.4 percent in 2000 to 15.1 percent in 2020 and 20.2 percent in 2040 (32). Even in the wake of the post-1970s pressure on social welfare spending, aging-related programs continued to fare both absolutely and relatively well. On balance, the biggest cuts came in the areas of unemployment, housing, and social services. This was due largely to continued popular support for maintenance and expansion of pension benefits (9, 33) and because, until quite recently, age-related benefits were widely perceived to be inadequate in many countries. Yet, even in the Great Britain where, according to the Luxembourg Income Study (reported in 34), 61 percent of elders have incomes below 125 percent of its poverty threshold, the argument carrying the day focuses on social security spending having grown at a rate five times the cost of living and twice the rate of overall economic growth since the Second World War. More generally, the Employment, Labor, and Social Affairs Committee of the OECD has called for increased "effectiveness and efficiency" in age-related programs, noting that (35):

> the increasing elderly population, with the numbers of the very old growing most rapidly, will bring with it increases in demands for income support, health care, long-term care, and other services. In the absence of significant increases in economic growth or other mitigating factors, the consumption of the aged will increase while contributions to the support of the aged may decline because of the reduced numbers of the potentially active population.

Relative Standing of the Old

Overall improvement in the well-being of the old has generated a "success vs. excess" debate throughout the industrialized world. To the degree that public pension benefits are assisting persons not demonstrably in need, calls are heard for better "target efficiency" and greater "fairness" between populations. As well, it is increasingly the case that the stark difference in well-being between younger and older populations is lessening. That is not to say all the elderly are doing well, just that from "a statistical point of view, the elderly [in the United States] are beginning to look at lot like the rest of the populations" (36, p. 48). More broadly, improvements in well-being among the old are such that—despite considerable variation—in only three of eight industrial countries is elderly poverty greater than child poverty, and in all but two countries severe poverty is higher among children than the old (34). Other recently emergent subpopulations are also in growing need of policy attention across a number of countries—unemployed youth, minority group members, and unwed mothers being three such groups.

Privatization and Market Pressures

Pressures to reassign responsibility for different social welfare functions to the private sector or to emphasize market-oriented equity principles are being applied to the old as well as to others. Where out-and-out privatization is taking place—as variously in Chile and Great Britain—principles of universalism are under direct attack; where the effort is to assure "fairness" in the return under publicly sponsored programs, the solidarity principle is increasingly more akin to Bismarck than to Beveridge. Thus, Eichenhofer notes an aim of the recent German pension reforms to strengthen "the contributional character and to weaken the distributional" (31). The emphasis on work-related incentives is also clearly tied to concerns about economic growth and the effects of social policy on it. Where the aged are concerned, the OECD (35) orientation is instructive. Stating that "systems of protection against certain risks are important for the economy" suggests the market-oriented pressures to which the old may be exposed. In the case of Danish pension reform, Nielson goes so far as to contend that the "protagonists on both sides of the struggle had long ago eliminated pensioner needs from the discussion," confining themselves to the "real struggle" between the merits of "popular capitalism" versus those of "fund socialism" (37, p. 128). In Great Britain, "state pensions were attacked as part of the general onslaught on public spending" (38, p. 26).

SOCIAL CONTINGENCIES AND SOCIAL RESPONSIBILITY

Those concerned with the well-being of the old today find themselves forced to respond to the alleged excesses of age-related allocations while being keenly aware how many of the old either have been excluded from policy's recent accomplishments or are facing risks largely unknown to earlier generations of elders. The new pressures require and the new diversity warrants reexamination of (*a*) what protections for the old should be expanded or could be curtailed and (*b*) how responsibility for different risks in old age should be shared.

Social Contingency Framework

Here and elsewhere (39), I propose a social contingency framework for addressing these questions. If, as argued earlier, aging today is no longer per se a contingent event, there is a need to redefine what indeed are the different protections that the aged require. To argue, as I will, that protections provided through the public sector might be reweighed is not to renege on commitments to universalism, adequacy, or equity. To do so, rather, says there is a need to refine the areas where these principles

Table 1

Policy typology of contingent events

Name of event	Criterion or response
Severity	Adequacy
Likelihood	Insurability
Variability	Assessibility

are applied. I propose a "policy typology of contingent events" designed to guide discussion of where more or less protection might be provided and by whom. Table 1, using reciprocal categories of event and response, places contingent events along three interrelated criteria.

The *severity* of an event is about the magnitude of outcome and is a function of the economic, psychological, and physical toll a negative event brings with it, although different events may be assessed differently depending on both the event and the afflicted party. Generally, elders have been treated sympathetically along this dimension. However, determination of severity is more straightforward in some areas than others. Income level can readily be determined, although the criterion one uses to judge its adequacy is critical: objective standard of need, relative to others, or relative to one's pre-retirement status. Severity can also be relatively clear cut in the case of acute illness where, as shown in the United States, diagnostic assessment protocols are in wide use. In most countries (17, 31, 40), there has been less recognition of the severity associated with chronic illness.

The *likelihood* of an event's occurrence conditions how it is understood and anticipated. One of the problems of private or "personal" welfare is that individuals, left to their own devices, often do not protect themselves against potentially devastating occurrences. As Aaron and Thompson (41) note, individuals tend to be least rational regarding widely separated events and contingencies with low probabilities. The coming of a third age and the heightened probabilities of living a very long life have changed aging-related contingencies in important ways. For some groups, old age itself is only recently a nonexceptional occurrence; for others who may have long taken a period of old age for granted, the vagaries of very advanced age are the new development. As the older population becomes more diverse, the distribution of these events varies in important ways across subpopulations, most notably by generation, class, race, and gender.

Variability refers to the difficulty in predicting an event's duration and its course. Life expectancy and the duration of certain events such as survivorship status and acute illness can be calibrated with considerable precision. However, much less firm estimates are possible in the case of chronic illness and functional incapacity. Geriatric assessment has increasingly moved toward the functionally centered approach and away from diagnostic ones, but predicting the duration of such impairments is a more difficult undertaking than is making determinations at one point in time (42). The vagaries of long-term care needs over time present clinicians, administrators, and insurers with dilemmas of client assessment, treatment, and coverage that are more problematic than in the case of other late-life contingent events.

Aging Policy and Contingent Events

The utility of these dimensions—severity, likelihood, and variability—lies in their providing a scale against which to assess the individual and collective costs of different events. For purposes of insurance, one would ideally like to have situations that are highly severe, very unlikely, and reliably assessed. These clear rank orderings can be seldom expected in real life; nor is there a common pattern of coverage cross-nationally. Nonetheless, the typology provides means for comparing the properties of different contingent events against existing programs and allocations.

Weighing of Contingencies. The need for retirement income has long been recognized by industrial nations and has been the central feature of aging-related policy. Most of these nations have also provided broad-based coverage against acute illness, but less attention has been paid to the growing volume of older (and younger) persons faced with long-term functional disabilities. Income security is obviously important, but it is not the sole determinant of economic security in old age. In fact, the growing need for health and social service intervention on behalf of increasing numbers of the very old suggests that income security is a less important component of overall economic security than it once was. Put differently, Heclo's (23) statement that social security is dependent on economic security which is in turn dependent on income security is not so nearly the case today as it may have been 20 years ago. In addition to normal consumption income, economic security is about adequate health and sickness coverage against potentially severe and unpredictable incapacities associated with very advanced age. Social security is about all that and, as well, a variety of housing and environmental supports that address questions of loneliness and isolation.

What holds for the United States, I believe, holds to a lesser degree for a number of industrial nations. Better protection is provided against events that are likely nonvariable, and *potentially* not severe. In Barr's (7) words, most countries do well in providing "income smoothing" for the old but less well in dealing with "unaccustomed drops." Pensions and income maintenance are about an "event" (retirement) that is near certain and whose course is broadly predictable, barring the onset of other late-life events that can appropriately be considered discretely. Most nations also protect well against acute illness, which is bounded and predictable, although not quite so neatly as retirement. Where most countries fall down is in the case of functional incapacity. Often being severe, unpredictable, and highly variable, these chronic conditions are unquestionably worthy of coverage. Doty's (17) review suggests that cross-national coverage is insufficient in this area, and Eichenhofer says of Germany what has certainly been true of the United States as well: "Handicapped people had not been covered by medical insurance because physical handicaps had not been conceived as 'physical impairment which needs medical treatment by physicians', which is how the covered risk 'sickness' is defined legally" (31, p. 77). As indicated earlier, difficulties in defining and delineating needed coverage in long-term care (7, 43) do present serious moral hazard problems—for both providers and clients—but there can be no doubt that the absence of such coverage represents an enormous and growing gap in social insurance protection for the old.

Differential Exposure to Risk. The blurring of the lines of what is—or need not be—genuinely contingent about old age may exacerbate inequities individuals bring to old age. This is especially true for older individuals who may not be officially poor, and thus eligible for supplemental benefits, but who do not have the private resources or family supports to protect themselves privately. These individuals have so few resources that they remain extremely vulnerable to unpredictable catastrophic events. Data from the Luxembourg Income Study, reported by Smeeding, Torrey, and Rein (34), show very considerable success by most countries in moving older people above 75 percent and even 100 percent of their cross-national poverty equivalency scale, but much less success in moving people to 125 percent of that level. In fact, 38.5 percent of the elderly in Australia, 29.8 percent in the former Federal Republic of Germany, 40.1 percent in Norway, 26.6 percent in the United States, and 61.1 percent in Great Britain remain below the 125 percent level.

Existing data support the supposition that persons of lower income not only have higher mortality rates—an especially inequitable feature when there are no dependents to whom survivors' benefits might be directed—but also have higher morbidity rates. Feinstein's (44) cross-national review finds the class/morbidity relationship holding consistently and cites Blaxter's (45) findings that the lowest classes in France and Denmark experience four times the rate of chronic illness of the highest classes, while there is less variation in Great Britain. In the United States, House, Kessler, and Herzog (46) find that the two lowest of four socioeconomic status groups manifest levels of chronic illness in their middle years (ages 45 to 64) that the two upper groups do not reach until after age 75.

These data suggest that most nations' relative success in boosting the majority of elders above an income threshold is eroded by that income not being sufficient to protect large numbers of "near poor" and lower-class individuals against identifiable incapacities that these populations bring to or prematurely become victim of in old age. But because most nations place relatively little emphasis on potentially severe and variable risks associated with long-term care needs, an otherwise precarious but protectable population is denied needed coverage. Put differently, the inefficiencies in modern social insurance programming may be less about *whom* we protect—those able to provide for themselves privately—than *what* we protect—reasonable amounts of income in the face of potentially overwhelming events. The argument is not that retirement income is too generous; rather it is that, as a matter of balance, nations provide too much protection for one type of age-related risk and not enough for another.

Social Contingencies and Social Sectors. As noted earlier, much attention is currently being devoted to what sectors may be less or more prepared to address social protection of different types. Most notable in this regard has been Great Britain, where a direct attempt was made to privatize the State Earnings-Related Pension Scheme (SERPS), to "residualize" the basic state pension, and to target resources on the poorest (8). Similar proposals have circulated widely in the United States in recent years (47). On actuarial grounds, there is a good case in favor of such moves; in a sense, retirement has almost ceased to be an insurable event, given that the overwhelming majority of individuals in "the pool" will live to make the claim. However, as a matter of either "citizenship" or social insurance, this new reality is essentially irrelevant: persons deemed unable to work should be collectively supported, most notably by those who are able to work.

Without prejudging whether or to what extent old age pensions might be privatized, my perspective here is that there are other risks in old age—mainly assuring protection against acute and chronic illness—which lend themselves considerably less to privatization than may be the case in assuring retirement income. The compulsory and universal feature of public insurance is essential in the former cases, first, because compulsion ensures that problems of adverse selection are overcome and, second, because of the breaking of the link between premium and risk noted by Barr (7). It is in just such areas as catastrophic and long-term illness that the progressive features of social insurance and citizenship principles are most required. The same benefit package can be offered to persons of different means, with questions of vertical equity being handled on the financing side of the equation rather than on the benefit side (48). The argument here is not that the private sector is equally or more capable of meeting a population's retirement income needs, although there clearly are many who believe that to be the case. Rather, the argument is that the private sector is ill-suited to addressing health and long-term care contingencies.

In the constrained environment of the contemporary welfare state, the logic of the argument here is that health-related allocations should be protected and, given the relative paucity of current support, provisions directed toward long-term care needs should be augmented. If political pressure requires that there be some degree of privatizing, income maintenance is the more legitimate area to explore. Indexed benefits, publicly assured inflation protection, and mandated availability of private coverage are non-negotiable items, but beyond these concerns a good case for private provision exists.

CONTINGENCY ANALYSIS AS THE PREFERRED APPROACH

The forces of "economic liberalism" are clearly in the ascendant among the OECD nations today. As a result, great pressures have been placed on social welfare schemes. However, as J. K. Galbraith has recently noted, the conservative attacks on socially liberal and progressive positions may have had the beneficial effect of provoking efforts in their defense and thus their reinvigoration.

The argument here is that with careful assessment of the risks which contemporary elders face, the values of universalism and adequacy as well as of equity can be preserved and built upon. All older persons (and preferably younger ones too, an option and topic beyond the scope of this chapter) would be assured protection against contingent events, and financing for programs addressing the most potentially severe and otherwise uninsurable would be on an inclusive and progressive basis. The contingency approach can serve to refine a "targeting within universalism" approach (49, 50) by suggesting both more appropriate targeting of benefits and reassessment of how protected groups might be constituted.

In most nations, this principle has been most successfully applied in the areas of retirement income and acute health care. Laudable as these successes are, the argument here is that it is imperative that coverage for chronic illness and functional incapacity be added to the list. Highly severe and unpredictable events that can destroy people financially demand both the most extensive group and the most progressive funding formula. By this standard, acute and long-term illness coverage is conceptually more compelling than is retirement income protection. As a midcourse option—and, thus, one unlikely to satisfy the proponents or detractors of current welfare state programming—the contingency approach represents something of an optimal course between residual, noncontributory, and stigmatizing means-tested programs on the one hand, and target-inefficient, potentially morally hazardous, citizenship-based programs on the other.

REFERENCES

1. Heclo, H. General welfare and two American political traditions. *Polit. Sci. Q.* 101(2): 179–196, 1986.
2. Sinfield, A. British social security policy during the eighties. In *Future Social Policy in Europe,* edited by B. Greve. Danish National Institute of Social Research, Copenhagen, 1992.
3. Quadagno, J. Generational equity and the politics of the welfare state. *Polit. Soc.* 17: 353–376, 1989.
4. Myles, J. Postwar capitalism and the extension of social security into the retirement wage. In *The Politics of Social Policy in the United States,* edited by M. Weir, A. Orloff, and T. Skocpol. Princeton University Press, Princeton, N.J., 1986.
5. Hibbs, D., and Madsen, H. J. Public reaction to the growth of taxation and government expenditures. *World Polit.* 33: 413–435, 1980.
6. Krieger, J. The British welfare state and Thatcher's new coalition. In *Remaking the Welfare State,* edited by M. Brown. Temple University Press, Philadelphia, 1988.
7. Barr, N. Economic theory and the welfare state. *J. Econ. Lit.* 30: 741–803, 1992.
8. Barr, N., and Coulter, F. Social security. In *The State of Welfare: The Welfare State in Britain since 1974,* edited by J. Hills. Clarendon, Oxford, 1991.
9. Greve, B. Introduction. In *Future Social Policy in Europe,* edited by B. Greve. Danish National Institute of Social Research, Copenhagen, 1992.
10. Marmor, T., Mashaw, J., and Harvey, P. *America's Misunderstood Welfare State.* Basic Books, New York, 1990.
11. Kohli, M., et al. (eds.). *Time for Retirement.* Cambridge University Press, Cambridge, England, 1991.
12. Smith, T. The polls: The welfare state in cross-national perspective. *Public Opinion Q.* 51: 404–421, 1987.
13. Estes, C. The Reagan legacy: Privatization, the welfare state and aging in the 1990's. In *States, Labor Markets, and the Future of Old Age Policy,* edited by J. Myles and J. Quadagno. Temple University Press, Philadelphia, 1991.
14. McConnell, G. *Private Power and American Democracy.* Vintage, New York, 1966.

15. Salamon, L., and Abramson, A. Governance: The politics of retrenchment. In *The Reagan Record,* edited by J. Palmer and I. Sawhill. Ballinger, New York, 1984.
16. Daatland, S. Stress and strategies in care systems: The Scandinavian experience. *Soc. Sci. Med.* 38: 867–874, 1994.
17. Doty, P. The Oldest Old and the Use of Institutional Long-term Care from an International Perspective. Paper presented at the conference on the Changing Face of Informal Caregiving, Berkeley Springs, W.Va., 1992.
18. Doty, P. Family care of the elderly: The role of public policy. *Milbank Q.* 63: 34–74, 1986.
19. Hokenstad, M., and Johansson, L. Swedish policy initiatives to support family caregiving for the elderly. *Ageing Int.,* pp. 33–35, 1990.
20. Andersen, B. The lessons from the welfare state. In *Future Social Policy in Europe,* edited by B. Greve. Danish National Institute of Social Research, Copenhagen, 1992.
21. Weale, A. Equality, social solidarity, and the welfare state. *Ethics* 100: 473–488, 1990.
22. Brandeis, L. Workingman's insurance—the road to social inefficiency. In *Proceedings of the National Conference on Charities and Correction.* New York, 1911.
23. Heclo, H. *Modern Social Politics in Britain and Sweden.* Yale University Press, New Haven, Conn., 1974.
24. Rubinow, I. *The Quest for Security.* Henry Holt, New York, 1934.
25. Graebner, W. *A History of Retirement.* Yale University Press, New Haven, Conn., 1980.
26. Quadagno, J. *The Transformation of Old Age Security, Class and Politics in the American Welfare State.* University of Chicago Press, Chicago, 1988.
27. Palme, J. Models of old-age pension. In *Needs and Welfare,* edited by A. Ware and R. Goodin. Sage, London, 1990.
28. Neugarten, B. Age groups in American society and the rise of the young-old. *Ann. Am. Acad. Polit. Soc. Sci.* 415: 178–198, 1974.
29. Laslett, P. The emergence of the third age. *Ageing Soc.* 7: 133–160, 1987.
30. Kohli, M. Ageing as a challenge for sociological theory. *Ageing Soc.* 8: 367–394, 1988.
31. Eichenhofer, E. Recent social policy development in Germany. In *Future Social Policy in Europe,* edited by B. Greve. Danish National Institute of Social Research, Cophenhagen, 1992.
32. Myles, J., and Quadagno, J. Introduction. In *States, Labor Markets, and the Future of Old Age Policy,* edited by J. Myles and J. Quadagno. Temple University Press, Philadelphia, 1991.
33. Brown, M. K. (ed.). *Remaking the Welfare State: A Comparative Perspective.* Temple University Press, Philadelphia, 1988.
34. Smeeding, T., Torrey, B., and Rein, M. Patterns of income and poverty: The economic status of children and the elderly in eight countries. In *The Vulnerable,* edited by J. Palmer, T. Smeeding, and B. Torrey. Urban Institute Press, Washington, D.C., 1988.
35. Organization for Economic Cooperation and Development, Employment, Labor, and Social Affairs Committee. *New Orientations for Social Policy.* Paris, 1992.
36. Schulz, J. *Economics of Aging.* Auburn House, Dover, Mass., 1992.
37. Nielson, F. The politics of aging in Scandinavian countries. In *States, Labor Markets, and the Future of Old Age Policy,* edited by J. Myles and J. Quadagno. Temple University Press, Philadelphia, 1991.
38. Walker, A. Thatcherism and the new politics of old age. In *States, Labor Markets, and the Future of Old Age Policy,* edited by J. Myles and J. Quadagno. Temple University Press, Philadelphia, 1991.
39. Hudson, R. Social contingencies, the aged, and public policy. *Milbank Q.* 73: 253–277, 1993.

40. Rice, T., and Gabel, J. Protecting the elderly against high health care costs. *Health Aff.* 5: 5–21, 1986.

41. Aaron, H., and Thompson, L. Social security and the economists. In *Social Security after 50*, edited by E. Berkowitz. Greenwood, Westport, Conn., 1987.

42. Kane, R., and Kane, R. *Assessing the Elderly*. Lexington Books, Lexington, Mass., 1981.

43. Zollner, D. Germany. In *The Evolution of Social Insurance*, edited by P. Kohler and H. Zacher. St. Martin's Press, New York, 1992.

44. Feinstein, J. S. The relationship between socio-economic status and health. *Milbank Q.* 71: 279–322, 1993.

45. Blaxter, M. A comparison of measure of inequality in morbidity. In *Health Inequalities in European Countries*, edited by J. Fox. Gower, Aldershot, England, 1989.

46. House, J., Kessler, R., and Herzog, R. Age, socio-economic status, and health. *Milbank Q.* 68: 383–411, 1990.

47. Haveman, R. *Starting Even*. Simon and Schuster, New York, 1988.

48. Wiener, J., Hanley, R., and Illston, L. Financing long-term care: How much private? How much public? *J. Health Polit. Policy Law* 17: 425–434, 1992.

49. Skocpol, T. Targeting within universalism. In *The Urban Underclass*, edited by C. Jencks and P. Peterson. Brookings Institution, Washington, D.C., 1991.

50. Hudson, R., and Kingson, E. Inclusive and fair: The case for universality in social programs. *Generations* 15: 51–56, 1991.

CHAPTER 19

Social Security:
Marketing Radical Reform

Eric Kingson and Jill Quadagno

"Entitlement fever" is hitting the nation, creating new opportunities for those seeking to radically alter the structure and terms of eligibility for Social Security. From the Concord Coalition's call to means-test Social Security, to the declaration of the 1995 Bipartisan Commission on Entitlement and Tax Reform that current federal commitments—largely to the elderly—unfairly burden the nation's children, to the furor over the balanced budget amendment, to the strident efforts of free marketers to privatize Social Security, efforts abound to legitimize radical change.

Although Social Security's projected financing problems are many years off, the Social Security rhetoric is already escalating to a feverish pitch. Testifying before the Bipartisan Commission, a self-appointed representative of "generation X" gleefully reports that more American adults under 35 believe in UFOs than in the future of Social Security (1). Writing in the *Boston Globe,* the columnist Jeff Jacoby (2) argues that Social Security is an immense Ponzi scheme that is slowly bankrupting young Americans in order to enrich their elders. The cover of *Time* advertises "The Case for Killing Social Security," the subject of a feature article that says "the numbers don't add up—and the politicians won't own up" (3, p. 24). And privatization advocates promise 100 million millionaires, a secure old age, and a thriving economy for all if workers' payroll tax contributions could be converted to private savings accounts (4).

To date, there has been much hyperbole, but little action. The Bipartisan Commission failed to agree on any proposals. Newly elected in 1985 as Speaker of the House, Newt Gingrich quickly professed that Social Security reform would remain off the table for at least six years, lest this potentially explosive issue derail the "Contract with America." The balanced budget amendment stumbled in the Senate amidst growing public fears that it would force large cuts in Social Security. And

This chapter is reprinted with permission from *The Future of Age-Based Public Policy,* edited by R. Hudson, published by The Johns Hopkins University Press, in press.

serious discussion of Social Security was conspicuously absent from the 1996 presidential campaign.

Even so, rhetoric matters, because how the problem is defined establishes parameters for possible solutions. The financing problems of Social Security provide an important window of opportunity for those seeking to advance an agenda of lower taxes and smaller government. What is occurring now is the contentious process of setting an agenda to decide the future of the nation's most successful social policy—Social Security, the Old Age, Survivors, and Disability Insurance (OASDI) program. Proposals previously associated with the far right (most notably, partial privatization and means-testing of Social Security) are now emerging as options requiring serious consideration. Indeed, the 1997 report of the Advisory Council on Social Security has seriously discussed—without reaching consensus—two plans which would redirect some portion of Social Security payroll tax contributions into private accounts. In this new political environment other changes that, while less extreme, are still drastic (for example, raising the normal retirement age to 70) have come to look like moderate alternatives. The potential consequences of such changes—for women, minorities, and the poor and also for the future of the middle class—are receiving little attention, a fact that should be of great concern.

In this chapter, we first review the existing Social Security financing problem and then examine the perception of Social Security as a program in crisis, including the marketing of the program as a burden to the young. Next, we examine selected proposals for cutting Social Security that arise from a definition of the program as unfair and unsustainable. We conclude by discussing real solutions for restoring the long-range solvency of the Social Security trust fund, including the Maintenance of Benefits plan (MB)—as advanced by 6 of the 13 members of the 1994–6 Advisory Council on Social Security—which seeks to address the financing problem while maintaining the basic promises and structure of OASDI.

THE SOCIAL SECURITY FINANCING PROBLEM

No doubt about it, there is a Social Security financing problem. Without any changes in current law, Social Security is projected as meeting its obligations for the next 33 years. But under intermediate cost assumptions, the Social Security trustees' report a projected shortfall of 2.17 percent of payroll over the 75-year period—1996 to 2070—over which long-range estimates are made. This represents a roughly 14 percent shortfall. Since the deficit years fall in the middle and at the end of the estimating period, the shortfalls in the out years are substantially larger than is suggested by the overall 2.17 percent-of-payroll estimate (4.86 percent of payroll from 2046 to 2070) (5).

However, while the projected financing shortfall must be addressed, it constitutes a warning, not a crisis. Tax returns (payroll tax receipts and receipts from taxation of benefits) will exceed outlays until 2012. Total income, including interest earnings, is expected to exceed expenditures through 2018 (by $60 billion dollars in 1995 alone) and the combined OASDI trust fund is projected as able to meet all its commitments through 2028, with sufficient revenues to meet 76 percent of all benefits promised thereafter (5). Of course, the projected shortfall may be larger or smaller, depending on economic and demographic changes.

A PROGRAM IN CRISIS?

The facts surrounding Social Security financing are not in dispute. The meaning attributed to the projected financing problem, however, is the source of lively debate. A new set of political circumstances has led to the definition of Social Security—both implicitly and explicitly—as a major problem, part of an "entitlement crisis" (6, 7). This view is incubated by budget politics and anxiety over the future and thrives in the presence of stereotypes of "greedy geezers," distortions about the value of Social Security, and a simplistic view of entitlements as a single entity. It is supported by a flawed but seemingly objective analysis of the size and implications of the federal deficit.

Crafting a Message of Fear

For some critics of Social Security, tying Social Security to the rhetoric of an "entitlement crisis" is a carefully conceived and executed strategy to shrink the federal government and advance the idea that radical reforms are needed in Social Security and other social programs. Frank Luntz (8), a pollster who worked on the Contract with America, advises in a memo to the new Republican congressional majority that the budget debate should be cast "in terms of 'the American dream' and 'our children's future'." To survive and prosper as a movement, Luntz says, Republicans must frame questions in *moral* terms, not in the heartless language of "budgeteers." And, he tells them, they must turn "the issue of 'fairness' against the Democrats," asking such questions as, "Is it 'fair' for Medicare recipients to have an even greater choice of doctors and facilities than the average taxpayers who are funding the system?"

Similarly, according to the final report of the Bipartisan Commission on Entitlement and Tax Reform: "Left unchecked, the Federal government's long-term spending commitments on entitlement programs . . . will lead to excessively high deficit and debt levels, unfairly burdening America's children and stifling standards of living for this and future generations of Americans" (9, p. ii).

Although Social Security, the "third rail of American politics," is often considered "too hot to touch," its framing as an out-of-control entitlement that benefits the "wrong people" (the poor, the rich, or the middle class, depending on the critic's argument) may provide a backdoor to radical restructuring of the program. Journalists, politicians, and budget advocates who approach the issue in this manner consistently highlight the program's various problems (financing, declining rates of return as the system matures, women's equity and adequacy concerns, declining public confidence) while ignoring its overall success. This image of the program as a drain on hard-working Americans and the young (as if they and their families do not face risks associated with disability, retirement, or death) is bolstered by analyses purporting to show that the growth of Social Security is part of a "unitary entitlement problem," which, left unchecked, will bankrupt the future. Thus the interim report of the Bipartisan Commission on Entitlement and Tax Reform contends that without "policy changes, entitlement spending and interest on the national debt will consume almost all federal revenues in 2010. In 2030, federal revenues will not even cover entitlement spending" (9, p. 4). Entitlements do indeed seem out of control.

Separate Programs, Separate Problems

Lumping all entitlements together, as one large problem, creates a false sense of crisis and places obstacles in the path of realistic reform of Social Security financing. There are many entitlement programs, each serving important social purposes and each in need of thoughtful ongoing review. The two major programs—Social Security and Medicare, which together account for 60 percent of entitlement spending—are both in need of reform, but for different reasons and in different ways. In fact, the entitlement "crisis" looks quite different when entitlements are separated according to specific programs. Social Security's outlay as a share of gross domestic product (GDP) is forecasted as growing from only 4.7 percent in 1996 to 6.4 percent by 2030. Even modest reductions in benefit levels would reduce that share. A 1.7 percent growth in share of GDP is not a terribly heavy price to pay for the retirement security of the baby boom cohort, whose education, employment, and housing needs we have been able to meet thus far without sacrificing economic security. What's more, many of our economic competitors presently devote a considerably higher proportion of GDP to public pensions without raising the panic that pervades Washington today. The percent of GDP spent on pensions ranges from 15.03 in Austria to 11.87 in Sweden to 4.79 in Japan, compared with the 4.8 percent figure for the United States (10).

The rest of the so-called entitlement problem is caused by other programs, mostly Medicare and Medicaid, and by interest on the debt. Projected long-term federal deficits are driven primarily by rapidly increasing health care costs and only secondarily by anticipated increases in Social Security expenditures. Medicare and Medicaid costs have been growing rapidly, and the Medicare Hospital Insurance trust fund is projected to be depleted in 2001.[1] Congress is presently considering measures to reduce health care inflation and bring the spiraling costs of Medicare and Medicaid under control. If any of these measures succeeds, the "crisis" lessens (11, 12).[1]

Notwithstanding the differing functions of the various entitlement programs and the differing challenges they face, the advocates of radical change prefer to talk about Social Security's financing problems as if Social Security, Medicare, Medicaid, and the many other entitlement programs were a single entity—all part of one big entitlement crisis. Proposals advanced by the Concord Coalition and by individual members of the Bipartisan Commission provide case examples of the solutions that emerge from this framework.

[1] Note: The 1997 budget agreement moved the projected date of exhaustion for the Hospital Insurance Trust Fund to 2007.

SOCIAL SECURITY REFORMS WITHIN THE
"ENTITLEMENT CRISIS" FRAMEWORK

Deficit politics are lending new legitimacy to proposals to reform Social Security by means-testing, privatization, and greatly scaling back benefits. While these proposals are often portrayed as a way to reduce long-run federal deficits, what gets lost is the human consequences of such proposals as well as their long-term effects on the future of the program. What follows is a look at some of these proposals, especially their impact on the Social Security program and on low-income workers, minorities, and women, groups that depend far more heavily on Social Security than do other recipient populations.

A Social Security Means Test

As the central feature of its deficit-cutting strategy, the Concord Coalition (13) has advanced Peter Peterson's proposal of a comprehensive means test (also known as "affluence test") of Social Security and many other entitlements. The coalition is proposing to reduce Social Security and other benefit payments for higher-income beneficiaries. In contrast to most means-tested programs, which rely on welfare bureaucracies to determine who is poor enough to receive social benefits, the new approach would use an income test applied through the tax system to reduce benefits for more affluent beneficiaries of Social Security and a variety of other federal social insurance and public assistance programs (13). Income from Social Security, unemployment insurance, welfare programs, selected veterans' benefits, and farm payments and the insurance value of Medicare would be subject to a graduated reduction—ranging from 10 to 85 percent—when income from all sources exceeded $40,000. Households with $55,000, $95,000 and $120,000 in income would lose 15, 55, and 85 percent of their benefits, respectively. In no case would the reduction exceed 85 percent (13, 14). Peterson (14, p. 58) suggests that an "affluence test" would strengthen Social Security while meeting the fairness challenge of achieving "large fiscal savings without hurting low-income Americans." But would it?

Indeed, this approach goes a long way toward answering two criticisms of means-tested programs—that they are administratively complex and that they stigmatize beneficiaries (15). But it does not address the main criticisms—that means-testing (even "affluence-testing") would initiate a process that is likely to pull apart America's most successful social policy and, in the long-run, to be particularly harmful to low- and moderate-income households (15, 16). Failure to provide some reasonable return to higher-income people who contribute to Social Security over their entire work lives would inevitably lead to demands by these people to withdraw from the program. Social Security is already criticized by some higher-income workers as not giving them their "money's worth"; means-testing would further fuel their discontent. Without the political support and participation of the affluent, there would be no way to sustain the progressivity of the program's benefit formula, which provides roughly twice as much in return to low-income people as to high-income people while simultaneously extending broad protection to the middle class (17). Also, means-testing Social Security, Medicare, and other social insurance entitlements would discourage savings (18–23) and would introduce a new level of uncertainty into retirement income planning. By reducing Social Security, Medicare, and other social insurance benefits of savers by as much as 85 percent, the government would be sending a message that it values consumption over retirement savings. Moreover, Quadagno notes that by providing a different set of incentives for higher-income persons, means-testing (and privatization efforts) threaten to undermine the income redistribution that takes place through Social Security, while also "undermining the moral framework that has sustained public support for Social Security by fracturing solidarity along lines of class and of generations" (7, p. 398).

Changes in Benefits and Eligibility Age

Senator J. Robert Kerrey (D-NE) and former Senator John Danforth (R-MO) have proposed a solution to the "entitlement crisis" that includes changing the Social Security benefit formula and raising the age of eligibility for benefits. The combined impact of their proposals would be a 43 percent cut in Social Security benefits. The burden of these cuts would be particularly damaging to people in low-income households.

The most problematic benefit cut involves a technical change in the benefit formula that, beginning in 1998, would index the Social Security "bend points" for inflation instead of for average wage growth. Under current law, two calculations are used to determine the amount of a worker's initial benefits.

First, the worker's average indexed monthly earnings (AIME) figure is calculated based on the worker's earnings record (of wages that were subject to the payroll tax). This calculation involves adjusting all covered wages for changes in average wages that have occurred since the year in which the wages were earned (indexed to age 60). These amounts are then averaged together with any wages for age 60 and after to produce the AIME. This procedure helps to ensure that benefits based on earnings keep pace with real wage growth, not just with inflation.

Second, the primary insurance amount (PIA) is calculated. The PIA is the basic monthly benefit, equivalent to the monthly benefit received by a worker retiring at normal retirement age. In 1996, the PIA benefit formula replaces 90 percent of the first $437 of AIME, 32 percent of the next $2,198 of AIME, and 15 percent of AIME in excess of $2,635.

The dollar amounts at which the percentage rates in this formula change are called "bend points." These bend points are also "wage-indexed"—increased annually by the growth in average wages. The percentage rates in the PIA formula do not change. The wage indexing of the bend points helps guarantee that over time, Social Security benefits reflect changes in average wages and replace a fairly constant proportion of preretirement earnings for workers at comparable wage levels.

Under the Kerrey/Danforth proposal, as real wages rise over time, all new beneficiaries would get pushed into a higher bend-point bracket, and thus replacement rates (and benefit amounts) would eventually decline, with the younger cohorts experiencing much greater reductions. This change would undermine protections extended to the poor because more of their income would be replaced at 32 percent, and less at 90 percent. The effect would be greatest on beneficiaries who receive a proportionately larger share of their incomes from Social Security—namely, the poor, aged widows of the future, and low-wage workers. Moreover, instead of stabilizing Social Security financing, tying bend points to changes in the consumer price index instead of changes in average wages would increase financing pressures during periods of high inflation and low growth. It would result in larger benefit increases during periods of low wage growth and high inflation.[2]

The Kerrey/Danforth Social Security proposal also includes a plan to gradually raise the normal retirement age to 70. Currently, the age of eligibility for full retirement benefits is 65. Beginning in the next century, it will gradually increase to 67 over a 27-year period. When fully implemented, early retirement benefits will be reduced, with benefits declining at age 62 from 80 percent of a full benefit to 70 percent, for example.

In many respects, it makes sense to raise the retirement age. People are living longer. Many have better health than in the past and are capable of working longer. The main effect of this option, however, would not be to delay retirement and keep older people in the labor force (23, 25). Simulations of the effect of the increase in the normal retirement age to 67 suggest that the average age of receipt of benefits will only increase by two to three months (26). Rather, the primary effect would be to produce long-run savings for Social Security by reducing early retirement benefits and the value of benefits at normal retirement age. Increases in the normal age of retirement will also result in benefit reductions for aged spouses and aged widow(er)s. Reductions in benefits for the latter group are especially problematic given their economic insecurity.

An increase of the retirement age to 70 would mean a 40 percent cut in benefits for workers retiring at age 62. The burden of the proposed change would fall most heavily on lower-income early retirees (23), most notably older workers in poor health, older workers who are functionally limited (but not totally disabled), minority older workers, unemployed older workers, and early retirees in "downsizing" industries. While this is arguably a relatively small proportion of early retirees, it is difficult to justify from a social justice perspective. The combined impact of the benefit formula and retirement age changes would be a whopping 43 percent cut in Social Security benefits.

More recently, Senator Kerrey teamed up with former Senator Alan Simpson (R-WY) to offer a revised version of the Kerrey/Danforth plan, termed the Personal Investment Plan Act of 1995. While still raising the retirement age to 70 and containing a substantial reduction in benefits via benefit formula changes, the revised plan includes huge reductions in cost-of-living (COLA) protections. By

---

[2] The Kerrey/Danforth cuts also incorporate another benefit formula change, one that was originally proposed by former Congressman Dan Rostenkowski (D-IL) as part of a financing package that included both deficit reductions and tax increases (23). When fully phased in over 50 years, this option would completely replace the current 15 percent bracket with the 10 percent bracket, and part of the 32 percent bracket with the 15 percent bracket (9). This option looks as though it would only affect the affluent. Ultimately, however, the benefits of average earners would be reduced by 8.4 percent and those of high earners by just over 20 percent. Combined with the proposal to change the indexing of bend points, these benefit formula changes would mean enormous benefit cuts.

limiting full COLA protection to the portion of an individual's benefit that is equal to 30 percent of the median Social Security benefit (i.e., the individual's Primary Insurance Amount), this proposal would impair the economic security of elderly persons, especially formerly middle-income women living to advanced old age. On average, the combined impact of the Kerrey/Simpson bill would be a 33 percent cut in benefits, but even greater for today's young and those who are likely to live to advanced old age.

Why cut so deep when modest measures (for example, a 14 percent cut or equivalent payroll tax increase) would solve the problem? The answer lies in the next "crisis" reform option—privatizing Social Security.

Privatization

Big benefit cuts are needed, according to the Kerrey/Danforth approach, to fund a giant step in the direction of privatizing Social Security—a 1.5 percent payroll tax decrease (2 percent under Kerrey/Simpson) for everyone under 55 along with a requirement that this money be placed in a personal savings/IRA-like account. Contributions to the individual personal account would not be deductible and earnings on the account would be taxed upon withdrawal. Withdrawal would be allowed only upon disability or retirement.

Because the Social Security trust fund will become insolvent in 2029, the logical solution to restoring solvency might be to raise payroll taxes sometime in the future. But this option would cut payroll taxes by 1.5 percent (by 2 percent under Kerrey/Simpson)! The rationale for cutting payroll taxes is based on the argument that such a cut would promote savings and personal responsibility. Right now, there is little evidence that privatization of benefits would have any effect on national savings, since it would merely shift funds from public to private accounts. Also, there is no evidence that this reduction in payroll taxes would provide an adequate substitute for Social Security benefits. Rather, past experience suggests that people would be likely to withdraw these funds and use them as family needs arose, unless the system were highly regulated. The real impact would simply be to jeopardize the trust funds and reduce income security in old age.

Even so, privatization proposals are proliferating. The CATO Institute, a conservative think tank, has initiated its Project on Social Security Privatization and is advocating consideration of the Chilean approach as a vehicle for privatizing the U.S. Social Security program. Two plans emerging out of the 1994–6 Advisory Council on Social Security—the Individual Account (IA), supported by two (of 13) members, and the Personal Security Account (PSA), supported by five members—would also radically depart from the 60-year tradition of gradual Social Security reform. Both would introduce mandatory private savings through individual accounts into Social Security.

The IA plan would raise the normal retirement age and scale back replacement rates for higher-income workers (27). The PSA plan would dramatically alter Social Security by phasing-in a two tier system—a universal flat benefit equal to two-thirds of the poverty line and individual accounts whose value would reflect the outcome of the earnings and investment decisions of workers. Both plans, especially the PSA, address the thorny transition problems posed by privatization proposals by reducing benefit commitments under the basic OASDI program while also increasing revenues. The IA plan would mandate a 1.6 percent payroll charge. The PSA plan contains a 75-year transition payroll tax of 1.5 percent with additional borrowing from general revenues during the first third of the 21st century. Besides addressing the financing problem, their proponents see the plans as promoting the savings habit and assuring younger workers that their Social Security investments will come to fruition. Their opponents see these plans as reducing—dramatically so in the PSA plan—benefits payable under the Social Security program, shifting additional risks associated with economic fluctuations onto individuals and compromising the anti-poverty role of Social Security. By explicitly separating out the individual equity and adequacy components of OASDI, these plans are seen by some as potentially undermining political support for the program, especially its poverty-reduction features (27–29).

Relatively little thought has been given to what the private retirement accounts would look like, how they would be managed, and what fees might be charged by private investors to manage the accounts. These issues have implications both for the income security of retirees and for the economy. Will there be any government supervision of how workers invest these funds? Or will workers be able to simply take the extra dollars and invest them as they please? Some proposals imply that the only penalty on workers for withdrawing funds from these accounts is that they will be taxed. If early withdrawals are allowed, experience suggests that workers may take the money out to pay off other debts due to life events such as illness or divorce and pay the tax penalty. If withdrawals are not allowed, what gigantic government agency will be put in place to monitor the private savings accounts of millions of individuals?

To keep the Social Security trust fund solvent, the payroll tax cut must be accompanied by the benefit cuts discussed above. The implicit assumption is that returns from private investments will make up the difference in retirement income. Perhaps some workers would do better, but others may lose all their money through poor or unlucky investments or bad advice. Thus, retirement savings could decline further rather than increase.

Senator Alan Simpson and Congressmen Alex McMillan and Porter Goss have proposed an alternative privatization plan in the Bipartisan Commission's final report. Their plan would make opting out of payroll taxes voluntary. If opting out becomes voluntary, then one must consider the effect on the entire system. Presently, the taxes of higher-income workers subsidize the benefits of low-income workers. One likely scenario is that high-income workers would opt out, but low-income workers would remain under the present system. That is in fact what happened in Great Britain because the set-up costs of the optional plans made opting out too costly for low-income workers (30).

If high earners opt out, would there still be sufficient tax contributions to pay low-income retirees what they are presently promised? If opting out makes it impossible to pay promised benefits to low-income retirees, where would the money come from? General revenues? An increase in payroll taxes? If opting out isn't established as some form of a mandatory defined contribution plan, then the proposal could merely amount to a payroll tax decrease for those workers who opt out. Under a voluntary system, how would opting out be operationalized? Employers' book-keeping would become much more complex. Firms would have some workers paying full payroll taxes and others paying reduced payroll taxes. Further, workers could choose to opt out at various points in time. Administration would also become more complex for the Social Security Administration. These administrative costs need to be factored into the estimates of how this option would affect the federal budget and how it would affect firms.

Discussion of options like those reviewed above are just beginning to take place in a public forum. Some, such as retirement age increases, are perfectly reasonable to consider as part of a balanced package, but taken together, "solutions" such as those advanced in the Kerrey/Danforth and the Kerrey/Simpson packages do much more than is needed to restore the trust funds to actuarial balance. What these proposals and many other privatization proposals have in common is one more version of rolling back the federal government. Instead of returning programs to the states, however, they return income security in old age to the private sector, providing clear benefits to some (for example, investment portfolio managers), increased uncertainty for many, and clear losses to those with little protection beyond Social Security.

REAL OPTIONS FOR SOCIAL SECURITY REFORM

In criticizing approaches to Social Security reform that rely on inflated claims of impending financing crises,[3] we do not intend to suggest that the projected financing problem should be ignored. Quite the contrary. While no immediate crisis exists, there is a need to thoughtfully advance policies—perhaps some combination of benefit reductions and tax increases—that will put the program back into actuarial balance. Changes affecting the income of future retirees should be put in place with sufficient lead time for workers to adjust their retirement expectations and savings behavior. Moreover, postponing action for many years would further undermine public confidence in the program and serve as an invitation to crisis mongering and sensational news reporting.

The Social Security trust fund can be restored to long-range solvency with relatively modest adjustments rather than a major restructuring of the program. Robert Ball (31), former commissioner of Social Security, notes that "there are many ways of bringing Social Security into long-range balance within the principles of the program." What might a plan look like?

The Maintenance of Benefits Plan

Six of the 13 members of the Advisory Council on Social Security support one such plan, the MB plan. This plan begins with four proposals essentially supported by almost all members of the council:

[3] The authors do not want to suggest that the IA plan is based on distorted claims of financing problems.

- Extending coverage to new state and local government employees (most are already covered).
- Reducing benefits by roughly 3 percent by computing average earnings of future beneficiaries based on 38 years of earnings (instead of 35).
- Taxing Social Security benefits in roughly the same manner as income from contributory defined-benefit plans.
- Adjusting the COLA to reflect the Bureau of Labor Statistics estimate that the Consumer Price Index over-adjusts for inflation by 0.21 percent.

Together, these changes would reduce the projected financing problem by about 1.06 percent of taxable payroll—that is, they would address nearly one-half of the projected 75-year average annual deficit of 2.17 percent of taxable payroll.

Additionally, the MB plan would:

- Direct (by 2020) all income generated from taxing OASDI into the combined OASDI trust fund. (A portion of these receipts are credited currently to the Medicare Hospital Insurance trust fund.)
- Schedule a 1.6 percent payroll tax increase (0.8 percent on employer and employee) near the middle of the 21st century.
- And, very importantly, gradually invest two-fifths of OASDI trust fund assets in broad, passively-managed index funds (e.g., Wilshire 5000). (This change would indirectly increase rates of return to individuals while also eliminating 40 percent (+0.90 percent of taxable payroll) of the projected financing problem.)

Proponents of this plan note that it addresses financing problems (leaving a margin of safety) and improves the rate of return on Social Security contributions, while maintaining the basic promises and structure of OASDI (27).

These options would solve the problem. They aren't the only options. And they should be subject to the same analysis of consequences as those we have discussed above. Computing benefits over 38 years instead of 35 years would primarily represent a benefit cut for higher-income people, who begin work later in life than do blue-collar workers. The practice could disadvantage some women, however, who leave the labor force to care for children or elderly parents. Similarly, a 1.6 percent payroll tax increase is an increase in a regressive tax, and investing trust fund assets in the private sector would introduce new volatility in trust fund financing.

Other Reforms that Preserve Social Security

Even if one does not like the MB plan, it is important to recognize that many other reforms could address the financing problems of the program without dramatically altering the distribution of benefits and obligations or the structure of the program. Starting with the four common elements of the three Advisory Council plans (−1.09 percent of taxable payroll savings), here are some other incremental changes that are consistent with the existing Social Security program.

The share of aggregate household income going to the upper quintile increase from 45.1 percent in 1983 to 48.3 percent in 1993; and from 17.1 to 20 percent for the top 5 percent of the income distribution. This widening of the income gap could be viewed as providing a rationale for adjusting the taxable maximum ceiling, set at $62,700 in 1996. During the 1980s, as the income distribution widened (with more people being pushed well above average wages), the proportion of wages covered by the payroll tax dropped from roughly 90 to 88 percent. It is projected to drop further, to 85.5 percent ten years hence. One proposal would restore and maintain the proportion of wages covered by the payroll tax at the 90 percent level by 2000, addressing about 14 percent of the projected financing problem (0.31 percent of taxable payroll).

In a similar vein, one could argue that an increased burden should be placed on firms offering disproportionately high salaries (and indirectly on such employees) by subjecting 100 percent of the employer's payroll to FICA taxation. This approach is also consistent with the view that the employer's contribution is part of a pool of funds that promotes the social goals of Social Security, including proportionately larger benefits for low- and moderate-income beneficiaries. As such, there is no need to increase benefits for future beneficiaries as would be the case for proposals that would eliminate the maximum taxable ceiling from both employers and employees. If implemented in 1998, lifting the ceiling on the employer share would address about half of the projected problem.

Still, in place of raising the maximum taxable ceiling, one could select from among the plethora of moderate reform alternatives—raising the retirement age to 68, reducing the percentage of the last bend point, or cutting the spouse benefit—and still restore actuarial balance. Others might treat some portion of fringe benefits as taxable for Social Security purposes, or return to an entirely pay-as-you-go system (with a floating tax rate). The point is, as the MB plan illustrates, the financing problem can be addressed without privatizing, means-testing, or otherwise altering the basic structure of the program. And many benefit changes can be made without making wrenching cuts and without the destabilizing effects of switching to a consumer price index measure for bend-point adjustments or greatly reducing cost-of-living protections.

Assuming modest growth (for example, 1.3 to 2 percent real growth) over the next 30 to 60 years, the United States should be able to respond to the strains in program financing that will accompany population aging without placing undue burden on future cohorts of workers. If the economy grows at rates that are greater than anticipated, then it will be easier to respond to financing challenges. If growth is slower, further adjustments in Social Security will be needed. Perhaps the most realistic way of responding to the inevitable uncertainties that surround financial projections is to time one set of changes (for example, some combination of payroll tax increases and benefit reductions) to be put in place around 2020 when, as currently expected, we will begin to draw down trust fund reserves. A second set of changes could be scheduled in 2035, structured in such a way as to capture greater savings in the out years when the gap between anticipated income and costs is expected to be largest. Having scheduled such adjustments, we should expect to return to Social Security financing many times before 2070, to make changes as future experience proves better or worse than currently anticipated.

In sum, the Social Security trustees have sounded a warning bell, not a fire alarm as the program's opponents are fond of suggesting. Social Security can be brought into long-range actuarial balance without destroying a system that has reduced poverty and provided income security in old age, survivor's insurance to nearly every American, and protection during disability—all without ever missing a payment. Public discourse needs to move past the tendency to reduce discussions about Social Security to mere accounting exercises that focus only on program costs, overlooking the benefits this program provides and the real consequences to the well-being of individuals and families that various possible changes may have.

Social Security is an institution that has strengthened the nation's families and communities. In a very fundamental way, it is an expression of the moral commitment of our nation to serve as our brothers', sisters', fathers', mothers', and our own keepers. In the process of addressing long-term financing problems, we should lose sight of neither the economic implications of various policy options nor the moral dimensions of this program, which is one of the joining institutions of our society.

REFERENCES

1. Lukefahr, R. Testimony Before the Bipartisan Commission on Entitlement and Tax Reform, September 23. Washington, D.C., 1994.
2. Jacoby, J. The Social Security scam. *Boston Globe,* December 20, 1994.
3. Church, G. J., and Lacayo, R. Social Security: The numbers don't add up—and the politicians won't own up. *Time,* March 20, 1995, pp. 24–32.
4. Beard, S. *Restoring Hope in America: The Social Security Solution.* Institute for Contemporary Studies, San Francisco, 1996.
5. Board of Trustees, Federal Old-Age and Survivors Insurance and Disability Insurance Trust Funds. *Annual Report of the Federal Old-Age and Survivors Insurance and Disability Insurance Trust Funds.* Government Printing Office, Washington, D.C., 1996.
6. Quadagno, J. The Myth of the Entitlement Crisis. Paper presented at the American Sociological Association's Congressional Briefing, Washington, D.C., March 6, 1995.
7. Quadagno, J. Social Security and the myth of the entitlement crisis. *Gerontologist* 36(2): 391–399, 1996.
8. Luntz, F. Memorandum to the Republican Conference, January 9, 1995. Reprinted in *New York Times,* February 5, 1995.
9. Bipartisan Commission on Entitlement and Tax Reform. *Final Report to the President.* Washington, D.C., 1995.
10. Organization for Economic Cooperation and Development. *New Orientations for Social Policy.* Paris, 1994.
11. Moon, M. Medicare: An appropriate age-related program? *Generations* 19(3): 54–57, 1995.
12. Kutza, E. Medicaid: The shifting place of the old in a needs-based health program. *Generations* 19(3): 58–62, 1995.
13. Concord Coalition. *The Zero Deficit Plan.* Washington, D.C., 1993.
14. Peterson, P. G. Reform Proposal of Commissioner Peter G. Peterson. In *Final Report to the President,* Bipartisan Commission on Entitlement and Tax Reform. Washington, D.C., 1995.

15. Kingson, E. R., and Schulz, J. H. Should Social Security be means-tested? In *Social Security in the 21st Century,* edited by E. R. Kingson and J. H. Schulz. Oxford University Press, New York, 1977.
16. Kingson, E. R. Testing the boundaries of universality: What's mean? What's not? *Gerontologist* 34(6): 735–739, 1994.
17. Ball, R. M., and Aaron, H. J. The myth of means testing. *Washington Post,* November 14, 1993, p. C4.
18. Ball, R. M. Testimony Before the Bipartisan Commission on Entitlement and Tax Reform, July 15. Washington, D.C., 1994.
19. Bernstein, M. C. Social Security: Continued entitlement or new means test? An issue of program stability. *Res. Dialogues* 26: 1–8, July 1990.
20. Myers, R. J. Testimony Before the Bipartisan Commission on Entitlement and Tax Reform, July 15. Washington, D.C., 1994.
21. Steuerle, C. E. Testimony Before the Bipartisan Commission on Entitlement and Tax Reform, July 15. Washington, D.C., 1994.
22. Walker, D. Testimony Before the Bipartisan Commission on Entitlement and Tax Reform, July 15. Washington, D.C., 1994.
23. Sammartino, F. J. The effect of health on retirement. *Soc. Sec. Bull.* 50: 41, February 1987.
24. Rostenkowski, D. The Social Security Trust Fund Will Be There When You Retire. Mimeo. Washington, D.C., 1994.
25. Leonesio, M. V. Social Security and older workers. *Soc. Sec. Bull.* 56(2): 47–58, 1993.
26. Gustman, A. L., and Steinmeier, T. L. The 1983 Social Security reforms and labor supply adjustments of older individuals in the long run. *J. Labor Econ.* 3(2): 237–253, 1985.
27. Gramlich, E. Different approaches for dealing with Social Security. *J. Econ. Perspect.,* 1997, in press.
28. Ball, R. M. Bridging the centuries: The case for traditional Social Security. In *Social Security in the 21st Century,* edited by E. R. Kingson and J. H. Schulz. Oxford University Press, New York, 1997.
29. Quinn, J. F., and Mitchell, O. S. Social Security on the table. *Am. Prospect,* May-June 1996, pp. 76–81.
30. Daykin, C. Occupational Pension Provision in the United Kingdom. Paper presented at the 1994 Pension Research Council Symposium, "Security Employer-Based Pensions: An International Perspective," Wharton School, University of Pennsylvania, May 5–6, 1994.
31. Ball, R. M. Letter to members of Bipartisan Commission on Entitlement and Tax Reform. January 9, 1995.

CHAPTER 20

Women and Productive Aging:
Troubling Implications

Martha Holstein

The phrase a "productive aging society" captures in a few words a normative vision or, at a minimum, a provisional cultural ideal about appropriate roles and norms for older people in the United States in the late 20th century. It builds upon pictures of health and wellness, and upon perceived social and personal needs. This image attempts to achieve simultaneously several ends. First, it informs: Older Americans are already productive. Productive individuals are neither frail nor disabled; its proponents intend this image to reverse the decline-and-loss paradigm that has traditionally dominated thinking about old age. It also counteracts "greedy geezer" stereotypes; productive older people are contributing to U.S. society and therefore are not selfish consumers of socially scarce resources. Second, it advocates: This society must open more opportunities to permit its older members to continue participating in productive activities. Third, it affirms a cultural ideal: It is good and desirable for U.S. culture to elevate productivity as a ruling metaphor for a "good" old age.

In this chapter, I will specifically challenge this third end, suggesting that it is neither good nor desirable to elevate a "productive aging society" as the regnant image of what society should be like as the next century approaches; I will touch upon the others. For stylistic purposes, I will use the terms, "productive aging" and a "productive aging society" interchangeably; however, there is a significant difference between accepting the value of productivity—in its broadest meaning—as an important good and promoting a "productive aging society" as a normative image for aging and for society. Such a normative goal suggests that productivity, with all its linguistic connotations and metaphoric images, is what aging "ought" to be about. Whether its advocates intend this normative interpretation, they cannot control how others render their "text." And that rendering will inevitably be linked to one's political, social, and philosophical perspectives. It is, therefore, important to probe for the implications of what it might mean if a "productive aging society" became a new—desired and perhaps dominant—image of aging. Whose image will prevail? What are the potentially unintended and often negative consequences of this well-meaning phrase? Is it possible or probable, given the uncertainty of whose interpretation will prevail, that this cultural image can differentially affect older people in terms of race, gender, class, and health status? In particular, what could this cultural ideal mean for women? How likely is it that such an ideal will negatively influence patterns of dominance and oppression?

My argument will center on three themes: the risk that cultural, political, and economic forces will reduce an enriched notion of productivity to paid work; the particular implications this move can have for women; and, a more general cultural analysis that probes the effect of a productivity agenda on the individual lives of many older people, especially those who suffer from chronic impairments. I will stress that gender, reinforced by class and race, as a category of analysis, reveals otherwise hidden implications of the productive aging scenario much as the language of family caregiving neutralizes its specific genderized features. My approach is contextual and hermeneutical. This perspective holds that there is no definitive, universally accepted, noncontingent interpretation of any "text" or even word. A word like "productivity" is historically and culturally shaped and interwoven with other shared social meanings—for example, about citizenship and responsibility. As such, it cannot be detached from these other social meanings. Productivity is thus a quintessentially embedded concept, so embedded that its meaning cannot be easily reinvented. Further, as noted above, texts, once in the public domain, have many interpreters. While certain interpretations often become hegemonic, no one individual or group can control how any given text will be used and applied. For this reason, a "productive aging society" must be understood contextually; the prevailing moral and political economies will suggest whose definitions are likely to predominate. They will also define the boundaries within which political and other actors will negotiate the meaning and enactment of productivity.

Specifically, an analysis based on an historically sensitive political economy framework can unmask contemporary structural and ideological conditions and the power relationships they sustain. Such an analysis can offer useful insights. In addition to suggesting whose interpretation is most likely to prevail, it also will suggest why and how a vigorous endorsement of the "productive aging society" scenario—in today's particular historical context—will differentially affect specific individuals and groups, particularly women. Women, for example, encounter a "productive aging society" scenario encumbered by their specific backgrounds and their cohort history, often structured by low wage, intermittent work histories, and caregiving responsibilities. This history establishes the conditions of possibility for the future. In these last years of the 20th century, when the dominant moral economy assumes that, with rare exceptions, the market can respond adequately to individual needs, their difficulties are compounded. Its recognition of obligations toward those whom the market economy serves poorly is minimal.

Cultural analysis reinforces the critique of a productive aging society developed through the lenses of moral and political economy. Such analysis serves two important purposes. When paired with historical considerations, it speaks to commonly accepted understandings of productivity, especially its association with paid work. It also provides insight into cultural influences on self-perception and self-valuation. Individuals come to understand themselves and others within a specific cultural context. To borrow from cultural anthropologist Richard Shweder (1), "thinking through culture" affirms that we can only experience ourselves and others within a world of shared and preconstituted cultural meanings. Productivity has meaning in this society because it quickly translates into images, valuations, and actions that help crystallize one's self-assessments. Individuals raised in the United States value productivity as a good in itself, but it also serves larger purposes. Productivity connects to a whole complex of feelings that relate to self-respect and dignity. Being "productive" generally means receiving approbation. Yet, trapped in its own web of cultural meanings, in particular its embeddedness in the publicly esteemed world of economic "man," it is an inadequate instrument to serve the larger purposes of bestowing dignity and self-respect for many older people.

In sum, then, the risk that productive aging, as a cultural norm, can become coercive and reinforce patterns of domination and oppression and, in this case, buttress the rule of the relatively unimpeded market, forms the central problematic this chapter addresses. Explicitly historical, ideas about productivity are not free floating; they are shaped, interpreted, and enacted in a context—the particular circumstances that are structuring our contemporary political, economic, and moral universe.

THE POLITICAL AND MORAL ECONOMY:
A SHIFTING FRAMEWORK

There is nothing inevitable about either the moral or political economy in any given historical moment. Today, U.S. society marginalizes—and increasingly blames—individuals who do not work—that is, do not "produce" in economic terms. This view places "nonproductive" individuals in conditions of double jeopardy. Entry into the needs-based system of distribution is tightening just as the political economy makes it difficult for the work-based distributional system to adequately provide for individuals and families.

While heavily imbued with the work ethic, this country's social response to non-workers has had a checkered history. For much of the 19th and 20th centuries a certain system of reciprocal relations prevailed. This system permitted three population groups—veterans; widows, mostly but not entirely native-born women, and their children; and older people—to withdraw from or never enter the workforce, that is, to be economically nonproductive. This state of "deservingness" did not, however, extend to most black women, many of whom served as domestics. A public response to their need would, in effect, provide alternatives to low-paid domestic work and reduce the power of employers. For the groups considered "deserving," the state assumed some modicum of financial obligation. Thus, in the second and third decades of this century, most states passed legislation authorizing "mother's pensions" for "worthy" women and their dependent children. States and counties intended these relatively meager pensions to compensate for the loss of a male breadwinner and to permit mothers to stay at home to raise their children. The state's response was not unconditional. It assumed dependency and facilitated paternalistic interventions, and invidious distinctions based on notions of worthiness. Nonetheless, the ascendant moral economy, reflecting assumptions about a woman's "proper place" (at least for certain women), supported a public response to their needs. Intervening in the market economy, an important contributor to her poverty, was not an available option. While these mothers gained society's permission to be economically dependent, the nature of the relatively unimpeded market and the state's paltry payments often pushed marginal women into the workforce in spite of their "deserving" status (2, 3). For the most part, however, at least for this group, shared social assumptions about reciprocity called for a minimalist, needs-based response, with need defined by well-intentioned, white, middle-class women who, implicitly, reserved the right to define worthiness.

Comparably, a needs-based response to the inability (and reluctance) of the market to provide adequate resources for older people evolved during the crises of the Depression. Explanations abound about the birth of the Social Security system and the particular form it took. At a minimum, the generalized economic insecurity of the period, the broad sweep of the Depression's devastations, the apparent destitution of the elderly, and the limited number of jobs available were seen as providing the immediate stimuli for public responsiveness. While the Social Security program also served other needs, the immediate crisis was instrumental in forging a response. In that historical moment, the need for some income security for a particular segment of the population became socially recognized in a specifically formative and determinative way. As it turned out, the enactment of the Social Security Act in 1935 helped to institutionalize the life course by introducing a formalized period when it was socially acceptable and, for many, economically possible to withdraw from the workforce (4). Of equal importance, it transformed the period after age 65, for most wage earners, into a time of acceptable leisure uniquely vested in old age. Until quite recently, this social contract with older retirees had few opponents.

These historical examples illustrate how the underlying moral economy responded to needs- and merit-based claims through providing commonly held social goods. Indirectly, these responses also mitigated market control over individual lives. The important point, for the argument of this chapter, is that the prevailing moral economy provided rough notions about which needs would be met and, subject to political negotiation, to what extent and how they would be met. It paired perceptions of need with obligations to respond. The political economy, alternatively, determined that the dominant economy and its related ideologies and power relationships would marginalize mothers and older people. Thus, in the case of mothers, deserving by the standards of the time (read white and native-born), and older workers, other considerations temporarily overrode the traditional American work ethic. While the politics of need worked differently for those groups, in effect, each received permission to be non-workers and, tacitly, nonproductive (in an economic sense) and also, therefore, tacitly devalued.

These examples also illustrate how taken-for-granted economic assumptions and structural conditions reinforced cultural norms that women—and later, older people—were noncontributing, economically dependent members of society. That construction was the price they paid to never enter or to withdraw from the "productive" workforce. There were other costs: social devaluation and often economic hardship. Women's historical role as caregivers for the ill and the old was irrelevant to this understanding of what it meant to be productive. Caregiving and caregivers remained politically and economically unrecognized, especially as the less advantaged generally served as society's paid or unpaid carers (5). Public policy supported these assumptions and conditions. Contemporary advocacy for a productive aging society arose partly in response to this construction of older people as nonproductive, albeit with social permission, socially marginal, and "useless." Insisting on a productivity agenda, however, inadvertently but nonetheless culpably, can reinforce traditional assumptions about worthiness.

In contemporary society, the removal of two groups of adults from market control established earlier in this century is now falling out of favor as the market regains its privileged place. Increasingly, "not the consensual generation of norms but money and power have become modes through which individuals define the social bond and distribute social goods" (6). Women and older people, including older women, are increasingly subjected to market forces and market discipline regardless of the particular conditions of their lives. As responsible human action becomes more stringently focused on work, even for those once excused from this ethic, this nation's moral and political economy will also be renegotiated. It is within this context of market resurgence and reassessment of the former protected status of women and older people that the notion of a productive aging society must be situated, understood, and evaluated. As the market's pervasiveness spreads, it affects certain groups most immediately and powerfully. As the needs-based system erodes—and the sense of obligation on which it rested—the work-based alternative will, most likely, be unable to replace it. This likelihood will reinforce economic definitions of productivity, to which I turn next, even as advocates of a productive aging society seek to impose an enriched definition. In this way, the political economy reinforces cultural meanings. As the powerful feel less obligated to respond to need, the choices open to older people will also be reduced.

PRODUCTIVITY AND PAID WORK

Productivity, understood culturally, is closely linked to paid work, a link that will be difficult to sever. This link constitutes both problem and potential. As I shall discuss shortly, contemporary views tend to base value on economic exchange, what Hendricks and Leedham (7) describe as a moral economy grounded in exchange value where evaluations of individuals rest on their capacity for economically productive labor. With the exceptions noted above, in the 19th and most of the 20th century, U.S. culture upheld work as an economic necessity and a moral good. As Anson Rabinbach (8) has pointed out, modernity itself has been grounded in a producing subject; one's occupation provided the anchor for social identity—except for women. For much of U.S. history, cultural norms relegated women to the private sphere of home and family. Work done in that arena did not count as productive labor.

In contemporary society, the "work ethic" is an important social good. "Members of the commonweal who work, who earn an income, are viewed as productive citizens, those who do not are viewed as lesser citizens, either because they are wards of the state or because they have no public self" (5, p. 166). Sanctification of economic and self-interested motives as the fundamental explanation for human behavior and the basis for determining the public good (9, 10) buttresses arguments about the work ethic. This view relegates noneconomic activity to a secondary and, at best, private role. In a society dominated by economic ideas that tend to measure worth by quantifiable measures of productivity (the United States measures its well-being through calculating the gross national product; it does not assess air and water quality, access to good medical care, or excellent parenting), it is hard to resist associating productivity with work.

Advocates of a productive aging society, who appropriately insist that productivity means more than paid work, thus encounter deeply entrenched cultural ideas that equate productivity to work. The recent debate over welfare and raising the Social Security retirement age displays this tendency. For women on welfare, economic productivity is becoming the new coercive standard; for many retired people, such a standard may be imminent should the retirement age continue to creep upward. Not unlike earlier periods in U.S. history, government places few if any explicit demands for economic and social changes that might facilitate work roles for women and older people, who often cannot readily conform to standard demands. Few in positions of power are asking if real work opportunities and a fundamentally altered workplace will be created, or if the economy can and will absorb both older workers and younger women.

If these are the general risks of an economic standard, women face more specific risks. Women, who are least likely to define the meaning of productivity and who would benefit most profoundly from a re-imagining of old age, will be particularly vulnerable to the effects of a work-related standard, especially if it becomes a social expectation. It is to the particular effects on women of an economic definition of productivity that I now turn.

WOMEN AND WORK: A MIXED BLESSING

The work ethic, as it has been shaped by public language both in the past and in the present, is generally blind to the possibilities for exploitation. With the exception of minimum wage laws, child labor laws, the Family Leave Act, and other protective strategies, government generally assumes that the possibilities for and conditions of work are by and large beyond the scope of policy interventions. In a labor market, where labor is just another cost of doing business and lay-offs a fact of everyday life, and where a growing number of formerly excluded groups are expected to enter the labor market, the power of these groups to negotiate suitable working conditions is negligible. People, especially women and the poor, take whatever jobs are available.

Older women have experienced and will continue to experience the problem most profoundly. Fewer women than men have adequate retirement incomes; it is thus likely that they would most immediately feel the effects of changing expectations about an extended work life. Their work histories and the changing marketplace for lesser skilled workers limit their work options. Taking what jobs are available can mean additional years of unrewarding, low-income work while closing off the possibilities for other areas of chosen productive engagement. As Hendricks and Leedham note, "reducing early benefits that force the elderly to remain in the labor force without creating opportunities for meaningful employment can only increase the conditions for hardship" (7, p. 61). Given the fundamental inequalities that still mark our society, women are more likely than men to be practically affected by a political reinterpretation of what it means to live in a productive aging society.

This universalistic perspective about the value of work, approximating a moral prescription, relegates caregiving and other forms of "productive" activity to a secondary status. Thus, the recent welfare bill imposes work responsibilities on mothers of young children. Part of the underlying argument is that middle-class women are working, so why should society exempt "welfare mothers" from work. This argument omits obvious differences; poor women bear heavier burdens than middle-class women—dangerous neighborhoods, inadequate child care, and long commutes with uncertain transportation are just a few of these burdens. This insistence on work also assumes that caring work will be done, whether the recipients are children or older people—an odd assumption when juxtaposed to "family values" which ostensibly esteem what family members do for one another. They are tangential to what really matters. *Paid* work counts.

In the economic sector, an older woman's market value and contribution to the system of economic productivity are already negligible. The work culture she has faced and would face has been largely unsupportive and has reflected historical patterns of inequality. But many older women may need (for economic reasons) and want (because it is a recognized way to gain social recognition) to work. Work, in a practical if not an optimal sense, will remain a critical option until (and if) their needs are met through improved income support programs or alternative ways to achieve social approbation and community. Yet, in their quest for meaningful work experiences, women often encounter a work environment defined by male norms (11) and/or job opportunities clustered in only 20 of the Department of Labor's 480 job categories (12). Women have always dominated the low-wage service sector and as they age, especially if they are widowed or divorced, their need for employment will compel many of them to take whatever jobs are available; often these jobs are part-time, a symbol of their role as the "shock absorbers" of an economy marked by marginal working conditions (13). If current employment patterns and economic downsizing continue, it is questionable whether older workers will find a place in the primary economy. It may be a dubious "privilege" for older women to choose between the kind of work that might be available or exclusion because of age, particularly if it interferes with efforts to assure an income sufficient for a decent standard of living. Yet, many women want and need such employment, a commentary not only on the financial problems older women face but on the limited way our society supports and values individuals.

By hailing a productive aging society, advocates may be offering tacit approval to work situations that reinforce patterns of inequality and allow the continued exploitation of women—emblematic of that troublesome middle ground where noble goals give birth to practical and somewhat baser policies. By conflating the availability of such low-wage work with the larger, value-laden goal of a productive aging society, less sympathetic voices can transform what may be an economic necessity for older women into a newly honored social norm. What is a coincidental—and perhaps transitory—juxtaposition between the economy's need for low-wage workers and the experiences of many women that prepare them for such work can shape new work expectations, particularly if these expectations are supported by policy shifts.

However, it would be irresponsible to ignore the very real need that many women have for jobs. Hence, instead of conflating this practical need into a normative conception of goals for old age, advocates should rather concentrate on an explicit jobs strategy. Such a strategy avoids confusion and potentially negative consequences while serving the effort to create better jobs that are more sensitive to the gifts of many women. In this way, the practices that arise from women's lives— caring, nurturing, maintaining relationships (5, 14)—can become a valid part of the socially sanctioned, and therefore socially supported, definition or foundation for new images of old age.

If participation in that work culture becomes a new and valued norm for old age and if opportunities to work became expectations to work (see below), women will have few opportunities to explore alternative paths to social recognition and personal meaning. Often freed from family and work responsibilities for the first time, older women's rich life experiences can make significant contributions to the community. While advocates within gerontology include voluntarism among productive activities, there is little room to be sanguine that other interpreters, with other agendas, will so readily incorporate this understanding of productivity. A work-oriented definition of productivity can obscure diversity, establish new standards for an acceptable old age, and support someone else's vision of social and economic needs.

THE CRITICS OF OLD AGE, POLITICS, AND PRODUCTIVITY

As noted in the introduction, words assume meanings in specific historical and cultural contexts. The analysis offered above argued that productivity has had a long historical and cultural association with paid work and that those excluded from this arena often paid the price of social disapproval and disregard. Using a political economy of aging framework, I further argued that such a definition would most likely harm women. They are already at a material disadvantage compared with men and have arrived at old age in a society where jobs for women occupied a narrow slice of the economic pie in which pay was low and employment often sporadic. Turning to a moral economy framework, I want to consider how contemporary attitudes toward old age and patterns of reciprocity can reinforce the more troubling aspects of the productive aging scenario.

In a society witnessing a shift in both its political and moral economics, the productive aging scenario can become the unintended handmaiden for a political agenda that delegitimizes old age benefits. By emphasizing health and vigor, by pointing to the availability of jobs without consideration of the quality of such jobs, and by ignoring the inherent gender biases in such a strategy, a job-oriented view of productivity can threaten the already tenuous economic status of older women.

In this environment, efforts to qualify and so "prove" older people's productivity can have decidedly mixed consequences. Caregiving serves as a good example. While it is important to alert legislators and others about older people's contributions to society, it is equally important for them to recognize that caregiving comes with a price. Viewed by most women as a personal responsibility, it is nonetheless the fulcrum of long-term care policy. Women, who continue to be economically deprived as a group, lose more ground as individuals when they assume caregiving responsibilities (15).

By assuming the desirability of productivity and reducing the vision of an aging society to it, advocates by-pass a critical task—to understand aging in all its manifestations and to respect people not only when they are contributing in any way elucidated to date, but also when they become more dependent. For example, contrasting productivity with dependency (one is good, the other is not; one is socially valued, the other devalued) reinforces a dichotomous view of aging (16). This view upholds only its positive pole and hinders the search for meaning even as dependencies arise. The ideal of a productive aging society reinforces the positive pole and is held hostage to the instrumental, accomplishment-driven orientation of our society.

CULTURE, MEANING, AND A PRODUCTIVE AGING SOCIETY

Carl Jung once suggested that no person would live to 70 or 80 if there were no special purpose to that period of life. Where once individuals were embedded in webs of religious and social meanings that envisioned spiritual growth in spite of physical or mental loss, those webs of meaning hold far less power in late 20th century America. Yet, as Callahan notes (17, p. S10):

> Every society has traditions and practices that affect the way the elderly think about themselves and the way they are thought about by others. The meaning of old age for individuals—what they make of their aging and how they come to value themselves—will be in part a function of the various messages society has conveyed to them in word and deed, and what the elderly themselves bring to their own aging. The social significance of aging—the societal role assigned to the elderly and the public programs developed in their behalf—will not only influence the self-perception of the aged, but will also project a picture of the value placed on them by society. From that latter picture will come most of the elements that determine, overtly or covertly, the amount and kind of resources made available to the elderly.

The reigning ideals of individualism and youthful vitality make frailty a condition to be shunned. Productive aging further reinforces the negativity associated with chronic illness or chronic impairment. As such, it can reinforce the threats to meaning that individuals who are impaired confront. While many older people can find meaning in spite of these cultural messages, how much better if these messages would be supportive rather than obstacles to overcome. Work in cultural psychology, anthropology, and philosophy suggests that cultural messages which elevate an ideal of productive aging can easily subvert—or, at a minimum, complicate—an older person's ability to find coherence and purpose in the face of frailty and disability. This discussion will focus on the personal and existential losses that can issue from an emphasis on productive aging and the cultural ideal of a productive aging society.

Cultural ideals, images, and metaphors provide the frameworks within and against which we define ourselves and find meaning. "Cultures supply the motivational patterns and symbolic interpretations in light of which individuals think of narrative histories, project their visions of the good life, interpret their needs and the like" (6, p. 55). "Not to have a framework," noted philosopher Charles Taylor, "is to fall into a life which is spiritually senseless" (18). Such cultural frameworks organize a way of life in pursuit of the end (or telos) in question: "To think, feel, judge within such a framework is to function with a sense that some action, or mode of life, or mode of feeling is incomparably higher than the others which are more readily available to us" (18).

The commitments we hold define the self and give it its sense of coherence and purpose. We are free to choose and to change, to stand before possibilities, to alter the status quo, and to adopt an attitude toward events, but only within the constraints of culture and our own social location and physical and mental well-being. This culture is constitutive, without being deterministic of who we are; it provides a publicly shared symbolic system essential for constructing meaning and dealing with anomaly. Thus, the self arises "not from an 'inner' essence relatively independent of the social world, but from experiences in a world of meanings, images, and social bonds" (19). To further quote cognitive psychologist Jerome Bruner: "The symbolic systems that individuals used in constructing meaning were systems already in place, already 'there' deeply entrenched in culture and language. They constituted a very special kind of communal tool kit whose tools, once used, make the user a reflection of the community" (19, p. 11).

If the political economy of aging paradigm alerts us to how external conditions—race, gender, ethnicity, class—influence how we grow old, then culture helps shape the way we interpret and act upon (or do not act upon) these conditions. The flow, however, goes two ways; while culture is shaping it is also continuously reshaped by the stories we tell. We both influence and are influenced by some defining community (18).

What, then, does U.S. culture offer the older person? At every stage of human life, even our culturally diverse society has forged socially sanctioned roles and norms to guide behavior (20). Tacitly, these roles and norms affirmed the social value of that life stage. We must learn, begin to work, marry, raise the next generation. Those who do not conform to these expectations are marginalized; the contemporary welfare debate judges those who do not conform. Yet, U.S. culture may not give older people the "tool-kits" needed to make sense of the particular untoward events of later life. Americans may need a culturally supported way to feel that life has a coherence and purpose in spite of loss and the nearness of death. The "third age" is that stage of life whose meaning has yet to be determined, at least on a collective level, by society as a whole. There seem to be no cultural expectations for old age—except perhaps to be as much like a middle-aged person as possible.

But many older people are not just like middle-aged people, only older. They face many leavings but no socially sanctioned beginnings and so live in a state of perpetual liminality. This loss is particularly true in a society with a Faustian image of endless possibilities, with the self infinitely open to change without boundaries. Thus, it is useful to pose the question: Ought there to be cultural expectations? Should old age have any special purpose and, in particular, a purpose that programs and policies can help support?

In his 1987 work, *Setting Limits: Medical Goals in an Aging Society*, Dan Callahan (21) raised this question and offered his suggestions for purposes of discussion. His critics largely ignored this effort and instead responded to his practical proposal for age-based rationing of health care. More recently Charles Fahey and Martha Holstein (20) argued that a normative vision for old age was a worthy subject for public discussion; they highlighted the roles that elder could play as moral leaders.

ANSWERS OR QUESTIONS?

The call for a productive aging society thus provides answers before old and young together have systematically asked questions about the meanings of old age. Available cultural messages have real consequences. They provide the frameworks in which individuals strive to locate themselves, in which they try to reconcile or at least make sense of the incongruity of social images of old age with their own self-images. If productivity becomes a dominant goal, at least for those under 75, U.S. society will have lost an opportunity for a vigorous engagement with questions about meaning and purpose. By risking the establishment of narrow standards for the good life, our society can negate, albeit unintentionally, an exploration of how to best use an often invisible and sometimes denigrated gift of age—relative freedom. To affix an easily misconstrued label—as a symbolic cue as well as a practical guide—to an inherently complex time in human life limits us. Since productivity sees so clearly a continuation of the values of the middle years, it begs the question as to whether old age is a unique time in human life, intrinsically valuable and fundamentally different from the period that came before. An emphasis on productivity can devalue the relational activities—often displayed in women's demanding roles as primary caregivers—that encroaching dependencies often demand, and obscure the creativity and moral integrity that are developed and realized in these relationships. A narrow understanding of productivity, especially when paired with the scapegoating of the old, can compound the psychological damage to female caregivers if their burden remains unacknowledged and unregarded as part of productivity's essential meaning. Moreover, emphasizing the productive contribution of women as a result of their caregiving activities, although recognizing the burden, does nothing to alleviate it. It may indeed have the opposite effect; such valorization removes an incentive to provide assistance while not assuring that society respects the women who provide care.

A corollary risk is that those older women who may not conform to the new rosy image of a productive old age may blame themselves and not the underlying social conditions that influence so dramatically their experience of old age. The historical tendency to individualize the experiences of old age renders invisible the political and economic conditions that shape the choices available. This notion of productivity can impose a negative value on those who are not productive in the traditional sense or who do not maintain youthful vigor and independence. It can also intensify the prejudice that already marks social attitudes toward the elderly who have physical or mental impairments (22). Thus, in the most basic way it is important to ask whether productivity is one of the deepest goods we should wish for in old age. It is only if that is true that we should consider risking the negative consequences of setting this goal.

Imagine the following productive aging scenario. The "gatekeepers of ideas" (23) will equate productivity with paid work. Emphasizing the productive capacities of the "healthy old," they will translate opportunities to work into expectations to work in whatever jobs become available. To reinforce these expectations, society will retrench from the social welfare policies that have created the retirement wage (24). As the standard retirement age creeps upward without a supportive change in disability benefits, individuals who are unhealthy will suffer disproportionately. Women will not be exempt from these newly developed norms or their traditional and evolving caregiving roles—to children, to spouses, and to the children of their sons and daughters who are unable or unwilling to provide care. They will continue to perform those roles with limited public support and social recognition. For many, a lifetime of working the "second shift" will continue unabated (25). Older women, at best, will be at the fringes of a gender-biased workplace, which will remain unyielding in its maintenance of male norms of achievement, success, communication, and style (11, 26, 27). These older women will hold low-paid, part-time jobs in the service economy protected by few health or retirement benefits. The workplace will continue to reflect, in a microcosm, the place that women and older people occupy in society at large. Yet, other means of contributing to society and gaining social approbation through means other than work will be underestimated or unexplored. The dichotomies between the "vigorous" and the "frail" will be underscored (28). Societal ageism will be displaced, directed to those who are least like middle-agers (22). Individuals who are disabled, and thus nonproductive by typical definitions, will be even further marginalized.

THINKING ABOUT ALTERNATIVES

This scenario, only slightly exaggerated, highlights the dangers of adopting "productive aging" or a "productive aging society" as a primary ideal for old age, particularly for older women. But work in productive aging reminds us that symbolic language—or ideals—can be the first step to action. It is a worthy goal to develop a substantive image or images of the last stage of life that respond to both individual and societal needs. If a productive aging society is a troublesome ideal, it nonetheless invites us to continue engaging in public conversation. We cannot have what we cannot name and describe. It is worth remembering that productivity is a metaphor for other deeply personal needs—self-respect, dignity, and social validation. The goal might then be to discover how to achieve these ends in other ways.

To begin, interested individuals and groups can think about old age as an important and unique period of human life when the facticity of finitude is an ever-present reality. In this view, older people are often "trapped between life and death, personal experience, and social time" which puts them in a unique cultural-symbolic space (29). With this understanding, we acknowledge the specialness of old age when the ability to live by our former meanings may be compromised and no other state awaits this transformation. It encourages reflection about what U.S. society offers older people when they can no longer meet the norms of productivity or other socially valued dimensions of human purpose. It helps us enter the world of those people who are no longer able to live in their habitual ways, for whom the gap between their former worlds of meaning and the abilities they now have has been severely disrupted.

Hence, the following questions may be starting points to encourage such conversation. Does our definition of old age encourage the development of new opportunities for personal growth, development, a more intense interiority, and the chance to exercise moral agency however limited our physical or mental capacities? Does it stimulate participation in both formal and informal interactions? Can it capture Malcolm Cowley's (30) experience of "sitting like a snake on a sun-warmed rock"? Can it simultaneously serve society and the older person? Can it honor the relational values that women have so long acted upon in the private sphere, oriented toward process as well as product? Does it serve existential ends and aid in the confrontation with human limits? Does it emphasize respect for the person more than respect for what the person does? Does it permit a complex understanding of old age, an understanding that permits mystery as well as mastery (16)?

What I'd like to suggest are a series of steps, from a feminist perspective, that might facilitate movement toward a positive response to these questions. I would ask us to think about the possibilities that old age is unique and possesses special gifts, some of which we are familiar with and others of which are awaiting discovery. The new norms that help establish a cultural meaning for old age will arise both deductively and inductively. They'll bubble up from the individual decisions of thousands of older people (31), but because ideas can have considerable power, a new vision of what old age can be like might open some new possibilities. Recall the feminism of the 1960s and 1970s.

In particular, what would happen if women's, especially older women's, voices were heard with a new clarity? Women might choose new ways to use their affiliative histories; their flexibility learned in years of balancing home, work, and other demands; their ability to deal with ambiguity and complexity; and their potential for growth once they have more freedom (32, 33). Women might exercise leadership roles as social critics based on social acceptance of their styles and a robust respect for their wisdom nurtured by their diverse lifetime experiences. Women might ask for a chance to test, in larger spheres, their ways of behaving, seeing, and acting so that these typically devalued ways function not as the sources of oppression but as part of the restructuring of the dominant culture (27).

Women could bring into public life those behavioral and emotional patterns that have been reserved historically for the private sphere. These patterns might include, for example, a new emphasis on personal (not only functional) relationships for life fulfillment, the value of work well done for its own sake, the norm of helpfulness to others, and an emphasis on care and responsibility (5, 20).

CONCLUSION

For today's older woman, it is important to counteract the ageist, sexist stereotypes that have distorted women's efforts to achieve a consistently satisfying sense of self-worth and social approbation without replacing them with an alternative mandate of how they should lead their lives. For those who need to work, a sustained effort to crumble the barriers to the kind of employment they want, and to create work that serves their needs as well as those of business, must be addressed. At times there may be synchronicity; at other times there will be none. The fundamental challenge will be to construct new ways of imagining work and life that sustain the values that women have often had to suppress. However well-intentioned, the move toward "productivity" as an important defining characteristic of a good old age, rather than helping this process, may be one more barrier to a rich and feminist appreciation of old age's gifts.

It is also fundamentally troubling within the context of the contemporary moral and political economy. As the work ethic and the market intrude upon people formerly exempt from these demands, women, people of color, and those with low income will inevitably pay the heaviest price. Decontextualized perceptions about work can further reinforce the devalued status of women and the poor, also mostly women. Once again, as in the 19th century, society will locate responsibility for their status almost singularly within the individual. Unfortunately, the productive aging vision, despite its important reminders about the strengths of old age, can easily reinforce this scenario.

REFERENCES

1. Shweder, R. *Thinking Through Culture: Expeditions in Cultural Psychology.* Harvard University Press, Cambridge, Mass., 1991.
2. Abramovitz, M. *Regulating the Lives of Women: Social Welfare Policy from Colonial Times to the Present.* South End Press, Boston, 1988.
3. Skocpol, T. *Protecting Soldiers and Mothers: The Political Origins of Social Policy in the United States.* The Belknap Press of Harvard University, Cambridge, Mass., 1992.
4. Kohli, M. Retirement and the moral economy. *J. Aging Stud.* 1: 125–144, 1987.
5. Tronto, J. *Moral Boundaries: A Political Argument for an Ethic of Care.* Routledge, New York, 1993.
6. Benhabib, S. *Situating the Self: Gender, Community and Postmodernism in Contemporary Ethics.* Routledge, New York, 1992.
7. Hendricks, J., and Leedham, C. Dependency or empowerment: Toward a moral and political economy of aging. In *Critical Perspectives on Aging: The Political and Moral Economy of Growing Old,* edited by M. Minkler and C. Estes. Baywood, Amityville, N.Y., 1991.
8. Rabinbach, A. *The Human Motor.* Basic Books, Harper Collins, Scranton, Pa., 1990.
9. Daly, H., and Cobb, J., Jr. *For the Common Good.* Beacon Press, Boston, 1989.
10. Lux, K. *Adam Smith's Mistake: How a Moral Philosopher Invented Economics and Ended Morality.* Shambala, Boston, 1990.
11. Kessler-Harris, A. *A Woman's Wage: Historical Meanings and Social Consequences.* University of Kentucky Press, Lexington, 1990.

12. Pateman, C. The patriarchal welfare state. In *Democracy and the Welfare State,* edited by A. Gutman. Princeton University Press, Princeton, N.J., 1988.
13. Nussbaum, K. Social insecurity: The economic marginalization of older women workers. In *The Aging of the Workforce: Problems, Programs, Policies,* edited by I. Bluestone, R. Montgomery, and J. Owen. Wayne State University Press, Detroit, Mich., 1990.
14. Gilligan, C. *In a Different Voice.* Harvard University Press, Cambridge, Mass., 1982.
15. England, S., Keigher, S., and Linsk, N. Community care politics and gender justice. In *Critical Perspectives on Aging: The Political and Moral Economy of Growing Old,* edited by M. Minkler and C. Estes. Baywood, Amityville, N.Y., 1991.
16. Cole, T. *The Journey of Life: A Cultural History of Aging in America.* Cambridge University Press, New York, 1992.
17. Callahan, D. What do we owe the elderly? Allocating social and health care resources. *The Hastings Center Report,* Suppl., March-April 1994, pp. S1–S12.
18. Taylor, C. *Sources of the Self: The Making of the Modern Identity.* Harvard University Press, Cambridge, Mass., 1989.
19. Bruner, J. *Acts of Meaning.* Harvard University Press, Cambridge, Mass., 1990.
20. Fahey, C., and Holstein, M. Toward a philosophy of the third age. In *Voices and Visions: Toward a Critical Gerontology,* edited by T. Cole, W. A. Achenbaum, P. Jakobi, and R. Kastenbaum. Springer, New York, 1993.
21. Callahan, D. *Setting Limits: Medical Goals in an Aging Society.* Simon and Schuster, New York, 1987.
22. Minkler, M. Aging and disability: Behind and beyond the stereotypes. *J. Aging Stud.* 4(3): 245–250, 1990.
23. Epstein, C. *Deceptive Distinctions: Sex, Gender, and the Social Order.* Yale University Press and Russell Sage Foundation, New Haven, Conn., 1988.
24. Myles, J. *Old Age and the Welfare State,* Revised Ed. University of Kansas Press, Lawrence, 1989.
25. Hochschild, A., and Machung, A. *The Second Shift: Inside the Two-Job Marriage.* Viking Press, New York, 1989.
26. Fuchs, V. *Women's Quest for Economic Security.* Harvard University Press, Cambridge, Mass., 1988.
27. Markus, M. Women, success, and civil society. In *Feminism as Critique: On the Politics of Gender,* edited by S. Benhabib and D. Cornell. University of Minnesota Press, Minneapolis, 1987.
28. Cole, T. The specter of old age: History, politics, and culture in an aging America. *Tikkun* 3(5): 93–95, 1988.
29. Hazan, H. *Aging: Constructions and Deconstructions.* Cambridge University Press, Cambridge, England, 1994.
30. Cowley, M. *The View from 80.* Viking Press, New York, 1980.
31. Riley, M. Women, men, and the lengthening of the life course. In *Gender and the Life Course,* edited by A. Rossi. Aldine, New York, 1985.
32. Friedan, B. Changing sex roles: Vital aging. In *Productive Aging: Enhancing Vitality in Later Life.* Springer, New York, 1985.
33. Gottlieb, N. Families, work, and the lives of older women. *Women as They Age: Challenge, Opportunity, and Triumph.* Haworth Press, New York, 1989.

Concluding Note

Meredith Minkler and Carroll L. Estes

A recent *Newsweek* magazine cover, boldly captioned "Mediscare," depicted a young man being crushed under the weight of a heavy-set elderly woman in a wheelchair. Across the Atlantic, a British billboard pictured the "two faces" of former Prime Minister John Major on the subject of social security, suggesting that workers and retirees best watch carefully lest the historic promise of public pensions be broken.

As this book goes to press, the themes of devolution, fiscal crisis, and the targeting of already marginalized groups for still harsher treatment appear, in many advanced capitalist nations, to increasingly be shaping the health and social policies that will follow us into a new century. In the United States, these developments have reached a particularly troubling level, with millions of Americans, including many elders, losing vital health and social benefits, and with states potentially "racing to the bottom" in long-term care rather than risking the fiscal responsibility of more generous health and social service provision.

Within this context, social inequalities based on race, class, gender, and age are likely to become even more pronounced, and already devalued groups, such as caregivers, may be further stigmatized and penalized. Schemes such as vouchers for Medicare and the privatization of Social Security, viewed not long ago as unrealistic proposals of the far right, may erroneously come to be perceived as "the inevitable adaptation of a responsible government to the constraints imposed by limited resources" (1, p. 134). Within such a climate, as Piven and Cloward prophetically pointed out during the early Reagan years, trends such as decentralization may "tend to become invisible as political issues and instead may appear to be merely the limits of the possible" (1, p. 132).

In the face of such developments, a political economy framework, which views the "problem" of old age in structural rather than individual terms (2), is particularly relevant. This relevance is underscored as the legitimacy of the state is attacked and welfare reform removes hundreds of thousands of legal immigrants from entitlement to cash or health assistance.

Yet, as we have suggested in this volume, narrow mechanistic versions of political economy are less helpful than broader, more inclusive approaches—approaches that recognize, with Cornell West (3), that "culture is as much structural as the economy or politics." As we look ahead to a new century, we anticipate and hope for an increased accent on culture in political economic analyses of aging in our increasingly heterogeneous societies.

The broader approach to political economy developed and applied in this volume has embraced a focus on moral economy that highlights the collective societal assumptions about fairness and reciprocity underlying many of our most basic policies and programs for the old. As we enter the 21st century, the careful examination of these foundational assumptions will prove crucial if we are to separate "bedrock" values and concerns from the rhetoric of ideological shifts that conservative policymakers in many nations are using to legitimate new rounds of cutbacks and mean-spirited policies.

The linking of political and moral economy perspectives, such as we have attempted in this book, also is important inasmuch as gerontologists have tended to be "notoriously unreflective" about their craft (2, 4). As part of a discipline that evolved during the scientific era of the 1940s and beyond, gerontologists have tended not to ask such questions as: What are the ends of our work? Does it matter? Does our work really contribute to the lives of older people (4)? And conversely, does it sometimes contribute to the *disempowerment,* rather than the empowerment, of the old? If so, how might the dominant paradigms and taken-for-granted assumptions be turned on their heads?

Political and moral economy pose these and related questions as we seek to understand the social construction of aging and to build on and apply new theoretical formulations in this undertaking. Popular notions such as "productive aging" and "successful aging," the false dichotomy of "dependence" and "independence" in old age, and the impoverishment of public discourse about reciprocity and the common good are among the areas ripe for rethinking as we enter a new century. Similarly, exaggerated notions of "senior power" and "intergenerational conflict" are in need of careful reexamination. We must pay far more attention to social inequities based on the intersections of gender, race, class, and age. Our analyses need to move away from the kinds of "add-and-stir" (5) approaches that use gender, age, or any other single dimension as the primary prism or lens through which to understand and explain oppressions that are in fact interlocking and multicausal.

Through scholarship, critical gerontologists can help place in clearer relief some of the dramatic policy shifts that are being attempted in many advanced capitalist nations and the unprecedented cutbacks being imposed upon the elderly and other vulnerable groups. Yet a theme linking many of the chapters in this book has been the need for gerontology to move beyond reflection and analysis, embracing praxis, or action based on critical reflection, as a vital part of our *raison d'être*. Borrowing from critical theorists (6, 7) who embrace the role of the intellectual in transformative change, we would argue that the "big project" for our scholarship needs to include both "critical empirical analysis" and praxis aimed at "improving the conditions of elders and the experience of aging in society" (8). Whether through historical studies, policy analysis, qualitative or quantitative research, or other undertakings, gerontologists must share what they have learned, in as personal a way as possible, and work for programs and policies that address poverty in old age, the medicalization and commodification of the needs of elders, and the disempowerment of the old through these and other means (9). "Questions of empowerment and the promotion of gender and ethnic justice need to be on the research agenda" as scholars "challenge and reframe the questions that have defined the mainstream" (Chapter 8, p. 212). In contrast to mainstream gerontological assumptions that view the elderly as "separate and different," the reframed questions of critical gerontology will play an important role in demonstrating the cross-generational stake in policies and programs such as social security and the need for reclaiming the sense of community that reminds us—young and old alike—of our intimate interdependence.

REFERENCES

1. Piven, F. F., and Cloward, R. A. *The New Class War: Reagan's Attack on the Welfare State and Its Consequences.* Pantheon Books, New York, 1982.
2. Estes, C. L., Swan, J. H., and Gerard, L. Dominant and competing paradigms in gerontology: Toward a political economy of aging. *Ageing Soc.* 2(Pt 2): 151–164, 1982.
3. West, C. *Race Matters.* Vintage Books, New York, 194.
4. Holstein, M. Critical gerontology: Implications for Theory, Research and Practice. Presentation at the Annual Meeting of the American Society on Aging, Nashville, Tenn., March 24, 1997.
5. Andersen, M. L. *Thinking About Women: Sociological and Feminist Perspectives.* Macmillan, New York, 1983.
6. Gouldner, A. *The Coming Crisis of Western Sociology.* Basic Books, New York, 1970.
7. Gramsci, A. *Selections from the Prison Notebooks,* edited and translated by Q. Hoare and G. Nowell Smith. Lawrence and Wishart, London, 1971.
8. Estes, C. L., Linkins, K. W., and Binney, E. A. The political economy of aging. In *Handbook of Aging and the Social Sciences,* Ed. 4, edited by R. H. Binstock and L. K. George, pp. 346–361. Academic Press, New York, 1995.
9. Minkler, M. Critical perspectives on ageing: New challenges for gerontology. *Ageing Soc.* 16: 467–487, 1996.

Contributors

PHILLIP G. CLARK is professor and director of the Program in Gerontology and the Rhode Island Geriatric Education Center at The University of Rhode Island in Kingston. As a visiting professor in Canada at the Universities of Toronto and Guelph during 1988–1989, he focused on comparative U.S. and Canadian geriatric health care policy. He is the author of "Public Policy in Canada and the United States: Individual Lives, Familial Obligation, and Public Responsibility" (in *The Remainder of Their Days: Domestic Policy and Older Families in the United States and Canada*, edited by J. Hendricks and C. Rosenthal, Garland, 1993); "Moral Discourse and Public Policy in Aging: Framing Problems, Seeking Solutions, and 'Public Ethics' " (*Canadian Journal on Aging*, 1993); and "Ethical Dimensions of Quality of Life in Aging: Autonomy vs. Collectivism in the United States and Canada" (*The Gerontologist*, 1991).

THOMAS R. COLE is professor and graduate program director at the Institute for Medical Humanities, University of Texas Medical Branch in Galveston. He received his Ph.D. in history from the University of Rochester in 1981. Dr. Cole's many articles and books on the history of aging and humanistic gerontology include *The Journey of Life: A Cultural History of Aging in America* (Cambridge University Press, 1992), which was nominated for a Pulitzer Prize. He is senior editor of *What Does It Mean to Grow Old?* (Duke, 1986); the *Handbook of Humanities and Aging* (Springer, 1992), and *Voices and Visions: Toward a Critical Gerontology* (Springer, 1993), and is coeditor of the *Oxford Book of Aging* and the biannual newsletter, *Aging and the Human Spirit*. Dr. Cole's recent research centering on mental illness, oral history, civil rights, and race relations in Texas has culminated in a book, *No Color Is My Kind: The Rediscovery of Eldrewey Stears and the Integration of Houston* (University of Texas Press, 1997), and a documentary film, *The Strange Discovery of Jim Crow: How Houston Integrated Its Public Accommodations, 1959–1963*.

PAULA DRESSEL is associate provost for academic programs and professor of sociology at Georgia State University in Atlanta. Her research focuses on the intersection of gender, race/ethnicity, and class in issues of poverty and social welfare policy. Most recently these interests have been applied to understanding grandparent caregivers of grandchildren whose mothers are incarcerated. She has published this work in *The Gerontologist* and has guest-edited a special issue of *Generations* (Spring 1996) on grandparenting at century's end.

CARROLL L. ESTES is professor of sociology in the Department of Social and Behavioral Sciences, School of Nursing, University of California, San Francisco, and director of the Institute for Health and Aging. Dr. Estes, whose Ph.D. is from the University of California, San Diego, conducts research on aging policy, health and long-term care policy, older women, fiscal crisis, and devolution. She is the author of *The Decision-Makers: The Power Structure of Dallas* (1963) and *The Aging Enterprise* (Jossey-Bass, 1979); coauthor of *Fiscal Austerity and Aging* (Sage, 1983), *Political Economy, Health and Aging* (Little, Brown, 1984), and *The Long Term Care Crisis* (Sage, 1993); and coeditor with Phillip Lee of *The Nation's Health* and with Charlene Harrington of *Health Policy and Nursing* (1997). She is past-president of the Gerontological Society of America, The American Society on Aging, and The Association for Gerontology in Higher Education.

CHARLENE HARRINGTON is professor of sociology and nursing in the Department of Social and Behavioral Sciences, School of Nursing, University of California, San Francisco. She is an R.N., a fellow in the American Academy of Nursing, and a member of the Institute of Medicine, where she serves on the Quality of Care Roundtable. Dr. Harrington received her Ph.D. in sociology and higher education from the University of California, Berkeley. She has been the principal investigator for several large national research studies on state policies in long-term care and their effects on utilization and expenditures, funded by the Health Care Financing Administration and the Agency for Health Care Policy and Research. Currently, she is the principal investigator of a study to develop a Nursing Home Consumer Information System and is conducting a descriptive study of Medicare consumer complaints. Her many publications include a coedited book, *Health Policy and Nursing* (2nd edition; Jones and Bartlett, 1997).

MARTHA HOLSTEIN is a research scholar at the Park Ridge Center for the Study of Health, Faith and Ethics in Chicago and directs the Center's Program on Aging. Her Ph.D. in the medical humanities is from the University of Texas Medical Branch in Galveston. While continuing her long interest in public policy and aging, she is also a historian of dementia and a student of meaning and old age, ethics and aging, and normative public policy. Among other works, she has coedited *A Good Old Age? The Paradox of Setting Limits* (Simon and Schuster, 1990), an exploration of categorical age-based rationing of health care. She now serves on the Board of Illinois Older Women's League and on the editorial board of the *Journal of Aging and Identity,* and is the immediate past chair of the Humanities and Arts Committee of the Gerontological Society of America.

ROBERT B. HUDSON is professor and chair of the Department of Social Welfare Policy, Boston University, School of Social Welfare. He received his Ph.D. in political science from the University of North Carolina at Chapel Hill and has written widely on the design and implementation of aging-related policies, the changing risk profile of contemporary older Americans, and the political and policy consequences of an aging society. Dr. Hudson serves as editor of *The Public Policy and Aging Report,* the publication of the National Academy on Aging, and on the editorial boards of *Generations, The Gerontologist,* and the *Journal of Aging and Social Policy.* In 1995 he delivered the Arthur S. Flemming Lecture at the National Association of State Units on Aging annual meeting, and in 1996 he received the Donald P. Kent Award from the Gerontological Society of America.

MALCOLM L. JOHNSON has been professor of health and social policy and director of the School for Policy Studies at the University of Bristol in England since 1995. From 1984 to 1995 he was professor and dean of the School of Health and

Social Welfare at the Open University. The author or editor of eight books and over 100 other publications—over half on aging and old age—Professor Johnson was also the founding editor of the international journal *Ageing and Society* (1980–1993). He served as secretary of the British Society for Gerontology from 1977 to 1984. His research interests in gerontology include biographical analysis, long-term care, ethical aspects of aging societies, death and dying, and intergenerational relations.

JAE KENNEDY is an assistant professor of health policy and administration in the Department of Community Health, University of Illinois in Urbana-Champaign, and director of the Long-Term Care Statistics Project in the Disability Statistics Research and Training Center, University of California, San Francisco. He received his doctorate in health services and policy analysis at the University of California, Berkeley. His research interests include disability policy, home and community-based long-term care, health care reform, and program evaluation. He is currently studying the socioeconomic consequences of family caregiving.

ERIC KINGSON is an associate professor of social policy at the Boston College Graduate School of Social Work. He directed the Emerging Issues Program of the Gerontological Society of America in 1984–1985 and served as policy advisor to the 1982–1983 National Commission on Social Security Reform and the 1994 Bipartisan Commission on Entitlement and Tax Reform. He is primary author of *Ties That Bind: The Interdependence of Generations* (Seven Locks Press, 1986) and *Social Security and Medicare: A Policy Primer;* author of *The Diversity of the Baby Boom: Implications for Their Retirement Years* (AARP, 1992); and coeditor of *Social Security in the 21st Century* (Oxford University press, 1997).

KAREN W. LINKINS is a doctoral candidate in medical sociology in the Department of Social and Behavioral Science, University of California, San Francisco, and a research associate and project coordinator at the Institute for Health and Aging. Her dissertation is entitled "Access to Community Based Long Term Care: Political, Community and Organizational Influences." Ms. Linkins has coordinated two national studies of community-based long-term care and mental health services that specifically address the influence of federal, state, and local policy changes on the delivery of services for the elderly and people with disabilities. She is currently coordinating a national, multilevel study of the politics of long-term care policy that addresses the role of grassroots activists, state and national coalitions, the media, and other influentials involved in the policy formation and implementation process. In addition, she and Dr. Carroll Estes are conducting a review of the policy research capacity of the Social Security Administration's Office of Research Evaluation. Ms. Linkins earned her B.A. in sociology from Smith College. She is coauthor of several articles, including a chapter in *The Nation's Health* (Sage, 1997).

MARTY LYNCH is executive director of the Over 60 Health Center in Berkeley, California, and a lecturer at the Institute for Health and Aging, University of California, San Francisco. He received his Ph.D. in sociology at UCSF in 1996 with a dissertation on the disabled elderly in managed care, and an M.P.A. in health policy at the John F. Kennedy School of Government at Harvard University in 1987. Dr. Lynch was one of ten recipients of a Robert Wood Johnson Community Health Leadership Award in 1995. His recent research has been in the areas of long-term care reform, medical services in social/health maintenance organizations, and managed care for the elderly.

MEREDITH MINKLER is professor and chair of Community Health Education at the School of Public Health, University of California, Berkeley. She holds a doctorate in public health. Her research interests include the political economy of aging and health and intergenerational issues. Dr. Minkler's publications include a coauthored book, *Grandparents as Caregivers: Raising Children of the Crack Cocaine Epidemic* (Sage, 1991); the coedited books, *Readings in the Political Economy of Aging* (Baywood, 1984) and *Critical Perspectives on Aging* (Baywood, 1991); and most recently, the edited volume *Community Organizing and Community Building for Health* (Rutgers University Press, 1997).

JONATHAN OBERLANDER is an assistant professor in the Department of Social Medicine, University of North Carolina at Chapel Hill. He received his Ph.D. in political science from Yale University. From 1995 to 1997 he was a visiting scholar and Robert Wood Johnson fellow in health policy at the University of California, Berkeley. His research interests include welfare state politics, federal health policy, and aging policy. He is currently completing a book on Medicare politics from 1965 to the present.

OLDER WOMEN'S LEAGUE (OWL), a nonprofit membership organization founded in 1980, is the only national organization to focus solely on midlife and older women's concerns. OWL strives to achieve economic and social equity for midlife and older women. It was founded by two California women, Tish Sommers and Laurie Shields, whose earlier work helped create the displaced homemakers movement. OWL's national agenda includes education and advocacy around a variety of issues, including Social Security reform, pension rights, job discrimination, universal access to health care, long-term care, eradicating domestic violence, and federal budget priorities. Through approximately 72 chapters and its headquarters in Washington, D.C., OWL consistently acts on its motto: "Don't agonize, organize!"

CHRIS PHILLIPSON is a professor of applied social studies and social gerontology and director of the Centre for Social Gerontology, University of Keele in England. His research interests include social theory and aging, social change and the family, and work and retirement. He has recently completed a large-scale study of kinship and old age in urban environments. He is the author of *Capitalism and the Construction of Old Age* (Macmillan, 1982) and coauthor of *The Sociology of Old Age* (1988), *Changing Work and Retirement* (1991), and *Elder Abuse in Perspective* (1995), all published by the Open University Press.

JILL QUADAGNO is professor of sociology at Florida State University in Tallahassee, where she holds the Mildred and Claude Pepper Eminent Scholar Chair in Social Gerontology. In 1994 she served as senior policy advisor on the President's Bipartisan Commission on Entitlement and Tax Reform. She is president-elect of the American Sociological Association and recipient of the 1994 Distinguished Scholar Award of the ASA Section on Aging. Her seven books on aging and social policy issues include *The Transformation of Old Age Security; State, Labor Markets and the Future of Old Age Policy;* and *The Color of Welfare: How Racism Undermined the War on Poverty.* The latter received the 1996 award for the Outstanding Book on the Subject of Human Rights from the Gustavos Meyers Center for the Study of Human Rights in North America. Dr. Quadagno is presently engaged in a study of the effect of downsizing on the long-term income security and savings behavior of older workers.

ANN ROBERTSON is an assistant professor in the Department of Behavioral Science, University of Toronto. She received her Dr.P.H. in health policy from the University of California, Berkeley, after several years in health promotion practice in Canada. Dr. Robertson is a coinvestigator with the National Network on Environments and Women's Health, one of five Canadian Centres for Excellence in Women's Health. Her research interests focus on a critical social science perspective on gerontology, discourses on health and risk, and women's health.

DEBRA STREET is a postdoctoral fellow in the Robert Wood Johnson Foundation Scholars in Health Policy Research program, School of Public Health, University of Michigan, Ann Arbor. She received her Ph.D. in sociology from Florida State University in 1996. Her research has recently appeared in *Social Problems, The International Journal of Sociology and Social Policy,* and *The Canadian Journal of Aging.* In 1995, she and Jill Quadagno coedited a reader in social gerontology entitled *Aging for the 21st Century,* and she is currently working on a book on the political economy of health and pension reform in Canada, Great Britain, and the United States.

STEVEN P. WALLACE is an associate professor in the Department of Community Health Sciences, University of California, Los Angeles, School of Public Health. He is the Borun Scholar of the Anna and Harry Borun Center for Gerontological Research at UCLA and associate director of the UCLA Center for Health Policy Research. He received his Ph.D. in sociology from the University of California, San Francisco. Dr. Wallace's research focuses on the impact of race and ethnicity on the use of long-term care and the consequences of public policies for the health and quality of life of racial and ethnic minority elderly. He has published his research in journals such as *The Gerontologist, Journals of Gerontology: Social Sciences, American Journal of Public Health,* and *The Journal of Aging Studies.* His current research includes projects on assessing the scope and directions of health promotion programs for the elderly in local and state health departments; determining the consequences of managed care on access to health care by minority elderly; and evaluating the health promoting activities of older Samoan women in Los Angeles.

JOANNA K. WEINBERG is an adjunct associate professor in the Department of Social and Behavioral Sciences and the Institute for Health and Aging, University of California, San Francisco, and an adjunct professor at Hastings College of Law. She is a graduate of Harvard Law School; she received an L.L.M. from Columbia Law School and a B.A. in sociology from Brandeis University. Dr. Weinberg teaches courses on Ethics, Law and Health Care at UCSF and on Public Benefit Law at Hastings Law School. She studies the devolution of welfare state policies, caregiving responsibilities of midlife and older women, and ethical aspects of health policies, with respect to vulnerable or disenfranchised populations. Her current research addresses the impact of managed care on at-risk populations, focusing on the issue of conflict within managed care settings and in the Medicare system. She also serves on the Board of the National Association on HIV Over 50, a research and advocacy organization concerned with AIDS and aging, and has been a visiting scholar at the Center for the Study of Law and Society at the University of California, Berkeley, and at the Murray Center for the Study of Society at Radcliffe College, Harvard University.

VALENTINE M. VILLA is research associate/lecturer in the Department of Social Welfare, University of California, Los Angeles, School of Public Policy and Social Research. Dr. Villa's research interests include the investigation of health status differentials among minority and non-Hispanic white populations, with an emphasis on the role of socioeconomic status, culture, health care utilization, and health practices in determining health status among older populations.

IRENE YEN has a master's degree in public health and a Ph.D. in epidemiology from the School of Public Health, University of California, Berkeley. She is also a research associate at the California Department of Health Services' Human Population Laboratory. Ms. Yen's research interests include the influence of neighborhood socioenvironments on health behaviors and health status, and urban design as it relates to health promotion.

Index